Teacher's Manual for
Lands of Hope and Promise
A History of North America

Catholic Textbook Project, Ventura, California

Catholic Textbook Project

Dear Catholic Educator,

Thank you for undertaking the education of the next generation of American Catholics in a century filled with both perils and promise. Christ offers our youth a challenge and a hope no other religion or philosophy permits. We, their teachers and parents, cannot allow our children to be ignorant of the origins of the Faith or of the beliefs of other cultures in an increasingly challenging world. We must know our history and teach it to our children. They must know why we are different from our neighbors in the world, and why our neighbors have developed as they have. Teaching history is teaching God's providential care for his people and his promise to the rest of the world. We must teach our children hope!

But as teachers of long experience, our editors have learned that in the matter of teaching history, there is a clear paradox: *Less is more*. Students learn better and learn more when they are taught the facts of history through the stories of the past, the legends of heroes, the tales of noble causes, and the lives of saints and holy men and women. Long lists of facts—names, dates, products, and causes—fade in the memory, but the stories remain and form the character and the understanding of a child. We encourage teachers to tell the stories, to expect the questions, and to offer a skeleton of key dates. What came before what, or after what, is more important to the learning mind than memory of the exact dates involved. All history is really a true and interesting story.

May our books bring both story and facts to life for our students, and for their teachers.

Michael Van Hecke, President
Catholic Textbook Project
P.O. Box 4638
Ventura, California 93007

Introduction

How to Use This Manual
How to Use This Book

In *Lands of Hope and Promise*, the authors have adopted a pedagogy different from that assumed by most modern textbooks. The conviction underlying this book is that history is, first and foremost, a story— an enjoyable story, a story filled with drama. We have written this book, therefore, as if we were writing a story—in this case, a continuation of the story of Christendom/Western Civilization in North America and its interaction with native cultures there. Our hope is that students, approaching history as a story, will learn to love history and will, thus, retain more historical knowledge than is normally the case with the more customary textbook style.

The difficulty is that the story approach to history often includes more information than what a teacher would expect most students to retain. To insist that students retain every detail, every date, would be to undermine a chief purpose of the book—to make the reading of history a matter of joy. We want students to approach history in a leisurely fashion, to read it as they would read a story, not a record of dry facts. Of course, one hopes that students will leave each chapter with more than the required knowledge, but this is best left to the capabilities of each student. Those historical facts every student should know are listed in the section, "What Students Should Know," in this teacher's manual. Beyond these basic facts, teachers should merely see that their students retain the chief outlines of the stories they will study in the book. (A teacher, however, should encourage students to stretch themselves beyond what they assume to be their own capabilities.)

How to Use *Lands of Hope and Promise* in the Classroom

We propose that the chief occupation of classroom sessions on the book be spent in having students recite, in their own words, what they remember from their assigned reading in the book and to discuss the ideas presented in the text among themselves and with the teacher. The teacher may call on different students to recount what they have read in the text or to tell what they know about the various characters or concepts they have encountered in their reading. This will help students solidify what they have learned and give them the opportunity to practice their language skills. The teacher may then patiently correct any false impressions the students may have or any inaccuracies in their presentations. Such exercises should be seen as merely educational exercises without the threat of grading. Each chapter in the book has, as well, an activities section to help students deepen their knowledge of the time period each chapter covers.

We also recommend that teachers use the timeline provided in the teacher's manual as a reference to help students make their own timelines for each chapter. After students have completed their own timelines, the teacher may use the timeline we have provided to help students correct and fill out the timelines they have drawn up.

A teacher may bring into the classroom pictures illustrative of the time period being studied or show educational videos. The assignment of fictional works of historical events will also help students get a feel for the time period they are studying. Recordings of period music—such as traditional folk, popular music, and classical music—help create for students the "mood" of historical epochs. Learning to sing simple folk or popular songs from these time periods will, perhaps, be even more effective. This teacher's manual provides a list of suggested works of historical fiction as well as period music.

Another Way to Use *Lands of Hope and Promise* in the Classroom

Some teachers may find it helpful to supplement the above method of using *Lands of Hope and Promise* with readings of the text in the classroom. Hearing the text read aloud can be helpful to students who are more auditory than visual in the way they take in information.

Teachers could assign readings of portions of the text to various students, or read them aloud themselves. After such a reading, the teacher could engage the students in conversation about the information found in the text or discuss with students the meaning of the ideas presented in the text. Such classroom readings should be seen as a reinforcement, not a replacement, of the reading each student does on his or her own. By reading the text aloud, students, too, can learn to pronounce unfamiliar words.

Contents of This Teacher's Manual

Scope and Sequence
Provides a general outline of the text and the contents of each chapter.

Period Music
Offers suggestions of period music and composers

Some Key Terms at a Glance
Puts in one place the various historical terms, persons, events, and vocabulary highlighted in each chapter, with their definitions.

What Students Should Know
Presents the minimal knowledge of persons, places, events, and dates students should retain. We have provided, for the teacher's convenience, a brief review for each important fact.

Questions for Review
Provides, for the teacher's convenience, the answers for each question presented in the "Chapter Checkpoint" section at the end of each chapter.

Ideas in Action
Gives suggestions for doing each activity, where necessary, plus explanations and reference material, where applicable.

Chapter Quizzes and Tests
Suggests questions for quizzes for different sections of each chapter, as well as a chapter test. Since our approach in *Lands of Hope and Promise* is literary, our quizzes and tests ask mostly short answer or short essay questions. We think it is important that students develop the ability to express their thoughts in complete sentences. Teachers, however, should not feel obligated to use these quizzes and tests either whole or in part or in the manner we have presented them. Teachers should feel free to mix questions from the tests or compose examinations of their own.

Essays
Offers essay topics to help students more deeply understand the time period they are studying. Teachers may wish to offer these essays as assignments in conjunction with the quizzes and tests, or use them in lieu of a more formal examination.

Resources for Further Reading or Investigation
This section gives suggestions for further student reading on each period covered in the text.

Timeline
The timeline presents in a linear manner the historical events recounted in this volume. The timeline is meant to aid teachers in helping students make their own timelines either individually or as a class.

Scope and Sequence

Chapter 1: Explorers and Conquistadors

The Genovese Mariner
Columbus' background
Columbus' first voyage to the Indies
Columbus discovers the New World
Columbus' second voyage to the New World
Columbus governs the New World
Columbus' third voyage

Other New World Explorers
Juan Ponce de León
Vasco Nuñez de Balboa
Juan Sebastián Elacano

The Conqueror of Mexico: Hernán Cortés
Cortés sails to Mexico
The Aztecs
Cortés wages war on Montezuma
The Aztecs defeat Cortés
Cortés marches on Mexico again and conquers the Aztecs

Quest for the Cities of Gold: Hernando de Soto
De Soto sets out to find the legendary Cities of Gold
De Soto's discoveries in North America
The Pueblo Indians

Francisco Vasquez de Coronado
The purpose of Coronado's expedition
The lands Coronado explored

Chapter 2: The Progress of Spanish America

In Search of Justice: Improving the State of the Indians
Treatment of the Indians in New Spain
Las Casas' labors to bring justice to the Indians
The Franciscans
The missionaries' attempts to Christianize and civilize native cultures through learning

New Mexico
Early attempts at settlement in New Mexico
Juan de Oñate settles New Mexico

La Florida
Spain's discovery and settlement of Florida
Indians of Florida rebel against the Spaniards

Chapter 3: France Settles the New World

First Voyages
Why France settled the New World
The explorations and discoveries of Giovanni da Verrazzano
Jacques Cartier's explorations and discoveries

The Founding of New France

The Natives of New France
The Mohawks
The Iroquois
The Huron

Missionaries of New France

North American Martyrs
Jean de Brébeuf
Isaac Jogues

New France Grows
French colonization in North America

The Church in New Spain

The Missions of Pimería Alta
Padre Kino
Rebellion in the Pimería missions
The Pimería after Kino

The Missions of Alta California
Fray Junípero Serra
Fray Junípero establishes missions
Conversion of the Indians
Martyrs in California

A Passage to New Mexico
Don Juan Bautista de Anza's explorations

Chapter 8: The Causes of the American Revolution

Life and Society in the English colonies
Westward expansion

Revolutionary Ideas
Liberalism and Republicanism
The Great Awakening

Kindling the Flames of Rebellion
The Stamp Act
The Revenue Act
Patrick Henry's "Resolves"
Reaction to and repealing of the Stamp Act
The Townshend Acts
The Boston Massacre
The Boston Tea Party

Chapter 9: The American Revolution

Growing Discontent
The Coercive and Quebec Acts
The first Continental Congress
The *Declaration and Resolves*
The New England Restraining Act

The War Begins
The Battle of Lexington
Ticonderoga
The second Continental Congress
Bunker Hill

The Declaration of Independence
Thomas Paine's *Common Sense*
Thomas Jefferson drafts the Declaration of Independence
The colonies become the United States

The War Continues
Saratoga
Alliance with France
The dark years of the war
The tide turns
Yorktown and victory

Chapter 10: A New Nation

Revolutionary Governments
Bills of Rights
The Articles of Confederation
Republican reforms
Enactments of religious freedom

Religion in the New Republic

The Struggle for a New Government
Problems with the Articles of Confederation
Other troubles
The Northwest Ordinance
Rebellion in Massachusetts

A New Constitution
Writing of the new constitution
The small states fight back
The Connecticut Compromise

The Fight for Ratification
The Federalist

The First President

George Washington's first and second terms

Chapter 11: The First Test of the Union

The Revolution of 1800
The Naturalization, Alien, and Sedition Acts
The election of 1800

Disintegration of Society
Love of commerce
Breaking of societal ties
The Second Great Awakening
Voluntary societies

Jefferson's Presidency
Marbury v. Madison
The Louisiana Purchase
Lewis and Clark

The War of 1812
War at sea
The war in the south
The defense of New Orleans and the end of the war

Chapter 12: Revolution in New Spain

The "Golden Age" of California
Life and society in California

Progress and Decline in the Missions
Troubles with the mission Indians

Revolution in Mexico
Prelude to the revolution
Padre Hidalgo
Vicente Guerrero

More Revolution
The bloodless revolution
Iturbide's revolution

Mexico independent
Liberalism in Mexico
Emperor Agustín
The Republic of Mexico

Chapter 13: Good Feelings and Hard Times

The Catholic Church in the Early 19th Century
Crisis in the American Church
Bishop John England
The Church on the frontier

The "Era of Good Feelings"
The Patriot War

The Death Knell of the Union
Business panic
The Tallmadge amendment
The slavery question
Political rivalry between North and South
Controversy over Missouri
The Monroe Doctrine

The Democratic Revolution
Andrew Jackson's election
The Tariff of Abominations and Nullification

The Trail of Tears
Black Hawk
The Five Civilized Tribes
Indian removal from the East

Chapter 14: Mexico and Manifest Destiny

An Unstable Republic
Mexico begins to lose her economic freedom to northern Europe
Santa Anna rebels and Congress proclaims Vincente Guerrero president
Spain tries to reconquer Mexico
Another rebellion

Santa Anna becomes president

The New Constitution
Conservatives call for the expulsion of Liberals
Congress replaces the Constitution of 1824 with a new constitution

The Alamo
Texian discontent with rule in Mexico
Rebellion
The battle of the Alamo

More Wars
The Pastry War
Santa Anna becomes dictator of Mexico
California's oath of allegiance to Mexico
California's civil conflicts

The Draw of the West
The Mountainy Men
Oregon Fever
Mormonism

Manifest Destiny
The United States' "Manifest Destiny"
John C. Frémont
The Bear Flag Revolt
War with the United States
Treaty of Guadalupe Hidalgo

Chapter 15: On the Eve of Disunion

Progress in the United States
Increased productivity and industrialism
Growth of eastern cities
19th century inventions
Immigration

The Sectarian Spirit
New religions and sects

Reform Movements
Free public schools

The search for Utopia

The South
Life and society in the South
Slavery in the South
Nate Turner's rebellion

The Gold Rush
John Marshall finds gold in California
California becomes a state
Anti-foreigner feeling in California
The fate of the Indians in California

Chapter 16: A House Divided

Abolition and Antislavery
William Lloyd Garrison
Theodore Dwight Weld
Angelina Grimké
Frederick Douglass
Sojourner Truth
Southern retaliation
The Catholic position

The Fight over the Territories
The Wilmot Proviso
Calhoun and Webster
Clay's Compromise
The Fugitive Slave Law

The 1850s
The Young Americans
Filibustering
The Ostend Manifesto
The Kansas-Nebraska Act

Bloody Kansas

A House Divided
The Dred Scott case
John Brown
Lincoln-Douglas debates
Lincoln wins the election of 1860
Secession

CHAPTER 1: Explorers and Conquistadors

Chapter Overview

♦ The year 1492 was an important year for Spain because Queen Isabel and King Fernando concluded the 700-year war that Christians on the Iberian Peninsula had been waging against the Muslims.

♦ Both Portugal and Spain desired to reach Indiaand establish a direct spice trade with East Asia, and so they sent out explorers to find a route.

♦ Columbus saw himself as destined to carry the Catholic faith to the heathens overseas. He also longed to find gold, however, and it was these two things that drove him to set out for the Indies. He hoped to reach the Indies by sailing westward across the Atlantic Ocean.

♦ Columbus reached what he thought was the Indies on October 12, 1492. He attempted to establish colonies there. The first colony he founded on Hispaniola was destroyed by the native Indians after his return to Spain.

♦ In 1513, by crossing the Isthmus of Panama (Darien),Vasco Balboa discovered a new ocean, thus showing theSpanish that they had not reached the Indies.

♦ In 1522 Juan Elcano, by circling the world, discovered how far the supposed Indies were from the real Indies.

♦ Hernán Cortés discovered what is now Mexico on April 21, 1519, and commenced to try to conquer the Aztecs who dwelt there.

♦ In 1520, while Cortés was absent from Tenochtitlán, the Aztecs rose up against the Spaniards. After Cortés' return, the Aztecs drove the Spaniards and their Indian allies from the city.

♦ Cortés returned with his own men and their Indian allies to Tenochtitlán. They conquered the city in August 1521.

♦ Hernando de Soto joined the Pizzaro brothers in their conquest of Peru. Beginning in 1539, he lead an expedition in the exploration of Florida, going all the way to the Mississippi, where de Soto died.

What Students Should Know

1. **The goals and accomplishments of Portuguese exploration in the 15th century.**

   Since 1415, under the impetus of Dom Henrique (Prince Henry the Navigator), Portugal had been engaged in navigation. Hoping to forge an alliance against the Muslims with the legendary Christian monarch, Prester John, Dom Henrique had sent ships southward along the coast of Africa to see what lay around the continent's great western cape. After Dom Henrique's death in 1460, Portugal's interest turned more to by a desire to reach India and establish a direct spice trade with East Asia. In the 1470s, Portuguese mariners discovered the Gold and Ivory Coasts of Africa, and kept pushing south. By 1488, Bartolomeu Días had rounded the southern tip of Africa, the "Cape of Good Hope." Ten years later, in 1498, another Portuguese captain, Vasco da Gama, followed this route to the port of Calicut in India.

2. What was Columbus' "Enterprise of the Indies"

The Enterprise of the Indies" was Columbus' conviction that one could reach the Indies by sailing west across the Atlantic. His conviction was based on a miscalculation – he had underestimated the circumference of the earth by reckoning the earth's circumference to be 25 percent smaller than it actually is and exaggerating the eastward stretch of Asia. He thus concluded that the distance from the Canary Islands to Japan would be some 2,400 nautical miles. It is actually 10,600 nautical miles.

3. What Columbus wanted to accomplish with his Enterprise

Columbus believed himself called to a special task – to carry the Catholic faith to the heathen oversea. He hoped, too, to find gold in the Indies both to enrich himself and the monarch he served. He hoped his monarch would finance with this wealth a new crusade against the Muslims to recover the Holy Sepulcher in Jerusalem for Christendom.

4. The events of Columbus' first voyage

Columbus set sail on August 3, 1492, with a crew of 90 men and boys and a fleet of three small ships, or caravels – the *Santa María*, the *Pinta*, and the *Niña*. A lookout on the *Pinta* first sighted land on October 12, 1492. On the same day, Columbus and his men went ashore on a small island the natives called *Guanahani*. Columbus claimed the land for the Spanish monarchs and for Christendom. He named the island San Salvador. From San Salvador, he set sail and discovered the islands of Cuba and Hispaniola. On the latter island, he established the first Spanish settlement in the New World, Navidad. Then Columbus set sail on the *Niña*

(with the *Pinta*) for Spain, where the ships arrived after a stormy crossing.

5. The character of the native cultures with which Columbus came in contact

The first native people Columbus met were the Taino. They had come to the Caribbean islands originally from South America, pushing back and enslaving the indigenous Siboney people of Cuba, Jamaica, and the Bahamas. The Taino did not have an advanced culture. They grew corn, yams, and other root crops, and they made cassava bread from the yucca plant. They excelled in pottery and used shells to make ornaments and utensils. Their shelters were simple, of wooden frame and palm leaf thatch. Taino men and women both went about with no other covering than a loincloth. The Taino were in the main peaceful and hospitable. This was not true of another Caribbean people Columbus encountered – the Caribs. The Caribs led slaving raids on the Taino and engaged in cannibalism.

6. The purpose and provisions of the papal bull, *Inter Caetera*, and the Treaty of Tordesillas

Portugal's king, Dom João, was not pleased with the news of Columbus' discoveries, for it appeared that Spain had reached the Indies before the Portuguese had. The king feared what this meant for Portugal's interests in Asia. To maintain peace between Spain and Portugal, Pope, Alexander VI sought to appease Dom João and in 1493 issued the bull, *Inter Caetera*, setting a demarcation line in the Atlantic. All lands west of the demarcation line, decreed the pope, would fall to Spain; those east of the line, to Portugal. This,

Alexander thought, would forestall disputes between Spain and Portugal.

Spain and Portugal later confirmed Pope Alexander's decision in the Treaty of Tordesillas. To further appease Dom João, Isabel and Fernando agreed to place the demarcation line 370 leagues to the west of the pope's line. This treaty secured Brazil, which juts out east of the line, for Portugal.

7. What were Queen Isabel and King Fernando's objectives for Columbus' second voyage

In their instructions for his second voyage, Isabel and Fernando insisted that the expedition's first objective was the conversion of the natives to the Catholic faith. The second was the establishment of a trading colony. The sovereigns said that Columbus must see that the "Indians" were treated "well and lovingly" so that friendly relations would prevail between them and the Spaniards. Columbus should punish anyone who mistreated the Indians.

8. The character of Columbus' government of the Indies

Columbus was more of sea captain and explorer than a governor. When, because of Spanish abuses, the Taino killed some Spaniards, Columbus decreed that in any conflict between Spaniards and Indians, he would consider the Indians the guilty party and the Spaniards innocent. He would punish any Indian who killed a Spaniard, no matter the provocation. "Guilty" Indians were to be hunted down, punished, and enslaved. Fearful that, without a significant discovery of gold, the Spanish monarchs would abandon further exploration and settlement of the Indies, Columbus commanded every native, 14 years and older, to pay him a tribute of gold dust every three months. Those who refused would be punished with death. He instituted an

Indian slave trade, a move which angered Queen Isabel.

9. When continental America was discovered

Columbus discovered the continent of South America (sailing along the coast of Venezuela) in August 1498.

10. The derivation of the name, "America"

In 1501, Amerigo Vespucci, a native of Florence, Italy, but living in Spain, wrote a letter in which he claimed to have been part of an expedition that had landed on the mainland of the New World one year before Columbus had first sailed along the coast of Venezuela and eight days before the English explorer John Cabot had touched the coast of Cape Breton Island far to the north.

Though its account was almost certainly fabricated, Vespucci's letter was published in 1504 and was widely read throughout Europe. Because Vespucci claimed to have been the first to have seen the New World, Europeans began to call the new lands after the latinized version of his Christian name, Americus.

11. The voyage and discoveries of Juan Ponce de León

In 1513, Juan Ponce de León set sail for an island called Bímini, in search of the fountain of youth. Landing on that "island's" eastern coast on Easter Sunday (*Pascua Florida* in Spanish) 1513, he named the new land, Florida. Starting from what is today known as the St. John's River, he explored the eastern coast of Florida south of Cape Canaveral and the western coast as far north as Tampa Bay. Later, in 1521, Ponce de León attempted a settlement at

Charlotte Harbor, but the Indians drove him off. He died of a wound he received in the battle.

12. Vasco Nuñez de Balboa's discovery and its importance

In 1513, Vasco Nuñez de Balboa, with 170 men, plunged into the interior of Darien (Panama). From a mountaintop, Balboa sighted a new ocean that he called the South Sea – the Pacific Ocean. Balboa's discovery of the Pacific showed the Spanish that they had not reached the Indies but that a vast ocean separated the new lands from East Asia.

13. Magellan and Elcano's achievement and what it demonstrated about America

Juan Sebastián Elcano had been part of the expedition under Fernando Magellan, whom in 1519 the new king of Spain, Carlos I, had commissioned to circumnavigate the globe. After crossing the Atlantic from Spain, Magellan had sailed southward along the coast of South America. Rounding Cape Horn, Magellan crossed to the Hawaiian Islands, from whence he sailed to Guam and then the Philippines. In the Philippines Magellan died from a poisoned arrow in a battle with the natives in April 1521. Elcano, taking command of the voyage, continued south and then west into the Indian Ocean. Rounding the Cape of Good Hope, he returned in triumph to Spain. The expedition proved that what had come to be called "America" was not even on the outskirts of the Indies, but was itself an entirely new world.

14. The purpose of Cortés' expedition into Mexico

In 1518, news reached Cuba of discoveries made by Juan de Grijalva off the coast of Yucatán and Mexico. Hungry for adventure and riches, Cortés sought and obtained from Velásquez the position of captain general of an expedition (funded by both), the sole purpose of which was to further explore and exploit the riches of the new region. In Mexico, however, Cortés said the primary purpose of the expedition was the conversion of the Indians to the true God from the worship of idols.

15. The character of the natives of Mexico

The Indians Cortés and his men found in Mexico, the region the natives called Anahuac, were not primitive like the Taino. They raised buildings and temple pyramids of stone instead of dwellings of stick and thatch. They were very numerous, too, and dwelt in ordered towns surrounded by well-cultivated fields of maize, or Indian corn. They were warlike and formidable opponents in war

16. The main points of the history of the Aztecs

According to their own history, the Aztecs had come from the northwest, from a region called Aztlán. In the 14th century they arrived at the shores of a lake in the high mountain valley of Mexico, where they settled and built their city, Tenochtitlán. In 1418, a barbaric tribe, the Tepanecs, invaded and conquered Tenochtitlán and its neighboring city, Texcuco. Later the Aztecs joined the king of Texcuco, and drove out the invader. As a reward, they received the Tepanec lands.

In the 15th century, Tenochtitlán and Texcuco grew in power. Until about 1500, Texcuco was predominant. But by the time Montezuma II became king (in 1502), the Aztecs were the masters of Texcuco. In his 17-year reign, Montezuma conquered the tribes of Anahuac. He ruled the subject tribes through fear, laying upon them heavy taxes and tributes.

17. The culture and civilization of the Aztecs

The Aztecs had learned civilization from Texcuco. By the 16th century, the Aztecs had advanced in agriculture and architecture; they planted beautiful gardens and raised a lordly city. Aztecs excelled in metal work, especially the delicate craftsmanship of gold ornaments. The exact observation of the stars allowed the Aztecs to make a solar calendar of 18 20-month days. In their hieroglyphic, or picture writing, they recorded history and wrote beautiful poetry. Like all other American peoples, however, the Aztecs never invented the wheel.

The Aztecs worshiped many gods. Among the most important of their gods were Huitzilpochtli, the god of war, and Quetzalcoatl ("feathered serpent"), god of the air. Quetzalcoatl was said to have instructed men in agriculture, in the use of metals, and in government. Under this god a golden age had flowered. But having incurred another god's anger, he left Anahuac, going east over the sea to the land of Tlapallan. Quetzalcoatl, who was said to have white skin, dark hair, and a flowing beard, promised his followers that, one day, he would return to Anahuac from the east, over the sea.

With his return, Quetzalcoatl would abolish religious human sacrifice. The Aztecs solemnized every festival with the sacrifice of men they had taken in war. Gathering victims for sacrifice was among the chief purposes of their wars. It is recorded that the Aztecs sacrificed about 20,000 victims each year.

18. The course of events leading to the conquest of Tenochtitlán

Cortés with 400 Spaniards and 6,400 Indian allies was welcomed into Tenochtitlán by Montezuma and shown every hospitality. But mistrusting Montezuma, Cortés had him captured and held prisoner. In the spring of 1520, Cortés left his men in Tenochtitlán under the command of Alvarado and went to Vera Cruz, where he brought Spanish forces under Pánfilo de Narvaez under his command. In Tenochtitlán, however, the Aztecs rose against the Spaniards and Indians under Alvarado after he had attacked Aztec men celebrating a religious festival. Cortés, with reinforcements, entered the city and led his men in a series of assaults on the Aztecs. But he saw the situation was desperate, and on the night of June 30-July, 1520, he withdrew from the city with great losses (the night called *la noche triste*). Finding refuge among the Tlaxcalans, Cortés prepared his return to Tenochtitlán. On December 28, 1520, the Spanish army and its Indian allies began the march to Mexico. Cortés' army took Texcuco on December 31, 1520. From Texcuco, he sent contingents of his troops to subdue the cities surrounding the lake of Mexico. On April 28, 1521, the assault on Tenochtitlán began. As they launched the brigantines, the Spaniards broke forth in a joyous *Te Deum*.

The advance into the city was slow, and to prevent attacks on his men, Cortés reluctantly commanded them to destroy every building they encountered in their advance. When Cortés' army had reached the marketplace, seven-eighths of the city had been laid waste. Though his people suffered from famine and their had been greatly reduced by smallpox, the Aztec king, Guatemozin, refused to surrender. Finally, Cortés ordered a major assault on the Aztec position, and the Spaniards overwhelmed what remained of the Aztec defenders.

19. Cortés' character as governor

Cortés was as much a builder as a conqueror, a governor as well as a general. Using forced Indian labor on the ruins of Tenochtitlán, Cortés raised Mexico City. Cortés urged many Spaniards to settle in Mexico and encouraged them to mingle and intermarry with the Indian population. Cortés extended Spanish power in America.

20. The regions Hernando de Soto explored in North America

De Soto with nine ships and 1,000 men, landed at Espiritu Santo (now Tampa) Bay in May 1539. De Soto explored the western Florida peninsula and subjugated Apalachee (the northwest part of Florida on the Gulf of Mexico). From Florida, he headed north in search of gold and explored what is now eastern and northern Georgia. From Georgia, de Soto turned south, and arrived at what is now Mobile, Alabama. From this region, he led his men northwest. They reached the Mississippi River in what is now northern Mississippi. Crossing the river, they explored into what is now Arkansas and wintered on the Ouachita River. In June 1542, de Soto died, and his men returned to Mexico by way of the Mississippi.

21. The culture of the Pueblo Indians

These peoples are called "Pueblo" (the Spanish word for "town") because they dwelt in compact, permanent settlements, unlike other native peoples of the region, such as the Apache and Comanche, who led a wandering life. Pueblo Indian towns were a congeries of rectangular structures made from adobe brick or limestone blocks. Each pueblo had one or two underground ceremonial chambers, called *kivas*, where religious rites were carried out and men could meet and carry on casual conversation. Pueblo men were hunters; the women farmed, cultivating maize, squash, beans, and cotton, and gathered wild plants. Each pueblo was politically autonomous, ruled by a council of men drawn from each of the pueblo's religious societies. The culture of the Pueblo peoples was diverse, and they spoke a number of different languages. The religion of the Pueblo peoples was a form of spirit worship. They believed that hundreds of *kachinas*, the spirits of ancestors or divinities, act as intermediaries between themselves and God. They deemed their yearly rituals were necessary to prevent the cosmos from breaking down.

22. The purpose of Coronado's expedition and the lands he explored

The viceroy of Mexico sent Coronado into the distant north to discover whether reports about the "Seven Cities of Cibola," filled with gold, were true. The viceroy, too, wanted Coronado to establish a settlement. Coronado discovered that the Seven Cities were settlements of the Pueblo people and possessed no gold. Different portions of the expedition discovered the Colorado River and the Grand Canyon and pushed into northwest Texas and Kansas. Coronado established a settlement in the region he named New Mexico, but he with most of the expedition returned to Mexico in April 1542.

Questions for Review

1. Columbus saw himself as called to carry the Christian Faith the heathens overseas. He was also eager to find gold in the Indies.

Key Terms at a Glance

Enterprise of the Indies: Columbus' belief that one could reach the Indies by sailing west across the Atlantic.

Treaty of Tordesillas: the treaty between Spain and Portugal in which they agreed to a decision by Pope Alexander VI to set a demarcation line in the Atlantic. Everything east of the demarcation line would fall to Portugal, while everything west of the line fell to Spain.

teocalli: the great pyramid temple of the Aztecs.

---

2. **Why was Columbus turned down so often, and what finally convinced Isabel to finance his journey to the Indies?**

The king of Portugal was focused on his own mariners' attempts to reach the Indies by saling around Africa. Fernando and Isabel were occupied with the conquest of Granada and were advised against Columbus' project. Luis de Santangel finally convinced Queen Isabel to finance Columbus' journey.

3. **What prompted the bull, *Inter Caetera*, that led to setting a demarcation line in the Atlantic?**

Portugal was displeased that Spain had reached the Indies before Portugal, and Pope Alexander VI, in order to stop a challenge of Spain's claim to the Indies, set up the demarcation line to appease Portugal.

4. **How did Columbus fail to carry out the king and queen's command to establish a trading colony? Why did he fail?**

Columbus proved to be a poor governor, and while he was away exploring other lands, the Indians in his settlements were mistreated by the Spaniards. This failure was prompted mainly by his desire to find gold.

5. **How did Columbus fall out of royal favor?**

Columbus fell out of the royal favor because of his poor showing as a governor, as well as slanders leveled against him. Ferdinand was disappointed with the poor revenue from the new lands, and Isabel was angry with Columbus' treatment of the Indians.

6. **What was Juan Ponce de León's motivation for exploration in the Indies?**

Juan Ponce de León's motivation for exploration of the Indies was that he had fallen in love and wanted to find on the island of Bimini a fabled fountain that supposedly restored youth.

7. **Who discovered that the new lands were not the Indies, and how did he discover it?**

Vasco Nuñez de Balboa discovered that the new land was not the Indies by discovering a new ocean, thus showing that the Spanish had not reached the Indies.

8. **How was it discovered how far the new lands were from the real Indies?**

Juan Elcano circumnavigated the world, thus demonstrating how far the supposed Indies were from the real Indies.

9. **What prompted Cortés to search for new lands and so discover Mexico?**

Columbus' discoveries, as well as hunger for adventure and riches, prompted Cortés to search for new lands.

10. **What is *la noche triste*. Describe the events it names**

La noche triste is "the night of sorrows", when, during the Spanish conquest of Mexico, Cortés and his men fought their way out of the Mexican capital after the death of Montezuma II. During this retreat, the Spanish lost many men (Indians and Spaniards) as well as the gold they had acquired in Tenochtitlán.

11. **Describe some of the atrocities that Cortés and his men inflicted on the Aztecs, and some of the good that they accomplished in Mexico.**

Cortés and his men slaughtered many natives during their conquest of Mexico and forced the Indians to labor. Cortés rebuilt the capitol of Mexico and encouraged Spaniards to settle in the new land. The Spanish moreover brought an end to human sacrifice and established the Catholic faith in the new lands.

12. **What do the lives of the discoverers and conquistadors tell us about human nature?**

The lives of the discoverers and conquistadors tell us that historical characters are rarely pure heroes or mere villains and how men often act from mixed motives.

Ideas in Action

1. Imagine that you are a member of either Columbus' or Cortés' expeditions, and write about your first impressions of the New World. Or imagine that you are a native Indian or Aztec, and write about your impressions of the Spanish.

Students should write about 2-5 pages from the viewpoint of a Spaniard or an Aztec. Stories should be written creatively and not just be reiterations of the chapter.

2. Read some historical fictional accounts of the discovery of either America or Mexico, and reflect on the complexity of the characters of the discoverers and conquistadors.

Students should consider the character's motivations, actions, and the consequences of those actions, and reflect on how these go together to make a complex character.

3. Read some Spanish poetry written at the time, or listen to the music of the time.

While reading or listening, students should consider how the ideas and actions of the time period are reflected in the poetry or music.

4. Read the bull *Inter Caetera*. (you may find it on the internet). Do you think it permitted the conquest of the native peoples? Why or why not?

You may find the document on the internet.

Sample Quiz I (pages 1-8)

Please answer the following in complete sentences.

1. What was Columbus' "Enterprise of the Indies," and what did he hope to accomplish by it?

2. What were the main goals of Portuguese exploration?

3. Where was Columbus' first settlement in the New World?

4. What were the differences between the first two native peoples Columbus met?

5. Why was the bull *Inter Caetera* written?

6. What was the objective of Columbus' second voyage?

7. What was the character of Columbus' government of the Indies?

8. Why was the new continent called "America"?

Answer Key to Sample Quiz I

Students' answers should approximate the following.

1. The Enterprise of the Indies" was Columbus' conviction that one could reach the Indies by sailing west across the Atlantic. He hoped to carry the Catholic Faith to the heathen oversea and find gold.

2. Portugal hoped to forge an alliance against the Muslims with Prester John. At first, under Dom Henrique, Portugal sent ships southward along the coast of Africa to see what lay around the continent's western cape. After Dom Henrique's death Portugal's interests turned more to a desire to reach India and establish a spice trade with East Asia.

3. Columbus' first settlement, Navidad, on the island of Hispaniola.

4. The Taino were mostly peaceful and hospitable. The Caribs were not peaceful and engaged in cannibalism.

5. Portugal was displeased that Spain had reached the Indies before Portugal, and Pope Alexander VI, in order to stop a challenge of Spain's claim to the Indies and forestall disputes between Spain and Portugal, issued the bull *Inter Caetera*, setting up a demarcation line in the Atlantic.

6. The objective of Columbus' second voyage was the conversion of the natives to the Catholic faith and to establish a trading colony.

7. Columbus was not a very good governor, and abuses arose. He demanded tributes from the Indians and instituted an Indian slave trade.

8. The new continent was named "America" after Amerigo Vespucci who claimed to have discovered America before Columbus.

Sample Quiz II (pages 8-22)

Please answer the following in complete sentences.

1. Why did Juan Ponce de León set sail, and what did he discover?

2. What did Vasco Nuñez de Balboa discover, and what did his discovery show?

3. What did Magellan and Elcano's achieve that proved something new about America?

4. Why did Cortés lead an expedition into Mexico?\

5. How were the natives of Mexico different from those found by Columbus?

6. How was Tenochtitlán conquered?

7. What regions did de Soto explore in North America?

8. What was the culture of the Pueblo Indians like?

9. What was the purpose of Coronado's expedition, and what lands did he discover and explore?

Answers to Sample Quiz II

Students' answers should approximate the following.

1. Juan Ponce de León set sail in search of the fountain of youth. He discovered what is now Florida.
2. Balboa discovered the Pacific Ocean, which showed the Spanish that they had not reached the Indies.
3. Magellan and Elcano circumnavigated the world, thus showing how far America was from the Indies.
4. Cortés led an expedition into Mexico to further explore and exploit the riches of the new region, although he said it was for the conversion of the Indians.
5. The Indians in Mexico had a highly developed civilization and lived in ordered towns with well-cultivated agriculture. The Taino and Caribs, on the other hand, had a more primitive society.
6. Cortés assaulted the city, laying waste to it as he advanced. The Aztec king refused to surrender until Cortés ordered a major assault on the Aztec position, thus overwhelming the Aztec defenders and forcing them to surrender.
7. De Soto explored from the western Florida peninsula up to Georgia, Alabama, Mississippi, and Arkansas.
8. The Pueblo Indians dwelt in compact, permanent settlements. They were hunters and farmers. Each pueblo was ruled by a council of men drawn from the pueblo's religious societies. They had a diverse culture and a form of spirit worship.
9. Coronado set out to discover whether reports of the "Seven Cities of Cibola" were true. He discovered that these Seven Cities were the settlements of the Pueblo people, who possessed no gold. He also discovered the Colorado River, the Grand Canyon, and pushed into Texas and Kansas. He established a settlement in New Mexico.

Essays

Instructions to be given to the students: Write in complete sentences. Underline your thesis. Give three supports or examples that explain why you think what you do and that support your thesis.

1. Write an essay on the complexity of historical characters. How can we know if someone was a hero or a villain? Choose one character from this chapter and show from his actions whether you think he was a hero or a villain, or if neither of those, how and why.

2. What, for the Spaniards, was the main purpose of exploration and settlement of new lands? How did this play out with the natives, of the Americas? Did other other objectives the Spanish had conflict with what they said was the primary purpose of their exploration? How and why?

Sample Test

Please answer the following in complete sentences.

I. Short Essay – Answer two of the following:

1. **What did Columbus hope to achieve through his explorations? How were his motives mixed in what he hoped to achieve?**

2. **How was the goal of Columbus' second voyage like the purpose of his first, and how was it different?**

3. **How did the discoveries of Balboa, Magellan, and Elcano add to Columbus' discovery?**

4. **What was the objective of Cortés' expedition, and how did it play out?**

II. Short Answer:

1. Who were the first Indians Columbus met and where were they from?

2. What was the purpose of the bull *Inter Caetera*?

3. What did *Inter Caetera* do?

4. Give two instances where Columbus angered the Spanish monarchs.

5. Who were the natives that Cortés met, and where did they originally come from?

6. Who was Montezuma II?

Answer Key to the Chapter Test

Students' answers should approximate the following:

I.

1. Columbus thought it his special task to carry the Catholic Faith to the heathen oversea, as well as to find gold in the Indies to enrich both himself and Spain. He hoped the Spanish monarchs would use the gold he would find to finance a new crusade, but he also sought riches for himself. His motives were thus not purely spiritiual.

2. In his second voyage, Columbus' main objective was still to convert the heathen natives to the Catholic faith and to discover gold. This time, however, Columbus was to establish a trading colony with the Indians, and to govern them so that friendly relations could exist between the new world and Spain.

3. Balboa's discovery of the Pacific Ocean showed the Spanish that the new land was not the Indies, but was separated from East Asia by a vast ocean. Magellan and Elcano's circumnavigation of the globe proved that the land that had come to be called "America" was not even on the outskirts of the Indies, but was an entirely new world.

4. Cortés was hungry for adventure and riches, and his expedition was funded for the purpose of further exploring and exploiting the riches of the new region of Mexico. Cortés said that the primary purpose of the expedition was the conversion of the Indians the Faith. While in Mexico, however, Cortés was more eager to conquer than convert the Aztecs. Once the Indians were conquered, he rebuilt the capitol and furthered Spanish power in the new world.

II.

1. The first Indians Columbus met were the Taino, and they were originally from South America.

2. The purpose of the bull *Inter Caetera* was to prevent any disputes between Spain and Portugal regarding the newly discovered lands.

3. *Inter Caetera* set up a demarcation line, dividing the newly disovered lands between Spain and Portugal.

4. Columbus angered the Spanish monarchs (*possible answers*):
   a. by ignoring Spanish abuses and putting the blame for violence on the Indians
   b. commanding every native 14 years and older to pay him a tribute of gold dust
   c. instituting a slave trade.

5. The natives Cortés met were the Aztecs, and they were from a northwest region called Aztlán.

6. Montezuma II was the ruler of the Aztecs at the time of the conquest of Mexico.

CHAPTER 2: The Progress of Spanish America

Chapter Overview

◆ In 1496 Columbus pacified a revolt in Hispaniola by giving rebels free land grants and Indian slaves. This led to many problems concerning slavery and abuse of the Indians in the Spanish New World dominions.

◆ The Spanish government established the Law of Burgos in 1512, which placed regulations on Indian labor in an attempt to reduce the abuse of Indians on *encomiendas*.

◆ In 1513 Spain established the *Requiriemento*, a document requiring Indians to acknowledge Spanish overlordship and permit the Catholic faith to be preached to them.

◆ Cortés departed for Spain, and the Reign of Terror began in Mexico. The *Audiencia Real*, sent to investigate the conquistador's administration of New Spain, imposed heavy taxes on the Indians and persecuted them in many violent ways.The Spanish priest Bartolomé de Las Casas labored hard for the passage of the *Nuevas Leyes* (New Laws) of 1542, forbidding slavery and perpetuation of encomienda. These laws angered colonists and resulted in a bloody civil war in Peru.

◆ King Carlos I revoked the New Laws in 1545. A debate took place in which it was discussed whether Indians are natural slaves or not. This conference of Valladolid resulted in the Basic Law in 1573, which said that Spaniards were not to "conquer" but to "pacify" the Native Americans.

◆ The era of the Spanish missionaries began as an attempt to evangelize and civilize the Indians.

What Students Should Know

1. **The origins and nature of the *encomienda* system**

An *encomienda* was a "complimentary land grant" the Spanish crown gave to individuals in return for the fulfillment of certain conditions. The grantee, called an *encomendero*, was given the right to compel Indians on his *encomienda* to labor, both in the fields and in mines. In return, *encomenderos* were to provide their charges suitable religious instruction and to train them in the ways of European civilization. In Mexico, Cortés permitted Indians to live in their villages under their native chiefs, and he enacted laws regulating the number of hours an Indian should work and how much he must be paid. Columbus initiated *encomiendas*, called *repartimientos* – "partitions." Later, when the Spanish crown regulated the *repartimientos*, they were called *encomiendas*.

The abuses of the *encomienda* were numerous. Being unused to the sort of labor required of them, and having no immunities for European sicknesses, thousands of natives died. *Encomenderos* often did not fulfill the conditions for holding *encomiendas* and treated their Indian charges as slaves.

2. How the Spanish crown viewed the inhabitants of the New World and how it worked to remove abuses against them

The Spanish crown recognized the Indians as equals to the Spanish colonists and so forbade their enslavement. But the crown had made slavery the punishment for rebellion and cannibalism, and unscrupulous Spaniards would simply claim that Indians were rebels and cannibals and so enslave them. In 1512, the crown enacted the Laws of Burgos that placed regulations on Indian labor, required that colonists work to convert the natives, and decreed that no one may insult Indians. The crown's *Requiriemento* of 1513 required that Indians acknowledge Spanish overlordship and permit the Faith to be preached to them. Conquistadors had to read the *requiriemento* when entering an Indian village and subjugate the natives only if they resisted. But this law was frequently abused. In 1542, the crown enacted the *Nuevas Leyes,* "New Laws," which forbade Indian slavery and the perpetuation of the *encomienda* system. But when a bloody civil struggle erupted in Peru after the Spanish governor attempted to enforce the New Laws, King Carlos I revoked some of the New Laws in 1545. In 1573, the Basic Law promulgated by the crown, decreed that Spaniards were not to "conquer," but to "pacify," the Indians. They were never to enslave them or exact tribute from them but to explain to them the benefits of submitting to the Spanish crown. Force could be used if the Indians refused to cooperate, but conquerors were to use as little force as possible. In preaching the Gospel, missionaries, said the law, should deal gently with the Indians' vices "so as not to scandalize them or prejudice them against Christianity." The Basic Law however did not abolish the *encomienda* system.

3. Who Bartolomé de las Casas was and what he accomplished

Bartolomé de las Casas was a Spanish lawyer who came to the New World in 1502, received an *encomienda*, and became a priest, later joining the Dominican order. King Carlos I appointed him bishop of Chiapas in 1544. Las Casas' conscience awakened to the plight of the Indians in the New World. In 1517, he was in Spain to protest the *encomienda* system and was appointed "Protector General of the Indians." Though he initially supported replacing Indian laborers with African slaves, he later repudiated this. As a Dominican, Las Casas spent the next 40 years insisting that Indians, as human beings, had the same rights as Spaniards and the Spanish crown had no right to conquer the Indians by force. He thought the crown could exercise dominion over the Indians but he insisted that it could not abolish Indian tribal governments or enslave natives. He declared the *encomienda* system was little better than slavery and should be abolished. He opposed using force in preaching the Gospel and objected to those missionaries who baptized converts without first giving them sufficient instruction in the Faith.

4. What the "Black Legend" is and how it originated

The Black Legend was an account embraced by Spain's enemies that Spanish conquest and rule of the Americas was peculiarly cruel. Its source was Bartolomé de las Casas' work, *A Short Account of the Destruction of the Indies*, that contained gross exaggerations of Spanish cruelty.

5. Who Juan de Zumárraga was and what he accomplished

Juan de Zumárraga was the first bishop of Mexico and the Protector of the Indians. When he first came to Mexico, he had to contend with New Spain's first *Audiencia Real,* the Royal Audience, that served as a court of appeals. Zumárraga was able to inform the crown of the cruelties perpetrated by the *audiencia,* and the king sent a new audience to Mexico.

6. **What effect the apparition of Our Lady of Guadalupe had on Indian conversions**

The apparition of the Virgin in 1521 brought on an amazing increase in native baptisms. The Spanish government had not been remiss in trying to convert the Indians of Mexico, but because of the brutality of the Spaniards, many Indians had remained aloof from the Church.

7. **What the *patronato real* was and what powers it granted to the Spanish crown**

The *patronato real,* the "royal patronage," was the right the Spanish king had to select all bishops and abbots in the Spanish domains and to publish papal decrees in the New World. Pope Julius II granted it to the Spanish kings in 1508. In return, the king was responsible for funding all missionary endeavors and for founding churches and monasteries.

8. **The purpose and the methods of the Spanish missionary endeavor**

The Spanish missionary endeavor was twofold – to evangelize and civilize. In accomplishing the first, the missionaries worked to adapt Church teaching to the native mind. They learned native tongues and used drama. They erected churches on the sites of pagan temples that had ordered destroyed. They could be ruthless in stamping out paganism (and along with it, much of native culture) but preserved much of what was good in the Indians' culture and attempted to find in it a new Christian meaning. Some missionaries saw the conversion of the Indians as an opportunity to renew Christian civilization and thus not only toiled to save souls but labored to found a new Christendom.

9. **Spanish efforts with education in the New World**

New Spain's missionaries sought to Christianize and civilize native cultures by founding institutions of learning. In New Spain, every church and convent had its school where the children of the rich and poor learned writing, music, and Latin, as well as practical arts, such as tailoring, carpentry, and painting. At the college of Santa Cruz in Mexico City (founded 1536), students studied native American languages. Bishop Zumárraga founded eight schools for girls in Mexico. A school opened in Mexico City for about 1,000 children offered study in religion, music, singing, and Latin. Mexico City offered a school for fine arts and practical trades as well as a college for higher studies. The Spaniards established the first universities in the New World, the oldest being the University of St. Thomas Aquinas in Santo Domingo, founded by the Dominicans in 1538.

10. **What the Reductions of Paraguay were and how they ended**

In the early 17th century, the Jesuits sought and obtained permission to separate the mission field of Paraguay from the Spanish colony of Peru. In Paraguay they established Indian republics, or "reductions," which they kept isolated from the influences of the Spanish colonists. In this way, the Jesuits hoped to preserve Indians from the influence of lax Christians and protect them from injustice and slavery. The Indians on a reduction held and farmed their lands in common, though each family had its own house and garden. Indian leaders, elected by their communities, helped the Jesuits govern the villages. To protect the villagers from raids carried out by other Indians and by Portuguese slavers from Brazil, the Jesuits oversaw the military training of the village men. The Reductions became quite prosperous between 1650 and 1720 and presented such a unique and humane way of colonization that they even earned the praise of some of the Church's enemies in Europe. The Reductions came to an end after Spain signed a treaty with Portugal January 1750 that granted Portugal seven districts of Paraguay. Once in control of Paraguay, the Portuguese ordered the 30,000 or so Indians on the Reductions to abandon their lands. In 1759, Portugal expelled the Jesuits from its colonies.

11. Who the first martyr was in what was to become the United States of America

The first martyr in what was to become the U.S. was the Franciscan missionary, Fray Juan Padilla, who was martyred by members of the Aciales tribe near what is now Dodge City, Kansas, on November 30, 1542.

12. The establishment and progress of New Mexico

Juan de Oñate led 200 soldiers and colonists, a contingent of Christian Indians from Mexico, seven thousand head of livestock, and eight Franciscan friars, to settle New Mexico. On Ascension Thursday, April 30, 1598, he took possession of the land in the name of the king of Spain and then established a settlement at the confluence of

the Río Grande and Chama rivers. By the end of 1598, the friars who had accompanied Oñate had established three missions for the Pueblo Indians of the region. In 1598, the Spanish put down a revolt by the Indians of Ácoma, the last major rebellion in New Mexico for about 80 years. Still, the new settlement was not prosperous and settlers were discontent. In 1608, King Felipe III decided to withdraw the settlers; but, hearing reports of the great number of converts among the Indians in New Mexico and the growth of the missions, he relented. Instead, he made New Mexico a royal province. In time the province flourished. Its chief city, Santa Fé (Holy Faith), was founded in 1610.

13. Why the Spanish crown established settlements in Florida

Learning that French Huguenots had settled on the eastern coast of Florida, Spain's King Felipe II in 1565 sent Menéndez de Avilés to establish a settlement in Florida and to drive out the Huguenots. Menéndez founded a settlement on the small bay he had discovered, naming it San Agustín. Menéndez defeated the French forces and captured their settlement, Fort Caroline.

14. The establishment, struggles, and expansion of the Florida missions

By the 1590s, Franciscans had set up missions in Florida, and northward into the region of the Guale people, in what is now southern Georgia. Missionary work in the region was not easy, for the Indians had to learn a whole new culture and morality, including monogamy. Indian men had multiple wives and so found the Christian teaching on marriage difficult to embrace. Still, the Franciscans made progress in this and other areas, and many Indians became Christian. Restrictions against polygamy inspired a rebellion by the Christian cacique, Juanillo, that destroyed the Guale missions. The rebellion ended after Juanillo was killed. The Guale missions were subsequently reestablished and Franciscans established new missions among the Timucuan Indians in Florida's interior. In the 1630s, Franciscans established missions among the Apalachee Indians in western Florida, baptizing nearly half the population by 1639.

Disputes between the Franciscans and the governor of Florida over who had jurisdiction over the missions and their Indians stirred up discontent. The governor's policy of forced labor on the Indians, coupled with a drastic decrease in Indian population on account of disease, inspired rebellions among the Apalachee and Timucuan peoples in 1647 and 1656. The rebellions were quelled, the offending governor punished by the crown, and the years following the rebellion saw a period of expansion in the missions.

Questions for Review

1. **What situation in the New World brought about the establishment of the *repartimientos* and the *encomiendas*?**

   Columbus returned to Hispaniola to find the Spanish colonists in revolt, and instead of crushing the rebellion, he pacified the rebels by giving them free land grants, called *repartimientos*, and Indian slaves.

2. **What abuses arose from the establishment of the *encomiendas*, and why did so many of the Indians on the *encomiendas* die?**

   While the Indians were not slaves, the colonists often forced them to work in the fields and labor in the mines. Being unused to such labor, and having no immunities for European sicknesses, thousands of natives died.

3. **What role did Cortés play in the establishment of *encomiendas*?**

Key Terms at a Glance

repartimientos: land grants and Indian slaves given to the rebels in Hispaniola

encomiendas: complimentary land grants given to Spanish colonists in which the Indians were not slaves but were forced to labor for the colonists, who were required to civilize and evangelize them

Laws of Burgos: a law passed in 1512 that put regulations on Indian labor and required the Spaniards to convert the Indians

Requiriemento: a document written in 1513, requiring Indians to acknowledge Spanish overlordship and permit the Catholic faith to be preached to them

Audiencia Real: the Royal Audience of Spain, which served as an appeals court

secular priest: a diocesan priest; a priest that does not belong to a religiouis order.

Reductions: Indian republics founded by the Jesuits in Paraguay to isolate new Indian converts from Spanish settlers, many of whom were lax Christians, and to prevent injustice and slavery

As governor of New Spain, Cortés established *encomiendas* which he sought to regulate justly.

4. **What were the benefits of the Laws of Burgos?**

The Laws of Burgos placed regulations on Indian labor, required that colonists work to convert the natives, forbade whipping and beating the Indians, and forbade calling them names.

5. **What were supposed to be the benefits of the *Requiriemento*, but what abuses did it lead to?**

The *Requiriemento* required the Indians to acknowledge Spanish overlordship and permit the Faith to be preached to them. The The conquistadors had to read the *requiriemento* when entering an Indian village; only if the Indians resisted the *requiriemento's* demands could conquistators subjugate them by force and enslave them as rebels.

But since unscrupulous conquistadors recited the *requiriemento* in Spanish (which the Indians did not understand), and often out of earshot of the Indians, the conquistadors often used it as an excuse to inflict violence on them.

6. **Why did the establishment of the New Laws result in civil war in Peru? Why were the New Laws revoked?**

The New Laws forbade Indian slavery and the perpetuation of the *encomienda* system. This enraged the colonists, and the Spanish crown revoked the laws.

7. **Explain the controversy that climaxed in the Conference of Valladolid. Who were the two main opponents involved?**

Bartolomé de las Casas engaged in a controversy with the Spanish jurist Juan Ginés de Sepulveda. Sepulveda had never visited America; still, he had written a treatise that argued that Indians were "natural slaves" and as such could be conquered and reduced to servitude. Las Casas disagreed. Their controversy climaxed in a famous debate --- at a conference held at Valladolid in 1550.

8. **Why were the missionaries so avid in their preaching and evangelizing?**

The missionaries saw themselves as conquerors of the souls of men, submitting them to the rule of Christ.

9. **Name two ways in which the missionaries evangelized and civilized the Indians.**

The missionaries worked to adapt Church teaching to the native mind. They learned native tongues and used drama to convey the message of Christ. They also preserved much of what was good in the Indians' culture and attempted to find in a new Christian meaning.

10. **What events led to the revival and expansion of the missions in Florida?**

After a rebellion in Florida, the Spanish royal government investigated Governor Diego de Rebolledo's administration of Florida. Uncovering a number of abuses, the crown removed Rebolledo as governor and brought him to Spain to stand trial. The years following these events saw a period of revival and expansion in the missions.

Ideas in Action

1. **Research the lives of the early Spanish-American saints and martyrs.**

Students should choose or be assigned one early saint or martyr and research his or her life. A short presentation on the saint or martyr can be given in class or special event.

2. **Choose a mission church of colonial Mexico and research its founding and mission.**

Students should choose or be assigned one mission church and research it. A short presentation can be given on the chosen mission in class or special event.

3. **Look up the art and music of the Spanish missions. Listen to composers such as Ignacio de Jerusalem y Stella and Manuel de Zumaya. Look up the works of artists such as Sebastían López de Arteaga and Fray Alonso López de Herrera.**

Sample Quiz I (pages 25-31)

Please answer the following in complete sentences.

1. Explain what the *encomienda* system was.
2. How did the Spanish crown view the inhabitants of the New World?
3. How did this view affect the Indians?
4. Who was Bartolomé de las Casas?
5. What was the "Black Legend"?
6. What is the apparition of Our Lady of Guadalupe?
7. What was the *patronato real?*
8. What was the purpose of the Spanish missionary endeavor?
9. Name some of the methods used by the Spanish missionaries in their evangelization of the New World.
10. What were the Reductions of Paraguay?

Answers to Sample Quiz II

Students' answers should approximate the following.

1. An *encomienda* was a "complimentary land grant" the Spanish crown gave to individuals in return for the fulfillment of certain conditions. The grantee, called an *encomendero*, was given the right to compel Indians on his *encomienda* to labor, both in the fields and in mines. In return, *encomenderos* were to provide their charges suitable religious instruction and to train them in the ways of European civilization.
2. The Spanish crown recognized the Indians as equals to the Spanish colonists.
3. Because the Spanish crown recognized the Indians as equals to the Spanish colonists, it forbade their enslavement and atempted to make sure they were not treated unjustly.

4. Bartolomé de las Casas was a Spanish lawyer who worked to protect the Indians in the New World from the abuses of the *encomienda* system.
5. The Black Legend was an account embraced by Spain's enemies that Spanish conquest and rule of the Americas was peculiarly cruel. Its source was Bartolomé de las Casas' work, *A Short Account of the Destruction of the Indies*, that contained gross exaggerations of Spanish cruelty.
6. The apparition of Our Lady of Guadalupe was the appearance of Our Lady in 1521 to an Indian, Juan Diego. Our Lady asked Juan Diego to request the Bishop to build a church on Tepeyac hill – the site where an Aztec temple to the goddess Tonantzin had once stood.

7. The *patronato real*, the "royal patronage," was the right the Spanish king had to select all bishops and abbots in the Spanish domains and to publish papal decrees in the New World. In return, he had to finance and promote evangelization in the New World.
8. The Spanish missionary endeavor was twofold – to evangelize and civilize.
9. The Spanish missionaries learned native tongues, used drama, and preserved much of what was good in the Indians' culture and attempted to find in it a new Christian meaning.
10. In the early 17th century, the Jesuits sought and obtained permission to separate the mission field of Paraguay from the Spanish colony of Peru. In Paraguay they established Indian republics, or "reductions," which they kept isolated from the influences of the Spanish colonists.

Sample Quiz II (pages 31-35)

Please answer the following in complete sentences.

1. Who was the first martyr in what was to become the United States?
2. What was the first Spanish settlement in Florida?
3. Why was missionary work in Florida so difficult?
4. Identify Pedro Menéndez de Avilés
5. What inspired a rebellion of the Indians in Florida?

Answers to Sample Quiz II

Students' answers should approximate the following.
1. The first martyr in what was to become the U.S. was the Franciscan missionary, Fray Juan Padilla.
2. The first Spanish settlement in Florida was San Agustín in a small bay of the same name.
3. Missionary work in Florida was so difficult because the Indians had to learn a whole new culture and morality.
4. Spanish explorer whom King Felipe II sent to settle Florida and drive out the Huguenots there.
5. Restrictions against polygamy inspired a rebellion of the Indians in Florida.

Essays

Instructions to be given to the students: Write in complete sentences. Underline your thesis. Give three supports or examples that explain why you think what you do and that support your thesis.

1. Write an essay on the affects of Spanish rule in the New World. In what ways did it help the Indians, and in what ways did it not? Use specific examples.
2. Compare and contrast the Spanish missionaries and the conquistadors.

Sample Test

Please answer the following in complete sentences.

I. Short Essay – Answer two of the following:
1. How did the *encomienda* system affect the Indians?
2. How according to Bartolomé de las Casas should the Indians have been treated?
3. What was the purpose of the Spanish missionary endeavor, and what methods did it use?

4. What difficulties did the Spanish missionaries come across in Florida, and why?

II. Short Answer:

1. Identify the following:
   a. *encomienda*
   b. *Requiriemento*
   c. New Laws
   d. *patronato real*

2. What did Juan de Zumárraga do to help the Indians?

3. What was the result of the apparition of Our Lady of Guadalupe?

4. What was the first university established in the New World?

5. What was the purpose of the Reductions of Paraguay?

6. Why did the Spanish establish settlements in Florida?

Answers to Chapter Test

Students' answers should approximate the following:

I.

1. The *encomienda* system gave the land owner, or *encomendero*, the right to compel Indians on his *encomienda* to labor both in the fields and mines in return for suitable religious instruction and training in the ways of European civilization. The system, however, brought about many abuses, and the *encomenderos* often enslaved the Indians and forced them to labor in conditions that they were unused to. This, along with lack of immunity to European diseases, caused the natives to die by the thousands.

2. Bartolomé de las Casas insisted that Indians, as human beings, had the same rights as Spaniards and the Spanish crown had no right to conquer the Indians by force. He thought the crown could exercise dominion over the Indians, but he insisted that it could not abolish Indian tribal governments or enslave natives. He thought the *encomienda* system was little better than slavery and should be abolished. He opposed using force in preaching the Gospel and objected to those missionaries who baptized converts without first giving them sufficient instruction in the Faith.

3. The Spanish missionary endeavor was twofold – to evangelize and civilize. In accomplishing the first, the missionaries worked to adapt Church teaching to the native mind. They learned native tongues used drama. They erected churches on the sites of pagan temples, which they had ordered destroyed. They could be ruthless in stamping out paganism (and along with it, much of native culture) but preserved much of what was good in the Indians' culture and attempted to find in it a new Christian meaning. Some missionaries saw the conversion of the Indians as an opportunity to renew Christian civilization and thus not only toiled to save souls but labored to found a new Christendom.

4. The Spanish missionaries found work in the region of Florida difficult because the Indians had to learn a whole new culture and morality, including monogamy. Indian men had multiple wives and so found the Christian teaching on marriage difficult to embrace. Restrictions against polygamy even inspired a rebellion that destroyed the Guale missions.

II.

1.

   a. a complimentary land grant the Spanish crown gave to individuals in return for the fulfillment of certain conditions.

b. a law that required that Indians acknowledge Spanish overlordship and permit the Faith to be preached to them.

c. laws which forbade Indian slavery and the perpetuation of the *encomienda* system.

d. the right the Spanish king had to select all bishops and abbots in the Spanish domains and to publish papal decrees in the New World. In return, the king had to sponsor all missionary work in the New World.

2. Juan de Zumárraga informed the Spanish crown of the cruelties perpetrated by the Royal Audience in New Spain.

3. The apparition of Our Lady of Guadalupe brought on an amazing increase in native baptisms.

4. The first university established in the New World was the University of St. Thomas Aquinas in Santo Domingo.

5. The purpose of the reductions was to preserve the Indians from the influence of lax Christians and protect them from injustice and slavery.

6. Spain's King Felipe II learned that French Hugeunots had settled on the eastern coast of Florida, so he sent men to establish a settlement in Florida and drive out the Huguenots.

CHAPTER 3: France Settles the New World

Chapter Overview

◆ François decided that, since Spain had not yet discovered a westward sea route to the true Indies, the rumored "Straits of Anian," he would send Giovanni da Verrazzano, one of his privateers, to find it. Verrazzano chose a northern route to avoid Spanish lands.

◆ Verrazzano first landed on the coast of what is now North Carolina and then went on to what is now New York harbor, Narragansett Bay, and then along the coast of Maine to Newfoundland. He failed to discover the Straits of Anian.

◆ Ten years later François sent out the pirate Jacques Cartier to find the Straits of Anian. Cartier landed on Prince Edward Island. He also discovered the St. Lawrence River and the place that would become Montreal. He gave the name "Canada" to the lands he had discovered along the St. Lawrence.

◆ In 1608, the royal geographer, Samuel de Champlain, established the first settlement at Québec, which became a center for fur trading. This brought not settlers but mostly fur traders, to New France.

◆ The Canadian Indians were found to be farmers and showed their highest achievement in government.

◆ The first missionaries to New France were Jesuits, sent by the Duchesse d'Aiguillon in 1611. Jesuits and Franciscan Recollects founded and staffed missions throughout New France and, later, Louisiana. Among the Jesuit missionaries were Jean de Brébeuf, Issac Jogues, and others whom we remember as the Norh American martyrs.

◆ King Louis XIV, desirous of having France as the greatest power in Europe, needed a great amount of money, so he sent Louis Jolliet and Jacques Marquette to find a route from New France to the silver mines of Mexico. The two explorers discovered the "Great Water" – the Mississippi.

◆ Lord de La Salle planned to protect the trade of New France from the inroads of the English and the Dutch by building a string of forts and missions along the waterways of New France. On his expedition down the Illinois

What Students Should Know

1. **Why France pursued colonization in the New World**

   France's king, François I, feared the power of Carlos I, king of Spain and Holy Roman Emperor, and did what he could to weaken his power. In particular, he thought that, since Spain had not yet discovered a westward sea route to the true Indies, France would send an explorer to find it. Because Spain had not yet discovered a westward sea route to the Indies, François I wanted a French explorer to find it.

2. **What Verrazzano discovered on his voyage**

   Verrazano landed on the coast of what is now North Carolina and was the first European to enter what would one day be called New

York harbor. Still heading northward, he sailed into Narragansett Bay, and then along the coast of Maine, to Newfoundland.

3. What Cartier discovered and the significance of his voyages for France

Cartier landed at Prince Edward Island and from there sailed into Chaleur Bay. On his second voyage, Cartier discovered the St. Lawrence River. He sailed up the St. Lawrence beyond the site of what would become Montreal. Cartier gave the name "Canada" (from the native word *kanata*, which means village or settlement) to the lands he explored along the St. Lawrence. In Chaleur Bay, Cartier discovered what would one day become the source of France's new world wealth – furs.

4. The significance of Champlain's career in Canada

In July 1608, Samuel de Champlain established a dwelling and storehouse at Québec, and it became a center for fur trading and the nucleus around which a village and fortress grew up. Champlain was able to attract about 400 French farmers to Québec. From Québec, Champlain explored the rivers that flow into the St. Lawrence. On one expedition he discovered the large lake, today called Champlain, that today straddles the border of New York and Vermont. In 1609, on the shores of Lake Champlain, near Ticonderoga, Champlain joined the Huron and Algonquin in a battle against the Iroquois nation. Defeated by this combination of Indians and French, the Iroquois became the implacable enemies of New France. In other explorations, Champlain continued down the St. Lawrence. In 1615, Champlain, with a small band of French soldiers, crossed Lake Ontario. A devout Catholic, Champlain, in 1614, brought four Franciscan Recollect

missionaries to Québec.

5. Who settled New France

Champlain found it difficult to convince anyone to settle as farmers in New France. Besides a few missionaries, the French in Canada were content to be fur traders: licensed traders, called *voyageurs*, and unlicensed traders, called *coureurs de bois*. Both sorts of traders became adept at woodcraft. Often they married Indian women and lived more like Indians than Frenchmen. Though some traders were unscrupulous, selling brandy to the natives and corrupting their morals by bad example, others, for their fairness and kindness, earned the Indians' trust.

6. The native cultures of Canada

The natives of Canada survived by fishing and hunting and wandered far afield in search of game, but they also practiced agriculture. In extensive fields surrounding their villages, Indian women (the men were the hunters and warriors) farmed maize, beans, squash, and tobacco. Their villages, congeries of "longhouses" formed from saplings and covered with elm bark, were more or less fixed in a location and, during war, were protected by wooden palisades. Two major tribal groupings inhabited Canada: the Iroquois and the Huron.

7. The character of Iroquois society

The Iroquois were originally a league of five Indian nations: the Mohawk, Oneida, Onondaga, Cayuga, and Seneca. In 1715 the Tuscarora of North Carolina, who had moved north to New York, joined the Iroquois, forming what was thenceforth known as the League of Six Nations. The league was formed, according to legend, sometime in the late 16th century. The individual tribes federated under a council of leaders and by the practice of common ceremonies. The member tribes of the Iroquois League sent delegates, chosen by the clans within each tribe, to the common council. No important decisions were reached unless every delegate agreed to the proper course of action. Every tribe of the nation had its own chiefs' council, made up of the leaders of the tribe. A woman's council, formed from the mothers of the tribe, had a say in all important matters affecting the tribe, including who sat on the chiefs' council.

Unlike other eastern tribes, the Iroquois were monogamous, though divorce was common among them. The Iroquois religion was polytheistic. They believed in two gods, one of winter and the other of spring, who were in continual conflict.

The Iroquois waged ruthless, bitter warfare on surrounding tribes. Some they enslaved, but others they admitted to the tribe to replace family members who had died. The Iroquois were skilled strategists, displaying a considerable talent for organization; when they attained guns in the mid-sixteenth century, they became nearly invincible. By 1656 they had swept over the Huron, Tionontati, the Neutrals, and the Erie. In the 18th century, the Iroquois conquered the Lenape nation and the Illini and harassed the English colony of Virginia.

The Iroquois were implacable enemies of the French, who were allied with the Huron and Algonquin. The Iroquois later allied themselves with the English and the Dutch.

8.   The character of Huron society

The Huron (also called the Wyandot), who lived north of the St. Lawrence, were of the same stock as the Iroquois and shared most of their culture. Like the Iroquois, the Huron lived in longhouses, gathered in palisaded settlements. Hunting and fishing supplemented the Huron diet, which came chiefly from farming, in which both men and women engaged. The Huron, however, lacked the Iroquois' genius for political organization. Still, like the Iroquois, the Huron governed by a council or assembly, which made all-important decisions. Women selected the leaders of the tribe. The chiefs' role was to announce the council's decisions to the clans, though no chief had the power to enforce compliance. There was no police force or threat of punishment for anyone who refused to go along with the council; a chief had to rely on his eloquence to sway his warriors. The Huron believed that the world is filled with good and evil spirits whose favor they sought to curry by sacrifice. The French missionaries said the Huron seemed to have some concept of a supreme being, though they offered him no worship. The Iroquois eventually crushed the Huron, with their kin, the Algonquin, and their villages were scattered.

9.   Who the North American martyrs were

The North American martyrs were the Jesuit priests Jean de Brébeuf, Isaac Jogues, Antoine Daniel, Jean Lalende, and Gabriel Lalement. All these were martyred by the Iroquois.

10.   How French colonization spread in North America

French colonization in North America spread through the efforts of fur traders and missionaries. Traders and missionaries often accompanied each other into the wild.

11.   The character of the government and society of New France

Key Terms at a Glance

Straits of Anian: the rumored western sea route to the Indies
fur trade: an industry dealing in the acquisition and sale of animal fr
voyageur: French name for licensed fur traders
coureurs de bois: French name for unlicensed fur traders
Iroquois or League of Six Nations: the alliance of the Mohawk, Oneida, Onondaga, Cayuga, Seneca, and Tuscarora tribes
North American Martyrs: eight men killed for the Faith during the the warfare between the Iroquois and the Huron in Canada

A governor general, appointed by the king, oversaw the French settlements of Acadia, Montreal, and Trois Rívìeres, each of which had its own local governor. Under the governor-general were an *intendant*, who looked after the colony's finances, and an administrator of justice. In 1659 the king appointed a bishop for Québec, who, together with the governor-general and the *intendant*, administered the colony. The three were aided by a council like the Spanish *audiencia*.

The settlement of New France followed an almost feudal pattern. As in Europe, the farmers, called *habitants*, were organized under a local lord, called the *seigneur*. French *habitant* settlements differed from those of the English further south, in that English colonists dwelt on isolated farmsteads, while the *habitants* gathered in villages from which they went out to work their fields. The *habitants* paid rent to the *seigneur* for their land and gave him six days of free labor a year.

12. How Louisiana was established

King Louis XIV of France needed funds to finance his desired expansion of French power and territory, and his finance minister, Jean-Baptiste Colbert, sought a route that would connect New France with the silver mines in Mexico, via the Pacific. The *intendant* of New France commissioned the fur trader, Louis Jolliet, to discover this route, who was joined by Jacques Marquette a Jesuit priest seeking new mission territory. This expedition, which began in 1673, left the Great Lakes region and traveled west via the Wisconsin River, which flowed into the Mississippi. It followed the Mississippi to a point just south of the Arkansas River, and then turned back. Thus, the French discovered and explored the northern reaches of the Mississippi River, the major artery of what would become Louisiana.

In 1677, King Louis XIV approved a plan to build a string of forts and missions along the waterways of New France, including the Mississippi. To accomplish this, he granted René Robert-Cavelier, Lord de La Salle, the right to explore the Mississippi to its mouth, to govern all the territory he should discover, and to own the Mississippi fur trade. La Salle's expedition got underway in 1681. By April 1682, the expedition had reached the Mississippi Delta, and at a spot where the great river made a wide turn, La Salle planned a city that would become the Paris of the New World. Reaching the mouth of the river, La Salle claimed the river and all the land on its banks, and along the banks of its tributary rivers, for King Louis of France, calling these lands "Louisiana" in honor of Louis XIV. La Salle began erecting forts in the new territory.

By 1712, settlements dotted the lower Mississippi Valley. Missionaries, Jesuits and Franciscan Capuchins, began working among the Indians. In 1717, New Orleans, which would become the most important center for trade and French culture in the New World, was established.

Questions for Review

1. What was François I's motivation for finding the Straits of Anian?

François I wanted to find a route to the Indies, and the Straits of Anian seemed the natural direction to go. It would, he hoped, avoid the Spanish-controlled regions of the newly discovered lands.

2. What events induced France to colonize North America?

Jacques Cartier's discovery of furs in North America and the luctrativeness of the fur trade encouraged France to colonize the New World.

3. What event caused the Iroquois tribe to become the implacable enemies of New France?

The Iroquois became implacable enemies of the French because of their alliance with the Huron and Algonquin.

4. In what ways did the Indians of Canada differ from those of Mexico and Peru?

The Indians of Canada lived in dwellings of wood and bark, and they were a simpler, more primitive people than the Indians of Mexico and Peru.

5. In what did the Canadian Indians excel?

Unlike the Indians of Mexico and Peru, who built great cities and had an advanced civilization, the natives of Canada survived by fishing and hunting and wandered far afield in search of game, but also practiced agriculture. But though they did not have the advanced civilization of Mexico and Peru, Canadian Indians excelled in the art of government.

6. What is the League of Five Nations, or the Iroquois?

The League of Five Nations, or the Iroquois, was an alliance of five Indian nations: the Mohawk, Oneida,Onondaga, Cayuga, and Seneca.

7. How did the Iroquois become the League of Six Nations?

The Tuscarora of North Carolina, who had moved north to New York, joined the Iroquois, forming what was thenceforth known as the League of Six Nations.

8. Describe the government of the League of Six Nations and how it was formed.

The member tribes of the Iroquois League sent delegates, chosen by the clans within each tribe, to the common council. No important decisions were reached unless every delegate agreed to the proper course of action. Every tribe of the nation had its own chiefs' council, made up of the leaders of the tribe. A woman's council, formed from the mothers of the tribe, had a say in all important matters affecting the tribe, including who sat on the chiefs' council.

9. Describe the government of the French settlement in Canada.

A governor general oversaw the French settlements of Acadia, Montreal, and Trois Rívìeres, each of which had its own local governor. Under the governor-general were an *intendant*, a bishop, and an administrator of justice. The three were aided by a council that acted like the Spanish *audiencia*. The settlement of New France followed an almost feudal pattern.

10. **Why did Jolliet and Marquette set out to find a route along the "Great Water" to Mexico?**

King Louis XIV wanted France to be the greatest power in Europe, for which he needed huge expenditures of money. He sent Jolliet and Marquette to find a route from New France to the silver mines of Mexico.

Ideas in Action

1. Look at a map of the Mississippi River and chart Jolliet and Marquette's route of exploration.

2. Read the lives of the early North American saints and martyrs, including St. Isaac Jogues and St. Kateri Tekakwitha.

3. Read some of the folktales of the American Indians of Canada and the Mississippi River regions.

Sample Quiz I (pages 39-44)

Please answer the following in complete sentences.

1. **What part did Spain play in France's pursuit of colonization in the New World?**

2. **Describe the route Verrazzano took in his explorations.**

3. **What was Jacques Cartier's biggest discovery?**

4. **What was to become France's New World wealth?**

5. **What made the Iroquois the implacable enemies of New France?**

6. **Which Indian nations were part of the League of Five Nations?**

7. **In what ways were the Huron like the Iroquois?**

8. **In what way did the Huron differ from the Iroquois?**

Answer Key to Sample Quiz I

Students' answers should approximate the following.

1. France's king, François I, feared the power of Carlos I, king of Spain and Holy Roman Emperor, and did what he could to weaken his power. In particular, he thought that, since Spain had not yet discovered a westward sea route to the true Indies, France would send an explorer to find it.

2. Verrazzano landed on what is now North Carolina in New York harbor. From there he sailed into Narragansett Bay, and then along the coast of Maine, to Newfoundland.

3. Jacques Cartier's biggest discovery was the lands which he named "Canada."

4. Furs would become France's New World wealth.

5. The Iroquois became the implacable enemies of New France when the French and other Indians defeated them in a battle on Lake Champlain.

6. The Indian nations that were part of the League of Five Nations were the Mohawk, Oneida, Onodaga, Cayuga, and Seneca.

7. The Huron were like the Iroquois in that they were of the same stock and shared much of the same culture. The Huron, like the Iroquois, lived in longhouses, gathered in palisaded settlements.

8. The Huron were different from the Iroquois in that they lacked the Iroquois' genius for political organization.

Sample Quiz II (pages 44-50)

Please answer the following in complete sentences.

1. Who of the following was *not* a North American martyr?
   a. Jean de Brébeauf
   b. Isaac Jogues
   c. Jacques Aubert
   d. Antoine Daniel
   e. Gabriel Lalement
   f. Jean Lalende

2. How did French colonization spread in North America?

3. Identify the following:
   a. *intendant*
   b. *habitant*
   c. *seigneur*

4. Who were Louis Jolliet and Jacques Marquette?

5. For whom was Louisiana named?

Answer Key to Sample Quiz I

Students' answers should approximate the following.

1. (c.) Jacques Aubert was not a North American martyr.

2. French colonization spread in North American through the efforts of fur traders and missionaries.

3.
   a. A government official who looked after a colony's finances
   b. French name for a farmer in the feudal system
   c. French name for a local lord in the feudal system

4. Louis Jolliet and Jacques Marquette were a fur trader and a Jesuit priest who were commissioned to discover a route to Mexico. They discovered the northern reaches of the Mississippi river and what would become Louisiana instead of a route to Mexico.

5. The new land of Louisiana was named for King Louis XIV of France.

Essays

Instructions to be given to the students: Write in complete sentences. Underline your thesis. Give three supports or examples that explain why you think what you do and that support your thesis.

1. Compare and contrast the cultures of the Iroquois and the Huron.

2. Choose one of the characters in this story, excluding the saints. In your opinion, is he a hero or a villain? Support your theory with specific examples.

Sample Test

Please answer the following in complete sentences.

I. Short Essay – Answer two of the following:

1. What was the significance of Champlain's career in Canada?

2. Describe the native cultures of Canada.

3. Describe the character of the government of New France.

4. Describe the society of New France.

II. Short Answer:

1. What prompted France to pursue colonization of the New World?

2. What does the name "Canada" mean?

3. What sort of people mostly settled in Canada at the beginning of French colonization?

4. What was the League of Five Nations?

5. What made the League of Five Nations become the League of Six Nations?

6. How did French colonization spread in North America?

Answer Key to the Chapter Test

Students' answers should approximate the following:

I.

1. Champlain established a dwelling and storehouse at Québec, and it became a center for fur trading and the nucleus around which a village and fortress grew up. Champlain was able to attract about 400 French farmers to Québec. He explored the rivers that flow into the St. Lawrence, and discovered the large lake which today is called Lake Champlain.

2. The natives of Canada survived by fishing and hunting and wandered far afield in search of game, but they also practiced agriculture. In extensive fields surrounding their villages, Indian women (the men were the hunters and warriors) farmed maize, beans, squash, and tobacco. Their villages, congeries of "longhouses" formed from saplings and covered with elm bark, were more or less fixed in a location and, during war, were protected by wooden palisades. Two major tribal groupings inhabited Canada: the Iroquois and the Huron.

3. A governor general, appointed by the king, oversaw the French settlements of Acadia, Montreal, and Trois Rívìeres, each of which had its own local governor. Under the governor-general were an *intendant*, who looked after the colony's finances, and an administrator of justice. In 1659 the king appointed a bishop for Québec, who, together with the governor-general and the *intendant*, administered the colony. The three were aided by a council that acted like the Spanish *audiencia*.

4. The settlement of New France followed an almost feudal pattern. As in Europe, the farmers, called *habitants*, were organized under a local lord, called the *seigneur*. French *habitant* settlements differed from those of the English further south, in that English colonists dwelt on isolated farmsteads, while the *habitants* gathered in villages from which they went out to work their fields. The *habitants* paid rent to the *seigneur* for their land and gave him six days of free labor a year.

II.

1. That Spain had not yet discovered a westward sea route to the Indies prompted France to pursue colonization of the New World.

2. The name "Canada" means village or settlement, from the native word *kanata*.

3. In the beginning, fur traders mostly settled in Canada.

4. The League of Five Nations was a league of five Indian nations: the Mohawk, Oneida, Onondaga, Cayuga, and Seneca.

5. The League of Five Nations became the League of Six Nations when the Tuscarora of North Carolina joined the league.

6. French colonization in North America spread through the efforts of fur traders and missionaries.

CHAPTER 4: England Comes to America

Chapter Overview

* Like Spain, England tried to find a route to the Indies but did not succeed. When news came of Columbus' discovery, however, England abandoned the quest for the Indies and sent ships out under the direction of John Cabot and thus established for England a future claim to Canada and what would become the northeast United States.

* In 1535, King Henry VIII broke off from the Catholic Church after Pope Clement VII refused to annul his marriage to Catherine of Aragon. Henry VIII declared himself head of the Church of England and denied the pope's authority.

* Elizabeth I encouraged trade with foreign lands, and she sent the privateer Sir Francis Drake to circumnavigate the globe. In 1578 he sailed to North America, plundering and pillaging along the way. He landed on the northwestern coast and claimed the land for Elizabeth, naming it "New Albion." The first Protestant services in North America were celebrated here.

* In 1584 Elizabeth sent Sir Walter Raleigh to colonize North America. Raleigh sent men to Roanoke Island. He named this land "Virginia" after Queen Elizabeth, the "Virgin Queen." Raleigh did not succeed in colonizing Virginia, but he succeeded in whipping up interest in America.

* In 1606 Bartholomew Gosnold organized a trading company called the London Company, which sold investments in America. In the same year King James I granted a charter to Gosnold and others to found a colony in Virginia. This colony almost failed due to the settlers' refusal to work and bad government of the colonists, but John Smith managed to pull it together, and by 1609 he had established a solid foundation for the colony.

* In 1610 John Rolfe provided what would be Virginia's economic salvation – tobacco. He brought tobacco seeds from the Caribbean and made tobacco a cash crop in Virginia. He married Pocahontas, the daughter of the chief of the Algonquin Indians, thus bringing about peace between the English and the Algonquins.

* In 1609 the Dutch became interested in finding a route to the Indies, and Henry Hudson was sent to find one. He touched North America at Newfoundland, then proceeded south to a great waterway along the coasts of Nova Scotia, Maine, and Massachusetts. He thought he had discovered the northwest passage to the Indies. He found that his passage was merely a river, however, which was later named the "Hudson" for him.

* In 1623, the Netherlands formed a province on the northern Hudson River to carry on the fur trade and establish trading posts in North America. They called this province the "New Netherlands."

* Peter Minuit became New Netherland's governor in 1626 and established a new plan of colonial settlement, called the patroon system.

* In 1609 a group of Protestants, the Puritans, left England to escape persecution. They went to Amsterdam for ten years, but finding it not to their liking, they were given a charter to establish a settlement in Virginia. They did not

make it to Virginia, however, and landed on the coast of Massachusetts, establishing a settlement called Plymouth.

What Students Should Know

1. **The significance of Cabot's expedition for England**

   Cabot's discoveries established for England a future claim to Canada and what would become the northeast United States.

2. **Queen Elizabeth's maritime policies**

   Elizabeth, who became queen in 1558, encouraged merchants to form companies to open trade with distant markets. English merchants began to trade with Russia and Poland for timber, pitch, and tar, for shipbuilding. With their growing fleet of trading ships, the English plied the waters of the Atlantic and the Mediterranean. Soon, some adventurers were carrying on a trade with the Spanish colonies in the West Indies. Such trade was illegal. Elizabeth encouraged piracy against the Spanish to obtain for England a portion of Spain's New World riches.

3. **Who Sir Francis Drake was and what he accomplished**

   Sir Francis Drake was a privateer, a pirate commissioned by the government of England. From a base in Darien (Panama) he conducted raids along the Spanish Main. Commissioned by Queen Elizabeth, Drake in 1577 commenced his circumnavigation of the world. On this expedition, he raided Spanish settlements in America, desecrating Catholic churches. Somewhere along the coast of California, Oregon, or Washington (no one is certain where) Drake's ship anchored in a bay, where he and his men celebrated the first Protestant religious service in North America,

and Drake laid claim to the land for Queen Elizabeth, naming it "New Albion." Drake arrived in Portsmouth harbor on September 26, 1580, where Queen Elizabeth knighted him.

4. **What was the first motivation for English colonization of the New World**

   Sir Humphrey Gilbert conceived of English colonies in America where the queen's subjects could establish themselves and farm the land. These colonies could in turn enrich those who invested in them.

5. **What was Sir Walter Raleigh's role in English colonization of America**

   Sir Humphrey Gilbert's half brother, Sir Walter Raleigh, shared his ambitions and became a major protagonist of early English settlement in America. Raleigh financed attempts at settlement in North America, including the two failed colonies on Roanoke Island. It was Raleigh who gave the lands emanating out from the Roanoke region the name "Virginia," after Queen Elizabeth, the "Virgin Queen." Though his own colonization schemes were failures, he did succeed in whipping up English interest in America.

6. **Motivations for English settlement in America**

   For English merchants, an American colony meant increased trade. For the government, it meant an outlet for the large number of idle soldiers lately returned from the Spanish wars. For Christian ministers, it meant an opportunity to convert the heathen.

7. **The story of Jamestown's founding**

   The navigator Bartholomew Gosnold organized a trading company – called the

Virginia Company of London, or just the London Company – and sold investments, called "bills of adventure." Soon a number of Englishmen, mostly members of the merchant class, were buying the bills. In April 1606, King James I granted a charter to found a colony in Virginia. On April 26, 1607, three ships landed at Cape Henry at the entrance to Chesapeake Bay. After landing in April, the colonists had followed the path of a wide river, which they named the James in honor of the king. On a small peninsula jutting out into the river, they built a fort and established a settlement, Jamestown. The area was swampy, and through the hot, humid summer of 1607, swamp fever killed many of the colonists. Jamestown suffered from attacks by the local Algonquin Indians. Jamestown it appeared would fail, not only because of disease and Indian attacks, but because over half the colonists were gentlemen who refused to work the fields.

8. How Captain John Smith saved Jamestown

By April 1608, only 38 of the original 105 colonists were still alive at Jamestown. That month, another ship, the *Phoenix*, arrived, bringing 120 more settlers. But the influx of new settlers did not solve the colony's problems. It was John Smith who did. Becoming president of the colonial council, Smith subjected the colonists to military discipline. He forced the lazy to work in the fields and to build new storage barns. By the spring and summer of 1609, Smith could claim he had established a solid foundation for the colony. Smith's policy of forcing food from the Indians, however, led to a deterioration of the colony's relations with the natives.

9. How John Rolfe saved Jamestown and Virginia

The London Company was disappointed with the returns on its investments in Virginia. None of the industries tried in Jamestown were deemed successful enough. It was John Rolfe, who came to Virginia in 1610, who provided Virginia's economic salvation – tobacco. In 1610, Rolfe brought smuggled Caribbean tobacco seed into Virginia. Tobacco became Virginia's cash crop and made the colony pay. Rolfe's marriage to Powhatan's daughter, Pocahontas, brought about peace between the English colonists and the Indians.

10. The founding of New Netherlands

In 1610, Amsterdam merchants began outfitting ships to trade for furs in the regions of America discovered by the explorer Henry Hudson. The business in furs was soon so lucrative that, in 1614, the Dutch government chartered a trading company, the New Netherland Company, to carry on the fur trade and establish trading posts in America. The company established Fort Nassau on the northern Hudson River where Albany currently stands, and another post on the southern tip of Manhattan Island. In 1623, the government of the Netherlands formed its New World settlements into a province, called New Netherlands. Some of the colonists chose to remain on Manhattan Island, while the rest followed the Hudson River north to Fort Orange (which had replaced Fort Nassau) and founded the settlement which would become Albany.

11. A description of the Dutch patroon system

A *patroon*, or "patron," was a man to whom the government granted land if he could fund the passage of 50 colonists to New Netherlands. The land grant, purchased from the Indians, was 16 miles on one side of a river or along the seashore, or eight miles on both sides of a river. It included as much land into the interior as the *patroon* could possibly use. The *patroon* received all rights to the plants, minerals, and springs within his land grant. He controlled rights to fishing, hunting, and the milling of grain. The *patroon* system was similar to the Spanish *encomienda* except that a Dutch land grant did not include Indians as laborers. Since the Dutch West India Company dealt in the West African slave trade, Indian laborers were unnecessary; the company promised "to supply the colonists with as many blacks as they possibly can." *Patroons*, however, preferred white laborers, "indentured servants," whose passage they would pay in return for a specified number of years of labor.

12. Who the "Saints" were

The "Saints" were a Protestant religious group, called Separatists by their countrymen in England because, in obedience to their convictions, they had separated themselves from the Church of England. The Saints belonged to a larger movement in Protestantism called Puritanism. While other Puritans remained within the Church of England and tried to reform it by "purifying" it of all Catholic practices, the Saints believed they could only follow their pure doctrines and practices outside the established church. In Scrooby, in Nottinghamshire, England, some Puritans came together to form a church of their own. They made a "covenant," or solemn promise, with each other to form an independent congregation of true believers. Under this covenant, leaders were elected by the men in the community of Saints. To observe their religious beliefs in freedom, the Saints went to live in Holland.

13. Why the Saints left Holland

After ten years of living in Holland, the Saints decided to seek refuge in America. Since they worked at low paying jobs, the Saints lived under the threat of poverty. Moreover, the 12-year truce between the Netherlands and Spain was about to expire, and the Saints feared a renewal of war. Moreover, their children were adopting Dutch ways and being influenced by "corrupt" manners. The Saints wanted their children to remain English and Puritan.

14. What King James' terms for the Saints' settlement in New England were

The Virginia company agreed to finance the Saints' expedition to "Virginia" but required that merchant adventurers accompany them to Virginia. King James issued a charter allowing the company to establish a settlement in what was to be called New England. But when the company approached James with the Saints' request for freedom of religion, the king replied that no subject of his was free to worship outside the Church of England. If, however, the Separatists decided to remain separate, the king said he would tolerate it.

15. What the Mayflower Compact said and its importance

The Mayflower Compact said the settlement was "undertaken for the glory of God, and advancement of the Christian faith and honor of our king and country." The covenant said the Saints and their fellow colonists did "solemnly and mutually, in the presence of God and one of another, covenant and combine ourselves together into a civil body politic, for our better ordering and preservation and furtherance of the ends aforesaid; and by virtue hereof to enact, constitute, and frame such just and equal laws, ordinances, acts, constitutions, offices from time to time as shall be thought most meet and convenient for the general good of the colony." The Mayflower Compact thus allowed adult males except those who were servants or hired men, to establish a government without the explicit permission of the king. This compact became the precursor of what would be characteristic of government in English America. Unlike the old European nations that were governed more by tradition and custom, English American states would be governed by written laws that were seen as covenants or contracts the people made between themselves and their government.

16. **The role of the Indians in the founding of Plymouth colony**

Through Samoset, an Abenaki from Maine, the Plymouth colonists were introduced to Massasoit, the chief of the Wampanoag tribe, who lived around Plymouth. The colonists and Massasoit signed a peace treaty with the colonists and told his people to befriend them. The Indians taught the colonists how to farm in the new country and introduced them to new crops: maize (corn), beans, squash, and Jerusalem artichokes. They suggested what fields to turn and how to fertilize crops.

17. **Describe the culture of the Wampanoag of New England**

The name Wampanoag means "eastern people," or "people of the dawn." The Wampanoag were divided into family groups that gathered together in winter to hunt and in spring to fish. In summer they would separate again so their women could cultivate corn, beans, squash, watermelon, Jerusalem artichokes, and other crops on individual plots. The men were the hunters and warriors, not the farmers. There was no

private property as we know it among the Wampanoag; rather, the entire community held their property in common and divided it among families to use. Like the Huron, Wampanoag sachems (chieftains) did not govern by force. They needed to be eloquent to convince tribesmen to follow their lead. Wise men, or *pow-waws*, also held great influence over the tribe.

Questions for Review

1. **What part did John Cabot play in bringing England to America, and what did he establish there?**

   Cabot's discoveries established for England a future claim to Canada and what would become the northeast United States.

2. **What is King Henry VIII so famous for?**

   King Henry VIII is famous for leading the Church of England into schism with the Catholic Church.

3. **What did Elizabeth I encourage that led to Sir Francis Drake's exploration?**

   Elizabeth I encouraged privateering against Spain, which ultimately brought about Drake's circumnavigation of the world.

4. **Name two things that Walter Raleigh accomplished.**

   Raleigh financed attempts at settlement in North America, and whipped up English interest in the New World.

5. **What did the London Company achieve in America?**

   The London Company sold investments to land in America, called "bills of adventure," to Englishmen.

6. **What was happening in the Virginia Colony to bring it into danger of failing?**

The Virginia Colony was in danger of failing from Indian attacks, and from a failure to find a lucrative source of trade with the mother country.

7. **Who saved the Virginia Colony, and what did he do to save it?**

Through smuggling tobacco seed to America and making it a cash crop, John Rolfe saved the Virginia Colony from failing.

8. **What did the patroon system establish in America?**

The *patroon* system brought Dutch colonists to America and the establishment of the New Netherlands.

9. **Who were the "Saints," and why did they leave England?**

The "Saints" were a Protestant religious group, called Separatists by their countrymen in England because, in obedience to their convictions, they had separated themselves from the Church of England. They left England in order to observe their religious beliefs in freedom.

10. **What was the "Mayflower Compact," and why is it important to law and government in America?**

The Mayflower Compact was a covenant that the Pilgrims and their fellow colonists signed that bound them into a civil body. The compact became the precursor of what would be characteristic of government in English America.

Ideas in Action

1. **Look up the names of the original colonies in America. What do these name mean?**

2. **Read some accounts of the Pilgrims in America.**

Sample Quiz I (pages 53-61)

Please answer the following in complete sentences.

1. **What is the significance of John Cabot's expedition for England?**

Key Terms at a Glance

charter: a document granting certain specified rights, powers, privileges, or functions from a sovereign state power to an individual or organized group

patroon: (patron) a man to whom the Dutch government granted land if he could fund the passage of 50 colonists to New Netherlands. The patroon received all rights to whatever was within his land grant, but he was not allowed Indians as laborers.

indentured servants: white laborers whose passage to America was paid in return for a specified number of years of labor

Puritanism: a sect of Protestants who tried to reform the Church of England by "purifying" it of all Catholic practices

Saints: a group of Puritans who believed they could only follow their pure doctrines and practices outside the established church

2. Why did Queen Elizabeth encourage piracy against the Spanish?

3. Identify the following:
   a. Sir Francis Drake
   b. Sir Walter Raleigh
   c. John Smith

4. What did Queen Elizabeth commission Sir Francis Drake to do?

5. What was Virginia named for?

6. What was the English merchants' motivation for settlement in America?

7. What was the English government's motivation for settlement in America?

8. Identify the Virginia Company of London.

Answers to Sample Quiz I

Students' answers should approximate the following.

1. Cabot's expedition established for England a future claim to Canada and what would become the northeast United States.

2. Queen Elizabeth encouraged piracy against the Spanish to obtain for England a portion of Spain's New World riches.

3.
   a. English privateer commissioned by Elizabeth I to raid Spanish ships
   b. English explorer who financed attempts at settlement in North America and gave Virginia its name.

   c. Admiral of New England who saved Jamestown from failing

4. Queen Elizabeth commissioned Sir Francis Drake to circumnavigate the world.

5. Virginia was named for Queen Elizabeth, the "Virgin Queen."

6. For English merchants, an American colony meant increased trade.

7. For the government, it meant an outlet for the large number of idle soldiers lately returned from the Spanish wars.

8. The Virginia Company of London was a trading company that sold investments to land in America.

Sample Quiz II (pages 61-67)

Please answer the following in complete sentences.

1. Identify the following:
   a. John Rolfe
   b. *patroon*
   c. "Saints"

2. What did John Rolfe introduce into Virginia that proved to be the colony's economic salvation?

3. What was the purpose of the New Netherland Company?

4. What did a *patroon* have to do to be granted land?

5. What was the Saints' covenant?

6. Why did the Saints leave England?

7. Who were the Indians who helped in the founding of Plymouth colony?

Answers to Sample Quiz II

Students' answers should approximate the following.

1.
   a. English settler in America who saved Jamestown and Virginia

   b. Dutch name for a patron
   c. A Protestant religious group, part of the larger Puritan movement who believed they could only follow their pure

doctrines and practices outside the established church.

2. John Rolfe introduced tobacco to America.

3. The purpose of the New Netherland Company was to carry on the fur trade and establish trading posts in America.

4. To be granted land, a *patroon* had to fund the passage of 50 colonists to New Netherlands.

5. The Saints' covenant was form an independent congregation of true believers.

6. The Saints left England so that their children would remain English and Puritan.

7. The Indians who helped in the founding of Plymouth colony were Samoset and Massasoit.

Essays

Instructions to be given to the students: Write in complete sentences. Underline your thesis. Give three supports or examples that explain why you think what you do and that support your thesis.

1. Compare and contrast the motives of the English with those of the Spanish in settling America. Use specific examples.

2. How do you think the different cultures found in New England as opposed to New Spain contributed to the ease or difficulty in colonizing? How did the different religious motivations play a part?

Sample Test

Please answer the following in complete sentences.

I. Short Essay – Answer two of the following:

1. **What were the motivations England had for colonizing and settling in America?**

2. **Describe the *patroon* system.**

3. **Who were the Saints, and what did they believe?**

4. **Why is the Mayflower so significant to government in America?**

II. Short Answer:

1. **What was Sir Walter Raleigh's major achievement?**

2. **Why did it look like Jamestown would fail?**

3. **How was the Dutch *patroon* system different from the Spanish *encomienda* system?**

4. **How did the Saints differ from other Puritans?**

5. **What role did Indians have in founding the Plymouth colony?**

Answer Key to the Chapter Test

Students' answers should approximate the following:

I.

1. The motivation for colonizing America was so that the queen's subjects could establish themselves and farm the land. The colonies could in turn enrich those who invested in them. There were several reason why England wanted to settle in America. For English merchants, an American colony meant increased trade. For the government, it meant an outlet for the large number of idle soldiers lately returned from the Spanish wars. For Christian ministers, it meant an opportunity to convert the heathen.

2. A *patroon*, or "patron," was a man to whom the government granted land if he could fund the passage of 50 colonists to New Netherlands. The land grant, purchased from the Indians, was 16 miles on one side of a river or along the seashore, or eight miles on both sides of a river. It included as much land into the interior as the *patroon* could possibly use. The *patroon* received all rights to the plants, minerals, and springs within his land grant. He controlled rights to fishing, hunting, and the milling of grain.

3. The "Saints" were a Protestant religious group, called Separatists by their countrymen in England because, in obedience to their convictions, they had separated themselves from the Church of England. The Saints belonged to a larger movement in Protestantism called Puritanism. While other Puritans remained within the Church of England and tried to reform it by "purifying" it of all Catholic practices, the Saints believed they could only follow their pure doctrines and practices outside the established church.

4. The Mayflower Compact is significant to American government because it became the precursor of what would be characteristic of government in English America. Unlike the old European nations that were governed more by tradition and custom, English American states would be governed by written laws that were seen as covenants or contracts the people made between themselves and their government.

II.
1. Sir Walter Raleigh's major achievement was naming Virginia and whipping up English interest in America.

2. It looked like Jamestown would fail because of disease and Indian attacks and because over half the colonists were gentlemen who refused to work the fields. Too, Jamestown could not find a source of wealth to justify its existence with investors.

3. The Dutch *patroon* system was different from the Spanish *encomienda* system because a Dutch land grant did not include Indians as laborers.

4. The Saints differed from other Puritans because they believed they could only follow their pure doctrines and practices outside the established church, while the Puritans remained in the Church of England.

5. The colonists and the Massasoit signed a peace treaty; the Indians befriended the colonists, and taught them how to farm in the new country.

CHAPTER 5: The English Colonies

Chapter Overview

- Puritans in England, deciding that they could not turn old England into their model of a Puritan commonwealth, formed such a society in New England. In 1628, under the leadership of John Endicott, they settled in Salem.

- In 1641 Massachusetts adopted the "Body of Liberties," and Plymouth established the "General Fundamentals," both of which ensured free elections; trial by jury; the right not to be deprived of life, liberty, or property without due process of law; the right not to be taxed if not represented; and the right not to be forced to incriminate oneself in trial.

- New England was nearly destroyed by two wars: the Pequot uprising of 1637 and King Phillip's War of 1675-1676.

- In 1643 Massachusetts formed a loose confederation called the United Colonies of New England with Plymouth, Connecticut, and New Haven.

- With the disbanding of the Virginia Company, King James I made Virginia a crown colony --- a dominion.

- In 1675 Nathaniel Bacon started a revolt against the government of Virginia because it would not do anything about Indian attacks on settlements. Bacon soon controlled most of Virginia.

- In 1622 George Calvert, desiring to solve the problem of persecution of Catholics in England, sent English Catholics to a colony called Avalon in America. This colony did not last long, however, and Calvert received a charter from King Charles I to found another colony in America. When George Calvert died, the charter was confirmed to his son, Cecil. The colony became known as "Maryland."

- In 1649 Lord Baltimore directed the Maryland government to approve the Toleration Act, which said that all Trinitarian religions were to be respected in Maryland.

- In 1692, King William III established the Church of England in Maryland and required everyone to support it.

- King Charles II, because of a grudge he held against the Dutch, conquered the Dutch New World possessions and gave them to his brother, James, duke of York. Under the duke of York, New Amsterdam became New York City.

- In 1680 William Penn received a land grant west of New Jersey as a haven for persecuted Quakers and other religious groups. King Charles II named the settlement Pennsylvania. In 1682 Penn laid out his "city of brotherly love," which he called Philadelphia.

- Following a boundary dispute between Penn and Lord Baltimore, two surveyors named Mason and Dixon settled the boundary between Pennsylvania and Maryland.

What Students Should Know

1. **The character of the Saints and Puritans' society**

   The Puritan religion was dour. Following the Calvinist, or Reformed, tradition of Protantism, the Saints believed that man's nature is entirely corrupt --- which is why they tended to condemn even innocent pleasures or "vanities," as they called them. The Saints taught that God, according to his good pleasure, had "predestined," or chosen beforehand, that some, the "elect," would be saved and all others damned. No person could know for certain which he was. To get some assurance of his election, one needed continually to examine his life to see if he were truly virtuous; for virtue was a sign of God's good pleasure. But, according to Calvinist teaching, even the virtuous could not be sure of his election. The Saints recognized only three holy days: the Sabbath, the Day of Fasting and Humiliation, and the Day of Thanksgiving and Praise. The last two were not celebrated on fixed dates but only when God's wrath or his gifts were evident.

The doctrines of Puritanism emphasized the goodness of manual, as well as intellectual, labor. The Puritans honored industry and attached no stigma to wealth-making --- in fact, material prosperity was for them a sign of God's favor. The Puritans thought idleness a sin; they frowned on all amusements that were not profitable, and so their days became mere rounds of hard labor and prayer. Though they appreciated beauty, Puritans discouraged the ornate beauty found in traditional Catholic architecture, painting, and music. The Puritans enforced morality through their laws, punishing, for example, those who worked on the Sabbath or used profanity. The Puritans did not see their colonies as refuges from persecution but as an attempt to form a holy commonwealth, a great experiment in Christian society. They did not tolerate anyone who disagreed with them on the meaning of Scripture. Massachusetts Bay passed laws against the Baptists in 1644, and, from 1656 to 1662, persecuted members of the Society of Friends, or "Quakers," as they were called. A Quaker could be whipped, imprisoned,

branded with hot irons, or banished into the surrounding wilderness. During this period, Massachusetts Bay executed four Quakers.

2. Describe the "City on a Hill" concept

"City on a Hill" is a phrase coined by the Puritan leader John Winthrop. It signified that the Puritans had entered in a covenant or contract with God. If the Puritans fulfilled their side of the covenant they would become an example or model of an ideal commonwealth to all the world. Winthrop's "city on a hill" is a specifically religious concept.

3. Why the Puritans came to New England and what was the purpose of their settlement

Many Puritans decided that since they could not turn old England into their model of a Puritan commonwealth, they would form such a society in New England. In 1629, the Massachusetts Bay Company received a charter from King Charles I to settle Massachusetts Bay. This charter granted the members of the company permission to elect their own governor as head of the corporation. The stated principal purpose of the colony was to bring the natives of New England to the Christian faith.

4. The character of the government of Puritan New England and how it changed

Puritan society had a hierarchical government, but in practice it was rather egalitarian. Freemen (that is, everyone but slaves and indentured servants) who were members of the church elected all officials of government and members of the assembly, the body that made colonial laws. Periodically freemen voted out established leaders. It was not long before the people of New England wanted safeguards for their freedom. In 1641, Massachusetts adopted the

"Body of Liberties," and about the same time, Plymouth established the "General Fundamentals." Both documents guaranteed the traditional safeguards of English liberty: free elections; trial by jury; the right not to be deprived of life, liberty, or property without due process of law; the right not to be taxed if not represented; and the right not to be forced to incriminate oneself in a trial.

5. **The pattern of New England settlements**

The Puritans established the pattern of settlement that still characterizes New England. When groups began to feel too crowded in one place they, with the permission of the colonial assembly, established new townships. The townships were divided into lots surrounding a "meeting house" where townsmen worshiped and conducted government business. In this way, from the original settlement at Boston, the Puritans established other towns. To these townships migrated independent farmers and craftsman who made the Massachusetts Bay colony nearly self-sufficient in the material goods needed for living. Other Massachusetts emigrants followed the Connecticut River southwards, founding the towns of Wethersfield, Windsor, and Hartford in 1634-35 --- the nucleus from which grew the colony of Connecticut. Others founded the colony of New Haven in 1638.

6. **Who Anne Hutchinson was and what she accomplished**

Anne Hutchinson was a woman who objected to the regime in Massachusetts Bay Colony. She publicly declared that it was wrong for the leaders of Massachusetts Bay to use human laws to establish the kingdom of God. She believed that individuals could have direct contact with God. Those in whom the Holy Spirit dwelt had no need of laws, she said, though laws were useful for the unsaved. For these ideas, the authorities of Massachusetts tried Hutchinson for heresy and exiled her from Massachusetts. With the wealthy William Coddington and others, Hutchinson went south to Narragansett Bay where she established a settlement called Portsmouth, the first settlement on what became known as Rhode Island. This settlement, however, split, and Coddington formed his own settlement on Rhode Island, calling it Newport.

7. **Who Roger Williams was and what he accomplished**

Rogers Williams was a religious dissident who criticized the Puritans of New England for remaining in the Church of England. He said it was sinful that the Puritans required everyone "to attend the religious services provided by the state or be punished." He criticized the Massachusetts colony for stealing Indian lands. When the authorities tried to arrest him, Williams fled to the Indians. Later he moved to Narragansett Bay and founded the settlement of Providence, where he defended the Indians there from English settlers. In Providence Williams established a policy of religious toleration. In 1663, Williams' "Providence Plantation" received a charter from King Charles II.

8. **The condition of Christian Indians in Massachusetts**

While New England expansion led to conflicts with Indians, some natives adjusted to the European settlement. Among these were the "praying Indians," who lived in self-governing settlements, separated from those of the English Puritans.

9. **Causes of Indian discontent in New England**

Most Indians in New England tried to sustain their ancient patterns of life. They did not understand European notions of land ownership, so when governments purchased land from them, they did not think that they were giving it up forever but merely lending it. The Indians suffered from contact with unscrupulous whites, who cheated them and, worse, sold them the alcohol for which the nations had no tolerance.

10. **The causes of King Philip's War, its effects and significance**

Among the causes of King Philip's War was the discontent of Metacom ("King Philip"), chief sachem of the Wampanoag tribe, that he and his people had been ill treated and insulted by the Puritans of Massachusetts. The proximate cause was the murder of Sassamon, a Harvard educated Indian. Sassamon had been King Philip's secretary and had informed against him to Governor Winslow of Plymouth. When the Indians who murdered Sassamon had been tried and hanged, Metacom, on June 24, 1675, led an attack on the white settlement of Swansea. By the autumn of 1675, Metacom's braves had wiped out the western settlements. The war ended in August 1676, when Metacom was captured and killed. King Philip's War has been called the most violent war ever fought on New England soil.

11. **Changes in New England government under Cromwell, the Stuarts, and William of Orange**

In 1643, after the assassination of King Charles I, Massachusetts, with Plymouth, Connecticut, and New Haven, formed a loose confederation called the United Colonies of New England. Throughout the period of Cromwell's rule, from 1649 to 1659, the United Colonies could manage their own affairs. In 1660 King Charles I's son, Charles II, became king, and in 1662, King Charles II ordered the union of the colonies of Connecticut and New Haven, granting them a new charter that made no mention of royal or parliamentary control over the new colony, to be called Connecticut. But Charles annulled Massachusetts' charter and placed the colony under an unelected, royal governor. The new royal government annulled the power of the Puritan church. After 1685, colonists resisted the attempts of King James II to unite all of New England into one colony. In obedience to the king's wishes, Governor Andros visited Hartford in 1687 to annul Connecticut's colonial charter of 1662. However, during a meeting between Andros and the colonial leaders, someone extinguished the candles and in the sudden darkness took the charter and hid it in an oak tree. After 1688, when James II's daughter Mary and her husband, William of Orange, assumed the throne of England, the New England colonies were allowed to return to old charters and liberties.

12. **How Virginia's government changed when it passed from the Virginia Company's to royal rule**

The Virginia Company had established in Virginia a representative assembly, elected by all freemen, that shared power with the colonial governor appointed by the company. This "House of Burgesses" was the first representative assembly in the New World. The company had also granted the colonists all the freedoms that they had enjoyed in England, such as the right to trial by jury and due process. When he disbanded the Virginia Company, King James made Virginia a crown colony, or royal province --- a dominion. James appointed a governor who was to select a council to help him rule the colony.

The House of Burgesses remained, whose members the freemen of the colony continued to elect.

13.   The character of life in Virginia

Virginia's settlement differed markedly from New England's. While the Puritans formed tightly knit townships, the Virginians lived widely separated on farmsteads. This settlement pattern resulted from "head-right," a system whereby a settler was granted fifty acres for himself and for every person whom he brought to Virginia. Most settlers became small farmers with 100 to 200-acre holdings. Some men, however, were able to amass great estates by the head-right system and rise from middling circumstances to wealth. Politically, Virginians were royalists. During the civil war, nearly every Virginian stood behind Charles I; some even went to England to fight in his cause. After Charles I had been executed, the House of Burgesses acknowledged the reign of his son, Charles II. Virginians were devoted to the Church of England. Virginians were ardent Anglicans but with a very Puritan flavor. In their services they omitted Catholic-inspired sections of the *Book of Common Prayer*, their ministers were not ritually vested, and they received communion as a memorial (not as the Real Presence) around a table, just like the Puritans did. Their moral legislation, too, mirrored that of Plymouth and Boston. In every parish a governing body of vestrymen enforced church discipline through the offices of two churchwardens. But since Virginia parishes were so large and settlements so widely separated, it was much harder to enforce regulations. Virginia did not have the grammar school system that New England had developed. Virginia had only two free schools and "field schools" for the children of the tobacco planters, but many wealthy

students were sent to private tutors for their education. In 1693 that Virginia established a college --- the College of William and Mary, in Williamsburg. The Virginians were never so stern as the New Englanders. They enjoyed horse racing, drinking, and the fox chase. Theirs was not, first and foremost, a religious but an economic establishment. Their culture had a penchant for the genteel and aristocratic.

14.   The condition of slavery in Virginia in the 17th century

In the early years of the colony, indentured white servants provided most of the labor on Virginia plantations. Before 1681, the number of black slaves in Virginia was relatively small. Unlike the white servants, whose terms of service were limited to a specified number of years and who could, afterward, hope to obtain property, blacks remained slaves for life, unless their masters emancipated them. In the 17th century, emancipation was not rare. Some whites believed one could not hold a fellow Christian in slavery; so, when their slaves were baptized, they freed them.

15.   The causes and results of Nat Bacon's rebellion

Virginia suffered from various abuses in the late 17th century. Sir William Berkeley, who, deposed by Cromwell, had returned to power in 1660, controlled the workings of the colony and was bent on promoting agricultural schemes (as well as new taxes to pay for them) unpopular with most Virginians. There had been no elections for the House of Burgesses in 14 years. The burgesses favored Berkeley's policies.

On top of all these problems, there were Indian troubles. Virginia had settled a number of tribes on reservations; but many of the whites who had settled around the reservations wanted to drive the Indians out. Sir William, however, saw it as his duty as royal governor to protect them. Then in 1675, the Susquehannock rose and began raiding plantations on Virginia's northern frontier, but Berkeley did not take immediate action against the tribe. Discontented colonists gathered around Nat Bacon and rebelled. When Berkeley failed to deal with the Indians as Bacon saw fit, Bacon renewed the rebellion and came to control all of Virginia except the eastern shore. The revolt died when Bacon died on October 26, 1676. Reforms instituted by Berkeley because of the rebellion did away with some of the glaring abuses that had arisen in Virginia's government.

16. Why Lord Baltimore sought a colony for Catholics in America

Catholics had long suffered under serious legal and social disabilities in England. Sir George Calvert, Lord Baltimore, thought to solve the "Catholic problem" in England it was necessary to find Catholics a refuge in America, where they could worship and not disturb the Protestant way of life in England.

17. The Founding of Maryland

In 1632, Calvert received from the king a charter granting him and his descendants ownership of a portion of Virginia, including the Chesapeake Bay and lands west and north of the bay. George Calvert was made the "proprietor" of the colony, with princely powers over who should settle there and the making of laws. Under the king, Calvert held absolute sway over the new colony. When George Calvert died in April 1632, King Charles issued the charter to Calvert's son, Cecil, the second Lord Baltimore. Though he knew that both Calverts had planned the colony as a refuge for Catholics, he could not openly tolerate such an endeavor. The

charter, granted June 20, 1632, was thus so vaguely worded as to allow for a toleration of Catholics. The king granted Baron Baltimore the "Faculty of erecting and founding Churches, Chapels, and Places of Worship, in convenient and suitable Places within the Premises, and of causing the same to be dedicated and consecrated according to the Ecclesiastical Laws of our Kingdom of England…" The charter also named the region "Maryland" --- ostensibly in honor of King Charles' Catholic wife, Queen Henrietta Maria, but secretly in honor of the Mother of God.

18. The character of Maryland's government

Though it fell under Lord Baltimore's proprietorship, Maryland was to become the most self-governing of the English colonies. In addition to the governorship, Cecil Calvert established a house of burgesses. The function of the burgesses was to advise the governor and the proprietor, but it was not long before it began to vote to approve or reject laws proposed by the governor. Lord Baltimore decreed that all freemen, whether proprietors or not, had the right to vote for members of the burgesses.

19. The character of Maryland society

In many respects, Maryland society looked a good deal like Virginia. As in Virginia, a head-right system encouraged land settlement. Maryland had a somewhat feudal character, for Lord Baltimore gave to "lords of manors" judicial powers to settle disputes between tenants and servants and to mete out punishments for minor offenses. Workers and craftsmen settled Maryland, as well as a good number of indentured servants, whose numbers were so great that there seemed to be little need for black slaves to work the tobacco plantations that became the chief source of Maryland's wealth. As the indentured servants worked themselves into freedom, however, the number of black slaves increased. Still, the number of slaves was not great in Maryland until after 1700. The majority of Marylanders were Protestant, but the 20 richest and most influential men in the colony were Catholic. For at least the colony's first 15 years, Protestants and Catholics lived in harmony, for Lord Baltimore had decreed complete freedom of religion in Maryland. They used the same church for worship. The governor of Maryland took an oath that he would not discriminate against anyone in conferring offices, rewards or favors on account of religion. Lord Baltimore forbade anyone to insult another's religion under threat of a fine.

20.   What the Toleration Act was

The Toleration Act was an act promoted by Lord Baltimore and approved by the Maryland that Burgesses guaranteed tolerance for religious belief and practice for all those who believe in Jesus Christ. Those who denied the Trinity, however, were susceptible to punishment --- though no one was ever punished for such offenses in Maryland.

21.   Why religious tolerance of Catholics was doomed in Maryland's

Maryland's religious toleration was doomed, because Catholics remained a minority in Maryland, while the population of Protestants continually increased.

22.   Condition of Catholics in Maryland after toleration ended

In 1692 William established the Church of England in Maryland and required everyone, except Puritans and Protestant nonconformists, to support it. Penal laws appeared on the books. It was forbidden to celebrate Mass, and parents who taught their children the Catholic faith received heavy fines. If Catholic children became Protestant, they could seize their parents' property without compensation; but someone who converted a Protestant to the Catholic Church could be killed.

23.   The character of the Dutch America

The Dutch colony had a mixed population. There were Swedes and Finns, who introduced housing that would long be in use in North America --- the log cabin. There were also Puritan English who had come from Connecticut; the Dutch allowed these to govern themselves by their own laws. There were black African slaves who worked farms owned by the rich *patroons*.

24.   How England gained possession of Dutch America

On August 18, 1664, during a brief war between Great Britain and Holland, four British frigates, sailed into New Amsterdam harbor and demanded the surrender of the fortress. Unable to convince the Dutch to resist the English invaders, the Dutch governor surrender to the English. By the end of October, the English had taken New Amsterdam, Fort Orange, and Fort Casimir on the Delaware, which they renamed respectively New York, Albany, and Newcastle. New Netherlands thus became an English possession. King Charles II eventually gave the Dutch possessions to his brother, James, Duke of York, and it was renamed New York.

25.   Who William Penn was

William Penn was the son of Admiral Sir William Penn. In school, the younger Penn attended schools influence by Puritanism. At the age of 12, he claimed to have experienced an interior comfort where his room was filled with a visible glory. He was convinced man could enjoy union with God. Penn was a religious non-conformist and eventually became a Quaker and a Quaker leader. He formed a purpose to found a settlement for Quakers in America, where they could practice their religion freely.

26. The founding of Pennsylvania

King Charles II owed Penn's father money. When Admiral Penn died in 1670, the right to claim the debt passed on to his son. In 1680, the younger Penn asked the crown for a tract of land in America north of Maryland in lieu of money payment. The king agreed, and in a royal grant, dated March 1, 1681, he made Penn proprietor of the land that would extend from New Jersey westward and from the border of Maryland north to the border of New York. Penn wanted to name this grant "Sylvania" (woodland), but the king insisted on adding "Penn" to the name, in honor of the late admiral. Though Penn protested, the king's will prevailed. The new colony was named Pennsylvania.

27. Who settled Pennsylvania

Attracted by the promise of living in a colony offering complete religious toleration, many English and continental Europeans flocked to Pennsylvania. In 1682, Penn laid out his "city of brotherly love," Philadelphia, at the confluence of the Delaware and Schuylkill Rivers. Three years later, Pennsylvania could boast nearly 9,000 inhabitants. Among these were Mennonite Germans under Franz Daniel Pastorius who, in 1683, settled Germantown. Quakers from Wales and England settled the colony in great numbers.

28. Religious toleration, slavery, and Indian relations in Pennsylvania

William Penn saw his colony as a "holy experiment" in religious toleration. This toleration extended to all groups, even Catholics, who found Pennsylvania a refuge from Maryland's penal laws. Though he did not abolish slavery in the colony, Penn insisted on laws requiring the instruction of blacks and granting them the right to marry. By the time he made these recommendations, however, the colonial assembly, which now consisted of more than just Quakers, rejected the proposals. Penn called for justice for Indians in Pennsylvania. Penn's kindness was reciprocated by the Pennsylvania natives, who long remained on friendly terms with the proprietor and his successors.

Questions for Review

1. **Describe some of the beliefs of the Saints.**

The Saints believed that man's nature is entirely corrupt. They taught that God, according to his good pleasure, had "predestined," or chosen beforehand, that some, the "elect," would be saved and all others damned. No person could know for certain which he was. To get some assurance of his election, one needed continually to examine his life to see if he were truly virtuous; for virtue was a sign of God's good pleasure. But, according to Calvinist teaching, even the virtuous could not be sure of his election.

2. **How did the Saints regard their colony of Plymouth?**

The Saints saw Plymouth colony primarily as an attempt to form a holy commonwealth, a great experiment in Christian society.

3. **Why did John Winthrop speak of Salem colony as a City on a Hill?**

"City on a Hill" is a phrase coined by the Puritan leader John Winthrop. It signified that the Puritans had entered in a covenant or contract with God. If the Puritans fulfilled their side of the covenant they would become an example or model of an ideal commonwealth to all the world.

4. **What situation prompted the founding of Salem?**

Many Puritans decided that since they could not turn old England into their model of a Puritan commonwealth, they would form such a society in New England, and led by John Endicott they settled Salem.

5. **What are some of the beliefs of the Puritans, and how do they differ from those of the Saints?**

The doctrines of Puritanism emphasized the goodness of manual, as well as intellectual, labor. The Puritans honored industry and attached no stigma to wealth-making --- in fact, material prosperity was for them a sign of God's favor. The Puritans thought idleness a sin; they frowned on all amusements that were not profitable, and so their days became mere rounds of hard labor and prayer. Though they appreciated beauty, Puritans discouraged the ornate beauty found in traditional Catholic architecture, painting, and music.

The Puritans differed little from the Saints in their teachings: both were Calvinist. But while the Saints were mostly farmers and artisans, the Puritans were drawn from the richer merchant classes and from the country gentlemen of England. The Puritans valued education highly. Though as Calvinists both they and the Saints embraced individual interpretation of Scripture and the freedom of the individual conscience, the Puritans gave the direction of society over to their learned ministers.

6. **What two events nearly destroyed the colonies of New England?**

The two event that nearly destroyed the colony of New England were the Pequot uprising and King Phillip's War.

7. **What part did the "heretics" of New England play in New England's history?**

Key Terms at a Glance

General Fundamentals and Body of Liberties: two bodies of law approved respectively by the Plymouth and and Massachusetts Bay colonies that ensured free elections; trial by jury; the right not to be deprived of life, liberty, or property without due process of law; the right not to be taxed if not represented; and the right not to be forced to incriminate oneself in trial

King Phillip's War: a bloody war in 1675-1676 that nearly destroyed New England

Toleration Act: an act approved by Lord Baltimore and the Maryland colonial government guaranteeing the free exercise of religion for all Christian groups in Maryland

Quakers: the Society of Friends, a religious group that stresses the interior guidance of the Holy Spirit and rejects external religious rites and ordained ministry.

The New England "heretics" challenged the beliefs of the Saints and Puritans.

8. **What situation or events caused Nathaniel Bacon to revolt?**

Nathaniel Bacon started a revolt against the government of Virginia because it would not do anything to restrainIndian attacks against settlers.

9. **What effects did Bacon's revolt have on Virginia and its government?**

Bacon's revolt caused Virginia to do away with some of the glaring abuses that had arisen in its government.

10. **What was the "Catholic problem" in England that George Calvert wanted to solve? How did he solve it?**

The "Catholic problem" that George Calvert wanted to solve was that Catholics were not allowed to openly practice the Faith in England. He solved the problem by sending Catholics to America where they could freely practice their faith.

11. **Describe the situation that prompted the Toleration Act.**

The Toleration Act was prompted by the growing number of Maryland settlers who were not Catholic. Many settlers had come to Maryland as indentured servants; and these, when their term of service expired, obtained the right to vote. Most of these were not Catholic. Too, a number of Puritans, driven from Virginia by its royalist governor, settled in Maryland. Fearing the growing number of Protestants boded ill for the safety of Maryland's Catholics, Lord Baltimore directed the colonial government to approve the Toleration Act.

12. **Describe the beliefs of the Quakers and their mode of Church government.**

The "Society of Friends," or the "Quakers," as they were called, believed the final authority for a believer was not the Church, nor even the Bible, but the light of the Holy Spirit's presence in the soul. Since everyone was capable of having this inner light, all were equal, and so the Friends had no clergy or hierarchy. Quakers condemned all violence and were pacifists. They believed in complete religious toleration.

Ideas in Action

1. **Read Nathaniel Hawthorne's *The Scarlet Letter* and consider how it reflects Puritan ideas.**

2. **Write your own account of what you think it would have been like to be a Catholic in Protestant England and America in the 17th century.**

3. **Find out if your family was in America in the 17th and early 18th centuries and create a family tree. See if you can discover any family stories or any accounts written about your ancestors.**

Sample Quiz I (pages 71-82)

Please answer the following in complete sentences.

1. **What form of Protestantism did the Puritans follow?**

2. **What did the doctrines of Puritanism emphasize?**

3. **What did the "City on a Hill" idea indicate about the Puritan establishment?**

4. **Why did many Puritans come to New England?**

5. What did the Puritans establish that characterizes New England?

6. Identify the following characters and what they are known for:
   a. Anne Hutchinson
   b. Roger Williams

7. What caused Indian discontent in New England?

8. What happened to Virginia when King James disbanded the Virginia Company?

9. How did New England's settlements differ from Virginia's concerning land?

10. Who was Nathanial Bacon, and what did he do?

Answers to Sample Quiz I

Students' answers should approximate the following.
1. The Puritans followed the Calvinist, or Reformed, tradition of Protestantism.
2. The doctrines of Puritanism emphasized the goodness of manual, as well as intellectual, labor
3. The "City on a Hill" indicated that the Puritans had entered in a covenant or contract with God.
4. Many Puritans decided that since they could not turn old England into their model of a Puritan commonwealth, they would form such a society in New England.
5. The Puritans established the pattern of settlement that still characterizes New England --- the division into townships.
6.
   a. Anne Hutchinson was a New England "heretic" who objected to the regime in Massachusetts Bay Colony. Hutchinson went south to Narragansett Bay where she established a settlement called Portsmouth, the first settlement on what became known as Rhode Island.
   b. Roger Williams was a religious dissident who criticized the Puritans of New England for remaining in the Church of England. Later moved to Narragansett Bay and founded the settlement of Providence, where he defended the Indians there from English settlers. In Providence Williams established a policy of religious toleration.

7. The Indians did not understand European notions of land ownership and thought they were merely lending land sold to whites. They also suffered from contact with unscrupulous whites, who cheated them and, worse, sold them the alcohol for which the nations had no tolerance.
8. When he disbanded the Virginia Company, King James made Virginia a crown colony, or royal province --- a dominion.
9. New Englanders formed tightly knit townships, while Virginians lived widely separated on farmsteads.
10. Nathanial Bacon was a Virginia colonist who stirred up a rebellion against abuses in Virginia's government.

Sample Quiz II (pages 82-90)

Please answer the following in complete sentences.

1. What was the "Catholic problem"?

2. What was unique about the governorship of Maryland?

3. What is a head-right system?

4. What was the Toleration Act?

5. Why was religious tolerance of Catholics doomed in Maryland?

6. How did Dutch America become an English possession?

7. Who was William Penn?

8. What did Penn see his colony as?

Answers to Sample Quiz II

Students' answers should approximate the following.

1. The "Catholic problem" was that Catholics were not allowed to practice publicly their faith in England.
2. Maryland's governorship was unique because of all the English colonies, it was the most self-governing.
3. A head-right system is a system whereby a settler was granted fifty acres for himself and for every person whom he brought to Virginia.
4. The Toleration Act guaranteed tolerance for religious belief and practice for all those who believe in Jesus Christ.
5. Religious tolerance of Catholics was doomed in Maryland because Catholics remained a minority while the population of Protestants continually increased.
6. Dutch America became an English possession because the Dutch governor was unable to convince his people to resist the English during an attack on Amsterdam harbor.
7. William Penn was the Quaker founder of the colony of Pennsylvania.
8. Penn saw his colony as a "holy experiment" in religious toleration.

Essays

Instructions to be given to the students: Write in complete sentences. Underline your thesis. Give three supports or examples that explain why you think what you do and that support your thesis.

1. Write an essay on whether you think religious toleration as seen in America is a good or bad thing. Compare it to England's situation in the 16th-18th centuries. Use specific examples.

2. Compare and contrast the Puritans' society with other societies, such as Virginia's, or the Spaniards'. How do their beliefs form their societies and governments? Use specific examples.

Sample Test

Please answer the following in complete sentences.

I. Short Essay – Answer two of the following:

1. What did the Body of Liberties and the General Fundamentals say?
2. What was the pattern of settlement in New England?
3. What were the causes of King Philip's War?
4. Describe Virginia's government when it was under the Virginia Company's rule.
5. What were the abuses against which Nat Bacon rebelled?
6. What was the character of Maryland's government?

II. Short Answer:

1. What did the "City on a Hill" signify?
2. What brought many Puritans to New England?
3. Identify the following:
   a. Anne Hutchinson
   b. Roger Williams
   c. Nathanial Bacon
   d. William Penn

4. What was the "Catholic problem" in England?

5. What was the Toleration Act?

6. What did William Penn want his colony to be?

....

Answer Key to the Chapter Test

Students' answers should approximate the following:

I.

1. The Body of Liberties and the General Fundamentals guaranteed the traditional safeguards of English liberty: free elections; trial by jury; the right not to be deprived of life, liberty, or property without due process of law; the right not to be taxed if not represented; and the right not to be forced to incriminate oneself in a trial.

2. When groups began to feel too crowded in one place they, with the permission of the colonial assembly, established new townships. The townships were divided into lots surrounding a "meeting house" where townsmen worshiped and conducted government business.

3. Among the causes of King Philip's War was the discontent of Metacom ("King Philip"), chief sachem of the Wampanoag tribe, that he and his people had been ill treated and insulted by the Puritans of Massachusetts. The proximate cause was the murder of Sassamon, a Harvard educated Indian. Sassamon had been King Philip's secretary and had informed against him to Governor Winslow of Plymouth.

4. The Virginia Company had established in Virginia a representative assembly, elected by all freemen, that shared power with the colonial governor appointed by the company. This "House of Burgesses" was the first representative assembly in the New World. The company had also granted the colonists all the freedoms that they had enjoyed in England, such as the right to trial by jury and due process.

5. Sir William Berkeley, who, deposed by Cromwell, had returned to power in 1660, controlled the workings of the colony, and was bent on promoting agricultural schemes (as well as new taxes to pay for them) unpopular with most Virginians. There had been no elections for the House of Burgesses in 14 years. The burgesses favored Berkeley's policies. There were also Indian troubles that, it seemed, the government would do nothing about.

6. Maryland became the most self-governing of the English colonies. In addition to the governorship, Cecil Calvert established a house of burgesses. The function of the burgesses was to advise the governor and the proprietor, but it was not long before it began to vote to approve or reject laws proposed by the governor. Lord Baltimore decreed that all freemen, whether proprietors or not, had the right to vote for members of the burgesses.

II.

1. The "City on a Hill" signified that the Puritans had entered in a covenant or contract with God and that this settlement would become an example of righteousness to all the world.

2. Many Puritans decided that since they could not turn old England into their model of a Puritan commonwealth, they would form such a society in New England.

3.
    a. Anne Hutchinson was a New England "heretic" who objected to the regime in Massachusetts Bay Colony. She founded a settlement on Rhode Island.

b. Roger Williams was a religious dissident who criticized the Puritans of New England for remaining in the Church of England. He founded the settlement of Providence, Rhode Island.

c. Nathanial Bacon was a Virginia colonist who stirred up a rebellion against abuses in Virginia's government.

d. William Penn was the founder of the colony of Pennsylvania.

4. The "Catholic problem" was that Catholics were not allowed to publicly practice their faith in England.

5. The Toleration Act guaranteed tolerance for religious belief and practice for all those who believe in Jesus Christ.

6. Penn wanted his colony to be a "holy experiment" in religious toleration.

CHAPTER 6: The Struggle for a Continent

Chapter Overview

- Slave raids on the Spanish missions in Florida and Georgia began prior to, and continued through, Queen Anne's War. They led to the destruction of the missions along the Georgia coast and in Apalachee.

- In 1702 Queen Anne's War, the American branch of the War of Spanish Succession, began. It ended in 1713 with the Peace of Utrecht.

- In 1739 Spanish revenue cutters captured an English smuggler named Edward Jenkins and cut off his ear. When the British saw Jenkins earless, they declared war on Spain. This war became known as the "War of Jenkin's Ear."

- In 1744 the War of Jenkin's Ear merged with another European war, called the War of the Austrian Succession by Europeans and King George's War by Americans. King George's War ended in 1748 with the Treaty of Aix-la-Chapelle.

- The Albany Congress was founded in 1754 to discuss how to maintain the British colonies' alliance with the Iroquois and achieve greater colonial unity. Their plan of unity was never more than a proposal, however, since the colonies were not ready for it, and Great Britain was not ready to grant that much independence to the colonies.

- France joined an alliance with Austria, and Great Britain joined an alliance with Prussia. This resulted in the Seven Years' War, which raged not only in Europe but in Europe's colonies in India and America. In America this war was called the "French and Indian War."

- In 1760 the French governor, the Marquis de Vandreuil, surrendered Montreal and all of French Canada to the British. This effectively ended the French and Indian War.

- The war in Europe ended in 1763 with the Peace of Paris.

What Students Should Know

1. **The events that led to the demise of the Spanish missions in the Guale and Apalachee regions**

   Attacks on the Spanish missions of Florida began in 1680 when pagan Indians, encouraged and aided by English settlers at Charleston in Carolina, attacked a Christian village on St. Simon's Island in what is now Georgia. The Charleston settlers (primarily Huguenots and Scots) frequently crossed over into Spanish territory and formed an alliance with the power Yamassee tribe. Despite the Treaty of Madrid (between Spain and Great Britain), which placed the southern border of Carolina at the Savannah River, Carolinians and the Yamassee conducted slaving raids on the Guale missions in Spanish territory. Repeated Indian and pirate attacks on the Guale missions convinced the Spanish governor to evacuate all the missions on the coast north of Florida. By 1685, missions on the coast north of the St. Mary's River were no more. The Caronlians and their Indian allies next led slaving raids on the Spanish missions in Apalachee. With the beginning of Queen Anne's War in 1702, South Carolina's governor, James Moore, leading 600 Indians and 600 Carolinians, sacked San Agustín, destroying enroute the coastal missions south of the St. Mary's River. In 1704, Moore led South Carolinians and Creek Indians against Mission Concepción de Ayubale in Apalachee and forced its surrender. Following the surrender, Moore and his Carolinians brutally butchered the mission's inhabitants, scalping and mutilating men, women, and children. Following this butchery, the Spanish decided to abandon Apalachee and move the Christian Indian population to San Agustín. The Apalachee region lost 4,000 native inhabitants, and its 14 prosperous missions, with the surrounding Spanish ranchos and smaller Indian settlements.

2. What Queen Anne's War demonstrated about the English colonies

Though they were subject to Her Royal Majesty, Queen Anne, the English colonies could show a remarkable independence. For instance, as Queen Anne's War proved, the queen's government could not force colonists to serve in the army but were forced to ask colonial legislators to levy troops. If a colony refused, as did New York during Queen Anne's War, it remained neutral.

3. The results of Queen Anne's War in America

Queen Anne's War ended in 1713 with the Peace of Utrecht. France ceded Newfoundland, Acadia (renamed Nova Scotia – "New Scotland") to the English. England won the right to engage in the *asiento* (African slave trade with the Spanish colonies). The borders of French Canada, English America, and Spanish Florida remained unchanged.

4. Conflicts and problems in Spanish Florida

Christian Indians continued to suffer from slaver raids on their settlements. More problems followed from a feud among the Franciscans themselves. Friars from America, called creoles, assumed control of the Florida missions and offered little support to missionaries from Spain, called *peninsulares*. The creoles did not allow the *peninsulares* to hold positions of authority and assigned them the least desirable missions. Open dissension between the groups broke out, and the king of Spain had to intervene on behalf of the *peninsulares*. The controversy grew so bad that when the second auxiliary bishop of San Agustín, he found families in a bad state, drunkenness among the Indians, a broken-down parish church, and English traders openly preaching heresy on street corners. For the next ten years, this bishop worked to reform the Church in San Agustín.

5. What events led to the War of Jenkins' Ear

Spanish revenue cutters captured an English smuggler named Edward Jenkins and cropped one of his ears, because he was a smuggler. The Spanish were angry that for years the English had ignored the provision of the Treaty of Utrecht that allowed them, under the *asiento*, to send only one trading ship a year to Porto Bello in the Caribbean. Jenkins was but one of many English smugglers engaged in illegal trade. Members of Parliament were outraged over the loss of Jenkins' ear and declared war on Spain in October 1739 – a war that became popularly known as the "War of Jenkins' Ear."

6. The founding of Georgia

In 1733, General James Edward Oglethorpe with a group of philanthropists established a new colony, Georgia (after George II) as a refuge for debtors. This colony stretched from the Savannah River south to Florida – all land claimed by Spain, land where the coastal Guale missions once stood. The settlers of Georgia were not numerous. They were Germans from Salzburg, who founded

Federica, a settlement up the Savannah River from Oglethorpe's town of Savannah, as well as Scots Highlanders and English debtors who wanted to start life again in a new place.

7. The relation of the War of Jenkins' Ear and King George's War

In 1744, the War of Jenkins' Ear merged with another European war, called the War of the Austrian Succession in Europe but, in America, King George's War. France and Britain fought each other in Europe; their colonies fought each other in America.

8. What was the role of American Indians in King George's War

As in Queen Anne's War, the French, with their Indian allies, raided New England frontier villages and the town of Saratoga, New York, while England's allies, the Iroquois, raided Canada.

9. The results of King George's War

The Treaty of Aix-la-Chapelle in 1748 ended King George's War. Great Britain agreed to return Louisbourg to France in return for Madras in India, which the French had captured from the British. In return for a payment of money from Spain, Great Britain renounced her part in the *asiento*.

10. What happened to the Acadians in Nova Scotia

Ill feeling between French and English in America was exemplified by the Acadians, the French settlers of what the English now called Nova Scotia, but what the French had named l'Acadie. Since receiving l'Acadie in the Treaty of Utrecht in 1713, the English had been tolerant, allowing French Acadians to keep their language, practice their Catholic religion, and even rule themselves by their own laws. The Acadians, however, remained hostile to the British. Hopes that France would one day reconquer l'Acadie kindled the fires of their resentment against British rule. The English began to worry about the French when English settlements were established at Halifax and Annapolis Royal in Nova Scotia in 1749. After all, war with France could erupt at any time, and Britain did not want a hostile population within her colonies. So it was that England gathered those French Acadians who lived near militarily strategic centers and deported them from Nova Scotia. Their land having been confiscated, some 6,000 to 7,000 Acadians were sent to various parts of British America. A group of Acadians were allowed to settle in Louisiana, and their descendants, called Cajuns (a corruption of Acadians), remain in Louisiana.

11. British and French struggles over the Ohio Valley and what they led to

The French saw attempts by English land companies to settle English colonies in the Ohio River Valley as a threat; they could cut off communications between Canada and Louisiana. To forestall the English advance into the Ohio region, in 1749, the French governor of Canada sent Celeron de Bienville to take possession of the Ohio River Valley for France. Four years later, the governor erected a series of forts on the Allegheny and upper Ohio rivers. These fortresses worried Virginia, whose western boundary ran along the Ohio. Governor Robert Dinwiddie sent a lieutenant colonel named George Washington to deliver a formal protest to the French, who ignored it. The governor again sent Washington to the Ohio Valley with 150 soldiers to keep the French from building a fort near the confluence of the Allegheny and Monongahela rivers in western Pennsylvania. But the French built Fort Duquesne before

Washington could arrive and defeated Washington in a battle at Great Meadows.

12. Results of the Virginian defeat at Great Meadows

To the English colonists the defeat at Great Meadows made the French seem suddenly more powerful. The Iroquois, long enemies of the French, wavered in their alliance with the English. For many English colonials, Washington's defeat was proof that the colonies needed to act in a more unified fashion if they were to defend themselves against the French. So it was that a congress of colonial representatives met at Albany, New York, in June 1754, to discuss how to maintain their alliance with the Iroquois and achieve greater colonial unity.

13. What the Albany Congress decided. Why its proposals were not adopted

The Albany Congress approved a plan of union, introduced by Benjamin Franklin of Philadelphia and Thomas Hutchinson of Boston, that called for a kind of legislative assembly whose members would be appointed by the colonies, with a president appointed by the king. This quasi-government would have the powers to declare war, make peace, and conclude treaties with Indian nations in the name of all the colonies. It could raise armies, equip fleets, build forts – and raise the taxes necessary to pay for all this. The purchase of lands in the west would fall under this body, as well as the governance of the west, until the British government should decide to establish new colonies there. Though adopted by the Albany Congress, this plan was rejected by every colonial legislature. The colonies were jealous of their local independence and prerogatives. Moreover, even if they had adopted the plan of union, it is unlikely that the British government would

have approved it, since it would have given the colonies a significant degree of independence.

14. The Battle of Fort Duquesne and its results

General Braddock, with George Washington, led the British army against Fort Duquesne. On July 7, 1755, a combined force of French officers and regulars, French Canadian militia, and Indian braves, surprised Braddock on the Monongahela River near Fort Duquesne. Braddock's regulars panicked but had nowhere to run. Braddock himself was shot through the lungs and died soon after. Of his force of 1,459 men, 977 were killed or wounded. Washington and the colonial officers were hard pressed to rally the survivors and get them home. Because of this defeat, Braddock's successor decided to abandon the defense of the western frontier, thus putting many English settlements in mortal danger. Many Indian tribes now joined the French, and the Iroquois' fidelity to Great Britain wavered more. Suffering from repeated Indian attacks, settlers in the Shenandoah Valley fled east, abandoning all they had.

15. What resulted from the defeat at Duquesne and how the Old French and Indian War merged with the Seven Years' War

War, called the "Old French and Indian War," between the French and English in America followed the defeat at Duquesne, with a series of French victories. Though the French were defeated at Lake George on September 8, 1755, they were able to hold Crown Point on Lake Champlain and there raise a fortress – Fort Ticonderoga. In 1756, this Old French and Indian War became but another theater of the Seven Years' War, in America called the French and Indian War. The war, however, still went badly for the British. The course of the war changed in 1758 when William Pitt became secretary of state and prime minister of Great Britain. Pitt saw how Britain could win the war in America. The population of the English colonies (about 1,000,000) dwarfed the population of New France (only about 60,000); thus, without reinforcements from France, New France must in the end fall to the British. To block reinforcements coming to French America, Pitt used Great Britain's greatest advantage, her navy. Great Britain had the largest navy in the world. The French navy could not vie with it. In 1758, the British began winning victories against the French. Then in September 1759, British General Wolfe defeated the French in a battle on the Plains of Abraham, outside of Québec city, and the British captured Québec. The fortress of Québec and the Saint Lawrence, from the sea to Montreal, now belonged to the British. In September 1760, the French governor surrendered Montreal and all of French Canada to the British. Except for an Indian insurrection under Chief Pontiac in Michigan, Illinois, Indiana, and Ohio, the war in America was finished.

16. Results of the French and Indian War

The war concluded in 1763 with the Peace of Paris. According to the terms of the peace, France lost to Britain all of her North American colonies except a couple of small islands off Newfoundland, as well as Saint-Dominique and Guadeloupe in the Caribbean. The vast expanse of Louisiana passed to Spain. In return for Havana, which the British had taken, King Carlos III of Spain ceded Florida to the British.

17. What happened to Florida under British rule

Though they promised Catholics freedom of religion in Florida, the British seized all church property because, they claimed, it belonged to the king of Spain, not to the

Church, under the *patronato real*. Afterwards, few Catholics decided to remain in Florida.

Questions for Review

1. **Why was the attack on St. Simon's Island in 1680 so ominous?**

    The attack on St. Simon's was so ominous because the Indians were led by English settlers. It pesaged further English attacks on Spanish Florida

2. **Under what conditions did Queen Anne's War begin?**

    Queen Anne's War began as a branch of the War of Spanish Succession.

3. **What happened to the Catholic Indians of Georgia and Florida just before and during Queen Anne's War?**

    Colonists from Carolina and their Indian allies had been leading slaving raids on the Spanish missions in Apalachee in the years before Queen Anne's War. With the beginning of Queen Anne's War in 1702, South Carolina's governor, James Moore, with Indians and Carolinians, sacked San Agustín, destroying enroute the coastal missions south of the St. Mary's River. In 1704, Moore led South Carolinians and Creek Indians against a mission in Apalachee, and when it surrendered, butchered its inhabitants. Following this raid, the Spanish abandoned the Apalachee missions, moving the Christian Indians to San Agustín.

4. **Why did the Spanish cut off Edward Jenkins' ear, and why did this precipitate a war?**

    The Spanish were angry that for years the English had ignored the provision of the Treaty of Utrecht that allowed them, under the *asiento*, to send only one trading ship a

---

Key Terms at a Glance

Queen Anne's War: the American branch of the War of Spanish Succession

Peace of Utrecht: the peace treaty that ended Queen Anne's War

War of Jenkins' Ear: the war between Great Britain and Spain that was precipitated by the cutting off of Edward Jenkins' Ear

King George's War: the merging of the War of Jenkins' Ear with the War of the Austrian Succession

Treaty of Aix-la-Chapelle: the treaty that ended King George's War

Albany Congress: a congress of colonial representatives which met in Albany, New York

French and Indian War: the war between the British and the French in America. It ended with the surrender of Canada to Great Britain.

Peace of Paris: the treaty that ended the French and Indian War

---

year to Porto Bello in the Caribbean. Jenkins was but one of many English smugglers engaged in illegal trade, and had the poor luck to be caught. Members of Parliament were outraged at the way Jenkins had been treated, and declared war on Spain.

5. **What part did Georgia play in the War of Jenkins' Ear?**

The English settled a colony in Georgia, which was held by the Spanish. After being defeated by the Spanish, General James Oglethorpe withdrew to Georgia.

6. **Explain what the War of Spanish Succession was and who was involved.**

The War of Spanish Sucession began because the king of Spain, Carlos II, died, leaving his kingdom, not to his Austrian Habsburg cousin, Leopold I, but to Philippe, duke of Anjou, the grandson of King Louis XIV of France. Louis XIV was the most powerful monarch of Europe, and the English and other powers feared a union of Spain and France, with all their new world wealth, under the Bourbon family. Thus a war broke out – the English, the Dutch, and the Austrians against France and Spain.

7. **How was America involved in War of the Spanish Succession?**

The Americans were involved in Queen Anne's War, which was a branch of the War of the Spanish Succession.

8. **What was the purpose of the Albany Congress, and why did it fail?**

The Albany Congress approved a plan of union, introduced by Benjamin Franklin of Philadelphia and Thomas Hutchinson of Boston, that called for a kind of legislative assembly whose members would be appointed by the colonies, with a president appointed by the king. It failed because the colonies were jealous of their local independence and prerogatives.

9. **How did the Seven Years War begin, and what relation did the French and Indian War have to it?**

The Seven Years War started with France joining an alliance with Austria; and Great

Britain, already engaged in war with France in America, allied itself with Prussia. The French and Indian War was a theater of the Seven Years War in America.

10. **How did the Seven Years' War affect Florida?**

In return for Havana, which the British had taken, King Carlos III of Spain ceded Florida to the British. Though they promised Catholics freedom of religion in Florida, the British seized all church property because, they claimed, it belonged to the king of Spain, not to the Church, under the *patronato real*. Afterwards, few Catholics decided to remain in Florida.

Ideas in Action

1. Research the events of the counterpart wars to the wars in America mentioned in this chapter.

2. Find maps of Europe and America that refer to the time of the wars mentioned in this

chapter. Mark off the territories controlled by each major power at the beginning of each war. See how the map changes over the course of each war, and mark the territorial changes in a separate color.

Sample Quiz I (pages 93-98)

Please answer the following in complete sentences.

1. **How did the attacks on Spanish missions in Guale and Apalachee regions begin?**

2. **What convinced the Spanish governor to evacuate all the missions on the coast north of Florida?**

3. **What did Queen Anne's War demonstrate about the English colonies in America?**

4. **What was the *asiento***

5. **What event caused the War of Jenkins' Ear?**

6. **Why was Georgia founded?**

7. **What war was the War of Jenkins' Ear a part of?**

Answers to Sample Quiz I

Students' answers should approximate the following.

1. Attacks on the Spanish missions of Florida began in 1680 when pagan Indians, encouraged and aided by English settlers at Charleston in Carolina, attacked a Christian village on St. Simon's Island in what is now Georgia.

2. Repeated Indian and pirate attacks on the Guale missions convinced the Spanish governor to evacuate all the missions on the coast north of Florida.

3. Queen Anne's War demonstrated that the English colonies in America could show a remarkable independence.

4. The *asiento* was the African slave trade with the Spanish colonies

5. The cropping of the English smuggler Edward Jenkins' ear caused the War of Jenkins' Ear.

6. Georgia was founded as a refuge for debtors.

7. The War of Jenkins' Ear was part of the War of the Austrian Succession in Europe.

Sample Quiz II (pages 98-102)

Please answer the following in complete sentences.

1. **Who were the Acadians?**

2. **Why did the French see any attempts by the English land companies to settle English colonies in the Ohio River Valley as a threat?**

3. What did the Virginian defeat at Great Meadows inspire the colonies to do?

4. What did the plan of union that the Albany Congress called for consist of?

5. What war resulted from the defeat at Duquesne?

6. What happened to Louisiana and Florida after the French and Indian War?

7. What justification did the British give for seizing all church property in Florida?

Answers to Sample Quiz II

Students' answers should approximate the following.

1. The Acadians were the French settlers of what the English called Nova Scotia and the French called l'Acadie.

2. The French saw any attempts by the English land companies to settle English colonies in the Ohio River Valley as a threat because they could cut off communications between Canada and Louisiana.

3. The Virginian defeat at Great Meadows inspired a congress of colonial representatives to meet at Albany, New York, in June 1754, to discuss how to maintain their alliance with the Iroquois and achieve greater colonial unity.

4. The Albany Congress called for a kind of legislative assembly whose members would be appointed by the colonies, with a president appointed by the king

5. War, called the "Old French and Indian War," between the French and English in America resulted from the defeat at Duquesne.

6. After the French and Indian War, Louisiana passed to Spain, and Spain ceded Florida to the British.

7. The British seized all church property because, they claimed, it belonged to the king of Spain, not to the Church, under the *patronato real.*

Essay

Instructions to be given to the students: Write in complete sentences. Underline your thesis. Give three supports or examples that explain why you think what you do and that support your thesis.

1. How do you think the wars in this chapter affected Catholic life in North America? Use specific examples from one or two of the wars to illustruate your point.

Sample Test

Please answer the following in complete sentences.

I. Short Essay – Answer two of the following:

1. What events led to the demise of the Spanish missions in the Guale and Apalachee regions?

2. How did the English colonies in America demonstrate their independence during Queen Anne's War?

3. How did the War of Jenkins' Ear begin?

4. How did the Albany Congress' government work?

II. Short Answer:

1. What war did the War of Jenkins' Ear merge with?

2. What happened to the Acadians in Nova Scotia?

3. How did the English colonists see the French after the defeat at Great Meadows?

4. Why was the Albany Congress' pland of union rejected?

5. What resulted from the defeat at Duquesne?

Answer Key to the Chapter Test

Students' answers should approximate the following:

I.

1. The events that led to the demise of the Spanish missions in the Guale and Apalachee regions were attacks on the Spanish missions of Florida by pagan Indians and English settlers, slave raids on the Guale missions in Spanish territory, and repeated Indian and pirate attacks.

2. During Queen Anne's War, English colonies in America demonstrated their independence in several ways. For instance, the queen's government could not force colonists to serve in the army but were forced to ask colonial legislators to levy troops. If a colony refused, as did New York during Queen Anne's War, it remained neutral.

3. Spanish revenue cutters captured an English smuggler named Edward Jenkins and cropped one of his ears, because he was a smuggler. The Spanish were angry that for years the English had ignored the provision of the Peace of Utrecht that allowed them, under the *asiento*, to send only one trading ship a year to Porto Bello in the Caribbean. Jenkins was but one of many English smugglers engaged in illegal trade. Members of Parliament were outraged over the loss of Jenkins' ear and declared war on Spain in October 1739 – a war that became popularly known as the "War of Jenkins' Ear."

4. The Albany Congress' government would have the powers to declare war, make peace, and conclude treaties with Indian nations in the name of all the colonies. It could raise armies, equip fleets, build forts – and raise the taxes necessary to pay for all this. The purchase of lands in the west would fall under this body, as well as the governance of the west, until the British government should decide to establish new colonies there.

II.

1. The War of Jenkins' Ear merged with the War of Spanish Succession.

2. The Acadians in Nova Scotia were deported and sent to various parts of British America.

3. The defeat at Great Meadows made the French seem suddenly more powerful to the English colonists.

4. The Albany Congress' plan of union was rejected because the colonies were jealous of their local independence and prerogatives.

5. The "Old French and Indian War," between the French and English in America followed the defeat at Duquesne.

CHAPTER 7: Spanish America in the 17th and 18th Centuries

Chapter Overview

- On August 10, 1680, an Indian religious leader by the name of Popé started a large-scale rebellion in New Mexico. The Spaniards were forced to flee.

- In 1692 Diego Vargas retook Santa Fé and the surrounding countryside. With the Reconquest of Santa Fé, New Mexico entered a period of expansion.

- In the 17th and 18th centuries the Spanish crown tried to reform the *encomienda* system. In 1720 the Bourbon king Felipe V finally abolished the whole system in law though it continued to exist in practice.

- To address the continuing existence of the *encomienda system*, King Carlos III placed an official called the *alcalde mayor* over the Indians. This new system was abolished in 1786.

- Beginning in the late 1680s, the Jesuit priest, Eusebio Kino, began establishing missions in the Pimería Alta.

- In 1695 the Pima Indians rose in revolt. Lieutenant Antonio de Solís set off to crush the rebellion. Padre Eusabio Kino desired to keep peace, so he called the Indians to sign a treaty.

- Through a number of expeditions to the northwest to find a land supply route to missions in California, Kino proved once and for all that Baja California is not an island, but a peninsula.

- After Kino's death in 1711 and another revolt, the Pimería suffered from becoming a military camp. Division spread amongst the Pimas. The expulsion of the Jesuits from the the Spanish empire brought further suffering to the Pimería and other regions of the empire.

- As part of the Spanish king's reform of the missions, Count José de Gálvez brought in the Franciscans to attend to purely spiritual affairs. The reform did not work, however, and in 1769 the control of the missions was once again in the hands of the missionaries.

- In 1769 Fray Junípero Serra arrived at San Diego and began his zealous work of converting the Indians and building missions all over California. He was made *padre presidente*, or head, of all the California missions.

- In 1769, Don Gaspar de Portolá found Monterey as well as the bay of San Francisco.

- In 1774 Don Juan Bautista de Anza led an expedition to find a route from California to New Mexico.

What Students Should Know

1. **What troubles afflicted Spanish New Mexico in the 17th century**

   Internal and external conflicts affected life in New Mexico. The chief internal problem was a controversy over jurisdiction between the friars and the secular governor. As in Florida, so in New Mexico – the governor claimed authority over the entire missionary enterprise, while the friars demanded complete autonomy for themselves. The policies of the Spanish governors, who were wont to demand tribute and free labor from the Indians, inspired conspiracies among the natives. Raids by nomadic tribes, the Comanche and the Apache, on outlying settlements was the chief external threat throughout the 1660s. Christian Indians found it difficult to defend themselves, for many had died in epidemics that arose from a drought. Those Pueblo Indians, indignant over the suppression of their native religion, blamed these misfortunes to its abandonment. Many natives returned to pagan worship.

2. Causes of Popé's revolt

In 1669, Governor Juan Francisco Treviño, discovering a conspiracy among the Indians, seized and imprisoned its leaders. Forty-seven of these were sentenced to be whipped and then sold into slavery, while four others were to be hanged. But Governor Treviño, fearing threats from Indians, altered the punishments. After whipping the 47 prisoners, he released them. One of those released was Popé, a religious leader from Taos pueblo. Over the next ten years he worked to unite the pueblos in a revolt against the Spanish.

3. The course of Popé's revolt and how Spanish rule was restored to New Mexico

On August 10, 1680, the Pueblo Indians rose and slaughtered Christian men, women, and children, both laymen and missionaries. Fleeing to Santa Fé, settlers and natives found refuge in the presidio. When the Indians cut off the the *presidio's* water supply, the fugitives, surrounded by soldiers, abandoned Santa Fé, fleeing 70 miles south to the friendly Indians of Isleta Pueblo. From Isleta,

they removed farther south, to El Paso. For ten years, Popé and other tribal leaders ruled the pueblos, ending their traditional independence and forcing them to destroy all traces of Spanish civilization that they forbade anyone to use the fruits, vegetables, and livestock the Spanish had introduced into New Mexico. Without the threat of Spanish arms to cow them, nomadic tribes intensified their raids on the pueblo settlements. Discontent grew, and civil wars broke out among the pueblos. Some Pueblo Indians went south to El Paso to invite them back. In September 1692, the Spanish governor, Diego de Vargas led a contingent of 800 soldiers, along with colonists and Christian Indians, to New Mexico and, after a two-day battle, took Santa Fé. Over the next year, Vargas obtained the peaceful surrender of most of the pueblos, though some resisted.

4. The condition of New Mexico after the Spanish reconquest

Following the reconquest, New Mexico entered a period of expansion. Missions were rebuilt and Indian children baptized. More families from Mexico, with soldiers and Franciscan missionaries, settled the land. On June 14, 1696, Indians in 15 Pueblo villages again rebelled. During the three months the rebellion raged, Indians killed five Franciscans and 21 Spaniards and pillaged and destroyed churches and dwellings. By September, however, Vargas had crushed the revolt and punished those responsible.

5. The character of Spanish America

The kings of Spain saw their New World possessions, not as colonies to be exploited for the sake of the mother country, but as new kingdoms, equal to the old kingdoms of Spain. New Spain and Peru were domains of the king no wit inferior to Castile, León, and

Aragon. While the king took a portion (the royal fifth) of whatever gold or silver or other wealth was found in America, he expended great sums of money in maintaining the colonies. The kings of Spain saw the free inhabitants of America, both natives and transplanted Spaniards, as equal subjects of the crown. As a Catholic king exercising the *patronato real*, the Spanish king saw it as his duty to Christianize and civilize the natives of America so that they could become full and equal subjects of the crown and the Church. So, despite the expense, the king would maintain a colony as long as there was progress in Christianizing and civilizing the Indians. Because the bull, *Inter Caetera*, granted much of the New World in some fashion to the king of Spain, all New World lands were called *hacienda real*, the "royal estate." All land was king's land, his exclusive possession and all lands were held under his authority.

The king of Spain maintained a firm control over the government of his New World possessions. The highest authority in each "kingdom" was the king, who exercised his rule through a representative called a "viceroy." Since the viceroy occupied the place of the king, he was forbidden to own land in his viceroyalty so he would work in the king's and not his own interest. At the end of his six-year term of office, the viceroy's administration had to undergo a detailed review by the next viceroy.

Alongside the viceroy was the court called the *audiencia real*. While the viceroy looked to the administration of the viceroyalty, the *audiencia* administered justice. Each province within the viceroyalty had its own *gobernador* (governor) and *audiencia*. Below the governor were a number of lesser officials. In the pueblos, or "towns," some of these officials were elected, while others were appointed. Since those rich enough could buy the office,

the Spanish established the office of the *visitador real*, the "royal visitor," who inspected the acts of officials to see that they conformed to law.

Spanish New World officials were governed by an elaborate system of laws that attempted to cover every conceivable situation. When a situation arose not covered by the laws, one had to consult either the governor, the viceroy, or even Madrid to know what he should do. Royal government was thus slow and inefficient, and private initiative was often thwarted.

6. The social classes in the Spanish New World

To break down the barriers that separated European settlers from the American natives, the royal government encouraged intermarriage between Spaniards and natives. From this intermingling of the races – what the Spanish called *mestizaje* – came a new racial type, the *mestizo*. The *mestizos* came to form the largest single class in Spanish American society. Spanish American society was divided into racial classes. The most influential and powerful group was the European-born Spaniards, called *peninsulares*, who controlled all the higher offices of government in Spanish America. Below the *peninsulares* were the creoles, who were pure Spaniards, but born in America. Though excluded from the highest political offices, creoles occupied less influential and powerful ones. Later, they were able to buy their way into higher offices and a few served as viceroys.

Mestizos, the largest social class, began to occupy many of the lowest offices, such as elective offices in the pueblos. Next after the *mestizos* in the social order were the Indians. Though considered full subjects of the king, Indians were often treated like a subject race and exploited. The crown and some viceroys sincerely tried to protect the Indians. Luis de Velasco, who was viceroy of New Spain from 1550 to 1564, freed some 160,000 Indians from forced labor service.

By 1808, Black slaves numbered about 700,000 out of a population of 15 million and suffered cruel treatment throughout Spanish America. Such treatment, however, violated the Spanish Laws of the Indies that sought to rein in the power of slave-owners and decreed that slaves had a right to own property. The law declared that the Church had to catechize black slaves and administer the sacraments to them, including sacramental marriage. The king required masters to teach their slaves the Catholic faith and give them elementary instruction in reading and mathematics. The crown regulated how much labor a master could require of his slaves and how he treated them. Just as with Indians, Spaniards intermarried with blacks, from which unions came another social group, the mulattos. The *zambos*, or *sambos*, came from intermarriages between blacks and Indians. Since slaves could buy their freedom, there came to be many free blacks and free black communities in Spanish America.

7. Attempts to reform the *encomienda* system

In the 17th and 18th centuries, the crown again tried to reform the *encomienda* system. Laws passed in 1612 and 1620 decreed that all *encomiendas* that had lapsed or had terminated (for instance, if an *encomendero* had no heir) would become crown property. King Felipe V in 1720, abolished the whole system in law, though it continued to exist in practice. To remedy this, King Carlos III (1759-1788) placed an official called the *alcalde mayor* over the Indians. However, because these *alcaldes* began to behave just

like the *encomenderos*, the king abolished the office in 1786 and appointed royal representatives called sub-delegates to handle Indian affairs.

8. The character of life in New Spain

By the 17th century, Spanish America had large, thriving cities with universities, theaters, mansions, and beautiful public buildings. Outside the large cities were many pueblos that grew from settlements of Spanish colonists or from missions. The towns were surrounded by ranches and farms where cattle and crops were raised. At first, the colonists of Spanish America preferred mining to any other industry – for it was a quick way to wealth. However, as time passed, agriculture became increasingly more important to the economy of the Americas. The Spanish crown strictly regulated trade between the America and Europe, and even between its American realms. All colonial products for foreign markets had to be shipped first to Spain, and from Spain to foreign or colonial ports. These cumbersome regulations meant that colonials often resorted to illegal trade with foreign powers. Partly to curtail this smuggling, the king of Spain eventually relaxed some of the trading regulations. The Spanish government laid burdensome taxes on all Spanish citizens whether in Europe or America. Though most of the tax money benefited America (the cost of colonization was always high for Spain), still they were hard to bear.

9. The culture and arts of New Spain

Spanish America had a rich culture. It was a Spanish, European culture, modified after a time by American influences. Throughout the land rose churches, cathedrals, monasteries, and palaces built in all the European styles – Gothic, Renaissance, and Baroque. Moorish influences were evident, too, in the design of doorways, windows, and fountains. The dark churches were filled with colorful statuary and paintings. Much of the art of Spanish America was done in service of the Church. Mexican composers composed church and secular music in the Baroque style, as well as in the Classical style of the late 18ᵗʰ century. Spanish American cities had theater for the performance of non-sacred music. Spanish America did not excel in literature, though it did produce a poet much admired today – Sor (sister) Juana Inés de la Cruz – who wrote both secular and religious poetry, novels, and comedies. Collecting a library of about 4,000 books, she engaged in scientific and classical literary studies.

10. The role of the Church in Spanish America

The Church influenced all of Spanish American society. Pueblos were built around parish churches. Priests and religious worked to civilize the Indians, teaching them how to engage in civic life and how to farm. The Church opposed exploiting or exterminating the Indians. From the beginning the Church upheld the dignity and rights of the American natives, especially after 1537 when Pope Paul III issued a bull that called Indians "real men" and forbade their enslavement. Missionary work was carried out by religious orders – primarily the Dominicans, the Franciscans, and the Jesuits – under the patronage, and control, of the Spanish king. It was the Church that had the care of the poor and the sick. Bishops, priests, and religious orders founded and staffed schools and hospitals, as well as missions. Endowed by the crown to carry out works of charity and social justice, the wealth of the colonial Church multiplied, making it one of the largest landholders in America. The Inquisition – a state institution staffed by

churchmen – was a court that tried cases having to do with heresy and certain kinds of immorality. The Inquisition had jurisdiction over foreign heretics, Jews, witches, and bigamists; they had no authority over the Indians. Condemnations and executions were relatively few; more common were *autos-de-fe*, public acts of faith, in which accused heretics publicly confessed their errors.

11. Why the Spanish government decided to open a missionary territory in the Pimería Alta

The Pimería Alta was a region covering what is today northern Sonora and southern Arizona. For years the Pima Indians had been asking for missionaries – and the government was now eager to send them some, for the Pimería had become economically and politically important. The Spaniards had discovered, and were exploiting, the rich silver mines in the region; but the settlements there were in danger. It had been only six years since the Pueblo rebellion in nearby New Mexico. The Apaches were a continual menace, and the government feared that the Pima Indians might also revolt. If they were converted, the Pima might form an important buffer between the silver mines of Sonora and the wild nomadic tribes of the north.

12. Who Eusebio Kino was and what he did in the Pimería Alta

Eusebio Kino, a native of the Tyrolese Alps, was a priest missionary of the Society of Jesus. In 1681, a mapmaker, he was in Mexico and sent to explore the region of California. Hoping to be sent as a missionary to what is now Baja California, Kino, to his disappointment, learned that he was, instead, to be sent to the Pimería Alta. At the Pima village of Corsari in modern Sonora, Kino established his first mission, Nuestra Señora de los Dolores (Our Lady of Sorrows) – the first in a string of missions that eventually spread out over the southern Pimería. Aided by a number of Jesuit priests, Kino, a man of untiring energy and zeal, taught the Indians not only the Faith but the rudiments of civilization. The Pimas were already a farming folk, but the Jesuits taught them better ways of farming and introduced them to European crops and domesticated animals. The Pimería, an arid desert land, became a flourishing garden through the labor of the native Pimas and Jesuit priests and brothers.

13. Padre Kino's explorations

In 1692, at the age of 47, Kino went on the first of the long explorations that would occupy him almost until his death. Kino undertook these journeys, partly to preach and seek out sites for new missions, and partly to discover if there were a land route from the Pimería to California. A land route would make it easier to supply new missions. Kino's journeys took him into what is now southern Arizona, where, near Tucson, he established missions at Guevavi, Tumacácori, and Bac. Bac was the largest Pima village in the region and later would boast a fine mission – San Xavier del Bac. From 1697 to 1703, Kino went on a number of expeditions to the northwest to find the junction of the Gila with another great river of which he had heard. He went also to discover whether there was a land supply route to the missions in California. By these expeditions, Kino proved once and for all that Baja California was not an island, but a peninsula.

14. The threats to the missions of the Pimería after Kino

In 1736, an ambitious *alcalde mayor* took over the administration of the northwest of New Spain. Because of a discovery of silver in an arroyo near the Pima settlement of Arizonac, the *alcalde mayor* decided to exploit the mineral wealth of the region. Soon settlers and adventurers swarmed into the Pimería. The Jesuits protested, fearing the settlement's ill effects on the Pimas, but their protests went unheeded. Within 15 years, the settlers had so disrupted Pima life that the Pima Indian governor, Luis Oacpicogigua, was able to ignite a rebellion against the Spaniards. The Pimas assaulted both *reales* (as Spanish settlements were called) and missions, and many Spanish miners and settlers were killed. The Spaniards eventually crushed the rebellion and restored the expelled padres to their missions.

15. The effects of the revolt and suppression on the Pimería

The revolt and its suppression of the Pima revolt had dire effects on the Pimería. For one, the Spanish decided that a stronger military presence was needed there, and so the once peaceful Pimería was reduced to a military camp. Because of all the injustices they had suffered, the Pimas were divided into factions, and long established tribal alliances were broken. Without a strong, united Piman front, the Apaches could carry their raids deep into Sonora.

16. King Carlos III's reform measures for the missions and their results

It was King Carlos III who expelled the Jesuits from his realms, including the Pimería. He wanted to establish a more "modern" and "rational" form of government over his domains and saw the Jesuits as an obstacle to his plans. The "rational" governing favored by King Charles involved changing the mission system. The Indians, according to the new policy, were to take their place as equal subjects of the Spanish crown. They were no longer to be administered by missionaries but incorporated into Spanish *pueblos* and ruled by Spanish officials. Missionaries or, better yet, secular priests, would serve only their spiritual needs. It soon became apparent that Gálvez's system did not work. Without missionary control over the mission lands and buildings, many churches and convents were collapsing. Finally, the government had to relent. In 1769, total control of the missions passed once again into the hands of the missionaries.

17. **The exploration of Alta California and why Spain decided finally to establish settlements there**

Spain's claim to Alta California dated back to 1542 when Juan Rodríguez Cabrillo explored the coasts of the North Pacific. Cabrillo reached a large, well-sheltered bay north of the Baja California peninsula and then sailed further north to discover Santa Catalina Island and the Santa Barbara Channel. Sixty years later, Sebastián Vizcaíno explored the same coast, landing at the first bay Cabrillo had discovered (and naming it San Diego); he then proceeded north to discover another, though less sheltered bay, which he called Monterey. At Monterey, Vizcaíno erected a stone altar where the first Mass on the Alta California coast was offered. When he returned to Mexico, Vizcaíno encouraged the Spanish authorities to settle the coast of what became known as Alta California. But 160 years passed before the Spanish government, in the person of Count José de Gálvez, conceived of colonizing California. Two powers – Russia and Great Britain – seemed to be showing an interest in the west coast of North America. Count Gálvez thought that, unless Spain strengthened her claim to the land by settlement, Spain might lose upper California. His plan was to establish a string of missions supported by only a skeleton force of soldiers.

18. **Who Fray Junípero Serra was and what he accomplished**

Fray Junípero Serra, a native of Mallorca, was a Franciscan priest. A professor of philosophy, he decided, in 1749, to volunteer for the missions in Mexico. His first mission was the to the pagan Pame Indians of the Sierra Gorda, a mountainous region 175 miles north of Mexico City, where he remained for eight years. From 1758-1767, he worked as a home missionary for the the Franciscan missionary College of San Fernando. He then was appointed *padre presidente* of the Baja California missions. In 1768, he was appointed to found the mission system in Alta California. In 1769, Fray Junípero established his first mission in Alta California at San Diego. At Monterey, in 1770, with Don Gaspar de Portolá, he took formal possession of Alta California for the king of Spain. By the time he died in 1784, Fray Junípero had established nine missions along the coast of California, from San Diego to San Francisco.

19. **How the Franciscans ran the California missions**

The California missions were set up as large agricultural and cattle raising concerns. The Indians were not forced onto the missions, but invited; once they came and were baptized, however, they were under the authority of the missionaries and were forbidden to leave. The missionaries taught the natives not only the Catholic faith but various crafts, the art of farming, and cattle raising. The missionaries treated the Indians as children, with the aim to educate and train them so that the mission pueblo and farms could eventually be turned over to them, and the missionaries replaced with secular priests. Mission Indians lived a highly regimented life.

20. The culture of the California Indians

California natives spoke at least 135 different languages. Divided into small clans, the natives were highly disunited and engaged in bloody feuds with each other. The natives lived by gathering acorns, pine nuts, and wild grains. They hunted, sneaking quietly up on their prey to shoot it at close range with bow and arrow. Their weapons, though accurate, were tipped with stone or bone. Their houses were small, made from reeds and branches of willow, though they did construct tight wood structures called sweat lodges. Native California arts, too, were primitive: for instance, they used stone mortars and *metates* to grind acorns and nuts. On the other hand the coastal tribes, such as the Chumash, chiseled out great urns from soft stone and built long boats in which they braved the seas, paddling out on expeditions to the Santa Barbara Channel Islands, about 15 miles offshore. Everywhere, too, the California Indians crafted exquisitely beautiful baskets with intricate designs and so tightly woven that they held water. When the Indians needed hot water, they heated stones in a fire until they grew quite hot and then cast them into the water-filled baskets. The Franciscans found the California natives to be quick learners, easily mastering the crafts the friars taught. They learned to play European musical instruments, and Indian choirs and orchestras in the missions performed complex works. Visitors to California in the early 19th century commented on the precision and beauty of these Indian musical ensembles. The friars trained and employed Indian artisans in adorning the mission churches.

21. The effect of disease on the California Indians

As in the rest of America, so in California: European diseases took their toll on the Indian population. Though such diseases as tuberculosis and syphilis were prevalent among the Indians before the coming of the Europeans (and this may be one reason for the relatively small number of natives in California), new diseases decimated the Indian population. Despite efforts by the friars to stem disease, the Indian population continued to decline during the mission period. By the 1820s, however, it seemed to begin to rebound as subsequent generations developed immunities to the diseases.

22. Spanish exploration of the Southwest

In their early days, the missions in California depended on supplies brought from Mexico by the sea route from San Blas. The supply route was long and somewhat precarious, and so it was that Fray Junípero suggested to the viceroy that a second supply route, a land route from Sonora and New Mexico, should be opened to facilitate supplying the missions. Fray Francisco Garcés had already explored and charted much of the Colorado River down to where it poured into the Gulf of California. Now, all that was needed was an expedition to chart a land route from New Mexico to the coast of Alta California. Don Juan Bautista de Anza was chosen to lead this expedition Accompanied by Fray Francisco Garcés, who was well known and liked by the Yuma Indians on the Colorado, Anza left Tubac in what is now Arizona in January 1774. Winning the friendship of the Yumas with gifts, Anza's men passed into the forbidding deserts of Southern California. From the barren desert, the expedition crossed the heights of the San Jacinto Mountains and passed into the dry, inland

Key Terms at a Glance

hacienda real: the "royal estate": the lands in the New World claimed by the king of Spain

gobernador: Spanish word for "governor"; the title for an official in Spanish America, the chief executive officer of a province

visitador real: the "royal visitor" who inspected the acts of officials in the New World

mestizaje: the result of the intermingling of Indian, black, and European races in the New World

peninsularees: European-born Spaniards, the highest racial class in America,

creoles: pure Spaniards, but born in America

mestizos: those in Spanish America of mixed European and Indian blood

neophyte: a new convert

valleys now occupied by the suburbs of Los Angeles. The expedition arrived at mission San Gabriel in March 1774.

23. The founding of pueblos in Califorrnia

The year 1777 saw the founding of the first Spanish pueblo in California, San José de Guadalupe, near Mission Santa Clara de Asís. The pueblo was founded to promote agriculture so that California settlers need not rely so heavily on Mexico for supplies. In 1781, eleven families under Captain Rivera founded another settlement on the coastal plain, not far from Mission San Gabriel. In this settlement, El Pueblo de Nuestra Señora Reina de Los Angeles de Porciuncula (the Pueblo of or Our Lady Queen of the Angels of Porciuncula) each family received a plot of land on which it could build a house.

Questions for Review

1. **What were the conditions in New Mexico that led to the destruction of the Spanish settlements there?**

The Indians were indignant that their native culture was being suppressed, and under Popé, a religious leader, they rebelled against Spanish rule, killing thousands of Spaniards and Christian Indians, and burning churches.

2. **How did the kings of Spain regard their New World possessions and the inhabitants of America?**

The kings of Spain saw their New World possessions, not as colonies to be exploited for the sake of the mother country, but as new kingdoms, equal to the old kingdoms of Spain.

3. **In what ways did the government of Spanish America differ from that of the English colonies?**

The English government saw its Spanish possessions as colonies to be exploited for the sake of the mother country, while the Spanish government did not, but as kingdoms or realms coequal to the realms of Spain. Though both England and Spain had economic motives to their colonization, religious concerns played a more prominent role with Spain than with England.

4. **Name and describe the social classes of Spanish America.**

    Peninsulares: European-born Spaniards, the most influential and powerful group who controlled all the higher offices of government in Spanish America.

    Creoles: pure Spaniards, but born in America. Though excluded from the highest political offices, creoles occupied less influential and powerful ones. Later, they were able to buy their way into higher offices and a few served as viceroys.

    Mestizos: the mestizos came from the intermingling of the Spaniards and natives. They were the largest single class in Spanish American society.

    Indians: the natives. Full subjects of the king, they were often treated like a subject race and exploited.

5. **Describe the government of Spanish America.**

    The king of Spain maintained a firm control over the government of his New World possessions. The highest authority in each "kingdom" was the king, who exercised his rule through a representative called a "viceroy." Alongside the viceroy was the court called the *audiencia real*. While the viceroy looked to the administration of the viceroyalty, the *audiencia* administered justice. Each province within the viceroyalty had its own *gobernador* (governor) and *audiencia*. Below the governor were a number of lesser officials. In the pueblos, or "towns," some of these officials were elected, while others were appointed. Since those rich enough could buy the office, the Spanish established the office of the *visitador real*, the "royal visitor," who inspected the acts of officials to see that they conformed to law.

6. **Explain how Spain and Europe benefited from America.**

    Spain and all Europe in turn benefited from American arts and agriculture. The Spanish carried back to Europe a rich storehouse of foods from the agriculture of the Americas. Native American farmers contributed to Europe's cuisine pink and Lima beans, the potato, yellow squash and acorn squash, chili pepper, maize corn of many types, chocolate, and the tomato.

7. **What are some of Spanish America's contributions to art and the Church?**

    Spanish America had left behind a legacy of hroughout the land rose churches, cathedrals, monasteries, and palaces built in all the European styles. The dark churches were filled with colorful statuary and paintings. Much of the art of Spanish America was done in service of the Church. Mexican composers composed church and secular music in the Baroque style, as well as in the Classical style of the late 18th century. Spanish America did not excel in literature, though it did produce a poet much admired today --- Sor Juana Inés de la Cruz

8. **What was the social role of the Catholic Church in America, and how is an understanding of the Church helpful in understanding New Spain?**

    Priests and religious worked to civilize the Indians. The Church opposed exploiting or exterminating the Indians and upheld the dignity and rights of the American natives. Missionary work was carried out by religious orders under the patronage, and control, of the Spanish king. It was the Church that had the care of the poor and the sick. Bishops, priests, and religious orders founded and staffed schools and hospitals, as well as missions. One cannot properly understand

New Spain without understanding the social role of the Catholic Church in Spain's New World dominions because the Church influenced all of Spanish American society.

9. **What did Padre Kino accomplish in America?**

Padre Kino established missions in the Pimería Alta region and turned it into a flourishing garden. Through his explorations in California Padre Kino proved once and for all that Baja California was not an island, but a peninsula.

10. **What did Junípero Serra accomplish in America?**

Fray Junípero Serra was a Franciscan priest who volunteered for the missions in Mexico. His first mission was to the pagan Pame Indians of the Sierra Gorda, a mountainous region 175 miles north of Mexico City, where he remained for eight years. From 1758-1767, he worked as a home missionary for the the Franciscan missionary College of San Fernando. He then was appointed *padre presidente* of the Baja California missions. In 1768, he was appointed to found the mission system in Alta California. In 1769, Fray Junípero established his first mission at San Diego. At Monterey, in 1770, with Don Gaspar de Portolá, he took formal possession of Alta California for the king of Spain. By the time he died in 1784, Fray Junípero had established nine missions along the coast of California, from San Diego to San Francisco.

11. **How did the Indians of California and the Pimería compare to the Indians of eastern North America? What especially were the western Indians skilled in?**

The Indians of the west, unlike those of the east, were highly disunited, and lived by hunting and gathering. The Indians of the

west were skilled in basket making, some in a simple agriculture, and others by the manufacture of boats that could ride the ocean. Eastern Indians too practiced some agriculture but seemed more adept at political organization. On the whole, eastern Indians were more highly advanced in technology than the Indians of California and the Pimería.

Ideas in Action

1. **Research the missions of California and the saints they are named after.**

Students can give a short presentation on a mission and its patron saint.

2. **Read Willa Cather's *Death Comes for the Archbishop* or a biography of Junípero Serra.**

3. **Read some of the works of Sor Juana Inés de la Cruz.**

4. **Discuss whether the methods Serra used in attracting the Indians to the mission were right in light of natural justice and the demands of the Gospel.**

5. **Compare Serra's misssionary methods with those of the Jesuits in New France. Which were more effective? Why?**

Sample Quiz I (pages 105-111)

Please answer the following in complete sentences.

1. **What was the chief internal problem afflicting Spanish New Mexico in the 17th century?**

2. **What caused Popé to revolt against the Spanish?**

3. What happened to New Mexico after the Spanish reconquest?

4. How did the kings of Spain see their New World possessions?

5. Identify the following:
   a. *Audiencia Real*
   b. *visitador real*
   c. *Peninsulares*
   d. Creoles
   e. *Mestizos*
   f. *Sambos*

6. What did the bull that Pope Paul III issued in 1537 say about the Indians?

7. Why was it so important the Spanish government to open a missionary territory in the Pimería Alta?

8. Who was Eusebio Kino and what did he do?

9. Why did the Pima revolt against the Spaniards?

10. Why did King Carlos III expel the Jesuits from his realms?

Answers to Sample Quiz I

Students' answers should approximate the following.

1. The chief internal problem was a controversy over jurisdiction between the friars and the secular governor.

2. After being seized for a conspiracy against the Spanish government, the Spanish governor had Popé whipped and then released. Indignant at at punishment, Popé worked to unite the pueblos in a revolt against the Spanish.

3. After the Spanish reconquest, New Mexico went through a period of expansion.

4. The kings of Spain saw their New World possessions, not as colonies to be exploited for the sake of the mother country, but as new kingdoms, equal to the old kingdoms of Spain.

5.
   a. A court in New Spain that administered justice
   b. The "royal visitor" who inspected the acts of officials to see that they conformed to law.
   c. European-born Spaniards who controlled all the higher offices of government in America.
   d. Pure Spaniards, but born in America

   e. *Mestizos* came from the intermingling of the Spaniards and natives. They were the largest single class in Spanish American society.
   f. The *sambos* came from the intermarriage of blacks and Indians.

6. The bull that Pope Paul III issued in 1537 said that the Indians were "real men" and forbade their enslavement.

7. It was important to open a missionary territory in the Pimería Alta because if they were converted, the Pima might form an important buffer between the silver mines of Sonora and the wild nomadic tribes of the north.

8. Eusebio Kino was a Jesuit missionary who established missions in the Pimería Alta region and through his explorations proved that Baja California was not an island but a peninsula.

9. The Pima revolted against the Spanish because settlers and adventurers disrupted Pima life.

10. King Carlos III expelled the Jesuits from his realms because he wanted to establish a more "modern" and "rational" form of government over his domains and saw the Jesuits as an obstacle to his plans.

Sample Quiz II (pages 119-126)

Please answer the following in complete sentences.

1. Why did the Spanish government finally decide to settle Alta California?

2. Who was Fray Junipero Serra, and what did he accomplish?

3. How did the California missionaries treat the Indians?

4. What did the California Indians make that they were particularly known for?

5. How did the Indians respond to the missionaries' teaching of the arts?

6. Why did the Indian population decline with the coming of the Europeans?

7. Why did Fray Junípero suggest a second supply route to the California missions?

8. Why did the desire for a land route to California lead to exploration of the Southwest?

9. Why was the first Spanish pueblo in California founded?

Answers to Sample Quiz II

Students' answers should approximate the following.

1. The Spanish government finally decided to settle Alta California because Russia and Great Britain seemed to be showing an interest in the west coast of North America, and the Spanish were afraid that if they did not strengthen their claim to the land by settlement, they might lose upper California.

2. Fray Junipero Serra was a Franciscan priest who became *padre presidente* of the Baja California missions, and founded the mission system in Alta California.

3. The missionaries treated the Indians as children, with the aim to educate and train them so that the mission and its lands could eventually be turned over to them, and the missionaries replaced with secular priests.

4. The California Indians crafted exquisitely beautiful baskets with intricate designs and so tightly woven that they held water.

5. The Indians adapted quickly to what the missionaries taught them and mastered the crafts taught them.

6. The Indian population began to decline with the coming of the Europeans because of diseases the Europeans brought to which the Indians had no immunities.

7. Fray Junipero suggested a second supply route to the California missions because the only existing supply route was long and precarious.

8. Because a land route had to be charted from New Mexico to the coast of Alta California.

9. The first Spanish pueblo in California was founded to promote agriculture so that California settlers need not rely so heavily on Mexico for supplies.

Essays

Instructions to be given to the students: Write in complete sentences. Underline your thesis. Give three supports or examples that explain why you think what you do and that support your thesis.

1. Do you think the Spaniards' method of converting the Indians by suppressing their native gods and ceremonies was the right way to go about converting them? Explain why or why not, using specific examples.

2. Compare and contrast how the kings of Spain saw their New World possessions to how the kings of England saw theirs.

Sample Test

Please answer the following in complete sentences.

I. Short Essay – Answer two of the following:

1. Describe the events that brought about an Indian rebellion in New Mexico and then the restoration of Spanish rule.

2. Who was Padre Eusebio Kino, and what did he accomplish during his life?

3. Who was Fray Junipero Serra, and what did he accomplish during his life?

4. How did the Franciscans run the California missions?

II. Short Answer:

1. How did the kings of Spain see their New World subjects, both natives and transplanted Spaniards?

2. Name the four social classes of the Spanish New World.

3. What was the role of the Church in Spanish America?

4. How were the California missions set up?

5. Why was the first California pueblo founded?

Answer Key to the Chapter Test

Students' answers should approximate the following:

I.

1. In New Mexico, the Indians were indignant that their native culture was being suppressed, and under Popé, a religious leader, they rebelled against Spanish rule, killing thousands of Spaniards and Christian Indians, and burning churches. For ten years, Popé and other tribal leaders ruled the pueblos, ending their traditional independence and forcing them to destroy all traces of Spanish civilization. Discontent grew, and civil wars broke out among the pueblos. Some Pueblo Indians went south to El Paso to invite the Spanish back. In September 1692, the Spanish governor, Diego de Vargas led a contingent of 800 soldiers, along with colonists and Christian Indians, to New Mexico and, after a two-day battle, took Santa Fé. Over the next year, Vargas obtained the peaceful surrender of most of the pueblos, though some resisted.

2. Padre Eusebio Kino was a Jesuit missionary and mapmaker was sent to explore the region of Pimería Alta in California. He established his first mission there, the first in a string of missions that eventually spread out over the southern Pimería. He taught the Indians not only the Faith but the rudiments of civilization. He explored a route from Pimería to California, and through his explorations proved that Baja California was not an island but a peninsula.

3. Fray Junipero Serra was a Franciscan priest who volunteered for the missions in Mexico. His first mission was to the pagan Pame Indians of the Sierra Gorda, a mountainous region north of Mexico City, where he remained for eight years. He was appointed *padre presidente* of the Baja California missions and then to found the mission system in Alta California. He established his first mission at San Diego and took formal possession of Alta California for the king of Spain. By the time he died in 1784, Fray Junípero had established nine missions along the coast of California, from San Diego to San Francisco.

4. The California missions were set up as large agricultural and cattle raising concerns. The

Indians were not forced onto the missions, but invited; once they came and were baptized, however, they were under the authority of the missionaries and were forbidden to leave. The missionaries taught the natives not only the Catholic faith but various crafts, the art of farming, and cattle raising. The missionaries treated the Indians as children, with the aim to educate and train them so that the mission pueblo and farms could eventually be turned over to them, and the missionaries replaced with secular priests. Mission Indians lived a highly regimented life.

II.

1. The kings of Spain saw their New World subjects as equal subjects of the crown.

2. The four social classes of the Spanish New World were: *peninsulares*, creols, *mestizos,* and *sambos.*

3. The Church influenced all of Spanish American society through its participation in every aspect of life in the colonies --- education, aid to the poor, care of the sick, etc.

4. The California missions were set up as large agricultural and cattle raising concerns.

5. The first California pueblo was founded to promote agriculture so that California settlers need not rely so heavily on Mexico for supplies.

CHAPTER 8: The Causes of the American Revolution

Chapter Overview

- In the 18th century the British colonies in America went through a population explosion. As a result of this population explosion and the expansion of new territory, the social classes began to merge and society began to tear apart.

- New ideas also began to tear society apart. Liberalism and republicanism took root in America. Liberalism made men think that natural, not divine, laws should govern and direct human societies. Republicanism made them doubt that anyone had a divine right to rule.

- Beginning in 1734, Jonathan Edwards' preaching inspired the "Great Awakening." This Great Awakening revived Puritanism and made it into a distinctively American expression of religion. The personal character of the Great Awakening fueled popular sentiment against the establishment of an Anglican bishop for the colonies. The common man saw himself as equal to the educated ministers of the church, which gave rise to another strain of political thought – democracy.

- In 1760 the government of George III tired to strengthen the Acts of Trade and Navigation passed by Parliament to regulate colonial trade.

- Parliament passed the Stamp Act in 1765, and Patrick Henry gave his famous speech against it. The Stamp Act inspired unrest in the colonies.

- The passage of the Stamp Act in 1765 caused the Virginia House of Burgesses to pass a set of "Resolves" against the Stamp Act, saying that the colonies possessed all the liberties and privileges possessed by the people of Great Britain. The "Sons of Liberty" formed to protest the Stamp Act and incited mobs against "enemies of liberty."

- Parliament repealed the Stamp Act in 1766 but passed the Declaratory Act, stating that the king and parliament of Great Britain could "bind the colonies in all cases whatsoever."

- In 1767, Charles Townshend levied external, not internal taxes, on the colonies, placing new duties on English manufactured items entering America. The colonists did not balk at this, but John Dickinson saw through Townshend's scheme and pointed out that there was a distinction between Parliament regulating trade and Parliament levying taxes to raise revenue for the British government. External taxes for the sake of raising revenue, Dickinson said, compromised the colonies' liberty.

- The colonies entered into the Non-Importation Movement, which boycotted all British and West Indian goods. In 1770, however, the king chose Frederick Lord North as his prime minister, and North repealed all the Townshend Acts, but kept a tax on tea.

- The Boston Massacre took place on March 5, 1770. This, along with other events, turned public opinion against the British.

• In 1773 Parliament passed a law that allowed the British East India Company to sell its tea directly to the colonies, creating what the colonists thought was an illegal monopoly on tea. In Boston, a tea ship entered the harbor, and when Governor Hutchinson refused to turn it away, a band of men dressed as Mohawk Indians boarded the ship and emptied the tea overboard.

What Students Should Know

1. The economic life of the English colonies

Most colonists made their living by farming. Their farms ranged from small family subsistence farms (where the bulk of the produce went to support the family, with the remainder sold on the market), to larger, more prosperous "middle-class" farms, and then to the large tobacco and rice plantations of the South. The smaller farmers tended to plant a variety of different crops, since they were feeding themselves as well as selling to markets. The large plantations, however, planted only one crop – such as tobacco or rice or wheat – that they would sell for cash. This kind of farming, called "monoculture," was damaging to farmland, since the continual planting of the same crop depleted the soil. But that was not seen as a problem in America's colonial period – there was so much new land for the taking. One could always move on.

After a while, some colonists pursued other avocations than farming. In Virginia, Pennsylvania, New Jersey, and Massachusetts, men set up works for smelting iron. Iron working became a thriving colonial industry – so much so that even Parliament's Iron Act in 1750 forbidding colonial iron mills from producing certain kinds of iron, didn't hurt

their business. The colonists, too, simply ignored Parliament. Colonists in the larger coastal towns traded with other parts of the British Empire and with Europe and non-British colonies. And, of course, they carried on an illegal trade with other European countries and their colonies. Though Parliament had laws against smuggling, the British government generally ignored it in the colonies.

2. Cities in the colonies

British colonial folk were on the whole country folk. Cities there were, but not even the three largest towns – Boston, New York, and Philadelphia – came anywhere near the population and size of London. In England, nearly half a dozen cities had populations of 30,000; there were none of such size in English America. England had over twenty cities with populations of at least 10,000; America had only three. The colonies could boast of only about six cities of over 5,000 people; and Philadelphia, the largest colonial city, had about 20,000 people.

3. The slave trade in the colonies

By the middle of the 18th century, a brisk and profitable slave trade flourished in the colonies. Every major port, from New England to the Carolinas, engaged in the African slave trade. North Carolina, in particular was the biggest importer of African slaves. The use of African slaves was increasing throughout the colonies, but particularly in the South, where the hot, humid climate and the disease-ridden cultivation of sugar and rice in the swampy coastal lowlands convinced whites that they themselves were not fit for such labor. By 1720, black slaves began to outnumber white, indentured servants in every colony south of Maryland. Not all southern whites approved of slavery: the Germans and the Scots Presbyterians of the Blue Ridge and Piedmont areas of North Carolina despised it.

4. The order English society in the 18ᵗʰ century

British society was *hierarchical*. At its head was the king, from whom all authority in society came. In Great Britain, all power and authority were seen as coming from the top down through descending levels of authority to the lowliest member of society. British society had a defined class structure. The upper and lower classes in Britain differed significantly in their mode of life. The "gentlemen" of the aristocracy and gentry led a life of leisure; the lower classes did not. Leisure signified activity carried on for reasons other than feeding and clothing oneself. Leisurely activities included governing, military service, intellectual pursuits, and even the practice of medicine (as long as it was done in a leisurely fashion – that is, not for a living.) A sense of honor marked the gentleman. To insult him was not merely to question his own personal goodness but his very position in society. The chief distinction between gentlemen and others, then, was not wealth, but family and leisure. However wealthy they might be, those outside the aristocracy and gentry were not thought "gentle" because they did not come from a gentle family and, moreover, they *had* to work for a living. Their pursuits were thought honorable, because they fulfilled functions necessary to society, as did those of the gentry. Their pursuits were just different from those of the gentry. By the 18ᵗʰ century, however, the practical distinction, though, between the

gentry and the professional classes was often less than clear.

Paternalism characterized the attitude of gentlefolk towards their inferiors. Just as the king was thought the "father" of all British subjects, so gentlemen were to be fathers to those below them on the social ladder. Gentlemen would grant favors to those lower on the social ladder. What the gentleman asked in return was good crops, a certain respect or deference, and loyalty. The social order was thus based on an *interdependence* between all ranks of society.

5. How English society was realized in the American colonies

The characteristics of British society applied only imperfectly to America. There was really no upper aristocracy, no titles (dukes, counts, marquises, etc.) in the North American colonies. Gentlemen there were, but they were never as rich or as leisurely as gentlemen in Great Britain. In America, gentlemen had no steady source of income; they had to engage in ungentlemanly activities, such as trade or farm work, to keep up gentlemanly appearances. In England and colonial America, interdependence not only characterized relations between superiors and inferiors, but everyone was seen as depending on every other member of society. Villages and towns had "warning out" laws. One belonged to his family, and families took care of their own. If they did not want to, laws and customs forced them to. People in a community were knitted together by mutual trust. Someone could rise in the colonial social order, but generally he had to enlist the help of a gentleman patron to do so.

6. Social changes in the British colonies

Unlike in England, it was relatively easy to obtain land in the colonies. Following the French and Indian War, settlers began moving into the region around Lake Champlain and into central New York. In the 1760s, frontiersmen began pushing their way southwest over the Appalachians. The most famous of these wandering hunters and trappers was Daniel Boone. In 1769, Boone began to explore the Kentucky country and opened up the Wilderness Road, from western Virginia, through Cumberland Gap in the Appalachians and into Kentucky. This road became a major route for emigrants heading west.

The availability of land began tearing colonial society apart. Lured by the hope of ever cheaper land, men began to leave their homes; families dissolved as their members sought their fortunes away from the paternal hearth. Old, established families left neighborhoods and towns, and new families moved in. Since so many were changing place, it became increasingly harder to maintain that everyone had to keep to his place, that he belonged somewhere and to someone. Trust between neighbors weakened. Gentlemen became less paternal and more businesslike in their relations with their tenants. Because society was becoming less stable, traditional bonds, mutual trust, and friendship were disintegrating.

Due to increased trade with England and other parts of Europe, the mid-eighteenth century was a period of waxing material prosperity in America. Everywhere people of all social groups were looking to better their circumstances. Often this took the form of buying more luxuries and comforts – silver tea sets, fancy clothes, carriages, fine linens. The family home and farm began to be seen, not as a patrimony to hand down to one's

children, but as a commodity to sell for a profit.

7. Liberalism and Republicanism

Liberalism and Republicanism were not political, social, or religious philosophies alone – they were all of these. Liberalism and Republicanism arose during a period called the Enlightenment. Men of the Enlightenment rejected what they considered the darkness and superstition of Europe's religious past in favor of a worldview founded solely on reason and science. What could not be proven by reasoning and logic was not to be believed; scientific experimentation and mathematical measurement and deduction should be the sole bases of human life. One had simply to discover the "natural laws" that govern and direct the world to explain the phenomena – what one saw and experienced in the world around him. The belief that by identifying natural laws, one could interpret all reality had an effect on religion. Some began to think that since laws governed the universe, one didn't need God as an explanation for what one did not understand. Some became atheists and agnostics and denied all religion. Others, the Deists, believed in a God who made the world to run by certain natural laws and left it to operate by itself. Deists essentially denied the concept of God's providence.

When men began to seek for the natural laws that govern and direct human societies, they arrived at Liberalism. Enlightenment thinkers, such as the English philosopher John Locke, said that at one time men had lived in what was called a "state of nature," a period when there was no government and each man was truly free and equal to his neighbor. As Locke argued in his *Two Treatises on Government,* in the state of nature each individual possessed all rights, especially the three most important rights – life, liberty, and property. Such rights are "inalienable" because no one has the right to take away (or "alienate") another's life, or his liberty, or his property. For Liberals, the possession of rights in freedom is the foundational good of human life and the good men cherish most.

Liberals held that governments arose because of the colliding of certain "natural" forces. In the state of nature, stronger men had begun to violate the rights of weaker men – they took their wives and children, they seized their fields; at times they enslaved or killed the weak. To protect their inalienable rights, therefore, men formed governments, to which they gave up lesser, "alienable" rights so that their life, liberty, and property would be protected. So government, according to Locke and others, originally derived its right to rule from the governed; government is merely the representative and voice of the people, established by the people so they could enjoy security in the free possession of their rights. This was the core conviction of Republicanism.

Republicanism thus contrasted with the understanding of governmental authority that came out of Catholic medieval Europe. Medieval political thought said the *authority* to rule is not derived from the governed but from God. A ruler's right to command obedience did not come simply from the fact that the people had chosen him but from the nature of political authority, which has been established by God. The ruler is the representative of God for his people. This does not mean (as those who proposed the Divine Right of Kings insisted) that the ruler has absolute power over his subjects; indeed, medieval thinkers said emphatically a king's

power or authority is limited to the specific tasks of promoting and protecting the common good of the whole people; he may not interfere with other authority in society, whether that of lords, cities, guilds, families, or, especially, the Church. Nevertheless, what authority he has is not derived from men but from God.

Locke wrote his *Two Treatises* in defense of the regime established by the Glorious Revolution of 1688. James II, the Stuart king of England, had, like his ancestors, championed the "divine right of kings." – the notion that, since a king derives his authority from God as the father of the people, the people, in return, owe the king absolute obedience. Divine Right was dealt its death blow in England when Parliament invited William of Orange and his wife Mary (James II's daughter) to take the throne of England, forcing James to flee to France. This "Glorious Revolution," as it was called, established the principle that kings only rule by the good pleasure of Parliament – the representatives of the English people.

8. The effect of the Glorious Revolution on political thought

The Glorious Revolution raised the question, if the king's authority is not sacred, how permanent or how sacred are other authorities in society? Throughout the 17th century, and into the 18th, republican political thinkers began to doubt that anyone had a divine right to rule anyone. The Glorious Revolution confirmed in many minds the idea that the right to rule comes from those who are ruled – that political authority arises from the people. Republicanism moreover attacked kinship relationships, hierarchy, patriarchy, and dependence – the very foundations of the monarchical social order.

9. The effect of Republicanism on traditional society both in England and America

Republicanism wreaked havoc on traditional society by denying that noble birth granted anyone a natural right to govern others. Not birth but talent, said republicans, recommends someone to political office. Not birth but virtue, republicans claimed, made someone worthy of political authority. But though they believed in the radical equality of all men, republicans were not egalitarian; they did not think the common man should direct public affairs. Mechanics, craftsmen, merchants – anyone employed by another – were not financially independent and thus unfit to govern. Though some commoners could at least be allowed the suffrage, they were, thought republicans, too bound up by their own self-interest to possess the public spirit required to look out for the good of society. Republicans wanted to replace the hereditary gentleman with the enlightened gentlemen. Enlightened gentlemen, went the republican theory, would form a "natural aristocracy." The people, freed from traditional government, entrenched in forms of hierarchy and family relations, would easily identify these natural aristocrats and vote them into office. Society and the state would then be ruled by only the best men. Republicanism caught on in the English American colonies, where the distinctions between the aristocracy and the people were not so pronounced as in England.

10. The Great Awakening and its effects

The "Great Awakening" was a great Protestant religious revival that hit the English colonies in the 18th century. It arose as a response to the decay of orthodox Calvinist Puritanism in New England into Arminianism and Unitarianism. Jonathan Edwards, a minister at Northampton, Massachusetts, was at the center of the revival. A stout Calvinist, Edwards fought Arminianism with spoken word and pen. He called for conversion so eloquently and ardently that, by 1735, hundreds were moved to conversion. In the Connecticut River Valley, he held "revival" meetings that everywhere saw enthusiastic and emotional conversions. The effects of the Awakening spread through America, England, and even into Germany and inspired others to follow Edwards' example.

The Great Awakening had several important effects on colonial life. For one, it revived Puritanism for a time, preserving it from decaying into a vague, this-worldly religion like Unitarianism, and gave rise to a distinctively American type of religious expression – the revival. It led to the establishment of three new universities: the College of New Jersey (Princeton), Dartmouth in New Hampshire, and Brown in Rhode Island. It fueled popular sentiment against the establishment of an Anglican bishop for the colonies, for it created a popular religion based on the notion that each individual achieved salvation through a personal relationship with God. The Great Awakening gave the common man a new interest in religion. The common man now saw himself as equal to the educated ministers of his church – and if he were equal to his superiors as regards religion, why not in other areas as well? Thus, the Great Awakening influenced the development of another strain of political thought in America, besides Republicanism – democracy.

11. Who Patrick Henry was

Patrick Henry was a Virginian and member of the Virginia House of Burgesses. In 1765 he urged the burgesses to take action against the Stamp Act. He would remain an ardent proponent of resistance to what he deemed British tyranny against the North American colonies.

12. What the Stamp Act was and why colonists opposed it

The Stamp Act was legislation approved by Parliament in 1765 that placed tax fees on all legal documents, diplomas, licenses, newspapers, and other documents. The documents had to bear an official mark or stamp, for which the tax was paid. Patrick Henry and other colonists condemned the act because it was the first internal tax ever placed on the colonies in their history. Until 1765, colonists had had to pay fees, or duties, on certain products brought into the American colonies – on external trade; but the Stamp Act was different, for it was laid on internal commerce – transactions between people within the colonies.

13. British policy regarding the colonies before and after the French and Indian War

Prior to 1765, a working balance of imperial power and local control had been established between Britain and her colonies. Parliament controlled foreign affairs, issues involving war, and all trade between America, Britain, British dominions, and foreign countries. Colonial assemblies all internal affairs – the appointment of government officials and the payment of their salaries; the commissioning of military officers; the raising of troops; and the administration of schools, churches, and allotment of lands – as well as taxation. When Great Britain had intervened in colonial affairs, it had been only to protect minority groups against an encroaching

majority and smaller colonies against larger ones.

During and after the French and Indian War, however, the British government began passing measures to bring colonial governments more into line with the wishes of king and Parliament. One of the reasons the British government had begun to tighten up on the colonies was that it had incurred a large debt fighting the Seven Years War. Much of this debt arose from Britain's warring in Europe, but a respectable portion came from acquiring French Canada and Florida. Not all the colonies had contributed equally to the cost of a war that, Great Britain argued, was fought in their defense. If it had not been for British troops, the French and their savage Indian allies would have overrun the colonies – or so went the royal argument.

14. British measures, other than the Stamp Act that created discontent in the colonies

British tightening down of parliamentary and crown control over the colonies created much discontent in the colonies. Prior to 1760, judges in colonial courts held their offices "during good behavior" – that is, colonial assemblies could remove judges if they thought them bad or incompetent or inconvenient. When George III came to the throne in 1760, however, he insisted that all colonial judges hold their offices "during the king's good pleasure" – that is, as long as the king desired that they hold it. Colonial leaders protested, for they said the Glorious Revolution of 1688 assured that, in England, judges would hold office only "during good behavior." The colonists thought they were not being treated as full subjects of the British crown. Beginning in 1763, the government of George III tried to strengthen the Acts of Trade and Navigation passed by

Parliament to regulate colonial trade and to raise revenue by the imposition of new taxes that affected, especially, New England. Stricter enforcement of trade laws, moreover, put a crimp in all smuggling, a customary New England pursuit. The crown now allowed customs officials to obtain a "writ of assistance" – legal permission – to search private premises for smuggled goods that went beyond what had been allowed before. Parliament ruled that those accused of smuggling would be tried not in local courts but in an "admiralty court," located in faraway Halifax, Nova Scotia – that is, not by a jury of their peers – thus denying them another right guaranteed to Englishmen.

15. Colonial reaction to the Stamp Act and the British government's response

Among the colonial reactions to the Stamp Act was a set of "Resolves" issued on May 30, 1765 by the Virginia House of Burgesses. The Resolves said that only the colonial assembly could impose taxes on Virginians, and thus Virginians owed no obedience to "any law or ordinance whatever, designed to impose any taxation whatsoever upon them" other than what the colonial assembly approved. In every colonial coastal town, middle class colonists, called "Sons of Liberty," seized and destroyed stamp paper, forced its distributors to resign their jobs, and incited mobs to attack anyone deemed an enemy of "liberty."

The Massachusetts assembly summoned the other colonies to send delegates to a Stamp Act Congress in New York City. Nine colonies sent delegates, and in October 1765 the congress passed a series of resolutions that insisted that the colonists were entitled to all the rights and liberties of native-born Englishmen (including trial by jury), that no taxes be passed on the king's subjects

without their consent, and that only their own local assemblies could impose taxes on them.

Seeing that it could not enforce the Stamp Act, Parliament finally backed down and repealed it in March 1766. But Parliament, after repealing the Stamp Act, passed the Declaratory Act that stated that the king and parliament of Great Britain could "bind the colonies in all cases whatsoever." In other words, the act said the colonists held their rights only at Parliament's pleasure.

16. Who Sam Adams was

Samuel Adams was one of the most radical of the colonists who protested the policies of the British government. Born in Boston of a middle class family, Adams had attended Harvard where he earned a master's degree. Adams was unsuccessful in business. He failed both as a brewer and a tradesman; and for a time he was a very inefficient tax collector. Adams' real niche was political action. In 1765 he was elected to the Massachusetts legislature and became a prominent figure during the Stamp Act controversy. A student of the classics and an admirer of Roman virtue, Adams was a thoroughgoing republican who wrote numerous articles and tracts defending American liberty. He was also a clever politician and a true revolutionary who used pageantry, rather than argument, to enflame the masses.

17. The Townshend Acts and colonial reaction

The "Townshend Acts," passed in June 1767, placed new duties on English manufactured items entering America – including tea imported by the British East India Company. The acts removed other taxes on colonial grain and whale oil entering England, and so encouraged colonial trade with the mother country. Bounties were placed on the production of colonial hemp, flax, and timber. Townshend strengthened the Acts of Trade and Navigation. The money from all this was to go toward military defense of the colonies and the salaries of royal governors and judges. Though colonists could object to British government salaries for colonial governors and judges (thus limiting colonial influence on these officials), it seemed they could not object in principle to acts that regulated external trade – for too many colonial writers had asserted that Parliament had constitutional control over external trade.

18. John Dickinson's response to the Town-shend Acts

John Dickinson, a lawyer from Pennsylvania, came up with a solution to show that the Townshend Acts were unconstitutional. Parliament, he said, has the legal authority to regulate the trade of Great Britain and the colonies, but it was, he argued, an "innovation" that Parliament impose duties in America "for the purpose of raising a revenue."

19. How Massachusetts protested the Townshend Acts and the results of that protest

In February 1768, Samuel Adams and James Otis drafted a circular letter to the colonies, adopted by the Massachusetts assembly. While affirming Parliament's "supreme legislative power over the whole empire," this letter, sent to every colonial legislature, denied that Parliament could take a man's property (that is, tax him) without his consent. Having seen the letter, Lord Hillsborough, the British secretary for the

colonies, ordered the Massachusetts assembly to rescind the letter. When the Massachusetts assembly refused to rescind it, Lord Hillsborough suspended the legislature. Not long after, two regiments of British troops from Halifax occupied Boston, after a Boston mob attacked a crown customs official who had falsely accused John Hancock of smuggling in Madeira wine.

20. How the controversy over the Townshend Acts finally played itself out

Events in other colonies injected life into the resistance movement against the Townshend Acts. In 1766, when two regiments of British had arrived in New York, an act of Parliament, the Quartering Act, required the New York legislature to provide lodging and supplies for the troops. When the legislature voted to provide the lodging and all the supplies, but not beer and rum, Lord Hillsborough suspended it. To force Parliament to listen to colonial protests, colonial merchants entered into voluntary agreements to boycott all British and British West Indian goods. But, because too few merchants and colonists participated, the boycott had no serious effect on British trade. It was King George III that finally took action, but only because he wanted to master Parliament. In 1770, the king's new prime minister, Frederick, Lord North, repealed all the Townshend Acts, except for the tax on tea to show that Parliament still claimed the absolute right to "bind the colonies in all cases whatsoever."

21. What other events whipped up colonial resistance to the British

The "Boston Massacre" was one event that stirred up colonial resistance after a brief period of calm. On the evening of March 5,

Key Terms at a Glance

hierarchy: a social arrangement in which members of society are designated above and below in the order of rank, honor, power, or authority

paternalism: the practice of treating people in a fatherly manner, especially in regard to their material welfare

interdependence: a relationship in which each member of a society is dependent on another

gentleman: a word derived from the Latin word for "family" or "clan"; a man of a prominent family

Liberalism: a political and social philosophy that emphasizes the freedom of individuals to follow their own desires in their social, religious, and economic life

Republicanism: a political ideology that holds that government derives from the authority of the people and is merely the representative and voice of the people, established by the people so they could enjoy security in the free possession of their rights.

Great Awakening: a Protestant revival in Colonial America that sparked new interest in religion

1770, British soldiers in Boston fired on a mob that had been pelting them with snowballs and stones, killing three of the mob outright and mortally injuring others. Sam Adams and the Sons of Liberty used the event for propaganda purposes, calling it the "Boston Massacre." Thereafter, every year on March 5, they led a procession in remembrance of it. The silversmith Paul Revere produced a very inaccurate engraving of the "massacre," showing British forces firing on a small group of passive, respectable Boston citizens. Then in June 1772 a revenue cutter, the *Gaspee*, that had been successfully capturing smugglers in the Narragansett Bay, ran aground on a sandbar while chasing a smuggler craft. A group of patriots boarded the ship, beat up the crew and captain, and burned their vessel. The government searched eagerly for the culprits and threatened to send them to England to stand trial. This simple threat to send any colonial to England for trial aroused colonists into a fury of indignation, for they saw it as a violation of the English right to trial by jury. In response to this affront, the Virginia burgesses voted to set up a committee of correspondence for their colony. And Virginia was not alone. By early 1774, twelve colonial assemblies had established committees of correspondence of their own.

22. The Boston Tea Party and its significance

In May 1773, Parliament passed a law that allowed the British East India Company to sell its tea directly to the colonies, without having to pass through middlemen in England. In this way, the East India Company tea, even with the Townshend tax, could undersell even smuggled tea in the colonies. The East India Company was to sell its tea only to merchants who had no ties to the Sons of Liberty. When colonial agitators accused the government of establishing an illegal monopoly on tea, the ships bringing the tea were turned back before they entered the New York and Philadelphia harbors. In Boston, Governor Hutchinson allowed the tea ship into harbor. After a Sam Adams and a Son of Liberty convention sent a message to Governor Hutchinson, demanding that he force the tea ship to leave the harbor (which would be illegal), and he refused, a band of men dressed as Indians and paint-darkened as Negroes, numbering together about 150 emptied 342 large chests of tea into Boston Harbor. This "Boston Tea Party" was the final provocation that determined Parliament to take more stringent measures to break colonial resistance to its authority.

Questions for Review

1. **How did the population expansion of the 18th century contribute to the disintegration of society in colonial America?**

    The population expansion of the 18th century brought more immigrants and encouaged the search for land in the West. The movement of people from established places of residence loosened the roots and ties in society.

2. **Describe the three elements of English society (hierarchy, paternalism, and interdependence) and why they did fully take root in colonial America.**

    British society was *hierarchical*; in Great Britain, all power and authority were seen as coming from the top down through descending levels of authority to the lowliest member of society. *Paternalism* characterized the attitude of gentlefolk towards their inferiors. Just as the king was thought the "father" of all British subjects, so gentlemen

were to be fathers to those below them on the social ladder. What the gentleman asked in return was good crops, a certain respect or deference, and loyalty. The social order was thus based on an *interdependence* between all ranks of society.

These three elements did not work in colonial America because there was really no upper aristocracy, no titles (dukes, counts, marquises, etc.) in the North American colonies. In America, gentlemen had no steady source of income; they had to engage in ungentlemanly activities, such as trade or farm work, to keep up gentlemanly appearances. Social classes lacked a sense of interdependence because the availability of land allwed common peole to own land rather than rent it from a lord.

3. **How did Daniel Boone's explorations contribute to the disintegration of society in colonial America?**

    When Daniel Boone opened up the Wilderness Road, the availability of land began tearing colonial society apart. Lured by the hope of ever cheaper land, men began to leave their homes; families dissolved as their members sought their fortunes away from the paternal hearth. Old, established families left neighborhoods and towns, and new families moved in. Since so many were changing place, it became increasingly harder to maintain that everyone had to keep to his place, that he belonged somewhere and to someone. Trust between neighbors weakened. Gentlemen became less paternal and more businesslike in their relations with their tenants. Because society was becoming less stable, traditional bonds, mutual trust, and friendship were disintegrating.

4. **What effects did increased trade with England have on society in America?**

Due to increased trade with England and other parts of Europe, the mid-eighteenth century was a period of waxing material prosperity in America. Everywhere people of all social groups were looking to better their circumstances. Often this took the form of buying more luxuries and comforts. The family home and farm began to be seen, not as a patrimony to hand down to one's children, but as a commodity to sell for a profit.

5. **Explain what Liberalism is and how it led to formation of revolutionary ideas in America.**

When men began to seek for the natural laws that govern and direct human societies, they arrived at Liberalism. Enlightenment thinkers, such as the English philosopher John Locke, said that at one time men had lived in what was called a "state of nature," a period when there was no government and each man was truly free and equal to his neighbor. As Locke argued in his *Two Treatises on Government*, in the state of nature each individual possessed all rights, especially the three most important rights – life, liberty, and property. Such rights are "inalienable" because no one has the right to take away (or "alienate") another's life, or his liberty, or his property. For Liberals, the possession of rights in freedom is the foundational good of human life and the good men cherish most. These principles were adopted by the founders of the United States as the "self-evident" truths on which the political order is founded.

6. **Explain what republicanism is and how it led to the formation of revolutionary ideas in America.**

No government, according to Locke and others, originally derived its right to rule from the governed; government is merely the representative and voice of the people, established by the people so they could enjoy security in the free possession of their rights. This was the core conviction of republicanism. The "Glorious Revolution" in England established the principle that kings only rule by the good pleasure of Parliament – the representatives of the English people. hese principles were adopted by the founders of the United States as the "self-evident" truths on which the political order is founded.

7. **Compare republicanism with the Catholic medieval view of government.**

While republicanism established the principle that kings only rule by the good pleasure of Parliament – the representatives of the English people, medieval political thought said the *authority* to rule is not derived from the governed but from God. A ruler's right to command obedience did not come simply from the fact that the people had chosen him but from the nature of political authority, which has been established by God.

8. **What are the three most important rights that Locke argues for? How do they form the basis of Liberalism?**

Locke argued that each individual possessed all rights, especially the three most important rights – life, liberty, and property. Such rights are "inalienable" because no one has the right to take away (or "alienate") another's life, or his liberty, or his property. For Liberals, the possession of rights in freedom is the foundational good of human life and the good men cherish most.

9. **What effects did the Great Awakening have on colonial life and revolutionary ideas?**

The Great Awakening had several important effects on colonial life. For one, it revived Puritanism for a time, preserving it from decaying into a vague, this-worldly religion like Unitarianism, and gave rise to a distinctively American type of religious expression – the revival. It fueled popular sentiment against the establishment of an Anglican bishop for the colonies, for it created a popular religion based on the notion that each individual achieved salvation through a personal relationship with God. The Great Awakening gave the common man a new interest in religion. The common man now saw himself as equal to the educated ministers of his church – and if he were equal to his superiors as regards religion, why not in other areas as well? Thus, the Great Awakening influenced the development of another strain of political thought in America, besides Republicanism – democracy.

10. **List each of the acts passed by Parliament. Why did these acts incite rebellion in the colonists.**

The Stamp Act was legislation approved by Parliament in 1765 that placed tax fees on all legal documents, diplomas, licenses, newspapers, and other documents. The documents had to bear an official mark or stamp, for which the tax was paid. Patrick Henry and other colonists condemned the act because it was the first internal tax ever placed on the colonies in their history.

The government began by strengthening enforcement of the Sugar Act of 1733, which placed a heavy tax on sugar and molasses imported from the non-British West Indies.

The new "Revenue Act" of 1764 lowered the duty on molasses and placed new duties on foreign sugar and some luxury items.

The Stamp Act showed that Parliament was not ready to heed protests from colonial assemblies. The burgesses' "Resolves" claimed that the right to impose internal taxes belonged to the people of His Majesty's "most ancient and loyal Colony"; thus the only body that could impose such taxes on Virginians was the colonial assembly.

The "Townshend Acts," passed in June 1767, placed new duties on English manufactured items entering America – including tea imported by the British East India Company. John Dickinson, a lawyer from Pennsylvania, came up with a solution to show that the Townshend Acts were unconstitutional. Parliament, he said, has the legal authority to regulate the trade of Great Britain and the colonies, but it was, he argued, an "innovation" that Parliament impose duties in America "for the purpose of raising a revenue."

11. **How did the colonists think they should be treated by the British government.**

The colonists wanted simply to be recognized and treated as Englishmen, with all the rights that Englishmen possessed. When they were not, they rebelled.

Ideas in Action

1. **Read St. Thomas' treatise *On Kingship* and compare his views on government with those of the colonial Americans.**

2. **Read some accounts, fictional and non-fictional, of the Boston Tea Party. Do you think it was a just and proper reaction to Parliament's actions? Why or why not?**

3. Read Patrick Henry's most famous speeches. Do these speeches betray the influence of Liberalism and republicanism? Be able to cite specific passages.

Sample Quiz I (pages 129-139)

Please answer the following in complete sentences.

1. How did the smaller farmers differ from the large plantations in regards to crops?

2. What was the condition of slavery in the mid 18th century?

3. Identify the following:
   a. hierarchy
   b. paternalism
   c. interdependence

4. Why did the characteristics of British society apply only imperfectly to the American colonies?

5. Who was Daniel Boone, and what is he known for?

6. How did the Enlightenment thinkers arrive at Liberalism?

7. What was the main principle of Republicanism?

8. What question did the Glorious Revolution raise?

9. How did Republicanism wreak havoc on traditional society in England and America?

10. What political movement did the Great Awakening influence?

Answers to Sample Quiz I

Students' answers should approximate the following.

1. The smaller farmers differed from the large plantations in that they tended to plant a variety of different crops, while the large plantations planted only one crop.

2. By the middle of the 18th century, a brisk and profitable slave trade flourished in the colonies.

3.
   a. a social arrangement in which members of society are designated above and below in the order of rank, honor, power, or authority
   b. a practice in treating people in a fatherly manner, especially in regard to their material welfare
   c, a relationship in which each member of a society is dependent on another

4. The characteristics of British society applied only imperfectly to the American colonies because there was really no upper aristocracy, no titles (dukes, counts, marquises, etc.) in the North American colonies.

5. Daniel Boone was a hunter and trapper who explored the Kentucky country and opened up the Wilderness Road. Social clases moreover lacked a sense of interdependence because of the availability of land allowed common people to own land and not rent land from a lord.

6. When Enlightenment thinkers began to seek for the natural laws that govern and direct human societies, they arrived at Liberalism.

7. Republicanism established the principle that kings only rule by the good pleasure of the people.

8. The Glorious Revolution raised the question, if the king's authority is not sacred, how permanent or how sacred are other authorities in society?

9. Republicanism wreaked havoc on traditional society in both England and America by denying that noble birth granted anyone a natural right to govern others.

10. The Great Awakening influenced the development of democracy.

Sample Quiz II (pages 139-148)

Please answer the following in complete sentences.

1. **What was the Stamp Act?**

2. **Why did the British government began to tighten up on its governance of the colonies?**

3. **What did the reaction to the Stamp Act, the "Resolves," say?**

4. **Identify the following:**
   a. **Patrick Henry**
   b. **Sam Adams**
   c. **John Dickinson**

5. **What were the Townshend Acts?**

6. **What was the purpose of the boycott on British goods?**

7. **Why did the boycott fail?**

8. **What happened during the Boston Massacre?**

9. **What was the law that prompted the Boston Tea Party?**

Answers to Sample Quiz II

Students' answers should approximate the following.

1. The Stamp Act was legislation approved by Parliament in 1765 that placed tax fees on all legal documents, diplomas, licenses, newspapers, and other documents.

2. The British government began to tighten up on the colonies because it had incurred a large debt fighting in the Seven Years War and from acquiring French Canada and Florida.

3. The Resolves said that only the colonial assembly could impose taxes on Virginians, and thus Virginians owed no obedience to "any law or ordinance whatever, designed to impose any taxation whatsoever upon them" other than what the colonial assembly approved.

4.
   a. Patrick Henry was a member of the Virginia House of Burgesses who urged the burgesses to take action against the Stamp Act. He would remain an ardent proponent of resistance to what he deemed British tyranny against the North American colonies.
   b. Samuel Adams was one of the most radical of the colonists who protested the policies of the British government. He wrote numerous articles and tracts defending American liberty.
   c. John Dickinson, a lawyer from Pennsylvania, came up with a solution to show that the Townshend Acts were unconstitutional.

5. The Townshend Acts placed new duties on English manufactured items entering America – including tea imported by the British East India Company. The acts removed other taxes on colonial grain and whale oil entering England, and so encouraged colonial trade with the mother country.

6. The purpose of the boycott on British goods was to force Parliament to listen to colonial protests.

7. The boycott failed because too few merchants and colonists participated.

8. During the Boston Massacre, British soldiers in Boston fired on a mob that had been pelting them with snowballs and stones,

killing three of the mob outright and mortally injuring others.

9. The law that prompted the Boston Tea Party allowed the British East India Company to sell its tea directly to the colonies, without having to pass through middlemen in England. The East India Company was to sell its tea only to merchants who had no ties to the Sons of Liberty.

Essays

Instructions to be given to the students: Write in complete sentences. Underline your thesis. Give three supports or examples that explain why you think what you do and that support your thesis.

1. Were the revolutionary ideas in America influenced by Enlightenment thinking? Why or why not?

2. Explain why or how an Enlightenment thinker would think that each of the acts and laws passed by the British government opposed the ideas of Liberalism, and republicanism.

Sample Test

Please answer the following in complete sentences.

I. Short Essay – Answer question 1 and 2, and one more:

1. **What is Liberalism?**

2. **What is republicanism?**

3. **Explain the three elements of English society (hierarchy, paternalism, and interdependence.)**

4. **How did the availability of land begin tearing colonial society apart?**

5. **How did the Great Awakening influence the development of democracy?**

II. Short Answer:

1. **How did most colonists make their living?**

2. **Why did Patrick Henry and other colonists condemn the Stamp Act?**

3. **Explain in one sentence what the Declaratory Act said.**

4. **Who were the Sons of Liberty?**

5. **What is the significance of the Boston Tea Party?**

Answer Key to the Chapter Test

Students' answers should approximate the following:

I.

1. When men began to seek for the natural laws that govern and direct human societies, they arrived at Liberalism. Enlightenment thinkers, such as the English philosopher John Locke, said that at one time men had lived in what was called a "state of nature," a period when there was no government and each man was truly free and equal to his neighbor. As Locke argued in his *Two Treatises on Government*, in the state of nature each individual possessed all rights, especially the three most important rights – life, liberty, and property. Such rights are "inalienable" because no one has the right to take away (or "alienate") another's life, or his liberty, or his property. For Liberals, the possession of rights in freedom is the foundational good of human life and the good men cherish most.

2. No government, according to Locke and others, originally derived its right to rule from the governed; government is merely the representative and voice of the people, established by the people so they could enjoy security in the free possession of their rights. This was the core conviction of Republicanism. The "Glorious Revolution" in England established the principle that kings only rule by the good pleasure of Parliament – the representatives of the English people. Republicanism moreover attacked kinship relationships, hierarchy, patriarchy, and dependence – the very foundations of the monarchical social order.

3. British society was *hierarchical*; in Great Britain, all power and authority were seen as coming from the top down through descending levels of authority to the lowliest member of society. *Paternalism* characterized the attitude of gentlefolk towards their inferiors. Just as the king was thought the "father" of all British subjects, so gentlemen were to be fathers to those below them on the social ladder. What the gentleman asked in return was good crops, a certain respect or deference, and loyalty. The social order was thus based on an *interdependence* between all ranks of society.

4. Lured by the hope of ever cheaper land, men began to leave their homes; families dissolved as their members sought their fortunes away from the paternal hearth. Old, established families left neighborhoods and towns, and new families moved in. Since so many were changing place, it became increasingly harder to maintain that everyone had to keep to his place, that he belonged somewhere and to someone. Trust between neighbors weakened. Gentlemen became less paternal and more businesslike in their relations with their tenants. Because society was becoming less stable, traditional bonds, mutual trust, and friendship were disintegrating.

5. The Great Awakening gave the common man a new interest in religion. The common man now saw himself as equal to the educated ministers of his church – and if he were equal to his superiors as regards religion, why not in other areas as well? Thus, the Great Awakening influenced the development of another strain of political thought in America, besides republicanism – democracy.

II.

1. Most colonists made their living by farming.

2. Patrick Henry and other colonists condemned the act because it was the first internal tax ever placed on the colonies in their history.

3. The Declaratory Act said that the colonists held their rights only at Parliament's pleasure.

4. The Sons of Liberty were middle-class colonists who organized themselves to take direct action against the Stamp Act.

5. The Boston Tea Party was the final provocation that determined Parliament to take more stringent measures to break colonial resistance to its authority.

CHAPTER 9: The American Revolution

Chapter Overview

- Parliament passed the Coercive acts in March of 1774, incensing the colonists, and causing the creation of the Continental Congress and the collection of arms and training of a militia in the colonies.

- Parliament passed the Quebec Act in June of 1774, further incensing the colonists.

- The Continental Congress met on September 5 to discuss what steps to take against the Coercive and Quebec Acts. This was the second time the colonies attempted to act as one. Congress soon after endorsed the Suffolk Resolves, which condemned the Coercive Acts. Congress also passed the Declaration and Resolves, which stated the rights of the colonists.

- In March of 1775 Parliament passed the New England Restraining Act, which forbade the colonies from trading with anyone but England and Ireland. This act further chipped away at whatever loyalty was left for the king and Parliament in the colonies.

- British General Gage needed a British victory that would turn public sentiment towards the British government. He heard of rebels caching arms and ammunition at both Worcester and Concord and sent out forces to capture those arms. On April 19 Gage's army met with an army of minutemen in Lexington. The rebels fired shots at the British, and the British retaliated with a murderous volley, killing ten minutemen and wounding nine others.

- Benedict Arnold, leading a colonial army, took Ticonderoga from the British in May of 1775.

Meanwhile, the Second Continental Congress convened in Philadelphia to discuss what was to be done. The Congress designated the troops the provisional army of the United Colonies, and made George Washington its commander-in-chief.

- The British defeated the colonial army in the costly battle of Bunker Hill in June of 1775.

- On July 6, 1775, Congress issued the "Declaration of the Causes and Necessity of Taking Up Arms," and two days later, the "Olive Branch Petition." The king was not moved by the last petition and issued a declaration calling on all his subjects to withstand and suppress the rebellion and bring the traitors to justice.

- Thomas Jefferson drafted the Declaration of Independence in June of 1776. Congress approved the declaration on July 3, 1776, and John Hancock as president of the Congress signed the Declaration on July 4. By August 2, 1776, all of the members of Congress had signed it.

- The Americans and the British met in the battle of Saratoga on September 19, 1777, and the British were defeated through Benedict Arnold's strategy.

- The French signed two treaties of friendship and commerce with Congress on February 6, 1778.

- In 1780 Benedict Arnold, angry because he was convicted of two trivial offenses, betrayed the Americans to the British.

- The siege of Yorktown began on September 28, 1781. On October 17 British General Cornwallis surrendered to the Americans. Two treaties between Great Britain and the United States were signed on November 30, 1782 and September 3, 1783.

What Students Should Know

1. **What the Coercive Acts were**

    The Coercive Acts were the British government's response to Boston's continued rebellion, culminating in the Boston Tea Party. The acts were aimed at punishing Boston. The Coercive Acts included the Boston Port Act, the Quartering Act, and the Massachusetts Government and Administration of Justice Act. The Boston Port Act ordered the closing of the port of Boston until the city paid for the dumped tea and for the property of royal officials destroyed by mobs, and said the port would remain closed until the king was satisfied that peace and due obedience to the laws were reestablished. The Quartering Act required Boston citizens to house and board the British soldiers that occupied the city. The Massachusetts Government and Administration of Justice Act revoked part of the Massachusetts Bay charter that provided for the popular election of members of the colonial council.

2. **What were the effects of the Coercive Acts?**

    The Coercive Acts angered the Bostonians, but the Massachusetts Government Act inspired discontent in the Massachusetts countryside. Colonists outside the Bay Colony joined in their countrymen's outrage. Bostonians drafted a message to the other colonies, calling upon them to join Massachusetts in a "Solemn League and Covenant neither to export to Great Britain, nor to import goods from there." Colonial centers throughout New England voiced

their support for Massachusetts protesters, and opposition to the Coercive Acts spread to other colonies outside of New England. Colonial leaders, such as George Washington, said the colonies should stand with Boston. On May 24, 1774, the Virginia House of Burgesses adopted a resolve, drafted by Patrick Henry, Richard Henry Lee, George Mason, and Thomas Jefferson, denouncing the "hostile invasion" of Boston by British regulars and designating June 1 as a day of fasting, humiliation, and prayer. As a result, the governor of Virginia dissolved the assembly. Reconvening at the Raleigh tavern in Williamsburg, the burgesses instructed the Virginia committee of correspondence to contact other colonial committees with a view to summoning a congress of the colonies. "Patriots" in New York voiced their support for such a congress, and soon other colonies followed suit. This "Continental Congress," as it was called, was set to convene on September 5, 1774.

3. **What the Quebec Act was. It's significance.**

    In late June of 1774, Parliament passed the Quebec Act which, among other provisions, guaranteed to the French in Quebec the freedom to practice the Catholic Faith. It also allowed the French to govern Quebec according to French, not British, laws. A final provision extended the southern border of Quebec to the Ohio River, thus cutting off colonial settlers and land speculators of the 13 seaboard colonies from the rich lands west of the Appalachian and Allegheny Mountains. British colonists vigorously protested the Quebec Act, claiming it would mean that Catholics would be treated by the British government as the equals to Protestants and would surround the English colonies with "a Nation of Papists and Slaves." Sam Adams and the Sons of Liberty claimed that George III was secretly thinking of becoming Catholic and so would become as dangerous as the Catholic James II.

4. The First Continental Congress and its significance

As planned, representatives of the various colonies from Massachusetts to South Carolina gathered in Philadelphia on September 5, 1774 to discuss what steps the colonies, acting together, should take in the face of the Coercive and Quebec acts. This "Continental Congress" was a significant meeting, since it was only the second time in their history that the various colonies attempted to act as one. The delegates had to forge a common mind and intent among colonies that had very different histories and customs and were used to looking out for their own interests alone.

Loyalists, including Joseph Galloway, tried to turn the congress away from radical measures and make sure the colonies remained in the British Empire. Galloway, for instance, suggested the establishment of an American parliament, called the "Grand Council," whose members, elected by the colonists, whose consent would be required before Parliament could pass laws and levy taxes. More radical delegates pushed for a non-importation, non-exportation agreement in solidarity with Boston. Against Galloway and other Loyalists, the congress endorsed the Suffolk Resolves (approved by several Massachusetts towns) that condemned the Coercive Acts for violating the British constitution, proclaimed Massachusetts a free state, and called on the people of the colony to take up arms if Parliament did not repeal the Coercive Acts. Congress then recommended imposing a non-importation, non-exportation agreement, called the "Association," on the colonies.

5. To what authorities the Continental Congress appealed to defend what they saw were colonial rights

The congress appealed to the British constitution, colonial charters, and to the Liberal republican thinkers among them called "natural law." In a Declaration and Resolves adopted by the delegates on October 14, 1774, the congress spoke in the language of the social contract: English colonists, says the Declaration and Resolves, "are entitled to life, liberty, and property, and they have never ceded to any sovereign power whatever, a right to dispose of either without their consent." The declaration appealed to the British constitution and the colonial charters, when it argued that Americans are guaranteed all the constitutional rights of Englishmen, especially since they "by no means forfeited, surrendered, or lost any of those rights" by their emigration to America.

6. How Parliament responded to the Declaration and Resolves

Though the British House of Commons, saw a bill introduced that would have made the Continental Congress a permanent legal body and repealed all the troublesome acts, Parliament, in March 1775, passed another coercive bill, the New England Restraining Act. This act forbade the New England colonies from trading with anyone but England and Ireland; even Scotland was off limits. The act struck a crippling blow to the New England fishing industry by closing off the banks of Nova Scotia and Newfoundland to New England fishermen. It further eroded whatever loyalty many American colonists still felt for king and Parliament.

7. What factions existed among the colonists

Not all colonists were in favor of the measures taken by the Continental Congress. Throughout 1774 and 1775, and even long into the war that followed, only about a third of the colonists strongly supported the more radical partisans of American rights. Among the reluctant, some who initially believed the colonies had genuine grievances later so strongly opposed the actions of the Continental Congress that they threw in their lot with Britain and King George. Loyalists made up from 20 to 30 percent of the population. Most other colonists, however, were neither loyalist nor strongly patriot, but indifferent.

8. How the Association was enforced

Enforcing the Association for non-importation was a matter of some concern to the Continental Congress. Not only was most of the population indifferent or opposed, but the congress itself had a very doubtful legal status. To enforce compliance with the Association, Congress authorized local Committees of Safety to investigate the conduct of citizens suspected of being unsympathetic with its aims. These committees were to administer a "pledge" to honor non-importation; any who refused to take the pledge could be held up to public scorn, threatened with the loss of livelihood or property (or worse consequences), and ostracized from society. The Committees of Safety, of course, were seen to have even less legal authority than the Continental Congress. Neither the committees nor Congress could claim that they derived their powers from the consent of the people as a whole, or even from the majority of the people. In each town the committees were usually composed of self-appointed Sons of Liberty. Committees investigated private papers; they spied on their neighbors; they used informers.

9. What happened at Lexington and Concord, and its significance in the coming struggle for American independence

British General Gage in Boston wanted a resounding British victory that could definitively turn the tide of public sentiment towards the British government and against the British. Learning from spies that the rebels had cached arms and ammunition at both Worcester and Concord, Gage wanted to get an operation against Concord underway secretly, to seize some valuable munitions and capture some important rebel leaders as well. Gage however could not keep his plans a secret, and by April 16, 1775, rebels in Concord had been warned to hide their armaments. On April 18, when Gage's advance troops were set to embark, the general finally learned that his plan was well known in Boston. He ordered the advance regardless.

On Wednesday, April 19, "minutemen" militia gathered in Lexington and there engaged in a skirmish with a British force under Major John Pitcairn. British Lieutenant Colonel Smith's troops continued the march to Concord, where they met and fought two battalions of militia that had already gathered. The British then began a retreat toward Boston. Along the line of retreat toward Lexington, rebel forces fired on the British from behind trees and stone walls. When the British finally made it back to the safety of Boston, their losses were 73 killed and 200 wounded. Of the Americans, 49 were killed, 41 wounded.

The Battles of Lexington and Concord were the first battles of what became the American Revolution. News of the battles spread quickly to all the colonies. Soon contingents from other colonies joined the Massachusetts militia in laying siege to Boston.

10. **What the Second Constitutional Congress was and what significant acts it did in the early part of the war**

The Second Continental Congress was the second gathering of representatives from the the 13 colonies that met in 1775. It accepted the Benedict Arnold and Ethan Allan's conquest of Ticonderoga and Crown Point. Though the congress protested it was not bucking for independence, it began to act very much as if it were a sovereign government. It designated the troops around Boston and at Ticonderoga the provisional army of the United Colonies and made George Washington of Virginia its commander-in-chief. It commissioned Benedict Arnold to go north to Maine and organize patriot resistance in Canada. On the diplomatic side, Congress sent ambassadors to European countries. Three departments of Indian affairs were created, and a treaty was signed with the Shawnee and Lenape Indians.

11. **Why Quebec did not join the colonial resistance to the British government**

Congress cherished hopes that Canada would join the struggle against Britain. In hopes of such an alliance, in May 1775, Congress sent an address "to the oppressed Inhabitants of Canada," drafted by John Jay of New York, that spoke of "the fate of the protestant and catholic colonies" as being "strongly linked together." It reminded the "Quebeckers" that "the enjoyment of your very religion, in the present system, depends on a legislature [Parliament] in which you have no share, and over which you have no control, and your priests are exposed to expulsion, banishment,

and ruin, whenever their wealth and possessions furnish sufficient temptation." The French Canadians, however, had not forgotten that the First Continental Congress had protested the "establishing of the Roman Catholick Religion in the province of Quebec," or that John Jay's October 1774 "Address to the People of England" expressed "our astonishment that a British Parliament should ever consent to establish in that country [Canada] a religion that has deluged your island in blood, and disbursed impiety, bigotry, persecution, murder and rebellion through every part of the world." The Canadians, bolstered in their opposition by Bishop Briand of Quebec remained loyal to King George III.

12. **The effect the Battle of Bunker Hill (Breeds Hill) had on the Revolution**

The victory at the Battle of Bunker Hill inspired the rebels with new confidence. In the wake of the battle, on July 6, 1775, Congress issued a "Declaration of the Causes and Necessity of Taking Up Arms." Drafted by John Dickinson and Thomas Jefferson, the declaration listed all the events leading up to the conflict between Great Britain and her colonies.

13. **The events that led to the Declaration of Independence**

Even after the Battle of Bunker Hill, Congress declared that it meant not to dissolve its union with Great Britain. Even at the close of 1775, George Washington and his officers still drank toasts to King George III – and embraced the illusion that Parliament alone, not the king, was behind all the measures to "suppress their liberties." By the spring of 1776, however, attitudes had changed.

As the progress of war intensified bitter feelings between the colonies and Great Britain, ever more colonists began to entertain thoughts of independence. By the spring of 1776, Washington wrote that he was convinced that independence was the only possible course for the colonies. An important factor in the changing of American opinion about independence was Thomas Paine's tract, *Common Sense*, published in 1776.

14. What *Common Sense* said

Thomas Paine's book is an eloquent summary of the social contract theory of government. In *Common Sense*, Paine calls human society a "blessing," but even the best government "but a necessary evil." If men were perfectly virtuous, Paine insisted, they would not need government; but because men are vicious, governments are necessary to assure freedom and security. But not any form of government is desirable; according to Paine; only republican governments of elected representatives of the people are just. All other governments – aristocracies, monarchies – are nothing but tyrannies. Paine said Great Britain had abandoned all other means but force to compel the colonies to union. America, he said, does not need Great Britain or Europe – but they need America, for its agricultural produce. The king of Britain, argued Paine, had used the colonies solely for his own benefit; he did not act like a father but a tyrant. America had come of age and no longer needed the guidance of Great Britain. In America, said Paine, not George III nor any merely human ruler, but the law is king.

15. What ideas and interests motivated the loyalists or Tories. How they suffered.

Loyalists included not only former agents of the British government (such as customs men), Anglican clergymen, and some of the very rich, but small farmers, poor craftsmen, fugitive slaves (to whom King George promised freedom if they abandoned their rebel masters), and some scoundrels. They represented a cross-section of society. Some remained loyal to the British crown out of self-interest but others out of conscience. Anglican clergymen would not renounce the head of their church; others thought they should not break oaths they had taken to remain the king's faithful subjects. Some loyalists tried to remain neutral, while others joined loyalist regiments that served with the British against the rebels. Independence brought an era of repression against loyalists, who could now be accused of treason. Active loyalists could expect death; but those who tried to stay neutral in the conflict had cause to fear death, exile, or just ill treatment.

16. The events that led to the Congress' declaration of independence

Common Sense and the continuing war were undermining whatever reverence English Americans felt for the king. Though the New England delegates to the Continental Congress were somewhat hesitant, it was not long before they joined Virginia's delegates in calling for independence. The New York and Pennsylvania delegates, however, openly opposed independence. But by clever politicking, Richard Henry Lee and the two Adamses got Congress to pass a resolution over the protests of New York and Pennsylvania – that the king had abdicated his authority by his prosecution of the war. Between mid-May and early June 1776, the southern colonies, from Georgia to Virginia, all endorsed independence, as did the four New England colonies. Only the Middle

Colonies (New York, New Jersey, Maryland, Pennsylvania, and Delaware) held back. Nevertheless, a committee of five – Thomas Jefferson, John Adams, Benjamin Franklin, Roger Sherman, and Robert Livingston – were appointed to draw up a declaration of independence. The youngest member of this committee, the 33-year-old Thomas Jefferson, was given the task of drafting the document. When the vote for independence was taken on July 2, twelve colonies voted for independence, while the New York delegation abstained. Congress then adopted Jefferson's draft of a declaration of independence. After emending the document, all the delegates, except John Dickinson, voted to adopt it, and John Hancock as president of Congress signed it the next day, July 4, 1776. Over the next month the Declaration was sent to the various colonial legislatures for their approval. Finally, on August 2, the members of Congress signed their names to the document.

17.   What the Declaration of Independence said

The Declaration of Independence is a catalog of the causes that, Congress claimed, compelled the colonies to seek independence from Great Britain. It is a "self-evident" truth, the declaration said, that all men are created equal, and "that they are endowed by their Creator with certain unalienable Rights, that among these are Life, Liberty and the pursuit of Happiness." This language was drawn from Locke, though Jefferson substituted the phrase, "pursuit of Happiness," for Locke's "property." Jefferson may have derived his language from another document with which he was doubtless familiar – the first article of the Virginia Bill of Rights, drafted by George Mason and adopted June 12, 1776 by Virginia. Once it has established a basis for

human liberty and equality, the declaration, in the language of the social contract, goes on to justify political revolution. Governments exist to secure the people's rights and derive their "just powers from the consent of the governed." When a "form of government becomes destructive of these ends, it is the Right of the People to alter or to abolish it, and to institute new Government." No people should do this lightly, however, but only "when a long train of abuses and usurpations, pursuing invariably the same Object evinces a design to reduce them under absolute Despotism." Then, it is the people's "right," "it is their duty, to throw off such Government and to provide new Guards for their future security." The Declaration then lists the alleged "injuries and usurpations" of the king of Great Britain against the colonies and formally declares independence.

18.   George Washington as general

Washington did not win most of the battles in which he engaged, but he was probably the best choice for commander-in-chief. He inspired confidence with his quiet, reflective, aristocratic Virginian manner. His genuine devotion to the cause for which he fought, combined with his evident concern for the good of his men, inspired their devotion. Many times, when supplies ran short for the army, Washington provided for his men from his own relatively modest Mount Vernon estate.

19.   The Battles of Freeman's Farm, or Saratoga, and their significance

British Major General John Burgoyne was concocting plans for an invasion of New York and New England in the spring of 1777. He himself would lead his army south by way of Lake Champlain and the Hudson, while General Howe was to send forces north by way of the Hudson and join with Burgoyne's forces – thus effectively cutting New England off from the other colonies. The American army under General Horatio Gates and the British under Burgoyne met in a major battle at Freeman's Farm near Saratoga, New York, on September 19, 1777. Under Gates' command, Benedict Arnold led the attack, and with sound tactical skill and daring, defeated the British forces. But in writing up his report of the battle for Congress, General Gates neglected to mention Arnold's decisive role and, instead, gave himself credit for the victory. When Arnold protested, Gates removed him from command.

After his defeat at Freeman's Farm, General Burgoyne's position worsened day by day. He couldn't retreat and his Indian allies were abandoning him. On October 7, Burgoyne took the only course left open to him – he attacked the American position. In the Second Battle of Freeman's Farm, Arnold took unofficial command of the New England regiments and with them routed the British. Unable to advance or retreat, Burgoyne surrendered to General Gates ten days later. In this way, the British were prevented from severing communication between New England and the other colonies.

20. Why France made an alliance with the United States and what were its effects on the American Revolution

The French people warmly supported the American Revolution. This in part was on account because of the French and Indian War and the Treaty of Paris that gave all of Canada to Great Britain, and many of the French and their king wanted to see England humbled. French intellectuals, and many aristocrats, too, were ardent republicans who looked to America as an experiment in political freedom. The Continental Congress

wanted a military alliance with France and sent Benjamin Franklin as its ambassador to the court of Louis XVI. But France was reluctant to acknowledge American independence openly – though she sent cargoes of clothing and munitions to Congress and allowed American privateers and naval ships to use French ports. But with Burgoyne's defeat, the French government worried that the military defeat might move the British government to seek peace with America – and indeed on November 7, 1777, a "conciliatory bill" was introduced into Parliament that basically granted the Americans everything the First Continental Congress had asked for in 1774. On February 6, 1778, the French government signed two treaties of friendship and commerce with Congress. Under the terms of the treaties, France joined the United States in their bid for independence. France agreed not to claim Canada (which many Americans were eager to annex to the United States), though she would be able to keep her West Indian island possessions; and France and America would grant each other special privileges in trade.

The United States received little help from France for several years. French aid, however, was decisive in the battle that ended the Revolution, at Yorktown, in 1781.

21. The role of Congress in the revolutionary struggle

The United States Congress provided a common government for the colonies, but its influence on events was often negative. Congress would choose military commanders rather than permit Washington to do so. And Congress' choices were often unfortunate (for instance, sending Horatio Gates into the South). An added problem was that Congress could not induce the states to send in their quotas of money and men for the army. The

United States army was therefore in a dismal state. The men were hungry, ill-clothed, and at times owed two to three years' back pay.

22. Why the years 1778-80 are called the "Dark Years" of the Revolution

These years witnessed mostly American defeats at the hands of British and loyalist troops. For instance, by the spring of 1779, the British had reinstated the royal governor in Georgia and had occupied Savannah. The next spring, Charleston surrendered to the British. Following the American defeat at Camden in August 1780 came the news that Benedict Arnold had betrayed the American cause and joined the British. Bright spots during this period included the sea victories of John Paul Jones and the American victory at King's Mountain, North Carolina, over a loyalist force on October 7, 1780. This loyalist defeat forced British General Lord Cornwallis to abandon an invasion of North Carolina.

23. The significance of General Nathaniel Greene

General Horatio Gates, who had commanded American troops in the South, had been a disaster. He had been Congress' choice, not Washington's. With the threat of an invasion of North Carolina by Cornwallis in 1781, Congress allowed Washington to choose the southern commander – and he chose Nathaniel Greene. An excellent strategist, and a man who inspired loyalty, Greene lost most of his battles while inflicting greater casualties on the enemy than he himself sustained. At the battle of Guilford Courthouse in North Carolina on March 15, 1781, Greene's forces had to retreat – but with far fewer casualties than Cornwallis, who lost 30 percent of his army. Cornwallis retired to Wilmington. In the summer of 1781, Greene advanced into South Carolina and forced the

British and loyalist forces to withdraw into Charleston.

24. What happened at Yorktown

In June 1781, Cornwallis sent out raiding expeditions and began moving his own force toward Williamsburg, Virginia. Throughout July, General Clinton sent Cornwallis a series of conflicting orders, eventually commanding him to establish a fortified naval station in Virginia. Cornwallis chose Yorktown, situated on a long peninsula formed by the York River, to the north, and the James River, to the south. On August 2, the British entered Yorktown and began building fortifications. Cornwallis had hoped Clinton would join him for a general assault on the South, but from New York Clinton dispatched his refusal. Though the French alliance had been a disappointment to the Americans, the summer of 1781 brought the good news that King Louis XVI promised to commit a major part of his navy to the American cause. Twenty line-of-battle ships under Rear Admiral le Comte de Grasse set sail for the West Indies, where four more ships and 3,000 soldiers awaited him.

It was de Grasse who chose to attack Cornwallis at Yorktown rather than Clinton at New York. Washington, French General Rochambeau, and de Grasse converged on Yorktown in early September 1781. There was no aid for Cornwallis, for General Clinton remained in New York, deceived by false reports (instigated by Washington) that the Americans and French would attack the city. On September 5, de Grasse's fleet met a British fleet of 19 ships off Cape Charles at the entrance to the Chesapeake Bay and defeated it. The British fleet, forced to sail to New York for repairs, left Cornwallis without support from the sea. On September 28, 1781, the siege of Yorktown began. Cornwallis' 8,000 men, blocked seaward by de Grasse's

---

Key Terms at a Glance

Tories: Patriot name for the colonists loyal to King George III

Continental Congress: the body of delegates who spoke and acted collectively for the states during the American Revolution

Minutemen: militiamen trained to gather quickly on notice of a British attack

Declaration of Independence: document approved by the Continental Congress on July 4, 1776, which announced the separation of the American colonies from Great Britain

---

fleet, could not escape by ship; nor could they move by land, surrounded as they were by Rochambeau's 8,000 French troops and Washington's 5,645 regulars and 3,200 Virginia militia. An experienced soldier, Cornwallis knew when he was beaten; on October 17 he sent out the white flag. Two days later, Cornwallis formally surrendered his entire army to the Americans.

25. The two Treaties of Paris and what they said

The first Treaty of Paris concluded between the United States and Great Britain on November 30, 1782, acknowledged American independence and granted the young republic all lands from the Appalachians to the Mississippi River and (except for Florida) from the Gulf of Mexico to the Great Lakes. The second, the formal treaty signed September 3, 1783, involved not only the United States and Great Britain but Holland, France, and Spain, all whom had waged war on Great Britain. In this treaty, France received little, while Spain received Florida and was assured of the continued possession of Louisiana. Over eight months after the Peace of Paris, on November 25, 1783, the British regiments evacuated New York City while Washington and his troops marched in to take possession.

Questions for Review

1. **Name and explain the three Coercive Acts and what effects they had on the colonies.**

The first of these acts, the Boston Port Act, ordered the closing of the port of Boston until the city paid for the dumped tea and for the property of royal officials destroyed by mobs. Even if Boston fulfilled these conditions, said Parliament, the port would remain closed until the king was satisfied that peace and due obedience to the laws were reestablished. To enforce this act, the British fleet would blockade Boston while regulars of the British army occupied the city. Later, Parliament passed the Quartering Act, requiring Boston citizens to house and board soldiers and officers. The Massachusetts Government and Administration of Justice Act revoked part of the Massachusetts Bay charter that provided for the popular election (albeit subject to the governor's veto) of members of the colonial council. Instead, the act mandated that all councilors, as well as all inferior court judges, marshals, justices of the peace, and sheriffs were to appointed by the governor.

The Boston Port Act proved a great blow to the port city, whose economy depended on trade and fishing.

2. **What was the Continental Congress and how was it formed?**

The Continental Congress was a representative body that spoke for all fo the colonies in their struggle against Great Britain. The first Continental Congress gathered in Philadelphia on September 5, 1774 to discuss what steps the colonies, acting together, should take in the face of the Coercive and Quebec acts. It was formed of representatives of the various colonies from Massachusetts to South Carolina. The Second Continental Congress gathered in the crisis following the Battles of Lexington and Concord.

3. **What are the rights listed in the Declaration and Resolves, and what authority did they claim as the basis of their demands?**

The Declaration and Resolves appealed to the Social Contract theory, saying that all people "are entitled to life, liberty, and property, and they have never ceded to any sovereign power whatever, a right to dispose of either without their consent." The declaration appealed to the British constitution and the colonial charters, as when it argued that Americans are guaranteed all the constitutional rights of Englishmen, especially since they "by no means forfeited, surrendered, or lost any of those rights" by their emigration to America. These rights are held by the immutable laws of nature, the principles of the English constitution, and the several charters or compacts.

4. **What effects did the New England Restraining Act and the Quebec Acts have on the growing rebellion?**

Such legislation further chipped away at whatever loyalty many American colonists still felt for king and Parliament. Indeed, most Americans had not wanted rebellion, much less independence. Even the most radical leaders (with the exception of some like Sam Adams) still hoped for reconciliation between the colonies and the mother country. But reconciliation seemed more and more remote as each side hardened its position.

5. **What events led to the battle of Lexington?**

British General Gage in Boston wanted a resounding British victory that could definitely turn the tide of public sentiment towards the British government and against the Bostonians. Learning from spies that the rebels had cached arms and ammunition at both Worcester and Concord, Gage wanted to get an operation against Concord underway secretly, to seize some valuable munitions and capture some important rebel leaders as well. Gage however could not keep his plans a secret, and by April 16, 1775, rebels in Concord had been warned to hide their armaments. On April 18, when Gage's advance troops were set to embark, the general finally learned that his plan was well known in Boston. He ordered the advance regardless. His plan of campaign would take his troops by way of Lexington and then to Concord. It was at Lexington that the British first came to passage of arms with the colonial militia.

6. **Why were the Canadians so opposed to joining forces with the Americans?**

The Canadians were so opposed to joining forces with the Americans because the French Canadians had not forgotten that the First Continental Congress had protested the "establishing of the Roman Catholick Religion in the province of Quebec," or that John Jay's October 1774 "Address to the People of England" expressed "our astonishment that a British Parliament should ever consent to establish in that country [Canada] a religion that has deluged your island in blood, and disbursed impiety, bigotry, persecution, murder and rebellion through every part of the world."

7. Why was the battle of Bunker Hill important to the revolution, and what document did it inspire?

The battle of Bunker Hill gave the rebels new confidence, and inspired the "Declaration of the Causes and Necessity of Taking Up Arms."

8. What was the chief difficulty the American army faced during the revolution?

The hardest thing the American army faced was lack of money, food, and clothing.

9. Briefly summarize Thomas Paine's *Common Sense* and explain why it was so influential.

In *Common Sense*, Paine calls human society a "blessing" and even the best government "but a necessary evil." If men were perfectly virtuous, Paine insisted, they would not need government; but because men are vicious, governments are necessary to assure freedom and security. But not any form of government is desirable; according to Paine; only republican governments of elected representatives of the people are just. All other governments – aristocracies, monarchies – are nothing but tyrannies. Paine said Great Britain had abandoned all other means but force to compel the colonies to union. America, he said, does not need Great Britain or Europe – but they need America, for its agricultural produce. The king of Britain, argued Paine, had used the colonies solely for his own benefit; he did not act like a father but a tyrant. America had come of age and no longer needed the guidance of

Great Britain. In America, said Paine, not George III nor any merely human ruler, but the law is king. This pamphlet convinced the colonists that independence was the only possible course for the colonies.

10. Briefly summarize the Declaration of Independence, what it was calling for, and the principles it cited as the basis for its claims.

The Declaration of Independence is a catalog of the causes that, Congress claimed, compelled the colonies to seek independence from Great Britain. It is a "self-evident" truth, the declaration said, that all men are created equal, and "that they are endowed by their Creator with certain unalienable Rights, that among these are Life, Liberty and the pursuit of Happiness." Once it has established a basis for human liberty and equality, the declaration, in the language of the social contract, goes on to justify political revolution. Governments exist to secure the people's rights and derive their "just powers from the consent of the governed." When a "form of government becomes destructive of these ends, it is the Right of the People to alter or to abolish it, and to institute new Government." No people should do this lightly, however, but only "when a long train of abuses and usurpations, pursuing invariably the same Object evinces a design to reduce them under absolute Despotism." Then, it is the people's "right," "it is their duty, to throw off such Government and to provide new Guards for their future security." The Declaration then lists the alleged "injuries and usurpations" of the king of Great Britain against the colonies and formally declares independence.

11. Explain the two treaties of Paris in 1782 and 1783.

The first Treaty of Paris concluded between the United States and Great Britain on November 30, 1782, acknowledged American independence and granted the young republic all lands from the Appalachians to the Mississippi River and (except for Florida) from the Gulf of Mexico to the Great Lakes.

The second, the formal treaty signed September 3, 1783, involved not only the United States and Great Britain but Holland, France, and Spain, all whom had waged war on Great Britain. In this treaty, France received little, while Spain received Florida and was assured of the continued possession of Louisiana.

Ideas in Action

1. Read historical fiction or eyewitness accounts of the American Revolution.

2. Read about and discuss the Social Contract Theory on which the Declaration of Independence is based. What positive and negative effects does the Social Contract Theory have on government and the society of America?

3. What would have happened if Cornwallis had not surrendered at Yorktown? Some historians, such as Page Smith, author of *A People's History of the American Revolution*, argue that Great Britain could not have prevented American independence, even if the United States had received no aid from the French. Research and discuss whether the French alliance was decisive to the securing of American independence from Great Britain.

4. Study the claims of patriots, for, and loyalists, against, American independence, and research what Catholic thinkers have said about the right to revolution. In light of Catholic tradition, who had the better cause — patriots or loyalists

Sample Quiz I (pages 151-157)

Please answer the following in complete sentences.

1. What was the purpose of the Coercive Acts?

2. What is the most important of the effects of the Coercive Acts?

3. Why did British colonists protest the Quebec Act?

4. Why was the first Continental Congress a significant meeting?

5. To what three authorities did the Continental Congress appeal?

6. What effect did the New England Restraining Act have?

7. Why was enforcing the Association for non-importation a matter of concern for the Continental Congress?

8. How did the Congress enforce compliance with the Association?

9. Why were the battles of Lexington and Concord so important?

Answers to Sample Quiz I

Students' answers should approximate the following.

1. The Coercive Acts were the British government's response to Boston's continued rebellion, culminating in the Boston Tea Party.

2. The most important effect of the Coercive Acts was the forming of the Continental Congress.

3. British colonists protested the Quebec Act, claiming it would mean that Catholics would be treated by the British government as the

equals to Protestants and would surround the English colonies with "a Nation of Papists and Slaves."

4. The first Continental Congress was a significant meeting, since it was only the second time in their history that the various colonies attempted to act as one.

5. The Continental Congress appealed to the British constitution. Colonial charters, and to what the Liberal republican thinkers among them called "natural law."

6. The New England Restraining Act further eroded whatever loyalty many American colonists still felt for King and Parliament.

7. Enforcing the Association for non-importation was a matter of concern to the Continental Congress because not only was most of the population indifferent or opposed

to the struggle against Great Britain, but the congress itself had a very doubtful legal status.

8. To enforce compliance with the Association, Congress authorized local Committees of Safety to investigate the conduct of citizens suspected of being unsympathetic with its aims. These committees were to administer a "pledge" to honor non-importation; any who refused to take the pledge could be held up to public scorn, threatened with the loss of livelihood or property (or worse consequences), and ostracized from society.

9. The battles of Lexington and Concord were so important because they were the first battles of what became the American Revolution.

Sample Quiz II (pages 157-177)

Please answer the following in complete sentences.

1. Why did the French Canadians refuse to join the colonial resistance to the British government?

2. On what theory are the arguments in Thomas Paine's *Common Sense* based?

3. How did U.S. independence effect the lives of loyalists in America?

4. What reason did the writers of the Declaration give to convince the hesitant states to to embrace the cause of independence?

5. What, in brief, is the Declaration of Independence?

6. What was General Burgoyne trying to achieve in the battles of Saratoga?

7. What were some reasons why France supported the American Revolution?

8. Why was Congress' influence on events during the revolution often negative?

9. Why was General Nathaniel Greene so significant?

10. What was the outcome of the battle of Yorktown?

Answers to Sample Quiz II

Students' answers should approximate the following.

1. The French Canadians refused to join the colonial resistance to the British government because they had not forgotten that the colonists had protested the Quebec Act.

2. Thomas Paine's *Common Sense* is based on the social contract theory of government.

3. Independence brought an era of repression against loyalists, who could then be accused of treason. Active loyalists could expect death; but those who tried to stay neutral in

the conflict had cause to fear death, exile, or just ill treatment.

4. The reason that the writers of the Declaration gave to convince the hesitatnt was that since the king had excluded "the inhabitants of the United Colonies" from his protection, he had basically abdicated his authority over them; thus, all the powers of government should be taken up under the authority of the people of the colonies.

5. The Declaration of Independence is a catalog of the causes that, Congress claimed, compelled the colonies to seek independence from Great Britain.

6. General Burgoyne was trying to sever communication between New England and other colonies in the battles of Saratoga.

7. France supported the American Revolution partly because the French and Indian War and the Treaty of Paris had given all of Canada to Great Britain, and many of the French and their king wanted to see England humbled. French intellectuals, and many aristocrats, too, were ardent republicans who looked to America as an experiment in political freedom.

8. Congress' influence on events was often negative because it would choose military commanders rather than permit Washington to do so, and Congress' choice was often unfortunate. An added problem was that Congress could not induce the states to send in their quotas of money and men for the army.

9. General Greene was an excellent strategist, and a man who inspired loyalty. He lost most of his battles while inflicting greater casualties on the enemy than he himself sustained.

10. The outcome of the battle of Yorktown was that General Cornwallis formally surrendered his entire army to the Americans.

Essays

Instructions to be given to the students: Write in complete sentences. Underline your thesis. Give three supports or examples that explain why you think what you do and that support your thesis.

1. Is Thomas Paine's idea of the nature of government correct? Why or why not?

2. Compare and contrast the ideas of the Declaration of Independence and *Common Sense* with the ideas of the Enlightenment. How do the documents express those ideas, and how do they not?

Sample Test

Please answer the following in complete sentences.

I. Short Essay – Answer two of the following:

1. **Describe the Coercive Acts.**

2. **Describe the factions that divided the colonists.**

3. **What does *Common Sense* say about the nature of government and human society?**

4. **What were the provisions of the two Treaties of Paris.**

II. Short Answer:

1. **What was the purpose of the first Continental Congress?**

2. **Why was the First Continental Congress so significant?**

3. Give two reasons why loyalists or Tories remained loyal to the king.

4. What effect did *Common Sense* and the continuing war have on the attitudes of many English Americans toward the king and Great Britain?

5. What made the French finally decide to fully support the American Revolution?

Answer Key to the Chapter Test

Students' answers should approximate the following:

I.

1. The Coercive Acts included the Boston Port Act, the Quartering Act, and the Massachusetts Government and Administration of Justice Act. The Boston Port Act ordered the closing of the port of Boston until the city paid for the dumped tea and for the property of royal officials destroyed by mobs, and said the port would remain closed until the king was satisfied that peace and due obedience to the laws were reestablished. The Quartering Act required Boston citizens to house and board the British soldiers that occupied the city. The Massachusetts Government and Administration of Justice Act revoked part of the Massachusetts Bay charter that provided for the popular election of members of the colonial council.

2. Not all colonists were in favor of the measures taken by the Continental Congress. Throughout 1774 and 1775, and even long into the war that followed, only about a third of the colonists strongly supported the more radical partisans of American rights. Among the reluctant, some who initially believed the colonies had genuine grievances later so strongly opposed the actions of the Continental Congress that they threw in their lot with Britain and King George. Loyalists made up from 20 to 30 percent of the population. Most other colonists, however, were neither loyalist nor strongly patriot, but indifferent.

3. In *Common Sense*, Paine calls human society a "blessing" but even the best government "but a necessary evil." If men were perfectly virtuous, Paine insisted, they would not need government; but because men are vicious, governments are necessary to assure freedom and security. But not any form of government is desirable; according to Paine; only republican governments of elected representatives of the people are just. All other governments – aristocracies, monarchies – are nothing but tyrannies. Paine said Great Britain had abandoned all other means but force to compel the colonies to union. America, he said, does not need Great Britain or Europe – but Great Britain and Europe need America, for its agricultural produce. The king of Britain, argued Paine, had used the colonies solely for his own benefit; he did not act like a father but a tyrant. America had come of age and no longer needed the guidance of Great Britain. In America, said Paine, not George III nor any merely human ruler, but the law is king.

4. The first Treaty of Paris concluded between the United States and Great Britain on November 30, 1782, acknowledged American independence and granted the young republic all lands from the Appalachians to the Mississippi River and (except for Florida) from the Gulf of Mexico to the Great Lakes. The second, the formal treaty signed September 3, 1783, involved not only the United States and Great Britain but Holland, France, and Spain, all whom had waged war on Great Britain.

II.

1. The purpose of the first Continental Congress was to discuss what steps the colonies, acting together, should take in the face of the Coercive and Quebec acts.

2. The first Continental Congress was a significant meeting, since it was only the second time in their history that the various colonies attempted to act as one.

3. *Possible answers*: Some loyalists remained loyal to the British crown out of self-interest but others out of conscience. Anglican clergymen would not renounce the head of their church; others thought they should not break oaths they had taken to remain the king's faithful subjects.

4. *Common Sense* and the continuing war undermined whatever reverence English Americans felt for the king.

5. The French finally decided to fully support the American Revolution because with Burgoyne's defeat, the French government worried that the military failure might move the British government to seek peace with America.

CHAPTER 10: A New Nation

Chapter Overview

* With the Declaration of Independence, colonial governments began acting as state governments, each with its own constitution.

* In 1776 George Mason wrote the Virginia Bill of Rights, adopted by the state of Virginia the same year. Other states followed Virginia's example.

* In 1776, John Dickinson, in an attempt to get the states to agree on a constitution for the new national government, introduced in Congress the Articles of Confederation and Perpetual Union. All of the states but Maryland approved the Articles of Confederation by 1779. Maryland ratified them in 1781.

* Following the revolution, religion in the United States underwent changes. In 1786 the Virginian assembly passed Jefferson's Statute of Religious Liberty. The American churches cut off ties with their mother churches in Europe, forming distinctly American groups. In 1784, John Carroll was named prefect apostolic of the Catholic Church in the United States, and bishop in 1789.

* Congress was facing many problems fulfilling its obligations to both Britain and its own people, so many Americans began to see the need for a stronger national government.

* In 1786, Massachusetts farmers, led by Daniel Shays, rose in rebellion against the high debts and taxes that were troubling them. The rebellion was crushed by 1787. This troubled many in America, as they were convinced that the current national government was insufficient to keep the peace.

* In 1787 Congress adopted the Northwest Ordinance, which governs United States territories to this day.

* Virginia and Maryland called for a convention of all the states to meet in September 1786 to discuss revisions to the Articles of Confederation. When only very few delegates came to attend, in February of 1787 Congress called for another convention to discuss revisions to the Articles. During the convention, two factions arose. One faction, the nationalists, called for a strong central government that would dominate the states, with proportional representation of the states in the legislature. The other faction favored a weak central government, the preservation of state sovereignty, with equal representation of the states in the legislature.

* Roger Sherman suggested the "Connecticut Compromise," a plan that called for proportional representation in the lower house and equal representation in the senate. The compromise was agreed upon and passed, and a committee drafted the new constitution on August 6.

* When 12 out of 13 states had approved the new constitution, Congress formally ratified it and called for presidential and congressional elections

* George Washington was elected the first president of the United States on April 30, 1789, with the entire electoral vote.

* Washington chose Thomas Jefferson and Alexander Hamilton to serve in his cabinet. Around these two men, who had very

different visions for the new republic, grew up two parties, the Republicans and the Federalists.

- Congress approved a bill of rights, a series of checks on the federal government. By December 15, 1791, the required number of states approved ten of the 12 provisions in the Bill of Rights, and these became formally part of the Constitution.

- Washington was reelected in 1792, again with a unanimous electoral vote. He retired in 1797, and John Adams became president, with Jefferson as his vice president. Washington died in 1799.

- Washington chose Thomas Jefferson and Alexander Hamilton to serve in his cabinet. Around these two men, who had very different visions for the new republic, grew up two parties, the Republicans and the Federalists.

- Congress approved a bill of rights, a series of checks on the federal government. By November 1791, the required number of states approved ten of the 12 provisions in the Bill of Rights, and these became formally part of the Constitution.

- Washington was reelected in 1792, again with a unanimous electoral vote. He retired in 1797, and John Adams became president, with Jefferson as his vice president. Washington died in 1799.

What Students Should Know

1. **Variations in state constitutions after the Revolution**

   With the Congress' declaration of independence, existing colonial governments began to function as state governments with little or no change to their constitutions.

Virginia's constitution – a legislature that dominated government, a council whose members were appointed by the legislature, and a governor whose veto power had to be supported by the council – became the model for several other states.

In 1779, John Adams drafted a new state constitution for Massachusetts, which established a house of representatives, elected by the people; a senate, which represented the wealthier citizens; and a popularly elected governor, who could veto acts of the legislature and appoint state officials. The governor appointed the members of an independent judiciary that could decide on the constitutionality of acts passed by the government. Adams' constitution reflected a strain of republican thought that held that pure forms of government inevitably became corrupt: monarchies became tyrannies; aristocracies hardened into oligarchies; and popular governments collapsed into anarchy. Adams thought the best government is one that has a mixtre of monarchical, aristocratic, and popular elements. Such a government would allow each element to check the power of the others.

Pennsylvania stood at the opposite end of the political spectrum from Massachusetts, having adopted a unicameral (one-house) legislature with no governor. Many radical thinkers thought this the only proper form of government for a republic. The people ruled through the legislature, they said – so what need was there for another governmental body to check the will of the people? The people's representatives were the best safeguard for popular liberties.

2. **How the suffrage differed from state to state**
   The states differed in their qualifications for the suffrage. All the states limited the

suffrage to white males, except for New Jersey, where women who held property and free blacks could vote. Seven states allowed every white male taxpayer to vote, while the rest established property requirements for voting. Almost every state permitted only property owners to vote for members of the upper house of the legislature. A few states, such as New Hampshire, had test oaths of loyalty for office-holders to keep Catholics and loyalists from holding office.

3. **The character of the Virginia Bill of Rights and its effects**

On June 12, 1776, the Virginia House of Burgesses adopted a bill of rights, authored by George Mason. The Virginia Bill of Rights declared "that all men are by nature equally free and independent, and have certain inherent rights, of which, when they enter into a state of society, they cannot by any compact deprive or divest their posterity." These rights, wrote Mason, are "the enjoyment of life and liberty, with the means of acquiring and possessing property, and pursuing and obtaining happiness and safety." The Virginia Bill of Rights further declared "that a power is vested in, and consequently derived from, the people; that magistrates are their trustees and servants, and at all times amenable to them." The Virginia bill listed as rights trial by jury, protection from searches without a warrant, and the freedom of the press. Without disestablishing the Anglican Church, the bill guaranteed "the free exercise of religion, according to the dictates of conscience." Other states followed Virginia's example and adopted bills of rights.

4. **When the Articles of Confederation were introduced and when they were adopted**

In July 1776, John Dickinson introduced into Congress the draft of a constitution called the Articles of Confederation and Perpetual Union. On November 15, 1777, Congress approved the Articles of Confederation and submitted them to the state legislatures for approval. It wasn't until February 1779 that all the states but one approved the articles. Maryland alone held out. When Maryland at last ratified the Articles, they went formally into effect on March 1, 1781, only seven months before Cornwallis surrendered at Yorktown.

5. **The provisions of the Articles of Confederation**

The Articles of Confederation gave the new government power to declare war and make peace, conclude treaties, regulate the coining of money, and decide in disputes between states. The articles, however, were drawn with special attention to state sovereignty. Article two stated that "each state retains its sovereignty, freedom and independence, and every Power, Jurisdiction and right, which is not by this confederation expressly delegated to the United States, in Congress assembled." To protect the sovereignty of each, every state, whatever its population, received one vote in Congress. The articles granted Congress no power to collect taxes; instead, Congress had to rely on state contributions for its revenue. Nor did Congress have the power to place duties on foreign trade. Any important decisions – such as declaring war, making treaties, and borrowing money – had to garner the agreement of nine of the thirteen states. Further, any change in the articles had to draw the unanimous consent of all the state legislatures.

6. **Political reforms in the states after the Revolution**

Following the Revolution, Virginia abolished primogeniture when an owner died intestate and entailment. Several northern states had movements to abolish slavery. Yet slavery was only abolished in those northern states where it was no longer economically viable – and, even then, many slaves were sold south and not freed at all. A Massachusetts court, however, freed a slave, Quock Walker, saying the state's bill of rights demanded it. Other northern states, Connecticut, New Hampshire, and Pennsylvania, declared the children of slaves to be free. Virginia, Delaware, Maryland, along with all the northern states, prohibited the foreign slave trade.

7. Effects of the Revolution on religious establishments

Like most European nations, most of the states had long had established churches – churches recognized by law and supported by taxes. In some cases, governments required attendance at church services. Following the revolution, however, New York, Maryland, and both Carolinas disestablished the Anglican Church. Thomas Jefferson and other republicans called for the disestablishment of state churches. Jefferson wanted not only freedom for all religions but what he called in an 1802 letter he wrote to the Baptists of Danbury, Connecticut, a "wall of separation" between church and state. Central to Liberalism is the conviction that religion is a purely private affair. It has nothing to do with the state, or the state with it. This conviction was rooted in another assumption – that religion is not about truth but is merely private opinion. The Virginia Bill of Rights had called for the "free exercise of religion, according to the dictates of conscience," but tax monies still went to support the established Anglican Church.

Jefferson fought vigorously for the disestablishment of the Anglican Church in Virginia. In 1777, the Virginia assembly repealed all laws requiring church attendance and universal support for the established Anglican Church. But Jefferson wanted to go further. In January 1786, the Virginia assembly passed Jefferson's Statute of Religious Liberty that disestablished the Anglican Church in Virginia. In New England, the Congregational Church remained quasi-established, since townships appointed ministers to local congregations.

8. Religion in America after the Revolution

Because, in New England, town selectmen tended to appoint more liberal-minded, this-worldly Unitarian ministers instead of the old hard-line Puritans, to lead congregations, Calvinists began setting up their own churches, supported by their members, not the state. Almost everywhere in the states, churches cut off ties with their mother churches in Europe and formed distinctly American groups. The state of the Catholic Church in America was not robust. In all there were about 25,000 Catholics in the United States, centered for the most part in Maryland and Pennsylvania; about 1,500 Catholics lived in New York and 200 in Virginia. Catholics in Pennsylvania, who were mostly English with a few Germans and a growing number of Irish, had benefited from Pennsylvania's traditional religious tolerance. But before the revolution, Catholics in Maryland had lived in fear of the penal laws. The priests in America were Jesuits who, because their flocks could not support them, were forced to make their living as planters. The Catholics in English America were under the authority of the bishop of London, called the "vicar-apostolic." Both priests and the Catholic faithful were opposed to the appointment of a Catholic bishop for America, fearing it would spark a persecution against them. Yet, because of the revolution, attitudes towards Catholics had begun to grow more positive in the United States. Still, Catholics who had suffered centuries of persecution, or the threat of persecution, continued to tread warily.

9.   Who John Carroll was and how he became the United States' first bishop

Both John Carroll and his cousin, Charles Carroll, belonged to an aristocratic family of Maryland. Both went to school in France; but while Charles turned to the study of law, John pursued studies for the priesthood as a member of the Jesuit order. A advocate for American independence during the revolution, John Carroll in 1776 accompanied his cousin, Charles, Benjamin Franklin, and Samuel Chase to Quebec in the unsuccessful attempt to convince the Canadians to join the rebellion. After the Revolution, in 1783, Father Carroll with five other priests issued a declaration to Rome stating that no bishop was needed in the United States but asked one of their number be appointed to serve as a superior. Carroll was nominated, and in 1784, Carroll was named prefect apostolic of the Church in the United States, with the faculties to administer the Sacrament of Confirmation.

As prefect apostolic, Carroll lacked priests, and the priests he received from Europe were often unworthy. He had to struggle with a peculiarly American form of Church government – trusteeship – where Catholic laymen, designated trustees, established and funded Catholic congregations and paid priests' salaries. Because of their status, it was not long before trustees began to see themselves as the final authorities in Church matters, hiring priests and firing them at will

if they did not approve of them. Such troubles convinced Carroll that the American Church needed a bishop; and, after he had been elected by the priests of America, on November 6, 1789, Pope Pius VII appointed Carroll bishop of Baltimore with jurisdiction over the entire United States.

10.   Issues faced by the Catholic Church in the United States

The problems in the American Church did not end because it now had a bishop. Trustees continued to assert their authority, and Carroll still had to rely on foreign priests to staff the churches. Revolution in France was driving a number of priests to American shores. Many of these were worthy men; some were not. The former Jesuits in the U.S. were attacked by a disgruntled priest of living like lords on estates worked by slaves, whom the priests treated cruelly. The former Jesuits did own slaves. They did not live in luxury, nor did they treat their slaves cruelly. Racial tensions affected the Catholic Church in the U.S., when German Catholics wanted a German bishop, and well-established parishes balked at submitting to a bishop's authority. But in 1791 four French Sulpician priests and five English-speaking students established a seminary for the United States and the Sulpician priests also staffed the first Catholic college in America, Georgetown College (now in Washington, D.C.

11.   The weaknesses of the Articles of Confederation

States had been unwilling to compromise their newly won independence by giving too much power to the national government, and they would not cooperate with it once it was established. Since Congress could not tax but only requisition money from the states, it relied on the willingness of state legislatures to supply needed revenues, but these were often not forthcoming. Attempts to enhance Congress' taxing power through amendments failed because it could not garner the consent of all the states. Congress' weaknesses meant it could not fulfill its obligations under the peace bargain with Great Britain, such as protection of loyalists. When Congress protested Great Britain's violation of the Treaty of Paris by retaining forts in the American northwest, the British government retorted that the United States had not honored the treaty, either: debts to Britain had not been paid, and the property of loyalists had not been returned. Congress could do little to settle state conflicts that threatened to tear the fledgling union apart.

12. The provisions and importance of the Northwest Ordinance

The Northwest Ordinance divided the Northwest (the territories north of the Ohio River and west of the Appalachians) into five regions, each of which eventually became a state. When any of these regions attained a population of 5,000 free males, Congress was to establish a territorial government for it. The government consisted of a representative assembly, elected by the people of the territory; a governor, appointed by Congress; and a council of five chosen by Congress from names submitted by the territorial assembly. All townships in the territories were to be surveyed six miles square and divided into 36 sections, each a mile square, that were to be sold at auction. Section 16 in every township was reserved for the support of public schools. When a region attained a population of 60,000 freemen, it could become a state, equal in rights and privileges to the original states. The Northwest Ordinance included a sort of bill of rights. Congress guaranteed territorial inhabitants

religious freedom. Settlements had to provide for schools, since, said the ordinance, "religion, morality, and knowledge" are "necessary to good government and the happiness of mankind." The Northwest Ordinance called for respect to be shown to Indians and their property rights and forbade slavery within the territories – though the ordinance included a fugitive slave provision.

13. How Shays' Rebellion accelerated the movement to revise the Articles of Confederation

Shays' Rebellion was troubling to many in America, confirming their conviction that the current form of the national government was insufficiently powerful to keep the peace. Though the Massachusetts militia had proved quite capable of handling the rebellion, some pointed out that the federal government had been powerless to help. Leaders throughout America were deeply worried about the future of the American union.

14. The course of events leading to the Constitutional Convention

When, in 1785, delegates from Virginia and Maryland met to settle their disputes over oyster fisheries and the Potomac boundary, they realized they could not reach a resolution on these questions without the cooperation of Delaware and Pennsylvania. The process of addressing such issues was haphazard and difficult under the Articles of Confederation, for it possessed no way to force states to come to an agreement on controversial points – and having come to an agreement, observe it. Virginia and Maryland called for a convention of all the states to meet in Annapolis, Maryland. But when the convention met in September 1786, only five states had sent delegates. The called for another convention. Congress concurred and on February 21, 1787 invited the states to send delegates to a convention that was to meet in Philadelphia "for the sole and express purpose of revising the Articles of Confederation" so that they might "render the federal constitution adequate to the exigencies of government, and the preservation of the Union." The convention was set to open on May 14, 1787; but, by that date, only a few delegates had appeared in Philadelphia. Eleven days later, delegates from only seven states were present. Delegates from Vermont, New Hampshire, Connecticut, and Maryland trickled in over the next few months. Rhode Island's delegates never showed up.

15. The provisions of the Virginia Plan

Introduced by Edmund Randolph of Virginia, the Virginia Plan called for a bicameral (two-house) national legislature. Both the lower and upper houses would represent the states according to population (proportional representation). The plan provided that the people would elect members of the lower house, while members of the upper house, the Senate, would be appointed by the lower house from lists provided by the states. The Virginia Plan provided for a national executive and a national judiciary. The Virginia Plan said the legislature should make laws "in all cases to which the separate States are incompetent, or in which the harmony of the United States may be interrupted by the exercise of individual legislation." It would further have the right "to negative all laws passed by the several States, contravening, in the opinion of the National Legislature the articles of Union; and to call forth the force of the Union against any member of the Union failing to

fulfill its duty under the articles thereof." To assuage the fears of delegates who were wary of a strong national government, the plan provided for a Council of Revision that could overturn any acts of the national government that it deemed violated the rights of the states.

16. The provisions of the New Jersey Plan

The New Jersey Plan was introduced into the convention by William Paterson of New Jersey on June 15, 1787. It opposed proportional representation and called for a mere revision of the Articles of Confederation and for equal representation of states in the legislature.

17. What compromise was reached

When delegates from Delaware, New Jersey, and Maryland threatened to leave the convention, Roger Sherman of Connecticut offered a compromise plan that he had offered earlier – proportional representation in the lower house, equal representation in the senate. The vote on the "Connecticut Compromise," as it was called, was five to five; nevertheless, it was recorded as passing.

18. The provisions of the new constitution

The draft of the new constitution, released on August 6, 1787, contained the Connecticut Compromise – the lower house, the House of Representatives, would have proportional representation, while the Senate would admit two representatives from each state. The executive, called the president, would be elected indirectly by the people – that is, the people would vote for electors who, in turn, voted for the president. The number of electors for each state was to be proportional to its population. The president would be commander-in-chief of the armed forces and would have veto power over congressional legislation. Only a two-thirds majority in both houses of the legislature could override a president's veto. Finally, the draft established a supreme court whose members, appointed for life by the president with the consent of the Senate, would serve during good behavior. The draft elicited more controversy over immigration, a standing army, paper money, property qualifications for public office, and the slave trade. For the slavery question, the convention adopted a compromise that allowed the foreign slave trade for another twenty years, after which time it would be illegal. Another controversy arose over the coercive powers of the federal government. The resolution is found in Article 6 of the Constitution – the national government could not resort to force but only to the courts of law if states refused to comply with congressional acts.

What resulted from all the debates was a "federal" model of government that more or less defined the areas where the national and state governments exercised sovereignty. The United States was to have two sovereigns – the states in regards to their internal affairs, and the national government in relation to national matters, such as war and peace, treaties with foreign nations, and international and interstate trade. As one aspect of this sovereignty, the national government would have the authority to lay taxes directly on citizens, bypassing state legislatures and thus freeing it from monetary dependence on the states.

19. When the Constitution was signed

The delegates signed the Constitution on September 17, 1787.

20. Who opposed the Constitution and why

Winning approval from the states for the new constitution was not automatic or easy. A vigorous opposition awaited the "federalists," as the supporters of the Constitution called themselves. Their foes, the "antifederalists," came from a variety of backgrounds and opposed the new constitution for a variety of reasons. In some cases, they represented the proponents of democracy, optimistic about human nature and hoping for the birth of an ideal age. These feared a strong centralized government with the power to tax; such a government, they thought, would become the tool of the few for the oppression of the many. Others opposed the new government for less worthy reasons, and many opposed it for a variety of reasons that cannot be easily cataloged. A common division was based on age – younger men tended to support the constitution while the older, more established men opposed it. This was true especially in the South, where the strongest opposition to the constitution came from the settled tidewater regions, while the raw western counties supported it.

Some antifederalists criticized the Constitution for its failure to outlaw slavery and because it did not forbid government offices to non-Christians. Those who thought liberty was preserved only if representatives served one-year terms objected to the two-year term for representatives and the six-year term for senators. Patrick Henry criticized the constitution because he said delegates had exceeded their authority in drawing it up. The office of president, he said, "squints toward monarchy" and the new taxing power would allow the Congress to obtain dictatorial powers. Chiefly, Henry feared that the new government would compromise America's fledgling liberty. George Mason questioned whether the Constitution could govern so wide a territory as the United States while preserving liberty.

21. The *Federalist Papers* and their importance

To counter New York opposition to the Constitution, Alexander Hamilton and John Jay, joined by the Virginian, James Madison, wrote, under the pen name "Publius," a series of articles for New York journals in defense of the Constitution. These articles, later collected into a volume called *The Federalist*, developed the themes of the insufficiency of the Articles of Confederation and the advantages of the Constitution. This collection, written by men who had participated in the constitutional convention, has since gained a quasi-official status as an authoritative interpretation of the Constitution.

22. The Bill of Rights, their ratification and contents

In part to appease the antifederalists, Washington in his inaugural address hinted that Congress should approve a bill of rights. Accordingly, twelve amendments were presented to Congress, which approved them and sent them on to the states for ratification. By November 1791, the required number of states had ratified ten of the twelve amendments, and they became part of the constitution.

The Bill of Rights was seen as a series of checks upon the power of the federal government. Thus, while Article I forbids Congress from making a "law respecting an establishment of religion, or prohibiting the free exercise thereof," it does not forbid state governments from doing so. Article II protects a state's right to a militia and so forbids the federal government from infringing on "the right of the people to keep and bear Arms." Article X enshrines a

principle dear to the antifederalists – the separation of powers in American government, mandating that "powers not delegated to the United States by the Constitution, nor prohibited by it to the States, are reserved to the States respectively, or to the people." Neither this amendment nor any part of the constitution, however, clearly delineates the respective powers of the federal government or the states – assuring that the question would serve as the grist for future debates both inside and outside of Congress.

23. What the Judiciary Act did

An important task for Washington was composing the Supreme Court. Although the constitution established the judiciary as the third branch of government, it did not specify how many justices should sit on the court. Thus, on September 24, 1789, Congress passed the Judiciary Act, setting the number of justices at six – one chief justice and five associates. (The number was later increased to nine.) The act also established 13 district courts and three circuit courts.

24. What precedents the Jay Court established

The Supreme Court presided over by John Jay, the republic's first chief justice, is significant for establishing precedents for what later became known as "judicial review" – the court's critique of the legal acts of states and the federal government. The first of these precedents was the Supreme Court's decision that a law passed by the Connecticut assembly was unconstitutional; the second was the court's refusal to execute a law passed by Congress. In the latter case, the court said that it was unconstitutional for the federal courts to act as the agents of Congress.

25. Alexander Hamilton's ideas and politics

Alexander Hamilton became Washington's most trusted adviser. Hamilton's goal was to see the new federal government well-established and strong. An admirer of the British government, Hamilton worked to set the financial affairs of the federal government upon principles already established in the mother country. For Hamilton, the wealthy (cultured and established families, prosperous merchants, creditors, and successful financiers) were the solid pillars upon which to erect the federal government. He thought that if the federal government established policies favorable to the wealthy, the wealthy would in turn lend their support to the federal government over state governments, which Hamilton wanted to see weakened.

Hamilton advocated a number of policies to put the new government on a sound financial footing. He promoted repayment of both the foreign and domestic debt. He convinced the president and then Congress that, instead of having each state pay its own debts, the federal government should assume and pay off all state debt. Under Hamilton's leadership, the federal government by 1795 had paid off the foreign debt. Hamilton also suggested and lobbied for the creation of a federal bank – the Bank of the United States.

Key Terms at a Glance

trusteeship: an American form of church government in which Catholic laymen established and funded Catholic congregations and paid priests' salaries.

Articles of Confederation: the first United States constitution

Northwest Ordinance: a body of laws adopted by Congress in 1787 to govern the territories

nationalists: those who favored a strong, central government that would dominate the states

Connecticut Compromise: the compromise promoted by Roger Sherman that provided for a dual system of representation in the legislature and was used as the basis of the existing Constitution

federalists: supporters of the new Constitution to replace the Articles of Confederation

antifederalists: opponents of the new Constitution

strict construction: a principal of interpreting the Constitution that says that the federal government only possesses those powers clearly granted it by the Constitution and may do only what is strictly necessary to the carrying out of the powers

loose construction: a principal of interpreting the Constitution that says that the federal government has the authority to act on any measure that bears an obvious relation to a power given by the Constitution to the federal government and is not forbidden by any part of the Constitution

26. Thomas Jefferson's opposition to Hamilton, and his ideas

Thomas Jefferson differed most from Hamilton in his ideas on society and government. Jefferson repudiated Hamilton's favoritism of the wealthy and his admiration for British government – Jefferson was horrified to learn that Hamilton had even been heard to say that he thought corruption an essential part of effective government. Jefferson represented the American democratic idealist. He hoped that the change to republican government and manners would draw mankind to new perfections. He favored the common man, the small farmer, whose independence he thought would form the foundation for free government. While it is true that he did not trust the common man's wisdom and believed that a republican government would foster a "natural aristocracy" that would direct the affairs of the nation, he also believed that defects in the common man could be remedied by free public education. Finally, unlike Hamilton, Jefferson wanted agriculture to be the economic foundation of the United States and mistrusted manufacturers and the artisan and merchant classes.

27. Strict and loose construction of the Constitution

Jefferson argued for a strict construction of the Constitution. He said that while the Constitution allowed Congress "to make all laws necessary and proper" to carry out the federal government's designated powers, it did not allow Congress to do what is merely convenient. For instance, a national bank, said Jefferson, was not necessary to federal finance and therefore was unconstitutional.

Hamilton's theory of constitutional interpretation is called loose construction. He said if some measure had "an obvious relation" to a power given by the Constitution to the federal government, and was not forbidden by any part of the Constitution, then "it may safely be deemed to come within the compass of the national authority." Thus, a national bank, according to Hamilton's reasoning, would be constitutional because, even though it was not necessary to federal finance, it had an obvious relation to it, since it facilitated the operation of a constitutional power of the federal government.

28. The rise of the Federalist and Republican political factions

The differences in American politics, exemplified by Jefferson and Hamilton, but including John Adams, Washington, and James Madison, crystalized in two political divisions. Jefferson's party, called Republican, was strict constructionist in interpreting the Constitution. They claimed to stand for the common man against the wealthy. It included former antifederalists, and looked kindly on the French Revolution. The Federalists, on the other hand, were loose constructionists and wanted to rest the republic on the the the foundation of the powerful and wealthy, and looked to Great Britain as an example of government. This division into two factions characterized what became representative of American government -- the two party system.

29. What the Whiskey Rebellion was. Its results

The Whiskey Rebellion, an uprising of farmers in western Pennsylvania, was an early challenge to federal power. In 1791, Congress had laid an excise tax on whiskey, which affected the farmers of the Appalachian region, who could only transport their corn by distilling it into spirituous liquors. When farmers in western Pennsylvania refused to pay the tax and rose in revolt, the Jeffersonian Republican governor of Pennsylvania, Thomas Mifflin, did nothing. With Washington's urging, however, Congress called up the militia of four states. Led by Washington, who was accompanied by Hamilton, the militia dispersed the farmers, putting an end to what was jokingly called the "Whiskey Rebellion."

30. The provisions of the Jay Treaty and opposition to it

Jay's Treaty was a treaty signed between the United States and Great Britain on November 19, 1794 in which the British agreed to evacuate all their forts on United States territory by 1796 and granted American ships a limited right to trade with the British West Indies; and while the United States agreed to pay back debts, the British offered a large sum in reparation for the illegal capture of American ships. But other parts of the treaty, Washington knew, would only stoke Republican ire – and they made even Washington wince. For one, the treaty forbade American ships from carrying, as they long had been doing, certain products, including cotton, molasses, and sugar, from the British West Indies to America. It did not press the British to compensate slave owners for slaves taken at the end of the war. Finally, the treaty made no mention of the impressing of American sailors – one of the chief complaints against the British. Republicans strongly opposed the treaty, which came to be one incident that illustrates the growing partisanship in the politics of the new republic. Even before the treaty, Republican attacks against not only the Federalists but even Washington himself had been

increasing in frequency and bitterness. The treaty only exacerbated this tendency.

31. What Washington said in his farewell address on September 17, 1796

In his farewell address, Washington expressed the hope that the happiness of the United States would be so preserved as to "acquire to them the glory of recommending it to the applause, the affection and adoption of every nation which is yet a stranger to it." He spoke of the value of the union and the importance of cultivating a national patriotism over local sympathies. Because of his deep regard for the union, Washington warned against factions, against altering the Constitution except by "an explicit and authentic act of the whole people," and against "the spirit of party in general." Washington praised religion and morality as instruments conducive to political prosperity. "A volume could not trace," he said, "all their connections with private and public felicity… reason and experience both forbid us to expect that national morality can prevail in exclusion of religious principle." The president added praises for "institutions for the general diffusion of knowledge," since, he said, they are "essential that public opinion should be enlightened."

Questions for Review

1. What was the significance of the Virginia Bill of Rights?

The Virginia Bill of Rights was the first bill of rights to be adopted by a state government. It states that that all men are by nature equally free and independent, and have certain inherent rights, of which, when they enter into a state of society, they cannot by any compact deprive or divest their posterity.

Other states followed Virginia's example and adopted bills of rights.

2. **What was Maryland's reason for not ratifying the Articles of Confederation, and how was the problem solved?**

Maryland held back on ratifying the Articles of Confederation because a powerful cadre of land speculators, who had formed the Illinois-Wabash company, had convinced the Maryland legislature to delay ratification of the Articles until the settlement of a land dispute with Virginia. When Virginia agreed to cede her western lands to the United States, Maryland ratified the Articles.

3. **What were some of the political and social reforms realized in the United States after the Revolution?**

Following the Revolution, Virginia abolished primogeniture when an owner died intestate and entailment. Several northern states had movements to abolish slavery. Other northern states, Connecticut, New Hampshire, and Pennsylvania, declared the children of slaves to be free. Virginia, Delaware, Maryland, along with all the northern states, prohibited the foreign slave trade.

4. **Why did republicans call for the disestablishment of state churches?**

Some republicans called for disestablishment of state churches because central to Liberalism is the conviction that religion is a purely private affair. It has nothing to do with the state, or the state with it. This conviction was rooted in another assumption – that religion is not about truth but is merely private opinion.

5. **Briefly explain Jefferson's Statute of Religious Liberty.**

Jefferson's Statute of Religious Liberty says that "... no one shall be compelled to frequent or support any religious worship, place or ministry whatsoever, nor shall be enforced, restrained, molested, or burthened in his body or goods, nor shall otherwise suffer on account of his religious opinions or belief; but ... all men shall be free to profess, and by argument to maintain, their opinion in matters of religion, and that the same shall in no wise diminish, enlarge or affect their civil capacities."

6. **What were the problems Father John Carroll faced as prefect apostolic of the Church of the United States? Give a brief description of each.**

As prefect apostolic, Carroll lacked priests, and the priests he received from Europe were often unworthy. He had to struggle with a peculiarly American form of Church government – trusteeship – where Catholic laymen, designated trustees, established and funded Catholic congregations and paid priests' salaries. Because of their status, it was not long before trustees began to see themselves as the final authorities in Church matters, hiring priests and firing them at will if they did not approve of them.

7. **What were the inadequacies of the Articles of Confederation?**

States had been unwilling to compromise their newly won independence by giving too much power to the national government, and they would not cooperate with it once it was established. Since Congress could not tax but only requisition money from the states, it relied on the willingness of state legislatures to supply needed revenues, but these were often not forthcoming. Attempts to enhance Congress' taxing power through amendments failed because it could not garner the consent of all the states. Congress' weaknesses meant it could not fulfill its obligations under the peace bargain with Great Britain, such as protection of loyalists. Congress could not settle conflicts threatening the union between the states.

8. **What did the Northwest Ordinance do for the United States?**

The Northwest Ordinance divided the Northwest (the territories north of the Ohio River and west of the Appalachians) into five regions, each of which eventually became a state and organized these territories. The Northwest Ordinance governs the United States to this day.

9. **What is the significance of Shay's Rebellion? How did it contribute to the call for a new constitution?**

Shay's Rebellion accelerated the movement to revise the Articles of Confederation because it confirmed the conviction that the current form of the national government was insufficiently powerful to keep the peace.

10. **Describe the two factions that divided the delegates to the Constitutional Convention.**

One faction was the nationalists, those who favored a strong, central government that would dominate the states. The other faction, which favored a weak central government and the preservation of state sovereignty, was at first disorganized and unable to stop the forward momentum of the nationalists. The second faction represented the small states.

11. **What was the Connecticut Compromise?**

The Connecticut Compromise was a constitutional plan that proposed proportional representation in the lower house of the national legislature, equal representation in its senate.

12. **List the factors that made it difficult for the new Constitution to be ratified?**

Those who opposed the new Constitution, the "antifederalists," feared a strong centralized government with the power to tax; such a government, they thought, would become the tool of the few for the oppression of the many. Others opposed the new government for less worthy reasons.

13. **What is the Bill of Rights and what did it seek to clarify?**

As part of its ratification, the Massachusetts convention requested the addition of a bill of rights to the constitution. The Bill of Rights sought to clarify the rights of citizens by providing a series of checks upon the power of the federal government.

14. **What were some of the problems that Washington faced as the first president?**

Washington had to turn a written constitution into a working government over a people, many of whom still opposed it. He had to deal with political factions among members of his own cabinet and in the country at large.

Ideas in Action

1. **Read and discuss the Constitution and the Bill of Rights. (Copies of these may be found on the Internet.) How have the ideas presented in these documents played out in the history of the United States?**

2. **Study the arguments of the anti-federalists. Have their predictions of the kind of government and society the Constitution would create come true? Why or why not?**

3. Debate the merits of the ideas of the strict and loose construction of the Constitution.

4. Read Washington's Inaugural and Farewell addresses (also found on the Internet).Does the United States today live up to the iedals that Washington espoused?

Sample Quiz I (pages 181-193)

Please answer the following in complete sentences.

1. With the Declaration of Independence, how did existing governments function?

2. What rights did the Virginia Bill of Rights list?

3. What powers did the Articles of Confederation give the new government?

4. How did the Articles of Confederation protect state sovereignty?

5. What political/social reforms were made in the states after the revolution?

6. Why did Thomas Jefferson and others want to disestablish state churches?

7. What happened to many churches after the revolution?

8. Who was John Carroll, and what is he known for?

9. What convinced Carroll that the American Church needed a bishop?

10. Describe the model of territorial government established by the Northwest Ordinance.

11. How did Shay's Rebellion accelerate the movement to revise the Articles of Confederation

Answers to Sample Quiz I

Students' answers should approximate the following.

1. With the Congress' declaration of independence, existing colonial governments began to function as state governments with little or no change to their constitutions.

2. The Virginia Bill of Rights listed as rights "the enjoyment of life and liberty, with the means of acquiring and possessing property, and pursuing and obtaining happiness and safety."

3. The Articles of Confederation gave the new government power to declare war and make peace, conclude treaties, regulate the coining of money, and decide in disputes between states.

4. According to the Articles of Confederation, to protect the sovereignty of each, every state, whatever its population, received one vote in Congress.

5. Following the Revolution, Virginia abolished primogeniture when an owner died intestate and entailment. Several northern states had movements to abolish slavery.

6. Thomas Jefferson and others wanted to disestablish state churches because they believed that religion is a purely private affair. It has nothing to do with the state, or the state with it.

7. After the Revolution, almost everywhere in the states churches cut off ties with their mother churches in Europe and formed distinctly American groups.

8. John Carroll was a Jesuit who was named prefect apostolic of the Catholic Church in the United States, and later made bishop of the United States.

9. Troubles with trustees who began to see themselves as the final authorities in Church matters, hiring priests and firing them at will if they did not approve of them, convinced Carroll that the American Church needed a bishop.

10. The government of the Northwest Ordinance consisted of a representative assembly, elected by the people of the territory; a governor, appointed by Congress; and a council of five chosen by Congress from names submitted by the territorial assembly.

11. Shays' Rebellion accelerated the movement to revise the Articles of Confederation because it convinced many in America that the current form of the national government was insufficiently powerful to keep the peace.

Sample Quiz II (pages 193-209)

Please answer the following in complete sentences.

1. **What event caused states to call for a revision of the Constitution?**

2. **Explain the Connecticut Compromise.**

3. **What resulted from debates over the new Constitution?**

4. **What are some reasons why the anitfederalists opposed the new Constitution?**

5. **What was the purpose of the *Federalist Papers*?**

6. **What is the Judiciary Act?**

7. **What was the significance of the John Jay Supreme Court?**

8. **What was the Whiskey Rebellion?**

9. **What was the Jay Treaty?**

10. **What did President Washington warn against in his farewell speech?**

Answers to Sample Quiz II

Students' answers should approximate the following.

1. When, in 1785, delegates from Virginia and Maryland met to settle disputes, they realized they could not reach a resolution on these questions without the cooperation of Delaware and Pennsylvania. Since the process of addressing such issues was haphazard and difficult under the Articles of Confederation, states began to call for a revision of the articles.

2. When delegates from Delaware, New Jersey, and Maryland threatened to leave the Constitutional Convention, Roger Sherman offered a compromise plan that he had offered earlier – proportional representation in the lower house, equal representation in the senate. This is called the "Connecticut Compromise."

3. What resulted from all the debates over the new Constitution was a "federal" model of government, that more or less defined the areas where the national and state governments exercised sovereignty.

4. Some antifederalists opposed the new Constituion because they feared a strong centralized government with the power to tax; such a government, they thought, would become the tool of the few for the oppression of the many. Some antifederalists criticized the Constitution for its failure to outlaw slavery and because it did not forbid government offices to non-Christians.

5. The *Federalist Papers'* purpose was to develop the themes of the insufficiency of the Articles of Confederation and the advantages of the Constitution.

6. The Judiciary Act set the number of justices in the Supreme Court at six and established 13 district courts and three circuit courts.

7. The Supreme Court presided over by John Jay, the republic's first chief justice, is significant for establishing precedents for what later became known as "judicial

review" – the court's critique of the legal acts of states and the federal government.

8. The Whiskey Rebellion, an uprising of farmers in western Pennsylvania, was an early challenge to federal power. In 1791, Congress had laid an excise tax on whiskey, which affected the farmers of the Appalachian region, who could only transport their corn by distilling it into spirituous liquors. Farmers in western Pennsylvania refused to pay the tax and rose in revolt.

9. Jay's Treaty was a treaty signed between the United States and Great Britain on November 19, 1794 in which the British agreed to evacuate all their forts on United States territory by 1796 and granted American ships a limited right to trade with the British West Indies.

10. In his farewell speech, Washington warned against factions, against altering the Constitution except by "an explicit and authentic act of the whole people," and against "the spirit of party in general."

Essays

Instructions to be given to the students: Write in complete sentences. Underline your thesis. Give three supports or examples that explain why you think what you do and that support your thesis.

1. Referring to the ideas of the Enlightenment, explore the idea of the disestablishment of Church and state. What does the Catholic Church say about this idea? (See the *Catechism of the Catholic Church*, paragraphs 2244-2246 and 2104-2109.)

2. Do you think the rights listed in the Bill of Rights are true human rights? Why or why not?

3. Compare the government of the United States with previous and more traditional governments. How does the United States' government improve on traditional government? How does it not?

Sample Test

Please answer the following in complete sentences.

I. Short Essay – Answer two of the following:

1. What were the weaknesses of the Articles of Confederation?

2. Explain the basic form of the government established by the Constitution in terms of the president, Congress, and judiciary.

3. Explain what is meant by strict and loose construction of the Constitution.

4. Explain the two political divisions of the early republic: Federalist and Republican.

II. Short Answer:

1. How many state votes were needed before Congress could make a major decision under the Articles of Confederation?

2. What assumption lies behind the conviction that religion has nothing to do with the state?

3. What particularly American problem did John Carroll have to deal with?

4. Identify the following:
   a. Federalist
   b. Antifederalist

5. What was the Bill of Rights meant to do?

Answer Key to the Chapter Test

Students' answers should approximate the following:
I.
1. States had been unwilling to compromise their newly won independence by giving too much power to the national government, and they would not cooperate with it once it was established. Since Congress could not tax but only requisition money from the states, it relied on the willingness of state legislatures to supply needed revenues, but these were often not forthcoming. Attempts to enhance Congress' taxing power through amendments failed because Congress could not garner the consent of all the states. Congress' weaknesses meant it could not fulfill its obligations under the peace bargain with Great Britain, such as protection of loyalists and payment of debts. Congress could do little to settle state conflicts that threatened to tear the fledgling union apart.

2. The draft of the new constitution established a congress with two houses – the lower house, the House of Representatives, would have proportional representation, while the Senate would admit two representatives from each state. The executive, called the president, would be elected indirectly by the people – that is, the people would vote for electors who, in turn, voted for the president. The president would be commander-in-chief of the armed forces and would have veto power over congressional legislation. Only a two-thirds majority in both houses of the legislature could override a president's veto. The Constitution established a supreme court whose members, appointed for life by the president with the consent of the Senate, would serve during good behavior.

3. Jefferson argued for a strict construction of the Constitution. He said that while the Constitution allowed Congress "to make all laws necessary and proper" to carry out the federal government's designated powers, it did not allow Congress to do what is merely convenient. Congress, according to the strict contructionist argument, could only do what the Constitution expressly allowed it to do. Hamilton's theory of constitutional interpretation is called loose construction. He said if some measure had "an obvious relation" to a power given by the Constitution to the federal government, and was not forbidden by any part of the Constitution, then "it may safely be deemed to come within the compass of the national authority."

4. Jefferson's party, called Republican, was strict constructionist in interpreting the Constitution. They claimed to stand for the common man against the wealthy. It included former antifederalists, and looked kindly on the French Revolution. The Federalists, on the other hand, were loose constructionists, wanted to rest the republic on the the foundation of the powerful and wealthy, and looked to Great Britain as an example of government.

II.
1. Under the Articles of Confederation, any important decisions – such as declaring war, making treaties, and borrowing money – had to garner the agreement of nine of the thirteen states.

2. The conviction that religion has nothing to do with the state is rooted in the assumption that religion is not about truth but is merely a private affair.

3. John Carroll had to struggle with a peculiarly American form of Church government – trusteeship.

4.
   a. Federalists were supporters of the new Constitution
   b. Antifederalists opposed the new Constitution

5. The Bill of Rights was meant to serve as a series of checks upon the power of the federal government.

CHAPTER 11: The First Test of the Union

Chapter Overview

- In 1797, the XYZ Affair gave President Adams and the Federalists the impetus to put through their program of national defense.

- The small American fleet began to win battle against the French. But when President Adams found out that the French had no desire for war, he reestablished friendly relations with them.

- In response to fears of foreign infiltration, President Adams and the Federalist Congress passed three acts in 1798: the Naturalization Act, the Alien Act, and the Sedition Act. The Republicans responded with the Kentucky and Virginia Resolves, written respectively by Thomas Jefferson and James Madison.

- Running for the Republicans, Thomas Jefferson won the 1800 election. He saw this election, or "Revolution," as he called it, as marking a fundamental change in American government.

- American society after the revolution was undergoing significant social changes. The traditional social order was disintegrating.

- The Second Great Awakening began in 1799 with a camp meeting in Kentucky. This Second Great Awakening gave Americans the belief that the United States was a Protestant Christian nation. This religious revival affected politics and laws.

- In an attempt to create new communities in the disintegration of traditional bonds, Americans began to start organizations for certain specific purposes; such organizations have become a hallmark of American society. But these organizations did not solve the problems of social distintegration.

- Under President Jefferson, James Madison withheld from William Marbury the commission of his appointment as justice of the peace, and Marbury sued Madison. The Supreme Court declared that the president had no right to withhold a commission, but no body of government could force the president to issue a commission. In this decision, the Supreme Court asserted that it had the constitutional authority to nullify laws passed by Congress and signed by the president.

- In 1803 the Spanish government transferred Louisiana to France, and France in turn sold the territory to the United States.

- In 1804 Lewis and Clark set out on their expedition to explore the lands encompassed by Louisiana. After making their way across the Rocky Mountains to the Oregon Country, the expedition returned in 1806.

- In the election of 1808, Jefferson's hand-picked successor, James Madison, was elected president, keeping the federal government under Republican control.

- The impressment of American sailors by the British, as well as a sea battle between the American ship, the *President*, and the British ship, the *Little Belt*, whipped up a clamor for war in the United States. In June 1812, Congress declared war on Great Britain. The war waged until the signing of a peace treaty at Ghent on December 24, 1814.

What Students Should Know

1. What the XYZ Affair was and its signficance

Federalists and Republicans were divided over their opinion of France and its revolution. The Republicans were pro-French; the Republicans, anti-French. An event in 1797 only served to confirm Federalist opinion of France. The new French government called the Directory had been trying to bribe three American commissioners to Paris – Elbridge Gerry, John Marshall, and Charles Cotesworth Pinckney. In what came to be called the XYZ Affair, three French ministers (hiding their identities under the pseudonyms, X, Y, and Z) told the American ministers that they could not negotiate with the French foreign minister, Talleyrand, until they paid him $250,000 and guaranteed the Directory a loan of $10 million. News of this "XYZ Affair" incensed the American public. The French-friendly Republicans were embarrassed; Adams and his Federalists, bolstered by public opinion, pushed through their program of national defense that was opposed by the Republicans.

2. What the Naturalization, Alien, and Sedition Acts were

Though a little cowed by the XYZ Affair, the Republicans did not let up in their attacks on Adams and the Federalists. Using a network of newspapers, Republicans harshly attacked the president and the Federalist members of Congress. Since many of the editors of these papers were foreign immigrants, the Federalists counterattacked by accusing the Republicans of wanting to give the country over to foreign powers.

The Federalist Congress and President Adams responded to fears of foreign infiltration by passing three acts in 1798. The first, the Naturalization Act, extended from five to 14 years the time a foreigner must reside in the United States before he could

become a citizen. The Alien Act gave the president power for two years to expel any foreigners he wished. The more controversial Sedition Act made it a crime to say or write anything critical of the president or government of the United States "with the intent to defame" or "to bring into contempt or disrepute." The crime was punishable by fine or imprisonment.

President Adams justified the Sedition Act by arguing that when the leaders of government are abused, government itself loses its dignity and force. Twenty-five men were arrested and ten convicted under the act, including several Republican editors.

3. What the Kentucky and Virginia Resolves were and said

The Kentucky and Virginia Resolves were two important critiques of the Alien and Sedition Acts, and the Constitution itself. The first of these, the Kentucky Resolves (adopted by the Republican-dominatd Kentucky legislature on November 16, 1798), was written anonymously by Thomas Jefferson. The states, said the Kentucky Resolves, did not unite "on the principle of unlimited submission" to the federal government; rather, they formed a "compact" by which they "constituted a general government for special purposes" and "delegated to that government certain definite powers, reserving each State to itself, the residuary mass of right to their own self-government." Since the national government, said said the Resolves, was created by a compact among equals – itself and the states – it could not be "the exclusive or final judge of the extent of the powers delegated to itself, since that would have made its discretion, and not the Constitution, the measure of its powers." Since the parties that agreed to the Constitution set up no person or body to stand as a judge between them, "each party," said the Resolves, "has an equal right to judge for itself, as well of infractions as of the mode and measure of redress." Thus, if a state government thought an act of the federal government was unconstitutional, it could refuse to recognize – that is, *nullify* – the act until a convention of states could gather to decide on its constitutionality. The Virginia Resolves, composed by James Madison, was a shorter document that basically followed Jefferson's reasoning.

4. **How John Adams assured a continued Federalist presence in government, though defeated by Jefferson in the election of 1800**

In January 1801, with only two months left in office, President Adams began to appoint Federalists to the federal courts. When Chief Justice Oliver Ellsworth retired from the Supreme Court, Adams nominated John Marshall of Virginia (Thomas Jefferson's cousin) to succeed him. Though even many Federalists opposed Marshall, the Senate confirmed him in late January. By such appointments, Adams assured the continuance of Federalist principles in what would become an increasingly important branch of the federal government: the Supreme Court.

5. **The significance of the election of 1800 according to Jefferson**

Jefferson saw the election of 1800 as marking a fundamental change in American government – he even called it a "revolution." "The Revolution of 1800," he later wrote, "was as real a revolution in the principles of our government as that of 1776 was in its form, not effected by the sword, as that, but by the rational and peaceable instrument of reform, the suffrage of the people."

6. **Why Americans began to turn against the founders' republican thought and the "natural aristocracy"**

The Republican (party) victory in 1800 was merely one aspect of greater changes in American society that had begun shortly after the surrender at Yorktown. In the name of the equality of all men, the Founding Fathers had rebelled against a traditional, hereditary aristocracy in favor of a "natural aristocracy" of talent and achievement (which included themselves). Birth, they insisted in good republican fashion, should not confer any privilege; a man should rise in society only if he prove himself worthy of honor and trust. By insisting that all men are created equal, the founders did not mean to imply that men were to remain equal. American colonial society had never been as traditional or as hierarchical as European society. Colonial society had always been somewhat tumultuous. Common, uneducated, and "unenlightened" men, however, began to ask why the "natural aristocracy" should have all the privileges – after all, they asked, were not all men created equal? Were not all men supposed to pursue happiness? Throughout the northern states in the 1790s, mechanics, tradesmen, and working men organized Republican societies, which took up the cry against educated men – the natural aristocracy of the founding fathers. Not only learning but the life of leisure was condemned. Leisure became equated with idleness. Rather than leisure, a life of labor became the ideal, at least in the North. To hold his head up in society, one needed to say that he worked for a living.

7. **The role of the love of commerce in post-revolutionary America**

In the American attack on aristocracy, there was no attack on wealth as such – even though the period following the revolution witnessed greater inequality of wealth than had prevailed before the revolution. Especially in the northern states, common people had become engrossed in the pursuit of wealth and hoped that they, too, might become rich. The race to obtain the wealth that purchased luxuries accelerated in the 1780s. After the war it became increasingly evident that internal trade – trade within and between states – could be very profitable. Farming families began to engage in home-based industries along with agriculture to take advantage of this trade.

8. The effect of the love of commerce in post-revolutionary America

Since commercial activity required an ability to read and cipher, the passion to engage in commerce led to higher literacy rates. It also led to "internal improvements," such as new roads and canals for internal transportation. The desire to engage in adventurous, entrepreneurial business enterprises necessitated a ready access to money. To ease transactions, states began issuing paper notes, which could be redeemed by national gold and silver currency. Banking grew at a phenomenal rate as men demanded more credit. While banking gave people a sense of independence (since they owed no personal gratitude to a bank), it involved them in an impersonal system that did not treat them as neighbors or dependents but as mere agents in a business transaction. Banks were harder and more unrelenting on borrowers than gentleman lenders had been. The desire for prosperity fueled emigration.

9. The effects of increased emigration on American society

With the opening of the western lands after the revolution, settlers, lured by the hope of richer soil, began pouring across the Appalachians into Ohio, Kentucky, Tennessee, and lands further west. Population growth in the West was swift. Such emigration meant that people were frequently moving. Established settlements in the East saw their old families pack up and leave. Houses and lands ceased to be homes and became merely commodities to buy and sell. It was not unusual for a family to move at least three or four times, each time selling the farm for a profit. Such movement promoted a greater sense of equality among people while it broke apart the social bonds that held them together. Just as the mobility of American society broke the predominance of the old aristocracy, it dispersed families, undermining the extended family and kinship relationships characteristic of traditional society. With the breaking apart of the traditional societies of the village and the family, society lost the glue that held people together. The lack of social cohesion began to show itself in the rising number of murders, suicides, thefts, and mobbings in the cities. Street riots increased as did tavern rowdiness, labor strikes, and racial conflicts. The poor grew resentful of the upper classes and were stung to anger at times by political propaganda. A spirit of competition began to dominate social life. Self-interest seemed to dominate the American spirit. The value of self-interest was loudly proclaimed; it was seen as the great equalizer, since everyone was motivated by it; and to receive a favor from someone motivated by self-interest did not carry with it the responsibility of gratitude or deference. Self-interest, or improving one's own lot, would remain an important component of the American ideal of rugged individualism.

10. **What the Second Great Awakening was, and its effects**

The Second Great Awakening was a religious revival that began in Logan County, Kentucky at the "Red River Revival," in the Summer of 1799. The revival was a preaching marathon meeting that resulted in displays of religious enthusiasm. Other such "camp meetings" occurred, both in the West and the East the most famous being the Cane Ridge Revival in Kentucky. The revivals represented an attempt by ordinary folk to deal with the revolutionary changes in their society. Those affected rejected the deistic, rationalistic philosophies of the Enlightenment and the "orthodox," overly intellectual Protestantism of the Anglicans or the New England Calvinists. Common Americans wanted a direct experience of God, an experience that made a rough life comprehensible. The religion of the camp meetings rejected the old Calvinist predestination and emphasized man's free will. The Second Great Awakening had its moral aspects, as well. Converts were to live upright lives, to reject selfishness and practice disinterested benevolence. Some preachers began to emphasize social justice themes, which led some to found antislavery, temperance, and Bible societies. And as women were often the controlling forces in these societies, their status and importance in society grew. The Second Great Awakening gave Americans the belief that the United States was a (Protestant) Christian nation; thus politics were not left untouched by revival. The more deistic, rationalistic leaders began to give way to leaders who gave at least lip-service to more traditional Protestant Christianity.

The Great Awakening, however, ultimately succumbed to rugged American individualism. The camp meetings ended in creating a large number of new sects, further shattering Protestant Christianity. The revival was also profoundly individualistic. Finally, preachers began appealing to people's self-interest. Thus was born among Americans the idea of "enlightened self-interest," that one should do good because it improves one's prospects in this world, as well as the next. It was not long before the idea of virtue for many degenerated into a useful policy one needs to follow to attain worldly advantage.

11. **How and why voluntary societies developed in the United States**

As the traditional bonds of their society disintegrated, Americans began to create new communities by joining together in organizations founded for certain specific purposes. So numerous were these organizations that they became a hallmark of American society. No other country in the world could boast so many volunteer benevolent organizations as the United States. Churches and other religious groups began to form societies for various charitable purposes. Though at first wealthy "aristocrats" headed up these societies, in time Americans of more moderate means came to direct them. The purpose of these societies was to serve as watchdogs of virtue. Though often their immediate purpose was to supply for the material wants of men, their goal was ultimately moral – to improve the character of the unfortunate. As time went on, the moral aspect gained even more importance.

Voluntary societies ultimately failed to replace the traditional ligaments of society. After a time, membership in them did not involve attending meetings or joining others in common action. Instead, members participated merely by lending monetary support.

12. The commercial society and it effects on American society

Commerce in American society unified the disparate regions of the federal union, but the new commercial society was severing the bond between past and present – the bond of tradition. Men were looking less and less to the past for orientation but always to what they thought would be a more hopeful and better future. The notion of what constituted an education changed under democratic influences. Unlike their European ancestors, Americans did not think that the point of education is to lead men to the knowledge of the truth and the enjoyment of beauty; rather, a good middle class education in America emphasized what is useful.

13. How a secular version of Winthrop's "City on a Hill" developed during this period

For many, the wonder of America lay in the fact that this vast mass of people, composed of individuals pursuing only their private interests, could come together with a common will. Many ascribed this to Providence – that God had a peculiar interest in the progress of the United States. The idea behind Winthrop's old "city on the hill" metaphor, now secularized, was applied to the young republic. It became almost a religious belief that America had a special destiny among the nations of the world.

14. Reactions of the founders to societal change

Though Charles Carroll of Carollton was optimistic about the United States, amidst these societal changes, not all the founders share his optimism. Benjamin Rush grieved that the revolution had changed "the principles and morals" of Americans and had brought government under the control "of the young and ignorant and needy part of the community." In 1812 he bemoaned that America was "a bebanked, a bewhiskered, and a bedollared nation." Nearly every revolutionary leader ended his life in disappointment. Even Alexander Hamilton and Thomas Jefferson came to despair of the future of the country they had helped form. Both felt like strangers in the new order. Jefferson's hopes in the common man were disappointed – the common man was more self-seeking, more superstitious (that is, religious) than ever, said Jefferson. Instead of progressing toward greater enlightenment, people seemed to be growing more barbaric, Jefferson thought. John Adams thought the prosperity of the states was corrupting the people with an inordinate desire for gain.

15. *Marbury v. Madison*, its importance and effects

Jefferson entered office hoping to reconcile Republicans and Federalists. He did not want to remove Federalists from the government offices; but because his party supporters clamored for rewards, Jefferson replaced some Federalists officeholders with Republicans. He called Adams' last minute appointments of Federalist justices an "outrage to decency" because he thought they violated the will of the people, who he said clearly had voted for Republican, not Federalist, ideas to prevail in the government. Jefferson thus instructed his secretary of state, James Madison, to withhold several commissions to Adams' appointees, including one William Marbury, whom Adams in the last days of his presidential term had appointed a justice of the peace.

Marbury, however, refused to back down to Jefferson. He sued James Madison, requesting the Supreme Court to command the secretary of state to issue the commission. Marbury appealed to the Congress's 1789 Judiciary Act that authorized the Supreme Court to issue a "writ of mandamus."

Though it seemed a simple matter, much was at stake in this case, *Marbury v. Madison*. Jefferson and the Republicans objected to any assertion of the the Supreme Court's power over the elected branches of government; rather, they thought the court should submit to the will of the people, expressed through their elected representatives. *Marbury v. Madison* thus seemed to offer the Republicans a golden opportunity to knock the court down to size. It seemed as if, whatever the result, they could not lose. If the Supreme Court issued a writ of mandamus in the case and the president defied it, the court could lose prestige. If the court refused to issue the writ, it would look like it was backing down to the president, and so lose prestige. Whatever happened, it seemed Jefferson would be able to strike a blow against the power of the Supreme Court.

But then, in 1803, Chief Justice Marshall laid down his decision in *Marbury v. Madison*. First, Marshal declared that the president had no right to withhold Marbury's commission; nevertheless, the chief justice conceded that no body of government could force the president to issue the commission, for the Judiciary Act of 1789, in authorizing the court to issue writs of mandamus, was unconstitutional and, therefore, void. By declaring a portion of the Judiciary Act unconstitutional, the Marshal court had implicitly asserted that it had the constitutional authority to nullify laws passed by Congress and signed by the president. In other words, in *Marbury*, Marshall asserted the principle established by Chief Justice John Jay – that the Supreme Court has the authority under the Constitution to review laws passed by Congress and declare on their constitutionality. In this way, the Supreme Court became the supreme interpreter of the Constitution.

16. How the Louisiana Territory became part of the United States

In return for some European territories, Spain secretly ceded Louisiana back to France, under the government of First Consul Napoleon Bonaparte in 1800. This secret cession became public in 1802 and worried Jefferson and other Americans – Republicans and Federalists alike – for they feared French control of Lousiana would hinder American expansion westward as well as American commerce on the Mississippi. When in 1803 the Spanish governor of Louisiana forbade Americans in the West the right to ship their goods through the port of New Orleans, Jefferson sent James Monroe to France as envoy extraordinary to help the American consul Robert Livingston negotiate an understanding with France. Napoleon, who was mobilizing for war with Britain, directed Talleyrand to approach Livingston and Monroe on April 11, 1803 with an offer to sell the whole of Louisiana to the United States. Nineteen days later Livingston and Talleyrand signed an agreement in which France agreed to sell Louisiana to the United States for the bargain price of $15 million. On November 30, 1803, the Spanish government formally transferred Louisiana to France. Three weeks later, France transferred the territory to the United States. By the stroke of a pen, Jefferson had doubled the size of the country.

17. The purpose of the Lewis and Clark expedition. When it set out and when it returned.

President Thomas Jefferson commissioned his friend, Meriwether Lewis, with William Clark, to lead an expedition into the newly purchased Louisiana territory, following the Missouri River and crossing the continent all the way to the Pacific Ocean. These two adventurers gathered a company of over 40 men, the "Corps of Discovery," including soldiers, two French hunters and interpreters, experienced river men, and Clark's black slave, York. Jefferson spoke of commerce in his instructions to Lewis and Clark; but more important to the president was scientific knowledge. The Corps of Discovery was to gather information on the animals and plants, the minerals and soil, of the lands through which they passed. The corps was also to describe the culture, religion, mores, traditions, and languages of the Indian tribes it encountered. Though always hungry for knowledge, Jefferson had a practical motive for such research: the president thought the Indians were capable of "progress"; but any attempts at civilizing them must take into account their character and ways. Lewis and Clark began their voyage up the Missouri from St. Louis on May 14, 1804. After the reached the Pacific Ocean, and wintered in Oregon, they set out again toward home, arriving back in St. Louis on September 23, 1806.

18. The character of the Indian nations Lewis and Clark encountered on the Missouri

The Indians Lewis and Clark would encounter along the Missouri River belonged to two families of tribes, each family having similar languages and customs. One, the Algonquin family, had originally inhabited the eastern seaboard but had been pushed west by the Iroquois. The other, the Siouan, comprised a number of tribes that also had been pushed west by the Iroquois. The Algonquian and Siouan tribes were almost always at war with each other and among themselves. After the expedition passed the mouth of the Osage River, it came across a settlement of the Siouan Osage, a tribe that originally inhabited the region of North Carolina and Virginia. The Osage were both hunters and farmers, cultivating pumpkins, corn, and beans. They lived in semi permanent villages, in dome-shaped houses made of saplings and mud. Their warriors, which numbered about 1,500, were tall, handsome men, said Clark, with "fine military capacities." After passing the muddy Platte River, the expedition crossed into Pawnee territory. The Pawnee were star-watchers who worshiped the morning and evening stars; and though they believed in many lesser gods, they worshiped a single, omnipotent god, and Mother Earth. The Pawnee lived by both agriculture and hunting buffalo. They had been pushed across the Mississippi by the Iroquois and forced further west by the Osage.

The expedition was now passing over the Great Plains, where ran multitudinous herds of buffalo, the prey of the Plains Indians, who hunted them by stampeding the herds over the edges of cliffs overlooking the Missouri. From the carcasses, the Indians would cull what they needed of hides and meat. The first of the Dakota or Sious people the explorers wet were the Yankton Sioux. Clark described the Yankton Sioux as having "a certain air of dignity and boldness." Fond of decoration, they wore "paint and porcupine quills and feathers ... with necklaces of white bear claws three inches long." According to Clark, the Sioux "camps are handsome of a Conic form Covered with Buffalo Robes painted different colors and all compact & handsomely arranged." He was describing, of course, the tipi, a kind of housing used only by the Plains Indians. The Sioux lived by hunting buffalo and were excellent horsemen. They frequently raided other tribes to steal their horses. The next of the Sioux nation the exploration met were the Teton Sioux, who lived by hunting buffalo and raiding their enemies, the Mandans, for horses. The Teton had once manufactured pottery but had given it up for the horse-trade. They maintaned friendly relations with their neighbors, the Arikaras, who were farming folk and supplied the Teton with corn. The farmers among the Arikara were the women, who cultivated the soil with digging sticks made from the shoulder blades of antelope and buffalo and rakes made from reeds fastened to a long handle. The Tetons' enemies, the Mandan, lived in villages were made up of permanent "lodges" centered around a sacred cedar post that represented a village hero. Like other tribes, the Mandan believed in "medicine" – a personal spirit or intercessor before the Great Spirit. There was "good medicine" (beneficial spirits) and "bad medicine" (maleficent spirits).

In the Rocky Mountains, Lewis and Clark met the Shoshone people. A Plains tribe that the Sioux had pushed into the mountains, the Sioux were short in stature and wore a costume of animal skins; tufts of their defeated enemies' hair fringed their boots. Though Shoshone held absolute sway over their wives and daughters, their government, wrote the explorers, was "perfectly free from restraint. Each individual is his own master, and the only control to which his conduct is subjected, is the advice of a chief supported by his influence over the opinions of the rest of the tribe."

The Indians of the Pacific were different from those of the Plains. They were, according to Clark, short and bowlegged. They lived in long, wooden plank lodges — sometimes over 200 feet long – that housed sometimes several families. They plied the rivers in long canoes, expertly made from redwood, hunting salmon. Lewis and Clark discovered that women had a higher station among these tribes than among those east of the Rockies – "they were permitted to speak freely before the men, to whom indeed they sometimes address themselves in a tone of authority." Chinook, Tillamook, Kalamath, and Clatsop were the names of some of these Pacific coast nations.

19. **The role of the federal government before 1812**

The federal government of the early 19th century was not powerful nor did it always evoke loyalty – especially in those who thought their interests were threatened by it. In those days it would have been relatively easy for a state or a group of states to separate from the union, for the federal government took care of only a certain limited number of concerns; the rest fell to the states. Moreover, the patriotism of most Americans still centered on their local region or states. They had not yet developed an American consciousness. So it was that in 1804 certain New England Federalists, fearing the policies of Jefferson and his Republicans, contemplated separating from the Union and forming a "Northern Confederacy of New England and New York."

20. What tensions existed between the United States and European powers during Jefferson's administration

The struggle between Great Britain and France's Napoleon Bonaparte affected neutral countries like the United States. Because of various maritime acts passed by Britain and France, American ships found themselves barred from most foreign ports. Tensions increased between Great Britain and the United States when, on June 22, 1807, the British warship, the *H.M.S. Leopard*, fired on the *U.S.S. Chesapeake* ten miles off the coast of Virginia. Americans were outraged; the Federalists clamored for war. Then France began seizing neutral ships – including American vessels. Unwilling to go to war with both Britain and France (or with either of them alone), Jefferson chose instead the more peaceful expedient of an embargo. On December 22, 1807, Congress passed the Embargo Act, which forced all American ships in port to remain in port, lest they be taken by British and French ships. The act struck the port cities of New England and New York hard. Ships sat idle in the shipyards; small ship owners were ruined.

21. Who Tecumseh was and how he tried to stem the advance of the Americans into Indian lands

The Shawnee chief, Tecumseh, was among the defeated at Fallen Timbers in 1794; but unlike his fellow chiefs, he had refused to sign the Treaty of Greenville, which handed millions of acres of land over to the United States government for a mere $10,000. Hoping to stop the advance of the whites, Tecumseh worked to join his people in an alliance of the northern tribes with the southern tribes. By 1808 he had formed an alliance with tribes of the western Ohio River Valley. He established the capital for this alliance at Tippecanoe, a settlement on the Wabash River in the Indiana Territory. At Tippecanoe, warriors gathered and trained for war. In 1809, Tecumseh met with the William Henry Harrison to convince him to void a treaty the U.S. government had signed with several tribes, a cession of three million acres in southern Indiana and Illinois, but Harrison rebuffed him. In 1811 Tecumseh went south to draw the Chickasaw, Choctaw, Creek, and Cherokee peoples into his alliance. To overawe the Indians or beat them into submission before Tecumseh's return, Harrison gathered 1,000 volunteers and regulars and stealthily moved against the Indian encampment at Tippecanoe. On November 7, 1811, Tenskwatawa, Tecumseh's brother, led an attack on Harrison's camp just before dawn. Though surprised by the onslaught, Harrison was able force the Indians back and the battle ended in a draw, with Tenskwatawa withdrawing by night. This Battle of Tippecanoe ended Tecumseh's hopes for an alliance of Indian nations. Instead, he turned to an alliance with the British in Canada.

22. What events led up to the War of 1812

Relations between the United States and France and Great Britain had been deteriorating. Great Britain refused to repeal the Orders in Council and continued to board American ships and impress American seamen. Under assurances from Napoleon that French ships would cease seizing American merchantmen, Madison moved Congress to renew the nonintercourse bill (which had lapsed the previous year) against Great Britain but to maintain trade with France. In response to the renewal of nonintercourse, the British navy began blockading the American coast. Madison ordered John Rodgers, commander of the

U.S.S. President, to protect American shipping. One evening, Rodgers, sailing the 44-gun *President* out of Chesapeake Bay, sighted in the growing darkness what he thought was a British warship. The a British warship, the *H.M.S. Little Belt*, attacked the *U.S.S. President, and in* a 15-minute battle, the *President* crippled the *Little Belt* and left 32 British dead or wounded. This battle whipped up a feverish clamor for war throughout the United States. Members of Congress, called "War Hawks" called for a declaration of war to show what free men could do against tyrants – and, as a side benefit, to add British-held Canada to the United States. In April 1812, Congress passed a bill establishing a 60-day embargo against Great Britain. If at the end of that period the British did not remove the Orders in Council and cease the impressment of American sailors, Congress would declare war.

On June 1, 1812, President Madison asked Congress for a declaration of war. On June 4, the House of Representatives voted 79 to 49 to declare war on Great Britain, and on June 19 the Senate voted to support the declaration.

23. Events of the War of 1812

Though the United States was not prepared for war, its navy scored some victories early in the war. The land war was not so successful; when U.S. troops attempted an invasion of Canada, it was driven back, and British forces captured Detroit in July 1812. Other attempts to invade Canada, from Buffalo, New York, also failed. With Detroit in British hands, the frontier from Ohio to George lay open to attacks from Tecumseh's warriors. But Oliver Hazard Perry's naval victories on Lake Erie forced the British to abort an invasion of Ohio and to abandon Detroit and Fort Malden in the spring of

1813. In Ontario, in October, the Americans won a victory in which Tecumseh was killed and American navy sacked Toronto (then York), and an American force captured Fort Niagara. But the Americans did not follow up these victories with an invasion of Canada, and the British tightened their blockade of American ports, bottling up even the U.S. navy. American privateers, instead, waged the war at sea.

In the South, the War of 1812 was not a struggle against the British but a war waged against the Creek nation. Following a massacre by a band of Creeks, called the Red Sticks, of white settlers at Fort Mims on the Alabama River, Andrew Jackson of Tennessee led an enlistment of men against the Red Sticks in their fortress on the Coosa River in Alabama and decisively defeated them.

Following the defeat of Napoleon at Waterloo, the British could dedicate more of their forces to the war in America. The British navy attacked American coastal towns. British forces invaded New York, though the Americans were able to maintain control of Lake Erie. In August 1814, British forces marched into Washington and set fire to the capitol, the White House, the navy yard, and the treasury building. They then attacked For McHenry in Baltimore, but were unable to reduce the fortress. Instead the British army and fleet set sail to the West Indies to prepare a powerful land and naval force to assault New Orleans. In January 1815, a large British force attacked New Orleans, but Andrew Jackson forced it to withdraw.

24. What the Hartford Convention was

The War of 1812 was highly unpopular in New England – so much so that New England governors refused to raise troops for service in the U.S. army. Many had opposed the policies of both Presidents Jefferson and Madison, and even hoped that Louisiana would go to Britain so the West would be forced to separate itself from the union, leaving the thirteen original states to operate according to the rules and character of their original constitutional compact.

Some New Englanders went further; they wanted their own states to secede from the union. Caleb Strong, Federalist governor of Massachusetts, sent an emissary to the British to discuss a separate peace between the Bay State and the mother country. In the fall of 1814, the Massachusetts legislature called on the other New England states to send delegates to a convention that would discuss their position in relation to the union. The hope was that, in time, a convention of all the states could be called to revise the Constitution. Though many feared the Hartford Convention (so named because it

was held in Hartford, Connecticut) would call for the secession of New England states from the union, it turned out to be a mild affair. Far from calling for secession, the convention only reiterated the grievances of the New England states. When the convention adjourned, New England was no closer to secession than she was before.

25. Peace between the U.S. and Great Britain and what it entailed

On Christmas Eve, December 24, 1814, two weeks *before* the Battle of New Orleans, the U.S. and Great Britain signed a peace treaty at Ghent, in Belgium. The Treaty of Ghent, however, accomplished nothing else but peace. Britain did not repudiate the impressment of sailors on American ships, and neither side gained any new territory. Things were just as they were when the war began. Yet, though the war achieved none of

Key Terms at a Glance

Naturalization Act: the act that extended the time a foreigner must reside in the United States before becoming a citizen

Alien Act: the act giving the president power for two years to expel any foreigners he wished

Sedition Act: the act that made it a crime to say or write anything critical of the president or government of the Unites States

Kentucky Resolves: an act, authored by Thomas Jefferson, of the Kentucky legislature that said the federal government is not the final judge of the extent of its own powers under the Constitution and asserted a state's right to nullify a federal law it deems unconstitutional

Second Great Awakening: a religious revival that swept the United States in the early 19th century and affected American society and government

embargo: a legal prohibition by a government restricting the departure of ships from some location to another location or country

commerce: a branch of production which deals with the exchange of goods and services from a producer to a consumer

the War Hawks' goals, it did have some beneficial effects. It led to better relations between the United States and Great Britain. Britain had learned to respect American soldiers and sailors, and both countries realized how much each relied on the other for trade. In the United States, the war created a new spirit of national unity. All sections had helped in the war effort; even New England had contributed her privateers. Though sectional problems would remain and become more intense as the years passed, the war had given Americans a common focus and a mutual endeavor, for the results of which (whatever those were) they were all responsible.

Questions for Review

1. **What was the "Revolution of 1800," and what were its effects?**

The Revolution of 1800 was when the Republicans won control of both the House of Representatives and the Senate and Thomas Jefferson was electedpresident. Thomas Jefferson called it a revolution because it was "a real revolution in the principles of our government." This "revolution" brought Republican policies to the fore and established a "dynasty" of Virginian presidents, beginning with Thomas Jefferson and continuing with James Madison.

2. **What is the significance of the XYZ Affair?**

News of the "XYZ Affair" incensed the American public. The French-friendly Republicans were embarrassed; Adams and his Federalists, bolstered by public opinion, pushed through their program of national defense that was opposed by the Republicans.

3. **What situation prompted John Adams and Congress to pass the Naturalization, Alien, and Sedition Acts?**

After the XYZ affair, using a network of newspapers, Republicans harshly attacked the president and the Federalist members of Congress. Since many of the editors of these papers were foreign immigrants, the Federalists counterattacked by accusing the Republicans of wanting to give the country over to foreign powers. The Federalist Congress and President Adams responded to fears of foreign infiltration by passing the three acts.

4. **Describe the differences between the Republicans and the Federalists.**

The Republicans strict constructionist in interpreting the Constitution. They claimed to stand for the common man against the wealthy. The Federalists, on the other hand, were loose constructionists and wanted to rest the republic on the the foundation of the powerful and wealthy, and looked to Great Britain as an example of government.

5. **What was President Jefferson trying to express in his inaugural address when he said, "We are all Republicans – we are all Federalists"?**

Jefferson was saying that, despite their political differences all citizens were united by being Americans and were deeply united in that they held essentially the same political and social ideals.

6. **How did commerce in America bring about the disintegration of traditional society?**

Love of commerce brought about the disintegration of traditional society because people felt more independent, and began to move about more. Men began looking less to the past for orientation and more to the future, which, they thought, held more hope and opportunity.

7. **Why did emigration and the mobility of American society contribute to the disintegration of traditional society?**

Commerce dispersed families, undermining the extended family and kinship relationships characteristic of traditional society.

8. **What was the social and political significance of the Second Great Awakening?**

The Second Great Awakening gave Americans the sense that the United States was a Protestant Christian nation – and this influenced politicians, who felt compelled to adopt traditional Protestant ways of speaking and acting and leave Enlightenment agnosticism behind. Since it was profoundly individualistic, the Second Great Awakening brought about the idea of "enlightened self-interest," that one should do good because it improves one's prospects in this world, as well as the next.

9. **What did Comte de Tracy mean by calling America "the hope and example of the world?" What did he mean when he said that "commerce and society are one and the same thing"?**

Comte de Tracy called America "the hope and example of the world" because the United States had given free reign to commerce. By saying that "commerce and society are one and the same thing" he meant that since in America the bulk of all trade was between states and regions, commerce was one way to keep the union together. Moreover, he held that, in general, it is commerce that unites peoples and nations.

10. **Explain *Marbury v. Madison* and its significance.**

Jefferson instructed his secretary of state, James Madison, to withhold several commissions to Adams' appointees, including one William Marbury, whom Adams in the last days of his presidential term had appointed a justice of the peace. Marbury, however, refused to back down to Jefferson. He sued James Madison, requesting the Supreme Court to command the secretary of state to issue the commission. The Supreme Court refused, saying doing so would exceed its authority. The court, moreover, orvverturned the Congress' Judiciary Act of 1789. *Marbury v. Madison* is important because Chief Justice Marshall asserted the principle established by Chief Justice John Jay – that the Supreme Court has the authority under the Constitution to review laws passed by Congress and declare on their constitutionality. The Supreme Court, thus, is the supreme interpreter of the Constitution.

11. **What did Jefferson hope to accomplish by sending Lewis and Clark on an expedition through the new uncharted American territory?**

The Corps of Discovery was to gather scientific information about the lands they passed through and the peoples they found in those lands. Jefferson also had a practical motive for such research: the president thought the Indians were capable of "progress"; but any attempts at civilizing them must take into account their character and ways.

12. **How was the War of 1812 begun? What events led up to the declaration of war?**

Relations between the United States and France and Great Britain had been deteriorating. Great Britain refused to repeal the Orders in Council and continued to board American ships and impress American seamen. Under assurances from Napoleon that French ships would cease seizing American merchantmen, Madison moved Congress to renew the nonintercourse bill (which had lapsed the previous year) against Great Britain but to maintain trade with France. In response to the renewal of nonintercourse, the British navy began blockading the American coast. Then the *H.M.S. Little Belt* attacked the *U.S.S. President*, whipping up public anger in the U.S. atainst Great Britain. In April 1812, Congress passed a bill establishing a 60-day embargo against Great Britain. If at the end of that period the British did not remove the Orders in Council and cease the impressment of American sailors, Congress would declare war.

13. **What did the War of 1812 accomplish?**

The War of 812 led to better relations between the United States and Great Britain. Britain had learned to respect American soldiers and sailors, and both countries realized how much each relied on the other for trade. In the United States, the war created a new spirit of national unity.

Ideas in Action

1. Read portions or all of the *Journals* written by Meriwether Lewis and William Clark. While reading the text, map out the path of their expedition.

2. Read Thomas Jefferson's Kentucky Resolves (available on the Internet). Do the ideas expressed in the document make sense given the nature of U.S. government.

3. Read all four verses of Francis Scott Key's "The Star Spangled Banner." What did Key want to express about America in the poem?

Sample Quiz I (pages 213-227)

Please answer the following in complete sentences.

1. **What was the XYZ affair?**

2. **How did the Federalist Congress and President Adams respond to fears of foreign infiltration?**

3. **What were the Kentucky and Virginia Resolves?**

4. **What was the significance of the election of 1800 according to Jefferson?**

5. **What were the societal effects in America of the questioning of the concept of a natural aristocracy in the early 19th century?**

6. **What are some of the effects of love of commerce?**

7. **What was the social effect of increased emigration in the United States in the early 19th century?**

8. **Why did voluntary societies develop in the United States?**

9. **How did the American founders react to societal change?**

10. **What was the result of *Marbury v Madison*?**

Answers to Sample Quiz I

Students' answers should approximate the following.

1. In what came to be called the XYZ Affair, three French ministers (hiding their identities under the pseudonyms, X, Y, and Z) told the American ministers that they could not negotiate with the French foreign minister, Talleyrand, until they paid him $25,000 and guaranteed the French government a loan of $10 million.

2. The Federalist Congress and President Adams responded to fears of foreign infiltration by passing three acts in 1798: the Naturalization Act, the Alien Act, and the Sedition Act.

3. The Kentucky and Virginia Resolves were two important critiques of the Alien and Sedition Acts, and the Constitution itself. They contended that states were equal authorities with the federal government in interpreting the Constitution.

4. Jefferson saw the election of 1800 as marking a fundamental change in American government – he even called it a "revolution."

5. When people questioned natural aristocracy, not only learning but the life of leisure was condemned. Leisure became equated with idleness. Rather than leisure, a life of labor became the ideal, at least in the North. To hold his head up in society, one needed to say that he worked for a living.

6. Some of the effects of love of commerce were: higher literacy rates, internal improvements (new roads and canals), the issuance of state paper notes that could be redeemed by national gold and silver currency. Commerce tended to unite the disparate parts of the union, but to separate Americans from a reverence for the past.

7. Increased emigration promoted a greater sense of equality among people while it broke apart the social bonds that held them together. Just as the mobility of American society broke the predominance of the old aristocracy, it dispersed families, undermining the extended family and kinship relationships characteristic of traditional society.

8. As the traditional bonds of their society disintegrated, Americans began to create new communities by joining together in organizations founded for certain specific purposes.

9. Not all founders were optimistic about the changes. Many came to despair of the future of the country they had helped form and ended their lives in disappointment. Jefferson thought that instead of progressing toward greater enlightenment, people seemed to be growing more barbaric. John Adams thought the prosperity of the states was corrupting the people with an inordinate desire for gain.

10. In *Marbury v Madison,* Chief Justice Marshall tacitly asserted the principle that the Supreme Court has the authority under the Constitution to review laws passed by Congress and declare on their constitutionality.

Sample Quiz II (pages 228-249)

Please answer the following in complete sentences.

1. Who were Meriwether Lewis and William Clark?

2. What were Jefferson's reasons for the Lewis and Clark expedition?

3. Why did New England Federalists contemplate separating from the Union?

4. How did the struggle between Great Britain and France's Napoleon Bonaparte affect neutral countries like the United States?

5. Why did Congress pass the Embargo Act?

6. Who was Tecumseh, and what did he accomplish?

7. What were the conditions of the 60-day embargo against Great Britain?

8. How did the New England states react to the War of 1812?

9. What beneficial effects did the war have on Britain and America?

Answers to Sample Quiz II

Students' answers should approximate the following.

1. Meriwether Lewis and William Clark were adventurers who President Jefferson commissioned to lead an expedition into the newly purchased Louisiana territory.

2. Jefferson hoped to garner scientific knowledge about the people and places of the West, but he also had a practical motive for the expedition: he thought the Indians were capable of "progress"; but any attempts at civilizing them must take into account their character and ways.

3. New England Federalists contemplated separating from the Union because they feared the policies of Jefferson and the Republicans.

4. Because of the struggle between Great Britain and France's Napoleon Boneparte, American ships found themselves barred from most foreign ports.

5. Congress passed the Embargo Act because Jefferson was unwilling to go to war with both Britain and France over their violations of the rights of American ships at sea, and chose the more peaceful route of an embargo.

6. Tecumseh was a Shawnee chief who, hoping to stop the advance of the whites, worked to join his people in an alliance of the northern tribes with the southern tribes.

7. If at the end of the embargo the British did not remove the Orders in Council and cease the impressments of American sailors, Congress would declare war.

8. The War of 1812 was highly unpopular in New England. New England governors refused to raise troops for service in the U.S. army. Many had opposed the policies of both Presidents Jefferson and Madison, and even hoped that Louisiana would go to Britain so the West would be forced to separate itself from the union, leaving the thirteen original states to operate according to the rules and character of their original constitutional compact. Some New Englanders wanted their own states to secede from the union.

9. The war led to better relations between the United States and Great Britain. It also gave Americans a common focus and a mutual endeavor that encouraged a sense of greater unity.

Essays

Instructions to be given to the students: Write in complete sentences. Underline your thesis. Give three supports or examples that explain why you think what you do and that support your thesis.

1. Write a paper on the effects of increased commerce on society. Use examples from the chapter and from your own experience.

2. Do you think it is a good thing for society to be mobile – for people and families to move frequently to new homes and regions? Use specific examples from the chapter or your own experience to show why or why not.

Sample Test

Please answer the following in complete sentences.

I. Short Essay – Answer two of the following:

1. Explain the three acts Congress passed in 1798 in response to the XYZ Affair.

2. Explain the concept of natural aristocracy.

3. What did the Kentucky and Virginia Resolves say?

4. What events led up to the War of 1812?

II. Short Answer:

1. What did the XYZ affair allow Adams and his Federalists to do?

2. What was the purpose of the voluntary societies?

3. What did the new commercial society sever?

4. Which of the following were *not* tribes that Lewis and Clark encountered?
   a. Algonquin
   b. Pawnee
   c. Otomí
   d. Shoshone
   e. Sioux

5. How did the War of 1812 differ in southern America from what it was in the North?

6. What did the Treat of Ghent accomplish?

Answer Key to the Chapter Test

Students' answers should approximate the following:

I.

1. Naturalization Act extended from five to 14 years the time a foreigner must reside in the United States before he could become a citizen. The Alien Act gave the president power for two years to expel any foreigners he wished. The more controversial Sedition Act made it a crime to say or write anything critical of the president or government of the United States "with the intent to defame" or "to bring into contempt or disrepute." The crime was punishable by fine or imprisonment.

2. In the name of the equality of all men, the Founding Fathers had rebelled against a traditional, hereditary aristocracy in favor of a "natural aristocracy" of talent and achievement (which included themselves). According to a concept of "natural aristocracy," birth should not confer any privilege; a man should rise in society only if he prove himself worthy of honor and trust. By insisting that all men are created equal, the founders did not mean to imply that men were to remain equal. American colonial society had never been as traditional or as hierarchical as European society. But there was to be a hierarchy of talent and intelligence at the top – the "natural aristocracy."

3. The Kentucky Resolves said states did not unite "on the principle of unlimited submission" to the federal government; rather, they formed a "compact" by which they "constituted a general government for special purposes" and "delegated to that government certain definite powers, reserving each State to itself, the residuary mass of right to their own self-government." If a state government thought an act of the federal government was unconstitutional it could refuse to recognize – that is, *nullify* – the act – until a convention of states could gather to decide on its constitutionality. The Virginia Resolves was a shorter document that basically followed the same reasoning.

4. Great Britain refused to repeal the Orders in Council and continued to board American

ships and impress American seamen. Under assurances from Napoleon that French ships would cease seizing American merchantmen, Madison moved Congress to renew the nonintercourse bill (which had lapsed the previous year) against Great Britain but to maintain trade with France. In response to the renewal of nonintercourse, the British navy began blockading the American coast. A battle between a British warship, the *H.M.S. Little Belt* and the *U.S.S. President* whipped up a feverish clamor for war throughout the United States. In April 1812, Congress passed a bill establishing a 60-day embargo against Great Britain. If at the end of that period the British did not remove the Orders in Council and cease the impressment of American sailors, Congress would declare war.

II.
1. Because of the XYZ affair, Adams and his Federalists, bolstered by public opinion, pushed through their program of national defense that was opposed by the Republicans.
2. The purpose of the voluntary societies was to serve as watchdogs for virtue.
3. The new commercial society severed the bond of tradition.
4. (c) The Otomí are not one of the tribes Lewis and Clark encountered.
5. In the South, the War of 1812 was not a struggle against the British but a war waged against the Creek nation.
6. The treaty accomplished nothing but peace. The grievances that led to the declaration of war in 1812 went unaddressed.

CHAPTER 12: Revolution in New Spain

Chapter Overview

♦ From the late 1780s to 1848, California enjoyed its "golden age" and attracted the interest of foreigners. In 1812, the Russians came to California and built a settlement at Fort Ross.

♦ In the early 1800s, the California missions went through a period of progress during which many Indians were converted. The missions also experienced difficulties resulting from runaway neophyte Indians and the bad influence of lax Spanish Catholics. In 1810 government payments and support for the California military garrisons ceased, so the missions began to supply the garrisons, bringing strain on the Mission Indians.

♦ The society of Spanish America was tarnished by injustice, structural problems, and political corruption. The ideas of Enlightenment and the examples of the American and French Revolutions drew people to embrace Liberal republican political philosophies.

♦ In the mother country, Spain, civil war was beginning. Napoleon pressured Carlos IV and his son, Fernando VII, to relinquish all claim to the Spanish throne, and made his own brother, Joseph Bonaparte, king of Spain. Indignation broke out against the French, and *juntas* were formed to oppose them. New Spain also rejected Joseph's rule, and the town council of Mexico City asked the viceroy, José de Iturrigaray, to assume the powers of government of New Spain in the name of Fernando VII. Iturrigaray was a greedy man, however, and his action drew the opposition of the *audiencia* of New Spain, as well as of the

Volunteers of Fernando VII, who broke into the viceregal palace and took Iturrigaray prisoner.

♦ During this early period of unrest in New Spain, *Caballeros Racionales* began meeting in Mexico to discuss revolutionary doctrines.

♦ In August of 1810, the priest, Miguel Hidalgo, and the Querátero group of *Caballeros Racionales* planned to capture key government officials and set up a revolutionary government. They were betrayed, but Hidalgo still chose to call for resistance, and by September 21, Hidalgo had amassed an army of 50,000. The army marched on Guanajuato on September 28 and slaughtered many inhabitants of the town. By October, Hidalgo had gained control of much of central Mexico. Hidalgo was captured in March 21, 1811, and later tried and executed.

♦ After the death of Hidalgo, Padre José María Morelos took command of the revolution. In 1813 Morelos abandoned any pretense that he was fighting for the rights of Fernando VII. He proclaimed that Mexico's dependence on the Spanish throne had ceased forever and been dissolved. He laid out his ideas for the government of an independent Mexico. The congress adopted his plans and set about drawing up a constitution.

♦ In 1814 Napoleon was defeated, and Fernando VII returned to the Spanish throne. He suppressed the constitution adopted by the Spanish Cortes in 1812.

♦ In 1816 the rebel general Luis Mier y Terán dissolved Morelos' revolutionary congress. In April of that same year, Juan Ruiz de Apodaca became viceroy and offered amnesty to the remaining revolutionaries.

- Revolution in Spain in 1820 forced Fernando VII to restore the Constitution of 1812. Liberals then demanded reform and determined that union with Spain was dangerous. They began to plot independence.

- Agustín de Iturbide published his *Plan de Iguala* with its "Three Guarantees," a blueprint for independence, in 1821. In July of that year a new Spanish viceroy, Juan O'Donojú, arrived in Veracruz, but the city was besieged, so he could not leave. In August he agreed to the *Plan de Iguala*, and the revolution was over, leaving Mexico independent.

- Iturbide began to set up his government, but the Spanish king would not recognize an independent Mexico. In 1822 a mob demanded that Iturbide take up the government of Mexico as emperor. Things did not go well with the new government, and Agustín's empire was falling apart. Congress began calling for a centralist government. Antonio de Santa Anna organized a rebel army against the new emperor, and on March 19, 1823, Emperor Agustín offered his resignation.

- After the fall of Iturbide, moderates took control of the government and declared Mexico a republic. Miguel Ramos Arizpe assumed leadership of a new congress and drafted a constitution patterned on that of the United States. The constitution was proclaimed on October 2, 1824.

What Students Should Know

1. **The character of *Californio* society**

   California was a hierarchical society with clearly demarcated levels of authority. At the pinnacle of the social/political structure was the Spanish governor. Though appointed by the viceroy in Mexico and formally subject to him, the California governor, because of the great distance from Monterey to Mexico City, was practically independent. Hardly any checks were placed on his actions. His power was absolute over all California society, except the missions, which answered to the *padre-presidente* alone.

   California's social structure was aristocratic. At the top of the social pyramid were the *gente de razón*, the families of more or less pure Spanish blood that included families of government officials and the increasing number of rancho dons. Indians who married into this group became members of the *gente de razón* by association.

   The *Californio* aristocrats were noted for their generosity and love of ease. Money meant little to them; they measured their wealth in lands and cattle. The *Californio* don was a proud man who despised all manual labor as beneath his dignity. The only occupations he would countenance were herding cattle and military service. Though there were some educated dons and *doñas*, no public system of education existed in California. Some families employed friars to teach their children, while others sent them to school in Hawai'i or the United States.

   Below these aristocrats were other "whites," many of whom were illiterate, some of whom were released criminals. The latter made the *pueblos* of Los Angeles, San José, and the short-lived Branciforte wild, unruly places. The number of these "whites," including the *gente de razón*, was never large.

   The Indians of California were divided between those who lived on the missions and those who did not. Of the former, there were 7,353 neophytes in 1790; over 10,000 by 1800. Earlier estimates of non-neophyte Indians reported around 133,000 souls ; more recent estimates, about three times that number.

2. **How the Spanish government dealt out land in California**

Theoretically, the king of Spain held all land titles in California; in practice, land was dealt out to its inhabitants. According to Spanish law, the Indians were to receive all land necessary to sustain them. Indeed, the vast mission lands, the best in California, were to be turned over to the Indians when the process of civilizing and Christianizing them was complete. Beginning in 1786, the king's government began granting land grants to non-Indians, having distributed 16 ranchos by 1795. Eventually, the rancho would become the predominant social institution in California.

3.   The Russian presence in California's

California inevitably attracted the eyes of foreigners. Alexander Baranov, the head of the Russian American Fur Company, took up a plan to establish a settlement in California. In March 1812, a large Russian ship brought to California native Alaskan fur hunters and a small number of Russian overseers, who began to construct a fort and settlement on a bluff overlooking a stream that became known as the Russian River. When finished, this settlement, called Fort Ross, consisted of a palisade built from large tree trunks surrounded by sixty buildings, orchards, gardens, grain fields, and villages for Alaskans and the local Kashaya Pomo people. Later, the settlers built a Russian Orthodox chapel. Until 1820, the Russians and Alaskans at Fort Ross were harvesting valuable sea otter pelts. When the number of sea otters drastically decreased because of overhunting, the settlers turned to growing grain and vegetables, which they sent north to Russian Alaskan settlements. Most of the settlers were not Russian, and among those that were, many intermarried with the Alaskans and the local natives.

4.   Charges of cruelty in the California missions and the friars' response

Though some have charged the mission system with cruelty, there is little evidence of it, at least until 1810. Despite the runaways, the Indians displayed no violent opposition to the missionaries. True, some tribes resisted the friars' invitations to join the missions, but even these showed no deadly hate. The first charges of cruelty came in 1798 when a friar who had been dismissed on charges of insanity after only two months in California, along with four Spanish military commanders wrote attacks on the missions. They charged that the friars forced pregnant women to work in the fields from six to nine hours a day and to engage in other hard labor. The friars, it was charged, did not give Indians sufficient time to gather wild fruits, punished them with the stocks and heavy floggings, and deprived them of water. Fray Fermín Lasuen, third president of the missions, and three other Calfornia missionary friars refuted the charges. They admitted that flogging, deprivation of water, the stocks were indeed applied, but only after repeated offenses; and only at Santa Barbara had women been flogged. After an investigation, the viceroy exonerated the missionaries. California governor, Don José Joaquin Arrillaga wrote that the friars treated their Indian neophytes as if they would their own children. In his refutation, Fray Fermín wrote that the "chastisement which we inflict on the Indians is in keeping with the judgment with which parents punish their own beloved children."

Governors of California allowed the friars the use of soldiers to pursue escaped neophytes, and the captured runaway was flogged – but only, said Lasuén, if they committed second offense of running away.

Repeat offenders could also be placed in the stocks or shackled.

5. Why the friars generally opposed Spanish settlements in California

Whatever difficulties the missionaries had with their neophytes were compounded by the Spanish settlers, whose encroachments on mission lands the friars had periodically to oppose. The friars had a poor opinion of the founding of ranchos and other non-Indian settlements. In California, such settlements, they said, did not add to the country's prosperity, they said, and were a detriment to missionary work.

6. The neophyte death rate in California and its causes

The death rate among the California Indians remained extremely high in the first two decades of the 19th century. Diseases such as dysentary, pleurisy, pneumonia, and measles decimated Indian populations in California. A major cause of sickness and death was syphilis, which, the friars said, was spread by the Indians' promiscuous habits. As the number of the coastal Indians that were yet unconverted decreased, missionaries had to go farther afield to find pagan tribes. Soldiers and friars began making expeditions over the Coast Range mountains into the great Central Valley to search out sites for new missions and to roundup fugitive neophytes. In the Tulares, among the lakes and sloughs of the Central Valley, were gentile *rancherías*; some of these were willing to receive the Gospel and welcomed the prospect of missions, but not all.

7. Why the numbers of runaways from the missions increased in the early 19th century

With the onset of revolution in Mexico in 1810, government payments and support for the California military garrison ceased. The missions, with their abundant crops, numerous livestock, and general prosperity, began to supply the garrisons. Such conditions seem to have brought added strain on the Mission Indians, and the second decade of the nineteenth century witnessed an atmosphere of greater tension in the missions. Also many, if not most, of the Indian oral traditions alleging cruelty on the part of the friars date back to this period. This was also the period (especially the second decade of the 19th century) of increased runaways from the missions. One opinion expressed by a contemporary friar was that the presidial troops did not pursue rebellious and runaway Indians. Another friar blamed the influence on the Indians of undisciplined and irreligious soldiers and that the burden of the soldiers' material support fell on the missions, and, thus, the Indians.

8. The character of life in New Spain by the 19th century

New Spain had a rich and beautiful culture that had developed since the days of Cortés. But like in any society, New Spain suffered from injustice and structural problems. By 1800, the *peninsulares* or *gauchupines*, those born in Spain, though still relatively few in number, controlled the majority of all political offices in New Spain. The creoles, American-born persons of Spanish blood, were many times the number of the *gauchupines*; yet, the Creoles had nowhere near the *gauchupines'* power and influence in government. This, of course, was source of deep discontent among the creoles, who had come to think they should occupy a position in society that accorded with their dignity and their numbers. The *mestizos* – those of mixed Indian and Spanish blood – had even less political power than the creoles, though the number of *mestizos* greatly exceeded that of the Creoles. It is not surprising that many of them thought themselves oppressed by the Spanish colonial system. The lot of the Indians had changed little since the days of Cortés – they remained, for the most part, laborers with little chance of social advancement. Political corruption was commonplace in New Spain. Offices were bought and sold, and bribery was widespread. Taxation was heavy. Both the government and the Church levied taxes. This hindered private initiative and inspired ill will among some towards both government and Church. The Spanish government maintained economic controls on New World dominions, forcing them to trade almost exclusively with the mother country. Colonial industries that would compete with established industries in Spain were forbidden. The Church provided what we today call "social services" – relief for the poor, hospitals, and schools.

Though from the beginning the Church had sponsored schools and universities, illiteracy remained high in New Spain. Folk traditions – song, legend, and plastic art – however were vibrant, forming a rich cultural substratum from which a refined civilization could arise. Among the literate, however, new ideas were stirring. Enlightenment and republican philosophies had begun to influence the ruling classes and the creole intellectuals; but because of the Inquisition they had to hold meetings in secret. And because of the *Index of Forbidden Books*, the works of Enlightenment thinkers could not be sold or distributed publicly. But like many a contraband item, these books were smuggled in, abridged into pamphlet form, and widely distributed. The examples of the American and French Revolutions drew many in Spanish America, especially creoles, to embrace Liberal republican political philosophies.

9. How at least many Spaniards viewed such institutions as the *Index of Forbidden Books* and the Inquisition

The Spanish saw both these institutions as necessary to protect society from false opinions. Error, it was thought, is worse than poverty, worse than death, for error leads men away from what gives life to the soul – truth and moral virtue. Since, according to Catholic tradition, human society exists not simply to ensure material benefits but to help men become good and attain eternal life, error undermines the very purpose of society and government and thus destroys both. In a society that accepted the Catholic faith as absolutely true, it was thought necessary to protect from opinions that would lead men away from the truth and, perhaps, condemn their souls to eternal death.

10. What events led to the first revolutionary movements in New Spain

The mother country, Spain, was rocked with civil war. These civil conflicts were sparked when in May 1808, Napolen Bonaparte pressured Carlos IV and his son, Fernando VII, to relinquish all claim to the Spanish throne, and, in their place, made his brother, Joseph Bonaparte, king of Spain. All over Spain, *juntas* were formed to oppose the French. At the end of September 1808, the *juntas* formed themselves into a national *Junta* and formed a *cortes* (parliament) to represent both Spain and America. New Spain also rejected Joseph's rule, and the town council of Mexico City asked the viceroy to assume the powers of government of New Spain in the name of Fernando VII. But when the viceroy proved corrupt, a group of 300 *gauchupines* who called themselves the Volunteers of Fernando VII overthrew the viceroy. When the successor the Volunteers chose proved incompetent, the

Volunteers asked the national *Junta* in Spain to appoint a new viceroy. Buy when the *Junta's* choice proved no better, in December 1809, some creoles formed a plot to overthrow the government, but it failed. In August 1810, the new viceroy arrived in Mexico.

11. How Hidalgo's rebellion began

A group of creole intellectuals and army officers had been meeting secretly in Querétaro, a town about 200 miles northwest of Mexico City, ostensibly to discuss literature but really to plot to overthrow *gauchupine* power and make Mexico independent of Spain, still officially faithful to Fernando VII. Among the conspirators was the 57-year old *cura* of the nearby village of Dolores, Miguel Gregorio Antonio Ignacio Hidalgo y Costilla. Padre Hidalgo had long had a reputation for radicalism; a French scholar, he had been drawn to the works of French Enlightenment thinkers, such as Rousseau and Montesquieu. As *cura* of the village of Dolores in Guanajuato, Hidalgo took great interest in the material welfare of the Indians. By August 1810 Hidalgo and the Querétaro group had a plan for a *coup d'état;* but when Hidalgo learned that the *coup* had been discovered, he gathered his Indian parishioners, and from the pulpit he gave the *grito de Dolores*, the "Cry of Dolores" to overthrow the gauchupine government.

12. How Hidalgo's rebellion progressed, and how it ended

Follow Hidalgo's *grito*, his peasant army, 50,000 strong, and led by Ignacio Allende and Juan Aldama, marched toward Guanajuato. Enroute, they brutally slaughtered any Europeans, *gauchupines*, or creoles they found in the villages. When the army reached Guanajuato on September 28, Hidalgo pledged that he would spare all Europeans if the city surrendered; but when it did not, Hidalgo's army captured the city's Alhóndiga and murdered everyone who had taken refuge in it. Ostensibly to rein in such violence in the future, Hidalgo issued "Nine Laws to Avoid Disorder and Bloodshed," though they called for stern measures against those who resisted the revolution. Following the capture of Guanajuato, the bishop-elect of Michoacán excommunicated Hidalgo and all his followers.

During October 1810 Hidalgo gained control of much of central Mexico west of Mexico City. Everywhere, the same mob violence was repeated. Hidalgo's tolerance of violence convinced creoles, whom Hidalgo had hoped would rise with the Indians, to instead joined forces with the *gauchupines*. From Valladolid, Hidalgo moved against Mexico City. On October 3, at Monte de Las Cruces in the foothills overlooking the capital, Hidalgo's 80,000 joined battle with 6,000 Spaniards under General Torcuato Trujillo and forced them to retreat to Mexico City. Allende and others encouraged Hidalgo to strike the city, but Hidalgo hesitated and instead decided to retreat northwest, toward Guadalajara. Demoralized by the loss of a victory that seemed so clearly within their reach, thousands abandoned the rebel army. On November 7, 1810, Spanish troops under General Félix Calleja defeated Hidalgo's remnant of 40,000 men at Aculco.

After he entered Guadalajara, Hidalgo, with the lawyer Ignacio López Rayón, established a government and issued a proclamation granting freedom to slaves and the surrender to the Indians of the lands they cultivated. The Guadalajara government pledged its fidelity to King Fernando VII. But on January 14, 1811, Spanish forces forced Hidalgo to retreat and flee northeast. Allende removed Hidalgo from command of the army. Hoping to connect with rebels in the north and elicit aid from the United States, Allende, with Hidalgo and 1,000 men crossed into the hot and barren deserts of northern Mexico enroute to Texas. On March 21, 1811, near Saltillo, in Coahuilla, the small rebel force was defeated by a Spanish force and seized Allende and Hidalgo. Allende was later executed. After being degraded from the priesthood, Hidalgo was delivered to the state for execution. He was executed by a firing squad on July 30, 1811.

13.   Morelos and the course of his revolution

In 1810, Hidalgo appionted the priest José Teclo Morelos y Pavon to lead the revolution in the south. Unlike Hidalgo, who had come from a creole family, Padre Morelos was a poor *mestizo* from Valladolid. Having been sent by Hidalgo to Zacatula on the Pacific coast, Morelos organized a small force there. A skilled commander, Morelos favored the hit-and-run methods of guerilla warfare rather than Hidalgo's pitched battle strategy. In 1811, Morelos carried out several successful campaigns against Spanish forces and captured the regions from the valley of Mexico City to the Pacific Coast, failing only to take Acapulco. Joined by Padre Matamoros and other rebel leaders, Morelos organized four armies and sent them to various parts of Mexico. Beginning in March 1812, the Spanish lay siege to Morelos' army in Cuautla for 73 days. Finally, Morelos and his men fought their way out of Cuautla and moved south and west, capturing the towns of Huajuapan, Orizaba, and Oaxaca.

Unlike Hidalgo, Morelos had a genius for government. On September 1, 1813, he, with Ignacio Rayón, Carlos María Bustamante, and other revolutionary leaders, assembled a revolutionary congress at Chilpancingo. In September, Morelos delivered ideas for a constitution to the congress. The congress adopted the the ideas and proclaimed Mexico independent of Spain, and set about drawing up a constitution. The tide of war, however, began to turn against the rebels. In December 1813, Morelos tried to take Valladolid but was repulsed by the creole royalist commander, Agustín Cosme Damián de Iturbide. Morelos' army disintegrated. In January 1814, government forces under Iturbide forced the rebel army and the new representative congress to flee. When the congress reassembled at Tlacotepec, it removed Morelos as head of the army; after Valladolid, the Congress had lost confidence in him. Yet, without Morelos' leadership, the rebel forces began to break down into factions. In the fall of 1815, while the congress was fleeing southeast to Puebla, Morelos, who was escorting them, was captured and sent to Mexico City.

Both military and ecclesiastical tribunals tried Morelos and condemned him. Morelos then was delivered over to the Church court that would degrade him from the dignity of priest. Here the Inquisition intervened and demanded its own trial against Morelos, even though, as an Indian, he did not fall under its jurisdiction. On November 27, 1815, the court of the Inquisition repeated the old charges and added others. The Inquisition condemned Morelos. On November 28, 1815, the viceroy condemned Morelos to die by firing squad.

14.   Morelos' ideas of government in the *Sentimientos de La Nation*

In his document, *Sentimientos de La Natión*, Morelos laid out his ideas for the government of an independent Mexico. In the *Sentimientos* he abandoned any pretense that he was fighting for the rights of King Fernando VII; instead he proclaimed that

Mexico's "dependence upon the Spanish Throne has ceased forever and been dissolved."

In line with Liberal republican thought, Morelos declared that the sovereignty of the state proceeds "immediately from the people." Government, he said, should be divided into legislative, executive, and judicial branches. Congress should pass laws to "increase the wages of the poor" and improve "their standard of living, removing ignorance, violence and theft." The congress must abolish torture, said Morelos, and slavery should be "prohibited forever and also distinction between classes, leaving everyone equal, and Americans distinguished from one another only by their vice or virtue." Morelos opposed the disestablishment of religion. It is true that he wanted to end tax support for the Church; her ministers, he said, should "be supported by all with only their tithes and offerings, and the people [should not] need to give any more than their devotion and offerings." Yet, Morelos said the new state "neither professes nor recognizes any religion but the Catholic, nor will it permit or tolerate the practice, public or private, of any other." The decree pledged that the government "will protect with all its power, and will watch over, the purity of the Faith and its dogmas and the maintenance of the regular bodies." He further proclaimed December 12, the feast of Our Lady of Guadalupe, "the Queen of our liberty," a national celebration. And while he forbade military expeditions outside the country, an exemption was granted to those who would "extend our faith to our brothers in far away lands."

15. The factions of Mexican politics in the years following Hidalgo's fall

In 1814, King Fernando VII was restored to the throne of Spain and suppressed the Liberal government of Spain. In Mexico, this restoration of Bourbon rule angered not only the Liberals but also the conservative creoles who had come to enjoy certain of the new liberties. But a simple Liberal/conservative divide did not characterize Mexico in this period; instead, Mexican society was divided between four factions: *gauchupines*, who wanted the old monarchical order; conservative creoles, many of whom opposed the Liberal Constitution of 1812; Liberals who wanted this constitution restored; and radicals who favored independence.

16. How rebellion in Spain lead to the "Bloodless Revolution" in Mexico

Rebellion in Spain in 1820 forced Fernando VII to restore the Constitution of 1812. Once again Liberal reforms were imposed on Mexico. These included reforms calling for the seizure of Church property, an end to the Inquisition, and the abolition of the *fueros* (traditional privileges) for clergy and military, such as those that preserved the clergy and military from trial except in the ecclesiastical and military courts. The Liberals, of course welcomed the law; but many "clericalists" – conservative creoles and members of the clergy – began to fear that the older order they so loved would be entirely destroyed. Union with Spain, they determined, was dangerous to that order. They began to plot independence.

One of these conspirators was Don Agustín de Iturbide. A royalist commander noted for his harsh treatment of insurgents, Iturbide had lost his command when he was accused of extorting money. For the next four years, Don Agustín remained inactive. During a period of forced retirement, Iturbide underwent a kind of religious conversion and attended a retreat at the Jesuit convent at La Profesa, a church in Mexico City. It so happened that La Profesa was a meeting place for influential conservatives, churchmen, and government officials, who, with Don Agustín, began discussing the possibilities for Mexican independence. Iturbide made valuable friendships with many prominent clergymen, who became his advocates with the viceroy. Upon their recommendation, the viceroy gave Iturbide the command of a military expedition against the insurgent, Vicente Guerrero.

Having become the leader of a party that sought to preserve the old ways, oddly enough, by revolution. Iturbide marched out to do battle with Guerrero in December 1820. But after suffering a defeat from rebel forces, Iturbide changed his tactics and began negotiating with the rebel chieftain. In February 1821, he published his *Plan de Iguala*, a blueprint for independence, to which Guerrero signed on. The *Plan* offered "three guarantees": independence for Mexico, the preservation of the Catholic Church, and the equality of *gauchupines* and creoles. It thus could please all parties. Iturbide's revolution was not successful at first. In April 1821, however, many royalists and Liberals cast their lot with Iturbide. In May, the rebel army marched into Guanajuato, then into Vallodolid. Guadalajara joined the rebel movement, as did all of the north. In August 1821, a new Spanish viceroy agreed to the *Plan de Iguala*. The revolution was over, and Mexico was independent.

17. The aftermath of Iturbide's revolution

In the immediate aftermath of the revolution, Mexico was at peace. Iturbide's revolution established creole dominance in Mexico; yet, the creole class was deeply divided. Many creoles admired the federal system of the

United States and wanted to establish a similar government in Mexico. These "Liberals" met opposition from "conservative" creoles, who favored a centralized regime and still hoped that Fernando VII or some other Bourbon prince would occupy the throne of Mexico. Though at first Iturbide won the support of the more radical Guerrero and of the Liberal creoles, he began to ally himself with the conservative centralists.

The revolution encouraged *mestizo* ambitions, and many *mestizos* were influenced by Liberal republicanism. Chieftains rose to power in these regions and, despite the central government, held nearly absolute sway. A check to Liberal republican aspirations, the military maintained the *fueros* it held under Spanish rule. Military men were tried in their own courts, which often did not respect civilian rights when they were violated by military men. After the revolution, in many parts of Mexico, the military robbed and murdered civilians.

18. Mexican Liberals and the Church

The Church was a target of the Mexican Liberals. The Church maintained its *fueros*. Clergy retained the right to be tried only in their own courts and were free from taxation. The bishops were eager to maintain this state of things and allied themselves with the more conservative and wealthy creoles. Liberalism was fundamentally anti-Catholic, for it held that religion is merely a matter of personal opinion and thus should not impinge on the life of society and the state. For Liberals, the state is the highest society to which all things, including religion, should be subject. For Liberals, the greatest human good is individual liberty. Since all people are fundamentally free, government derives its authority from the people alone, not God.

Key Terms at a Glance

junta: a group controlling a government, especially following a revolution

Missouri Compromise: a bill voted into law by Congress in 1820 that allowed Missouri to submit its constitution, slavery and all, to Congress; at the same time, it admitted Maine as a free state. The compromise help quiet North-South sectional strife for another 30 years.

Monroe Doctrine: President James Monroe's declaration that any attempt by European nations to exercise hegemony in the Americas would be considered dangerous to the peace and safety of the United States **tariff:** a duty placed on the price of imported or exported goods **nullification:** a legal theory that a state has the right to nullify, or invalidate, within its borders any federal law that the state has deemed unconstitutional.

It had long been the contention of Catholic theologians and, indeed, of the Church's magisterium, that the Church is not and cannot be subject to the power of the state. The argument went like this. Since the Church is a true society, through which the greatest good comes to mankind – eternal salvation, union with God – the Church is supernatural, and thus superior to the state – a society whose purpose is merely to help citizens attain natural goods: peace, access to the means of subsistence, cultural achievement, and, finally, moral and intellectual virtue. Though she is ultimately a spiritual society, the Church nevertheless needs material goods to carry out her mission. Because the Church is superior to the state, the state has no direct authority or power over what belongs to the Church. The state, thus, may not justly confiscate Church property.

19. Who Iturbide's opposition was

The congress to which Iturbide had agreed was elected according to a formula that favored wealthy creoles – most of whom were *Borbonistas* (supporters of the royal Bourbon family and Fernando VII). But by the time the congress met for the first time, in February 1822, it was well known that neither Fernando VII nor any member of his family intended to ascend the throne of an independent Mexico. Disappointed in their hopes of a Bourbon king, the *Borbonistas* in congress began calling for a centralist republic. They joined forces with the Liberals in congress. Together, they opposed Iturbide. The conservatives (*Borbonistas* and others) had long been organized in Masonic lodges of the Scottish rite. Under the influence of the United States minister, the Liberals (republicans) organized themselves in Masonic lodges of the York rite.

20. Iturbide's career as emperor

With the Mexican congress aligned against him, Iturbide needed to act to protect his power. Calls has been made urging Iturbide to take up the crown of Mexico. On the evening of May 18, 1822, Iturbide's soldiers raised the cry: *"Viva Agustín I!"* Iturbide at first rejected the call; but, consulting the regents, he decided to accept the crown. Bells rang and guns were fired into the air in honor of the new king. While mobs threatened death to any who opposed Iturbide, the congress voted to proclaim Iturbide the emperor, Agustín I, of Mexico.

Though it had proclaimed him emperor, the congress remained Iturbide's enemy. When Emperor Agustín imprisoned the Liberal priest, Fray Servando Teresa y Mier and 15 other congressmen, the congress declared its opposition to him. In October 1822, Don Agustín dissolved the congress and replaced it with a smaller, 45-member *Junta Nacional Instituyente,* handpicked by the emperor from the old congress. But this new reduced congress resisted the emperor, refusing to write up a constitution and vote for taxes. Don Agustín's generals were also discontent with him because he could not pay them. The emperor issued paper money to pay them, but this only caused prices to rise fanning public discontent with the emperor.

In the fall of 1822, Antonio López de Santa Anna sent out a call for the overthrow of the empire and the establishment of a republic. Liberals joined Santa Anna. At first, the rebellion was a failure, but then Don Agustín's generals began to desert him. In February 1823, one general issued a plan demanding the restoration of congress. All of the emperor's generals signed on to the plan, and his troops in Mexico City deserted him. On March 4, Emperor Agustín summoned the old congress. Not wishing to submit the Church and his own office to the judgment of congress, on March 19, 1823, Iturbide offered his resignation. The congress accepted it and sentenced him to perpetual banishment.

21. How the Republic of Mexico was founded

The fall of Iturbide, left conservatives divided and weak. Moderates took control of the government and declared Mexico a republic. Congress proclaimed a new constitution, patterned on the constitution of the United States, on October 4, 1824. The constitution divided Mexico into 19 states and four territories; each state was to elect its own governor and legislature. Unlike the U.S. constitution, however, the Mexican constitution made no provision for trial by jury. Though it forbade the practice of any other religion except the Catholic, the constitution abolished the Church's exclusive control of schools. According to the new constitution, state legislatures were to elect the president and vice president of the republic. Their choice in 1824 was Guadalupe Victoria for the first office and Nicolás Bravo for the second.

Questions for Review

1. **Describe the chief characteristics of the "golden age of California"?**

The "golden age of California" is the period of California history, roughly from 1800 to 1846, that is imagined as a period characterized by holy padres teaching docile Indian converts, proud rancho dons, *caballeros* in colorful costume, and beautiful, dark-eyed *doñas* and *señoritas*. The picture, of course is inaccurate; but it gives wome idea of California life in the period.

2. **How was California a hierarchical society?**

At the pinnacle of the social/political structure was the Spanish governor who had absolute power over all California society except the missions. Under the governor were the captains of the *presidios* and civil officers, called *comisionados*. California's social structure was aristocratic. At the top of the social pyramid were the *gente de razón*, the families of more or less pure Spanish blood. Below the aristocrats were other "whites." At the bottom fo the social period were the Indians

3. **What were some of the difficulties the missionaries were experiencing with the Indians of the missions?**

The Franciscans not only had to teach the Gospel to the natives, but had to draw them from their stone-age cultures into a highly complex European civilization which contrasted sharply with the native culture. Many neophytes fled from the regimen of mission life. Bloody feuds among the gentile Indians often involved tribes to which mission Indians were connected, and the friars had to be on the watch to make sure that their converts did not run off to join their kindred's conflicts. Then the farmers had to deal with Spanish Catholic settlers, who were not a good example of Christian life for the Indians.

4. **What conditions led to the Mexican revolution?**

The mother country, Spain, was rocked with civil war, and civil war in Spain affected the Spanish colonies in the New World. Spanish governmental restraints on native industry in New Spain prepared the soil for a revolt among the Indians.

5. **How did Napoleon's actions in Europe encourage the Mexican revolution?**

Napolen Bonaparte pressured Carlos IV and his son, Fernando VII, to relinquish all claim to the Spanish throne, and, in their place, made his brother, Joseph Bonaparte, king of Spain. New Spain also rejected Joseph's rule, and the town council of Mexico City asked the viceroy to assume the powers of government of New Spain in the name of Fernando VII. But when the viceroy proved corrupt, a group of 300 *gauchupines* who called themselves the Volunteers of Fernando VII overthrew the viceroy.

6. **What did Hidalgo achieve during the Mexican revolution?**

Hidalgo goaded the Indians into rebellion against the European government. During the rebellion he gained control of much of central Mexico and established a government in Guadalajara.

7. **Describe Morelos' idea of government.**

In line with Liberal republican thought, Morelos declared that the sovereignty of the state proceeds "immediately from the people." Government, he said, should be divided into legislative, executive, and judicial branches. Congress should pass laws to "increase the wages of the poor" and improve "their standard of living, removing ignorance, violence and theft." The congress must abolish torture, and slavery should be "prohibited forever and also distinction between classes, leaving everyone equal, and Americans distinguished from one another only by their vice or virtue." Morelos opposed the disestablishment of the Catholic religion, though it also opposd taxes to support the Church.

8. **Describe the *Plan de Iguala* and its Three Guarantees.**

The *Plan de Iguala* was a blueprint for independence. The *Plan* offered "three guarantees": independence for Mexico, the preservation of the Catholic Church, and the equality of *gauchupines* and creoles.

9. **What were the factions and dissensions that threatened the newly independent Mexico?**

Many creoles admired the federal system of the United States and wanted to establish a similar government in Mexico. These

"Liberals" met opposition from "conservative" creoles, who favored a centralized regime and still hoped that Fernando VII or some other Bourbon prince would occupy the throne of Mexico.

10. **Explain why the Church cannot be subject to the power of the state.**

Since the Church is a true society, through which the greatest good comes to mankind --- eternal salvation, union with God --- the Church is supernatural, and thus superior to the state --- a society whose purpose is merely to help citizens attain natural goods: peace, access to the means of subsistence, cultural achievement, and, finally, moral and intellectual virtue.

11. **What events led up to Agustín I's resignation as emperor?**

When Emperor Agustín imprisoned the Liberal priest, Fray Servando Teresa y Mier and 15 other congressmen, the congress declared its opposition to him. In October 1822, Don Agustín dissolved the congress and replaced it with a smaller, 45-member *Junta Nacional Instituyente*. But this new reduced congress resisted the emperor, refusing to write up a constitution and vote for taxes. Don Agustín's generals were also discontent with him because he could not pay them. In the fall of 1822, Antonio López de Santa Anna sent out a call for the overthrow of the empire and the establishment of a republic. At first, the rebellion was a failure, but then Don Agustín's generals began to desert him. In February 1823, one general issued a plan demanding the restoration of congress. All of the emperor's generals signed on to the plan, and his troops in Mexico City deserted him.

12. **Describe the 1824 constitution of Mexico.**

The 1824 constitution divided Mexico into 19 states and four territories; each state was to elect its own governor and legislature. Unlike the U.S. constitution, however, the Mexican constitution made no provision for trial by jury. Though it forbade the practice of any other religion except the Catholic, the constitution abolished the Church's exclusive control of schools. According to the new constitution, state legislatures were to elect the president and vice president of the republic.

Ideas in Action

1. **Read the 1824 Constitution of Mexico (this can be found in the Internet) and compare it to the American Constitution. How did they differ and how are they alike?**

2. **Choose one of the California missions and research its founding, the region wherein it was built, the Indians who inhabited it, and the work the missionaries and the Indians did.**

Sample Quiz I (pages 253-268)

Please answer the following in complete sentences.

1. **What was supposed to happen to mission lands after a certrain time period, according to Spanish law?**

2. **Why did the friars generally oppose Spanish settlements in California?**

3. **Why was the neophyte death rate in the Calforina missions so high?**

4. **Why did the numbers of runaways from the missions increase in the early 19th century?**

5. **What caused discontent amongst the creoles in Mexico?**

6. **Who was Padre Hidalgo, and what did he accomplish?**

Answers to Sample Quiz I

Students' answers should approximate the following.

1. According to Spanish law, the Indians were to receive all land necessary to sustain them. The vast mission lands were to be turned over to the Indians when the process of civilizing and Christianizing them was complete.
2. The friars generally opposed Spanish settlements because they said that such settlements did not add to the country's prosperity and were a detriment to missionary work.
3. The neophyte death rate was so high because they contracted diseases to which they had no immunities.
4. With the onset of revolution in Mexico in 1810, government payments and support for the California military garrison ceased. The missions began to supply the garrisons. Such conditions seem to have brought added strain on the Mission Indians, and the second decade of the nineteenth century witnessed an atmosphere of greater tension in the missions. Thus, to escape these condisions, neophytes ran away.
5. The creoles were about ten times the number of the *gauchupines*; yet, the creoles had nowhere near the *gauchupines'* power and influence in government. This was source of deep discontent among the creoles, who had come to think they should occupy a position in society that accorded with their dignity and their numbers.
6. Padre Hidalgo was a *cura* of the village of Dolores who led a rebellion against the Spanish government. During this rebellion, he gained control of much of central Mexico and established a government in Guadalajara.

Sample Quiz II (pages 268-278)

Please answer the following in complete sentences.

1. **Who was Padre Morelos, and what did he accomplish?**

2. **Describe the four factions which divided Mexican society following Hidalgo's fall.**

3. **How did rebellion in 1870 in Spain lead to the "Bloodless Revolution" in Mexico?**

4. **Who was Agustin de Iturbide, and what did he accomplish?**

5. **How were the creoles divided politically after Iturbide's revolution?**

6. **Why was Liberalism fundamentally anti-Catholic?**

7. **What finally decided Iturbide to resign as emperor?**

8. **Describe the new constitution of 1824.**

Answers to Sample Quiz II

Students' answers should approximate the following.

1. Padre Morelos was a *mestizo* priest whom Hidalgo appointed to lead the revolution in the south. Morelos assembled a revolutionary congress which adopted proclaimed Mexico independent of Spain.

2. Following Hidalgo's fall, Mexican society was divided between four factions: *gauchupines*, who wanted the old monarchical order; conservative creoles, many of whom opposed Spain's Liberal Constitution of 1812; Liberals who wanted this constitution restored; and radicals who favored independence.

3. Rebellion in Spain in 1820 forced Fernando VII to restore the Constitution of 1812. Once again Liberal reforms were imposed on Mexico. The Liberals, of course welcomed the law; but many conservative creoles and members of the clergy began to fear that the older order they so loved would be entirely destroyed. Union with Spain, they determined, was dangerous to that order. They began to plot independence.

4. Agustin de Iturbide was a royalist commander who led a military command against the insurgent Vencente Guerrero and published the *Plan de Iguala*, a blueprint for independence. After winning independence for Mexico, Iturbide became head of state and then emperor of Mexico.

5. Many creoles admired the federal system of the United States and wanted to establish a similar government in Mexico. These "Liberals" met opposition from "conservative" creoles, who favored a centralized regime and still hoped that Fernando VII or some other Bourbon prince would occupy the throne of Mexico.

6. Liberalism was fundamentally anti-Catholic, for it held that religion is merely a matter of personal opinion and thus should not impinge on the life of society and the state.

7. Not wishing to submit the Church and his own office to the judgment of the re-summoned old congress, on March 19, 1823, Iturbide offered his resignation.

8. The constitution of 1824 was decentralist, patterned on that of the United States, divided Mexico into 19 states and four territories; each state was to elect its own governor and legislature. Unlike the U.S. constitution, however, the Mexican constitution made no provision for trial by jury. Though it forbade the practice of any other religion except the Catholic, the constitution abolished the Church's exclusive control of schools. According to the new constitution, state legislatures were to elect the president and vice president of the republic

Essays

Instructions to be given to the students: Write in complete sentences. Underline your thesis. Give three supports or examples that explain why you think what you do and that support your thesis.

1. Examine the ideas of Morelos' *Sentimientos de la Nation* (which can be found on the Internet) and compare them with the political and social ideas of the founders of the United States. How are they similar? How are they different?

2. Explain in depth how Liberalism and the ideas of the Enlightenment are fundamentally contrary to the teachings of the Catholic Church.

Sample Test

Please answer the following in complete sentences.

I. Short Essay – Answer two of the following:

1. **How did many Spaniards view such institutions as the *Index of Forbidden Books* and the Inquisition?**

2. **What events in Spain led to the first revolutionary movements in New Spain?**

3. **What were Morelos' views on government?**

4. **Explain the relation between Church and state as it was understood by Catholics in Mexico in the early 19th century.**

II. Short Answer:

1. How did the friars treat their Indian neophytes?

2. What drew many in New Spain to embrace Liberalism?

3. What did Morelos proclaim about his revolution in relation to Spain and her king?

4. Name the four political factions in Mexican society after Hidalgo's fall.

5. What were the "three guarantees" proclaimed by Agustín de Iturbide?

6. On what constitution was the Constitution of 1824 patterned?

Answer Key to the Chapter Test

Students' answers should approximate the following:

I.

1. The Spanish saw both these institutions as necessary to protect society from false opinions. Error, it was thought, is worse than poverty, worse than death, for error leads men away from what gives life to the soul – truth and moral virtue. Since, according to Catholic tradition, human society exists not simply to ensure material benefits but to help men become good and attain eternal life, error undermines the very purpose of society and government and thus destroys both. In a society that accepted the Catholic faith as absolutely true, it was thought necessary to protect from opinions that would lead men away from the truth and, perhaps, condemn their souls to eternal death.

2. The mother country, Spain, was rocked with civil war. These civil conflicts were sparked when in May 1808, Napolen Bonaparte pressured Carlos IV and his son, Fernando VII, to relinquish all claim to the Spanish throne, and, in their place, made his brother, Joseph Bonaparte, king of Spain. All over Spain, *juntas* were formed to oppose the French. New Spain also rejected Joseph's rule, and the town council of Mexico City asked the viceroy to assume the powers of government of New Spain in the name of Fernando VII. But when the viceroy proved corrupt, a group of 300 *gauchupines* who called themselves the Volunteers of Fernando VII overthrew the viceroy.

3. In line with Liberal republican thought, Morelos declared that the sovereignty of the state proceeds "immediately from the people." Government, he said, should be divided into legislative, executive, and judicial branches. Congress should pass laws to "increase the wages of the poor" and improve "their standard of living, removing ignorance, violence and theft." The congress must abolish torture, and slavery should be "prohibited forever and also distinction between classes, leaving everyone equal, and Americans distinguished from one another only by their vice or virtue." Morelos opposed the disestablishment of the Catholic Church, though he wanted to abolish tax payments ot the Church.

4. In the early 19th century in Mexico, it was generally thought, with Catholic theologians and, indeed, the Church's magisterium, that the Church is not and cannot be subject to the power of the state. Since the Church is a true society, through which the greatest good comes to mankind – eternal salvation, union with God – the Church is supernatural, and thus superior to the state – a society whose purpose is merely to help citizens attain natural goods: peace, access to the means of subsistence, cultural achievement, and, finally, moral and intellectual virtue. Though she is ultimately a spiritual society, the Church nevertheless needs material goods to carry out her mission. Because the Church is superior to the state, the state has no direct

authority or power over what belongs to the Church.

II.

1. The friars treated their Indian neophytes as if they were their own children. At times they used corporal punishment against recalcitrant neophytes.

2. The examples of the American and French Revolutions drew many in Spanish America, especially creoles, to embrace Liberal republican political philosophies.

3. Morelos proclaimed that Mexico's "dependence upon the Spanish Throne has ceased forever and been dissolved."

4. The four factions in Mexican society after Hidalgo's fall were the *gauchupines*, the conservative creoles, the Liberals, and the radicals.

5. The "three guarantees" were: independence for Mexico, the preservation of the Catholic Church, and the equality of *gauchupines* and creoles.

6. The Constitution of 1824 was patterned on the Constitution of the United States.

CHAPTER 13: Good Feelings and Hard Times

Chapter Overview

- After the death of her husband, Elizabeth Ann Seton became Catholic and opened a school for girls in Baltimore. She was joined by other women, and they adopted the rule of the Sisters of Charity of St. Vincent de Paul. John England, Catholic bishop of Charleston, South Carolina favored reforms that would render the expression of the Catholic faith better assimilated to American principles. His spirit of accommodation came to dominate a large section of the American Catholic Church.

- Other bishops, including Benedict Joseph Flaget and Demetrius Gallitzin, worked hard among the pioneer Catholics, founding seminaries and Catholic settlements.

- Florida was a troublesome place, and the government had problems with the Seminole and the blacks, particularly from the Negro Fort. U.S. troops destroyed the Negro Fort in 1816, but trouble again arose from the Seminoles. The war against the Seminoles finally ended in 1818, and Spain ceded all of East Florida to the United States. Florida formally became a territory in 1821.

- After the War of 1812, British products again flooded the American market, jeopardizing infant American industries. Many citizens demanded tariffs on imported goods and Congress approved a tariff bill.

- In 1816 Calhoun and Clay began supporting the rechartering of the Bank of the United States. In 1819, in *McCulloch v. Maryland*, Maryland argued that Congress had no power to charter a bank.

- James Monroe won the elections of 1816 and 1820. The Monroe years have been called "The Era of Good Feelings" because there was remarkable political unity and a generally good economy in the United States.

- The year 1819 awakened the rivalry between the North and the South. In the dispute over whether Missouri should be a slave or free state, Congress in 1820 passed a compromise bill (the Missouri Compromise) and allowed Missouri to submit its constitution, slavery and all, to Congress, while admitting Maine as a free state, thus maintaining an equal representation of North and South in the Senate.

- Fernando VII of Spain, with the help of King Louis XVIII of France, overthrew the power of the Spanish parliament, the Cortes. It was rumored that Fernando, with the French, would invade the New World, so Great Britain approached the United States in 1823 and suggested an alliance. This resulted in the Monroe Document, in which the United States told Europe that its days of colonizing the Americas were over.

- The election of 1824 saw several different factions dividing the Republican Party. John Quincy Adams won the election after it was thrown to the House of Representatives.

- Andrew Jackson defeated Adams in the election of 1828, and he purged the government of Adams' appointees. Such a thorough purge was something new, but it would become the standard practice in future administrations.

- South Carolina was struggling economically, which it blamed on tariffs on foreign imports. After Congress passed the Tariff of 1828, the "Tariff of Abominations," John Calhoun published his thoughts on a new political doctrine called "Nullification." Congress removed sections of the Tariff of Abominations, but this did not satisfy South Carolina, and a state convention passed an order of nullification. When South Carolina threatened secession, Congress passed a new tariff bill as well as a force bill in 1833. South Carolina repealed the ordinance of nullification.

- The election campaign of 1832 found the Republicans split into rival parties, with Jackson's wing calling itself the Democratic Party. The other wing called itself the National Republican Party.

- To destroy the Bank of the United States, which Congress rechartered in 1832, President Jackson ordered his treasury secretary to remove all government funds from the bank and deposit them in local banks. Without government deposits, the Bank of the United States could not operate, and it closed its doors.

- In 1830 Congress passed the Indian Removal Act to allow whites to settle in the west without the resistance of the native Indians. Many of the tribes went peacefully, but some of them fought back, including the Sauk and Fox under Black Hawk, the Cherokee, and the Seminole. All but the Seminole were finally forced to remove to the new Indian Territory in the west.

What Students Should Know

1. **What were the divisions in the Catholic Church in early 19th-century America**

The bickering of national factions, and American individualism, compromised the unity of the Catholic Church in the United States in the early 19th century. When John Carroll, archbishop of Baltimore, died in 1815, the largely Irish Catholic population east of the Appalachians fell under the rule of bishops who were mostly French, and this led to resentment among Irish Catholics. Among Irish clergy were several talented men, and they appeared less foreign than the French clergy. Bishops had to contend with parish trustees, who were unwilling to recognize episcopal authority over their parishes. The situation tended dangerously toward schism; trustees in Charleston, South Carolina, for instance, contemplated accepting a bishop consecrated by the schismatic bishop of Utrecht.

2. **Bishop John England, his policies and ideas**

Bishop John England was the bishop of South Carolina, a diocese that covered the states of South Carolina, North Carolina, and Georgia. His flock, however, was small, consisting of no more than 15,000 souls. As Bishop England saw it, his task was to acquiesce as much as possible in what he deemed his people's just demands while maintaining his episcopal authority. In particular, he hoped to assimilate the Faith to "American principles." To Rome, he wrote, "I do not know of any system more favorable to the security of religious rights and of church property than that of the American law…. I prefer it to the law of almost every Catholic country with which I am acquainted." In an address to Congress, he said, "We do not believe," said England, "that God gave to the Church any power to interfere with our civil rights, or our civil concerns…" One measure he adopted for his diocese was to set up a "congress," with purely advisory powers, made up of a Convocation of Clergy and a lay House of Representatives. Yet he attacked trusteeship; he cut off the trustees' financial power by abolishing the fees they charged people for occupying pews in church. His policy of assimilation created tension between England from his brother bishops. But Bishop England objected to these bishops as well. The French clergy, he thought, made the Catholic faith seem foreign, almost exotic, to most Americans.

England opened a seminary to train his own priests in Charleston. He worked diligently to advance not only the spiritual but the cultural good of his people. England cared for both the white and black members of his flock, even providing education for free black girls and religious instruction for female slaves. He asked his metropolitan, Archbishop Maréchal of Baltimore, to call a synod of bishops in Baltimore to discuss establishing uniform regulations for governing the dioceses of the Church in America. Maréchal called the First Council of Baltimore in 1829, but the American bishops ignored England's calls for uniform regulations for the Church in America.

3. **The condition of Catholic life on the American frontier in the late 18th and early 19th centuries**

In the late 18th century, most Catholics west of the Appalachians were French. Only two secular priests served them. Six other priests rode the rounds ministering to Catholics in Kentucky and Tennessee, who met in ten small log cabin churches. Because the scattered Catholic population could expect only rare ministrations from a priest, laymen took over many clerical functions – reading prayers on Sundays, administering baptism, and registering marriages. Sometimes these laymen exceeded their powers, for instance by giving homilies or spicing up the worship celebrations (for instance, in one case, with a brass band).

4. **Who Benedict Joseph Flaget was and what he accomplished**

Flaget was appointed bishop of Bardstown, Kentucky, in 1808. Like his priests, he made visits in his far-flung diocese, riding on horseback and lived like a poor peasant.

5. **Who Bishop Simon Bruté de Remur was and what he accomplished**

Bruté was a native of France who became a Sulpician priest and went to America. In 1834, when he was in his fifties, Bruté became bishop of Vincennes. In the West, he became a horseback priest and generously dispensed material goods to those in need, living himself on the barest necessities. In his short reign of five years, Bruté established two seminaries.

6. **Who Demetrius Augustin Gallitzin was and what he accomplished**

Gallitzin, born at the Hague in Belgium in 1770, was the son of a Russian ambassador and a Prussian mother who later in life became a fervent Catholic. Prince Gallitzin himself became Catholic at the age of 17, and in 1792 came to America, where he entered Bishop Carroll's seminary and was ordained a priest three years later. Taking the name, "Mr. Smith," in 1799 he headed west over the Alleghenies to work with Catholics in western Pennsylvania. There he founded a settlement, really a Catholic colony, called Loretto. Using his own wealth he bought land, selling it at one-fourth its price to lay Catholic settlers. He built a flour mill and a saw mill for the settlers.

7. What the Patriot War was, its causes and results

East Florida had been a troublesome place since 1812 when, with the secret encouragement of Washington, a group of Anglo settlers (mostly from Georgia) had settled there. Calling themselves the "Patriots," these settlers had seized Amelia Island with the aid of U.S. gunboats and then marched on San Agustín, protected by a garrison of only 400 Spanish soldiers. Then Seminole Indians, suffering from Anglo-American inroads on their lands, and a group of blacks who had escaped from plantations in Georgia began attacking plantations in southern Georgia. A bloody struggle ensued that pitted the Patriots, federal troops, and Georgia state militia against blacks and Seminoles under the chieftain Bowlegs. The war ended in 1816 when the Patriot leader, Buckner Harris, was killed and the remainder of his followers made peace with the Spaniards.

After the "Patriot War," trouble with blacks and Seminoles continued. In November 1814, an agent of the British government had built a fort on a bluff overlooking the Apalachiola River in East Florida. This fort became known as the "Negro Fort" when it was taken over by escaped black slaves who used it as a base from which they raided cattle and sheep ranches in Georgia, terrorizing white settlers. General Jackson, after warning the Spanish commandant at Pensacola, sent U.S. troops and boats that destroyed the fort. The Seminole then took to the warpath in the spring of 1817. General Jackson, with President James Monroe's permission, and in

conjunction with naval forces, captured St. Mark's and took possession of Apalachiola Bay. When the Spanish governor protested Jackson's invasion of Spanish territory, Jackson marched on Pensacola and captured the town, along with the governor and his troops. The "war" against the Seminoles formally ended in 1818, and a year later Spain ceded all of East Florida to the United States in return for $5 million and a settlement of the disputed border between the Louisiana Territory and Spanish Texas.

8. Why centralism advanced after the War of 1812

The Republicans began adopting policies championed by their defeated enemy, the Federalists, including Hamilton's policy on manufacturing. In 1816, the Republican-controlled congress rechartered the National Bank (which Republican opposition had killed) and voted for a tariff on foreign manufactured products – both strongly nationalist measures. Changes during and after the War of 1812 in part explain the transformation in Republican policies. To protect American industries from British imports, many citizens began demanding tariffs – duties added to the cost of the product – on imported goods that competed with goods American industries could produce in sufficient quantities. Leading Republicans, who had once opposed the Bank of the United States, now supported its rechartering, and in defending it, used language reminiscent of Hamilton's broad construction of the Constitution. In *McCulloch v. Maryland*, Chief Justice John Marshall used the "necessary and proper" clause of the Constitution and Hamilton's theory of implied powers to rule against the state of Maryland, which had taxed the Baltimore branch of the National Bank because, said Maryland, Congress had no authority to charter a bank.

9. How the North-South rivalry was kindled after the War of 1812, and how it was quieted, for a time

A bill introduced into Congress in 1819 awakened the rivalry between North and South. Formerly part of the Louisiana territory, Missouri had been settled by folks from the South who had been drawn by the good bottom land along the Missouri and Mississippi rivers. Since Missouri had been open to slavery, settlers brought their slaves with them; and so it was that in their proposed state constitution the people of Missouri forbade emancipation and prohibited free blacks from entering the state. Then Representative James Tallmadge of New York introduced an amendment to the Missouri bill that prohibited the further introduction of slaves into Missouri and provided that all children born to slave parents at the time the state constitution was established should be free when they turned 25. Southerners denounced what they called unconstitutional restrictions and restraints introduced as criteria for admitting new states. In 1820, the Senate passed a compromise bill that established the latitude 36 degrees, 30 minutes (the southern boundary of Missouri westward) as the division between slave and free territory, and allowed masters to retrieve any slaves who escaped into free territory. The House defeated a similar bill but approved an amended bill on account of House Speaker Henry Clay's cajoling and arm-twisting tactics. This "Missouri Compromise" allowed Missouri to submit its constitution, slavery and all, to Congress; at the same time, it admitted Maine as a free state, thus maintaining an equal representation of North and South in the Senate. The Missouri Compromise quieted sectional wrangling for another 30 years.

10. The roots of North-South rivalry over slavery in 1819-20

Southern opposition to the Tallmadge Amendment was rooted in the fear that if slaves could not be transported into the territories, or new slave states were not admitted to the union, then blacks would come to outnumber whites in the existing slave states (as they already did in some regions of the South). Once the slaves realized their power, a bloody slave revolt, so dreaded by southern whites, might come to pass.

Political rivalry exacerbated North/South relations. Because the North in 1820 had a population of 5,152,000 people, as opposed to the South's 4,485,000, in the House representatives of the the North outnumbered those from the South, 105 to 81. In the Senate, the number of southern and northern representatives was equal – eleven states each. The South feared that unless Missouri came in as a slave state, the North would end up dominating both the House of Representatives and the Senate; for Maine, a northern and "free" region, was seeking admission at the same time Missouri was.

Antislavery sentiment was not particularly strong in the North at this time. Though some in the North denounced slavery as unchristian and unconstitutional, it was the political rivalry that prevailed in the current contest. Some northerners saw the Missouri issue as a way of creating a "solid north" that would "snatch the scepter from Virginia." Desire for political dominance was thus the predominant factor inspiring northern opposition to the admission of another slave state to the union.

11. The cotton gin and its effect on the slavery question in the United States

The slavery question had arisen in the Constitutional Convention of 1787 and had been lulled to sleep by compromise. In 1819, however, controversy was more difficult to quiet than in 1787, when one could argue that slavery was growing obsolete and would die a natural death. But the invention of the cotton gin in 1791 by Eli Whitney of New Haven, Connecticut had changed all that. Suddenly the laborious and time-consuming task of separating seeds from cotton fiber was made simple, and slaves once again became profitable – at least in South Carolina, Georgia, and the Gulf states, where cotton was grown. The cotton gin, worked by slaves and fed by slaves harvesting cotton in greatly expanded fields, phenomenally increased production, and cotton became the source and the foundation of the wealth of the southern states.

12. What the Monroe Doctrine was

Worried that Spain under Fernando VII would restore her power in Latin America, Great Britain in 1823 suggested an alliance with the United States. But President James Monroe's secretary of state, John Quincy Adams, said the United States should issue terms to both France and Spain – and Great Britain as well. Monroe spelled out Adams' policy in the "Monroe Doctrine" in 1823. While the United States, Monroe said, would not interfere "with the existing colonies or dependencies of any European power," nevertheless, the American continents, "by the free and independent condition which they have assumed and maintain, are henceforth not to be considered as subjects for future colonization by any European powers." The United States, said Monroe, "should consider any attempt" of European

nations "to extend their system [of government] to any portion of this hemisphere as dangerous to our peace and safety." The Monroe Doctrine, in effect, said only the United States was henceforth to be the hegemon in the Western Hemisphere.

13. President John Quincy Adams, his character and policies

In the election of 1824, John Quincy Adams represented New England interests and the remnants of the old Federalist Party, though, officially, he belonged to the Republican Party. Though he came in second to one of his three opponents, Andrew Jackson, Adams was elected president by a vote of the House of Representatives. Adams was one of the last representatives of classical republican probity. On taking office, he not only refused to indulge in the "spoils system," removing political opponents from appointed offices, but even gave appointments to Jackson men. Adams was a thoroughgoing nationalist, a proponent of federally funded internal improvements and even scientific expeditions. He wanted to make Washington the national center of research and learning; but his efforts in this, and in trying to establish a naval academy, were thwarted by Congress at every turn.

14. Andrew Jackson and his "Democracy"

Andrew Jackson answered more to the spirit of the times in which he lived than did John Quincy Adams. Democracy, the rule of the common man, was everywhere in the air; the voice of republicanism with its "natural aristocracy" was drowned out by a discordant clamor about the rights of the people. Jackson led a party of men who had themselves risen from the bottom of society. They wanted to give the common man his chance to rise, unhindered by the pretensions of aristocracy, natural or otherwise. They were not the party of the downtrodden but of the poor, ambitious to rise in society. They called for the removal of property qualifications in voting, and a universal suffrage for all free, white males. They favored free public education.

15. Why the South, especially South Carolina, opposed national tariffs

South Carolina was undergoing hard times. The opening up of the Gulf Coast states to cotton growing had brought an increase in cotton production, leading to lower prices for cotton on the market and a decrease in profits for South Carolina growers. Because South Carolina planters had for years and years been planting only cotton on the same land, the soil had become depleted. Lower yields and decreasing prices spelled economic disaster for the South Carolina growers.

Added to this were the tariffs that, since 1816, Congress had been imposing on foreign imports to protect manufacturers in the North. Because the South had little manufacturing, southern growers were dependent on foreign imports, for which they had to pay increasingly higher prices because of ever-increasing tariffs that benefited primarily New England. The South Carolina growers began to blame the tariffs for their impoverishment. The Tariff of 1828 proved the final straw. Calling it the "Tariff of Abominations," South Carolinians denounced what they thought was an attempt to rob the South to benefit the North. A South Carolina senator claimed that because the tariff decreased profits Britain made from exporting goods to America, the British were forced to buy less cotton from the South. Great Britain was the South's biggest cotton customer.

16. John C. Calhoun's doctrine of Nullification

In response to the Tariff of Abominations, Vice President John C. Calhoun anonymously set forth a new theory of Nullification in his "South Carolina Exposition and Protest." Calhoun's Nullification was something of a development of Jefferson and Madison's nullification doctrine found in the Kentucky and Virginia Resolves. Calhoun said states were equal partners with the federal government in a social contract, whose terms were spelled out in the Constitution. As an equal partner to this contract, each state had as much right as the federal government to interpret the terms of the contract. If a state deemed a federal law contrary to the Constitution, said Calhoun, the state could nullify the federal law within its borders. Calhoun's nullification doctrine was more radical than anything the Kentucky and Virginia Resolves had proposed. Jefferson and Madison had held that a convention of states could nullify a federal law, not an individual state by itself.

17. Daniel Webster's vision of the union and his reaction to secession

Webster's eloquence presented the union as the safeguard of liberty. While Calhoun and other political thinkers saw the union as a threat to liberty, insofar as it curtailed the rights of states and made it harder for states to protect the interests of their own people, Webster saw the union as the only sure foundation for liberty. When, for instance, he spoke of the sun "shining on the broken and dishonored fragments of a once glorious Union; on States dissevered, discordant, belligerent; on a land rent with civil feuds, or drenched, it may be, in fraternal blood," Webster suggested that, without the union, the states would be reduced to a condition of warring powers. For Webster, liberty and union were "one and inseparable" – thus he could not tolerate the notion of secession. Webster referred to the United States as "the world's last hope."

18. The course of South Carolina's nullification controversy

Congress gave South Carolina grounds for testing Calhoun's theory in 1832 when a new tariff, pushed by Henry Clay, removed sections of the Tariff of Abominations, though maintaining its high duties on iron and textiles. On November 24, 1832, the South Carolina convention issued an order of nullification that forbade federal officers to collect customs duties in South Carolina after February 1, 1833 and threatened secession if the federal government tried to enforce the tariff. In response, President Andrew Jackson reinforced Forts Sumter and Moultrie in Charleston harbor, ordered revenue cutters to collect duties on imports if customs officials refused to do so, and on December 10 issued to the people of South Carolina a proclamation condemning the right of secession. In return, the South Carolina state legislature approved the nullification ordinance and raised a volunteer force. Jackson responded by saying he would send troops into the state at the first sign of resistance. Then on March 2, 1833, Congress adopted a proposal made by Henry Clay to scale down customs duties; at the same time, it debated a force bill that would grant Jackson the authority to use the army and the navy to collect customs duties if South Carolina refused to acknowledge the judgment of the courts. Congress passed the Force Bill, and Jackson signed it, along with Clay's tariff bill. On March 11, the South Carolina convention again met and repealed the ordinance of nullification.

19. When the Democratic Party was founded, and what it stood for

During the election campaign of 1832, the Republican Party had split into rival parties, with Jackson's wing organizing itself as the Democratic Party, which at its first convention nominated Jackson and Van Buren as its presidential and vice presidential candidates. This party championed states' rights and opposed the National Bank and became especially popular among westerners and southerners, who wanted easier credit and more paper money to fund the land speculation to which they were addicted. The Bank of the United States made both of these items harder to get. Jackson, however, was a firm opponent of both easy credit and paper money.

20. The sources of conflict between Americans and the western Indians

American frontiersman had a seemingly limitless hunger for land. Indian lands, though guaranteed by federal treaties, proved too tempting to the hordes of settlers who were continually crossing the Appalachians. Whites encroached on Indian lands, settled on them, and treated the "savages" cruelly, murdering them when it suited their purposes. The federal government was generally powerless to hinder violations of its treaties; its authority came from the very people who perpetrated the outrages. Intermarriage with Indians, as well as blacks, was repugnant to most Anglo-Americans.

21. Why Indian removal acts were pushed in Congress

Those in the U.S. government who were friendly to the Indians formulated the only policy they thought could save them from extermination. The government, they said, should give eastern tribes lands west of the Mississippi in return for the lands they vacated in the East. Such measures received some opposition, as from President John Quincy Adams, for humanitarian reasons. However, under President Jackson, the champion of the western frontiersman, the removal policy took on new life.

22. Black Hawk, the Sauk and Fox, and the Indian removal policy

In 1829, a portion of the Sauk and Fox nation in Illinois Territory had agreed to move west of the Mississippi. Black Hawk, a chief of the Sauk and Fox, however, refused to leave his ancestral tribal seat at the mouth of the Rock River in Illinois. Black Hawk made alliances with other tribes to resist the whites. When white settlers arrived at the Sauk village in 1831, Black Hawk prepared to drive them out; but threatened by state militia, he and his followers escaped across the Mississippi. At a peace conference, Black Hawk and his followers agreed to leave Illinois forever. In their new home, Iowa, a bitter winter and the threat of the Sioux reduced the Sauk and Fox to starvation. The following spring, looking for a place to plant corn to feed his people, Black Hawk recrossed the Mississippi. Illinois' governor, John Reynolds, called out the state militia and told Black Hawk to return to Iowa. Black Hawk refused, and federal forces with state militia went in pursuit of Black Hawk. Black Hawk defeated state militia forces twice and fled north into Wisconsin. When his peace overtures were ignored, Black Hawk and his people were attacked by whites at Wisconsins River on May 14, 1832. Retreating with his remaining warriors and the band of starving women and children, Black Hawk arrived at the confluence of the Mississippi and Bad Axe

Rivers, where the U.S. army, state militia, and their Indian allies annihilated Black Hawk's branch of the Sauk and Fox. Following Black Hawk's defeat, the United States government seized all Sauk and Fox land in Illionis and eastern Iowa. Terrified by what happened to Black Hawk and his people, other tribes fled Illinois and Wisconsin for the West.

23. Who the Five Civilized Tribes were

Unlike other Indian tribes in Anglo-America, the Choctaw, Creek, Chickasaw, Cherokee, and Seminole of the old South had adopted much of white culture; they had established farmsteads and, in many cases, embraced the Christian faith. The were thus called the Five Civilized Tribes.

The Cherokee were the most civilized of the Civilized Tribes. Cherokee lands lay in northern Georgia, eastern Tennessee, western North Carolina, and northern Alabama. George Gist, a half-breed whose Indian name was Sequoya, had invented a Cherokee alphabet, allowing his people to print the Bible, various books, and a weekly newspaper, the *Cherokee Phoenix*, all in the Cherokee language. Many Cherokees had become Christian and had built roads, houses, and churches. They drew up their own constitution and had an elected legislature to govern their affairs.

24. The removal policy and the Civilized Tribes

The Five Civilized Tribes, though civilized, were in the way of white settlement. Despite federal treaties, the states of Georgia, Alabama, and Mississippi claimed they had jurisdiction over tribal lands, and they doled them out to white settlers. As with the native peoples in the North, the removal of the southern tribes to the West brought with it suffering and death. The Choctaw in Mississippi were the first to accept the federal offer of resettlement in the Indian Territory and by 1833 had removed to their new lands in what is now Oklahoma. In 1832, the Creek in Alabama signed a treaty and followed the Choctaw west. Their case had been desperate: white settlers had encroached on their land, sold them whiskey, and destroyed their property. When false reports of a Creek uprising were spread about, federal troops rounded up the Creek and forced them to move west. The Chickasaw of Mississippi fared better, though many of their people died on the long trek to their new home.

25. Why the Cherokee were removed from their homeland

White settlers, however, had long been encroaching on Cherokee lands In 1828, gold was discovered in Cherokee country, and white encroachments on tribal lands increased until, by 1830, about 3,000 white settlers were occupying Cherokee lands. The legislature of Georgia for its part ignored a 1791 federal treaty that had acknowledged the Cherokee as an independent nation; instead, the state encouraged the dispossession of the Cherokee. In 1832, the Supreme Court under Chief Justice Marshall ruled that Georgia had no authority over the Cherokee, because they constituted a sovereign nation; but the state legislature denounced the court and ignored the ruling. President Jackson took Georgia's side. When a Cherokee council rejected a treaty of removal offered by the federal government, a period of terror followed. Whites, including justices of the peace, crossed into Cherokee territory; they destroyed property, assaulted and flogged Cherokee men and women with cowhide, hickory sticks, and clubs. Finally, in order to avoid intervening in state affairs and so risk another secession movement – and to save the Cherokee from extermination – the federal government decided to break its treaty with the Cherokee and force them to move west. In May 1838, General Winfield Scott, commanding U.S. forces, began the forced expatriation of the Cherokee to Indian Territory. By the time the Cherokee reached Indian Territory, about 4,000 of them had died.

26. The Seminole War

In Florida, the Seminole had also signed a treaty of removal with the U.S. government. But, since the treaty stipulated that all blacks living among them would be sold into

Key Terms at a Glance

Missouri Compromise: a bill voted into law by Congress in 1820 that allowed Missouri to submit its constitution, slavery and all, to Congress; at the same time, it admitted Maine as a free state. The compromise help quiet North-South sectional strife for another 30 years.

Monroe Doctrine: President James Monroe's declaration that any attempt by European nations to exercise hegemony in the Americas would be considered dangerous to the peace and safety of the United States

tariff: a duty placed on the price of imported or exported goods

nullification: a legal theory that a state has the right to nullify, or invalidate, within its borders any federal law that the state has deemed unconstitutional.

slavery, the Seminole chief, Osceola, refused to abide by the treaty. President Jackson told the Seminole that they must go willingly, or in chains. The Seminole would not go. The war that followed was bloody. Poorly armed, the Indians fought guerrilla-style in the swamps and thick forests against a vastly superior American force. Still, Osceola was able to destroy Fort King, killing its commander, Wiley Thompson, who had taken Osceola's half-black wife prisoner. Then began raids on plantations, so effective that the civilian population fled to the cities and area forts. In the fall of 1837, the American general met with Osceola under a flag of truce; but, during negotiations, American troops quietly surrounded the Seminole camp. Osceola and his men were taken prisoner and sent to Fort Moultrie in South Carolina. The capture of Osceola, however, did not end the Seminole resistance. The war would last another five years until the United States, in desperation, simply gave up the struggle. No peace treaty had been signed, so these Seminole remained officially at war with the United States well into the 20th century.

Questions for Review

1. **What are Elizabeth Ann Seton's greatest contributions to the American Catholic Church?**

Elizabeth Ann Seton founded a quasi-religious community that opened schools for poor children and orphans. She gave Catholics an example of charity and devotion to family and Church

2. **What compromised the unity of the American Catholic Church in the early 19th century?**

The bickering of national factions, and the governance of parishes by lay trustees who were protective of their status compromised the unity of the Catholic Church in the United States in the early 19th century.

3. **Why did Bishop England want to assimilate the Catholic faith to American principles?**

Bishop England wanted to assimilate the Catholic faith to American principles because he said that he "did not know of any system more favorable to the security of religious rights and of church property than that of the American law."

4. **Why did Congress agree to lay tariffs on trade with Britain?**

Congress passed tariffs on trade with Britain because Britain was importing goods that competed with goods American industries were producing. To foster the growth of American industry, Congress thoguht it needed to protect that industry from competition.

5. **What was the "Era of Good Feelings," and why is it so called?**

The elections of 1816 and 1820 displayed remarkable political unity that, together with a generally good economy, seemed to jusify calling the time, "The Era of Good Feelings."

6. **What was the predominant factor in the North's opposition to the admission of another slave state into the union in the early 19th century? Why did the South want Congress to continue to allow the admission of slave states to the union?**

Desire for political dominance was the predominant factor inspiring northern opposition to the admission of another slave state to the union. The South wanted the continued admission of slave states so that the South could maintain its power in the national government by keeping its equal representation in the Senate.

7. What was the Missouri Compromise and what did it accomplish?

In 1820, the Senate and House of Representatives passed a bill that established the latitude 36 degrees, 30 minutes (the southern boundary of Missouri westward) as the division between slave and free territory, and allowed masters to retrieve any slaves who escaped into free territory. This bill was called the "Missouri Compromise" because it was a compromise between the demands of northerners and southerners over the admittance of Missouri as state into the union. The bill allowed Missouri to submit its constitution, slavery and all, to Congress; at the same time, it admitted Maine as a free state, thus maintaining an equal representation of North and South in the Senate. The Missouri Compromise quieted sectional wrangling for another 30 years.

8. What aspects of the social and political life in the 1820s and '30s showed that Americans were moving away from the ideals of republicanism?

Republicanism as a political ideal emphasized virtue and high ideals in government. It eschewed partisanship and promoted disinterested public service. Though it rejected an aristocracy based on birth and privilege, it looked for the establishment of a natural aristocracy of virtue and talent. It was, thus, not deeply democratic, though it upheld the idea that virtue and talent were not class conditioned. The rise of Jacksonian democracy represented a rejection of these ideals. The Jacksonians often appealed to the baser passions of the poor who were eager to better their station. Instead of intellectual subtlety, they presented issues in thick strokes of black and white. They could encourage narrowness and bigotry among those they appealed to.

9. Explain Calhoun's doctrine of Nullification and how it differs from the similar doctrine espoused by Thomas Jefferson and James Madison.

Nullification was a constitutional theory put fort by Senator John C. Calhoun. The theory said that states were equal partners with the federal government in a social contract, whose terms were spelled out in the Constitution. As an equal partner to this contract, each state had as much right as the federal government to interpret the terms of the contract. If a state deemed a federal law contrary to the Constitution, said Calhoun, the state could nullify the federal law within its borders. Calhoun's nullification doctrine was more radical than anything the Kentucky and Virginia Resolves had proposed. Jefferson and Madison had held that a convention of states could nullify a federal law, not an individual state by itself.

10. Explain the views of both the proponents and opponents of the National Bank.

Proponents of the National Bank saw it was a way to fund internal improvements and stabilize currency. Opponents of the National Bank thought that it represented an invasion of states' rights and was a monopoly that would favor the rich and foreign investors over hardworking farmers, mechanics, and shopkeepers.

11. What is the Indian Removal Act, and why was it passed? How was it abused?

The Indian Removal Act gave eastern tribes lands west of the Mississippi in return for lands they vacated in the East. Those friendly to the Indians saw the act as the only way they could save the Indians from extermination. In some cases, the Indian Removal Act was abused when unscrupulous federal agents often cheated these Indians of the just compensation for their lands. Some agents got chiefs drunk and convinced them to sign away their lands; other agents simply did not pay them what their lands were worth. In the case of nations like the Cherokee, the federal government broke its treaty with the Indians and used force to push them from their lands.

Ideas in Action

1. Read the life of Elizabeth Ann Seton, Bishop John England, or any other Catholic figure mentioned in this chapter.

2. The question of whether or not to assimilate to American culture was to become very controversial to Catholics living in America. What dangers could arise for the Catholic faith from such assimilation? What benefits? Could one detect any of those dangers or benefits already in the early 19th century?

3. Based on your understanding of the United States Constitution as a "social compact," does Calhoun's theory of Nullification make sense? Was he right that states were equal partners in the compact and thus had as much right as the federal government to interpret its terms? Why or why not?

5. On a map, follow the routes of the various "Trails of Tears," marking the route each nation or tribe took to the Indian Territory.

6. What alternatives to Indian removal did the federal government have, given the character of American government at the time? Were there any alternatives?

Sample Quiz I (pages 281-292)

Please answer the following in complete sentences.

1. What compromised the unity of the Catholic Church in early 19th century America?

2. Who was Bishop John Ireland, and what is he known for?

3. Identify the following:
   a. Benedict Joseph Flaget
   b. Bishop Simon Bruté de Remur
   c. Demetrius Agustin Gallitzin

4. What caused the Patriot War?

5. What happened after the Seminole War?

6. Why did many American citizens begin demanding tariffs on goods from Great Britain?

7. What was the purpose of the Missouri Compromise?

8. What was the predominant factor inspiring northern opposition to the admission of another slave state to the union?

9. How did the cotton gin affect the continuation of slavery?

Answers to Sample Quiz I

Students' answers should approximate the following.

1. The bickering of national factions, and American individualism, compromised the unity of the Catholic Church in the United States in the early 19th century.

2. Bishop John Ireland the was bishop of South Carolina who attempted to assimilate the Faith to American principles. He attempted to unite the American bishops in a common purpose by convincing them to establish uniform regulations for all dioceses.

3.
   a. Benedict Joseph Flaget was bishop of Bardstown, Kentucky in 1808. He rode about on horseback attending his diocese and lived like a poor peasant.
   b. Bishop Simon Bruté de Remur was a Sulpician priest who ministered to those in need in the West. He established two seminaries.
   c. Gallitzin was the son of a Russian ambassaor and himself a Russian nobleman. After becoming Catholic, he came to the United States and was ordained a priest. With his own wealth (and that of others) he founded a settlement for Catholics in western Pennsylvania.
4. The Seminole Indians, suffering from Anglo-American inroads on their lands, and a group of blacks who had escaped from plantations in Georgia began attacking plantations in southern Georgia. bloody struggle ensued which pitted the a group of settlers called the Patriots, federal troops, and Georgia state militia against blacks and Seminoles.

5. A year after the Seminole War, Spain ceded all of East Florida to the United States in return for $5 million and a settlement of the disputed border between the Louisiana Territory and Spanish Texas.
6. Many American citizens began demanding tariffs to protect American industries form British imports which competed with American industries.
7. The Missouri Compromise allowed Missouri to submit its constitution, slavery and all, to Congress which admitting Maine as a free state, thus maintaining an equal representation of North and South in the Senate.
8. Desire for political dominance was the predominant factor inspiring northern opposition to the admission of another slave state to the union.
9. The cotton gin made the laborious and time-consuming task of separating seeds from cotton fiber simple, and slaves once again became profitable in the South.

Sample Quiz II (pages 292-303)

Please answer the following in complete sentences.

1. **What were President Adams' policies?**

2. **What were some of the goals of Jacksonian Democracy?**

3. **How did South Carolina see the "Tariff of Abominations"?**

4. **Why could Daniel Webster not tolerate secession?**

5. **What did the Democratic Party stand for?**

6. **What was the source of conflict between Americans and western Indians?**

7. **Who were the Five Civilized Tribes?**

8. **Why were the Cherokee removed from their homeland?**

9. **What caused the Seminole War?**

Answers to Sample Quiz II

Students' answers should approximate the following.

1. President Adams was a thoroughgoing nationalist, and a proponent of federally funded internal improvements and scientific expeditions.
2. Proponets of Democracy wanted to give the common man his chance to rise, unhindered by the pretensions of aristocracy, natural or

otherwise. They were not the party of the downtrodden but of the poor, ambitious to rise in society. They called for the removal of property qualifications in voting, and a universal suffrage for all free white males. They favored free public education.

3. South Carolinians saw the Tariff of Abominations as an attempt to rob the South to benefit the North.

4. For Daniel Webster, liberty and union were one and inseparable; to lose union would be to lose liberty. Thus, he could not tolerate the notion of secession.

5. The Democratic Party championed states' rights, opposed the National Bank, and wanted easier credit and more paper money.

6. Indian lands, though guaranteed by federal treaties, proved too tempting to the hordes of settlers who were continually crossing the Appalachians. Whites encroached on Indian lands, settled on them, and treated the Indians cruelly, murdering them when it suited their purposes.

7. The Five Civilized Tribes were the Choctaw, Creek, Chickasaw, Cherokee, and Seminole tribes who had adopted much of white culture.

8. In order to avoid intervening in state affairs and so risk another secession movement, as well as to save the Cherokee from extermination, the federal government decided to break its treaty with the Cherokee an force them to move west.

9. In Florida, the Seminole had signed a treaty of removal with the U.S. government. But, since the treaty stipulated that all blacks living among them would be sold into slavery, the Seminole chief, Osceola, refused to abide by the treaty. President Jackson told the Seminole that they must go willingly, or in chains. The Seminole would not go.

Essays

Instructions to be given to the students: Write in complete sentences. Underline your thesis. Give three supports or examples that explain why you think what you do and that support your thesis.

1. How do you view the assimilation of the Catholic Faith to American principles? Were Bishop England's ideas of assimilation basically correct or not? Defend your position.

2. Defend or argue against John C. Calhoun's doctrine of Nullification. Would it have benefited or compromised the union formed by the United States Constitution?

3. Does modern America reflect more the ideals of republicanism or those of Jacksonian Democracy? Defend your thesis with examples.

Sample Test

Please answer the following in complete sentences.

I. Short Essay – Answer two of the following:

1. **What were the social and political roots of North-South rivalry over slavery?**

2. **Explain the Monroe Doctrine.**

3. **Explain the theory of Nullification.**

II. Short Answer:

1. **What did Bishop Ireland hope to do with the Catholic faith in America?**

2. **What awakened the rivalry between the North and South?**

3. Why did Daniel Webster think the union so important?

4. Why did the U.S. government push the Indian removal acts?

5. Name the Five Civilized Tribes.

Answer Key to the Chapter Test

Students' answers should approximate the following:

I.

1. Southern opposition to attempts to limit slavery was rooted in the fear that if slaves could not be transported into the territories, or new slave states were not admitted to the union, then blacks would come to outnumber whites in the existing slave states. Once the slaves realized their power, a bloody slave revolt might come to pass. Political rivalry exacerbated North/South relations. In the Senate, the number of southern and northern representatives was equal – eleven states each. The South feared that unless Missouri came in as a slave state, the North would end up dominating both the House of Representatives and the Senate.

2. Worried that Spain under Fernando VII would restore her power in Latin America, Great Britain in 1823 suggested an alliance with the United States. But President James Monroe's secretary of state, John Quincy Adams, said the United States should issue terms to both France and Spain – and Great Britain as well. Monroe spelled out Adams' policy in the "Monroe Doctrine" in 1823. While the United States, Monroe said, would not interfere "with the existing colonies or dependencies of any European power," nevertheless, the American continents, "by the free and independent condition which they have assumed and maintain, are henceforth not to be considered as subjects for future colonization by any European powers." The United States, said Monroe,

"should consider any attempt" of European nations "to extend their system [of government] to any portion of this hemisphere as dangerous to our peace and safety." The Monroe Doctrine, in effect, said only the United States was henceforth to be the hegemon in the Western Hemisphere.

3. In response to the Tariff of Abominations, John C. Calhoun's Nullification was something of a development of Jefferson and Madison's nullification doctrine found in the Kentucky and Virginia Resolves. Calhoun said states were equal partners with the federal government in a social contract, whose terms were spelled out in the Constitution. As an equal partner to this contract, each state had as much right as the federal government to interpret the terms of the contract. If a state deemed a federal law contrary to the Constitution, said Calhoun, the state could nullify the federal law within its borders.

II.

1. Bishop Ireland hoped that the Faith would be assimilated to American Principles.

2. A bill introduced into Congress in 1819 awakened the rivalry between North and South.

3. Daniel Webster saw the union as a safeguard of liberty.

4. The U.S. government pushed the Indian removal acts because they thought removal the only policy that could save the Indians from extermination.

5. The Five Civilized Tribes were the Choctaw, Creek, Chickasaw, Cherokee, and Seminole tribes.

CHAPTER 14: Mexico and Manifest Destiny

Chapter Overview

♦ In 1828, Gómez Pedraza, running against Vincente Guerrero, won the election for president in Mexico. Antonio López de Santa Anna would not tolerate a conservative in power, and he mounted a rebellion against Pedraza. The rebellion ended in 1829. and Congress proclaimed Guerrero president.

♦ King Fernando VII sent troops to Mexico to reconquer the country for Spain. The Spanish troops were not used to the sultry, swampy Tamualipas coast, and they succumbed to yellow fever, and many died.

♦ In late 1829, the conservative party denounced Guerrero, and troops seized Mexico City, forcing Guerrero to flee, and making Vice President Bustamante president. Bustamante began to suppress the Liberals, and this combined with the execution of Guerrero in 1831, sparked rebellion in the northern states in 1832. Santa Anna seized Veracruz and proclaimed Pedraza the rightful president. Bustamante relinquished power and went into exile. Santa Anna was elected president, though he claimed to be ill and returned to his hacienda, Manga de Clavo. While he was gone, his vice president, Gómez Farías put through his radical Liberal agenda.

♦ In 1834, in response to Farías' actions, conservatives called for the expulsion of the Liberals and the protection of religion. Under the leadership of Santa Anna they completely purged the government of Liberals. Santa Anna called a new congress, which replaced the Constitution of 1824 with a new instrument that set up a *Poder Conservador* – a committee of citizens, who were to see to it that the executive, legislative, and judicial branches did not encroach on each other.

♦ Americans began to receive land grants in Texas from the Mexican government, and a large number of Anglo-American began to settle there. These settlers did not like the laws of Mexico, and trouble began to surface between them and the Mexicans in the mid 1820s. Santa Anna decided he had to do something about the Anglo settlers in Texas, so he sent in an army to enforce obedience to the law. Stephen Austin called on Texians to take up arms. In 1836 Santa Anna and his troops laid siege to the Alamo. All of the Texians defending the fort were slaughtered. Later at the battle of San Jacinto, Santa Anna was captured, and the war ended. To assure his release, Santa Anna promised to recognize the independence of Texas.

♦ In response to the property loss of French citizens at the hands of Mexicans, France demanded compensation from Mexico. When Mexico failed to comply, the Pastry War commenced. The war ended when Mexico paid the demanded amount to the French.

♦ In 1841 Santa Anna became dictator of Mexico when a revolt was raised against Bustamante. The first year of Santa Anna's reign was a constant fiesta, which drained the country's wealth, and discontent swelled. Santa Anna again retired to Manga de Clavo.

♦ Santa Anna again took power in 1844 when Texas again requested admission to the United States. This time his extravagance reached its limit, and a rebellion forced him into exile for ten years.

- In 1836 Liberal *Californios* rose in revolt and declared California an independent state. *Californios* in the south of California objected, however.

- "Mountainy" men, including Hugh Glass, Jedediah Smith, Thomas Fitzpatrick, and Jim Bridger, began to explore the Far West. Fitzpatrick discovered the South Pass through the Rockies, and Smith discovered a route through the Sierra Nevada.

- "Oregon Fever" struck white settlers in Iowa, Missouri, Illinois, and Kentucky, and thousands of people went west to settle the rich lands in Oregon's Willamette Valley.

- Mormonism arose in 1830, and the new group settled in Nauvoo, Illinois. When they earned the dislike of their neighbors, the Mormons went west with Brigham Young in 1846 to the "promised land," the basin of the Great Salt Lake of Utah.

- Convinced that it had a "manifest destiny" to stretch from the Atlantic to the Pacific, the United States decided it must seize California before any other country did so. President Polk offered to buy the region from Mexico but was refused. He decided he would have to go to war to get it, and he managed to manipulate matters so that it seemed as if Mexico had started a war against the United States. In 1846 the United States declared war on Mexico.

What Students Should Know

1. **How Mexico came under foreign economic domination**

   Great Britain's foreign secretary, George Canning, saw Mexico as a lucrative market for British business. When Spain, in a confederacy of European nations called the Holy Alliance, had threatened to reconquer Mexico, Canning recognized Mexico's independence. Canning's diplomat in Mexico, seeing Guadalupe Victoria's money problems, convinced the president to accept two loans of three million pounds each from British banking houses. Though much of the money never reached Mexico, and much of it was ill spent after it did, the loans did help shore up Victoria's unstable government. But the loans helped make Mexico a British economic satellite. Deeply in debt to Great Britain, Mexico had no choice but to allow British business interests to acquire large portions of Mexico's trade and to permit British capital to develop mines for extracting the country's rich mineral wealth. Soon, France and Germany too invested in Mexico.

2. **How Freemasonry contributed to the instability of the Mexican republic**

   The Mexican conservatives were organized in masonic lodges that followed the Scottish Rite (and so were called *Econcistas*). The U.S. ambassador, Joel Poinsett introduced York Rite masonry to help organize the Liberal faction in Mexican politics. Though the creole *moderados* (moderates) dominated the congress, the influence of the Liberals, called *puros* or *Yorkistas* (because they followed the York Rite of Freemansonry), was growing. The factions brought instability to the new republican government.

3. **Identify the following:**

   a. **Lucas Alamán:** the most prestigious of the Mexican conservatives, Alamán believed Mexico should continue its tradition of centralized government; he opposed the division of Mexico into states on the model of the United States. He favored bringing in a foreign monarch to rule Mexico; and if that weren't possible, he wanted to see the establishment of a home-bred authoritarian regime. Under President Bustamante, Alamán favored drastic measures against Liberals.

b. **Nicholas Bravo:** a leading conservative in Mexican politics, he had been an ardent supporter of independence and had served under Morelos. But Bravo did not favor radical social change. Fearing Poinsett's influence on the Mexican government, Bravo mounted a rebellion against Victoria's government, calling for a centralized government, the abolition of Masonic lodges, and the deportation of Poinsett. Vicente Guerrero, however, put down the rebellion, and Bravo went into exile. President Guerrero later pardoned Bravo, and he returned to the country. In 1838, Bravo, who served under Santa Anna as vice president, was driven from power by a Liberal revellion.

c. **Vicente Guerrero:** a Liberal revolutionary in Mexico, Guerrero had joined forces with Agustín Iturbide in his revolution that had established Mexico's independence from Spain. It was not long before he turned against Iturbide and helped in the establishment of the Mexican republic. Leading government troops, Guerrero put down Bravo's rebellion against President Guadalupe Victoria. A popular candidate in the presidential election of 1828, he conceded the election to Pedraza. Not long afterwards, Santa Anna proclaimed his support for Guerrero in a rebellion that drove Pedraza into exile. By the end of January 1829, congress proclaimed Guerrero preisdent, with Anastasio Bustamante vice president. When the Spanish attempted a reconquest of Mexico, Guerrero was given almost dictatorial powers. As president, he abolished slavery in Mexico. But in late

1829, Bustamante led conservative in seizing the capital, and Guerrero was driven into the mountains of the south. Guerrero continued his resistance to the government. After about a year, General Bravo defeated Guerrero in battle at Chilpancingo. Guerrero retired to Acapulco, where he took refuge on an Italian ship, the *Colombo*, commanded by a friend. But the captain took Guerrero prisoner and sold him to the government. Proclaimed mentally incapable of governing, Guerrero was imprisoned. On February 14, 1831, he died by firing squad in Cuilapa, in the state of Michoacán.

d. **Anastasio Bustamante:** a leading conservative who served as vice president under Vicente Guerrero. In 1829 he drove Guerrero from Mexico City. Despite a counter-revolution under Santa Anna, Guerrero attained the presidency of Mexico. As president, Bustamante issued a decree forbidding further Anglo settlement in Texas. With Alamán's encouragement, Bustamante took drastic measures against Liberals. In the name of public order, troops armed with bayonets and cannon surrounded congress. The army removed Liberal governors and legislatures in eleven states, suppressed newspapers, and jailed, shot, or exiled leaders of the Liberals. The execution of Guerrero and the repression of Liberals sparked a rebellion of the northern states in 1832. Seeing resistance hopeless, Bustamante relinquished power and went into exile. After Santa Anna's defeat at San Jacinto in Texas in 1836, Bustamante again became president. In 1838, during the Pastry War, Bustamante was again driven from power. After a brief Liberal government, Bustamante again took up the presidency. In 1841, Bustamante was driven from power in a Liberal revolt.

e. **Valentín Gómez Farías:** a physician and leader of the Liberals. In 1833, congress appointed him vice president under President Santa Anna, but when Santa Anna withdrew to Manga de Clavo, Farías assumed the powers of president and put through his radical agenda. He pushed through Congress a series of laws designed to weaken the Church's power, abolishing the compulsory payment of tithes to the Church, allowing monks and nuns to renounce their vows, transferring the oversight of education from the Church to the state, and secularizing the missions in California. The government enforced these measures even though the Constitution of 1824 had pledged Mexico to protect the Catholic religion "by wise and just laws, and prohibit the exercise of any other whatever." Under Gómez Farías, congress reduced the size of the army and the number of officers and deprived the military of its *fueros.* In April 1834, Santa Anna joined in a revolution against the government, and Gómez Farías fled to New Orleans. In 1838, Gómez Farías returned from exile and called for a restoration of the federal Constitution of 1824. But after 11 days fighting in Mexico City, Gómez Farías again went into exile and Anastasio Bustamante re-assumed the presidency. In 1846, Gómez Farías again became president, and maintained the office, though Santa Anna became the real power in Mexico. Following the Battle of Saltillo, Santa Anna removed Gómez Farías from power.

4. **The role of Antonio López de Santa Anna in the history of the Mexican republic**

Santa Anna was a general in the Mexican army and had the reputation of an effective commander. A political chameleon, he had from the beginning wavered between the conservatives and the Liberals, acting as the champion of either group when he sensed it was most likely to gain power. Thus, he was responsible for establishing both Liberal and conservative governments, of which he would serve as president. Santa Anna, however, would not long take an active role in government, but would retire, leaving his vice president in charge. He thus was a source of instability for the Republic of Mexico.

5. **The Anglo-American settlement of Texas**

In the last years of her rule, Spain had encouraged immigration of U.S. born Americans of English, Irish, and Scots Irish extraction to Texas, hoping by this means to keep the United States from seizing the largely unpopulated territory. In 1821, a Connecticut Yankee named Moses Austin had received a large land grant in Texas from the Spanish king; but he died six months later. In 1823, the Mexican government confirmed the grant to Austin's son, Stephen. The grant gave Stephen Austin the right to settle 300 families in Texas. Each family would receive 177 acres of rich farming land, plus 13,000 acres of prairie pasture. Austin, himself, would receive a bonus of 65,000 acres. In return, the settlers would have to become Mexican citizens and convert to the Catholic Church. Fifteen other *empresarios* (as the land grantees were called) received land grants along with Austin. They settled in the southeastern section of Texas, and over the years their numbers grew. Until 1829, Austin was the sole authority in the Texas colony, and, in the early days, he and other *empresarios* tried to conduct themselves as good Mexican citizens. But not every settler converted to the Catholic faith, since the decree ordering conversion was not strictly enforced. Most of the settlers were slave owners, attracted by the black loam that was so good for cotton growing. Though he opposed slavery, Austin permitted it in his colony. The Mexican Constitution of 1824 had abolished slavery; but, in 1827, the Mexican government gave Austin permission to permit slavery in Texas.

6. **What were Texian complaints about Mexican rule**

Anglo-Americans in the Mexican territory of Tejas were unhappy. The great upheavals in Mexico, along with the inefficiency of Mexican officials, annoyed and frustrated them. Then there was the sheer foreignness of Mexican law, which did not provide for trial by jury and had no common law. Tejas (Texas) was the northern portion of Coahuilla, and Anglo-Texans wanted to have their own government.

Ardent federalists, the Texians, along with many *Tejanos* (Spanish-speaking inhabitants of Tejas), bitterly disliked Bustamante's centralist regime. Texian leaders, including Stephen Austin, were Masons and had, in 1828, petitioned for the establishment of the York rite in Texas – thus showing their support for the supposedly Liberal Santa Anna's rebellion. The Texians were upset when Mexico ordered the collection of customs duties along the Texas/Louisiana border, thus burdening the trade of the Texians with the United States, and sent troops to enforce the decree and crackdown on smuggling. Among the chief motivations for Texian discontent with Mexican rule was the fear that the Mexican government might enforce the 1827 decree abolishing slavery

even in Texas. Texians hoped to reap great wealth from slave labor and they feared that talk of emancipation would inspire slave revolts.

7. **Identify the following:**

a. **Sam Houston:** Houston was an old friend of Andrew Jackson, had served in the Creek War, and had worked as an agent to help move a band of Cherokee from East Tennessee to Indian Territory. In 1818 Houston went to practice law in Nashville. After serving one term in Congress, Houston was elected governor of Tennessee in 1827; but two years later, after his wife of three months left him, Houston resigned his governorship and went to live among the Cherokee. The Indians adopted him as a member of their tribe and gave him the unflattering epithet, "Big Drunk." In 1832, at the age of 39, he went to Texas, where he became a Mexican citizen and a Catholic. Houston commanded the Texian army that defeated Santa Anna at San Jacinto. When Texas proclaimed its independence, Houston served as its first president.

b. **James Bowie:** a frontiersman, an illegal slave smuggler, and land speculator, Bowie had come to Texas in 1830. Shortly after coming to Texas, James Bowie was baptized a Catholic and married into a prominent San Antonio family. Over the next few years he gambled, engaged in land speculation, and earned the ill will of Stephen Austin, who thought him a charlatan. Bowie, though, had distinguished himself as a brave leader in the battle of Béxar against General Cos. He died during the Battle of the Alamo in 1836.

c. **David Crockett:** David Crockett arrived in Texas at the lag end of 1835. A legendary frontiersman, Crockett had fought in the Creek Wars and had served in Congress as a representative from Tennessee, where he distinguished himself as an opponent of Jackson's Indian removal policy. In 1835 he lost his congressional seat, left Tennessee, and went to Texas. He fought at the Alamo, where he died.

8. **What happened at the Alamo. Its significance.**

President Santa Anna had led an army into Texas to put down its revolution. On February 23, 1836, Santa Anna with 3,000 troops laid siege to the 150 defenders of the Alamo. For two weeks, Colonel Travis refused to surrender. Finally, in the early hours of March 6, the assault began. Almost all the defenders died within a few hours. The Battle of the Alamo gave the Texian revolutionaries a battle cry in their struggle against Mexico.

9. **What happened at San Jacinto. Its significance.**

The Texians had proclaimed Texas independence a few days before the Alamo massacre. Sam Houston, hearing that Santa Anna's army had turned east and was terrorizing the population as it advanced, ordered a general retreat. The entire population of Texas was in flight. Santa Anna, hearing that the provisional Texas government had removed to Harrisburg at the mouth of the San Jacinto River, thither led his force them to bag Houston's army and the rebellious government together. Santa Anna met Houston and his small army at Lynchburg Ferry on the San Jacinto, and a face-off ensued between the two armies. But while Santa Anna lay asleep in his tent, Houston attacked the Mexican position. Santa Anna barely escaped while Houston's small force destroyed the Mexican army. Santa Anna recognized Texas independence to secure his freedom.

10. **The attitude of the *Californios* toward the revolution in Mexico**

Spanish and royalist sentiment was strong among *Californios* as a whole, and especially strong among the Franciscans. Yet, the *Californios* were realistic enough to know that, if Spain did not hold Mexico, it could not hold California. Thus, they took the oath to the government and empire of Agustín Iturbide and the Mexican republic as well.

11. **The secularization of the California missions and its effects**

Secularization had always been the goal of the Indian missions throughout Spanish America. In 1813, the Spanish *Cortes* had ruled that all missions ten years old or older were to be secularized. This law, however, was never enforced in California. The California friars opposed secularization. The California Indians were very primitive when Serra arrived, and ten years could never have been a sufficient period of time in which to civilize them fully. When he became governor of California in 1825, Colonel José María Echeandía commenced a limited secularization of the missions, disrupting the life at missions in the south by creating discontent among the neophytes. In 1830, Echeandía introduced a plan to secularize all the missions, but his successor as governor, Colonel Manuel Victoria, who had been sent to California by conservative Anastasio Bustamante government in Mexico, halted Echeandía's plans.

Followng the overthrow of Victoria by the *Californios, t*he Liberal government of Gómez Farías sent General José Figueroa to California. Governor Figueroa came with the charge to secularize the missions by turning them into pueblos and giving their lands to the neophytes. In 1834, Figueroa, however, gave in to the demands of the California *diputación* and presented a plan that would turn mission lands over to *Californio mayordomos.* Under this secularization plan, half of the mission lands were to go to the Indians and half to the *Californios,* but this was not how things turned out. Not fully assimilated into European culture, most of the Mission Indians did not attempt to farm their lands, nor did they know how to manage them. In a few years, the mission lands, had become the possession of the *Californios,* while the mission Indians were scattered. The secularization of mission lands, along with the Mexican government's approval of more land grants to white settlers, increased the number of private ranchos in California. In 1835, the Mexican governor of California, Mariano Chico, informed the California government that the Mexican congress had suspended its earlier secularization decree and so nullified Figueroa's secularization act. But the *diputación* ignored Chico.

12. **Indian discontent in California and its results**

Indian neophytes at the missions could sense the changes brought about by the Mexican Revolution. Since the supply ship from San Blas had stopped coming in 1811, Indian laborers had borne the burden of feeding the soldiers and their families, and they were weary. Moreover, the soldiers, who had less fear of the friars, had grown more careless toward the Indians and at times mistreated them cruelly. The fact that the unconverted Indians, or gentiles, having learned the use of the horse, had grown emboldened in their attitude towards the Spanish population made the neophytes even more restless and discontent. This smoldering discontent flamed into violence on February 21, 1824 at Missions Santa Inés and La Purísima Concepcíon. Spanish troops engaged in violence against Indian neophytes at Mission Santa Barbara on February 22. All the revolts were put down and, the Indian revolt lost steam.

13. **Who the mountainy men were**

The mountainy men were hunters and trappers who pushed into the Great Plains and the mountains of the West in search of the haunts of the beaver, whose pelts the East coveted for hats, gloves, and other clothing. Clad in skins, the mountainy men lived like Indians, even taking Indian women to wife. They worked for various fur companies.

14. **Identify the following:**

a. **Thomas Fitzpatrick:** Fitzpatrick was a trapper and hunter. While trapping in the Wind River and Sweetwater regions, in what is now Wyoming, Fitzpatrick and his partner, Jedediah Smith, heard from Indians of the many beaver in the Green River Valley, in what is now eastern Utah. Fitzpatrick set off south and discovered a wide pass that made a graded ascent through the Rockies. This was the famous "South Pass" through which immigrant wagon trains would in a few years make their passage over the mountains enroute to the fertile lands of Oregon beyond.

b. **Jedediah Smith:** a fur trapper and hunter, Smith partnered with William

Sublette in buying William Ashley's Rocky Mountain Fur Company. But Smith was more interested in exploration than fur trading, and in the summer of 1826 he set out with a party to find a route through the Rockies to California. Crossing the Great Basin, the Mojave Desert, and the Southern California mountains, Smith arrived at Mission San Gabriel. But instead of returning, as the Mexican commandant commanded him, the way he came, Smith went north, crossed the Sierra Nevada at Tehachapi Pass, passed up the San Joaquin Valley, and crossed the Sierra Nevada into what is now Nevada. Only a few weeks after arriving at Bear Lake, Smith returned to California, traversing the Mojave Desert and the San Bernardino Mountains to San Gabriel, and then westward and northward into the San Joaquin Valley. He pushed ever northward through California's great Central Valley and crossed the Coast Ranges to Monterey. Thence Smith pushed north into Oregon where he wintered at British Fort Vancouver. In the spring, he and his men followed the Columbia eastward, then continued up the Snake River. At last they met some of Sublette's men at what is now Jackson Hole, Wyoming.

15. The pattern of American settlement in California

Jedediah Smith may have been the first Anglo-American to cross into California westward, over land. Other Anglo-Americans, however, had come to California before Smith's explorations, but by sea. Some of these Yankees settled in California, and though few in number, became influential by conducting the business end of things in the territory. A few married into prominent *Californio* families. As in Texas, a foreigner could remain in California if he swore allegiance to the Mexican government and became Catholic. Abel Stearns did both. On the trail Jedediah Smith had blazed through the Sierra Nevada, fur trappers came overland to California to hunt beaver. Dirty and unruly, the trappers were unwelcome to the Mexican authorities, who jailed them, when and if they caught them. Other Anglo-Americans emigrated overland to settle, illegally, in California.

16. The pattern of American settlement in Oregon

The Oregon Country had, since 1818, been held jointly by the United States and Great Britain. Before 1832, trappers of both the Rocky Mountain Fur and the Hudson's Bay Companies had been hunting beaver in the rivers and streams of this region. In 1834, American Protestant missionaries, Jason Lee and his companions, settled in the Willamette Valley near modern Salem. There they joined with former employees of the Hudson's Bay Company and began raising wheat and cattle. On July 5, 1843, at Champoeg, they drew up a compact for governing their small colony. White settlers then began leaving Iowa, Missouri, Illinois, and Kentucky in an emigration to the Willamette Valley. Gathering at Independence, Missouri, wagon trains of pioneers began the long, overland trek westward across what became known as the Oregon Trail. They generally gathered in May, pushed on to Fort Leavenworth in Kansas, and then followed the course of the River Platte to the Rockies. The pioneers crossed the Rockies through the easy gradient of South Pass; then traversing the Wyoming basin, they skirted the Gros Ventre and Teton ranges, following the westward flowing rivers. When at last they reached the Snake

River, many pioneers built rafts to float their wagons to the Columbia. The journey to Oregon was long and full of dangers from Indians, the elements, starvation, and disease. If all went well, settlers who left Independence in May could reach the Willamette Valley by November. Despite the dangers, however, 5,000 emigrants arrived in Oregon between the years 1842 and 1845.

17. The Mormons, their origins, and their western settlement

In 1830, a book appeared, purporting to be a revelation of Jesus Christ to the natives of North America. It was called the *Book of Mormon*, and its promoter, Joseph Smith, claimed to have received it in the form of golden tablets from an angel on a hilltop in New York state. The tablets, Smith said, conveyed a revelation of the restored gospel, lost for centuries; and, he averred, he was the prophet of a restored church, called the Church of Jesus Christ of Latter Day Saints.

The Latter Day Saints, or the "Mormons," were not welcome in New York, and so they moved on to Kirtland, Ohio, then to Missouri, and then, in 1839, to Nauvoo, Illinois. In Nauvoo, Smith received a "revelation" that God wanted to reestablish polygamy. Whether for this or for the promise that good Mormon men would one day become gods, the Latter Day Saints won converts in both the northern states and in England. Their swift growth, however, and their peculiar religious practices earned them the keen dislike of their neighbors, and in 1844 non-Mormons attacked Nauvoo and killed Joseph Smith. Brigham Young, who took on the office of prophet, organized groups called "Avenging Angels" and for two years waged bitter war on the "gentiles."

In 1846, Brigham Young led his followers on a journey west to the "promised land." In July 1847, the pioneer band of saints reached the basin of the Great Salt Lake, then a part of Mexico. Under Young's autocratic command, the Mormons built irrigation canals to bring water from the surrounding mountains and established a system of small farms. Young provided for foreign and domestic missions and helped finance transatlantic and transcontinental immigration to Deseret, as the Mormons named their new home. By the end of 1848, 5,000 Mormons had settled in Deseret.

18. How Texas entered the union

Southerners, including John C. Calhoun, feared an independent Texas could not maintain the institution of slavery by itself; and if, as it was feared, Great Britain should annex Texas, slavery would end there. No fugitive slave agreement, as the South had with the North, would exist with an independent Texas; and if slavery were abolished in Texas, slaves in the states could easily escape there. Some southerners, too, thought admitting Texas would provide a "release valve" for the tensions created by the large slave population in the southern states. Too, Calhoun and other southerners feared the political dominance of the North. If no more slave states were created, they argued, the North would come to dominate not only the House of Representatives but the Senate as well. The growing number of antislavery "abolitionists" in the North wanted to keep Texas out of the union. President Martin Van Buren, however, opposed the annexation of Texas because he was engaged in delicate negotiations with Mexico at the time, and Mexico was very sensitive about the issue.. The annexation issue was brought before Congress in 1838 and was defeated after a three-week anti-annexation speech by Senator John Quincy Adams. When John

Tyler became president, he joined John C. Calhoun and other Democrats and pressed for the annexation of Texas. Tyler resorted to a constitutionally questionable move – Congress approved the annexation, not by passing a bill of annexation but through a joint resolution. On February 28, 1845, just a few days before he left office, Tyler informed Sam Houston that Congress had approved Texas' admission into the union.

19. How the Oregon Country became part of the United States

Oregon Country was vast western territory that included modern British Columbia, as well as the states of Washington, Oregon, and Idaho. In 1818, the United States and Great Britain agreed to a joint occupation of the territory. During the Texas annexation fight, John C. Calhoun suggested linking the annexation of Oregon with that of Texas in order to appease the Northerners. In 1844, President Taylor had approached British prime minister, Lord Aberdeen, with a plan to divide Oregon along the latitude of 49 degrees. Aberdeen, however, refused to give up Fort Vancouver, which lay south of that line, on the Columbia River, and so the talks came to nothing. In 1845, President James K. Polk said all of the Oregon Country (from latitude 54 degrees 40 minutes southward) should belong tot he United States and asked Congress to end the 1818 joint occupation agreement with Great Britain. These measures would threaten war with Great Britain. But Polk was then contemplating war with Mexico; so, when Lord Aberdeen suggested that Oregon be divided along latitude 49 degrees north to Puget Sound, Polk accepted the compromise, but Senate expansionists pushed for all of Oregon, declaring, "54 40 or Fight!" But, at last, on June 15, 1846, the Senate accepted the compromise.

20. "Manifest Destiny" and the events that led to the U.S. declaration of war on Mexico

President James K. Polk was convinced that it was the United States' "manifest destiny" to stretch from the Atlantic to the Pacific. The conviction that the country's boundaries should reach ever westward – that it had almost a divine mandate to do so – had seeped into the popular mind in the U.S. Rich lands lay in Oregon and in fabled California. Many thought the latter was not ruled well by the Mexicans, who couldn't realize its potential. California was ripe for the taking, and rather than let France or England take it (rumor said they wanted it), the United States must seize it.

President Polk wanted California, but the Mexican government had broken off diplomatic relations with the United States over Texas and so would pay no attention to Polk's proposals to buy California. Polk suggested that Mexico should give California to the United States in lieu of the debt payment the Mexican government owed American citizens. Polk said that Mexico should recognize the Río Grande as the southern boundary of Texas and sell New Mexico to the U.S. for $5 million. When Mexico refused this offer, Polk decided he would have to resort to war to get California.

Polk in July 1845 had sent General Zachary Taylor and a detachment of the regular army to the Nueces River in Texas to guard the border with Mexico. On January 13, 1846, when he had learned of Mexico's refusal, Polk ordered Taylor to cross the Nueces and proceed to the Río Grande. This was a provocative act, for Mexico had never recognized Texas' claim to the Río Grande boundary but insisted that everything between the Río Grande and the Nueces belonged to Mexico. By late March, Taylor was on the Río Grande and was blockading Matamoros, a city at on the south bank of the Río Grande and clearly within Mexico's borders. On April 25, Mexican cavalry had crossed the Río Grande and skirmished with United States dragoons, leaving several Americans dead. In May 1846, Polk asked for, and Congress granted, a declaration of war against Mexico.

21. The Bear Flag Revolt and John C. Frémont's role in it

The context of the Bear Flag Revolt is the division in *Californio* government. In the north, at Monterey, José Castro held the office of military *commandante general*, while in the south, in Los Angeles, Pío Pico occupied the office of civil governor. Pico and Castro mistrusted each other. They were on the verge of leading troops against each other. Castro had had to deal with John C. Frémont's alleged "topographical mission" into California. Frémont had resisted Castro's demand that he leave California. When finally he set out toward Oregon, Frémont received news that convinced him that he should return to the Sacramento River.

On May 30, 1846, Frémont sent two messengers out to rouse Anglo-American settlers to his camp on the Sacramento, claiming that armed Spaniards were conducting a violent expedition into the Sacramento River. He called "every free man" to come to his camp. About a week later, news reached Frémont that some men sent by General Castro had requisitioned 200 horses at the rancho of Mariano Guadalupe Vallejo in Sonoma. Without delay, a band of Frémont's men, under Ezekiel Merritt, rode out and, the next day, captured the horses at Murphy's Rancho, south of Sutter's fort. After

driving the horses to Frémont's camp, Merritt gathered 21 men and rode to Sonoma. At Sonoma, Merritt and his men took General Mariano Vallejo prisoner, thus beginning a full revolt of American settlers in the north. The revolt might have dissipated had it not been for William B. Ide, a Massachusetts Yankee, who organized the disparate band. On the very day of Vallejo's capture, Ide raised a flag – white, with a red flannel horizontal stripe at the bottom, a star in the upper left-hand corner, and a rather pig-like grizzly Bear image to the right of the star– and proclaimed the independent "California Republic." On July 4, 1846, Frémont arrived in Sonoma and the next day took command of the Bears, saying he would lead them in the struggle to "free" California from the "usurper" Castro. Though Frémont was acting illegally, the capture of Monterey by Commodore John Drake Sloat, commander of the United States Pacific squadron, on July 7, gave him legal cover. Mexico and the United States were at war.

22. American reaction to the Mexican-American War

States bordering the Mississippi welcomed the war, but the original 13 states did not. Elder statesmen in the South thought the annexation of Texas was enough. Calhoun, for one, rightly foresaw that opening up new territories west of Texas would revive the controversy over slavery in the territories. Antislavery opposed the war, which, they said, was nothing more than a grab for more slave territory. The Whigs generally opposed it, including the Illinois Whig congressman, Abraham Lincoln, who condemned it as immoral.

23. General Zachary Taylor's role in the war

Following the attack on his forces, General Zachary Taylor had crossed over the Río Grande and engaged General Mariano Arista in battle, and General Arista withdrew from Matamoros. Taylor occupied Matamoros and sent dispatches to newspapers in the U.S. announcing his victory. Then, for two months, "Old Rough and Ready," as Taylor was called, refused to move. He waited in Matamoros for supplies and reinforcements while thousands of his men died from measles and dysentery. In September, having received a few reinforcements, Taylor moved against Monterey in Sierra León, capturing the city after a three-day battle. Then advancing into Coahuila, he encamped at an exposed position near Saltillo – and remained there for the next four months. Displeased with Taylor's lack of progress, President Polk made General Winfield Scott overall commander of the war in Taylor's place.

24. Antonio López de Santa Anna's role in the war

In August 1846, an insurrection pushed Mexico's President Paredes from power and placed Gómez Farías and the Liberals again at the helm of government. Gómez Farías made Santa Anna overall commander of the Mexican army. By January 1847, Santa Anna was leading an army against Taylor at Saltillo. There Santa Anna and Taylor's armies clashed in a bloody battle in which the Mexicans gained an initial advantage but were soon mowed down by the superior firing power of the American guns. When night fell, Santa Anna withdrew, leaving his fires burning. The Americans, fearing a renewal of the attack the following day, were relieved next morning to find their enemy had withdrawn. Taylor did not order a pursuit. When he returned to Mexico City, Santa Anna removed Gómez Farías from office and, with a loan from the Church, led an army against General Winfield Scott, who had landed at Veracruz.

25. The course of General Taylor's invasion of Mexico

On March 9, 1847, Scott's forces, transported by naval ships, landed at Veracruz, which surrendered after a siege and bombardment

---

Key Terms at a Glance

junta: a group controlling a government, especially following a revolution

puros: a name given to the Mexican Liberals

fueros: traditional rights and privileges accorded to certain groups in society, such as (in Mexico) the Church and the military

Poder Conservador: in Mexico, a committee of citizens whose job it was to see that the executive, legislative, and judicial branches of the government did not encroach on each other

common law: a body of law that arises from custom or the custom of interpreting law based on precedent (judicial interpretations of written law)

Manifest Destiny: the conviction that the United States had almost a divine mandate to stretch from the Atlantic to the Pacific

lasting two weeks. From Veracruz, Scott marched to the fortified mountain pass of Cerro Gordo, where, with the help of Captain Robert E. Lee, he was able to flank the Mexican forces and force them to retreat. Scott then moved on Puebla, and from there, toward Mexico City. There, confusion reigned, for all Mexican parties mistrusted Santa Anna. But Scott's approach to the city proved difficult and bloody. United under Santa Anna, the Mexicans fought doggedly for every inch of ground. Always in the forefront of battle, Santa Anna however would brook no competition for glory even if it spelled defeat. For instance, he ordered General Gabriel Valencia, who held a strong position, to retreat. When Valencia refused, Santa Anna removed his own troops from Valencia's control, leaving the general to his fate – an ignominious defeat. On August 20, 1847, Mexicans suffered heavly losses in the battle of Churubusco, less than ten miles from Mexico City. When Santa Anna refused a truce that Scott offered on September 13, the Americans stormed and took the fortress of Chapultepec, and on the same night, broke through the walls of Mexico City. Santa Anna retired to Guadalupe while American forces and the desperate Mexicans engaged in bitter street fights. Finally, on the morning of September 14, 1847, the city government let fly the white flag.

26. Who the San Patricios were

The San Patricios were mostly Irish immigrants, but they included Germans, Italians, French, Scots, Poles, and even escaped American slaves in their number. Most of them were Catholic. They had signed up with the United States army to fight in Mexico, but their Protestant officers had treated these immigrants with undue harshness. The United States army provided

no Catholic chaplains, and some officers forced the Catholics to attend Protestant services. Though some of the San Patricios may have been attracted by Mexican offers of land if they deserted, others had decided that they could not fight for a Protestant against a Catholic country. They bravely fought at Churubusco and inflicted heavy losses on the Americans. At the battle's end, Americans captured 83 San Patricios, 72 of whom were court-martialed for desertion. Of that number, 50 were sentenced to be hanged, while 16 were to be flogged and branded on the cheek with the letter "D" – for deserter.

27. The Treaty of Guadalupe Hidalgo and what it entailed

Though resistance to the Americans continued, Manuel de la Peña y Peña, chief justice of the Mexican supreme court and the acting president, opened up negotiations with the U.S. A treaty was ratified by U.S. and Mexican representatives on February 2, 1848 at the town of Guadalupe Hidalgo, about 150 miles north of the capital. In the Treaty of Guadalupe Hidalgo, the only treaty in U.S. history to open with an invocation of God, Mexico agreed to cede Alta California and New Mexico (including Arizona, western Colorado, Utah, and Nevada) to the United States for $15 million and affirmed the Río Grande as the southern boundary of Texas. In return, the United States agreed to assume all unpaid debts owed by Mexico to American citizens. The treaty guaranteed the rights of Mexicans residing in the ceded territories. Their property, said the treaty, "shall be inviolably respected," and they "shall be maintained and protected in the free enjoyment of their liberty and property, and secured in the free exercise of their religion without restriction." Grants of land made by Mexico to individuals, said the treaty, shall "preserve the legal value which they may possess; and the grantees may cause their legitimate titles to be acknowledged before the American tribunals." By this treaty, Mexico lost more than half her territory.

Questions for Review

1. **What events or situations sparked the rebellion of 1828 in Mexico? What was the outcome of the rebellion?**

When Gómez Pedraza won the election of 1828, Santa Anna would not tolerate the victory, and unfurled the banner of rebellion. The Liberals won and Congress proclaimed Vincente Guerrero president.

2. **What did Gómez Farías do to cause the rebellion of 1834 in Mexico?**

As vice president to the absent President Santa Anna, Farías put through his radical agenda against the Church and the military, angering many people.

3. **Why were the Anglo-Americans in Texas so opposed to Mexican government? How did this opposition lead to rebellion in Texas?**

Anglo-Americans in Texas were opposed to Mexican government because it was foreign to them, did not provide trial by jury, and had no common law. The Mexican government, too, was inefficient. The Texians feared that the government would interfere with slavery in Texas. Anglo-Texans wanted to have their own government, so they rose up in revolt against the Mexican government.

4. **What is the significance of the Pastry War?**

The Pastry War made Santa Anna a hero, and he was able to take control of the government again and put down a rebellion.

5. **Briefly describe the condition of California under Mexican rule.**

California took the oath of allegiance to Mexico because they knew that if Spain did not hold Mexico it could not hold California. Yet most Californians remained royalist at heart. Under Mexican rule, California suffered from civil and violent struggles between contending parties.

6. **Who instigated the secularization of the California missions? What were their motives? What were the results of the secularization?**

When he became governor of California in 1825, Colonel José María Echeandía commenced a limited secularization of the missions. In 1830, Echeandía introduced a plan to secularize all the missions, but his successor as governor, Colonel Manuel Victoria, who had been sent to California by the conservative Anastasio Bustamante government in Mexico, halted Echeandía's plans.

Followng the overthrow of Victoria by the *Californios, t*he Liberal government of Gómez Farías sent General José Figueroa to California. Governor Figueroa came with the charge to secularize the missions by turning them into pueblos and giving their lands to the neophytes. In 1834, Figueroa, however, gave in to the demands of the California *diputación* and presented a plan that would turn half of the mission lands over to the Indians and half to the *Californios*, but this was not how things turned out. Not fully assimilated into European culture, most of the Mission Indians did not attempt to farm their lands, nor did they know how to manage them. In a few years, the mission lands, had become the possession of the *Californios*, while the mission Indians were scattered. The secularization of mission lands, along with the Mexican government's approval of more land grants to white settlers, increased the number of private ranchos in California. In 1835, the Mexican governor of California, Mariano Chico, informed the California government that the Mexican congress had suspended its earlier secularization decree and so nullified Figueroa's secularization act. But the *diputación* ignored Chico.

7. **Who were the "mountainy men" and what did they achieve in the American West?**

The mountainy men were hunters and trappers who pushed into the Great Plains and the mountains of the West in search of the haunts of the beaver. They explored much of the West and blazed trails that would serve emigrants moving west to Oregon and California.

8. **What is the Manifest Destiny? What did it entail for California and Oregon?**

Manifest Destiny was the conviction that the country's boundaries should reach ever westward to the Pacific, and that it had almost a divine mandate to do so.

9. **What was the Bear Flag Revolt, and what was John Charles Frémont's role it?**

While on an alleged topographical expedition in California, Frémont claimed claiming that armed Spaniards were conducting a violent expedition into the Sacramento River. Such false reports stirred up a movement among Anglo-Americans in California called the Bear Flag Revolt. In Sonoma, the Bears proclaimed an independent California republic.

10. **What events or situations led to the United States declaring war on Mexico?**

President Polk wanted California, but he did not want to go to war for it. He suggested that Mexico give California to the United States in lieu of a debt payment. The proud Mexicans thought it an insult to their honor. Finally Polk decided he would have to go to war in order to get California. In order to make it look like Mexico had started the war he sent General Zachary Taylor to cross the Nueces and proceed to the Rio Grande. Taylor did so and blockaded Matamoros. Then Mexican cavalry crossed the Río Grande and skirmished with American troops. Polk used this event to whip up war fury against Mexico, and Congress declared war.

11. **Summarize the provisions of the Treaty of Guadalupe Hidalgo.**

In the Treaty of Guadalupe Hidalgo, Mexico agreed to cede Alta California and New Mexico (including Arizona, western Colorado, Utah, and Nevada) to the United States for $15 million and affirmed the Río Grande as the southern boundary of Texas. In return, the United States agreed to assume all unpaid debts owed by Mexico to American citizens. The treaty guaranteed the rights of Mexicans residing in the ceded territories. Their property, said the treaty, "shall be inviolably respected," and they "shall be maintained and protected in the free enjoyment of their liberty and property, and secured in the free exercise of their religion without restriction." Grants of land made by Mexico to individuals, said the treaty, shall "preserve the legal value which they may possess; and the grantees may cause their legitimate titles to be acknowledged before the American tribunals." By this treaty, Mexico lost more than half her territory.

Ideas in Action

1. Explore why Mexico's government was so unstable in the first half of the 19th century? What form of government, do you think, would have brought stability to Mexico? Why?

2. Using a map of the United States, chart the routes taken by the mountainy men in the West.

3. Read the histories of some of the regions mentioned in the history of the mountainy men.

4. Read stories or life accounts of such men as David Crockett and Jim Bowie.

5. Stage a debate on the morality of the United States' declaration of war on Mexico in 1846. Constult the *Catechism of the Catholic Church*, paragraphs 2258-2330.

Sample Quiz I (pages 307-324)

Please answer the following in complete sentences.

1. How did Mexico become a British economic satellite?

2. How did Freemasonry contribute to the instability of the Mexican republic?

3. Identify the following:
   a. Vincente Guerrero
   b. Valentín Gómez Farías

4. How was Santa Anna a source of instability for the Republic of Mexico?

5. Identify the following:
   a. Sam Houston
   b. James Bowie
   c. David Crockett

6. Why was the Battle of the Alamo significant?

7. Why did California take the oath of allegiance to Spain?

8. Why did the California friars oppose secularization?

9. What was the result of secularization of the missions?

10. Give three reasons why the California Mission Indians grew discontented after 1811.

Answers to Sample Quiz I

Students' answers should approximate the following.

1. Mexico became a British economic satellite because it was deeply in debt to Great Britain and had no choice but to allow British business interests to acquire large portions of Mexico's trade and to permit British capital to develop mines for extracting the country's rich mineral wealth.

2. Though the creole *moderados* (moderates) dominated the congress, the influence of the Liberals, called *puros* or *Yorkistas* (because they followed the York Rite of Freemansonry), was growing. Mexican conservatives united ner Scottish rite masonry and were called *Esconcistas*. The factions brought instability to the new republican government.

3.
   a. A Liberal revolutionary in Mexico who joined forces with Agustín Iturbide in his revolution that had established Mexico's independence from Spain. Guerrero became president of Mexico after the revolution of 1828.
   b. Leader of the Liberals who served as vice president under Santa Anna and pushed through a radical agenda that angered the conservatives and caused the rebellion of 1834.

4. Santa Anna was a source of instability for the Republic of Mexico because he was a political chameleon, acting as champion of either the Liberals or conservatives when he sensed it was most likely to gain power. He would not take an active role in government when he was made president, but was always ready to overthrow an existing government.

5.
   a. Houston commanded the Texian army that defeated Santa Anna at San Jacinto. When Texas proclaimed its independence, Houston served as its first president.
   b. Frontiersman, an illegal slave smuggler, and land speculator who died during the Battle of the Alamo. He is attributed with the invention of the Bowie knife.
   c. A legendary frontiersman, Crockett had fought in the Creek Wars and had served in Congress as a representative from Tennessee, where he distinguished himself as an opponent of Jackson's Indian removal policy. When in 1835 he lost his congressional seat, he left Tennessee, and went to Texas. He fought at the Alamo, where he died.

6. The Alamo was significant because it gave the Texian revolutionaries a battle cry in their struggle against Mexico.

7. California took the oath of allegiance to Mexico because they knew that if Spain did not hold Mexico it could not hold California.

8. The California friars opposed secularization of the missions because the California Indians were very primitive when Serra arrived, and they judged that enough time had not passed to allow them to civilize the Indians fully.

9. Not fully assimilated into European culture, most of the Mission Indians did not attempt to farm their lands, nor did they know how to manage them. In a few years, the mission lands, had become the possession of the *Californios*, while the mission Indians were scattered.

10. Reasons why the California Indians were discontented:
    a. Indian laborers had borne the burden of feeding the soldiers and their families, and they were weary.
    b. The soldiers, who had less fear of the friars, had grown more careless toward the Indians and at times mistreated them cruelly.
    c. The fact that the unconverted Indians, or gentiles, having learned the use of the horse, had grown emboldened in their attitude towards the Spanish population led the neophytes to greater resistance and discontent.

Sample Quiz II (pages 324-341)

Please answer the following in complete sentences.

1. Who were the mountainy men?

2. Identify the following:
   a. Thomas Fitpatrick
   b. Jedediah Smith

3. Who were the Mormons?

4. Why did Southerners want Texas annexed?

5. What was Manifest Destiny?

6. Why did the United States go to war with Mexico?

7. What was John C. Frémont's role in the Bear Flag Revolt?

8. What are some reason why Americans opposed the Mexican war?

9. What was Santa Anna's role in the war?

10. Why did the San Patricios decide to fight for Mexico instead of the United States?

Answers to Sample Quiz II

Students' answers should approximate the following.

1. The mountainy men were hunters and trappers who pushed into the Great Plains and the mountains of the West in search of the haunts of the beaver.

2.
   a. A trapper and hunter who discovered the famous "South Pass" through the Rockies.
   b. A trapper and hunter who made extensive explorations through California, Nevada, and Oregon.

3. The Mormons were followers of Joseph Smith, a "prophet" who claimed to have received the *Book of Mormon*, a revelation of the restored gospel, from an angel on a hilltop in New York State.

4. Southerners wanted Texas annexed for a number of reasons. They feared feared an independent Texas could not maintain the institution of slavery by itself. If Great Britain should annex Texas, slavery would end there. If slaver were abolished in Texas, slaves in the states could easily escape there. They also feared the political dominance of the North if no new slave states could be admitted into the union.

5. Manifest Destiny was the conviction that the country's boundaries should reach ever westward, and that it had almost a divine mandate to do so to expand all the way to the Pacific.

6. President Polk wanted California, but the Mexican government would pay no attention to Polk's proposals to buy California. Polk suggested that Mexico should give California to the United States in lieu of the debt payment the Mexican government owed American citizens. When Mexico refused this offer, Polk decided he would have to resort to war to get California.

7. While on an alleged topographical expedition in California, Frémont claimed that armed Spaniards were conducting a violent expedition into the Sacramento River. He took command of the Bears and said he would lead them in the struggle to "free" California from the "usurper" Castro.

8. Americans opposed the Mexican war for several reasons. Elder statesmen in the South thought the annexation of Texas was enough. Some foresaw that opening up new territories west of Texas would revive the controversy over slavery in the territories. Antislavery opposed the war, which, they said, was nothing more than a grab for more slave territory. Some thought the war immoral.

9. Santa Anna led an army against General Taylor at Saltillo. When Scott landed at Veracruz, Santa deposed the Mexican president and became overall commande of the Mexican army. He contested Scott's advance on Mexico City.

10. The San Patricios decided to fight for Mexico instead of the United States because they could not fight for a Protestant against a Catholic country. The had been mistreated in the U.S. army on account of their religion.

Essays

Instructions to be given to the students: Write in complete sentences. Underline your thesis. Give three supports or examples that explain why you think what you do and that support your thesis.

1. Describe the events that led up to the Mexican-American war.

2. How did Manifest Destiny influence the western expansion and the annexation of Texas and Oregon?

3. Describe Mormonism. What role did it play in America's westward expansion?

Sample Test

Please answer the following in complete sentences.

I. Short Essay – Answer two of the following:

1. What were Texian complaints about Mexican rule?

2. Explain the secularization of the missions and the results of secularization.

3. What events led to the declaration of war on Mexico?

4. Explain the Treaty of Guadalupe Hidalgo and what it entailed.

II. Short Answer:

1. Why did Prime Minister Canning recognize Mexico's independence?

2. Why did Spain encourage immigration from the U.S. to Texas?

3. Why did Santa Anna recognize Texas independence?

4. Why did John Calhoun suggest linking the annexation of Oregon to that of Texas?

Answer Key to the Chapter Test

Students' answers should approximate the following:

I.

1. Anglo-Americans in the Mexican territory of Tejas complained about Mexican rule for several reasons. The great upheavals in Mexico, along with the inefficiency of Mexican officials, annoyed and frustrated them. Then there was the sheer foreignness of Mexican law, which did not provide for trial by jury and had no common law. Anglo-Texians wanted to have their own government. Ardent federalists, the Texians, along with many *Tejanos*, bitterly disliked Mexican president Bustamante's centralist regime. Texian leaders, including Stephen Austin, were Masons and had, in 1828, petitioned for the establishment of the York rite in Texas – thus showing their support for the supposedly Liberal Santa Anna's rebellion. Among the chief motivations for Texian discontent with Mexican rule was the fear that the Mexican government might enforce the 1827 decree abolishing slavery even in Texas. Texians hoped to reap great wealth from slave labor and they feared that talk of emancipation would inspire slave revolts.

2. Secularization had always been an expectation of the mission system. The friars' function was not only to Christianize the Indians but to educate them to take their full place in Spanish society. When that was completed, the government would turn over mission lands to the Indians and replace the friars with secular clergy. In 1813, the Spanish *Cortes* had ruled that all missions ten years old or older should be turned over to the bishop "without excuse or pretext whatever, in accordance with the laws" – that is, they were to be secularized. Under the secularization plan, half of the mission lands were to go to the Indians and half to the *Californios*, but this was not how things turned out. Not fully assimilated into European culture, most of the Mission Indians did not attempt to farm their lands, nor did they know how to manage them. In a few years, the mission lands, had become the possession of the *Californios*, while the mission Indians were scattered. The secularization of mission lands, along with the Mexican government's approval of more land grants to white settlers, increased the number of private ranchos in California.

3. President James K. Polk was convinced that it was the United States' "manifest destiny" to stretch from the Atlantic to the Pacific. The conviction that the country's boundaries should reach ever westward – that it had almost a divine mandate to do so – had seeped into the popular mind in the U.S. Many thought California was not ruled well by the Mexicans, who couldn't realize its potential. California was ripe for the taking, and the United States must seize it. President Polk wanted California, but the Mexican government had broken off diplomatic relations with the United States over Texas and so would pay no attention to Polk's proposals to buy California. Polk suggested that Mexico should give California to the United States in lieu of the debt payment the Mexican government owed American citizens. Polk said that Mexico should recognize the Río Grande as the southern boundary of Texas and sell New Mexico to the U.S. for $5 million. When Mexico refused this offer, Polk decided he would have to resort to war to get California. Polk sent Taylor to the Río Grande. Taylor did so and blockaded Matamoros. Then Mexican cavalry crossed the Río Grande and skirmished with American troops. Polk used this event to whip up war fury against Mexico, and Congress declared war.

4. In the Treaty of Guadalupe Hidalgo, Mexico agreed to cede Alta California and New Mexico (including Arizona, western Colorado, Utah, and Nevada) to the United States for $15 million and affirmed the Río Grande as the southern boundary of Texas. In return, the United States agreed to assume all unpaid debts owed by Mexico to American citizens. The treaty guaranteed the rights of Mexicans residing in the ceded territories. Their property, said the treaty, "shall be inviolably respected," and they "shall be maintained and protected in the free enjoyment of their liberty and property, and secured in the free exercise of their religion without restriction." Grants of land made by Mexico to individuals, said the treaty, shall "preserve the legal value which they may possess; and the grantees may cause their legitimate titles to be acknowledged before the American tribunals."

II.

1. When Spain, in a confederacy of European nations called the Holy Alliance, had threatened to reconquer Mexico, Canning recognized Mexico's independence.

2. Spain encouraged immigration from the U.S. to Texas because it hoped by this means to keep the United States from seizing the largely unpopulated territory.

3. Santa Anna recognized Texas independence to secure his freedom after he ws captured in the Battle of San Jacinto.

4. Calhoun suggested linking the annexation of Oregon with that of Texas in order to appease the Northerners who wanted a free state if Texas were admitted as a slave state.

CHAPTER 15: On the Eve of Disunion

Chapter Overview

- By the 1850s in the northern United States, increased productivity and industrialism and the growth of eastern cities came with the dawn of the canals and the railroads. Manufacturing was accelerated with the invention of the sewing machine, the mechanical reaper, and the telegraph.

- By 1850, immigrants were flooding into the country, increasing the number of people in the cities. The immigrants often succumbed to poverty, disease, and violence. Some Irish immigrants became involved in politics, while many Germans founded their own communities. By 1850 New York had become the most democratic state when, before, it was the most aristocratic. The New York Democratic Party had fallen under the sway of what became known as the Albany Regency. The New York Democratic Party system became the model for all party systems across the union.

- The sectarian spirit took hold of the North and gave American Protestantism an exotic feel. Many Protestants formed new sects.

- Reform-minded Christians began to form various societies to improve the spiritual and material condition of the poor and society in general, including temperance, women's suffrage, women's dress, and asylums for the mentally insane.

- A movement arose in the first half of the 19th century that called for free public schools, partly to provide an education for all Americans, and partly to defend the Protestants against "papistry."

- Some reformers sought to create Utopias in order to reform society. These Utopias included Robert Owen's New Harmony, Charles François Marie Fourier's phalanxes, and George Ripley's Brook Farm. All of these experiments eventually failed.

- The spirit of sectarianism influenced the New England Renaissance in literature.

- Life in the South was very different from that of the North. The South not only had slavery but lacked the restlessness and spirit of growth that characterized the North. Southerners viewed themselves as conservatives and sought to preserve tradition to form an aristocratic society. The ideal of the southern gentleman was one who's wealth existed to support a particular mode of life, who was chivalric, hospitable, and faithful to his kindred.

- There were several classes of whites in the South: the gentleman, the yeoman farmer, the "poor white trash," and the "hillbillies" of the mountains. Literacy was low in the South, and religion was not as affected by a wild sectarianism. In politics, the interests of the people held sway.

- Slavery was a common institution in the South. Some slave owners treated their slaves well, while others were cruel and sadistic. By 1831 the Virginia legislature was considering a gradual abolition of slavery, which was voted down. In the same year, Nat Turner, a field slave, led a short but bloody insurrection against the whites in Virginia.

◆ In 1848 in California, a carpenter named John Marshall found a lump of gold while building a mill on the American River. His find prompted thousands of people to come to California to find gold. California grew very quickly in size, and chaos reigned.

◆ In 1850 California became a state. Californians did not take kindly to the "foreign" Hispanics, Chinese, Japanese, and Mexicans, and the state legislature placed a miner's tax on all foreigners, forcing Mexicans to leave the state.

◆ Many *Californios* held land grants; but since the boundaries of these grants were ambiguous, Congress passed a law that required a federal board or commission to approve all land grant titles. *Californios* had to sell off large tracts of their lands to carry on litigation.

◆ The Indians of California fared far worse than the *Californios*. The Yankees regarded them as useless, and often murdered them. Through the remainder of the 19th century, the Indian population in California dwindled significantly.

What Students Should Know

1. Social life the 19th-century American North by 1850

By 1850, Americans were living as they had at the turn of the century. Most engaged in subsistence farming – their produce went primarily to support the family; only the excess was sold on the market. Most others – merchants, storekeeprers, craftsmen, and small bankers – dwelt in the small towns and villages that dotted the countryside. Life in the North was a buzz of activity. Foreign visitors to America commented on how Americans had little regard for leisure or entertainments. The Puritan ethic prevailed almost everywhere, since much of the immigration into the old Northwest had come from New England. Others peopled the Northwest too – Pennsylvanians, Kentuckians and, increasingly, German and Scandinavian immigrants. New England's culture held sway. With the Indian threat pushed westward across the Mississippi, the states of the Old Northwest had grown more settled, civilized, and urbanized. The Old Northwest, by 1850 called the "Near West," prospered in trade and agriculture and grew in population.

2. Material progress in the North by 1850

Though, in 1850, most freight still traveled by way of canals, railroad traffic had been increasing. By 1856, rails connected New York City with Chicago and Philadelphia and Pittsburgh. Improved transportation allowed for increased industrial output. In the first half of the 19th century, over 1,000 textile factories rose along rivers to power large looms that wove cotton into cloth. Wool factories increased at a similar rate. Iron production in the United States grew more slowly. Other factories in the North produced machine tools, firearms, furniture, wooden clocks, and other products. Yankees produced a number of inventions: the sewing machine, the mechanical reaper, the electric telegraph (invented by Samuel F. B. Morse in 1832). Manufacture occurred in large factories and in home-based manufacture. With increased manufacture and transportation came the growth of eastern cities. Between 1820 and 1850, the combined populations of New York, Philadelphia, Baltimore, and Boston grew from 293,500 to over 943,000. Population increase in the cities during the 1840s outstripped westward migration in numbers and importance to the life of the nation. Though many native-born Americans moved to the cities, a goodly percentage of urban growth can be attributed to immigration of foreigners from England, Germany, and, especially, famine-ravaged Ireland.

3. Immigration in the first half of the 19th century

The United States had attracted immigrants from foreign countries since independence from England. By 1850, however, immigrants were flooding into the country when, only 30 years before, their numbers were a mere trickle. These immigrants were mostly Irish, followed by Germans, with a smattering of English. In the 1840s, however, the number of immigrants nearly tripled. Among the causes of increased immigration were the Irish potato famine in 1845 and wars and revolutions in Europe. Many of these immigrants came to America to escape dire poverty; some, such as the skilled craftsmen, came because they had fallen on hard times in their countries; others, because they thought that in America they would find greater opportunities for social advancement. Some, particularly Germans, sought a greater freedom than they had in their homeland to practice their religion.

4. How immigrants were received in America

In New York harbor, where most immigrants arrived, both native born Americans and, sometimes, even their own countrymen who had come over earlier, cheated and swindled them. Despised by both natives and earlier immigrants, the new immigrants often faced physical assault, beatings, and even murder. Forced to take the lowest-paying, most laborious, and often most dangerous work, immigrants dwelt in the worst parts of the city. Great numbers of immigrants died of disease, from bad liquor, or from being ground-down by heavy labor.

Americans blamed immigrants for disease, crime, the poverty of their ghettoes, and prostitution. Natives complained that a very large percentage of immigrants were unskilled laborers who only swelled the ranks of those requiring public aid. This was true, but these unskilled laborers also provided a pool of cheap labor for the capitalist class. Immigrants were guilty of violence against natives; but the American-born were often the instigators of violence, in part because large number of both German and Irish immigrants were Catholic.

Nativist fear gave rise to a new political party, called the American Republican Party. The American Republicans wanted tighter restrictions on immigration and a requirement that a foreigner live 21 years in the United States before he could apply for citizenship. (The law at the time required only five years' residence.) Anglo-American culture had a hard time not only with the Irish, but with the Germans as well. German immigrants were farmers and artisans; some were Liberal political refugees and intellectuals. German-speaking colonies arose in New York, Baltimore, Cincinnati, and St. Louis. By 1850, Milwaukee was predominately German. Germans and Scandinavian immigrants settled the land and farmed.

Germans were unwilling to assimilate often because they distrusted and feared the corrosive moral and individualistic tendencies of American culture. German religious colonies, both Protestant and Catholic, sought to shield themselves from a culture which they thought threatened the integrity of their own religious cultures.

5. Character of city life in the North to 1850

The growth of industry and the influx of foreign immigrants dramatically changed the character of the great northern cities. From relatively small provincial towns they grew into teeming metropolises and reverberated with a confusion of tongues. In the great cities of New York, Boston, and Philadelphia, opulence and middle-class respectability contrasted with abject poverty and destitution. The vast underclass lived in sordid conditions. Riots, caused by racial, religious, or class strife, were common, especially in Philadelphia, which was notorious for its sometimes near-lawless conditions. Northern American cities were torn by an acquisitiveness that extended even to religion. Poor neighborhoods were filled with drunkenness, filth, and prostitution; epidemics were rampant.

New York was a city that seemed to go through constant changes. It was a business center, and New Yorkers engaged in speculation, trade, and manufacturing. It had little truck with literature or the arts, though Edgar Allen Poe spent some time in New York as a literary editor. The poet William Cullen Bryant lived there, as did Walt Whitman. Samuel F.B. Morse founded the National Academy of Design in the city. Other notable New York literati were Washington Irving, James Fennimore Cooper, and Herman Melville.

Boston had about it a conservative and elegant staidness. Among Boston's literary figures were Henry Wordsworth Longfellow, who became America's favorite poet; Oliver Wendell Holmes, Sr.; and the poet James Russell Lowell.

6.   The character of political parties

The New York Democratic Party developed the structure that became typical of American political parties. The structure was in some ways not very democratic, though its leadership, the "Regency," protested that it

fought for "the people" against organized wealth. Nevertheless, it insisted that the people, for their own good, had to be controlled by powerful party "bosses." Each locality had its own caucus, and caucuses sent representatives to county conventions that, in turn, sent representatives to state conventions. There were also district conventions for congressional elections, and every four years, national conventions where the party would vote on its platform and choose its candidate for president. The strength of the caucus system was that it was able to bring to prominence rural leaders who might otherwise have had no opportunity to enter politics. But in the cities the caucuses were dominated by powerful bosses and were riddled with corruption.

7.   The development of Tammany Hall

Political bosses and corruption became the notorious marks of Tammany Hall, Aaron Burr's old Republican political "club" and the power base of the Democratic Party in New York City. No sooner had the New York state legislature passed a law permitting universal manhood suffrage (the right of all male citizens to vote) in 1827, than Tammany Hall began recruiting immigrants right off the boat. Party representatives would help immigrants find work and lodging and, in a matter of days, rush them through the naturalization process that, by federal law, was supposed to take five years. Tammany Hall and the New York City Democratic Party became dominated by Irish.

8.   The development of American religion

The region of central New York state along the Erie Canal was called "The Burned-over District" because it had experienced so many fiery religious revivals. Central New York also witnessed the birth of odd religious movements that would give American Protestantism a rather exotic look. Joseph Smith, founder of the Mormon sect, came from central New York. Mother Ann Lee of New Lebanon, New York, said God had revealed to her that the original sin was Adam's "knowing" of Eve, who founded colonies of men and women, who lived together in celibacy – the "Universal Friend," or "Shaker" communities. William Miller of Hampton, New York, said that Christ would return on October 22, 1843, and he convinced thousands to sell their goods, don white robes, and so await the advent of Christ – the Second Coming – on hilltops and rooftops. These were called Millerites or Adventists. John Humphrey Noyes of Vermont believed the Second Coming had already occurred and the Kingdom of God was already present on earth. At Oneida, New York, he founded a community where there was no marriage; instead, men and women indulged in "free love." The Oneida community included communal ownership of all property, common labor, and the common raising of children. Beginning in 1848 the Fox sisters of Rochester, New York, held *séances* in which they claimed they could communicate with spirits of the dead. This "Spiritism" spread throughout the country.

Revivalism still held sway in New York and throughout the North. Evangelist Charles Grandison Finney gave frontier revivalism a new twist by toning down its extreme emotionalism and injecting into it a concern for justice and the social order. Henry Ward Beecher, first in Indianapolis and later in New York, attacked corrupt judges from the pulpit and ardently denounced slavery.

In New England, Unitarianism was growing. Unitarians denied the central Christian doctrines of the Incarnation and the Trinity because they did not think them "rational" to the Unitarian. Unitarianism insisted on the unity of God; and against sin and grace, Unitarians taught the radical goodness of man and his ability to improve himself by his natural powers alone.

9. **Transcendentalism and the New England Renaissance**

Discontent with traditional New England Protestantism, Ralph Waldo Emerson became a Unitarian minister. Later abandoning the ministry altogether, Emerson became a sort of lay preacher for a movement called Transcendentalism. In his popular speeches and essays, Emerson emphasized that every individual could become enlightened and improved by his own efforts alone. He taught that "God is in every man" and that "life is an ecstasy."

Emerson's thought had a profound effect on the antebellum North and led to what is called the "New England Renaissance." Prominent among the Transcendentalists was Henry David Thoreau, the author of *Walden* (1854), a description of, and meditation on, his time spent in a small cabin on Walden Pond outside Concord, Massachusetts. Thoreau was a naturalist. He believed men had to simplify their lives to be aware of the world around them; only thus could they discover what is essential to human happiness and contentment. His essay, "On Civil Disobedience," written after a night spent in jail for refusing to pay his taxes (in protest of the Mexican-American War), would in future years inspire revolutionaries against oppressive regimes worldwide.

Though never a true Transcendentalist, Nathaniel Hawthorne, a native of Salem, Massachusetts, was associated with the movement. His short stories and novels explore the darker aspects of New England Puritanism.

10. American reform movements

In the first half of the 19th century, some American Christians turned their attention from mere soul saving and interior religion to engagement in crusades to right the wrongs of society. Missionary societies formed to spread religion among the lower classes but aimed as well to inculcate in them the values of the middle class, such as cleanliness. Reform-minded Christians formed various societies to improve the spiritual and material condition of the poor.

Other reform movements were not purely religious in character. One of the most influential was the movement to abolish slavery; another was Temperance. A vocal minority began to push for legislation forbidding the production, importation, possession, and use of alcoholic beverages. Between 1846 and 1856, several states in the North and the West passed laws either restricting or prohibiting entirely the sale and use of alcohol. Many of the women involved in Temperance were also advocates for women's suffrage, a movement that began in Seneca Falls, New York, in 1848. Leaders of this movement were Lucy Stone and Susan Brownell Anthony.

Two closely allied movements were anti-death penalty and prison reform. The former was partially successful – Maine abolished the death penalty in 1837, as did Rhode Island in the 1850s. The prison reform movement sought to make prisons more humane and to direct their efforts towards reform rather than punishment. Dorothea Lynde Dix of Maine began a campaign to reform insane asylums. Between 1845 and 1852 hospitals for the insane were founded both in the North and in nine southern states, and Dix convinced Queen Victoria and Pope Pius IX to reform asylums in Great Britain and the Papal States.

11. Horace Mann and the Common School Movement

Churches – both Catholic and Protestant – had been operating most schools in America, whether elementary, secondary or collegiate. In the early 19th century, there were more secondary academies and colleges in the South than in the North and almost all of them charged fees. In New England, some elementary and even secondary schools were free.

A growing number of people became convinced that the state should provide free schools for all citizens. Among these was Horace Mann, chairman of the Massachusetts board of education. Mann believed that no one, regardless of wealth, should go without education. He also believed that religious instruction – particularly Bible reading –should be part of the school day. To avoid a public espousal of the tenets of any one religious group, Mann said instruction should be in the "common truths" of Christianity alone – something rather like Unitarianism. It was for this reason that groups like the Episcopalians, the Presbyterians, and the Lutherans opposed Mann's nonsectarian schools. They supported, not free "common" schools, but public support of denominational schools. In 1841, John Hughes, the Catholic bishop of New York, led the fight for public funding of Catholic parochial schools. But other Protestant groups, like the Methodists, Baptists and Congregationalists, supported state-funded nonsectarian "common" schools. In part, this was because of nativist reaction to the Catholic Church. They opposed state funding of denominational schools because they did not want to fund Catholic as well as Protestant schools. Gradually, Protestants began to view free public schools as a defense against "papistry."

Despite opposition, the principles of the common school movement spread. Gradually many states provided free public elementary schools for all children, and after a time, free public secondary schools as well. But the Catholic and Missouri-synod Lutheran parochial school systems continued.

12. The founding of utopian communities

Some reformers were not content just to tinker with existing society but wanted to erect perfect communities that could be a example to all the world of how mankind should live. Such reforms were working to establish a Utopia. Unlike the communities founded by Noyes or the Shakers, however, many of the new Utopian communities were not religious in inspiration; they were founded on the conviction that men could recreate their world by their own natural powers, without God.

Among these Utopian communities was one founded in 1825 by Robert Owen – New Harmony, Indiana. At New Harmony, all land and the means of production were held in common. In order to learn more "enlightened" ways of behaving and thinking, children were raised and educated apart from their parents. Religion was to have no part at New Harmony and, after a time, Owen declared even marriage to be an anachronism. The community met its demise in 1828.

George Ripley founded the Institute of Agriculture and Education at Brook Farm, Massachusetts in 1841. He wished, he said, "to prepare a society of liberal, intelligent, and cultured persons, whose relations with each other would permit a more wholesome and simple life than can be led amidst the

pressure of our competitive institutions." Brook Farm became a haven for young Transcendentalists. Young farmers, seamstresses, and mechanics, along with intellectuals and artists, formed the community. Brook Farm concentrated much energy on education, trying to stimulate childrens' imaginations and expand their reasoning and intuitive faculties. Work on the farm was mixed with study; leisure time was enlivened by plays, concerts, poetry, and dramatic readings. Adults cultivated a spirit of concern for one another. Eventually, Brook Farm dispersed after a great fire in 1847.

13. Cultural differences between the North and South

Among the causes between the differences of North and South was the presence of slavery in the South. But slavery alone did not account for these differences. There cultural and economic causes as well. The Puritan spirit of New England but, more importantly, the New England mindset, dominated the North, along with the New England social and political organization. Puritanism had always implied a questioning and rejection of tradition and custom that led many New Englanders away from Puritanism's more rigid doctrines into Unitarianism and other systems; but the native distrust of received tradition remained and had been intensified by democracy. This spirit spurred emigration and induced men to become merchants and manufacturers. Though the North still remained largely agrarian, industrial concerns and interest in making money were becoming dominant there – even in agriculture. This was evident even in agriculture, where farmers were becoming speculators, buying farms only to improve them and sell them at a higher price.

Though the South had undergone its pioneer phase, and Southerners were still pushing west, yet throughout much of the South the pioneering spirit left behind a culture characterized by settlement and a sleepiness that contrasted with the rabid ferment of the North. Unlike in the North, where people seemed constantly on the move, families in the South settled down and became identified with the regions in which they lived. This rootedness in a place begat pride of family. In contrast to the North, the South was committed to s society conceived along the lines of traditional European arrangements. The South had rich agricultural lands, and this fact encouraged southerners to farming rather than trade and manufacture.

Town dwellers were relatively few in the South, for the simple reason that, unlike the North, towns were few and far between. The only cities of any size were Richmond, Virginia; Charleston, South Carolina; Atlanta, Georgia; and New Orleans, Louisiana. The rest were small towns or mere meeting places (such as churches or courthouses) for the surrounding farm families.

14.   The effect of cotton growing on the South

Cotton growing dominated a great deal of the South, from South Carolina into Georgia, throughout the black soil lands of the Gulf states into Texas, up the Mississippi, and along the Red River. Eli Whitney's invention of the cotton gin had allowed cotton growing to spread across the continent and made cotton the largest export, not only of the South, but of all the United States. By 1860, cotton made up two-thirds of all U.S. exports. This wealth of cotton helped keep the South an agricultural land. Growers did not invest money in trade or manufactures, or even in improving the buildings on their sometimes

vast plantations. Because cotton growing quickly depleted the soil, plantation owners were continually investing in new lands to replace the exhausted ones. As long as new lands were there for the taking, few cotton growers concerned themselves with wise management of the soil, and this contributed to the move westward, into the Gulf states and Texas. Too, the cotton gin had made slavery profitable, so much of a plantation owner's profits went into buying new slaves to work his expanding domain. The non-cotton southern states became supply depots for the cotton states, providing them with food, mules, and more black slave labor.

15.   The aristocratic ideal of the South

The people of the South regarded themselves as conservative and preservers of tradition. In particular, they saw themselves as carrying on the traditions of European, specifically English, aristocratic society – even to the point that many southern gentlemen believed themselves not merely descendants in spirit, but also in blood to English "cavaliers." Two books contributed to this belief: *The Cavaliers of Virginia*, written in 1832 by William A. Caruthers, and *Lettres sur l'Amérique du Nord*, written by Michel Chevalier in 1836. Chevalier argued that while northern Americans descended from Oliver Cromwell's Puritan Roundheads, the settlers of Virginia came from the cavaliers who followed the Stuart king, Charles I. This was not true; most southerners descended from English, Scots, and Irish of the middle and lower classes; others came north from England into America as indentured servants, scarcely above the status of slaves. The South actually had few "old families." Even most rich landowners, especially in the Gulf states, had been up-and-coming men who had made it rich on cotton. Some were even transplanted Yankees.

Yet, even though they were not blood descendants of European gentry, many a southerner strove to become an aristocrat. Southern society was a conscious attempt to continue Old World European social and cultural traditions in the New World. Since aristocracy was part of these traditions, it too had to be transplanted in American soil. The aristocrat was seen as different from the rich northern merchant, speculator, or industrialist. The southern aristocrat, it was thought, was wealthy, but he did not "chase the Almighty Dollar" like his northern counterparts. In fact, according to the southern aristocratic ideal, while wealth was necessary for one to live the leisurely life of a gentleman, wealth did not make him a gentleman. Unlike in the North, where the patterns of life and the social order were continually being altered to accommodate wealth-making, in the South wealth existed to support a particular model of life.

"Chivalry" summed up those traits that made a man a gentleman in southern eyes. The southern gentleman was to cultivate refined manners. He was to foster the spirit of *noblesse oblige* by which he showed kindness and deference to inferiors. He was to be hospitable towards guests and strangers. He was to show a lofty respect for women, at least white women. The southern gentleman's sense of honor could brook no insult to his name or family. A duel to the death was the proper way to erase an insult, though many resorted to less noble avenues of revenge, such as horse-whipping or stabbing. Though he could tolerate a good deal of laziness or shiftlessness from his "domestics," the southern gentleman could not countenance a slave who crossed him or resisted his will. Honor demanded that a gentleman aid both his rich and poor

kinsmen, even those distantly related to him. A southern gentleman's fidelity to family was to find its fulfillment in love for his country. He was to have a lofty public spirit that would compel him to military service or to a run for the legislature.

16. The reality behind the ideal

The reality of southern life rarely lived up to the aristocratic ideal. Except for a very few, southern gentlemen had little time for leisure. Rather, he was occupied with the affairs of his plantation and with the responsibilities arising from owning many slaves. Human weakness, too, and the inability fully to come to terms with the fact that southern society depended on the misery of men condemned to unending, involuntary servitude compromised the southern aristocratic ideal. The southern gentleman did not love slavery; but he saw it as a necessary foundation for the sort of life he cherished. This was not the only reason he defended slavery, but it was an important one

17. Southern social classes

Only about 15,000 southern families could be called "gentry"; yet, their ideals set the tone for southern society. To greater or lesser degrees, most southern whites followed the code of chivalry espoused by the gentry. Most southern white families belonged to the class of yeomen farmers. Such farmers owned their own land and the buildings on them. They raised cash crops – tobacco, sugar cane, or cotton – and grazed cattle, kept hogs, and grew much of their daily food. The farmer worked in the fields, alongside the half dozen or so slaves he might own; these shared their master's dinner, often at the same table with their master's family. But while many yeomen farmers were slave owners, thousands more were not. Most southern whites owned no slaves. Unlike the great planters, who relied on New York banks for loans to buy land and slaves, the yeoman farmer in the South lived fairly independently. The yeoman farmer and his family lived in a log cabin or a simple frame house. Like the gentry, the yeoman farmer did not read much beyond the Bible and the newspaper, if he read at all; schools of any sort were scarce in the South. The yeoman's entertainment was outdoor sports, hunting, and fishing.

Below the yeomen farmers was a class of people derisively called "poor white trash," "crackers," and other unfortunate names, who accounted for less than ten percent of the population of the South. Despised by more respectable whites, these illiterate, unskilled, and uncultured folks despised and envied their "betters" in turn. They hated blacks, many of whom lived in more dignity and orderliness than the "rednecks." They lived in tiny cabins with dirt floors, and had a bad diet.

Few foreign immigrants came to the South. Unwilling to compete with slave labor, or to be placed on the same social level as black labor, most foreign immigrants chose to settle in the North. The absence of manufacturing centers in the South needing cheap labor was another factor that kept many immigrants from settling there.

Though sometimes confused with "poor white trash," the mountaineers, or "hillbillies" of the South were an entirely different sort of people. Fiercely independent, they lived in the mountain valleys or on the hillsides of the Appalachians and, westward, in the Ozarks. There they subsisted by farming small plots of corn and by hunting and fishing.

18. Literature and learning in the South
Southern literary tastes tended toward the Romantic and medieval – such as the novels and poetry of Sir Walter Scott. The antebellum South experienced no renaissance of literature like that of New England and New York, though Edgar Allen Poe was a southerner, as was William Gilmore Simms, the writer of ten romances, including the historical novel, *The Yemassee*. The sparseness of southern literary works may be because the southern genius had long been turned toward political writing. The antebellum South did however produce a number of gentleman amateur scientists, including John James Audubon, author of *The Birds of America* and *The Quadrupeds of North America*, Dr. Edmund Ravenel of Charleston, a leading authority on shells, and Henry Ravenel, who published a book on fungi in 1853. The Georgia planter, Louis Le Conte, kept a botanical garden at his plantation. He was the father of the famous geologist, Joseph Le Conte. Edmund Ruffin studied soil chemistry and published a book on the subject in 1832. Ruffin agitated for better methods of cultivation to restore the fruitfulness of Virginia's tidewater soils. Finally, United States naval commander, Matthew Fontaine Maury of Virginia, published a highly respected and definitive book, *The Physical Geography of the Seas*, in 1855.

19. The character of southern religion
Southern religion had a decidedly democratic flavor. The Protestant Episcopal Church (the U.S. branch of the Anglican Communion) attracted mostly members of the old families and had since the Second Great Awakening remained stagnant in numbers. Except for Maryland and Louisiana, and outside of the larger cities, few Catholics lived in the South because of a live-and-let-live attitude

amongst Catholics and anti-Catholic prejudice. Instead, most middle class southerners flocked to evangelical sects, particularly the various Methodist and Baptist groups.

Though in the South, as in the North, Protestant groups had splintered into hundreds of sects, southerners, unlike northerners, did not form strange, fringe religious movements like Noyes' Oneida group and Miller's Adventists. They were not drawn to Unitarianism or movements that only stressed natural morality apart from God's grace. Though at times intensely emotional, southern religion was classically Bible-based Protestant and conservative. A kind of Puritan narrowness of morals descended on southern evangelicalism since the Second Great Awakening.

20. The character of southern politics

One place the aristocratic ideal of the South did not hold sway was in politics. Andrew Jackson of Tennessee had been quite popular in the South, and "Democracy" had inspired the yeoman farmer with the hope of achieving a higher social status; moreover, Jacksonian Democracy had spread the conviction that, since the common men were in the majority, they should have more than just a voice in government. They should control the government. So, even if one was an aristocrat, if he wanted public office he had to show himself a friend to radical democracy. In most parts of the South, this meant one had to be a candidate of the Democratic Party. The South had its Whigs, but on the whole, Jacksonian Democracy held sway.

But despite this democratic fervor, the ideal of aristocracy still held its own in the South. Though in Alabama and Mississippi the yeoman class controlled the government,

in other states one had to be connected to one of the great families to attain political office. Yet, even aristocrats had to show they were the willing servants of the public that elected them. This contradiction expressed and exacerbated a longstanding rivalry between large planters and yeoman farmers and backwoods mountaineers and poor farmers.

21. The character of southern slavery

Slavery was not everywhere the same in the South. Many slave owners were considerate and kind masters; others, if only a relative few, were cruel and sadistic. Many southerners believed that slavery was a benign institution and that it should be spread, through conquest, to Latin America. But though there were "good" mastersthere there were few checks on those masters who drove their slaves like beasts. And even the best of masters resorted to cruel floggings or mutilation to force his slaves to obedience. Unlike his counterpart in Spanish America, the Anglo slave owner exercised absolute power over his black slave. He could treat him well, or he could beat him till he was nearly dead. Some states had laws against excessive cruelty, but they were rarely enforced. Two forces kept slavery more or less humane, when it was humane: fear of retaliation from the slaves and ostracism by neighbors who treated their slaves well. The owner could sanction the marriage of slaves, or he could tear a family apart and sell the members to different masters far from their homes. Slaves dreaded being sold "down south" to the factory-like cotton plantations of the Gulf States where slaves labored long hours in work gangs and suffered the worst cruelties.

22. Social classes among blacks in the South

Slaves recognized different classes among themselves. Slaves distinguished themselves by how long they had been in America. Some slave families had been in America for 200 years; then there were blacks – "Gullahs" they were called – who had recently been smuggled illegally into the country from Africa. Slaves distinguished themselves by the work they did. Domestic slaves, such as butlers, maids, and "mammies" held a privileged place on the plantation. Below the domestic slaves were the skilled craftsmen and artisans – carpenters, blacksmiths, and barbers – who earned wages and could purchase their freedom with the percentage of the money they earned for their masters. Below these were field hands to whose lot fell all the hard, monotonous work on the plantation. Field hands made up the majority of the slave population. A small number of free blacks lived in the South. They were interspersed among whites in the cities and towns, and lower class whites often intermingled socially with their free black neighbors. Upper class whites, though they frowned on any interracial mixing, themselves had dealings with the few prosperous free blacks. A few free blacks owned slaves and looked down on enslaved blacks as much as any white man did.

23. Changing attitudes toward slavery in the South in the first half of the 19th century

Before 1822, southerners looked upon slavery as a necessary evil. Some, like George Mason and Thomas Jefferson, wanted to see a gradual emancipation of the slaves and their repatriation to Africa. Things began to change, however, in 1822. An attempted slave insurrection in Charleston awakened fears of slave revolt. The specter of Haiti, where black leader Jean Jacques Dessalines had massacred whites 15 years earlier, frightened southern whites. States began to tone up their "black codes" (laws governing the conduct of slaves). Blacks were forbidden to assemble or to leave their quarters after curfew; and bands of armed men patrolled roads by night. Every state, except Maryland, Kentucky, and Tennessee, passed laws forbidding masters to teach their slaves to read and write, since literate slaves learned to long for a better life. Despite the ease with which they mixed socially with their slaves, white southerners lived in fear of them. There were enough isolated cases of stealthy murder of white masters or mistresses to keep the fear alive.

A growing antislavery sentiment in the North spurred some southerners to a positive defense of slavery. They argued, for instance, that slavery had produced the civilizations of ancient Greece and Rome and that Scripture sanctioned slavery. Others said the black is less human than the white European or that civilization required a subject race. As late as 1831, the Virginia legislature was contemplating a gradual abolition of slavery. After 1831 all legislative attempts to abolish slavery in the South ceased because of Nat Turner's rebellion in Virginia.

24. How gold was discovered in California, and by whom

Johann Sutter had hired a carpenter named James Wilson Marshall to build him a saw mill on the American River near Sacramento, California. One day, January 24, 1848, Marshall saw in the millrace "something shining" that he thought might be gold. Marshall told Sutter of his find, and Sutter thought to keep the matter a secret. However, he told his servants, who spread word of the discovery.

25. The course of the Gold Rush in California

Word of the gold strike became widely known in California, and then spread by ship to Hawai'i, and then south into Mexico and Chile. In the fall of 1848, word of the gold discovery reached the East Coast of the United States. Gold fever brought tens of thousands of Americans to California, some by ship around Cape Horn, others via Panama and then along the Pacific Coast to San Francisco. Other gold seekers came by land to California – some in Conestoga wagons. The "Forty-niners" (so-called because they came in 1849) faced innumerable dangers – starvation, thirst, disease, wild animals, hostile Indians, and their own gullibility and foolishness. Gold-hungry adventurers followed the American River into the Sierra Nevada. They panned and sluiced gold out of the river and its tributary streams and knocked it out of rocks. Soon new gold strikes had been made north on the Sacramento River, and farther north on the Trinity and Humboldt Rivers, all the way to the Oregon border. The mining camps that sprang up overnight in the gold fields were colorful places where all ranks of society were reduced to a common level. The camps had professors, doctors, lawyers, even European nobility mixing with the common farmer and mechanic. Even blacks were accepted as equals in the comradery of the camps.

The miners who made their fortune were generally the clever or unscrupulous who organized and exploited the labor of others. Most miners however did not even break even. Some left the gold fields to become carters, run boarding houses, or operate stores. Though most came to California for only as long as it took them to strike it rich, many were so utterly ruined that they could not afford to return to their homes.

The height of the California gold rush was from 1849 to 1853. During this period, miners dug or panned or sluiced $220 million in gold out of California's waters and soil.

26. Social effects of the Gold Rush on California society

Hawai'ians, Mexicans, and Chileans had been the first to arrive at the California gold fields. Then came the thousands of Americans from the East Coast and the Middle West, and Europeans and hundreds of immigrants from Asia. The population of California in five years increased over tenfold, to 223,856 people. San Francisco grew from 500 in 1848 to over 25,000 - 35,000 people by 1850. Hastily constructed frame structures, some with canvas sides, covered the peninsula. Settlers erected schools, churches, theatres, and a public library. Enterprising individuals published magazines and newspapers. But the city had more than its share of saloons, brothels, and gambling parlors – and criminals and charlatans. Crime was so frequent that citizens finally organized a vigilance committee in 1851, by which San Francisco in a matter of a few months achieved a lower crime rate than even long-established cities in the East. Chaos however reigned everywhere else in California. It was not long before Sacramento, Oakland, and San Jose adopted vigilance committees. But in the camps and in the mining settlements crime was epidemic. Speculation set prices on all sorts of goods soaring.

California's population had grown so swiftly that in June 1849 the territorial governor called for a constitutional convention. The 48 delegates who gathered in Monterey in September included mostly older residents; among these were Mariano Vallejo and seven other *Californios*. Despite the large number of southerners in the region, the constitution the delegates crafted declared California a free state and adopted a clause from Mexican law that allowed married women to own property apart from their husbands. Only about 13,000 voters approved the new constitution in November, and it was sent to Congress for ratification; but even before ratification, elections were held for governor, state legislature, United States representatives and senators. In September 1850 word reached California that Congress had admitted the region as a state of the federal union.

27. The character of California society

Though the Gold Rush brought a large number of "foreign" miners to California, Anglo-American miners did not take kindly to them. In 1850, the state legislature placed a miner's tax – $20 a month – on all foreigners, and bands of Yankee miners made sure the foreigners paid it. It was not long before most

Mexicans left the state to escape the burdensome tax. The state legislature passed laws limiting the immigration of Chinese and Japanese into California.

In northern California, the influx of Yankee miners overwhelmed the old *Californio* population. The provision of the Treaty of Guadalupe Hidalgo that recognized old Mexican and Spanish land grants became a problem. For one, the ranchos covered immense tracts of land, and the old records describing the boundaries were ambiguous. Yankee emigrants, moreover, simply squatted on rancho lands. In 1851, Congress passed a law that required a federal board or commission to approve all land grant titles. To prove their claims to their lands, *Californios* had to carry on litigation in courts. To pay their lawyers' fees, they were forced to sell off large tracts of their land.

If Mexicans and *Californios* fared badly under American rule, the lot of the Indians

---

Key Terms at a Glance

Shaker: a member of the United Society of Believers in Christ's Second Appearing, founded by Ann Lee in the 19th century. Shaker teaching emphasized simplicity, celibacy, and work.

antislavery: the name referring to proponents of a gradual emancipation of the slaves

abolitionists: proponents of immediate emancipation of the slaves

Know-Nothings: the nickname of members of the American Party that opposed immigration, especially Catholic immigration, to the United States

Underground Railroad: a network of secret routes and safe houses that helped black slaves to escape to free states

Free-Soilers: member of the Free-Soil Party that opposed the introduction of slavery in the new territories

Popular Sovereignty: the political doctrine that said that a territory's settlers alone should decide whether it should or should not permit slavery

filibuster: to carry out revolutionary activities in a foreign country

was worse still. Under Mexican rule, even after the secularization of the missions, Indians, though often grossly mistreated, played a role in Californian society as *vaqueros* on the ranches. The Yankees, however, thought the Indians were poor laborers and decided they were useless. Yankees in the Sacramento Valley murdered Indians without provocation; and since California (unlike the Mexican) law would not allow Indians to testify against whites in court, such murders went unpunished. Violent tribes incited Yankee fears and vengeance; the Mojave, Yumas, and Apaches in the south, the Modocs, Klamaths, and Pit River Indians in the north, raided white settlements and killed miners. White retaliations were often brutal; they slaughtered not only the men, but the women, the old, and young children. The Indian population of California would decrease throughout the remainder of the 19th century, shrinking from 150,000 in 1845 to a mere 16,000 in 1900.

The Gold Rush and the great influx of population mostly affected the northern part of California. In the south, from San Luis Obispo to San Diego, life continued to center on cattle ranching. There were Yankee settlers in the south, and Los Angeles had as much violence and murder as any northern town; yet, outside the towns, the old rancho culture continued and even prospered for a short period. Cattle prices had risen, and *vaqueros* drove herds to the north where they sold them for a profit. But many a rancho don wasted his money in extravagant spending and in gambling, and some lost their lands to high interest rates on loans they had taken out to pay for their extravagance.

Questions for Review

1. **How did the Puritan ethic contribute to the spirit of industrialism?**

The Puritan ethic frowned upon leisure and entertainment, and promoted the supremacy of work instead.

2. **Name some of the hardships the immigrants faced in America, and why.**

Americans often cheated and swindled the immigrants, assaulted them, and sometimes even murdered them. The immigrants were forced to take the lowest-paying, most laborious, and often most dangerous work. They lived in the worst parts of the cities. Americans despised immigrants because they were afraid that immigrants would make the United States a "heterogeneous mass," and they thought the immigrants were the very scum and dregs of human nature.

3. **Why did Thomas Jefferson think that democracy in America needed to be protected against immigrants?**

Thomas Jefferson thought that democracy in America needed to be protected against immigrants because he was afraid the immigrants would "infuse in [the United States] their spirit" and "warp and bias its direction." In other words, he thought immigrants would compromise America's political tradition.

4. **What did nativist Americans fear immigrants?**

Native Americans hated the immigrants for what they thought were the immigrants' poverty, their ignorance, their foreign ways, and because of their religion. Many of the German and Irish immigrants were Catholic, and Americans saw them as threatening one of the safeguards of American liberty: the Protestant religion.

5. **How did the influx of immigrants change the character of the northern cities?**

    The influx of immigrants changed the character of the northern cities because they went from being relatively small provincial town to teeming metropolises, where various cultures and languages were represented and a sharp contrast was seen between opulence and destitution.

6. **What is the sectarian spirit, and how was it displayed in the United States?**

    The sectarian spirit was when people broke off into smaller sects and start their own churches or religious groups. It was displayed in America by a rapid splintering of Protestantism into an ever increasing number of groups, which in turn was a function of the disintegration of society.

7. **Briefly describe each of the sects mentioned in this chapter.**

    Shaker: the United Society of Believers in Christ's Second Appearing, founded by Ann Lee in the 19th century. Shaker teaching emphasized simplicity, celibacy, and work.

    Adventist: the Adventists were distinguished by their emphasis on the belief that the personal, visible return of Christ was close at hand

    Spiritism: the belief that the living are able to communicate with the spirits of the dead

    Unitarianism: a call for rationalism and a rejection of the doctrine of the Trinity

Swedenborgianism: the doctrine that God and Satan are engaged in an eternal struggle and that God is present in all things. Swedenborgianists reject Original Sin.

Transcendentalism: movement of writers and philosophers who believed in the essential unity of all creation, the innate goodness of man, and the supremacy of insight over logic and experience in the revelation of truths

8. **What were the traits that were thought to characterize the southern gentleman?**

    The southern gentleman was to be wealthy but not chase after wealth. He was to cultivate, refined manners and follow the code of chivalry and have a lofty respect for women. He was to hospitable towards guests and strangers. He was to have a high sense of honor that brooked no insult to his name or family. He had a strong sense of fidelity to his family and love of his country.

9. **Describe the different conditions under which slaves lived in the American South.**

    Slaves recognized different classes among themselves. Slaves distinguished themselves by how long they had been in America. Some slave families had been in America for 200 years; then there were blacks – "Gullahs" they were called – who had recently been smuggled illegally into the country from Africa. Slaves distinguished themselves by the work they did. Domestic slaves, such as butlers, maids, and "mammies" held a privileged place on the plantation. Below the domestic slaves were the skilled craftsmen and artisans – carpenters, blacksmiths, and barbers – who earned wages and could purchase their freedom with the percentage of the money they earned for their masters. Below these were field hands to whose lot fell all the hard, monotonous work on the plantation. Field hands made up the majority of the slave population.

10. **How did the Gold Rush change the character of California?**

The gold rush caused the population of California to multiply at a phenomenal rate. Chaos reigned in the hastily built cities, and crime was frequent. The Americans who came to California despised the Mexicans and Indians. The old Californian cultrue was submerged in an Anglo-American majority.

Ideas in Action

1. Read some of the literature of the New England Renaissance; for instance, esays by Emerson, Nathaniel Hawthorne's short stories, Henry David Thoreau's *Walden* or "On Civil Disobedience." Discuss how these works reflect Transcendentalism.

2. Read about Samuel Morse, and learn how to do Morse code.

3. Listen to the songs of Stephen Foster and other songwriters of the time – and, if you can, peform them yourself.

4. This chapter describes the cultural characteristics of the major sections of the United States by 1850. Do these characteristics still apply to these regions today? How and how not? What section do you think has been most influential? Why?

5. Did American society in 1850 reflect the kind of social order the founding fathers of the United States had envisioned for the new country? Why or why not?

Sample Quiz I (pages 345-360)

Please answer the following in complete sentences.

1. By the 1850s where did most Americans live and how did they make a living?

2. What effect did improved transportation brought about by the railroad have on industrial imput in America?

3. Give two reasons why immigrants came to America.

4. Why did many native Americans object to the immigrants?

5. What were Horace Mann's views on education?

6. What did Ralph Waldo Emerson say about how people can perfect themselves?

7. Why did many Protestants finally support state-funded schools?

8. Why did people in the North try to found Utopian communities?

··

Answers to Sample Quiz I

Students' answers should approximate the following.

1. By the 1850s most Americans lived in the country and engaged in subsistence farming – their produce went primarily to support the family; only the excess was sold on the market. Most others – merchants, storekeepers, craftsmen, and small bankers – dwelt in the small towns and villages that dotted the countryside.

2. One benefit of improved transportation brought about by the railroad was that improved transportation allowed for increased industrial output.

3. *Possible answers:* Many immigrants came to America to escape dire poverty; some, like skilled craftsmen, came because they had fallen on hard times in their countries; others, because they thought that in America they would find greater opportunities for social advancement. Some, particularly Germans,

sought a greater freedom than they had in their homeland to practice their religion.

4. Americans blamed immigrants for disease, crime, the poverty of their ghettoes, and prostitution. Natives complained that a very large percentage of immigrants were unskilled laborers who only swelled the ranks of those requiring public aid.

5. Horace Mann believed that no one, regardless of wealth, should go without education. He also believed that religious instruction – particularly Bible reading – should be part of the school day. To avoid a public espousal of the tenets of any one religious group, Mann said instruction should be in the "common truths" of Christianity alone.

6. Emerson emphasized that every individual could become enlightened and improved by his own efforts alone. He taught that "God is in every man" and that "life is an ecstasy."

7. Many Protestants finally supports state-funded schools because they saw free public schools as a defense against "Papistry" and the Catholic Church.

8. Some reformers were not content just to tinker with existing society but wanted to erect perfect communities that could be a example to all the world of how mankind should live. Others founded Utopias on the conviction that men could recreate their world by their own natural powers, without God.

Sample Quiz II (pages 360-377)

Please answer the following in complete sentences.

1. **How did cotton growing contribute to the South's move westwards?**

2. **How did the people of the South regard themselves?**

3. **Why did the reality of southern life rarely live up to the aristocratic ideal?**

4. **What is a possible reason for the sparseness of southern literary works?**

5. **How did slaves distinguish their social classes?**

6. **How did the attitude towards slavery change in the South during the first half of the 19th century?**

7. **How did the California Gold Rush begin?**

8. **What were the social effects of the Gold Rush on California Society?**

9. **How were the California Indians treated under American rule?**

Answers to Sample Quiz II

Students' answers should approximate the following.

1. Because cotton growing quickly depleted the soil, plantation owners were continually investing in new lands to replace the exhausted ones. As long as new lands were there for the taking, few cotton growers concerned themselves with wise management of the soil, and this contributed to the move westward, where new lands could be found.

2. The people of the South regarded themselves as conservative and preservers of tradition. In particular, they saw themselves as carrying on the traditions of European, specifically English, aristocratic society – even to the point that many southern gentlemen believed themselves not merely descendants in spirit, but also in blood to European "cavaliers."

3. The reality of southern life rarely lived up to the aristocratic ideal because, except for a very few, southern gentlemen had little time

for leisure. Rather, he was occupied with the affairs of his plantation and with the responsibilities arising from owning many slaves. Human weakness, too, and the inability fully to come to terms with the fact that southern society depended on the misery of men condemned to unending, involuntary servitude compromised the southern aristocratic ideal.

4. The sparseness of southern literary works may be because the southern genius had long been turned toward political writing.

5. Slaves distinguished themselves by how long they had been in America. Some slave families had been in America for 200 years; then there were blacks, Gullahs, who had recently been smuggled illegally into the country from Africa. Slaves distinguished themselves by the work they did. Domestic slaves, such as butlers, maids, and "mammies" held a privileged place on the plantation. Below the domestic slaves were the skilled craftsmen and artisans who earned wages and could purchase their freedom. Below these were field hands to whose lot fell all the hard, monotonous work on the plantation.

6. Before 1822, southerners looked upon slavery as a necessary evil. But this attitude began to change in 1822. An attempted slave insurrection in Charleston awakened fears of slave revolt. The specter of Haiti, where black leader Jean Jacques Dessalines had massacred whites 15 years earlier, frightened southern whites. States began to tone up their "black codes" (laws governing the conduct of slaves). A growing antislavery sentiment in the North spurred some southerners to a positive defense of slavery.

7. Johan Sutter had hired a carpenter named James Marshall to build him a saw mill on the American River near Sacramento, California. One day, January 24, 1848, Marshall saw in the millrace "something shining" that he thought might be gold. Marshall told Sutter of his find, and Sutter thought to keep the matter a secret. However, he told his servants, who spread word of the discovery.

8. During the Gold Rush, the population of California increased quickly. The cities were full of saloons, brothels, and gambling house. Crime was an epidemic. Speculation set prices on all goods soaring.

9. The Yankees thought the Indians were poor laborers and decided they were useless. Yankees in the Sacramento Valley murdered Indians without provocation, and since California law would not allow Indians to testify against whites in court, such murders went unpunished. The Indian population decreased throughout the remainder of the 19th century.

Essays

Instructions to be given to the students: Write in complete sentences. Underline your thesis. Give three supports or examples that explain why you think what you do and that support your thesis.

1. How did industrialism and the influx of immigrants change the character of northern U.S. society?

2. Explain how social and economic changes in American society encouraged the sectarian spirit and the forming of different religious sects. Be sure to use at least three sects as examples.

3. How did the North and South differ culturally in the first half of the 19th century? Give specific examples.

Sample Test

Please answer the following in complete sentences

I. Short Essay – Answer two of the following:

1. How did industry and the influx of foreign immigrants change the North?

2. Describe three of the religious sects discussed in this chapter.

3. Why and how did the North and South differ culturally?

4. Describe the Southern social classes.

II. Short Answer:

1. What was Tammany Hall?

2. Name four popular reform movements.

3. Why did Protestants oppose state-funded church schools?

4. How did the southern gentleman view slavery?

....

Answer Key to the Chapter Test

Students' answers should approximate the following:

I.

1. The growth of industry and the influx of foreign immigrants dramatically changed the character of the great northern cities. From relatively small provincial towns they grew into teeming metropolises and reverberated with a confusion of tongues. In the great cities of New York, Boston, and Philadelphia, opulence and middle-class respectability contrasted with abject poverty and destitution. The vast underclass lived in sordid conditions. Riots, caused by racial, religious, or class strife, were common. Northern American cities were torn by an acquisitiveness that extended even to religion. Poor neighborhoods were filled with drunkenness, filth, and prostitution; epidemics were rampant.

2. *Religious sects:*

   Shaker: the United Society of Believers in Christ's Second Appearing, founded by Ann Lee in the 19th century. Shaker teaching emphasized simplicity, celibacy, and work.

   Adventist: the Adventists were distinguished by their emphasis on the belief that the personal, visible return of Christ was close at hand

   Spiritism: the belief that the living are able to communicate with the spirits of the dead

   Unitarianism: a call for rationalism and a rejection of the doctrine of the Trinity

   Swedenborgianism: the doctrine that God and Satan are engaged in an eternal struggle and that God is present in all things. Swedenborgianists reject Original Sin.

   Transcendentalism: movement of writers and philosophers who believed in the essential unity of all creation, the innate goodness of man, and the supremacy of insight over logic and experience in the revelation of truths

3. Among the causes of the differences of North and South was the presence of slavery in the South. There were cultural and economic causes as well. The Puritan spirit of New England dominated the North; then there were New England's social and political organization. These helped inspire emigration and induced men to become merchants and manufacturers. Though the North still remained largely agrarian, industrial concerns and interest in making money were becoming dominant there. This was evident even in agriculture, where farmers were becoming speculators, buying farms only to improve them and sell them at a higher price. Though the South had undergone its pioneer phase, and

Southerners were still pushing west, yet throughout much of the South the pioneering spirit left behind a culture characterized by settlement and a sleepiness that contrasted with the rabid ferment of the North. Unlike in the North, where people seemed constantly on the move, families in the South settled down and became identified with the regions in which they lived. This rootedness in a place begat pride of family. In contrast to the North, the South was committed to traditional society along the lines of traditional European arrangements, including aristocracy. The South had rich agricultural lands, and this fact encouraged southerners to farming rather than trade and manufacture.

4. Some southern families could be called "gentry," and their ideals set the tone for southern society. Most southern white families belonged to the class of yeomen farmers. Such farmers owned their own land and the buildings on them. They raised cash crops – tobacco, sugarcane, or cotton – and grazed cattle, kept hogs, and grew much of their daily food. The farmer worked in the fields, alongside the half dozen or so slaves he might own; these shared their master's dinner, often at the same table with their master's family. But while many yeomen farmers were slave owners, thousands more were not. Most southern whites owned no slaves. Below the yeomen farmers was a class of people derisively called "poor white trash," "crackers," and other unfortunate names, who accounted for less than ten percent of the population of the South. Despised by more respectable whites, these illiterate, unskilled, and uncultured folks despised and envied their "betters" in turn. They hated blacks, many of whom lived in more dignity and orderliness than the "rednecks." They lived in tiny cabins with dirt floors, had a bad diet. The mountaineers, or "hillbillies" of the South were fiercely independent and lived in the mountain valleys or on the hillsides of the Appalachians and, westward, in the Ozarks. There they subsisted by farming small plots of corn and by hunting and fishing.

II.
1. Tammany Hall was a political club that came to dominate the Democratic Party in New York City. It was noted for its corruption.
2. Four popular reform movements: abolition, Temperance, anti-death penalty, and prison reform.
3. Protestants opposed state-funded schools because they did not want to fund Catholic as well as Protestant schools.
4. The southern gentleman did not love slavery, but he saw it as a necessary foundation for the sort of life he cherished.

CHAPTER 16: A House Divided

Chapter Overview

- The antislavery movement in the United States became a major political force. It included such antislavery proponents as Benjamin Lundy, William Lloyd Garrison, and Angelina Grimké, as well as former slaves such as Sojourner Truth and Frederick Douglass. The antislavery movement split into two factions, the "antislavery" and the "abolitionist." The movement made enemies in the southern states.

- In 1835 abolitionists began sending petitions to Congress asking it to abolish slavery in the District of Columbia. This caused Congress to pass the first of its "gag resolutions" in 1836, which, because of unrelenting abolitionist opposition, was repealed in 1844.

- James Birney organized the first antislavery party in the United States, the Liberty Party, in 1839.

- When David Wilmot submitted his "Wilmot Proviso" to Congress he awakened the sectional controversy over slavery in territories. The territories in question were the newly acquired territories from the war with Mexico.

- In January of 1850, Henry Clay proposed the Compromise of 1850. By September his bill had been cut into five separate bills. President Fillmore signed the bills that same month. The North greeted the Compromise with anger, especially the strengthened Fugitive Slave Law. The fortified Fugitive Slave Law especially frightened escaped slaves, who formed secret vigilance committees for mutual protection.

- In 1852, Harriet Beecher Stowe published a controversial book, *Uncle Tom's Cabin*, with its portrayal of what would become the standard of the cruel slave owner, Simon Legree. Stowe's book elicited a storm of protest in the South.

- The early years of the 1850s were prosperous for both the North and the South. American idealism was renewed with the "Young Americans." The president, Franklin Pierce, favored filibustering, and tried to instigate a war with Spain.

- In 1854, Jefferson Davis, who promoted a southern transcontinental railroad route, persuaded President Pierce to purchase from Mexico the territory south of the Gila River and west of the Rio Grande.

- In 1854, Stephen Douglas introduced a bill to divide and organize the Nebraska Territory into two separate territories – Kansas and Nebraska. Congress passed the Kansas-Nebraska Act on May 25, 1854. The territories were organized under the concept of Popular Sovereignty.

- In 1854, the anti-immigrant, anti-Catholic American or "Know-Nothing" Party became a powerful force in politics.

- Northerners feared that Popular Sovereignty might claim Kansas and Nebraska for slavery, so they organized emigrant aid societies to settle antislavery men in these territories. Soon the majority of settlers were Free soilers. Free-soiler and proslavery rivalry resulted in bloody warfare in Kansas.

- In 1857 the Supreme Court published its decision in the Dred Scott case. In his decision, Chief Justice Roger Taney said black men were excluded from the purview of the Constitution and are the property of their owners. In his decision, Taney nullified the Missouri Compromise, thus opening up all the territories to slavery. In 1858 Congress attempted to admit Kansas into the union under a proslavery constitution, thus creating a wider chasm between the North and South.

◆ In 1859, John Brown sought to instigate a violent revolution to free the slaves by assaulting the federal arsenal at Harper's Ferry, Virginia. Brown was arrested and hanged.

◆ Abraham Lincoln won the presidential election of 1860. Following the election, South Carolina seceded from the union, followed by seven other southern states. The congress of the new Confederate States of America drew up a provisional constitution and on February 9, 1861 elected Jefferson Davis and Alexander Stephens as provisional president and vice president.

◆ In 1860, the Confederate government demanded that the United States remove all its troops from forts in Confederate territory. When Fort Sumter in Charleston harbor refused to surrender to the Confederate government, Confederate troops fired on it on April 12, 1861, thus beginning the Civil War.

What Students Should Know

1. **Identify:**

   a. **William Lloyd Garrison and Benjamin Lundy**
   Garrison, a printer and writer, had been promoting total abstinence from alcohol in Boston when he met Benjamin Lundy. Lundy, who had founded an antislavery society in 1815, inspired Garrison to join the antislavery cause. A year later, in 1829, Garrison joined Lundy in Baltimore and with him edited *The Genius of Universal Emancipation*.

Lundy was a gradualist; that is, he believed slavery should be abolished, but slowly, over time. He also believed that Americans should colonize emancipated slaves somewhere outside the United States. Garrison, at first, accepted these ideas; but, as the years wore on, his mind began to change. He took to promoting immediate emancipation and argued that blacks should remain in America as full and equal citizens of the United States. By 1830, Garrison and Lundy had parted company, and, in 1831, Garrison, with Isaac Knapp, founded in Boston another journal – *The Liberator*. Garrison's rhetoric, southerners believed, posed a real threat to their safety. Moreover, Garrison's call for immediate emancipation of slaves, without compensation to their masters, struck at the very foundations of the southern economy. Such a course would have ruined the South, which depended on slave-harvested and processed cotton as its chief export. Other slavery opponents understood the practical problems of emancipation – and it was thus that they promoted gradual emancipation with compensation to the owners. The gradualists called themselves "antislavery" and distinguished themselves from the more radical men like Garrison, who became known as "abolitionists."

   b. **Theodore Dwight Weld**
   Theodore Dwight Weld of Connecticut was an antislavery gradualist. Weld had been converted to evangelical Christianity by Charles Grandison Finney. In 1833, after he had traveled to the Gulf of Mexico to observe slavery conditions first hand, Weld with others founded the American Antislavery Society, whose publication, *The Emanci-*

pator, became the most widely read of the antislavery journals. The society attracted the rich New York businessman, Arthur Tappan, and the poet John Greenleaf Whittier, who headed the society's New York branch. Standing upon the "Declaration of Independence and the truths of divine revelation," the society's "Declaration of Sentiments" admitted that the federal constitution did not grant the federal government the authority to interfere with slavery; so, instead of agitating for political change, the society dedicated itself to moral persuasion to change the hearts of both northerners and southerners. But such positions were no comfort to the South, since the society held that all laws that protected slavery were null and void.

c. **Angelina Grimké**
Angelina Grimké and her older sister, Sarah, the daughters of a Charleston, South Carolina, judge, had grown up in the South and so had witnessed slavery first-hand. Their experience made them prominent antislavery advocates; but Angelina, in particular, lent her energies to the "emancipation" of women as well. She thought the causes of women and slaves were connected. "Reformations," she said, are "bound together in a circle like the sciences; they blend with each other like the colors of the rainbow; they are parts only of our glorious whole and that whole is Christianity, pure practical Christianity."

d. **Oberlin College**
Oberlin College in Ohio (founded in 1833) was the center of antislavery and other reform causes. In 1834, Oberlin became the first U.S. college to admit black students. The college had also been the first in America to educate women together with men; in 1841, three women graduated from Oberlin with bachelor of arts degrees comparable to degrees men received in other universities.

e. **Frederick Douglass**
In the antislavery movement, former slaves worked with others for emancipation, traveling to antislavery conventions, telling of their experiences in slavery. One of these black speakers was Frederick Douglass, the son of a white man and a black mother. In Maryland, Douglass' master's wife had taught Douglass as a young man how to read and write. Douglass put his learning to practice and began forging passes for slaves who wanted to escape north. Though his master, William Freeland, was kind to him, Douglass himself attempted an escape in 1836, but was suspected and jailed. He was later released on lack of evidence. In the late 1830s, Douglass escaped by train to New York City. He ended up in New Bedford, Massachusetts and in 1841 gave an extempore speech before an antislavery meeting in Nantucket. This proved to be the beginning of his career as a lecturer in the antislavery circuit. Douglass' eloquence and learning led some to call him an imposter, and to refute the charge false, in 1845 Douglass published the *Narrative of the Life of Frederick Douglass, An American Slave*. From 1845 to 1847 he went to England and Ireland to lecture – and avoid capture.

f. **James Holly**
James Holly was a free black and Episcopalian minister who advocated that blacks move outside the boundaries

of the United States and set up a republic of their own. He wanted to show whites that blacks were capable of self-government. After his visit to Haiti, Holly encouraged free blacks to move there, advice he himself finally took in 1861.

g. Isabella Baumfree, "Sojourner Truth"

Isabella Baumfree, who called herself "Sojourner Truth" – had belonged to a New York slaveholder, who had raped her. When New York passed its manumission law, she became free. Sojourner said that she talked with God, who told her to preach against slavery. Leaving everything behind, she took to preaching against slavery. For Sojourner Truth, the fight for justice did not rely solely on human powers, but on God.

h. Elijah Lovejoy

Elijah Lovejoy became the most celebrated of abolitionist martyrs. He had left St. Louis, Missouri, to settle in Alton, Illinois, just across the Mississippi, to escape opposition to his church paper, *The Observer*, which carried his antislavery editorials. But a mob in Alton destroyed his printing press in 1837. Later, they destroyed a second press. When Lovejoy bought a third press, securing it in a warehouse under armed guard, a mob attacked the warehouse. Shooting broke out, one of the assailants was killed, and the mob withdrew. When Lovejoy opened the door of the warehouse, five shots rang out, and he fell, dead. The death of Lovejoy, and the sufferings of others abolitionists did not retard an increase in the ranks of antislavery societies. Their membership, by 1840, had swelled to 150,000.

i. Harriet Tubman and the Underground Railroad

Harriet Tubman was a slave in Maryland who fled to the North after she learned in 1849 that she was to be sold following her master's death. She reached Philadelphia but then returned a year later to bring out her family. In the ensuing years, she returned to the South 19 times. In all she led 300 slaves to freedom.

Tubman worked as part of the "Underground Railroad," an organized system that, in defiance of the Fugitive Slave Law, helped slaves escape north and thence into Canada. The Underground Railroad ran from Virginia and Kentucky along certain routes, house to house, into the North. An escaping slave followed the north star by night and hid by day until he met a conductor, who would by various disguises and stratagems, help him to the next station. It was a dangerous business. Slave-hunters and many other perils pursued escaped slaves. Since the Fugitive Slave Law allowed slave-hunters to pass the Mason-Dixon and the Ohio in pursuit of their quarry, the fugitive slaves were not safe until they reached Canada.

2. How southerners defended slavery

Southerners responded to abolitionist attacks and used the Bible to justify slavery. When abolitionists, unable to find a clear Biblical condemnation of slavery, began arguing that slavery violated the natural equality of man, some proslavery apologists took another tack. John C. Calhoun, for instance, argued that a subject race was needed to serve civilization and was "the most safe and stable basis for free institutions in the world." IN his book,

Cannibals All!, George Fitzhugh of Virginia pointed to northern hypocrisy. "We are all," Fitzhugh wrote, "North and South, engaged in the White Slave Trade, and he who succeeds best, is esteemed most respectable." By the "white slave trade," Fitzhugh meant the inhuman treatment of immigrant workers in northern factories. The "White Slave Trade," said Fitzhugh, "is far more cruel than the Black Slave Trade, because it exacts more of its slaves and neither protects nor governs them … The profits, made from free labor, are the amount of the products of such labor, which the employer … takes away, exacts, or 'exploitates' from the free laborer." The slave owner, however, receives smaller profits from slave labor, said Fitzhugh, "because the master allows the slave to retain a larger share of the results of his own labor." White slavery, said Fitzhugh, is more cruel, for it leaves "the laborer to take care of himself and family out of the pittance which skill or capital have allowed to retain." Fitzhugh argued slaves were better cared for than white laborers.

3. Northern reactions to antislavery and abolitionism

In general, northerners themselves were scarcely more welcoming of their antislavery men and abolitionists than were southerners. Most northerners, and even a great number of antislavery people, were opposed to full social and legal equality for blacks, slave or free. The very thought of intermarriage with blacks appalled them. Then there was the economic aspect of the question. Northern textile manufacturers benefited from the fruits of slavery – the abundant cotton crop of the South. Northern merchants, too, had, for a long time, been involved in the African slave trade, and continued, illegally, to smuggle in slaves from Africa. In the North,

free blacks occupied the lowest rung on the social ladder. They lived in squalid ghettoes, segregated from the predominately white community. They competed with poor whites, particularly Irish immigrants, for jobs and suffered periodically from riots and violence from the Irish and other groups.

4. Catholic reaction to antislavery and abolitionism

The Catholic position on antislavery was complicated by the fact that the Church in America had been founded in Maryland, south of the Mason-Dixon, and this tended to mold Catholic opinions on antislavery nationwide. Maryland Jesuits had owned slaves, as did some bishops and the Ursuline sisters of New Orleans. The "black code" of Louisiana, hearkening back to both French and Spanish law, held that masters were to respect the marriages of blacks and to provide them the freedom to observe holy days, which, in those days included freedom from manual labor. This code, though, was often ignored. Some Catholics engaged in slave smuggling – though the popes themselves had condemned it. The Catholic position on slavery can in part be explained by the fact that Catholics were engaged in their own struggles against nativist bigotry. Catholics, too, were for the most part Democrats, a party that had an enormous power base in the South. Further, though Catholic theologians taught that it is immoral to enslave an innocent free man, one is not, they said, necessarily bound to abolish a condition of slavery or to free people already reduced to a condition of slavery. If freeing slaves would lead to greater evils that would seriously harm the common good – if, say, their freedom meant economic ruin for all, both slave and free – then one was not bound to emancipate them. A master had to treat his slaves as human beings, not mistreat them, not buy and sell them, not forbid them to marry, divide families, or deprive them of the benefits of religion; but, he need not free them. With Bishop John England, most American Catholics thought abolition merely a political question, not a moral necessity.

In 1839, Pope Gregory XVI condemned the slave trade. Previous popes had condemned both slavery and the slave trade.

5. **The "gag resolutions" and the opposition to them**

The "gag resolutions" where resolutions passed by Congress, beginning in 1836, that declared that all petitions relating to slavery or abolition should be "laid on the table"; that is, ignored. John Quincy Adams, then a representative from Massachusetts, vigorously opposed the gag resolution, calling it "a violation of the Constitution of the United States, of the rules of this House, and the rights of my constituents." Galvanized into resistance against the gag, abolitionists sent tens of thousands of petitions into Congress, all of which were tabled. In the end, the sheer amount of unrelenting abolitionist opposition to the gag resolutions had its effect – Congress repealed the resolutions in 1844.

6. **Division in anti-slavery ranks over the question of whether or not to engage in politics**

By 1844 one could detect a definite split in the antislavery ranks. Some, like Garrison, eschewed politics; others, however, began to form organized political resistance to slavery. James Birney, a southerner converted by Weld to the abolitionist cause, organized the first antislavery party in the United States, the Liberty Party, in 1839. Birney ran for president the following year but garnered

only 7,000 votes. Four years later, though, he ran again and received 62,000 votes. Garrison's rejection of politics weakened his influence among antislavery people. Indeed, not only would Garrison not sully himself with politics, but he wanted nothing to do with the federal union, calling for "'no union with slaveholders, socially or religiously, and up with the flag of Disunion.'" Such rhetoric only served to distance Garrison further from the mainstream of the movement he had founded.

7. **The Wilmot Proviso and its effects**

As early as 1846, talk of what to do with conquered California, New Mexico, and Utah stirred up the question, would these territories be open to slavery or not? On August 8, 1846, Representative David Wilmot of Pennsylvania submitted his "Wilmot Proviso" to Congress – a proposal to forbid any introduction of slavery into territories where it did not already exist. Southern representatives protested the Wilmot Proviso. President Polk, trying to restore peace, proposed extending the Missouri Compromise line to the Pacific – territories north of that line being free, those south of it, open to slavery. On the antislavery side, many argued that Congress had a moral duty to forbid slavery in the new territories. Slavery, they said, should be confined to the southern states, where it would, eventually, die out. On the proslavery side, Senator John C. Calhoun declared the Missouri Compromise itself unconstitutional. Since the union, said Calhoun, was a partnership of northern and southern states, the territories belonged equally to all the states; Congress therefore could not forbid settlers from bringing their "common law property" into any territory. Congress, Calhoun concluded, had the constitutional duty to protect slave property, like any other property.

8. The Compromise of 1850 and its significance

The 73-year-old Henry Clay, sought to break the impasse over the admission of California. On January 29, 1850, he proposed a compromise, known to history as the Compromise of 1850. Congress, said Clay, should admit California into the union as a free state but organize territorial governments in New Mexico and Deseret (Utah) without any reference to slavery, thus allowing slaveholders to bring slaves into those territories. As a sop to the southerners, Clay offered a new, stricter fugitive slave law; and as a concession to the abolitionists, he proposed abolishing the slave trade in the District of Columbia. John C. Calhoun opposed Henry Clay's compromise. He said the union was "permanently and hopelessly [being] converted into the means of oppressing, instead of protecting" the South. His solution? The North must allow for a change in the Constitution, establishing two presidents, one for the South and one for the North. Only then, said Calhoun, would southern interests be secure. Senator William H. Seward of New York opposed the compromise. While he admitted Congress had the power to establish slavery in the territories, "there is a higher law than the Constitution which regulates our authority over the domain" – the law of God. He continued: "All measures which fortify slavery or extend it, tend to the consummation of violence; all that check its extension and abate its strength, tend to its peaceful extirpation."   By September 1850, Clay's compromise had been cut into five separate bills. Assisted by Stephen A. Douglas, the short, intensely ambitious

Democratic senator from Illinois, and by other Democrats, Clay was able to get enough support for the five bills to see them pass in the Senate and the House of Representatives in early September. President Fillmore signed the bills, and the Compromise of 1850 – the last great compromise between North and South – became law.

9. Reaction to the Compromise of 1850

In the North, outrage greeted the news of Clay's compromise. Though Democrats, on the whole, embraced it, Free Soilers and abolitionists denounced it, and many Whigs, whether antislavery or not, decried it. For antislavery folk and escaped slaves, the most vexing part of the compromise was the new, strengthened Fugitive Slave Law that effectively removed any legal protection runaway slaves had in the North. According to the law, an owner need not be present or sign any affidavit to prove that a black man seized in the North was indeed his slave – the claim of the slave hunter himself was sufficient evidence. The accused could not testify in court on his own behalf nor even call witnesses to testify for him. Even harder to take was the fact that slave hunters and the law could call on passersby to help capture a runaway; any who refused – even from conscience – could suffer heavy penalties. Helping a fugitive to escape, hiding him, or attempting to free him from custody, brought heavy fines or imprisonment. The Fugitive Slave Law spread terror among escaped slaves. Many fled north to Canada, where the slave hunters could not reach them. Others formed secret vigilance committees for mutual protection.

In the deep, cotton South, the two major parties, the Democrats and the Whigs, for a short time disappeared, to be replaced by a Southern Rights Party (which favored secession) and a Union Party (which did not). The Unionists, however, carried the day in every cotton state election, except one: South Carolina went for the Southern Rights Party.

10. *Uncle Tom's Cabin* and its importance

Uncle Tom's Cabin, by Harriet Beecher Stowe of Connecticut, was published in 1852. It told a story of black slaves, their white masters, and the misery that slavery thrust on all of them. Some of the southern slaveholders in Stowe's portrayal are kindly and good men – a fact, she wrote, she drew from real life. But the protagonist, Uncle Tom's last owner, Simon Legree, would become in the popular imagination the epitome of the cruelty of the slave system. Stowe wrote in the epilogue to *Uncle Tom's Cabin* that God's wrath would not be long withheld from America for the sin of slavery, a sin, she said, for which both the North and the South were responsible. She urged, however, that there was still time to right the wrong. The impact of *Uncle Tom's Cabin* was great. Southerners denounced the book, saying that Stowe had never visited the South (which was true, she had known only a few slaveholders) and could not know the true character of their "peculiar institution."

11. Who the Young Americans were

The "Young Americans" was a movement of men, old and young, that sought to find new ideals to inspire civic leadership, to support democratic revolutions the world over. By their inspiration, in 1849 the legislatures of New York, Ohio, and Indiana called for national action against Austria, where the Habsburg emperor had crushed a nationalist revolution in his kingdom of Hungary. Daniel Webster, at that time secretary of state under President Fillmore, reflected the spirit of the Young Americans by writing a condescending letter to Emperor Franz Josef:

"The power of this republic [the United States] at the present moment is spread over a region, one of the richest and most fertile on the globe, and in an extent in comparison with which the possessions of the House of Hapsburg are but a patch on the earth's surface." The Young Americans' ideals influenced President Franklin Pierce's cabinet. Pierce came to favor filibustering expeditions against Spanish Cuba. Secretary of State Jefferson Davis, like many southerners, wanted the United States to annex slave-holding Cuba as compensation to the South for the loss of California as a slave state. In 1848, Narciso López, a former Spanish general and ex-governor of Madrid, led an independence movement in Cuba against Spanish rule. Defeated, he fled to the United States. Two years later, López led a force of mostly American volunteers from New Orleans into Cuba but was defeated and captured. Spanish authorities executed the entire force.

12. What the Ostend Manifesto was

In response to American filibustering, Spanish authorities in Cuba began seizing suspicious American merchant ships. In 1854, they seized the American ship, *Black Hawk*, and detained it in Havana, confiscating its cargo of cotton. This was a pretext for war, according to Jefferson Davis. Pierce, who wanted Cuba, tried to incite the Spaniards to declare war on the United States, but the Spanish government did not take the bait; instead, it apologized for the seizure of the *Black Hawk*. Undaunted, Pierce called on his ambassadors to England, France, and Spain – James Buchanan, John Mason, and Pierre Soulé – to draw up a policy to govern the United States' relations with Cuba. The result was the Ostend Manifesto of 1854. The Ostend Manifesto declared Cubans were "now suffering under the worst of all possible governments, that of an absolute despotism." Moreover, and incidentally, this government made it impossible for the United States to suppress the African slave trade. The United States should buy Cuba from Spain, said the resolution; but (it continued), if Spain refused to sell Cuba, the U.S. would be justified "by every law, human and divine," and by the principle of self-preservation, in taking it from Spain. Yet, the manifesto's belligerent and self-righteous tone fell short of its desired effect. It did not lead to war with Spain.

13. The Transcontinental Railroad, the Gadsden Purchase, and the Kansas-Nebraska Act

With California and Oregon filling up with settlers, Americans began to dream of a transcontinental railroad. Different routes were proposed. A southern route seemed most promising. Secretary of State Jefferson Davis advocated the southern route because it would connect the South to the West. Because the route would pass through the Gila River valley, which was Mexican territory, Davis persuaded President Pierce to buy it from Mexico. Mexico agreed to the sale, and in 1854 the Gadsden Purchase (named for James Gadsden, the U.S. ambassador to Mexico) added the territory south of the Gila River and west of the Rio Grande (in what is now Arizona and New Mexico) to the United States.

But Davis' southern route met opposition from Senator Stephen A. Douglas, who had been speculating in western lands and in Chicago real estate. Douglas championed a central route for the transcontinental railroad. The railroad, however, needed to pass through organized territories, and the Nebraska territory between Missouri and Utah had no territorial government. In 1854,

Douglas introduced a bill to split and organize the Nebraska territory into two separate territories – Kansas and Nebraska. Douglas proposed that the territories should be organized without any reference to slavery. Instead, the people who settled the territories would decide whether they would accept slavery among them or forbid its introduction. This was called popular or "squatter" sovereignty.

Douglas' proposal implicitly overturned the Missouri Compromise; the new territories lay north of longitude 36 degrees, 30 minutes, from where slavery was supposedly forever banned. Douglas also took the further step of supporting a bill, presented in the Senate by Senator Dixon of Kentucky and Senator Atchison of Missouri, that would explicitly repeal the Missouri Compromise. In the end, Douglas' political engine broke through all opposition in Congress, and both houses passed the Kansas-Nebraska Act on May 25, 1854, and President Pierce signed the bill.

14. Reactions to the Kansas-Nebraska Act

Antislavery Democrats in Congress denounced the Kansas-Nebraska Act; they called the act a "gross violation of a sacred pledge." Citizens, they declared, might resist the act, "for the cause of freedom is the cause of God." Other Democrats showed their disgust for the Democrats' support for the Kansas-Nebraska Act by leaving the party. Throughout the North voices began to call for state conventions to stem the spread of slavery. A convention in Massachusetts drew up a platform for what they called the Republican Party. The platform proclaimed "that no man can own another man … That slavery must be prohibited in the territories … That all new States must be Free States … That the rights of our colored citizens going to other States must be protected." Fearing that popular sovereignty might claim Kansas and Nebraska for slavery, northerners organized emigrant aid societies to settle antislavery men in these territories.

15. What Know-Nothingism was

Charles B. Allen of New York had in 1849 founded a secret patriotic society called the Order of the Star Spangled Banner. Its goal was to support the election of anti-immigrant and anti-Catholic politicians to public office. Members of the order took oaths of secrecy; and, when asked anything about the order, were to reply "I know nothing" (for which they became knowns as the "Know-Nothings"). In 1852, the order showed some influence at the polls. By 1854, it had become a serious force in politics. That year the "Know-Nothing" Order organized itself into a political party, called the American Party. In the off-year elections of 1854, the American "Know-Nothing" Party almost won significant victories in the North, the South, and the West. It seemed that the American Party could become a real rival of the Democratic Party (for the Whigs Party had ceased to exist).

16. The events that gave Kansas the epithet, "bloody"

Even before the Kansas-Nebraska Act had been signed into law, Missourians had been crossing the border onto the plains of Kansas. The Missourians in Kansas were proslavery. But with the passage of the Kansas-Nebraska Act, settlers from the Northeast, funded by emigrant aid societies, poured into Kansas to make sure the territory would be free-soil, not slave. Soon, the majority of settlers were free-soilers, and desperate proslavery southerners saw Kansas slipping from their grasp. President Pierce appointed Andrew Reeder of Pennsylvania as the first territorial

governor of Kansas and Samuel Dexter Lecompte as the territory's first chief justice. As chief justice, Lecompte organized the first election for a territorial representative to Congress. Over 1,500 armed Missourians crossed the border to vote for proslavery candidates, overwhelming the votes of the free-soilers. During the election for the territorial legislature in March 1855, the same thing happened – Missourians assured a proslavery majority in the legislature. Hoping, however, to maintain peace in the territory, Governor Reeder dissolved the territorial legislature. But President Pierce, who favored the proslavery forces, removed Reeder and replaced him with a proslavery governor, William Shannon. The free-soilers, meanwhile, had set up their own legislature in Topeka that, in December 1855, drew up a free-state constitution that excluded all blacks, free or slave, from Kansas. The Topeka legislature chose state officials and sent a delegation to Congress.

In the midst of all this political wrangling, armed bands of proslavery men had been stopping wagons of emigrants from the Northeast, arresting free-soilers, and threatening anybody opposed to a proslavery future for Kansas. When President Pierce blamed the emigrant aid societies for all the trouble in Kansas and gave his full support to the proslavery Leavenworth assembly, emigrant aid societies began sending supplies of Sharps repeating-rifles to Kansas free-soilers.

The stage was now set for a full-scale bloody conflict. Major Jefferson Buford of Alabama, with 300 volunteers, marched into the territory to aid the proslavery forces. Governor Shannon welcomed Buford and designated his force the Kansas Militia. Strengthened by 500 more men, in May 1856, Major Jefferson Buford's "Kansas Militia" (recognized the by the governor) descended on Lawrence, a free-soil town, confiscated the arms of the citizens, and destroyed printing presses, the public library, and the Free State Hotel. Reaction to the attack on Lawrence was bloody. John Brown, , in retaliation for the sacking of Lawrence and the murder of free-soilers, led a party to the proslavery settlement at Dutch Henry's Crossing on Pottawatomie Creek, seized five men and gunned them down in a mass execution. For the next several months, Northern "Jayhawkers" pitted themselves against Missouri "border ruffians" with such names as Kickapoo Rangers, Doniphan Tigers, and Lecompton Guards.

17. The new Republican Party and the significance of the election of 1856

The Republican convention, meeting in June 1856, in Philadelphia nominated John C. Frémont, the "Pathfinder," as their candidate for president, the delegates approved a platform that struck out at both slavery and the Mormons, declaring that it is "both the right and the duty of Congress to prohibit in the Territories these twin relics of barbarism, polygamy and slavery." The delegates came up with a catchy party slogan for the campaign: "Free soil, free speech, and Frémont."

In the election, the Democratic presidential nominee, James Buchanan, carried every slave state, except Maryland, which fell to the Know-Nothing Party. In the North, he carried every state except Pennsylvania, Illinois, and Indiana. The final vote tally was 174 electoral votes for Buchanan to 114 for Frémont. The popular vote was close: 1,838,000 for Buchanan to 1,340,000 for Frémont. Only 1,200 of Frémont's votes came from slave-holding states. If Frémont had triumphed in every northern state, he could have beaten Buchanan. The seriousness of the possibility

was not lost on southerners. The North formed a block that could control, not only the House of Representative, but the presidency as well. If the South lost its footing in the Senate, it would be completely at the mercy of the North and its interests.

18. The Dred Scott decision and its significance

In the early 1840s, the slave Dred Scott's master, Dr. John Emerson, had followed his army commission to free territory, taking Scott and his wife with him. In 1843, Emerson died, and Dred Scott, his wife, and other property passed to Emerson's wife, who lived in Missouri. Dred Scott was convinced that because he and his wife had lived in free territory, they were free. A judge in Missouri agreed; but the Missouri Supreme Court agreed with Emerson's wife, who claimed Scott and his wife were still slaves. The United States Supreme Court agreed to hear the case in 1856. On March 6, 1857, the Supreme Court published its decision in the Dred Scott case. Writing for the majority, Chief Justice Roger Taney maintained that neither the Declaration of Independence nor the Constitution had the slave population in mind when it spoke of citizens and their rights. "All men," in the Declaration, said Taney, referred only to white, Europeans. As a black man, and therefore excluded from the purview of the Constitution, Dred Scott had no legal right to sue in the courts of Missouri, according to Taney. Whether or not Dred Scott had lived in free territory, he was still a slave, wrote Taney, for the Constitution guaranteed a man his property, and slaves were property. Taney declared that when the Constitution gave Congress the right to make laws for the territories, it referrred only to those territories lying east of the Mississippi River, since Louisiana had not yet been purchased. The Missouri Compromise was, thus, an unconstitutional exercise of congressional power.

The Dred Scott decision thus nullified the Missouri Compromise and so opened up all the territories to slavery – even those, like Oregon, which had been declared free. Furthermore, besides nullifying the Missouri Compromise, the decision toppled popular sovereignty in the territories, since it said the Constitution protected the "property" of any slaveholder anywhere, even in free territory. Many southerners were pleased with the decision, since it gave them what they sought – equal rights with the North in the territories. Northerners, whether antislavery or not, were outraged at what appeared an exercise of raw judicial power in favor of the "slaveocracy."

19. Why Abraham Lincoln opposed the extension of slavery into the territories

For Lincoln, the question of slavery in the territories was not fundamentally a practical or strategic one; it was a moral one. He did not demand immediate emancipation of the slaves, but he opposed any approval of slavery in the territories because he thought slavery a moral wrong. As a moral wrong, he said it should be confined to the places it existed in the hope that, eventually, it would die out there. Lincoln appealed to principles that were higher than any written law, higher even than the Constitution. Lincoln appealed to the "inalienable rights" of man as expressed in what was, for him, the creed that defined the United States – the Declaration of Independence. If all men were created equal and endowed with inalienable rights, then these rights belonged to all men, black as well as white. This high moral stance endeared Lincoln to antislavery folk throughout the North and contributed to his swift rise in the ranks of the Republican Party.

20. John Brown's attack on Harpers Ferry and its results

In Canada, John Brown of Kansas met with New England abolitionists who had become convinced that only violence could free the slaves. Brown laid out his plan. He would capture the federal arsenal and gun factory at Harpers Ferry, Virginia, and establish it as the center of a fugitive slave republic, from whence he would lead a general slave insurrection. On October 16, 1859, John Brown with 13 whites (including three of his sons) and five blacks assaulted the federal arsenal at Harper's Ferry. Killing an army major, they seized the arsenal and then proceeded to round up the prominent citizens of the town. Fifty slaves, freed by Brown, joined him in the railroad roundhouse where, the next day, the Jefferson Guards of the Virginia state militia besieged them. A bitter fight ensued in which, one by one, Brown's men fell dead around him. The next day, October 18, Colonel Robert E. Lee and a contingent of United States marines battered down the doors of the roundhouse and took a wounded Brown and three others prisoner. Lee delivered them to Richmond, where they were to stand trial for treason. Brown refused the insanity defense his lawyer had prepared for him, and the court condemned him to death. Unruffled and unrepentant, Brown addressed the court. No general slave revolt followed Brown's action or his execution by hanging on December 2, 1859. The South, however, reeled with fear of slave insurrection and blamed the radical agitation of abolitionists for Brown.

21. The election of 1860 and its results

His stirring speech at Cooper Union in New York City won Abraham Lincoln the Republican nomination for president. The Democratic Party was badly split between supporters of Senator Stephan Douglas and popular sovereignty and the southern members who insisted on an extreme proslavery platform. Among these southern Democrats were cotton state delegates, like Jefferson Davis, who hoped for a split convention. If there were two Democratic candidates, the election could be thrown to the House of Representatives. But others, "fire eaters" they were called – hoped the election would usher in a Republican president and so push the South to secede from the union.

When in April 1860 the Democratic convention gathered in Charleston, South Carolina, cotton state delegates led by Jefferson Davis, demanded a platform calling for the establishment of black codes in all territories. William L. Yancey of Alabama wanted another platform declaring for the morality of slavery. When the convention rejected an extreme proslavery platform, delegates from the eight cotton states withdrew. The remaining delegates could not agree on a candidate, and they adjourned to Baltimore, where, in June, they nominated Stephen Douglas for their presidential candidate. Those who had seceded at Charleston formed a rival convention, adopted an extreme proslavery platform, and nominated John C. Breckenridge of Kentucky for president and Senator Joseph Lane for vice-president.

The Republican convention met in Chicago in May and adopted a platform that enshrined the doctrine of the Declaration of Independence that all men are created equal, and condemned disunion. It proclaimed freedom to be "the normal condition of all the territory of the United States," and declared

Key Terms at a Glance

Shaker: a member of the United Society of Believers in Christ's Second Appearing, founded by Ann Lee in the 19th century. Shaker teaching emphasized simplicity, celibacy, and work.

Adventist: member of a group of Protestant Christian churches that are distinguished by their emphasis on the belief that the personal, visible return of Christ is close at hand

Unitarianism: the ideology of a religious sect that calls for rationalism and denies the Trinity

Transcendentalism: movement of writers and philosophers who asserted the essential unity of all creation, the innate goodness of man, and the supremacy of insight over logic and experience in the discovery of truth

New England Renaissance: the period beginning in the the 1830s when American literature came of age as an expression of the national spirit

suffrage: the right to vote

universal manhood suffrage: the right of all male citizens to vote

Utopia: an ideal community whose inhabitants exist under seemingly perfect conditions

that Congress should ban slavery in the territories. Beyond the slavery issue, the platform called for "appropriations by Congress for River and Harbor improvements of a National character"; a free land grant homestead act for the West; and for "adjustment" of "imposts as to encourage the development of the industrial interest of the whole country" – that is, increasing the tariff on foreign manufactured goods, which the South still vehemently opposed. These planks betrayed a purely northern sectional bent and a growing orientation toward the interests of commerce and manufacturing – the interests of the North.

Abraham Lincoln won the election of 1860, with a majority of the electoral votes, 180. Stephen Douglas, though he came second in the popular vote, finished last in the electoral college, capturing only Missouri's 12 electors. John C. Breckenridge finished second, taking all the cotton states, with 72 electoral votes, while John Bell won Virginia, Kentucky, and Tennessee, giving him 39 electoral votes.

The election of 1860 presents an interesting snapshot of the U.S. at the time. Though he won the election, most Americans did not favor Lincoln; the vote totals of the three other candidates combined exceeded Lincoln's by about one million. Lincoln also won by taking the North – hardly a vote was cast for him south of the Mason-Dixon line. The election of 1860 demonstrated that a solid North could capture and control the presidency.

22. How Lincoln's election led to the secession of southern states

With Lincoln's election, enthusiasm for secession was strongest in the cotton South, and at its most intense in South Carolina. There, the state legislature summoned a state convention to meet December 17 to discuss whether South Carolina should remain in the union. On December 20, 1860, the South Carolina convention voted unanimously that "the union now subsisting between South Carolina and other States, under the name of 'The United States of America' is hereby dissolved." Soon state conventions in Mississippi, Florida, and Alabama voted for secession, and on January 19, 1861, Alexander Stephen's state, Georgia, left the union. On January 26, Louisiana seceded, and on February 1, despite the pleas of Sam Houston, Texas severed its ties with the United States. The cotton South had left the union.

23. The formation of the Confederate States of America

President James Buchanan did nothing while state after state seceded from the Union. Though urged to action by General Winfield Scott, Buchanan did not threaten South Carolina with military intervention. Delegates from the eight seceded states met in Montgomery, Alabama, on February 8, 1861, to discuss how they would unite under their own federal government. They formed a provisional Congress of the "Confederate States of America" and drew up a provisional constitution that would prove little different from the permanent constitution adopted a year later. The Constitution of the Confederate States of America opened with the preamble, "We, the people of the Confederate States, each State acting in its sovereign and independent character..." to make it clear that states, not the people as a whole, established this government.

The new constitution differed little from the United States Constitution, except in lengthening the term of the president to six years and forbidding his reelection. Also, unlike the United States Constitution, it forbade tariffs and the appropriations of "money for any internal improvement intended to facilitate commerce." The Confederate constitution prohibited the passage of federal laws "denying or impairing the right of property in Negro slaves" and opened all territories to slave holders. However, despite the fire-eating dreams of some southerners for the revival of the foreign slave trade, the new constitution forbade the "importation of Negroes of the African race, from any foreign country, other than the slaveholding States or Territories of the United States of America." On February 9, the delegation of six states elected Jefferson Davis and Alexander Stephens as respectively provisional president and vice president of the new government.

24. Why Lincoln opposed secession

Lincoln opposed secession because, he said, it was unconstitutional. In his inaugural address of March 14, 1861, he said the union of the states "is perpetual. Perpetuity is implied, if not expressed, in the fundamental law of all national governments"; thus any attempt by one or a few states to secede was illegal, "insurrectionary and revolutionary, according to the circumstances." Further, if the federal government is a compact, said Lincoln, then, if it is to be dissolved, both sides in the compact must agree to its dissolution.

25. The events that led up to the Confederate firing on Fort Sumter

In his inaugural address, Lincoln had declared he would not surrender to the seceded southern states any property held by the federal government and would collect all federal duties and imposts; but, he said, "beyond what may be necessary for these objects, there will be no invasion – no using of force against, or among the people anywhere." Among the federal properties the Confederacy had taken was Fort Sumter in Charleston, South Carolina. Lincoln sent a telegraph message to Governor Pickens of South Carolina, informing him that he was sending provisions, but no reinforcements or armaments, to the garrison at Fort Sumter. Commanding Confederate forces around Charleston was General Pierre Gustav Toutant Beauregard of Louisiana. With news of the approach of a provision ship, the question over what to do with Sumter reached a crisis point, and President Davis telegraphed Beauregard to send a message to Major Robert Anderson, commander at Fort Sumter, demanding the surrender of the fort. If Anderson refused to surrender, he was to be informed that Confederate shore batteries would open fire on him at once. On April 11, a group of Beauregard's staff officers crossed by boat to Sumter. They presented their general's terms to Anderson, who replied he could not surrender Sumter without due instructions from his government. As the Confederate officers departed, Anderson admitted that his garrison, without new provisions, could hold out only a few days. Beauregard communicated this news to Davis, who replied that if they could get assurances from Anderson that he would surrender when his food supply ran out, then they would refrain from bombarding the fort.

But Anderson would give no assurance of surrender; he told the Confederates that he would surrender only if he were not reprovisioned in the next few days. The staff officers, thinking it pointless to confer with Beauregard on this reply, passed a written note to Anderson that he would open fire on the fort on the morning of April 12. Confederate batteries opened fire at the time specified. The firing continued throughout the day, with no casualties on either side. The relief ship arrived outside Charleston harbor; but being unable to reach the fort, it turned back. Finally, the next day, April 13, Anderson, his ammunition exhausted, surrendered.

Questions for Review

1. **How did the antislavery movement differ from the abolitionist movement, and what were the main ideas of each?**

The antislavery movement differed from the abolitionist movement in that the antislavery movement called for gradual emancipation of the slaves, while the abolitionists called for immediate emancipation. Some proponents of antislavery held that the emancipated slaves should be colonized somewhere outside the United States. Abolitionists held that the emancipated slaves should remain in the United States as free and equal citizens.

2. **How did George Fitzhugh's *Cannibals All!* Answer northern criticisms of southern slavery?**

Though *Cannibals All!* could not and did not justify southern slavery, it pointed out an inconsistency in many antislavery minds; they paid scant attention to the plight of free laborers --- black and white --- in the North in their concern for the black slaves of the South. He argued that "white slavery" – the labor system of the North – was far more cruel than black slavery.

3. **What was the position of American Catholics on slavery in the first half of the 19th century? What actions did the Church take or not take on slavery, and why?**

The Catholic position on slavery was complicated. While the popes condemned slavery, some Catholics in America owned slaves. Slave owners were supposed to respect the marriage of blacks and to provide them the freedom to observe holy days. These laws were often ignored, however. Though Catholic theologians taught that it is immoral to enslave an innocent free man, one is not necessarily bound to abolish a condition of slavery or to free people already reduced to a condition of slavery. A master had to treat his slaves as human beings, and not mistreat them. Many Catholics thought abolition was a political question, not a moral necessity. The Catholic position on slavery can in part be explained by the fact that Catholics were engaged in their own struggles against nativist bigotry.

4. **Explain the controversy between North and South over the new western territories. What constitutional and moral arguments did each side make?**

The controversy over the new western territories concerned the question of whether those territories should be admitted to the union as free or slave states. Anti-slavery people argued that, since slavery is immoral, it should be forbidden to spread outside the South, where it already existed. Pro-slavery men, such as John C. Calhoun, said that, since the union was a compact between equal parties, the states, the territories belonged equally to all states. Thus, Congress could not forbid settlers bringing their "common law property" into any territory.

5. **Did Henry Clay Compromise of 1850 solve the controversy between North and South over slavery? Why or why not?**

Henry Clay's Compromise of 1850 solved little, because neither the North or the South was happy with it. Southerners such as John C. Calhoun thought the compromise did not sufficiently protect the South, because it did not recognize the equality between states and their interests. Som northerners thought it immoral even to permit slvery into any territory. Others objected to the strengthened Fugitive Slave Law.

6. **Explain the importance of *Uncle Tom's Cabin* in the controversy over slavery?**

Because of the way it portrayed southern slavery, *Uncle Tom's Cabin* produced a reaction in the South. Southerners denounced the book because of the negative way it portryed slavery. The character, Simon Legree, became the epitome of the cruelty of slavery.

7. **Explain the controversy over the Kansas-Nebraska bill and how it contributed to the slavery controversy.**

The controversy over the Kansas-Nebraska bill centered on whether the territories should be slave or free, and whether there should be a southern or central railroad line. Fearing that popular sovereignty might claim Kansas and Nebraska for slavery, northerners organized emigrant aid societies to settle antislavery men in these territories. This led to violence when pro-slavery men in Kansas sought to hinder the entrance of free-soil settlers into that territory.

8. **How did the Dred Scott decision fuel the slavery debate? What effect did it have on the relationship between the North and the South?**

The Dred Scott decision fueled the slavery debate because it ruled that the Declaration of Independence and the Constitution addressed only white Europeans and free men. Moreover, it said slaves were property. Many southerners were pleased with the decision, since it gave them what they sought

-- equal rights with the North in the territories. Northerners, whether antislavery or not, were outraged at what appeared an exercise of raw judicial power in favor of the "slaveocracy." The chasm between North and South was widened.

9. **Briefly explain both Lincoln and Douglas' views on slavery as expressed in their debates during the Illinois senatorial campaign of 1858.**

Douglas said he was opposed to black citizenship because the government, he said, "was made on the white basis ... by white men, for the benefit of white men and their posterity." He held that black people were inferior to white people. Lincoln did not deny that, in certain respects, the black man might be inferior to the white man, but in their fundamental rights, black and white people are equals. As for the question of slavery in the territories, Douglas held to popular sovereignty. For Lincoln, though, the question of slavery in the territories was not fundamentally a practical or strategic one; it was a moral one. Though he refrained from demanding immediate emancipation, Lincoln appealed to principles that were higher than any written law, higher even than the Constitution. Lincoln appealed to the "inalienable rights" of man as expressed in what was, for him, the creed that defined the United States – the Declaration of Independence. If all men were created equal and endowed with inalienable rights, then these rights belonged to all men, black as well as white.

10. **Why did South Carolina decide to secede from the union?**

Lincoln's election caused great discontent in the South, most of which had opposed

Lincoln's candidacy. When he was elected president, South Carolina reacted by calling a convention to decide whether or not to remain in the Union.

Ideas in Action

1. Research the history of the Know-Nothings and their effect on the Catholic Church in the United States.

2. Study the history of the Underground Railroad and chart the paths slaves took to freedom.

3. Study the arguments for gradualism and immediate abolition and stage a debate between students who hold, one or some to gradualism, and one or some to immediate abolition.

4. Read a fictional or eyewitness account of the opening of the war. Compose your own imaginary eyewitness account of the war's opening from whatever perspective you wish.

5. In his first inaugural address, Abraham Lincoln said secession is illegal because the union "is perpetual. Perpetuity is implied, if not expressed, in the fundamental law of all national governments." Research what the secessionists thought about the right to secession; how would they have answered Lincoln? What constitutional arguments would they have used? Given what you know about the Constitution and the powers it grants to the federal government and reserves to the states, who do you think had the better argument — Lincoln or the secess

Sample Quiz I (pages 381-397)

Please answer the following in complete sentences.

1. What was the essential difference between abolitionist and gradualists?

2. How did George Fitzhugh defend slavery?

3. Why were many northerners opposed to antislavery and abolitionism?

4. Give one reason why the Cathlic Church did not have a clear position on slavery.

5. What were the "gag resolutions"?

6. Briefly explain the Compromise of 1850.

7. Why did many Northerners dislike the Compromise of 1850?

8. Who were the Young Americans?

9. Briefly explain the Ostend Manifesto.

Answers to Sample Quiz I

Students' answers should approximate the following.

1. Abolitionists believed in immediate emancipation of the slaves. Gradualists believed that slavery should be abolished, but slowly, over time.

2. George Fitzhugh said that the "white slave trade" – the immigrant workers in northern factories – was far more cruel than the black slave trade because it exacts more of its slaves and neither protects nor governs them. White slavery, he said, is more cruel, for it leaves the laborer to care for himself and family out of a pittance. He argued that black slaves were better cared for than white laborers.

3. Many northerners were opposed to antislavery and abolitionism for several reasons. They were opposed to full social and legal equality for blacks. Then there was the economic aspect, as northern textile manufacturers benefited from the fruits of

slavery, the cotton crop. Some northerners were involved in illegal slave trade.

4. *Possible answers:* The Catholic position was complicated by the fact that the Church in America had been founded in Maryland, south of the Mason-Dixon, and this tended to mold Catholic opinions on antislavery nationwide. Maryland Jesuits had owned slaves, as did some bishops and the Ursuline sisters of New Orleans. The "black code" of Louisiana, hearkening back to both French and Spanish law, held that masters were to respect the marriages of blacks and to provide them the freedom to observe holy days, which, in those days included freedom from manual labor. This code, though, was often ignored. Some Catholics engaged in slave smuggling – though the popes themselves had condemned it. Though Catholic theologians taught that it is immoral to enslave an innocent free man, one is not, they said, necessarily bound to abolish a condition of slavery or to free people already reduced to a condition of slavery. The Catholic position on slavery can in part be explained by the fact that Catholics were engaged in their own struggles against nativist bigotry.

5. The "gag resolutions" were resolutions passed by Congress, beginning in 1836, that declared that all petitions relating to slavery or abolition should be "laid on the table"; that is, ignored.

6. Henry Clay sought to break the impasse over the admission of California by presenting a compromise that called for admitting California as a free state but would organize territorial governments in New Mexico and Deseret without any reference to slavery, thus allowing slaveholders to bring slaves into those territories. He also suggested new, stricter fugitive laws, and abolishing the slave trade in the District of Columbia.

7. Northerners disliked the Compromise because of the new, strengthened Fugitive Slave Law. Others objected that, since slavery was immoral, it should not be allowed to spread outside the areas where it then existed – the South.

8. The Young Americans was a movement of men, old and young, that sought to find new ideals to inspire civic leadership, and to support democratic revolutions the world over.

9. The Ostend Manifesto was a policy drawn up to govern the United States' relations with Cuba. The Manifesto said that Cubans suffered under absolute despotism. It said the United States should buy Cuba from Spain, and if Spain refused to sell, the U.S. would be justified in taking it from Spain.

Sample Quiz II (pages 397-415)

Please answer the following in complete sentences.

1. **Who were the Know-Nothings?**

2. **What is the significance of the election of 1856?**

3. **What is the significance of the Dred Scott decision?**

4. **Why did Abraham Lincoln oppose the extension of slavery into the territories?**

5. **What was the result of the attack on Harper's Ferry?**

6. **How did the Confederate States of America's constitution differ from the United States'?**

7. **Why did Lincoln think succession was unconstitutional?**

Answers to Sample Quiz II

Students' answers should approximate the following.

1. The Know-Nothings were a secret patriotic society whose proper name was the Order of the Star Spangled Banner. Their goal was to support the election of ant-immigrant and anti-Catholic politicians to public office.

2. In the election of 1856, the North formed a block that could control, not only the House of Representatives, but the presidency as well. If the South lost its footing in the Senate, it would be completely at the mercy of the North and its interests.

3. The Dred Scott decision nullified the Missouri Compromise and opened up all the territories to slavery. Besides nullifying the Missouri Compromise, the decision toppled popular sovereignty in the territories, since it said the Constitution protected the "property" of any slaveholder anywhere, even in free territory.

4. Abraham Lincoln opposed the extension of slavery into the territories because he thought slavery a moral wrong. As a moral wrong, he said it should be confined to the places it existed in the hope that, eventually, it would die out there.

5. As a result of the attack on Harper's Ferry, the South reeled with fear of slave insurrection and blamed the radical agitation of abolitionists for Brown.

6. The Confederate States' constitution differed little from the United States Constitution, except in lengthening the term of the president to six years and forbidding his reelection. Also, unlike the United States Constitution, it forbade tariffs and the appropriations of "money for any internal improvement intended to facilitate commerce." The Confederate constitution prohibited the passage of federal laws "denying or impairing the right of property in Negro slaves" and opened all territories to slave holders.

7. Lincoln thought secession was unconstitutional because he said the union of the states is perpetual, so any attempt by one or a few states to secede was illegal. Further, if the federal government is a compact, said Lincoln, then, if it is to be dissolved, both sides in the compact must agree to its dissolution.

Essays

Instructions to be given to the students: Write in complete sentences. Underline your thesis. Give three supports or examples that explain why you think what you do and that support your thesis.

1. Explain the views of the abolitionists and those of the anti-slavery proponents. How were they alike, and how did they differ? Which view do you think is better, and why? Why is the other view not good?

2. Describe each of the important acts that led up to the war: the Compromise of 1850, the Kansas-Nebraska Act, and the Dred Scott decision. What was their importance? How did these acts contribute to the discontent between North and South, and finally culminate in war?

3. Explain how the new Republican Party and the elections of 1856 and 1860 were significant. Douglas' bill became law and implicitly repealed the Missour Compromise.

Sample Test

Please answer the following in complete sentences

I. Short Essay – Answer two of the following:

1. What was attitude of Catholic Americans on slavery? What aspects of Catholic life and thought influenced this attitude?

2. Explain the Kansas-Nebraska Act and the decisions that led up to it.

3. Explain the Dred Scott decision.

4. Explain the views of the Democratic and Republican parties during the election of 1860.

II. Short Answer:

1. Why were the gag resolutions finally repealed?

2. What was the Wilmot Proviso?

3. Why did *Uncle Tom's Cabin* so anger southerners?

4. What principle did Lincoln appeal to regarding slavery?

5. What did the election of 1860 demonstrate?

6. Why did Lincoln oppose secession?

....

Answer Key to the Chapter Test

Students' answers should approximate the following:

I.

1. The Catholic position was complicated by the fact that the Church in America had been founded in Maryland, south of the Mason-Dixon, and this tended to mold Catholic opinions on antislavery nationwide. Maryland Jesuits had owned slaves, as did some bishops and the Ursuline sisters of New Orleans. The "black code" of Louisiana, hearkening back to both French and Spanish law, held that masters were to respect the marriages of blacks and to provide them the freedom to observe holy days, which, in those days included freedom from manual labor. This code, though, was often ignored. Some Catholics engaged in slave smuggling – though the popes themselves had condemned it. Though Catholic theologians taught that it is immoral to enslave an innocent free man, one is not, they said, necessarily bound to abolish a condition of slavery or to free people already reduced to a condition of slavery. The Catholic position on slavery can in part be explained by the fact that Catholics were engaged in their own struggles against nativist bigotry.

2. Davis' proposal of a southern route for the transcontinental railroad met opposition from Senator Stephen A. Douglas, who had been speculating in western lands and in Chicago real estate. Douglas championed a central route for the transcontinental railroad. The railroad, however, needed to pass through organized territories, and the Nebraska territory between Missouri and Utah had no territorial government. In 1854, Douglas introduced a bill to split and organize the Nebraska territory into two separate territories – Kansas and Nebraska. Douglas proposed that the territories should be organized without any reference to slavery. Instead, the people who settled the territories would decide whether they would accept slavery among them or forbid its introduction. This was called popular or "squatter" sovereignty.

3. Dred Scott was a slave whose master took him to free territory. Scott was convinced that because he and his wife had lived in free territory that they were free. The Supreme Court under Chief Justice Roger Taney

disagreed, and said that neither the Declaration of Independence nor the Constitution had the slave population in mind when it spoke of citizens and their rights. As a black man, and therefore excluded from the purview of the Constitution, Dred Scott had no legal right to sue in the courts of Missouri. Whether or not Dred Scott had lived in free territory, he was still a slave, wrote Taney, for the Constitution guaranteed a man his property, and slaves were property. Taney declared that when the Constitution gave Congress the right to make laws for the territories, it referrred only to those territories lying east of the Mississippi River, since Louisiana had not yet been purchased. The Missouri Compromise was, thus, an unconstitutional exercise of congressional power.

4. When the Democratic convention gathered in Charleston, South Carolina, cotton state delegates led by Jefferson Davis, demanded a platform calling for the establishment of black codes in all territories. William L. Yancey of Alabama wanted another platform declaring for the morality of slavery. The Republican convention adopted a platform that enshrined the doctrine of the Declaration of Independence that all men are created equal, and condemned disunion. It proclaimed freedom to be "the normal condition of all the territory of the United States," and declared that Congress should ban slavery in the territories. Beyond the slavery issue, the platform called for "appropriations by Congress for River and Harbor improvements of a National character"; a free land grant homestead act for the West; and for "adjustment" of "imposts as to encourage the development of the industrial interest of the whole country" – that is, increasing the tariff on foreign manufactured goods, which the South still vehemently opposed.

II.
1. The sheer amount of unrelenting abolitionist opposition to the gag results caused Congress to repeal the resolutions.
2. The Wilmot Proviso was a proposal to forbid any introduction of slavery into territories where it did not already exist.
3. *Uncle Tom's Cabin* so angered southerners because they said Stowe could not know the true character of their "peculiar institution" and portrayed it in a bad light.
4. Lincoln appealed to the "inalienable rights" of man as expressed in the Declaration of Independence.
5. The election of 1860 demonstrated that a solid North could capture and control the presidency.
6. Lincoln opposed seccession because he thought it was unconstitutional.

CHAPTER 17: A Brothers' War

Chapter Overview

- Many at the beginning of the war believed it would be over swiftly. With that assumption, Lincoln called for 75,000 volunteers. General Winfield Scott wanted up to 100,000, but Lincoln would not follow his suggestion, thinking the uprising in the South a mere insurrection and that he could easily crush.

- Virginia seceded on April 17, 1861, and the Confederate government moved its capital from Montgomery, Alabama to Richmond, Virginia.

- The South was inferior to the North in numbers and industrial output and needed the support of foreign powers,

- The South was inferior to the North in numbers and industrial output and needed the support of foreign powers, Great Britain and France, to supply its arms. The South had an important bargaining chip, cotton. The South's greatest assets were the spirit of its men and its commanding officers, including Lt. Colonel Robert E. Lee.

- The North's greatest advantage was its navy. Lincoln planned to blockade the southern coast and seize control of the Mississippi River, therefore cutting off the South's trade with Europe and eventually starving the Confederates into submission.

- Lincoln's first task of the war was to secure for the Union the neutral border states of Maryland, Kentucky, Delaware, and Missouri. In order to silence secessionist voices in the divided state of Maryland, on April 27, 1861, Lincoln ordered the suspension of the writ of

habeas corpus "for the public safety" along the military line that ran through Maryland to Washington. This caused indignation in the state, and Chief Justice Taney said that only Congress could order suspension of the writ. But Lincoln would not heed him.

- In May the Confederate congress authorized the recruitment of 400,000 volunteers. Still, recruiters turned away southern men eager for the fight because there was just no room for them.

- In June, General George McClellan forced Lee to evacuate Virginia's western mountain counties which stood strongly for the Union. On June 11, western Virginia organized a pro-Union government and sent representatives to Washington.

- General Benjamin Butler, though he had supported nomination of Jefferson Davis in 1860, had more recently remade himself into a liberator of slaves. Slaves were crossing Union lines at Fortress Monroe on Chesapeake Bay, and Butler was not turning them away. By late spring he was using about 1,000 slaves for menial tasks around the fortress.

- At the first Battle of Bull Run, or Manassas, Confederate forces defeated the Federal army, which retreated toward Washington. This battle awakened people to the fact that war would not be a quick affair, but a long, drawn-out struggle.

- In September 1861, Confederate general Leonidas Polk marched his forces into Kentucky, thus ending the state's neutrality. The state went to the Union. When southern sympathizers in Maryland again agitated for secession, Lincoln arrested and jailed the mayor and 31 legislators, replacing them with a pro-Union majority.

- In January of 1862, Lincoln issued General War Order Number 1, commanding a general movement of all land and sea forces on February 22, 1862.

- The unconditional surrender of Forts Henry and Donelson made General Ulysses S. Grant a northern hero and opened the interior of Tennessee and Alabama to Federal armies.

- On April 16, 1862, the Confederate congress passed two laws. The first extended the enlistment of men already in arms for the length of the war, and the second conscripted all able-bodied men between the ages of 18 and 35 for three years' service. This conscription law met a storm of protest, and many states declared it was a violation of states' rights.

- General Johnston was wounded in the battle of Fair Oaks or Seven Pines and was forced to relinquish command of the Confederate army. President Davis chose Robert E. Lee to take his place. Lee renamed the army the Army of Northern Virginia to indicate his goal of retaking all of Virginia. He marched out to defend Richmond against the Federal army under the command of General George B. McClellan.

- Following the series of battles called the Seven Days, with fearful losses on both sides, McClellan asked Lincoln for more men or he could not beat Lee. Lincoln told him the numbers were not available, and he should return to Washington. The Army of the Potomac left Richmond.

- General Pope issued three general orders, and commanded his soldiers to "subsist off the countryside" – that is, to take what food they needed from Virginia citizens. This measure was enacted with vengeance, and Lee marched out to drive the "miscreant" from Virginia. The

two armies met in the Second Battle of Bull Run or Manassas, in which the Confederates were victorious.

- Lincoln began to turn his thoughts towards the antislavery movement. After a marginal victory in the Battle of Antietam or Sharpsburg, Lincoln issued the Preliminary Emancipation Proclamation on September 22, 1862.

What Students Should Know

1. **What were Lincoln's aims in the war**

Lincoln said his aim was to preserve the union, to save it, not to end or destroy slavery. Lincoln battled to maintain a union that he saw as "the city on the hill" – the messianic hope of the world.

2. **What were Jefferson Davis' aims in the war**

Davis' aim was to preserve the independence and continued existence of the Confederate States of America.

3. **What resources each side possessed**

The North had superior resources to the South. The white population of the North, for one, was 18.9 million in contrast with the South's mere 5.5 million. Northern industry could produce the arms and provisions needed by the Federal army. The North had a navy; the South did not possess one. The South had little industry. Southern wealth was in cotton and other agricultural products, which the South could use to purchase arms and provisions in Europe. But Europe was an ocean away. Perhaps the South's greatest asset was the spirit of many of its men, who saw themselves as fighting to protect their homes and native states. And Davis could place these men under the command of the cream of the United States army's officer corps, who had left the U.S. army to fight for the South.

4. What the "Anaconda" strategy was

It was the commander of the U.S. army, General Winfield Scott, who came up with this strategy. He advised Lincoln to use the navy to establish a blockade of the coast and seize control of the Mississippi in order cut off the South's trade with Europe and eventually starve the Confederates into submission. Lincoln adopted the policy as part of his greater war strategy, which would establish a blockade of the southern coast and capture key positions on the western rivers, while at the same time, three forces would invade the South: one, east of the Appalachians; another, west of the Appalachians and east of the Mississippi; and a third, west of the Mississippi.

5. Lincoln's policy toward the border states

Lincoln's first task was to secure for the Union the neutral border states – Maryland, Kentucky, Delaware, and Missouri. Delaware, with few slaves, had shown no signs of seceding. Kentucky, however, had a strong secessionist faction and could as easily go Confederate as remain in the Union. Lincoln thought an insistence that Kentucky contribute to the war effort against the South would goad that state into secession. He thus assured Kentucky that he would respect her neutrality. No federal troops would cross over onto Kentucky soil

Missouri was divided between southern and Union sympathizers, among the latter the numerous German population around St. Louis. Though in February 1861, a state convention voted to stay in the Union, Governor Clairborne Jackson refused to send troops to Lincoln and plotted to seize the federal arsenal in St. Louis. The commander

of the arsenal, Nathaniel Lyon, got wind of this and with federal troops broke up a state militia encampment at St. Louis. Promoted to brigadier general and to the command of Federal troops around St. Louis, Lyon then marched on Governor Jackson, driving him from the state capital, Jefferson City, into the southern regions of Missouri.

Maryland was a special worry for Lincoln, for if that state seceded, Washington would be cut off from the North. Lincoln had to secure Maryland at any cost. Maryland's governor, Thomas B. Hicks, stood stoutly for the Union, but the state had many secessionists. To forestall an irregular meeting of the state assembly, which secessionists would dominate, Hicks called a regular session of the assembly to meet on April 26. During the session, Hicks called for Maryland's neutrality, and the legislature decided that it had no legal right to call a state convention to consider secession. Still, Lincoln adopted harsher measures to silence secessionist voices in the state. On April 27, he ordered Scott to suspend the writ of *habeas corpus* "for the public safety" along the military line that ran through Maryland to When Chief Justice Taney sent a United States marshal with a writ of *habeas corpus* for a man the government arrested, Lincoln ignored Taney. Cadwalader's predecessor, Brigadier General Benjamin F. Butler, placed Baltimore under martial law and closed newspapers with a secessionist bent, confiscated arms, arrested men suspected of Confederate leanings, and imprisoned ministers who in church services omitted prescribed prayers for the president of the United States. The outcry against Butler was great, and he was removed from Baltimore; but the government did not undo what Butler had wrought, and martial law continued under his successor, Major General Cadwalader.

6. How the Confederacy lost West Virginia. The significance of this loss

In June 1861, General George Britten McClellan led a Federal force into Virginia's western mountain counties, which stood strongly for the Union. McClellan encountered a smaller force under Confederate General Robert E. Lee and forced the southern commander to evacuate the region. The battle pushed Lee into a desk job in Richmond and lost for the South a region rich in coal. On June 11, western Virginia organized a pro-Union government and sent representatives to Washington. The region would later secede from Virginia to form the state of West Virginia.

7. The First Battle of Bull Run or Manassas and its significance

The First Battle of Manassas or Bull Run, fought in July 1861, was the first major battle of the Civil War. The Federal army, under Irwin McDowell, marched from Washington against the Confederates, under General Joseph E. Johnston, at Manassas Junction. At first, the Federals pushed the Confederates back. But when the Confederates retreated to a new position on Henry's Hill, five Virginia regiments under Brigadier General Thomas J. Jackson rallied the retreating Confederates. With Jackson as its anchor, the Confederate line held. Reinforcements under Colonel Jubal Early arrived, and about 4 p.m. the Confederates counterattacked. The Union retreat became a rout; soldiers fled in confusion, casting away their weapons. The Battle of First Manassas or First Bull Run showed the North that the war would not be over quickly and that the South had the will to resist.

8. How the Confederacy lost Kentucky

Both Lincoln and Jefferson Davis thought it important to honor Kentucky's neutrality. Lincoln was especially concerned, for if Kentucky seceded, important points on the Ohio and Mississippi would fall to the Confederacy and threaten the success of Lincoln's western strategy. For Jefferson Davis, Kentucky, neutral or Confederate, stood as a buffer zone between the Northern armies and Tennessee. If Kentucky went fully to the Union, all of central Tennessee, along with Mississippi and Alabama, lay open to a Federal advance. Davis wanted to do nothing to tip Kentucky into the Union. But Confederate General Leonidas Polk was worried about the buildup of Federal forces in Illinois under Brig. General Ulysses S. Grant, massed at Cairo, lllinois, while Federal gunboats threatened from St. Louis. Fearing a Federal advance into Kentucky, Polk marched his forces into the state in early September and took and fortified Columbus, a city on a bluff overlooking the Mississippi. U.S. Grant quickly reacted to Polk's move and captured Paducah on the Kentucky side of the Ohio. The move was decisive, for now the Union controlled the mouth of the Tennessee River, which provided a road to the heart of the central Confederate states. And Grant had this advantage – it was Polk, not he, who first violated Kentucky's neutrality. Polk's invasion of Kentucky ended the state's neutrality. In September 1861, the strongly pro-union Kentucky legislature met and asked for Federal military aid against the Confederates.

9. The significance of the battle of the ironclads

The battle of the *Virginia* and the Monitor introduced a new era of naval warfare, the era of steam ships clad in steel.

10. How Lincoln stopped Maryland's secession

Emboldened by the Confederate victory at Manassas, southern sympathizers in Maryland again agitated for secession. In September the state assembly was set to meet in special legislative session, and Lincoln feared it would vote for Maryland's withdrawal from the Union. To forestall this, Lincoln sent troops into Baltimore and arrested and jailed the mayor and 31 legislators. Lincoln held them in jail for two months, long enough to assure the election of a pro-union majority to the legislature in November.

11. The significance of the Battles of Fort Henry and Fort Donelson

General Ulysses Grant's (and Commodore Foote's) victory at Forts Henry and Donelson opened up central Tennessee as well as Mississippi to Federal invasion. They also established Grant's reputation as a hard-fighting general.

12. What happened at Shiloh

The Battle of Shiloh was fought at Pittsburgh Landing on the Tennessee River in Tennessee in April 1862. Though the Confederates, first under Albert Sydney Johnson and then General Beauregard, were able to push the Federal forces under Grant to the banks of the Tennessee River, the arrival of Federal reinforcements under General Buell forced the Confederates to retreat to Corinth, Mississippi. Shiloh was the single most bloody battle of the war to that time.

13. The significance of the Union's capture of New Orleans

In addition to the capture by the Union forces of Fort Pillow and Island 10 on the Mississippi River and of Corinth in Mississippi state, the capture of New Orleans proved a serious blow to the Confederate war effort. An important sea port, New Orleans was captured by the Federal navy under the command of Admiral David G. Farragut on April 25, 1862. Once he had taken New Orleans, Farragut continued up the Mississippi, taking Baton Rouge, Port Hudson, and Natchez. Now, the only Confederate stronghold remaining in the Mississippi Valley was Vicksburg, Mississippi, that Jefferson Davis called the "nailhead [that] holds the South's two halves together."

14. The Confederate conscription act and the reaction to it

By mid-April 1862, the military prospects of the Confederacy looked grim. Faced with the unraveling of the war effort (and the end of their national existence), the Confederate congress passed two laws on April 16. The first extended the enlistment of men already in arms for the length of the war; the second conscripted all able-bodied men, ages 18 to 35, for three-years' service. This conscription act met a storm of protest throughout the South; it was viewed as a violation of states' rights. Though Jefferson Davis signed the law, Vice-President Stephens opposed it. One-half of those conscripted refused to sign up for military service.

15. The Battle of the Seven Days and its significance

By May 24, 1862, General George McClellan had drawn up the Federal army in lines five miles from Richmond, the Confederate capital. But he did not move against Richmond, for he falsely thought that the Confederates outnumbered him. Instead, McClellan awaited reinforcements – which did not arrive because they were occupied fighting Stonewall Jackson in the Shenandoah Valley. It was the Confederate commander, General Joe Johnston, who attacked the Federals in a brief, inconclusive engagement on May 31, in which Johnston himself was injured. General Robert E. Lee replaced McClellan as overall commander, and on June 26 commenced the series of battles collectively known as the Battle of the Seven Days. From June 26 to July 1, Lee's army, though itself suffering fearful casualties, was able to push the Federals back to the James River. By September, the Federals had completely withdrawn from Richmond and returned to Washington. In this way, Richmond was saved and the Confederacy was preserved from an early demise. Too, this battle brought Robert E. Lee into prominence.

16. What Pope's General Orders were and their effect

Lincoln appointed General John Pope as commander of a portion of the Federals in the East, and it was this general that put in place Lincoln's more stringent war policy that mandated that not just the Confederate army, but civilians were to suffer for secession. The General Orders, issued in July 1862, were three in number. First, citizens of Union-occupied territory in Virginia were to be held responsible for any guerrilla activity in their region – whether they were truly responsible for it or not. Second, any male citizen who refused to take an oath of allegiance to the United States would have to leave his home

and cross over to enemy lines; and if he returned, he would be "subjected to the extreme rigor of military law." Third, those who took the oath of allegiance, and then violated it, would be executed. Pope also issued orders commanding his soldiers to "subsist off the countryside" – that is, to take what food they needed from Virginia citizens. When the inevitable abuses arising from such an order occurred, Pope issued corrective orders. These were, however, not vigorously enforced, and Federal troops pillaged the Virginia countryside. Southerners roundly condemned Pope's orders; they had hoped the war could be fought according to civilized codes, and now Lincoln's government was removing the barriers civilization had erected to stave off the brutality of war.

17. What the Federal government did about slavery during the first part of the Civil War

Though Lincoln insisted that the war was being fought to preserve the Union, not to abolish slavery, Federal commanders and lawmakers began to move the war in the latter direction. Federal commanders, like Benjamin Butler, confiscated slaves in southern territory. Slaves, too, were finding freedom by fleeing to invading Union armies. Congress, dominated by extreme antislavery Republicans called the Radicals, passed a law in March 1862 that forbade army officers to return fugitive slaves to their owners. Later, in April, under Radical Republican influence,

Key Terms at a Glance

habeas corpus: a writ, or legal action that requires a person under arrest to be brought before a judge or into a court so that it might examine the reasons for imprisonment

Congress abolished slavery in the District of Columbia and, in June, prohibited slavery in the western territories.

18. **What Lincoln did about slavery during the first part of the war, and why he began to contemplate emancipation**

During the war, Lincoln had begun secretly contemplating a declaration to emancipate slaves in the rebellious states. He tried to abolish slavery in the border states by offering slaveholders there $400 for each slave along with expatriation of the freedmen to Africa or Central America. This offer, refused by slaveholders, was condemned by free blacks, who said that the United States, not Africa or Central America, was their home. Yet, Lincoln was not moved solely by humanitarian concern – emancipation, he thought, could further the war effort. By freeing the slaves in the Confederate states, Lincoln could strike a blow at the southern economy and, perhaps, prevent European nations from recognizing the Confederacy; for what king, prince, or president in enlightened Europe would wish to align himself against a fight for freedom?

19. **The significance of the Battle of Sharpsburg (Antietam)**

Lincoln decided to issue a proclamation freeing slaves in those states still in a state of rebellion against the Union. But to do so, he needed a military victory – for, without a victory, emancipation would appear a gesture of weakness, not strength. That victory was won by the Federal army under General McClellan at Sharpsburg on September 17, 1862. Though he did not destroy Lee's army, McClellan forced it to withdraw from Maryland. This was the victory Lincoln needed to proceed with his plan for emancipation.

20. **What the Emancipation Proclamation said, the reaction to it, and its significance**

On September 22, 1862 Lincoln issued the Preliminary Emancipation Proclamation – "preliminary," because it would not go into effect until January 1, 1863, and then only if the southern states were still "in rebellion against the United States." The proclamation freed slaves, but only those in rebellious states. Southerners condemned the Emancipation Proclamation. They thought it not only struck at their economy, but the safety of their women and children, by encouraging slave revolts. Many abolitionists were not satisfied with the proclamation, since it exempted the Border States. Others, though, saw its true import – it put slavery on the road to quick extinction; for how could the Border States maintain slavery when it was everywhere else abolished? It also changed the very character of the war. No longer was it a struggle for something called the "Union." It now became a fight for human freedom

Questions for Review

1. **What was Abraham Lincoln's main objective in the war?**

Lincoln's main objective in the war in the war was to preserve the union.

2. **Describe the personalities of Abraham Lincoln and Jefferson Davis and how they differed.**

Davis was a refined southern aristocrat, with all the vices and virtues of his class. He had honesty, a devotion to duty, a deep sense of honor, but was often aloof, overly sensitive on small points that touched on his dignity, impatient with those who opposed him, and tactless. Davis fought for his country's independence.

Lincoln was a rough westerner who peppered his conversation with homey stories and coarse jokes. He was willing to humble himself to subordinates to obtain a greater goal, somewhat unconcerned about using unworthy means to obtain a desired end, but acted with a keen, hard-headed astuteness. While Davis fought for his country's independence, Lincoln battled to maintain a union that he saw as "the city on the hill" – the messianic hope of the world.

3. **What were the South's greatest assets in the war?**

The south's greatest asset was the spirit of many of its men, who saw themselves as fighting ot protect their homes and native states. The south also possessed the cream of the United States army's officer corps, who had left the U.S. army to fight for the South.

4. **What were the North's greatest assets in the war?**

The north's greatest assets were it large population, its industry that could produce the arms and provisions needed by the Federal army, and its navy.

5. **Why did Lincoln find it necessary to secure the neutral states for the Union?**

Lincoln found it necessary to secure for the Union the neutral states because they could easily go to the North or the South.

6. **What significance did the First Battle of Bull Run (Manassas) hold for the war?**

The First Battle of Bull Run was the first major battle of the war. It showed the North that the war would not be over quickly and that the South had the will to resist.

7. **What was the significance of Vicksburg? How could its capture by the Federal army change the course of the war?**

Vicksburg was important, for if the Federals did not take it, they couldn't control the Mississippi, and if the Confederacy lost it, the southern nation would be split in half.

8. **Why did General Lee change the name of his army. What events led him do so?**

General Lee changed the name of his army after taking command to indicate his goal of retaking all of Virginia.

9. **Why did Lincoln decide to make slavery an issue of the war?**

Lincoln changed his mind about the slavery issue's relation to the war because he thought it could further the war effort by making it a crusade for liberty, against slavery.

10. **How did the Preliminary Emancipation Proclamation change the character of the war?**

The Preliminary Emancipation Proclamation changed the character of the war by making it into a crusade for liberty.

Ideas in Action

1. **Read some fictional or eyewitness accounts of civilians in the American Civil War and discuss the effects the war had on civilians both in the North and South.**

Suggestions for further reading: Mary Chesnut: *A Diary from Dixie: A Lady's Account of the Confederacy During the Civil War;* Michael Shaara, *The Killer Angels;* Stephen Crane, *The Red Badge of Courage;* Sarah Morgan, *Sarah Morgan: The Civil War Diary of a Southern Woman*

2. Stage a debate between students, with some taking the side of the South and others taking the side of the North over the right of the southern states to resist the military might of the Federal government. Might there have been another position than than these?

3. Did Lincoln violate the Constitution when he ordered the suspension of the right of *habeas corpus* in Maryland? Why or why not? Was his action morally justified?

4. Imagine you are a northerner or southerner, either a soldier or civilian, during the Civil War, and write an account of your experiences.

Sample Quiz I (pages 419-429)

Please answer the following in complete sentences.

1. What were Lincoln's aims in the war?

2. What was Jefferson Davis' aim or aims in the war?

3. What were the North's most important resources?

4. What were the South's most important resources?

5. Explain the "Anaconda" strategy.

6. Why did Lincoln order the suspension of *habeas corpus* in Maryland?

7. What was the significance of the loss of West Virginia on the Confederacy?

8. What was the significance of the First Battle or Bull Run, or Manassas?

9. What was important about the battle of the ironclads?

10. How did Lincoln stop Maryland's secession?

Answers to Sample Quiz I

Students' answers should approximate the following.

1. Lincoln's aim was to preserve the union, to save it, not to end or destroy slavery. Lincoln battled to maintain a union that he saw as "the city on the hill" – the messianic hope of the world.

2. Davis' aim was to preserve the independence and continued existence of the Confederate States of America.

3. The North's most important resources were its larger population, its industry, and its navy.

4. The South's most important resources were the spirit of its men and its commanders.

5. The "Anaconda" strategy was created by U.S. army General Winfield Scott. He advised Lincoln to use the navy to establish a blockade of the coast and seize control of the Mississippi in order cut off the South's trade with Europe and eventually starve the Confederates into submission.

6. Lincoln ordered the suspension of *habeas corpus* in Maryland to silence secessionist voices in the state.

7. The battle that lost West Virginia to the Confederacy lost the South a region rich in coal. On June 11, western Virginia organized a pro-Union government and sent representatives to Washington. The region would later secede from Virginia to form the state of West Virginia.

8. The First Battle of Bull Run, or Manassas, was the first major battle of the Civil War. This battle showed the North that the war would not be over quickly and that the South had the will to resist.

9. The battle of the *Virginia* and the Monitor was important because it introduced a new era of naval warfare, the era of steam ships clad in steel.

10. Lincoln stopped Marylands secession by sending troops into Baltimore and arresting and jailing the mayor and 31 legislators.

Lincoln held them in jail for two months, long enough to assure the election of a pro-union majority to the legislature in November

Sample Quiz II (pages 430-444)

Please answer the following in complete sentences.

1. Why was the Battle of Shiloh significant?

2. What was the significance of the Union's capture of New Orleans?

3. Why did the Confederate conscription act meet such a storm of protest?

4. Why was the Battle of the Seven Days significant?

5. Briefly explain Pope's General Orders.

6. Why did Southerners condemn Pope's Orders?

7. Why did Lincoln begin to contemplate emancipation of the slaves?

8. Why did Lincoln need a military victory in order to issue a proclamation freeing the slaves?

9. Why did many Southerners condemn the Emancipation Proclamation?

10. Why were many abolitionists dissatisfied with the Emancipation Proclamation?

Answers to Sample Quiz II

Students' answers should approximate the following.

1. Shiloh was significant because it was the single, most bloody battle of the war to that time.

2. The Union's capture of New Orleans was significant because now the only Confederate stronghold remaining in the Mississippi Valley was Vicksburg, Mississippi, that Jefferson Davis called the "nailhead [that] holds the South's two halves together."

3. The Confederate conscription act met with such a storm of protest because Southerners viewed it as a violation of states' rights.

4. The Battle of the Seven Days was significant because, on account of it, Richmond was saved and the Confederacy was preserved from an early demise. This battle also brought Robert E. Lee into prominence.

5. Pope's General Orders were part of Lincoln's more stringent war policy that mandated that not just the Confederate army, but civilians were to suffer for secession.

6. Southerners condemned Pope's orders because they had hoped the war could be fought according to civilized codes, and now Lincoln's government was removing the barriers civilization had erected to stave off the brutality of war.

7. Lincoln thought emancipation could further the war effort. He thought that by freeing the slaves in the Confederate states, he could strike a blow at the southern economy and, perhaps, prevent European nations from recognizing the Confederacy.

8. Lincoln needed a military victory in order to issue a proclamation freeing the slaves because without one, emancipation would appear a gesture of weakness, not strength.

9. Many Southerners condemned the Emancipation Proclamation because they thought it struck not only at their economy but at the safety of their women and children by encouraging slave revolts.

10. Many abolitionists were dissatisfied with the Emancipation Proclamation because it exempted the Border States

Essays

Instructions to be given to the students: Write in complete sentences. Underline your thesis. Give three supports or examples that explain why you think what you do and that support your thesis.

1. Was freeing the slaves a good idea? Why or why not? What do you think would have been a good way to go about it?
2. Compare and contrast the aims of Lincoln and Davis in the war. Which do you think was better, and why?

Sample Test

Please answer the following in complete sentences

I. Short Essay – Answer two of the following:

1. How did Lincoln plan to use the "Anaconda" strategy?
2. Why were both the Lincoln and Davis concerned about Kentucky's neutrality?
3. Explain the General Orders.
4. What did the Federal government do about slavery during the first part of the Civil War?

II. Short Answer:

1. What border states did Lincoln want to secure?
2. Why did Lincoln thik that keeping Maryland in the union was so important?
3. Why did the Confederacy issue a conscription act?
4. What did Lincoln say he was fighting for at first?
5. What is significant about the Battle of Sharpsburg, or Antietam?

Answer Key to the Chapter Test

Students' answers should approximate the following:
I.
1. Lincoln planned to use the navy to establish a blockade of the coast and seize control of the Mississippi in order cut off the South's trade with Europe and eventually starve the Confederates into submission. Lincoln adopted the policy as part of his greater war strategy, which would establish a blockade of the southern coast and capture key positions on the western rivers, while at the same time, three forces would invade the South: one, east of the Appalachians; another, west of the Appalachians and east of the Mississippi; and a third, west of the Mississippi.
2. Both Lincoln and Jefferson Davis thought it important to honor Kentucky's neutrality. Lincoln was especially concerned, for if Kentucky seceded, important points on the Ohio and Mississippi would fall to the

Confederacy and threaten the success of Lincoln's western strategy. For Jefferson Davis, Kentucky, neutral or Confederate, stood as a buffer zone between the Northern armies and Tennessee. If Kentucky went fully to the Union, all of central Tennessee, along with Mississippi and Alabama, lay open to a Federal advance. Davis wanted to do nothing to tip Kentucky into the Union.
3. The General Orders, issued in July 1862, were three in number. First, citizens of Union-occupied territory in Virginia were to be held responsible for any guerrilla activity in their region – whether they were truly responsible for it or not. Second, any male citizen who refused to take an oath of allegiance to the United States would have to leave his home and cross over to enemy lines; and if he returned, he would be "subjected to the extreme rigor of military law." Third, those who took the oath of allegiance, and then

violated it, would be executed. Pope also issued orders commanding his soldiers to "subsist off the countryside" – that is, to take what food they needed from Virginia citizens.

4. Though Lincoln insisted that the war was being fought to preserve the Union, not to abolish slavery, Federal commanders and lawmakers began to move the war in the latter direction. Federal commanders, like Benjamin Butler, confiscated slaves in southern territory. Slaves, too, were finding freedom by fleeing to invading Union armies. Congress, dominated by extreme antislavery Republicans called the Radicals, passed a law in March 1862 that forbade army officers to return fugitive slaves to their owners. Later, in April, under Radical Republican influence, Congress abolished slavery in the District of Columbia and, in June, prohibited slavery in the western territories.

II.

1. Lincoln wanted to secure Maryland, Kentucky Delaware, and Missouri.
2. Maryland was important for Lincoln to get for the North because if it seceded, Washington would be cut off from the North.
3. The Confederacy issued a conscription act because it was faced with the unraveling of the war effort.
4. Lincoln said he was fighting to preserve the Union, not to abolish slavery.
5. The Battle of Sharpsburg or Antietem is significant because it gave Lincoln the victory he needed to proceed with his plan for issuing the Emancipation Proclamation.

CHAPTER 18: To the Bitter End

Chapter Overview

- Northerners were growing weary of the war and wanted to let the South go its own way. Fathers and newspapers encouraged soldiers to desert. Lincoln thought such opposition required stern measures, and on September 24,, 1862, he ordered suspension of *habeas corpus* throughout the North. All who openly encouraged resistance to enlistment or disloyalty were subject to martial law.

- Southerners had quarrels with their own president, Jefferson Davis, who, apart from the conscription act, attempted to manage the war down to the last detail. In 1864, Davis asked Congress to suspend the writ of *habeas corpus*. The Confederate congress voted heavy taxes on the people of the South. The military requisitioned crops and impressed slaves; and prices went up in the cities.

- In May 1863, Lee defeated Hooker at Chancellorsville and lost Stonewall Jackson.

- Grant attempted to capture Vicksburg but was beaten back. Davis was worried and urged Lee to send General Longstreet to relieve Vicksburg. Lee had what he thought was a better idea: he would invade the North.

- In late May 1863, the Army of Northern Virginia commenced its invasion of the North. At Gettysburg, Lee was defeated by the Federal army under General Meade.

- On July 4, 1863, Vicksburg fell to Grant after a long siege. The Federals now controlled the Mississippi River and the South was divided in half.

- In March 1864, General Grant took on the rank of Lieut. General of all the Federal forces. In May, he commenced his campaign against Lee and the Army of Northern Virginia. The campaign ended in Grant laying siege to Petersburg, Virginia; a siege that lasted 10 months.

- William Tecumseh Sherman took Atlanta on September 1-2, 1 864. General Sheridan drove the Confederates out of the Shenandoah Valley in Virginia and laid waste to it. Because of these victories, Lincoln was reelected in 1864.

- After burning one-third of Atlanta, Sherman marched towards the sea and the seacoast town of Savannah, where he could reestablish contact with the North. Along the way he laid waste to the countryside. He captured Savannah on December 22, 1864.

- From Savannah, Sherman marched into South Carolina, devastating it as he had Georgia. He captured Columbia, the capital of South Carolina, on February 17, 1 865. The same day Fort Sumter fell to the Federal navy.

- With only a skeleton of his army left, Lee asked the Confederate government to induct black slaves. On March 13 the congress approved a call for the enlistment of 300,000 black soldiers.

- On April 2, 1 865, Grant's forces overran Lee's trenches before Petersburg. As the Confederate government removed to Danville, Grant's army captured Richmond.

- On April 6, after a battle at Sayler's Creek in which Lee lost nearly a third of his army, Grant sent him a message asking him to surrender his army. Lee refused. Enroute to Appomattox Court House, Lee, cut off by Sheridan in front and Meade behind, decided to meet with Grant. On April 9, Lee and Grant met at Appomattox Courthouse and Lee surrendered his army.

- John Wilkes Booth, a southern partisan, was determined to assassinate both Lincoln and Grant. While the president was enjoying a play at Ford's Theatre in Washington, Booth shot him in the back of the head. Lincoln died the next morning, April 15, 1865.

- On April 17, 1865, Johnston and Sherman, joined by Confederate secretary of war, John C. Breckenridge, signed a peace treaty that called for a generous reconciliation between the North and the South.

What Students Should Know

1. **When the Emancipation Proclamation went into effect and its effects.**

   The Emancipation Proclamation went into effect on January 1, 1863. Besides bringing joy to abolitionists and anti-slavery stalwarts, it led to little change in the South. Escaped slaves in Federal "contraband camps" were now free, and, as before the proclamation, many slaves continued to seek Union lines, while other slaves remained on their masters' plantations. No slave insurrections troubled the South, however; and thought the economy suffered, it was on account of the ever-tightening Union blockade rather than escaping slaves.

2. **Who the Copperheads were and what Lincoln's response to them was**

By 1863, the Midwestern states (in particular) were rife with opposition to the war, with fathers encouraging their sons to desert the army and newspapers publicly calling for military desertion. Many midwesterners did not want to fight t end slavery or for what they thought were the interests of New England manufacturers and merchants. Some of these "Southern sympathizers" were openly in favor of the Midwest joining the South in a struggle against the Northeast. Lincoln thought such opposition required stern measures. On September 24, 1862, Lincoln ordered the suspension of *habeas corpus* throughout the North. All who openly encouraged resistance to enlistment or were "guilty of any disloyal practice affording aid and comfort to the rebels" were to be subject to martial law. Lincoln was extending what he had done in Maryland to the entire North, and his military authorities throughout the North acted with zeal. Throughout the course of the war, 13,000 northerners would be imprisoned and have their right of *habeas corpus* denied them.

3. **The condition of the South, government and people, in 1863**

On the whole, the southern government was less vigorous than its northern counterpart, and was rife with controversy. Among the controversies that beset the South at this time was that between those supported a stronger central government and those who held to a strict doctrine of states' rights. Among the measures opposed by states' rights Confederates was the Confederate Congress' (under the urging of President Jefferson Davis) suspension of the writ of *habeas corpus* in Richmond and other areas of the South. This led to arbitrary arrests, but it was not prosecuted as vigorously as it was in the North by Lincoln's government The Confederate Congress voted taxes that weighed heavily on the people of the South. All landowners were required to pay one-tenth of their produce to the government in return for valueless Confederate paper money. Military agents who requisitioned cattle and crops impoverished farmers. Congress ordered the impressment of slaves from objecting rich landowners. With the scarcity of food and other necessities in the cities, merchants hiked prices to exorbitant levels. Not only merchants, but some rich planters continued to trade with Northern merchants, thus "aiding and abetting the enemy." To supply its army with arms and its people with food, the South used a small fleet of blockade runners that sneaked through the Union blockade to carry cotton to the British islands of Bermuda and New Providence and returned with manufactured goods, luxury items, and rifles. Southern women spun and weaved their own cloth to make "homespun" dresses for themselves and "homespun" uniforms for the army. Women collected the family's urine to make nitre for gunpowder. They gathered raspberry leaves for tea and ground chicory for coffee.

4. The significance of the Battle of the Wilderness

The Battle of the Wilderness, fought May 1-4, 1863, was a significant battle, for Robert E. Lee was able to beat back the destruction of his army to which the new Federal commander, Joseph Hooker, was committed. The defeat of the Federals allowed to Lee to carry the war outside of Virginia into Pennsylvania. The death of Stonewall Jackson, however, weakened Lee at the very moment when he needed all the advantages he could muster.

5. The significance of the Battle of Gettysburg

Robert E. Lee had carried the war into the North to spare Virginia further destruction and to supply his army with provisions, with which Pennsylvania was rich. Lee's Confederates and the Federal army under General George Meade met by chance at Gettysburg in southern Pennsylvania on July 1, 1863. The Federals were able to capture the high ground, from which Lee was unable to dislodge them. Following at desperate attempt to take the Federal center ("Pickett's Charge"), Lee ordered the withdrawal of his army on July 4. The battle was significant, for it marked the end of the advance of the Confederates in the East. Now, Lee was in withdrawal. The South needed a victory in the North if it was going to get foreign recognition of the Confederate government. With the defeat at Gettysburg (and the fall of Vicksburg the same day), such recognition would not be forthcoming.

6. The significance of Vicksburg and its surrender

The city of Vicksburg, set atop bluffs overlooking the Mississippi River, was the last remaining point at which the South controlled the Mississippi. Its loss would mean that the western Confederate states would be irrevocably split from the eastern Confederate states. In late May 1863, Federal forces under General Ulysses Grant invested Vicksburg but were unable to take the city. But Confederate troops and the citizens of Vicksburg suffered from hunger and want; and it was the judgment of Vicksburg's commander, General John Pemberton, that his troops would mutiny if the siege continued. Thus, on July 4, 1863 (the very day Lee withdrew from Gettysburg), Pemberton surrendered Vickburg to Grant. The fall of Vicksburg, along with the defeat at

Gettysburg, assured that Great Britain and France would not recognize the Confederacy and thus force Lincoln to seek peace. The Confederacy, too, was divided between West and East.

7.   The role of black soldiers in the war

Though the abolitionist, Frederick Douglass, claimed that blacks served in the Confederate army as soldiers, throughout most of the war, the Confederate Congress did not officially accept blacks into its armies. Nevertheless, thousands of blacks, free and slave, served in the Confederate ranks throughout the war, but mostly as servants and laborers; some blacks, however may have served as soldiers bearing arms. Following Gettysburg and Vicksburg, some prominent Confederate leaders proposed an official recruitment of blacks into the Confederate army, but they faced stern opposition, forcing Jefferson Davis to shelve the idea.

Lincoln supported recruiting blacks into the Federal army, but many Federal generals opposed it. The battle of Milliken's Bend, Louisiana, on June 7, 1863, however changed their minds. In this fight, Federal soldiers, both black and white, fought bravely against a superior force of Confederates. By the end of the war, free blacks from the North, along with escaped slaves from the border states and the Confederacy, had joined the Federal army to the number of 185,000. But though they had proven their worth in battle, these black soldiers still did not receive equal pay to the whites and were not given the same clothing allowances. White doctors, too, were loath to operate on black patients, and many black soldiers died for lack of attention. The Confederate government, too, did not recognize blacks who served in the Union army as soldiers and so refused to include them in prisoner exchanges. Instead, the Confederate government ordered that black Federals captured in battle were to be shot.

8.   Lincoln's conscription act: its causes and results

With the defeats at Gettysburg and Vicksburg, the increasing effectiveness of Federal blockade of the South, and the dying hope of European intervention on the side of the Confederacy, Lincoln needed another supreme effort, it seemed, to topple the Confederacy. The problem was, he needed more troops. In March 1863, Congress had passed a conscription act that allowed the president to draft into service men between the ages of 20 and 45. Lincoln enacted the conscription act, and in July 1863 called for 300,000 men to serve for three-year stints. Lincoln's conscription allowed for a $300 "commutation fee" for those who did not wish to serve. A draftee could also find another to serve in his place. The draft gave an occasion for all sorts of corruption. Brokers for substitutes set up shop, taking a fee to find substitutes for men with means. Some doctors for a large fee diagnosed non-existent diseases. It seemed the poor working class man alone would fill the ranks of the army and become cannon fodder for the Union. On July 11, 1863, Irish mobs attacked the draft office, destroyed files, and then razed the building. The riots continued until July 17, when Archbishop John Hughes of New York, appealed to his flock to stop the rioting. Federal troops restored order.

9.   Border warfare and its consequences

Bloody guerrilla struggles raged along the border of Missouri and Kansas. Against pro-Southern Missourians, Federal Brigadier General James H. Lane and his band of pro-Union *banditti* called "Jayhawkers" crossed the border into Missouri, raiding and setting fire to settlers' houses, burning and plundering towns. Missourians formed themselves into bands called "Bushwackers" and took revenge on the Jayhawkers and their supporters in Kansas. The most formidable and bloody Bushwacker band was led by Confederate Captain William Clarke Quantrill, whose Bushwack Raiders took and sacked Lawrence, Kansas on August 21, 1863.

To put an end of Quantrill and to keep Missouri settlers from supplying Bushwackers, General Thomas Ewing, Jr., who commanded Union forces in Missouri, issued General Order 11, commanding the inhabitants of three Missouri counties driven from their homes. Union troops forced 10,000 men, women, and children from their homes, which Jayhawkers then plundered and burnt. In response, General Sterling Price, leading 12,000 Confederate regulars, invaded Missouri in September, pushing as far as the northwestern part of the state. But at Westport on October 23, 1864, he met a powerful Federal army under General Samuel Curtis and was routed. Fleeing through eastern Kansas, Price and his men went to Texas. With Quantrill fleeing with Price, Westport was the last major Confederate offensive west of the Mississippi.

10. The significance of of Grant's victories at Missionary Ridge and Lookout Mountain

The victories of Grant at Missionary Ridge and Lookout Mountain in November 1863 forced the Confederates to abandon Chattanooga. The Confederates were thus forced to abandon Tennessee and the way stood open for Union advance into Georgia.

11. The leading ideas of the Gettysburg Address

The Gettysburg Address, given by Abraham Lincoln at a dedication of a Federal cemetery at Gettysburg, encapsulated Lincoln's vision of the federal union. According to Lincoln, other nations had been founded on a common culture or race, but the United States had been founded on a proposition – an idea demanding a response: human equality. Not culture, not race; not soil or blood, but a belief defined America. For Lincoln this belief had been set forth in a kind of creed, the Declaration of Independence. For Lincoln, the Civil War was significant not just for America, but for the world. It had universal significance. Could a nation, dedicated to the creed of equality, survive? The fate of the United States, the Union, (which Lincoln elsewhere called the "last best hope of earth") would be the test.

12. Grant's strategy for prosecuting the war as Lieut. General of the Union armies

Grant thought the Union armies had operated independently of one another for too long. He intended to coordinate all the Union armies, east and west, in a combined assault on the Confederacy. Grant would send General Franz Sigel to capture the Shenandoah Valley, the breadbasket for Lee's army, while Benjamin Butler moved up the James River toward Richmond. Grant himself, with General Meade and 110,000 men of the Grand Army of the Republic (as Grant's army was now called), would pursue the Army of Northern Virginia, 60,000 strong, while, in the west, Sherman advanced from Chattanooga to Atlanta, Georgia.

13. What Grant's strategy was in his march against Richmond. What Lee's strategy was in response to Grant's

Grant's strategy was to push toward Richmond, always moving south and east to get around Lee's flank. He would throw his superior numbers against Lee, though it meant enormous casualties. Lee knew he was up against something new in Grant – that at last he faced a relentless, vigorous campaigner. Outnumbered, Lee would try to hold fortified positions against which Grant must hurl and break his army. Lee hoped by this strategy to make the price of war so high in northern blood that the North would tire of the war and call for peace. Lincoln was up for re-election in November 1864; perhaps enough war tragedy would bring a new, more peaceminded president into office. The course of the war went basically as both commanders had foreseen – though Lincoln was not voted out of office. Grant lost enormous numbers of men, was defeated in nearly every battle, but forced Lee south until the Federal army lay siege to Petersburg and Richmond.

14. Description of Grant and Sherman's policy of total war

General William Tecumseh Sherman, commanding the 98,000-strong Grand Army of the West, had set out on May 6, 1864 from Chattanooga, Tennessee into Georgia. His goal was to capture Atlanta, the second most important manufacturing center of the Confederacy. In pursuit of this goal, Sherman advocated total war – war waged on civilians as well as the military. When he captured Atlanta, Sherman ordered one-third of the city burned. In its march to the sea, that began on November 16, 1864, Sherman's arm lay waste the countryside. Sherman had ordered that his troops respect private property, but nobody (not even he himself) took his order seriously. His troops committed acts of theft, destruction, and rapine. Sherman had said he wanted to "make Georgia howl." "We cannot change

the hearts of these people of the South," he wrote, "but we can make war so terrible … and make them so sick of war that generations [will] pass away before they again appeal to it." Sherman carried out a similar operation in South Carolina.

Grant carried out a similar policy in Virginia's Shenandoah Valley. In late August 1864, Grant told General Philip Sheridan, "if the war is to last another year, we want the Shenandoah Valley to remain a barren waste." The lieutenant general did not want the valley supplying the Confederate capital or its armies. Sheridan obeyed Grant with earnest thoroughness.

15. The major ideas of Lincoln's Second Inaugural Address

It his second inaugural, delivered March 4, 1865, Abraham Lincoln, speaking of the war that was drawing to its end, said both unionists and secessionists had "deprecated war, but one of them would make war rather than let the nation survive, and the other would accept war rather than let it perish, and the war came." He said the slave interest was somehow the cause of the war, and he noted that though his government had sought nothing more than to limit the "territorial enlargement" of slavery, "the insurgents in order to strengthen and enlarge that institution] would rend the Union even by war." The war, said Lincoln, had not realized the hopes of either side in the struggle. He indicated that war was the means by which "the providence of God" sought to remove the "offense" of slavery. Lincoln suggested that the fault of slavery rested not on the South alone; but North and South had to atone for it. He closed his address with a promise of reconciliation.

16. When Lee surrendered at Appomattox, and the terms of the surrender

Lee surrendered to Grant at Appomattox Court House in Virginia on April 9, 1865. Grant's terms were generous. No unconditional surrender. Lee's men, he said, could keep their side arms, their personal possessions, and their horses, for it was the time for spring planting. "Each officer and man will be allowed to return to his home, not to be disturbed by the United States authorities," as long as they were peaceful and kept the laws. Grant said he would provide rations for Lee's men.

17. When General Joseph Johnston surrendered to Sherman, the terms of the surrender, and the result

General Johnston surrendered to Sherman on April 17, 1865, in a log cabin outside Durham, North Carolina. The treaty Sherman offered Johnston allowed Confederate soldiers, from the Atlantic to beyond the Mississippi, to return home with their weapons, which they would deposit at their state capitals. There the weapons might remain so the states could defend themselves against rebel guerrilla insurgents. State governments should be reorganized, said the treaty, once state officers then holding office swore allegiance to the Constitution of the United States. The treaty guaranteed southerners "their political rights and franchises, as well as the rights of person and property as defined by the Constitution of the United States and of the states respectively." President Andrew Johnson rejected this treaty, which was more conciliatory even than Lincoln's proposals for reconstruction. The new president told Grant that Johnston must surrender under the same terms given to Lee. On April 26, Sherman met with Johnston again, and the Confederate general signed the new terms of surrender.

18. Who John Wilkes Booth was and why he assassinated Lincoln

John Wilkes Booth was a renowned Shakespearian actor as well as an ardent southern partisan. He thought Lincoln a tyrant and had warned that re-election would make him a king. Booth, it seems, had worked as a spy in the southern interest but had never entered the southern army, for which, as he confessed to his diary, he deemed himself a coward. Booth wanted to strike a blow for his country – at first, the kidnapping of Lincoln; but when this failed, he determined to carry out an assassination. Lincoln was assassinated at Ford's Theater in Washington, D.C., on Good Friday, April 14, 1865. Lincoln died the next morning.

19. What was Lincoln's plan of reconstruction

In 1863, Lincoln had enacted a reconstruction program for the conquered areas of Louisiana – a program, he thought, that might prove a model for the other states once the "rebellion" was over. This plan specified that if 10 percent of the people of Louisiana swore allegiance to the Union, they could establish a state government and constitution. In Louisiana, 12,000 people had done this. They had adopted a new state government and a new constitution; they had approved emancipation; they had established public schools for both whites and blacks; and they had empowered their legislature to grant the franchise to blacks. What's more, the Louisiana legislature had approved the 13th Amendment (to abolish slavery) to the Constitution.

20. What the 13th Amendment was and when it was ratified

The 13th Amendment abolished slavery throughout the United States. Congress approved the amendment in January 1865. It still, however, had to be ratified by the states.

Questions for Review

1. **Why were the people of the North growing weary of the war and encouraging soldiers to desert?**

    The North was growing wearing of the war and encouraging soldiers to desert because many midwesterners did not want to fight to end slavery or for what they thought were the interests of New England manufacturers and merchants.

2. **What hardships did the Confederate government and army place on the people of the South during the course of the war? How did these hardships affect the course of the war?**

    The southern government made arbitrary arrests and voted taxes that weighed heavily on the people of the South. Military agents requisitioned cattle and crops, impoverishing farmers. The high taxes and scarcity of food made merchants hike their prices to exorbitant levels. These policies brought about blockade runners, who would sneak goods from the North, and inspired the people of the south to make do with what they had and to support their army.

3. **What was Lee's objective in his invasion of the North?**

    Lee carried the war into the North to spare Virginia further destruction and to supply his army with provisions.

4. **Explain the significance of the battle of Gettysburg to the war.**

    The battle of Gettysburg was important because it marked the end of the advance of the Confederates in the East. The defeat meant, too, that Lee lost the opportunity for a victory in the North – which the Confederacy needed it if was ever to get foreign recognition.

5. **Explain the significance of the capture of Vicksburg to the Confederate war effort.**

    The loss of Vicksburg meant that the entire Mississippi River came under federal control, splitting the eastern Confederacy from its western states and territories. Along with Gettysburg, the fall of Vicksburg assured that Great Britain and France would not recognize the Confederacy and thus force Lincoln to sek peace.

6. **Briefly summarize the ideas Lincoln presented in his Gettysburg Address. Have they been influential?**

    The Gettysburg Address encapsulated Lincoln's vision of the federal union. According to Lincoln, other nations had been founded on a common culture or race, but the United States had been founded on a proposition – an idea demanding a response: human equality. Not culture, not race; not soil or blood, but a belief defined America. For Lincoln this belief had been set forth in a kind of creed, the Declaration of Independence. For Lincoln, the Civil War was significant not just for America, but for the world. It had universal significance. Could a nation, dedicated to the creed of equality, survive? The fate of the United States, the Union, (which Lincoln elsewhere called the "last best hope of earth") would be the test. The Gettysburg Address helped Americans define the character of their country.

7. **Considering that Lee was against slavery and secession, why did he fight for the Confederacy?**

Lee fought for the south because he believed his obligation was first to his people and his state, Virginia.

8. **Why was Sherman so ruthless in his campaigns in Georgia and South Carolina?**

    Sherman believed in "total war": the waging of war on civilians as well as the military. He thought the suffering of total war would dissuade the South from ever chosing warfare in a struggle against the union.

9. **Describe the main ideas of Lincoln's proposed reconstruction of the South.**

    Lincoln's reconstruction plan specified that if 10 percent of the people of a state swore allegiance to the Union, they could establish a state government and constitution.

10. **What was Booth's motivation for assassinating Lincoln?**

    Booth thought that Lincoln was a tyrant, and be believed that if Lincoln was re-elected he would become a king. He thought that striking out at Lincoln would help the Confederacy.

Ideas in Action

1. **Listen to the songs and music of both the North and the South created during the war. Discuss how these songs embody the spirit and the ideas of each.**

2. **Read and discuss the Gettysburg Address. How do Lincoln's ideas of America and the union reflect those expressed by Daniel Webster in his speeches? Do Lincoln's ideas of America influence Americans in our own day?**

Sample Quiz I (pages 447-462)

Please answer the following in complete sentences.

1. **What were the effects of the Emancipation Proclamation?**

2. **What was Lincoln's response to the Copperheads?**

3. **Name some ways the people of the south helped to arm the Confederate army and to feed themselves.**

4. **What is the significance of the Battle of the Wilderness?**

5. **Why did Lee carry the war into the North?**

6. **Why was the Battle of Gettysburg significant?**

7. **What kind of corruption did Lincoln's conscription act bring about?**

8. **What was the reason behind General Order 11?**

9. **What is the significance of Grant's victories at Missionary Ridge and Lookout Mountain?**

Answers to Sample Quiz I

Students' answers should approximate the following.

1. Besides bringing joy to abolitionists and anti-slavery stalwarts, the Emancipation Proclamation led to little change in the South. Escaped slaves in Federal "contraband camps" were now free, and, as before the proclamation, many slaves continued to seek Union lines, while other slaves remained on their masters' plantations. No slave insurrections troubled the South.

2. Lincoln's response to the Copperheads was to suspend *habeas corpus* throughout the North. All who openly encouraged resistance to enlistment or were "guilty of any disloyal

practice affording aid and comfort to the rebels" were to be subject to martial law.

3. To supply its army with arms and its people with food, the South used a small fleet of blockade runners that sneaked through the Union blockade and carried back goods. Southern women spun and weaved their own cloth to make "homespun" dresses for themselves and "homespun" uniforms for the army. Women collected the family's urine to make nitre for gunpowder. They gathered raspberry leaves for tea and ground chicory for coffee.

4. The Battle of the Wilderness was significant because Lee was able to beat back the destruction of his army to which Joseph Hooker was committed. Hooker's defeat allowed Lee to carry the war outside Virginia, into Pennsylvania.

5. Robert E. Lee had carried the war into the North to spare Virginia further destruction and to supply his army with provisions, with which Pennsylvania was rich.

6. The Battle of Gettysburg was significant because it marked the end of the advance of the Confederates in the East. It also spelled the end of any hope of foreign recognition of the Confederacy.

7. The draft gave an occasion for all sorts of corruption. Brokers for substitutes set up shop, taking a fee to find substitutes for men with means. Some doctors for a large fee diagnosed non-existent diseases.

8. General Thomas Ewing, Jr., issued General Order 11 to put an order to Bushwacker leader Captain Quantrill and to keep Missouri settlers from supplying the Bushwackers.

9. The victories of Grant at Missionary Ridge and Lookout Mountain in November 1863 forced the Confederates to abandon Chattanooga. The Confederates were thus forced to abandon Tennessee and the way stood open for Union advance into Georgia.

Sample Quiz II (pages 462-478)

Please answer the following in complete sentences.

1. What was Grant's strategy for prosecuting the war?

2. What was Grant's strategy in his march against Richmond?

3. What was Lee's strategy in response to Grant's?

4. Why did Sherman advocate total war?

5. What were Grant's terms of surrender?

6. Why did Booth assassinate Lincoln?

7. What were Booth's plans for "striking a blow for his country"?

8. What was Lincoln's plan of reconstruction?

9. What did the 13th Amendment do?

Answers to Sample Quiz II

Students' answers should approximate the following.

1. Grant thought the Union armies had operated independently of one another for too long. He intended to coordinate all the Union armies, east and west, in a combined assault on the Confederacy.

2. Grant's strategy was to push toward Richmond, always moving south and east to get around Lee's flank. He would throw his superior numbers against Lee, though it meant enormous casualties.

3. Outnumbered, Lee would try to hold fortified positions against which Grant must hurl and break his army. Lee hoped by this

strategy to make the price of war so high in northern blood that the North would tire of the war and call for peace.

4. Sherman wanted to make the cost of war so high in human blood and loss of property that the South would not choose the expedient of war in the future. Thus, he advocated total war.

5. Grant's terms of surrender were generous. No unconditional surrender. Lee's men, he said, could keep their side arms, their personal possessions, and their horses, for it was the time for spring planting. "Each officer and man will be allowed to return to his home, not to be disturbed by the United States authorities," as long as they were peaceful and kept the laws. Grant said he would provide rations for Lee's men.

6. Booth assassinated Lincoln because he thought that Lincoln was a tyrant, and be believed that if Lincoln was re-elected he would become a king.

7. Booth first planned to kidnap Lincoln, but when this failed he determined to carry out an assassination.

8. Lincoln's reconstruction plan specified that if 10 percent of the people of a state swore allegiance to the Union, they could establish a state government and constitution.

9. The 13th Amendment abolished slavery throughout the United States.

Essays

Instructions to be given to the students: Write in complete sentences. Underline your thesis. Give three supports or examples that explain why you think what you do and that support your thesis.

For both essays, students should consult the *Catechism of the Catholic Church*, 2263-2266 and 2302-2317.

1. Is total war a moral way of waging war? Why or why not? Students can bring in outside sources to answer this question.

2. St. Thomas says that for a war to be just, *"a just cause is required, namely that those who are attacked, should be attacked because they deserve it on account of some fault. Wherefore Augustine says (Questions. in Hept., qu. x, super Jos.): 'A just war is wont to be described as one that avenges wrongs, when a nation or state has to be punished, for refusing to make amends for the wrongs inflicted by its subjects, or to restore what it has seized unjustly.'"* Does the Civil War fall under this category? Why or why not? [For this essay, students should read St Thomas Aquinas *Summa Theologica, Part II Question 40.*]

Sample Test

Please answer the following in complete sentences

I. Short Essay – Answer two of the following:

1. **What was the condition of the South, government and people, in 1863?**

2. **Describe the condition of black soldiers, North and South, during the war?**

3. **What are the leading ideas of the Gettysburg Address?**

4. **How did Sherman put total war into effect?**

5. **What are the major ideas of Lincoln's Second Inaugural Address?**

II. Short Answer:

1. **When did the Emancipation Proclamation go into effect?**

2. **Why was Vicksburg important?**

3. What is "total war"?

4. When did Lee surrender at Appomattox?

5. When was Lincoln assassinated?

Answer Key to the Chapter Test

Students' answers should approximate the following:

I.

1. On the whole, the southern government was less vigorous than its northern counterpart, and was rife with controversy. Among the controversies that beset the South at this time was that between those supported a stronger central government and those who held to a strict doctrine of states' rights. Among the measures opposed by states' rights Confederates was the Confederate Congress' (under the urging of President Jefferson Davis) suspension of the writ of *habeas corpus* in Richmond and other areas of the South. This led to arbitrary arrests, but it was not prosecuted as vigorously as it was in the North by Lincoln's government. The Confederate Congress voted taxes that weighed heavily on the people of the South. All landowners were required to pay one-tenth of their produce to the government in return for valueless Confederate paper money. Military agents who requisitioned cattle and crops impoverished farmers. Congress ordered the impressment of slaves from objecting rich landowners. With the scarcity of food and other necessities in the cities, merchants hiked prices to exorbitant levels. Not only merchants, but some rich planters continued to trade with Northern merchants, thus "aiding and abetting the enemy."

2. Throughout most of the war, the Confederate Congress did not officially allow blacks to serve as soldiers in its armies. Nevertheless, thousands of blacks, free and slave, served in the Confederate ranks throughout the war, but mostly as servants and laborers; some blacks, however may have served as soldiers bearing arms. Following Gettysburg and Vicksburg, some prominent Confederate leaders proposed an official recruitment of blacks into the Confederate army, but they faced stern opposition, forcing Jefferson Davis to shelve the idea. Lincoln supported recruiting blacks into the Federal army, but many Federal generals opposed it. The battle of Milliken's Bend, Louisiana, on June 7, 1863, however changed their minds. In this fight, Federal soldiers, both black and white, fought bravely against a superior force of Confederates. By the end of the war, free blacks from the North, along with escaped slaves from the border states and the Confederacy, had joined the Federal army to the number of 185,000. But though they had proven their worth in battle, these black soldiers still did not receive equal pay to the whites and were not given the same clothing allowances. White doctors, too, were loath to operate on black patients, and many black soldiers died for lack of attention. The Confederate government, too, did not recognize blacks who served in the Union army as soldiers and so refused to include them in prisoner exchanges. Instead, the Confederate government ordered that black Federals captured in battle were to be shot.

3. The Gettysburg Address, given by Abraham Lincoln at a dedication of a Federal cemetery at Gettysburg, encapsulated Lincoln's vision of the federal union. According to Lincoln, other nations had been founded on a common culture or race, but the United States had been founded on a proposition – an idea demanding a response: human equality. Not culture, not race; not soil or blood, but a belief defined America. For Lincoln this belief had been set forth in a kind

of creed, the Declaration of Independence. For Lincoln, the Civil War was significant not just for America, but for the world. It had universal significance. Could a nation, dedicated to the creed of equality, survive? The fate of the United States, the Union, (which Lincoln elsewhere called the "last best hope of earth") would be the test.

4. When he captured Atlanta, Sherman ordered one-third of the city burned. In its march to the sea, that began on November 16, 1864, Sherman's army lay waste the countryside. Sherman had ordered that his troops respect private property, but nobody (not even he himself) took his order seriously. His troops committed acts of theft, destruction, and rapine. He carried out a similar operation in South Carolina.

5. It his second inaugural address, Abraham Lincoln, speaking of the war that was drawing to its end, said both unionists and secessionists had "deprecated war, but one of them would make war rather than let the nation survive, and the other would accept war rather than let it perish, and the war came." He said the slave interest was somehow the cause of the war, and he noted that though his government had sought nothing more than to limit the "territorial enlargement" of slavery, "the insurgents [for the strengthening and enlargement of that institution] would rend the Union even by war." The war, said Lincoln, had not realized the hopes of either side in the struggle. He indicated that war was the means by which "the providence of God" sought to remove the "offense" of slavery. Lincoln suggested that the fault of slavery rested not on the South alone; but North and South had to atone for it. He closed his address with a promise of reconciliation.

II.

1. The Emancipation Proclamation went into effect on January 1, 1863.

2. Vicksburg was important because it was the last remaining point at which the South controlled the Mississippi, and the last remaining linchpin connecting the western with the eastern Confederate states.

3. "Total war" is war waged on civilians as well as the military.

4. Lee surrendered at Appomattox on April 9, 1865.

5. Lincoln was assassinated on April 14, 1865.

CHAPTER 19: Liberalism Triumphs in Mexico

Chapter Overview

- The war with the United States had exhausted Mexico, and a sign of this was that there were no revolutions from 1848-1853. However, Mexico had fallen into chaos, and the Constitution of 1824 was insufficient to combat the chaos. States were breaking up into smaller and smaller states. Commerce was dead, and local caciques made laws as they saw fit.

- Lucas Alamán thought that Mexico needed order imposed by a powerful, central authority, such as a foreign prince. He and other conservatives negotiated with the Spanish court, but were told they needed to take control of the Mexican government first. The conservatives needs some dictator who would impose order and maintain it until the hoped-for prince would come. In desperation, the conservatives chose Santa Anna for their leader, and in January 1853 they overthrew President Arista. Santa Anna took control and reformed the government and removed Liberals everywhere. But when Alamán died, Santa Anna resumed his old, dissolute ways, and the country fell into ruin again and Liberals ran rampant.

- A change came in Mexican Liberalism. Some espoused the Liberal doctrines for the interest of the secular good, and not for self-interest. These believed that the Church and military where the chief obstacles to progress, and must be brought under the thumb of the state. The Church fought to maintain its lands and property, while the Liberals sought to make the state not only the highest but the only real authority in society.

- In 1854 *guerilleros* in the state of Guerrero rose against His Most Supreme Highness (Santa Anna), led by Juan Álvarez and Ignacio Comonfort. In March the rebel leaders issued the *Plan de Ayutla*. Santa Anna attempted to crush the rebellion. Comonfort refused to surrender, and Santa Anna contented himself with burning Indian villages and killing Liberals.

- In 1855, Northern Mexico declared for the *Plan de Ayutla*, and when the entire east coast joined the revolution, Santa Anna drove out of Mexico City and took a ship to Venezuela. Juan Álvarez marched in triumph into Mexico City on November 24, 1855.

- Ignacio Comonfort became president after Álvarez resigned in December. Comonfort was a moderate at heart, and he wanted to win over conservatives to his government. This became impossible because Álvarez's minister of justice, Benito Juárez issued two sets of laws, called the *Ley Juárez* and the *Ley Lerdo*. This proved to be disastrous. Creoles, churchmen, and many Indians rose in rebellion against the new laws, but were crushed in 1856.

- At the same time, a convention met in Mexico City to draw up a new constitution. The new constitution was merely a revision of the Constitution of 1824, and it further centralized the government.

- The 1857 constitution was completed on February 5. This was followed by a *pronunciamento* from the conservatives, and Pope Pius IX condemned the Liberal government and declared the new anti-clerical laws null and void and implicitly blessing resistance to the government. The Church in Mexico excommunicated all who swore allegiance to the constitution.

- In 1857 Félix Zuloaga captured Mexico City, proclaiming the *Plan de Tacubaya*, a Comonfort dictatorship, and declared an end to the Constitution of 1857. By that time, Comonfort was alienated from the Liberal party, but would not link fortunes with his former enemy. When the Liberals rose in resistance, Comonfort changed his mind and gathered an army to resist Zuloaga. Desertions rendered his army too small, and Comonfort went into exile to the United States in 1858.

- Declared president by the conservatives, Zuloaga repealed the laws of reform and marshaled clericalist generals to resist the Liberals under Tomás Mejía, Miguel Miramón, and Leonardo Márquez.

- In July, Juárez, wanting a share of the Church's riches that the conservatives controlled, issued the Laws of Reform.

- With the issuance of the Reform Laws, the civil war grew bloodier, and foreign-owned property was destroyed. This provided the opportunity for foreign intervention. France, Great Britain, and Spain recognized the conservative government, while the United States favored the Liberal cause. The United States sent arms and munitions to the Liberal Mexicans, even throughout the American Civil War.

- In spring and summer of 1860, the tide of war began to turn against the conservatives. In the autumn Liberal *guerilleros* converged on Mexico City. Miramón fled by night and went into exile in France. On January 1, 1861, Ortega entered Mexico City in triumph.

- As president, Juárez would not become dictator. He offered clemency to all those who had opposed him if they laid down their arms. He faced opposition from the Liberal congress. Fifty-one congressmen signed a petition demanding him to resign, but they were opposed by 52 congressmen, and Juárez escaped being overthrown by his own party.

- The conservatives rose again, but they were driven back by Liberals into the mountains. Added to that, Mexico owed an 80-million *peso* debt to France, Spain, and Great Britain, whose troops occupied the port of Veracruz. France seemed to want war, and tried to goad Mexico into an attack. Finally the British and Spanish withdrew, leaving Veracruz in the possession of the French.

- Empress Eugeníe, enamored of the Mexican exiles, introduced them to her husband, Napoleon III. Napoleon resolved to vindicate them and deliver Mexico from Liberal bonds. He had first to secure Mexico, so he sent in 6,000 troops under General Charles Ferdinand de Lorencez, ostensibly to secure repayment of debts but really to instigate a war.

- On May 5, 1862, Lorencez led his army against Ignacio Zaragoza in Puebla. Lorencez lost and was forced to withdraw to Veracruz. That day became the festival, *Cinco de Mayo*.

- In March of 1863 González Ortega surrendered Puebla to the new French commander, Élie Forey, after a long siege. Finding that he did not have enough men, Juárez withdrew from Mexico City on May 31, and on June 10 the French and Mexican army entered the capital.

- In October 1863, a delegation of Mexican exiles went to the Archduke Maximilian and offered him the throne of Mexico. Maximilian wanted a document proving that the majority of Mexican people wanted him to assume the throne. General Forey called a "Supreme Council" of conservatives, which was not the majority, who issued a call for Maximilian to take up the rule of Mexico. The archduke was fooled and in April 1864 accepted the imperial crown of Mexico.

- Maximilian did not understand the divisions that shattered Mexico, and since he had Liberal leanings, he built his government on the *moderados* instead of the conservatives who had brought him to Mexico. He refused to repeal the Laws of Reform when the Pope requested him to. Conservative opposition soon mounted against him. Despite setbacks, Maximilian's first year of rule showed encouraging signs, and as long as he had enough money from the French government, he could keep peace.

- After Robert E. Lee's surrender in 1865, the United States again turned its attention towards Mexico. It's policy was twofold – to fee Mexico from foreign domination and to aid Juárez. General Sheridan began amassing American troops on the Rio Grande, and with American support and arms, Juárez's army began to grow.

- When Maximilian found out that Napoleon was planning to withdraw French troops, he sent emissaries to Napoleon, to no avail. Napoleon ordered Bazaine to make one last attempt to crush Juárez. Bazaine urged Maximilian to be severe against the Liberals, and in October 1865 Maximilian published a decree ordering the execution of anyone caught resisting imperial forces. This decree harmed Maximilian's cause, however, and inspired universal indignation against the emperor.

- When French troops began to withdraw, Maximilian began to lose hope and contemplated abdication. His wife, Carlota, convinced him not to give up, and she went to France to plead with Napoleon, who made no promises. She went next to Rome and pleaded the pope's aid, which was refused to her. Reaching the end of her strenghth, she was pronounced insane. Again Maximilian contemplated abdication, but was again convinced not to abandon the throne.

- In 1867, without French aid, Maximilian and his small army fought against the larger Liberal army. Due to a traitor, Maximilian was forced to surrender. Juárez wanted to make an example of him, and he tried Maximilian in a rigged court and sentenced him to be shot on June 19, 1867. A few days later Porfirio Díaz took Mexico City, and the war was over.

- In 1871 when Juárez ran again for a fourth term as president, Porfirio Diaz, who had been snubbed by Juárez, declared that Juárez was trying to establish a dictatorship, and announced his own candidacy. When Juárez was again elected, rebellion broke out from the *porfirista* party and was quickly suppressed. Juárez died soon after on July 18, 1872, and Lerdo de Tejada, president of the supreme court, became president in his place.

- Lerdo soon lost the heart of the people, and when in 1876 he announced he was going to run for reelection, Díaz gathered money and recruits in the United States and proclaimed the *Plan de Tuxtepec*, calling for more local democracy and no reelection. In October Lerdo fled, and Díaz entered Mexico City and assumed the provisional presidency.

What Students Should Know

1. **Why Lucas Alamán supported the dictatorship of Antonio López de Santa Anna**

   The war with the United States had exhausted Mexico. The federal constitution, the Constitution of 1824, was insufficient to combat the chaos into which the country had fallen. Though Mexico's finances had improved, regions within states throughout the country were becoming increasingly more independent. Districts seceded from states to form new states; local caciques (political leaders) interpreted laws and made laws as they saw fit; and politicians sold themselves out for bribes. At the same time, commerce was dead, starvation wracked the capital while troops quartered in the city pillaged and plundered at will. Law and order broke down throughout Mexico. For example, in Yucatán, Mayan Indians and *hacendados* waged a brutal war against each other. Lucas Alamán thought Mexico needed order, and order through the rule of a foreign prince. But the Spanish court told Alamán and other conservatives to appoint first a dictator to bring law and order to Mexico. To Alamán, the only man who could summon up the authority to act as a dictator was Santa Anna – though he knew the problems with the man.

2. **How Liberalism in Mexico changed**

   The old Liberals – from the time of Morelos to the Mexican-American War – believed in a decentralized, constitutional government; they favored *laissez-faire* in economics. Though some had called for the secularization of Church lands as well as schools, many Liberals wanted to maintain the Catholic faith as the sole religion of Mexico and, like Morelos, professed themselves devout Catholics. The older Liberals rose mostly, though not solely, from the creole class.

   The new generation of Mexican Liberals, who rose to prominence after the Mexican-American War, had studied in secular schools and, instead of belonging to one of the creole families, were of the rising *mestizo* class. They basically accepted the older Liberalism's political and economic goals, but their class interests were different. Just as the creoles had coveted the political power of the *gauchupines*, so now the *mestizos* desired to possess the political power that accorded with their place in the population, the majority. For this reason, many *mestizos* sought to possess Church lands as a source of wealth for themselves. They thus were anti-clerical – favoring both the secularization of Church lands and schools as well as the disestablishment of the Catholic Church and the establishment of complete religious freedom and expression. Many local caciques joined the Liberal ranks, for a weak, decentralized national government would not interfere with the power they wielded in their regions.

   For the new Liberals, the chief obstacles to Mexico's progress were the Church and the military. Since both held *fueros*, they were seen as retarding individual enterprise and true political reform. Some Liberals attacked the Church for what they called her "superstitions." They thought both the Church and military – and indeed all organs of society – needed to be brought under the control of the state. Liberals wanted to eradicate from society any intermediate bodies between the state and the individual. The wanted the state to be not only the highest but the only real authority in society.

3. **What kind of society Mexico's conservatives sought to preserve**

Though the Mexican conservatives represented the generals, the wealthy creoles, and the clergy, as the character of Liberal policies became clearer through their effect on the lower classes, many Indians joined the conservatives. The conservatives stood for centralized authority, the maintenance of the hacienda system, and the preservation of military and ecclesiastical *fueros*. Such ideals did not favor only the wealthy, however; for not only the Church and the military possessed *fueros* but so did cities and Indian peoples. Since the time of Spanish rule, the Indians held *ejidos* – corporately owned lands – as a perpetual right. Liberal policies threatened not only the military and the Church, but the traditional rights of Indian peoples.

4. Why the Church fought so doggedly to preserve her possession of property

The Church fought for a principle when it contended that the state had no right to seize Church property. That principle was that the state does not have authority over the Church, that the Church is not the subject or the servant of the state. The Church could divest herself, if she wished, of lands and money – *temporalities*, as they were called; but no human institution had the authority to force the Church to make such a concession. The Church in Mexico was fighting for her independence.

5. What caused the Revolution of Ayutla. What its result was.

The corruption of Santa Anna's government as well as his suppression of Liberal leaders inspired the revolution that began with the issuing of the *Plan de Ayutla* in March 1854. One fruit of the revolution was that Santa Anna sold the Mesilla Valley (southern Arizona) to the United States for $10 million in the Gadsen Purchase on December 30,

1853. (The U.S. Senate ratified the sale on June 30, 1854.) In August 1855, Santa Anna fled Mexico City; and though the conservatives established a new government, it could not long survive. The Liberals under Juan Álvarez established a Liberal government in the capital in November 1855.

6. What "the Reform" was

Juan Álvarez's government did not last. In December 1855, Ignacio Comonfort became president. Though Comonfort was a moderate, his government established what became known as the Reform. The Reform consisted of two bodies of law. The first, the *Ley Juárez*, was issued by Comonfort's minister of justice, Benito Juárez. It restricted cases tried by ecclesiastical courts to members of the clergy and sought to break military *fueros*. In June 1856, the government issued the *Ley Lerdo* (drafted by Miguel Lerdo de Tejada, but inspired by Juárez). This law attempted to spur economic progress and increase government revenues by the secularization and sale of Church lands. According to the law, the Church was, henceforth, forbidden to own land, and all lands held by the Church were to be sold. Though the proceeds of the sales would go to the Church, the *Ley Lerdo* placed a heavy sales tax on all transactions, the proceeds of which were to go to the government. But *Ley Lerdo* did not just target Church lands; it forbade any corporate body to hold land. Henceforth, only individuals were permitted to own property. Cities, thus, had to sell their lands. Even *ejidos*, held by tribes since the time of Cortés, were to be broken up and sold to individuals.

7. What were the effects of the Reform

Though a few secular clergy bought Church-owned haciendas, most creoles refused to participate in the break-up of Church property. Mostly, it was foreign capitalists from Great Britain, France, Germany, and the United States who could afford Church lands and the taxes attached to their sale; these formed a new wealthy ruling class. Many a disappointed *mestizo*, unable to afford Church lands, "denounced" Indian *ejidos* to the government and bought the land for a pittance. Attempts by the government to remedy this situation were unsuccessful. The secularization of Church lands had a dire effect on the economy and society of Mexico. Church haciendas were generally better managed than those owned by lay *hacendado* families, who often squandered their patrimony in two or three generations. Moreover, the revenue from ecclesiastical haciendas did not go merely to enrich churchmen but funded public charities, hospitals, schools, and colleges. The Church also functioned as a sort of bank, loaning money at low rates of interest. Secularization swept away all these benefits.

8. The Constitution of 1857 and its provisions

The Constitution of 1857 was a revision of the Constitution of 1824 that created a more centralized government. The new constitution abolished the senate (seen as too aristocratic), reducing the congress to one house with the power to remove state governors for cause. The constitution gave the supreme court power to decide state elections and made all federal elections for president indirect – the people would vote for electors (government employees appointed by the president) who would, in turn, vote for the president. The new constitution enshrined *Ley Lerdo* and *Ley Juárez* and added further anti-clerical laws. According to a provision forbidding peonage, the government permitted monks and friars to break their vows; while another

provision removed education from the hands of the Church. The constitution contained neither a provision allowing religious liberty nor one establishing the Catholic Church as the religion of Mexico.

9. Conservative reaction to the Constitution of 1857

With the completion the new constitution in February 1857, conservative insurgents in Querétaro issued a pronouncement against it. Pope Pius IX condemned the anti-clerical provisions of the constitution, saying they would result in the corruption of manners and indifferentism. He declared the anti-clerical provisions null and void. The bishops and clergy of Mexico joined the pope in his condemnation.

10. How conservative reaction to the Constitution of 1857 resulted in the War of the Reform

Seeking to placate the conservatives, President Comonfort in the Autumn of 1857 asked Congress to suspend civil liberties and work on a reform of the new constitution. Congress refused, but in Tacubaya Félix Zuloaga proclaimed a revolution and, capturing Mexico City, established Comonfort as dictator. In response, Liberal forces declared Vice President Benito Juárez (whom Zuloaga had imprisoned) president. Comonfort, turning against Zuloaga but without Liberal support, eventually fled to the United States.

11. How Juárez and the Liberals triumphed in the War of the Reform

Though the conservatives initially had the advantage in funding and in military skill, the Liberals under Juárez controlled the port of Veracruz and the customs payments that flowed through that port. Juárez further alienated the conservatives by issuing in July 1859 the Laws of the Reform, ordering the complete confiscation of all Church lands, the immediate suppression of all monasteries, and the gradual demise of women's monasteries and convents. The Laws of the Reform ordered Church lands to be divided among small landowners – but the result was that they fell, instead, into the hands of new oligarchy. The Laws of the Reform heightened the violence of the war. The destruction of foreign property by both sides caused France, Great Britain, and Spain to side with conservative government under Miguel Miramon, while the United States supported Juárez's government. Throughout the course of the war, the U.S. sent Juárez tens of thousands of muskets. The conservatives' lack of funds ultimately undermined their war effort. Troops began to desert the conservative armies. In late December 1860, Liberal forces destroyed Miramon's conservative army at San Miguel Calpulalpan, 75 miles northeast of Mexico City. Miramón abandoned the capital.

12. The character of Juárez's first presidency

Despite the disastrous state of Mexico after the War of the Reform, Benito Juárez would not do as others might have done in his place: he would not become dictator. Seeing himself the defender and upholder of the Constitution of 1857, he would not violate it. He did banish five bishops from Mexico, but he offered amnesty to all conservatives who had resisted him in the War of the Reform, if they agreed to lay down their arms. Juárez allowed complete freedom for the press, even of anti-government publications. While he had to deal with a conservative insurgency, he faced opposition from the Liberal congress

that assembled in May 1861. The congress nearly removed him from office.

13. Why Great Britain, Spain, and France occupied Veracruz

Mexico owed an 80-million *peso* debt to France, Spain, and Great Britain – a debt for which Juárez suspended all payments. The three European powers would not accept this expedient and agreed they would together occupy the port of Veracruz. In December 1861, Spanish troops landed at Veracruz; in January, British and French forces joined them. Though Great Britain and Spain pledged not to make war on Mexico, France it seemed was trying to find a pretext for war. In April 1862, the British and the Spanish decided that the French wanted war, and they withdrew, leaving Veracruz in the possession of the French.

14. The course of the French conquest of Mexico

The plight of Mexican conservative exiles in Paris, both clergy and lay, appealed to the imagination of Empress Eugeníe, the wife of Emperor Napoleon III. Eugeníe introduced the exiles to Napoleon, who, eager to vindicate the honor of monarchy, decided to send an expedition to Mexico to free it from the Liberals. Thus, the 6,000 French troops iunder General Lorencez in Veracruz, along with conservative *guerrilleros* under General Márquez, began a campaign of conquest. They first marched on Puebla; but there Lorencez was defeated on May 5, 1862 by Mexican forces under Ignacio Zaragoza. This event the Mexican people honor as the festival, *Cinco de Mayo*. Napoleon sent more forces to Mexico; the French army numbered 34,000 and was joined by a force of 20,000 Mexican conservatives. In the late winter of 1863, Forey moved on Puebla and invested the city on March 16. On May 16, Puebla surrendered. Juárez withdrew from Mexico City to San Luis Potosí on May 31. On June 10, General Forey and his French and Mexican army entered the capital.

15. The character of the French occupation of Mexico City

Though the clergy and conservatives of Mexico City welcomed the entrance of French General Forey; they found he was not a conservative as they had hoped. Forey issued a proclamation declaring that confiscated Church lands would remain in the hands of those who currently possessed them. When the clergy threatened to suspend the public administration of the sacraments, Forey said he would blow open church doors with artillery.

16. How Maximilian von Habsburg became emperor of Mexico

When the French had taken Mexico City, a delegation of Mexican exiles visited the Habsburg archduke, Maximilian in his castle in Trieste. Maximilian wanted the delegation to assure him that the people of Mexico wanted him as their ruler. In Mexico, General Forey organized a "Supreme Council" of conservatives, who issued a call for Maximilian to take up the rule of Mexico. In April 1864, he accepted the imperial throne of Mexico.

17. The character of Maximilian's reign

Maximilian did not understand the divisions that had shattered Mexico. Though, as in Europe, Liberalism and conservatism in Mexico represented irreconcilable ideals. Maximilian wanted to rise above party divisions. The problem was that Maximilian, if not a Liberal, had Liberal leanings. He tried to conciliate men who would never accept conciliation and so ended up alienating his friends. Instead of building his government on the conservatives who had brought him to Mexico, Maximilian wanted to base his rule on the *moderados.* He refused the papal nuncio's request to repeal of the Laws of the Reform and restore Church lands. Maximilian contemplated granting Mexicans complete freedom of religion. Conservative and clerical opposition mounted against Maximilian.

It was not long before Maximilian understood that he had little real power in his empire. The French general François Achille Bazaine listened only to Napoleon. Without Liberal or conservative support, Maximilian was entirely dependent on the French emperor. Despite this, Maximilian and Carlota zealously threw themselves into their new imperial role. They threw lavish banquets, planned to build a theatre and an academy of sciences in Mexico City, and laid plans for the capital's beautification. They tried to become Mexicans in every way. Maximilian faced *juarista* guerrilla raids on the Valley of Mexico. Nevertheless, the Mexican people seemed to acquiesce to the emperor's rule. The French forces won important military victories, while, in the far north, Juárez barely held on. Without the aid of the United States, Juárez had no power – and the U.S. gave him little aid, because it was engaged in the Civil War.

18. How the United States aided Juárez against Maximilian

Following the end of the Civil War, the United States government could turn its attention to Mexico. The United States had begun to covet the wealth of the rich mineral mines in Mexico; it thus had to secure the good will of the Mexican people, lost during the Mexican-American war so that Anglo-American businessmen might invest in and develop the rich resources of Mexico. United States' policy was twofold – to free Mexico from foreign domination and to aid Juárez. Secretary of State Seward pressed Napoleon to withdraw his troops from Mexico, and Napoleon, who had found that his Mexican adventure had brought him no profit, was willing to agree with U.S. demands. Napoleon broke his promise of aid to Maximilian and assured Seward that he would begin withdrawal of the French army. Direct U.S. aid went to Juárez in the form of arms, and the *juarista* army began to grow.

19. How Maximilian's reign ended

Maxilimilian had not been consulted about the withdrawal of the French army. At the urging of General Bazaine, he published an edict ordering the execution of any captured "bandits"; but when this edict was used against a *juarista* general, public opinion in Mexico turned against the emperor. In March 1866, Bazaine began his withdrawal from Mexico, while Maximilian began forming a volunteer Mexican army. In February 1867, when Bazaine set sail with the French army from Veracruz, Maximilian had a force of 15,000 to 20,000 Mexicans, with some European volunteers.On May 14, 1867, At Queretaro, however, Maximilian, betrayed by one of his own men, surrendered to the *juaristas*. Despite pleas for clemency coming from the crowned heads of Europe, Juárez ordered Maximilian's execution. The emperor, with two his generals, died by firing squad on June 19, 1867.

20. How Juárez changed when he returned to power as president

On returning to power, Don Benito put aside some of his Liberal scruples. Though reelected president in 1867 by wide margins, Juárez faced constant opposition from the new Liberal congress. With an empty treasury and decreased foreign investment, Juárez could brook no opposition, constitutional or not. He began to interfere in congressional elections to obtain representatives favorable to him. He used all his popularity and prestige to force through congress an amendment to the federal constitution, adding a senate to congress. Juárez increased presidential power by another amendment that required a two-thirds vote to override a presidential veto. Juárez further centralized the Mexican government by taking power from local caciques.

21. The character of economic development under Juárez

Under Juárez, Mexico experienced the beginnings of industrial development and a growth of commerce that brought more money into the national treasury. Unfortunately, foreigners controlled much of this growth. The circulation of the money gotten from the seizure of Church lands along with the 3 million francs left in Mexico City by the French helped spur this development. In 1873, with Juárez's support, British engineers completed the railroad line running from Veracruz to the capital.

22. The character of educational reform under Juárez

The Laws of the Reform had removed education from the jurisdiction of the Church and placed it into the hands of the state. Juárez planned a system of free secular public schools. Juárez took the old Jesuit college of San Ildefonso in Mexico City and turned it into the National Preparatory School. He required *hacendados* to build schools on their estates.

23. Land tenure policy under Juárez and its fruits

Though, to some degree, the lot of the Indians did not worsen under Juárez (he gave up any attempt to turn them into farmer proprietors and protected their remaining *ejidos*), other *campesinos* (field workers) fared badly. Juárez's government needed money. He continued the old policy of refusing to turn Church lands over to the poor men who worked them, selling them instead to rich *hacendados* who had supported the Liberal cause. Many of the dispossessed field workers, along with anti-*Juarista* soldiers, were driven into banditry. Juárez faced revolts led, some by Liberal military leaders, some by peasants, some by Indians.

24. How Porfirio Díaz came to power

Following Juárez's death by heart attack in July 1872, Sebastián Lerdo de Tejada became president of Mexico. In the autumn of 1872, Lerdo was elected to a full four-year term as president. It was not long however before Lerdo lost the heart of the people. He was arrogant and overused the power of the state. Many believed that he gave too many concessions to United States railroad barons who wanted to penetrate into Mexico – though, in reality, he had forbidden them to extend their lines into Mexico, a move which cost him the support of the U.S. government.

In 1876, Lerdo announced he would run for reelection as president. Porfirio Díaz, banking on popular discontent with the president, gathered money and recruits in the United States, and called for more local democracy and no reelection of a president to a second consecutive term. In October 1876. Lerdo fled to the United States. Díaz entered Mexico City and assumed the provisional presidency. This was the beginning of *el Porfiriato*, the long dictatorship of Don Porfirio Díaz, that lasted 35 years.

Questions for Review

1. **How did Mexican Liberalism change after Santa Anna became dictator of Mexico?**

The new generation of Mexican Liberals after Santa Anna basically accepted the older Liberalism's political and economic goals, but their class interests were different. Just as the creoles had coveted the political power of the *gauchupines*, so now the *mestizos* desired to possess the political power that accorded with their place in the population, the majority. They thus were anti-clerical – favoring both the secularization of Church lands and schools as well as the disestablishment of the Catholic Church and the establishment of complete religious freedom and expression. For the new Liberals, the chief obstacles to Mexico's

---

Key Terms at a Glance

cacique: political leader

guerillero: member of a guerilla group

peonage: the condition where a person, called a *peon*, is held to perform labor for another

indifferentism: the belief that people do not have the duty to believe in God by worshiping according to and practicing the one true religion

progress were the Church and the military. Since both held *fueros*, they were seen as retarding individual enterprise and true political reform. Some Liberals attacked the Church for what they called her "superstitions." They thought both the Church and military – and indeed all organs of society – needed to be brought under the control of the state. Liberals wanted to eradicate from society any intermediate bodies between the state and the individual. The wanted the state to be not only the highest but the only real authority in society.

2. **How have the Mexican conservatives been characterized, and what did they really stand for?**

The conservatives were characterized as representing the generals, the wealthy creols, and the clergy. They really stood for centralized authority, the maintenance of the hacienda system, and the preservation of military, ecclesiastical, and other (Indian and local) *fueros.*

3. **Why did the Church fight to maintain control of land and privileges? What was the main principle behind the Church's defense of her rights?**

The Church fought for a principle when it contended that the state had no right to seize Church property. The Church in Mexico was fighting for her independence. The Church's main principle was that the state does not have authority over the Church, that the Church is not the subject or the servant of the state. The Church could divest herself, if she wished, of lands and money – *temporalities*; but no human institution had the authority to force the Church to make such a concession.

4. **What goals did the Mexican Liberals want to achieve?**

The Liberals thought both the Church and military – and indeed all organs of society – needed to be brought under the control of the state. Liberals anted to eradicate from society any intermediate bodies between the state and the individual. The wanted the state to be not only the highest but the only real authority in society.

5. **What were some of the effects of the secularization of Church lands on the economy and society of Mexico?**

The secularization of Church lands had a dire effect on the economy and society of Mexico. Church haciendas were generally better managed than those owned by lay *hacendado* families, who often squandered their patrimony in two orthree generations. Moreover, the revenue from ecclesiastical haciendas did not go merely to enrich churchmen but funded public charities, hospitals, schools, and colleges. The Church also functioned as a sort of bank, loaning money at low rates of interest. Secularization swept away all these benefits.

6. **Briefly describe *Ley Juárez* and *Ley Lerdo*, and what effects they had**.

Ley Juárez restricted cases tried by ecclesiastical courts to members of the clergy. Before, certain wealthy creoles had obtained the privilege to be tried in Church courts.

Ley Lerdo attempted to spur economic progress and increase government revenues by the secularization and sale of Church lands. According to the law, the Church was, henceforth, forbidden to own land, and all lands held by the Church were to be sold. Though the proceeds of the sales would go to the Church, the *Ley Lerdo* placed a heavy sales tax on all transactions, the proceeds of which were to go to the government. But *Ley Lerdo* did not just target Church lands; it forbade any corporate body to hold land. Henceforth, only individuals were permitted to own property. Cities, thus, had to sell their lands. Even *ejidos*, held by tribes since the time of Cortés, were to be broken up and sold to individuals.

7. What was France's motivation in helping Mexico?

France decided to intervene in Mexico in part because Empress Eugenie wanted to protect the rights of the Church and traditional society in Mexico. She, thus convinced her husband, Emperor Napoleon III, to intervene. Napoleon's motivations were not quite so noble; he wanted France to be able to obtain a portion of Mexico's wealth.

8. What was the United States' motivation in helping Mexico?

The United States had begun to covet the wealth of the rich mineral mines in Mexico; it thus had to secure the good will of the Mexican people, lost during the Mexican-American war so that Anglo-American businessmen invest in and develop the rich resources of Mexico

9. Why was Emperor Maximilian unable to secure the throne of Mexico?

Maximilian ws unable to secure the throne of Mexico for several reasons. First, he alientatedhis base of support – the conservatives and the Church. Secondly, Napoleon III decided to withdraw the French army from Mexico, thus leaving Maximilian to fend for himself. Thirdly, the emperor's opponent, Benito Juárez, received a good eal of aid from the United States, which allowed him to build up his army and armaments.

10. Were Juárez and the Mexican Liberals successful in achieving their goals for Mexico? Please explain.

Because the United States was engaged in the Civil War, it could give Juárez no aid, and so he lost his power.

11. How did Porfirio Díaz come to power in Mexico? Did he fulfil his promises to the Mexican people? Please explain.

In the autumn of 1872, Sebastián Lerdo de Tejada was elected to a full four-year term as president. It was not long however before Lerdo lost the heart of the people. He was arrogant and overused the power of the state. Many believed that he gave too many concessions to United States railroad barons who wanted to penetrate into Mexico – though, in reality, he had forbidden them to extend their lines into Mexico, a move which cost him the support of the U.S. government. In 1876, Lerdo announced he would run for reelection as president. Porfirio Díaz, banking on popular discontent with the president, gathered money and recruits in the United States, and called for more local democracy and no reelection of a president to a second consecutive term. In October 1876. Lerdo fled to the United States. Díaz entered Mexico City and assumed the provisional presidency. This was the beginning of *el Porfiriato*, the long dictatorship of Don Porfirio Díaz, that lasted 35 years.

Ideas in Action

Compare the ideas of the American Liberals with those of the Mexican Liberals. How are they the same and how do they differ, if at all?

Sample Quiz I (pages 481-490)

Please answer the following in complete sentences.

1. Why did Lucas Alamán support the dictatorship of Santa Anna?

2. Describe the political ideas of the old Liberals in Mexico.

3. Describe the political ideas of the new Liberals in Mexico.

4. What did the conservatives stand for?

5. What principle did the Church fight for in its struggles against Juárez and the Liberals?

6. What caused the Revolution of Ayutla.

7. What effect did the secularization of Church lands have on the economy and society of Mexico?

8. How did conservative reaction to the Constitution of 1857 result in the War of Reform?

9. What did the Laws of Reform seek to accomplish?

Answers to Sample Quiz I

Students' answers should approximate the following.

1. Lucas Alamán supported the dictatorship of Santa Anna because he thought Mexico needed order, and through the rule of a foreign prince. The Spanish court told Alamán to appoint first a dictator to bring law and order to Mexico. To Alamán, the only man who could summon up the authority to act as a dictator was Santa Anna.

2. The old Liberals believed in a decentralized, constitutional government; they favored *laissez-faire* in economics. Though some had called for the secularization of Church lands as well as schools, many Liberals wanted to maintain the Catholic faith as the sole religion of Mexico and professed themselves devout Catholics. The older Liberals rose mostly, though not solely, from the creole class.

3. The new Liberals thought the chief obstacles to Mexico's progress were the Church and the military. Some Liberals attacked the Church for what they called her "superstitions." They thought both the Church and military – and indeed all organs of society – needed to be brought under the control of the state. Liberals wanted to eradicate from society any intermediate bodies between the state and the individual. They wanted the state to be not only the highest but the only real authority in society.

4. The conservatives stood for centralized authority, the maintenance of the hacienda system, and the preservation of military, ecclesiastical, Indian, and local *fueros*.

5. The principle that the Church fought for was that the state does not have authority over the Church, that the Church is not the subject or the servant of the state.

6. The corruption of Santa Anna's government as well as his suppression of Liberal leaders inspired the revolution that began with the issuing of the *Plan de Ayutla* in March 1854.

7. The secularization of Church lands had a dire effect on the economy and society of Mexico. Church haciendas were generally better managed than those owned by lay *hacendado* families, who often squandered their patrimony in two or three generations. Moreover, the revenue from ecclesiastical haciendas did not go merely to enrich churchmen but funded public charities, hospitals, schools, and colleges. The Church also functioned as a sort of bank, loaning money at low rates of interest. Secularization swept away all these benefits.

8. Seeking to placate the conservatives, President Comonfort in the Autumn of 1857 asked Congress to suspend civil liberties and work on a reform of the new constitution. Congress refused, but in Tacubaya Félix Zuloaga proclaimed a revolution and, capturing Mexico City, established Comonfort as dictator.

9. The Laws of the Reform ordered the complete confiscation of all Church lands, the immediate suppression of all monasteries, and the gradual demise of women's monasteries and convents.

Sample Quiz II (pages 490–502)

Please answer the following in complete sentences.

1. **Why did Napoleon III decide to free the Liberals?**

2. **How did the French occupation government of Mexico City deal with confiscated Church lands?**

3. **What was the motivation behind the United States' aid to Mexico?**

4. **What economic developments occurred under Juárez?**

5. **What education reforms happened under Juárez?**

6. **What was the land tenure policy under Juárez?**

7. **How did Porfirio Díaz come into power?**

Answers to Sample Quiz II

Students' answers should approximate the following.

1. Napoleon III, who was, under his wife's influence, eager to vindicate the honor of monarchy, decided to send an expedition to Mexico to free from the Liberals. He also wanted France to have a part in Mexico's wealth.

2. French General Forey issued a proclamation declaring that confiscated Church lands would remain in the hands of those who currently possessed them. When the clergy threatened to suspend the public administration of the sacraments, Forey said he would blow open church doors with artillery.

3. The United States had begun to covet the wealth of the rich mineral mines in Mexico; it thus had to secure the good will of the Mexican people, lost during the Mexican-American war so that Anglo-American businessmen invest in and develop the rich resources of Mexico.

4. Under Juárez, Mexico experienced the beginnings of industrial development and a growth of commerce that brought more money into the national treasury. Foreigners, however, began to control mcuh of this growth.

5. The Laws of the Reform had removed education from the jurisdiction of the Church and placed it into the hands of the state. Juárez planned a system of free secular public schools. Juárez took the old Jesuit college of San Ildefonso in Mexico City and turned it into the National Preparatory School. He required *hacendados* to build schools on their estates.

6. Juárez continued the old policy of refusing to turn Church lands over to the poor men who worked them, selling them instead to rich *hacendados* who had supported the Liberal cause. But he protected the remaining Indian *ejidos*.

7. Porfirio Díaz, banking on popular discontent with President Lerdo, gathered money and recruits in the United States, and called for more local democracy and no reelection of a president to a second consecutive term. In October 1876. Lerdo fled to the United States. Díaz entered Mexico City and assumed the provisional presidency.

Essays

Instructions to be given to the students: Write in complete sentences. Underline your thesis. Give three supports or examples that explain why you think what you do and that support your thesis.

1. Compare and contrast the ideas and ideals of the old and new Liberals. Were the ideals of one group better than the other? Why or why not? Use specific examples.

2. Compare and contrast the ideas and ideals of the conservatives and the Liberals in Mexico.

3. How did the Reform change Mexico? Do you think it was beneficial? Why or why not? Use specific examples.

Sample Test

Please answer the following in complete sentences

I. Short Essay – Answer two of the following:

1. **In what condition did the war with the United States leave Mexico?**

2. **Explain the laws the Reform and what they did.**

3. **Describe the character of Maximilian's reign.**

4. **How did Juárez change when he returned to power as president?**

II. Short Answer:

1. **What did the new Liberals think were the chief obstacles to Mexico's progress?**

2. **Identify the following:**
   a. **Ignacio Comonfort**
   b. **Benito Juárez**
   c. **Maximilian von Habsburg**

3. **For what reasons did Pope Pius IX condemn the anti-clerical provisions of the Constitution of 1857?**

Answer Key to the Chapter Test

Students' answers should approximate the following:

I.

1. The war with the United States had exhausted Mexico. The federal constitution, the Constitution of 1824, was insufficient to combat the chaos into which the country had fallen. Though Mexico's finances had improved, regions within states throughout the country were becoming increasingly more independent. Districts seceded from states to form new states; local caciques (political leaders) interpreted laws and made laws as they saw fit; and politicians sold themselves out for bribes. At the same time, commerce was dead, starvation wracked the capital while troops quartered in the city pillaged and plundered at will. Law and order broke down throughout Mexico. For example, in Yucatán, Mayan Indians and *hacendados* waged a brutal war against each other.

2. The Reform consisted of two bodies of law. The first, the *Ley Juárez*, was issued by Comonfort's minister of justice, Benito Juárez. It restricted cases tried by ecclesiastical courts

to member of the clergy and sought to break military *fueros.* The second, *Ley Lerdo,* attempted to spur economic progress and increase government revenues by the secularization and sale of Church lands. According to the law, the Church was, henceforth, forbidden to own land, and all lands held by the Church were to be sold. Though the proceeds of the sales would go to the Church, the *Ley Lerdo* placed a heavy sales tax on all transactions, the proceeds of which were to go to the government. But *Ley Lerdo* did not just target Church lands; it forbade any corporate body to hold land. Henceforth, only individuals were permitted to own property. Cities, thus, had to sell their lands. Even *ejidos,* held by tribes since the time of Cortés, were to be broken up and sold to individuals.

3. Maximilian did not understand the divisions that had shattered Mexico. He wanted to rise above party divisions. The problem was that Maximilian, if not a Liberal, had Liberal leanings. He tried to conciliate men who would never accept conciliation and so ended up alienating his friends. Instead of building his government on the conservatives who had brought him to Mexico, Maximilian wanted to base his rule on the *moderados.* He refused the papal nuncio's request to repeal of the Laws of the Reform and restore Church lands. Maximilian contemplated granting Mexicans complete freedom of religion. Conservative and clerical opposition mounted against Maximilian. It was not long before Maximilian understood that he had little real power in his empire. Despite this, Maximilian and his wife, Empress Carlota, zealously threw themselves into their new

imperial role. They tried to become Mexicans in every way. The Mexican people seemed to acquiesce to the emperor's rule.

4. On returning to power, Don Benito put aside some of his Liberal scruples. Though reelected president in 1867 by wide margins, Juárez faced constant opposition from the new Liberal congress. With an empty treasury and decreased foreign investment, Juárez could brook no opposition, constitutional or not. He began to interfere in congressional elections to obtain representatives favorable to him. He used all his popularity and prestige to force through congress an amendment to the federal constitution, adding a senate to congress. Juárez increased presidential power by another amendment that required a two-thirds vote to override a presidential veto. Juárez further centralized the Mexican government by taking power from local caciques.

II.

1. For the new Liberals, the chief obstacles to Mexico's progress were the Church and the military.

2.
    a. Ignacio Comonfort: president of Mexico who established the Reform
    b. Benito Juárez: president of Mexico who established Liberalism in Mexico
    c. Maximilian von Habsburg: the first emperor of Mexico

3. Pope Pius IX condemned the anti-clerical provisions of the Constitution of 1857, because he said they would result in indifferentism and the corruption of manners.

CHAPTER 20: Reconstruction and the Gilded Age

Chapter Overview

♦ The Federal government promised parole to Confederate President Jefferson Davis, but he was viewed as a traitor, so he was kept in a prison cell at Fortress Monroe. While he was in prison he received a picture of Pope Pius IX with the inscription, "If any man will come after me, let him deny himself, and take up his cross, and follow me." This gift symbolized the sufferings of Davis and thousands in the South, where destitution reigned.

♦ In the South, the "Negro Question" was predominant during Reconstruction. The Southerners feared that their freed slaves would obtain too much political power; they especially feared miscegenation. The Federal government established the Freedmen's Bureau to pass out emergency rations of food and to integrate blacks into white society.

♦ Freedmen greeted wage earning at first with joy, but they soon learned the disabilities it carried. Before, slave owners cared for their slaves even when sick, but employers did not care for their workers. Freedmen earned very low wages.

♦ In the Federal government, opinions differed on how the South should be treated. Some, such as President Andrew Johnson, thought the South should be treated with kindness and gentleness and southern states admitted back into the union. Others, including Edwin M. Stanton, Charles Sumner, and Thaddeus Stevens, thought the South should be more severely punished for the war. In June 1865, President Johnson appointed provisional governors for each of the southern states, and told them to call conventions to draw up new state constitutions that had to declare secession illegal and abolish slavery. By January each southern state except for Texas had functioning state governments. The Radical Republicans objected because the new governments had a large number of former Confederate officers and they enforced blacks codes, laws to keep blacks "in their place."

♦ These black codes did not please Stevens and Sumner, who wanted immediate and complete equality for the blacks. Radical Republicans assailed President Johnson's reconstruction policy by passing the Freedmen's Bureau Bill in 1866, which President Johnson vetoed. Congress passed the Civil Rights Act in March, which President Johnson also vetoed. Congress overrode the president's veto on April 9, 1866.

♦ In April 1866, the Supreme Court decision, *Ex Parte Milligan*, ruled that Lincoln's wartime suspension of *habeas corpus* had been unconstitutional.

♦ In July the Radicals were able to override the president's veto of the Freedmen's Bureau, and in June of 1866 they inserted the 14th Amendment into the Constitution, linking state with national citizenship.

♦ Although President Johnson declared the end of the war on August 20, 1866, race riots still troubled the South. These riots not only assured the passage of the 14th Amendment but weakened northern support for Johnson. In 1867 the Radical Republicans took Reconstruction out of the hands of the president. In a Reconstruction Act, Congress disbanded all southern state governments and divided the South into five military districts under five generals.

- Under Congress' Reconstruction, there were more black than white voters, since only "loyal" whites could vote. In South Carolina, blacks (many of them educated men) dominated the state constitutional convention.

- The state elections of 1867 were the first in which blacks could vote. The number of blacks who voted far outnumbered the number of whites. Republicans came to dominate southern state legislatures.

- In 1865 a group of young, former Confederate soldiers decided to form a secret society (which they called the "Ku Klux Klan") merely for their entertainment. They dressed in white sheets and rode through the streets. Eventually the group became a sort of vigilante group, and the hooded men in white sheets began visiting black cabins to frighten the inhabitants to keep their place. They even killed blacks who presented any problems. The group died out on its own by 1870.

- Radical Republican congressmen wanted to impeach President Johnson, but they needed some offense on which to try him. In March 1867 Congress passed the Tenure of Office Act, which required the president to seek the advice and consent of the Senate when appointing and dismissing members. When Johnson violated this act, the Radicals called for his impeachment. The House of Representatives voted to impeach the president, but the Senate acquitted him. Although the Radicals had failed to oust the president, they had neutralized his power.

- By 1868, eight southern states voted to ratify the 14th Amendment and were admitted into the union. On July 9, 1868, the amendment became part of the Constitution.

- Ulysses S. Grant won the presidential election of 1868 for the Republicans. He was committed to centralization and expressed hopes for an international tribunal that would peacefully resolve disputes between nations. His espousal of a dominant national power reflected a new epoch in the United States history. The United States was becoming a consolidated nation.

- Grant called for the ratification of the 15th Amendment, extending the suffrage to blacks nationwide. Congress approved the amendment on February 26, 1869 and it was ratified the following year.

- The period after the war was characterized by political corruption, and Mark Twain called it the "Gilded Age." New York City was a major center of this corruption.

- After Grant's reelection in 1872, several scandals in his administration were brought to light. President Grant did little to stop the corruption, however.

- A frenzy for money resulted in a too rapid expansion of the economy which brought on the Panic of 1873.

- In the state elections of 1874, Democrats took control of several reconstructed state governments. Radical hopes were not dead, however, and Sumner again introduced his Civil Rights Act. On March 1, 1875, Congress approved it, and President Grant signed it into law.

In 1876 Rutherford B. Hayes became president. President Hayes removed federal troops from the state capital of South Carolina and evacuated federal troops from New Orleans. These acts ended Reconstruction in the South.

What Students Should Know

1. **The general condition of the southern states after the war**

   The South after the war was devastated economically and politically. Confederate veterans, some wounded, returned home to find their wives and children starving. Destitution was everywhere. To escape federal rule, a small number of southerners left their homes. Some of these expatriated to Brazil, taking with them whatever slaves who were willing to go with them; others went to fight for the Emperor Maximilian. Some moved north. Most remained in their native states, trying to rebuild their fortunes.

2. **The attitudes of Southern whites towards freedmen after the war**

   Many southern whites were determined that, if the black man was free, he need not be equal. Southern whites feared (as they had feared under slavery) that if blacks were not "kept down," they would perpetrate bloody war on whites. Though whites outnumbered blacks almost three to one in the South, in some areas blacks were in the majority. Whites wondered what would happen if those blacks gained political power. Southern whites feared miscegenation. They thought (as did most northerners) the black race inferior to the white; thus it was imperative that inter-racial marriages be avoided. To give equality to blacks, whether of pure or mixed ancestry, might, many feared, open up the door to legal, marital unions between whites and blacks and to a thorough mixing of the races. They thought this would degrade southern society.

3. **What the Freedmen's Bureau was**

   The desolation wrought by Federal armies in the South, the dislocation of many free blacks who had followed those armies and who now congregated around military outposts in the larger cities, produced great problems. The federal government established the Freedmen's Bureau (a branch of the war department) to pass out emergency rations of food (to both whites and blacks), and to integrate blacks into white society. The bureau founded schools for blacks throughout the South and helped support the founding of four black colleges. The bureau encouraged the many wandering freedmen to return to their former masters and work for wages. The bureau operated only in those areas occupied by Federal armies.

4. **Condition of blacks in the South after the war**

   The condition of blacks in the South varied. Some blacks had never left their old plantations, even when able to; others, following in the wake of the Union army, had fled from their old homes. Many blacks were eager to work for wages, while others equated freedom with idleness. Many black families suffered from starvation, as some whites were unwilling to hire black men who had children.

   Blacks had their own social classes. Those who had been house slaves or who had been freemen before the war had adopted more of white culture than those who had been field slaves. The habits of their less cultivated brethren embarrassed educated blacks. A black sub-culture was developing among the poorer, less-educated people from which the more "cultured" blacks were excluded, as they were by whites. Blacks more assimilated to white culture tried to raise the poorer blacks to what they thought a higher level of culture; but black preachers became the leaders of black society.

   Freedmen greeted wage earning at first with joy. But former masters, now employers, paid freedmen as small a wage as possible, which was often not enough for their needs. Unlike under paternalistic system of slavery, employers turned out the infirm to fend for themselves. Many freedmen, too, had little notion of the value of money and wasted it on luxuries bought at the plantation store, leaving them little for necessities. Despite its evils, slavery was a world built on personal relationships that somewhat softened its rigors. The new, wage-earning world could be cold and pitiless.

Outside those areas controlled by the Freedmen's Bureau, the lot of freedmen was not much changed; in fact, it was arguably worse. Fear of blacks led to violence against blacks. Freedmen who were too "uppity," who dared to assert their equality, or who even looked a white man in the eye, were beaten, often killed. The worst violence against blacks was found in parts of the South, such as eastern Tennessee, where there had been few plantations and where Unionist sentiment had been strongest during the war. Blacks, by and large, fared better among the "old master" class and in the plantation South. Poor whites saw blacks as competitors for their place in society and blamed blacks for the war and the subsequent destruction of their homes.

5. Divisions among southern whites after the war

White violence was not only directed against blacks but against other whites, as well. Unionists suffered in some parts of the South at the hands of Confederate veterans, and Confederates suffered in areas that had been predominately Unionist. Confederate hate was also directed against "scalawags"– southerners who cooperated with federal occupying forces, Republicans, or the Freedmen's Bureau. Southern whites also despised the "carpetbaggers" – Northerners who had moved South either to help freedmen or, more typically, to profit off southern misfortune. Named carpetbaggers because they were said to have come south with all their belongings in a satchel made from two squares of carpet, these northerners bought up old plantations at depressed prices or established businesses and built factories. Eventually they would play leading roles in southern politics while native southerners were excluded from voting and holding office.

6. The different opinions in government over how to carry out Reconstruction

President Andrew Johnson, along with Secretary of State William H. Seward and Secretary of the Navy Gideon Welles, wanted to restore the constitutional order of the United States to what it was before the war. Seward and Welles, in particular, were for clearly defined states' rights. They believed that, while the federal government might punish individuals for traitorous conduct, it could not punish states. On the other hand, Secretary of War Edwin M. Stanton, along with the Radical Republicans – especially Thaddeus Stevens in the House of Representatives and Charles Sumner in the Senate – thought the South should be more severely punished for the war. But more than revenge, this faction wanted to reconstruct the social order in the South, giving blacks full equality and voting rights with whites. To this end, they wanted to extend the power of the federal government beyond what many believed its constitutional limits.

7. President Johnson's Reconstruction program

In June 1865, President Johnson appointed provisional governors for the southern states.

These states, he said, were to call conventions to draw up new state constitutions that had to declare secession illegal and abolish slavery. Southern whites would be allowed to vote under the new constitutions, but not those who had served as civil officers in the Confederacy, had been governors of seceded states, had been general officers in the Confederate army and navy, or whose wealth had exceeded $20,000. Even among these groups, army and naval officers, and the rich, could obtain a pardon if they swore oaths of allegiance to the union. Johnson enacted his Reconstruction package without summoning Congress to a special session.

8. The behavior of southern state governments established under Johnson

By the time Congress assembled in December 1866, every southern state, except Texas, had held elections and by January had functioning state governments. That the new southern legislatures had a large number of former Confederate officers troubled the Radical Republicans. Some southern governors evinced a spirit of defiance of the Federal government. Among the measures approved by these Reconstructed governments were the black codes – laws passed by southern legislatures to keep blacks "in their place." The new governments, dominated by middle and lower class whites, passed laws that prohibited blacks from voting and from serving as jurors. Some of the black codes prohibited black men to assemble, made it illegal for them to own firearms, and established the pillory and flogging to punish them. The black codes contained elements of old laws against vagrancy and embodied in law the customs of slavery times. Some black codes, however, contained measures to protect freedmen's rights – for instance, to a

wage agreed on with an employer. The severity of black codes varied from state to state – Mississippi's, Louisiana's and Florida's were the harshest; those of Virginia, North Carolina, and Georgia were more benign. Because of strong Unionist influence, Tennessee had no black code at all.

9. What the Freedmen's Bureau Bill was and why President Johnson vetoed it

In February 1866, Congress passed the Freedmen's Bureau Bill, extending the life of the bureau and expanding its powers. In vetoing the bill, President Johnson said it was unconstitutional and did not secure freedom and security to freedmen. In particular, Johnson said the bill violated Article 6 of the Constitution by maintaining martial law in peacetime. Further, said the president, by passing a law governing 11 states, while refusing to seat their representatives, Congress was violating the principle of no taxation without representation.

10. What the Civil Rights Act was and why President Johnson vetoed it

In March 1866, Congress passed the Civil Rights Act: "All persons born in the United States and not subject to any foreign power … are hereby declared to be citizens of the United States." As citizens, such persons, regardless of their color or "previous condition of slavery," are guaranteed the "full and equal protection of the law." Johnson vetoed the act because, he said, state citizenship "is just as exclusively with the several states as the power to confer the right of Federal citizenship is with Congress." Johnson said the bill gave the federal government powers that had been "considered as exclusively belonging to the States. They all relate to the internal police and economy of the respective States." He said the bill was "another step, or rather stride, toward centralization and the concentration of all legislative powers in the National Government."

11. What the U.S. Supreme Court decided in *Ex Parte Milligan*

Doubts about the constitutionality of the Civil Rights Act were settled in April 1866 by the Supreme Court decision, *Ex Parte Milligan*. Lincoln appointee, Chief Justice Salmon P. Chase, with the entire court, ruled that Lincoln's wartime suspension of *habeas corpus* throughout the union had been unconstitutional. Since the Constitution applies to rulers and people both in peace and wartime, said the court, "martial rule can never exist when the Courts are open and in the proper and unobstructed exercise of their jurisdiction." This decision vindicated Johnson, who immediately suspended military court trials of civilians throughout the South.

12. What the 14ᵗʰ Amendment said, and its significance

The 14th Amendment, approved by Congress in June 1866, embodied the Civil Rights Act by linking state with national citizenship. "All persons," it read, "born or naturalized in the United States, and subject to the jurisdiction thereof, are citizens of the United States and of the State wherein they reside." Further, the amendment assured equal treatment for all citizens. It says: No State shall make or enforce any law which shall abridge the privileges or immunities of citizens of the United States; nor shall any State deprive any person of life, liberty, or property, without due process of law; nor deny to any person within its jurisdiction the equal protection of the laws. Striking out at President Johnson's

pardon of Confederate generals and soldiers, the amendment said only *Congress* "may by a vote of two-thirds of each House, remove such disability." In the clause, "The Congress shall have the power to enforce, by appropriate legislation, the provisions of this article," the 14th Amendment added language to the Constitution that would in the future give the federal government almost unlimited sway over the states.

13. How the Radical Republicans took control of Reconstruction

The new Congress that gathered in December 1866 had a larger, veto-proof Republican majority. From December to March 1867, the congressional Joint Committee on Reconstruction presented testimony after testimony of abuse of freedmen and Unionists, as well as southern lack of cooperation with the Freedmen's Bureau and the military. The committee recommended establishing in the South black manhood suffrage when many northern states still withheld the suffrage to blacks. Strengthened by the conclusions of the joint committee, Congress in a Reconstruction Act passed in March 1867 disbanded all southern state governments then functioning and divided the South into five military districts under five generals, all of whom answered to Ulysses Grant. The Reconstruction Act gave the military the authority to purge state governments of "disloyal" members, for Congress had ruled that ex-Confederates could not serve in public office. Under Congressional Reconstruction, southern states had to call conventions to draw up new state constitutions to guarantee black civil rights and the right to vote. Blacks would have a voice in choosing delegates to the constitutional conventions. Congress further decreed that before any reconstructed southern state could be readmitted to the union, its legislature had to ratify the 14th Amendment.

14. How southern state governments functioned under Congress' Reconstruction

Because of Congress' Reconstruction Act, many white Southerners lost the right to vote. South Carolina, Alabama, Florida, and Mississippi had more black than white voters. Blacks dominated the state constitutional convention in South Carolina and included such well educated and accomplished black men as Robert Brown Elliott, Francis Cardozo, William Whipper, and Martin Delany. The convention called for free public schools and compulsory education of children, the direct election of the governor, and the state's first divorce law. In the election of 1867, 700,000 blacks registered to vote in the South while white registered voters numbered only 40,000. Many whites, in protest against the Reconstruction governments, simply refused to register or to vote. The result was that southern governments became predominately Republican, with a large number of blacks serving in the state legislatures and on governors' staffs. Some of these blacks were competent to serve; others were not, and thus, white "carpetbaggers" used them as pawns in the greater political struggle.

15. The origins and role of the Ku Klux Klan

The Ku Klux Klan began as a club formed by young, former Confederate officers in Pulaski, Tennessee, in December 1865. The members adopted an elaborate but silly ritual and began riding through the streets of the town by night, dressed in white sheets. It was not long before the club morphed into a political and terrorist resistance movement for white supremacy. General Nathan Bedford Forrest, who became the first "Grand Wizard" of the order, described the Klan as "an institution of Chivalry, Humanity, Mercy and Patriotism" whose purpose was to resist the inroads of the northern conqueror into southern society. Since blacks were seen as the tools by which Yankee carpetbaggers were crushing white southerners, blacks would have to be warned to mind their behavior. Such warnings went beyond mere terrorizing into beatings and murders. Klansmen attacked white Unionists, carpetbaggers, and scalawags. The Klan formed an "Invisible Empire" that successfully resisted the attempts of Reconstruction governments to suppress it. In some counties, the Klan was the de-facto government. Though many southern whites deplored the Klan's violence, they welcomed its intervention. They saw blacks as tools of the northern radicals to undermine white southern culture and independence. Through 1868, and into 1869, Congress and Reconstruction governments adopted harsher measures to deal with the Invisible Empire, hunting down Klansmen and establishing martial law in Klan-dominated counties. In 1869, Bedford Forrest ordered the Klan disbanded, and it ceased to exist as a centralized organization, though local chapters continued. But the Klan was already growing obsolete died of its own accord in the mid 1870s.

16. Why Congress impeached President Johnson and the results of the impeachment

The Radical Republicans in Congress, led by Senator Thaddeus Stevens and Representative Benjamin Butler used President Johnson's dismissal of Secretary of War Edwin Stanton as the main pretext for removing him from office. The president, they said, had removed Stanton without the

Senate's advice and consent in violation of the Tenure of Office Act passed by Congress in March 1867. and had in his speeches attacked the Republican Congress. They claimed the president was responsible for racial and anti-Federal violence in the South. On February 24, 1868, the House of Representatives voted, 126 to 47, to impeach President Johnson "of high crimes and misdemeanors in office." Following the trial of the president in the Senate, however, on May 16, 1868, seven Republicans voted to acquit Johnson, bringing the vote to 35 Senators for conviction, 19 against – just one vote shy of the required two-thirds majority needed to convict a president. Yet, though he kept his office, Johnson's political power had been neutralized. The Radicals were triumphant. By the summer of 1868, eight southern states (North Carolina, South Carolina, Georgia, Florida, Alabama, Louisiana, Arkansas, and Tennessee) voted to ratify the 14th Amendment and were admitted into the Union. On July 9, 1868, the amendment had been ratified by enough states to become part of the Constitution.

17. The effect of U.S. expansionist goals and the Fenian raids on the development of Canada

U.S. leaders and citizens had long wanted to annex Canada to the United States. This and the Fenian invasions of Canadian territory from 1866 to 1871 strengthened the cause of the "Federationists," who had been calling for a certain degree of self-rule and independence from Great Britain. As an independent nation, Canada would have less to fear from United States expansionists. Canadian elections in 1866 brought Federationist victories in New Brunswick and Nova Scotia. These provinces, along with Ontario and Quebec, sent delegates to London to discuss the idea of a federation

with British government authorities. These meetings culminated in the British North American Act of 1867. Under this act, the "Dominion of Canada," as it was to be called, would have a two-house parliament and would be divided into provinces that would not be conceived as sovereigns (like the states of the U.S.) were but would function under governors appointed by the Canadian federal government. Canada would conduct its domestic affairs separately from Great Britain while remaining subject to Her Majesty, Queen Victoria. The British government, though, would still control Canada's foreign affairs. Parliament would appoint a governor general to represent the queen in Canada. The Dominion of Canada was inaugurated on July 1, 1867. Gradually other provinces joined the original provinces: British Columbia in 1871 and Prince Edward Island in 1873. In 1869, Canada obtained the Northwest Territories from the Hudson's Bay Company.

18. Social and political rifts in the United States after the Civil War

The Civil War had encouraged the idea that the only rift in the country was between the northern and southern states. This was not the case. The Appalachians marked another division between the increasingly industrialized Northeast and the predominately agricultural Middle West. One could also note gaping chasms in the large cities between the wealthy and the swarms of poor working men, many of whom were Irish immigrants. The Republican and Democratic parties represented other divisions. The Republican Party's championing of Negro suffrage and civil rights did not appeal to many westerners and poor working class Irish. The Republican platform favored the interests of the industrialists and bankers and speculators of the East by insisting that the value of money be based on gold and by calling for high tariffs on imported manufactured goods. Western farmers and small businessmen favored the paper currency that had been issued during the war because they thought that increasing the number of dollars in circulation benefited small shopkeepers and farmers. The Democrats attacked Reconstruction and the Republican disregard for states' rights. The Democrats called for amnesty for those who had fought against the Union during the war. It demanded the "abolition of the Freedmen's Bureau" and an end to the military occupation of the South. The Democrats favored a tariff only for the purpose of tax revenue, not for protection of industry, and called for the use of specie other than gold.

19. How Ulysses S. Grant's election as president mirrored the new order in the U.S. after the war.

Grant thought it belonged, not to the states, but to the federal government, to protect and foster the "greatest good of the greatest number." The states, in his opinion, were to function as instruments of the national government. In his commitment to centralization, Grant aligned himself with the Radical Republicans in Congress. Grant's espousal of a dominant national power reflected a new epoch in United States history, one inaugurated by the Civil War. Increasingly people would say the United States "is," instead of, as previously, the United States "are." This grammatical shift indicated that the United States "were" becoming a consolidated nation, not a union or confederation of sovereign states.

20. What the 15th Amendment proposed, who opposed it and why, when it was ratified

The 15th Amendment would extend the suffrage to blacks nationwide. Like the 14th Amendment, the proposed amendment extended the power of Congress over questions that had formerly been the domain of the states. It forbade the United States or any state to deny or abridge the right to vote purely "on account of race, color, or previous condition of servitude"; and decreed that "the Congress shall have the power to enforce this article by appropriate legislation." Congress had passed the 15th Amendment on February 26, 1869. But Charles Sumner and other Radicals had opposed the amendment because, they said, it did not go far enough to protect the rights of blacks. While the amendment did not allow states to withhold suffrage from blacks merely because of their race and color, it said nothing about discrimination based on other grounds – such as the ability to read or to pay a poll tax. Sumner argued that unless the amendment specified that a state could not discriminate in voting on account of education or wealth, it would become a dead letter. States would raise obstacles to voting that few blacks could overcome. The amendment was ratified in February 1870.

21. What the Force Acts were; their results

The Force Acts were laws passed by Congress in 1870, 1871, and 1872 to compel southern whites to respect the right of blacks to vote. The effect of the acts was to alienate some Republicans from the Radical cause. The German congressman from Missouri, Carl Schurz, for one, began to believe that federal interference was subverting republican government. He decried the interference of the "National Government into local affairs on every possible occasion," and "even to disregard and throw aside the most fundamental safeguards of popular rights for the correction of passing abuses." Schurz believed the doctrine of states' rights to be "the embodiment of true and general self-government," and was "convinced that this is the prevailing sentiment among the American people."

22. Why the period after the Civil War was called the "Gilded Age"

The period was called the Gilded Age because, though it was a time of material prosperity, this prosperity barely concealed the poverty in the cities and the corruption in government and business. It was a period too of increasing public immorality.

In large cities such as New York, government was complicit in criminal activity. Embezzlement of public funds was rife among office holders, while the poor lived in rank tenements and in shantytowns. Probably the most famous corruption ring was that of William Magear "Boss" Tweed in New York. From 1858 to 1871, Tweed established his power through the Democratic party political machine, Tammany Hall, and enriched himself through graft. With these funds he bribed public officials, civil servants, and others. The Tweed Ring reduced the taxes of some citizens to buy favors and issued bonds at high interest rates. By 1868, Tweed had gained control of the state Democratic Party. Now his influence spread to Albany, and some feared it would eventually reach all the way to Washington. Tweed's career came to an end in 1871 when the *New York Times* published evidence obtained from a city bookkeeper revealing the extent of Tweed's embezzlements.

23. The corruption in the Grant Administration and the federal and state governments

Corruption tainted nearly everyone in Grant's administration, even the members of his cabinet. In September 1872, during Grant's second administration, private letters revealed a huge scandal involving senators, representatives, and the Crédit Mobilier Company. Promoters of the Union Pacific Railroad had organized Crédit Mobilier to divert government funds from railroad construction to themselves. During Grant's first administration, Crédit Mobilier promoters distributed shares among members of Congress and to Vice President Schuyler Colfax, to keep them from investigating the company. Then, members of the "Whiskey Ring" in St. Louis, with Grant's private secretary and friend, General Orville Babcock, and treasury officers defrauded the government of millions of dollars. President Grant was personally untouched by the corruption. Still, he did little to stop it,

Corruption extended to members of Congress. Business interests (railroads, oil, textiles, iron, steel) "patronized" United States Senators – such leading Republicans as James G. Blaine of Maine. These party leaders became quite wealthy on such "patronage," which they justified by claiming it forged the bonds that Alexander Hamilton thought were so important between government and business. Graft, embezzlement, and bribery were found in state governments. Reconstruction governments spent extravagantly and racked up large debts.

24. What the Civil Rights Act of 1875 was and its effects

The Civil Rights Act, approved by Congress in 1875, had been promoted by Senator Charles Sumner since 1870. It entitled to everyone, regardless of race, the use of public facilities, such as theaters, inns, trains, and stages.

But the passage of this act was only a short-lived victory; it quickly became a dead letter.

25. How Reconstruction ended

In the election of 1876, it appeared that that the Democratic candidate, Samuel J. Tilden, had won the presidency against the Republican, Rutherford B. Hayes. But returns from Oregon were disputed, and in three southern states (South Carolina, Florida, and Louisiana) Reconstruction governors threw out thousands of Democratic votes, saying they were fraudulent. With these states, Hayes would have 185 electoral votes to Tilden's 184. It appears that a Congressional electoral commission of eight Republicans and seven Democrats that met to decide what to do about the disputed results from the South through "visiting statesmen" made a deal with southern Democrats. The Democrats agreed to recognize the election of Hayes if the Hayes administration agreed not to force the South to honor the 15th Amendment that guaranteed black voting rights. Hayes secured the presidency.

But even if no deal had been made with southern Democrats, President Hayes acted in their interest – for instance, he ordered the withdrawal of Federal troops that barred former Confederate general Wade Hampton from taking up the governorship of South Carolina after the state supreme court decided a disputed election in his favor. Hampton was one the "Redeemers" (advocates of southern white rule); his opponent, who claimed the election victory, was Federal general Daniel H. Chamberlain. Without the support of federal bayonets, Chamberlain could not maintain his claim, and Hampton became governor. Two weeks later, Hayes ordered the evacuation of federal troops from New Orleans, ushering in white southern rule in that city.

Such acts effectively ended Reconstruction. Except in Texas, state governments in the South fell under control of members of the Confederate officer class. "Redeemer" governors such as Wade Hampton, however, promised to respect the civil rights of blacks, and for almost two decades blacks in the South continued to vote in large numbers, and a few even sat in state legislatures.

Key Terms at a Glance

Reconstruction: the process by which the southern states were to be readmitted to the union after the Civil War; the period in which this reconstruction took place
miscegenation: the mixing of races, especially through marriage
scalawags: southerners who cooperated with federal occupying forces
carpetbaggers: northerners who moved South either to help freedmen or to profit off southern misfortune
poll tax: a fixed amount of money a person has to pay in order to vote
specie: money in coin
graft: gaining money or other gain in an illegal or dishonest manner

Questions for Review

1. **Describe the condition of the South after the Civil War.**

   The South was in a very bad state. The economy was devastated, and people were starving. Destitution was everywhere. Davis, in his humiliation, had become a symbol of the fallen southern nation.

2. **Describe the condition of blacks in the United States after the war.**

   The condition of blacks in the South varied. Some blacks had never left their old plantations, even when able to; others, following in the wake of the Union army, had fled from their old homes. Many blacks were eager to work for wages, while others equated freedom with idleness. Many black families suffered from starvation, as some whites were unwilling to hire black men who had children.

   Freedmen greeted wage earning at first with joy. But former masters, now employers, paid freedmen as small a wage as possible, which was often not enough for their needs. Unlike under the paternalistic system of slavery, employers turned out the infirm to fend for themselves. Many freedmen, too, had little notion of the value of money and wasted it on luxuries bought at the plantation store, leaving them little for necessities. Despite its evils, slavery was a world built on personal relationships that somewhat softened its rigors. The new, wage-earning world could be cold and pitiless.

   Outside those areas controlled by the Freedmen's Bureau, the lot of freedmen was not much changed; in fact, it was arguably worse. Fear of blacks led to violence against blacks. Freedmen who were too "uppity," who dared to assert their equality, or who even looked a white man in the eye, were beaten, often killed. The worst violence against blacks was found in parts of the South, such as eastern Tennessee, where there had been few plantations and where Unionist sentiment had been strongest during the war. Blacks, by and large, fared better among the "old master" class and in the plantation South. Poor whites saw blacks as competitors for their place in society and blamed blacks for the war and the subsequent destruction of their homes

3. **What was President Johnson's policy towards the South, and how did it embitter the Radicals towards him?**

   President Johnson appointed provisional governors for each of the southern states and told them to call conventions to draw up new state constitutions that had to declare secession illegal and abolish slavery. Some southern governors, too, were defiant of federal authority. Southern whites would be allowed to vote under the new constitutions, but not those who had served as civil officers in the Confederacy, had been governors of seceded states, had been general officers in the Confederate army and navy, or whose wealth had exceeded $20,000. Even among these groups, army and naval officers, and the rich, could obtain a pardon if they swore oaths of allegiance to the union. Johnson enacted his Reconstruction package without summoning Congress to a special session. The Radicals objected because the new governments had a large number of former Confederate officers and they enforced black codes, laws to keep blacks "in their place."

4. **What did the Radical Republicans think should be done with the South?**

   The Radical Republicans thought the South should be more severely punished for the war. But more than revenge, this faction wanted to reconstruct the social order in the South, giving blacks full equality and voting rights with whites. To this end, they wanted to extend the power of the federal government beyond what many at the time believed its constitutional limits.

5. **Why was the 14th Amendment so important for the Radical Republicans?**

The 14th Amendment linked state with national citizenship and gave Congress new power over the states. The 14th Amendment assured that the Radical Republicans' dream of equality would live on long after their political power ended. It embodies the Civil Rights Act that President Johnson had vetoedand thus kept states from denying ciitzenship to blacks. The 14th Amendment allowed the Radical Republicans to take Reconstruction out of the hands of the president. Congress passed a Reconstruction Act which disbanded all southern state governments then functioning and divided the South into five military districts under five generals, all of whom answered to Ulysses Grant. The Reconstruction Act gave the military the authority to purge state governments of "disloyal" members, for Congress had ruled that ex-Confederates could not serve in public office. Under Congressional Reconstruction, southern states had to call conventions to draw up new state constitutions to guarantee black civil rights and the right to vote. Blacks would have a voice in choosing delegates to the constitutional conventions. Congress further decreed that before any reconstructed southern state could be readmitted to the union, its legislature had to ratify the 14th Amendment.

6. **What is the Fifteenth Amendment? Did it affect both the North and the South? Please explain.**

The 15th Amendment would extend the suffrage to blacks nationwide. Like the 14th Amendment, the proposed amendment extended the power of Congress over questions that had formerly been the domain of the states. It forbade the United States or any state to deny or abridge the right to vote purely "on account of race, color, or previous condition of servitude"; and decreed that "the Congress shall have the power to enforce this article by appropriate legislation." The amendment affected both the northern and southern states. Previous to the amendment, northern states had withheld the suffrage from blacks. The amendment, however, did not specify that a state could not discriminate in voting on account of education or wealth.

7. **What were the various attitudes toward black equality both in the North and the South?**

Not all white Americans – even those who supported abolition – backed black equality. Some in the North supported the Radical Republicans' calls for complete equality, but southern whites feared that such equality would lead to miscegenation and the destruction of white society and culture in the South. The Republican Party's championing of Negro suffrage and civil rights did not appeal to many westerners and poor working class Irish.

8. **Briefly explain the Civil Rights Act.**

The Civil Rights Act entitled to everyone, regardless of race, the use the public facilities, such as theaters, inns, trains, and stages.

9. **How did the government of the Dominion of Canada differ from the government formed by the United States Constitution?**

The Dominion of Canada had a two-house parliament (the Uniteds States, too, had a two-house legislature) and was divided into provinces, just as the United States was made up of states. But the provinces were not conceived as sovereigns (like the states of the U.S.) were but would function under governors appointed by the Canadian federal government. Unlike the United States, which conducted its own foreign affairs, while Canada conducted its domestic affairs separately from Great Britain, the British government conducted Canada's foreign affairs. Parliament would appoint a governor general to represent the queen in Canada.

10. **What did President Grant's espousal of a dominant national power reflect? How did this affect the United States?**

Grant's espousal of a dominant national power reflected a new epoch in United States history, one inaugurated by the Civil War. Increasingly people would say the United States "is," instead of, as previously, the United States "are." This grammatical shift indicated that the United States "were" becoming a consolidated nation, not a union or confederation of sovereign states.

11. **What did Mark Twain mean by calling the post-war period the "Gilded Age"?**

Mark Twain called the post-war period the "Gilded Age" because it was a time of material prosperity, which, like a thin layer of gold covering a baser metal, hid a multitude of ills – moral, cultural, and political.

12. **What events caused the end of the Southern Reconstruction?**

President Hayes acted in the interests of the southern Democrats by ordering the withdrawal of Federal troops that barred former Confederate general Wade Hampton from taking up the governorship of South Carolina after the state supreme court decided a disputed election in his favor. Hampton was one the "Redeemers" (advocates of southern white rule); his opponent, who claimed the election victory, was Federal general Daniel H. Chamberlain. Without the support of federal bayonets, Chamberlain could not maintain his claim, and Hampton became governor. Two weeks later, Hayes ordered the evacuation of federal troops from New Orleans, ushering in white southern rule in that city. Such acts effectively ended Reconstruction.

Ideas in Action

1. **If you were the president of the United States, what would you have wanted to do with the South after the war? Come up with what you think would be a fair treatment and defend it.**

2. **Examine the U.S. Constitution in regards to what it says about the powers granted to the federal government and state governments. In light of this, defend whether you think that Radical Republican policies after the Civil War were in accord with the Constitution or not.**

3. **In light of what Catholic theology and papal teaching said about slavery at the time, were Radical Republican policies concerning the status of freedmen more in accord with Catholic teaching or not? Address the same question in light of subsequent Church teaching on human freedom (for instance, the *Catechism of the Catholic Church*, 1730–1742 and 2401–2449).**

Sample Quiz I (pages 507-521)

Please answer the following in complete sentences.

1. What was the general condition of the southern states after the war?

2. What did Southern whites fear from the freedmen?

3. What was the Freedman's Bureau?

4. Describe President Johnson's Reconstruction program.

5. Why did President Johnson veto the Freedmen's Bureau Bill?

6. Why did Johnson veto the Civil Rights Act?

7. Describe the Reconstruction Act under the Radical Republicans.

8. How did southern state governments function under Congress' Reconstruction?

9. Why did Congress impeach President Johnson?

Answers to Sample Quiz I

Students' answers should approximate the following.

1. The South after the war was devastated economically and politically. Destitution was everywhere. Some left for foreign countries; others moved north. Most remained in their native states, trying to rebuild their fortunes.

2. Southern whites feared that if blacks were not "kept down" they would perpetrate bloody war on the whites. They also feared miscegenation, which they thought would degrade southern society.

3. The Freedman's Bureau was a branch of the war department that passed out emergency rations of food to both whites and blacks. It helped to integrate blacks into white society through the building of schools for blacks.

4. President Johnson appointed provisional governors for the southern states. These states, he said, were to call conventions to draw up new state constitutions that had to declare secession illegal and abolish slavery. Southern whites would be allowed to vote under the new constitutions, but not those who had served as civil officers in the Confederacy, had been governors of seceded states, had been general officers in the Confederate army and navy, or whose wealth had exceeded $20,000. Even among these groups, army and naval officers, and the rich,

could obtain a pardon if they swore oaths of allegiance to the union.

5. In vetoing the bill, President Johnson said it was unconstitutional and did not secure freedom and security to freedmen. In particular, Johnson said the bill violated the Constitution by maintaining martial law in peacetime. Further, said the president, by passing a law governing 11 states, while refusing to seat their representatives, Congress was violating the principle of no taxation without representation.

6. Johnson vetoed the Civil Rights Act because, he said, conferring state citizenship "is just as exclusively with the several states as the power to confer the right of Federal citizenship is with Congress." Johnson said the bill gave the federal government powers that had been "considered as exclusively belonging to the States. They all relate to the internal police and economy of the respective States." He said the bill was "another step, or rather stride, toward centralization and the concentration of all legislative powers in the National Government."

7. Under Congressional Reconstruction, southern states had to call conventions to draw up new state constitutions to guarantee black civil rights and the right to vote. Blacks would have a voice in choosing delegates to

the constitutional conventions. Congress further decreed that before any reconstructed southern state could be readmitted to the union, its legislature had to ratify the 14th Amendment.

8. Because of Congress' Reconstruction Act, many white Southerners lost the right to vote. South Carolina, Alabama, Florida, and Mississippi had more black than white voters. Blacks dominated the state constitutional convention in South. The convention called for free public schools and compulsory education of children, the direct election of the governor, and the state's first divorce law. Many whites, in protest against the Reconstruction governments, simply refused to register or to vote. The result was that southern governments became

predominately Republican, with a large number of blacks serving in the state legislatures and on governors' staffs. Some of these blacks were competent to serve; others were not, and thus, white "carpetbaggers" used them as pawns in the greater political struggle.

9. The Radical Republicans in Congress cited President Johnson's dismissal of Secretary of War Edwin Stanton as the main pretext for removing him from office. The president, they said, had removed Stanton without the Senate's advice and consent in violation of the Tenure of Office Act and had in his speeches attacked the Republican Congress. They claimed the president was responsible for racial and anti-Federal violence in the South.

Sample Quiz II (pages 521-532)

Please answer the following in complete sentences.

1. What effect did U.S. expansionist goals have on the development of the Dominion of Canada?

2. Name some of the divisions in the United States after the Civil War.

3. What was President Grant's idea of how the federal government and the states should function?

4. Explain the grammatical shift between "is" and "are" in referring to the United States.

5. What did the 15th Amendment propose?

6. Why did Charles Sumner and other Radicals oppose the 15th Amendment?

7. Why was the period after the Civil War called the "Gilded Age"?

8. What was the Civil Rights Act of 1875?

Answers to Sample Quiz II

Students' answers should approximate the following.

1. U.S. leaders and citizens had long wanted to annex Canada to the United States. This and the Fenian invasions of Canadian territory from 1866 to 1871 strengthened the cause of the "Federationists," who had been calling for a certain degree of self-rule and independence from Great Britain. As an independent nation, Canada would have less

to fear from United States expansionists. This resulted in the Dominion of Canada.

2. The Appalachians marked a division between the increasingly industrialized Northeast and the predominately agricultural Middle West. One could also note gaping chasms in the large cities between the wealthy and the swarms of poor working men, many of whom were Irish immigrants. The

Republican and Democratic parties represented other divisions.

3. Grant thought it belonged, not to the states, but to the federal government, to protect and foster the "greatest good of the greatest number." The states, in his opinion, were to function as instruments of the national government.

4. After the Civil War, people would say the United States "is," instead of, as previously, the United States "are." This grammatical shift indicated that the United States "were" becoming a consolidated nation, not a union or confederation of sovereign states.

5. The 15th Amendment would extend the suffrage to blacks nationwide. Like the 14th Amendment, the proposed amendment extended the power of Congress over questions that had formerly been the domain of the states. It forbade the United States or any state to deny or abridge the right to vote purely "on account of race, color, or previous condition of servitude"; and decreed that

"the Congress shall have the power to enforce this article by appropriate legislation."

6. Charles Sumner and other Radicals had opposed the amendment because, they said, it did not go far enough to protect the rights of blacks. While the amendment did not allow states to withhold suffrage from blacks merely because of their race and color, it said nothing about discrimination based on other grounds – such as the ability to read or to pay a poll tax.

7. The period was called the Gilded Age because, though it was a time of material prosperity, this prosperity barely concealed the poverty in the cities and the corruption in government and business. It was a period too of increasing public immorality.

8. The Civil Rights Act of 1875 entitled to everyone, regardless of race, the use the public facilities, such as theaters, inns, trains, and stages.

Essays

Instructions to be given to the students: Write in complete sentences. Underline your thesis. Give three supports or examples that explain why you think what you do and that support your thesis.

1. Do you think the measures taken after the Civil War to integrate blacks into white society were good? How could it have been

done better, or why were the measures taken the best possible ones? Use specific examples.

2. How would you have carried out Reconstruction in the South? Explain your ideas and reasons in depth.

3. Do you think the corruption that occurred during the Gilded Age was a result of the Civil War or any of the new policies and events after the war? Explain why or why not, using examples.

Sample Test

Please answer the following in complete sentences

I. Short Essay – Answer two of the following:

1. **What was the condition of blacks in the South after the war?**

2. **What were the different opinions in the federal government over how to carry out Reconstruction?**

3. **Describe the corruption in the Grant Administration and the federal and state governments.**

4. How did Reconstruction end?

II. Short Answer:

1. Why did many southerners leave their homes after the war?

2. Against whom was white violence directed after the war?

3. What did the Supreme Court rule in *Ex Parte Milligan*?

4. What did the original Ku Klux Klan morph into?

5. What were the Force Acts?

Answer Key to the Chapter Test

Students' answers should approximate the following:

I.

1. The condition of blacks in the South varied. Some blacks had never left their old plantations, even when able to; others, following in the wake of the Union army, had fled from their old homes. Many blacks were eager to work for wages, while others equated freedom with idleness. Many black families suffered from starvation, as some whites were unwilling to hire black men who had children.

   Former masters, now employers, paid freedmen as small a wage as possible, which was often not enough for their needs, and they turned out the infirm to fend for themselves. Many freedmen, too, had little notion of the value of money and wasted it, leaving them little for necessities.

   Outside those areas controlled by the Freedmen's Bureau, the lot of freedmen was not much changed; in fact, it was arguably worse. Fear of blacks led to violence against blacks. The worst violence against blacks was found in parts of the South, such as eastern Tennessee, where there had been few plantations and where Unionist sentiment had been strongest during the war. Blacks, by and large, fared better among the "old master" class and in the plantation South. Poor whites saw blacks as competitors for their place in society and blamed blacks for the war and the subsequent destruction of their homes.

2. President Andrew Johnson, along with Secretary of State William H. Seward and Secretary of the Navy Gideon Welles, wanted to restore the constitutional order of the United States to what it was before the war. Seward and Welles, in particular, were for clearly defined states' rights. They believed that, while the federal government might punish individuals for traitorous conduct, it could not punish states. On the other hand, Secretary of War Edwin M. Stanton, along with the Radical Republicans – especially Thaddeus Stevens in the House of Representatives and Charles Sumner in the Senate – thought the South should be more severely punished for the war. But more than revenge, this faction wanted to reconstruct the social order in the South, giving blacks full equality and voting rights with whites. To this end, they wanted to extend the power of the federal government beyond what many believed its constitutional limits.

3. Corruption tainted nearly everyone in Grant's administration, even the members of his cabinet. In September 1872, during Grant's second administration, private letters revealed a huge scandal involving senators, representatives, and the Crédit Mobilier Company. Promoters of the Union Pacific Railroad had organized Crédit Mobilier to divert government funds from railroad construction to themselves. During Grant's

first administration, Crédit Mobilier promoters distributed shares among members of Congress and to Vice President Schuyler Colfax, to keep them from investigating the company. Then, members of the "Whiskey Ring" in St. Louis, with Grant's private secretary and friend, General Orville Babcock, and treasury officers defrauded the government of millions of dollars. President Grant was personally untouched by the corruption. Still, he did little to stop it, Corruption extended to members of Congress. Business interests "patronized" United States Senators, who became quite wealthy on such "patronage," which they justified by claiming it forged the bonds that Alexander Hamilton thought were so important between government and business. Graft, embezzlement, and bribery were found in state governments. Reconstruction governments spent extravagantly and racked up large debts.

4. In the election of 1876, a congressional electoral commission met to decide what to do about the disputed results in the presidential election from the South. It appears that some representtatives made a deal with southern Democrats that if they agreed to recognize the election of Hayes, the Hayes administration would not to force the South to honor the 15th Amendment that guaranteed black voting rights. Hayes secured the presidency. But even if no deal had been made with southern Democrats, President Hayes acted in their interest – for

instance, he ordered the withdrawal of Federal troops that barred former Confederate general Wade Hampton from taking up the governorship of South Carolina after the state supreme court decided a disputed election in his favor. Hampton was one the "Redeemers" (advocates of southern white rule); his opponent, who claimed the election victory, was Federal general Daniel H. Chamberlain. Without the support of federal bayonets, Chamberlain could not maintain his claim, and Hampton became governor. Two weeks later, Hayes ordered the evacuation of federal troops from New Orleans, ushering in white southern rule in that city. Such acts effectively ended Reconstruction.

II.

1. Many southerners left their homes after the war to escape federal rule.

2. After the war, white violence was directed against blacks and other whites, including Unionists and those who worked with the Freedman's Bureau.

3. The Supreme Court ruled in *Ex Parte Milligan* that Lincoln's wartime suspension of *habeas corpus* throughout the union had been unconstitutional.

4. The original Ku Klux Klan morphed into a political and terrorist resistance movement for white supremacy.

5. The Force Acts were laws passed by Congress to compel southern whites to respect the right of blacks to vote.

CHAPTER 21: A New America is Born

Chapter Overview

- As white settlers moved into the West, the question of what to do about the Indians came more to the fore. To solve the problem, the United States government made treaties with Indian nations to get them out of the way of white settlement. The Indians were moved to reservations and were given government subsidies and a sum of money for their land.

- The Arapaho and Cheyenne under Black Kettle signed a treaty in 1861 and were moved to a reservation. The reservation was so poor that the Indians were dying, and Cheyenne braves began raiding white ranches, causing the settlers to call out the militia. This led to a general uprising of the Cheyenne and Arapaho. Black Kettle signed a treaty in 1865 and went to a reservation. Dissatisfied Cheyenne continued the resistance.

- The Jesuit priest, Pierre De Smet, came to American in 1821 and began to work among the Indians. He had a powerful influence over the Indians, and they trusted him. He established missions in many of the Indian villages and made peace between warring nations.

- In 1862 the government delayed a yearly subsidy payment to the Sioux, and the nation rose in revolt under their chief, Little Crow. The government appealed to Father De Smet to pacify the Indians. When De Smet learned that the government had no intention of honoring its promise to the Indians, De Smet refused to negotiate any further.

- After the Civil War, the long cherished plan for a transcontinental railroad could be realized. The railroad would, however, have to pass through Indian lands, so it was imperative to make peace with the Indians.

- The army began building forts along the Bozeman trail, which ran through Sioux lands, to protect miners and settlers en route to gold fields in Montana. In 1866, Captain William Fetterman fell into an Indian ambush, and he and his men were slaughtered.

- Congress created a non-government organization called the Indian Peace Commission. In 1868 the commission recommended the hitherto untried policy of endeavoring to conquer the Indian by kindness. They called for a peace conference in 1868. The commissioners and the Sioux concluded the Treaty of Fort Laramie in May and concluded similar treaties with other nations.

- On May 10, 1869, the Union Pacific and the Central Pacific railroads met at Promontory Point in Utah and drove in a gold spike to mark the completion of the first transcontinental railroad.

- With the transcontinental railroad came an increasing number of settlers into the West, and the Indian problem became even more pressing. The early 1870s saw the rise of a number of Indian aid societies.

- When white settlers came to the lava beds of northeastern California and southeastern Oregon, they demanded the removal of the Modoc, the inhabitants of that region. The government complied and removed the Modoc to a reservation on the Klamath River.

This reservation was already shared by the Snake and Klamath tribes, who were enemies of the Modoc. The Klamath harassed the Modoc, and the Modoc chief, Captian Jack, demanded lands elsewhere, but he was refused. The Modoc fled to the dry lava beds on the shores of Tule Lake and were pursued by the U.S. army. Finally Captain Jack was betrayed by one of his own, Hooker Jim. The whites tracked Captain Jack down. He surrendered and was hanged.

• When Colonel Custer and his men found gold in the Black Hills, the government offered the Sioux money in return for the Black Hills. The price was not high enough, so the Sioux refused. The government decided there would be no further subsidies for food for those who refused to compromise. When Sioux warriors began to rally around Crazy Horse, Sitting Bull, and others, the Indian Bureau ordered all Cheyenne and Sioux to gather at Fort Laramie. Because of extreme cold, most of the tribes did not come to Fort Laramie. A war followed with the Sioux and Cheyenne. During this struggle, in which Colonel Custer and his men were slaughtered by Sioux led by Crazy Horse, and throughout the United States people clamored for revenge. Crazy Horse surrendered in May 1877, and Sitting Bull surrendered four years later.

• Before he died, Old Joseph, chief of the Nez Percé tribe, told his son never to sell the tribal lands in the Wallowa Valley. His son, Young Joseph, refused at first to sell the Wallowa Valley when in 1876 an army commission tried to persuade him to sell. The commission gave him a month to withdraw peacefully. Realizing he did not have enough men to fight, Chief Joseph left with his people. When some of his young warriors, angry at their loss, killed white settlers, Joseph fled over the Rockies with his people toward Canada. Along the way they were attacked several times by U.S. cavalry, and finally Joseph surrendered.

• After a long war with the United States, Cochise, chief of the Chiracahua Apache, surrendered and went to the reservation the government had set aside for his tribe. There he died. The Apache were unwilling to take to farming and made raids in Mexico. When the government ordered their removal to a desert region of Arizona, the Apache rose in revolt under Geronimo. Geronimo surrendered in 1844, and the Apache settled on the San Carlos reservation. Geronimo escaped several times until he was finally captured and removed to Florida.

• In the 1870s reformers called for civilizing the Indians. The reformers thought the best way to do that was to break up the tribes and give individuals their own plots of land. Congress passed the Dawes Act in 1887 that authorized the break-up of reservations into individual homesteads. The Indians, however, could not easily adjust to western civilization because they had no tradition of private ownership. This Dawes Act reduced tribes to greater destitution.

• When the Sioux began to practice the Ghost Dance to make themselves immortal, white authorities were frightened. This, coupled with growing Indian unrest, caused the authorities to fear that Sitting Bull would join the Ghost Dancers and further agitate them. On December 19, 1890, Sioux reservation police broke into Sitting Bull's cabin to arrest him. A fight ensued in which Sitting Bull was killed by one of his own people. The Sioux fled the reservation, pursued by soldiers. At Wounded Knee, the soldiers ordered the Indians to surrender their rifles, and a struggle ensued that ended in a massacre. This was the last armed engagement between the United States and the Indians.

- In the West the railroads helped create one of America's romantic legacies – that of the cowboy and the cattle drive. The brief epoch of the cattle drives became an image of freedom and strenuous activity.

- Western cattle and the railroads changed the agricultural economy of the United States. Farms were increasingly no longer subsistence farms and became larger due to the use of new machinery.

- With the harnessing of electricity came other new breakthroughs. In 1876 Alexander Graham Bell invented the telephone. Charles Brush developed a dynamo capable of providing power to arc lamps, replacing gas lamps with electric light. Thomas Edison developed the phonograph and the incandescent light bulb.

- In the business world of the North after the war, there was wild speculation and rapid production. Overproduction brought on financial panics.

- To stabilize the marketplace somewhat, manufacturers came up with the "trust." With his own trust, John D. Rockefeller controlled 90 percent of the oil refinery business in the United States.

- In order to combat abuses associated with trusts, Congress passed the first Interstate Commerce Act in 1887 and the Sherman Antitrust Act in 1890. Both were largely ineffective.

- The plight of the urban laborer was deplorable. Men, women, and children worked long hours for a mere pittance, and families lived in squalid conditions. In 1877 the "Great Strikes" disrupted business throughout the eastern United States. The strikes ended when President Rutherford Hayes sent in the United States army. The strike brought some benefits to workers, but still their situation was far from ideal.

- Labor groups called unions began to form in America, starting with the Knights of Labor. This group gave way to the American Federation of Labor in 1886. The AFL helped realize the passage of the eight-hour work day laws in many states.

- Religion began to take an interest in the labor issue, and the late 19th century saw a growing number of Christian justifications for unionism and even socialism. On May 15, 1891, Pope Leo XIII issued an encyclical letter, *Rerum Novarum*, presenting the Catholic teaching on property and labor.

What Students Should Know

1. **The U.S. government's intent in settling Indians on reservations; its actual effects**

   The U.S. government saw moving Indians to reservations as the first step in civilizing them, but it proved to be the beginning of their decline. It became harder for Indians to support themselves in the customary manner – by hunting wild game. They increasingly relied on government subsidies of food and clothing; but these were often not sufficient, and the Indians began to suffer hunger and want.

2. **Father Pierre-Jean De Smet's ideas on how to help the Indians**

   Father De Smet thought it was best for the Indians to abandon their nomadic, hunter life for the settled existence of farmer folk. Besides the benefits an agricultural life would bring in terms of civilization, De Smet thought that it was the only way the Indians could survive in a world increasingly dominated by white men. He favored the model of the Reductions of Paraguay – settled, self-ruled communities of Indians, separated from the influence of white men.

3.   Father De Smet's accomplishments

De Smet founded missions among various Indian tribes. His first was a mission to the Pottawatomies of Council Bluffs. He undertook missionary journeys to the western tribes, including the Flatheads, Pend d'Oreilles, Crow, and Gros Ventres. In 1841, with Father Nicholas Point, De Smet founded a mission among the Flathead; and later, after he made peace between the Blackfeet and the Crow and other tribes, the Blackfeet agreed to the establishment of a mission among themselves. De Smet had earned the trust of the Indians; thus the U.S. government at times asked him to pacify and help negotiate treaties with Indian tribes.

4.   What were the opinions about what to do about the Indians

Red Cloud's assaults on the Bozeman Trail forts kept the regiments posted in them in a constant state of fear. The government was at a loss what to do. Father De Smet, again working among the Indians, drew up a long list of Indian grievances that he sent to Washington. Peace with the Indians, he said, could be achieved if the government employed honest agents. The old abolitionist guard agreed with De Smet; but, since they had never lived amongst the western Indians, their prescriptions were more idealistic than the priest's. They favored a different tactic than that of the military, which believed that Indians had first to be pacified (conquered), then treated with fairness. The Eastern reformers wanted the government to take a conciliating approach towards the Indian – a position which earned them the ire of many a western settler who believed the only good Indian was a dead Indian. On the heels of the news of the Fetterman Massacre, Congress created a non-governmental organization called the Indian Peace Commission. The members of the commission included prominent reformers and General Sherman. In 1868, the commission came out with a report that recommended a "hitherto untried policy of endeavoring to conquer [the Indian] by kindness," while it warned of the serious threat that a "handful of savages" posed to the march of civilization and progress.

With the increase in Indian troubles after the building of the transcontinental railroad, the debate over the Indian question grew more intense. Some easterners echoed western calls for extermination. Others wanted to see an end to the reservation system and a break up of the Indian tribes so they could be absorbed by white society.

5.   The provisions of the Treaty of Fort Laramie

Commissioners and the representatives of the U.S. government concluded the Treaty of Fort Laramie in May 1868 with the Sioux. The treaty gave the Sioux an enormous tract of land, centering on the Black Hills (a sacred spot to the Sioux) in South Dakota, as well as a yearly subsidy of food and clothing. The treaty forbade all white settlement on Indian land. Any Indian who wanted to farm would be provided with 360 acres of land, plus seed and farming implements. The United States government, too, would provide schools to which the Indians agreed to send their children. In return, the Indians had to abandon any claim to lands that lay outside their reservation and agree to "withdraw all opposition to the construction of the railroads now being built on the plains." The commissioners concluded similar treaties with the Comanche, Kiowa, Arapaho, and Southern Cheyenne; with the Crow, the Ute, the Bannock, and the Shoshone; with the Navaho and the Snake.

6. The building of transcontinental railroads

The first transcontinental railroad ws the Union Pacific and Central Pacific. The construction of the Union Pacific set out from from Omaha going west. Work on the Central Pacific began from Sacramento, California, laying track across the Central Valley, over the Sierra Nevada, and into the Great Basin deserts. On May 10, 1869, the two railroads met at Promontory Point, near the Great Salt Lake in Utah. There they drove in a gold spike to mark the completion of the railroad that linked East and West. Over the next 15 years, Congress chartered other transcontinental railroads: the Northern Pacific, the Southern Pacific, and the Santa Fe Railroad.

7. Effects of the transcontinental railroads on American society

The railroads brought increased white settlement to the West. Railroad companies advertised for settlers to whom they sold land on credit, and whom they then transported to their property. Many new towns sprang up along the rail routes, and many older towns grew into cities. With increased white settlement, the question of what to do with the Indians became more pressing than ever before. Indian hostilities had not ceased on the plains. The railroads frightened away game and, most importantly, buffalo; they brought professional hunters who killed buffalos by the hundreds The loss of buffalo inspired new revolts among the Southern Cheyenne, the Comanche, and the Kiowa, halting westward traffic on the trails.

8. What were President Grant's reform ideas and measures

Grant saw the reservation system as a means to civilize the Indians. While the natives lived off rations and what they could produce for themselves, the government would provide them schools in which they could be trained in the rudiments of American culture. Grant removed the corrupt Indian agents, replacing them with Christian ministers. But, of the 43 ministers appointed, most were Quakers and only four were Catholic. Catholic Indians thus in some cases were placed under Protestant ministers.

9. The goals of those who wanted a reform of U.S. Indian policy

The reformers pointed out how the U.S. government had broken treaty after treaty with the Indians and settled them on the poorest lands. Indians were not improving, the reformers said, but growing more degraded. These reformers, who included the Colorado author, Helen Hunt Jackson, clergymen, and statesmen like Carl Schurz, said the government should strive to civiliize the Indians. Civilization meant Christianization. It meant teaching the Indians to read and write and cipher. It meant getting them to settle down as farmers. Many reformers thought this goal could best be achieved if the tribes were broken up and individuals were given their own plots of land to cultivate. Property ownership was the means, they said, to make the Indians into American citizens and, ultimately, assimilate them into white American culture.

10. The problems with the reform proposals

The problem with Indian policy reform proposals was that the Indians, with their tribal culture, could not easily adjust to western civilization. Indians had no tradition of private property ownership – all property belonged communally to the tribe. Another problem was that Indian men thought it an indignity to farm; they were hunters and warriors, not farmers. Whatever farming that was done was left to the women.

11. What the Dawes Act did, and its results

The Dawes Act , passed by Congress in 1887 (with the support of reformers and land speculators) allowed the president to authorize the break-up of reservations into individual homesteads when he received sufficient evidence that the Indians in question wanted it. Each family, said the act, would receive a homestead of 160 acres. Any reservation lands remaining after every family had received its allotment was to be sold to white settlers, the money from the sale to be held in trust for the tribe. The Dawes Act exempted the Five Civilized Tribes in Indian Territory from this break-up and allotment. The breaking-up of the reservations began in 1891. Within one year, Indian lands had been decreased by 12 percent. (By 1932, Indians had lost two thirds of the 138 million acres they possessed in 1887.) Though Indians received homesteads, they did not benefit from them. They knew nothing of the value of land, and land speculators easily took advantage of them. Though passed ostensibly to "improve" the Indians, the Dawes Act set in motion forces that would reduce tribes to even greater destitution.

12. What the Ghost Dance was and its significance

The Ghost Dacne was a ritual that spread among the Sioux, Cheyenne, Arapaho, and other plains tribes in 1889-90. It had come from a Nevada Paiute named Wovoka who had said that in 1889 he had been taken up into heaven where the Great Sprit told him of a soon-to-come renewal of the world – a great flood that would destroy the white men and all would return to what it was before they

came. Dead Indians, said Wovoka, would return to life; game would abound. Those who performed a ritual called the Ghost Dance would become immortal – the bullets of the white man could not penetrate their bodies. The Ghost Dance frightened white settlers and Indian agents, and it led to the killing of Sittlng Bull and the Battle of Wounded Knee.

13. The significance of Wounded Knee

Wounded Knee was the last violent encounter between American Indians and the U.S. military. It marked the end of America's Indian wars.

14. Identify:

a. *Kientpoos*: called "Captain Jack" by white settlers, Kientpoos was a chief of the Modoc, who lived in northeastern California and southeastern Oregon in the region of Tule Lake and the Lost River. Kientpoos and his Modoc followers refused to abandon their ancestral lands to make way for white settlement. Beginning in January 1873, Kientpoos and the Modoc became involved in a a war with the U.S. army that ended on June 1, 1873, when Kientpoos surrendered himself. He was hanged October 3, 1873 for the murder of a peace commissioner.

b. *George Armstrong Custer*: a colonel of the Seventh Cavalry, he had distinguished himself as an Indian fighter in the West. He led the reconnaissance of the Sioux reservation during which gold was discovered in the Black Hills. The government's attempts to force the Sioux to sell the Black Hills led to a war with the Sioux. During this war, Custer attempted to take a Sioux village on the

Little Bighorn River in what is now Montana, where he and all his men were slaughtered in June 1876 in the famous Battle of the Little Bighorn.

c. *Crazy Horse*: a Sioux chief who, with Sitting Bull and other chiefs leading 1,200 Sioux and Cheyenne warriors, refused to accept any sale of the sacred Black Hills to the U.S. government. When the Sioux and Cheyenne failed to appear as ordered at Fort Laramie, General Philip Sheridan, commanding the Seventh Cavalry, went in pursuit of them. Crazy Horse defeated Custer at the Battle of the Little Bighorn; but he and his allied chiefs suffered various defeats in the summer and fall of 1876. Crazy Horse surrendered to Colonel Nelson A. Miles in May 1877.

d. *Sitting Bull*: a Sioux shaman who joined Crazy Horse and other Sioux and Cheyenne chiefs in resistance to the U.S. government. Following a series of defeats in the latter part of 1876, Sitting Bull and his band fled to Canada. He surrendered to the U.S. government four years later. He settled on the Standing Rock reservation, where, in December 1890, he was killed by Sioux police.

e. *Chief Joseph*: Hinmaton-Yalatkit ("Rolling Thunder in the Mountains"), a chief of the Nez Percé and a Christian, who tried to keep peace with white settlers and the U.S. government. Joseph refused to leave his ancestral homeland, the Wallowa Valley in northeastern Oregon; but when the U.S. government threatened a forcible removal to the Lapwai Reservation in Idaho, Joseph gave in. But when some of his warriors killed white settlers, Joseph and his people fled,

hoping to reach Canada. Though successful in some skirmishes, Joseph at last had to surrender to General Nelson Miles, only 40 miles from the Canadian border in October 1876.

f. *Cochise*: the leader of th Chiracahua Apache in Arizona who, following an altercation over a kidnapping in which he was held complicit, went on the warpath, laying waste to white settlements in the region of the Gila River. He at last surrenderd when the U.S. government established a reservation for the Chiracahua in their homeland. Cochise died in a raid into Mexico in June 1874.

g. *Geronimo*: a Chiracahua Apache shaman who led a resistance to the U.S. government when it ordered his people to remove to the barren San Carlos reservation in Arizona. For six years, Geronimo and his warriors raided white settlements, spreading terror throughout the region. In January 1884, Geronimo surrendered, and his people settled on the San Carlos reservation. In May 1885, Geronimo and some of his people fled the reservation, but surrendered again in September 1886.

15. **The Homestead Act**

The Homestead Act, passed by Congress in 1862 and signed by President Abraham Lincoln, opened up the Great Plains to settlers. Under this act, the federal government granted 160 acres of public land to any settler who could afford to pay a small fee and resided on the land for five years. The Homestead Act (and the transcontinental railways) stimulated a new wave of agricultural growth.

16. How   western cattle raising, the trans-continental railroads, and new farm machine changed the East's agricultural economy

the East Traditionally, both in Europe and America, cattle had been raised in the areas where the people who consumed them lived. Now, with cattle shipped from the West, cattle raising declined in the East. Not just railroads, but industrial development in the East, would have its effect on agriculture as a whole. Except for the great plantations, most farms had had been subsistence farms – growing a number of different crops ,first, for the consumption of the farmer's family, then for sale on the market. To use the new farming machinery, farms had to become larger (for the machinery was expensive) and produce almost solely for the market. Instead of growing a number of crops, farmers increasingly specialized in one or a few crops – wheat and for, for example.

17. The growth of the steel industry in the United States

The Bessemer converter, invented in the 1850s by the English engineer Sir Henry Bessemer, converted iron ore into eteal at a relatively low cost. This method was brought to the United States, that had a rich lode of iron ore fields. In 1867, the United States produced 20,000 tons of steel. In the ensuing years, this number g rew exponentially, so that by 1895, the country produced 6 million tons of steel, and 10 million tons only five years later.

18. American inventions using electricity

In 1876, Alexander Graham Bell introduced the "telephone" at the Centen- Exhibition in Philadelphia. Later, Bell and his partner, Theodore Vail, organized the Bell Telephone Company. and provided telephone service in the cities. Charles Brush, developed a dynamo capable of providing power to arc lamps that were used to light cities. Thomas Alva Edison of Ohio developed a "phonograph" or "speaking machine": a cylinder covered with tin foil and turned by a crank. On October 21, 1879, Edison developed the incandescent light bulb.

19. The business climate of post-war America

The post-war era was a time of wild speculation, of rapid production, of ruthless competition. Railroad companies lowered rates and fares to drive each other out of business. Railroad and other companies manipulated state governments to control markets. Mining companies bribed judges who heard suits over rival claims. Since railroads had practically unlimited control over the regions through which they ran, they could raise and lower their rates at will, and the farmer or merchant had no other recourse than to pay them. Such activities helped bring instability to the market – companies rose and fell, the value of bonds plummeted, the rivalry of manufacturers led to overproduction, which brought a glut of products to the market resulting in dramatic falls in prices. These factors combined to create a financial "panic" (as depressions were then called) in 1873 and, another one twenty years later.

20. What trusts were

A trust is a combination in which companies or firms hand over, or "entrust," their securities and power to a central board of "trustees." Such trustees did not form a company incorporated under the laws of any state; thus, they were not subject to the same restraints as other companies. Thus, trusts, if they grew large enough, could dominate and control markets.

21. Who John D. Rockefeller was and what he did

John D. Rockefeller was a late 19th century businessman who built the Standard Oil Trust. In 1870, with his brother William and other partners, Rockefeller formed the Standard Oil Company. Rockefeller set out to group smaller companies together, to economize their business practices, and improve their technology. To do this, Rockefeller and his allied refiners organized the South Improvement Company and convinced the Pennsylvania, Erie, and New York Central railways to lower shipping prices for them while upping rates for competitors. South Improvement then offered to buy its competitors' companies (when they could no longer compete) by offering them money or stock in Standard Oil. By such methods, and by others (such as assailing competitors with lawsuits until they went bankrupt), Rockefeller had by 1878 gained control of over 90 percent of the oil refineries in the United States. In 1882, he formed the Standard Oil Trust, which, by 1882, governed 39 corporations in various states.

22. Who Andrew Carnegie was, and what he accomplished

In 1848, at age 13, Andrew Carnegie came from Scotland to America with his father. Employed by the railroad, the young Carnegie rose in the business world and was the first to introduce sleeping cars for the railroads. After observing the Bessemer process in Europe and foreseeing the coming demand for iron and steel, Carnegie invested in iron and in 1875 built the Edgar Thomson Steel Works near Pittsburgh. There he produced steel rails. By 1888, Carnegie had bought out the steel works in Homestead, Pennsylvania; and had gained control of coal and iron fields, a 425-mile long railway, and a line of Great Lakes steamships.

Carnegie recognized that the modern capitalist system brought great hardship to many while it enriched a relative few. He praised the "law of compeititon" because, he said, it brought about "wonderful material development." But, he added, that "while the law may be sometimes hard for the individual, it is best for the race, because it insures the survival of the fittest in every departrment." Though he opposed personal charity because he thought it violates the law of competition, he thought the wealthy should administer their wealth to form ties of brotherhood with the workers. The rich, he said, should use their excess wealth for the good of society. They should endow schools, museums and other cultural establishments to help the poor to better themselves. In his lifetime, Carnegie set up the Carnegie trusts to fund cultural and intellectual endeavors.

23. How Darwin's theory of natural selection influenced economic thought in the late 19th century

The evolutionary theory of the English naturalist Charles Darwin seemed a justification for the unregulated competition of the business world. According to Darwin, more complex life forms develop from less complex ones through a process of natural selection in which only the fittest, most adaptable, species survive. Many in the late 19th century thought that economics operated in the same manner; in business, they thought, only the fittest should survive. Far from implying any injustice, such survival led, it was thought, to the progress of human society.

24. **The *laissez-faire* and Darwinian theories of William Graham Sumner**

    Proponents of *laissez-faire* believed that businessmen should be able to pursue their economic interest as they wished with little or no government interference. An influential proponent of the Darwinian and *laissez-faire* school of economics was William Graham Sumner, a professor of sociology at Yale University. Sumner thought that populations inevitably grow too large for their food supply and thus suffer want and starvation. In order to overcome this natural state of affairs, he said, men invent things and engage in activities that lead to the further progress of the human race. To interfere with this natural cycle – say, by coming to the aid of the less fortunate – said Sumner, is to diminish man's potential. Sumner thought men should maintain the social institutions they have inherited and eschewed ideals, declaring that they (and religion, for that matter) were in conflict with science. Hard-nose scientific facts, thought Sumner, pointed to the soundness of the developing economic order.

25. **The sociological theories of Lester Ward**

    Lester Ward – called the father of American sociology – rejected the Darwininian, *laissez-faire* view of society. Ward thought that men by scientific investigation could come to understand how society works and learn how to order and direct it to ameliorate the disorderly effects of economic competition and diminish suffering. Religion, he thought, could not accomplish this, since it had hindered true morality by trying to make men good through fear. Ward thought society (that is, government), armed with scientific knowledge, could create an "organization of happiness." "It is the duty of society, in its collective capacity," he wrote, "so to regulate the phenomena of the social aggregate as to prevent, as far aspossible, the advancement of a small class at the expense of a large one."

26. **State government attempts to control trusts and why they failed**

    Faced with the power that trusts possessed to corner and control markets, states began to try and break these combinations. They were largely unsuccessful. New York, for instance, sued a branch of the Sugar Trust, only to have it regroup later under a new organization and a new name – the American Sugar Refining Company – and eventually control 85 percent of sugar production in the United States. New York's attorney general, David Watson, tried to break up Standard Oil but failed to force Standard Oil to sell off many of its holdings. Rockefeller simply gave the controlling board a new name – "liquidating trustees" (board members entrusted with selling property) – and business went on as before. Beginning in 1886, too, courts began to overturn state attempts to regulate business on the basis that they violated the freedom of contract.

27. **Federal attempts to regulate business and their results**

    In 1887, Congress passed the first Interstate Commerce Act to regulate "unreasonable" railroad rates and the pooling of companies across state borders. The act established the Interstate Commerce Commission. When, however, the federal courts said the commission could review railroad rates, but not fix them, it lost its teeth. In 1890, Congress passed the Sherman Anti-Trust Act, which declared illegal monopolies and business combinations that hindered interstate trade illegal. This act also was largely ineffectual; the five years following the passage of the act saw the formation of at least 25 new trusts throughout the country.

28. The lot of laborers in late 19th-century America

Workers labored long hours (12 to 14 hours a day) for little pay, in dirty and dangerous conditions. Their labor was monotonous and was deprived of the opportunity to achieve true craftsmanship. Not only a father, but his wife and even his young children (eight years old and up) labored in factories. Children between eight and 14 years old performed the labor of men, ten to 11 hours a day. Women worked long hours as well, in miserable conditions. Woman and children, who were paid less, often replaced men. Periods of unemployment, caused either by slumps in the business cycle or by the introduction of labor-replacing machinery, threatened workers with homelessness and starvation. Just as an industrialist would try to pay the lowest price possible for his machines, so he would pay the lowest wage possible to his employees. Since there were so many men who wanted work, the employer could always find someone who would work for what he wanted to pay and he could be careless about the safety of his factories; for if an employee was injured, there were always others to replace him or her.

This conditions of industrial life put new pressures on family life, for each family member went about his own individual task, and long hours of labor separated parents from their children, who then grew up without guidance. Gangs of youth roamed the streets, and the young fell into dissolute living and, too often, crime. Women who were single or who had lost their husbands and had no extended family, sometimes cohabited with men not their husbands or, in their desperation, turned to prostitution.

29. Changes in emigration and immigration in the late 19th century

After the war, new laborers, such as farmers' sons escaping to the city and discharged soldiers, entered the industrial workforce. In the 1860s, the number of immigrants from the British Isles began to decrease while the number of immigrants from the European continent grew. Russians, other Slavs, Italians, and southern and eastern Europeans, as well as laborers from China, made up an increasing share of the swelling number of immigrants entering the United States.

30. Who the Molly Maguires were and what they did

The Molly Maguries were a small group of Irish Catholic mine workers who took to agitating for better working conditions and better wages. When "coal and iron police" under the employ of the Anthracite Board of Trade committed murders and other crimes to intimidate their opposition, the Molly Maguires, during the "Long Strike" of 1875, used threats, beatings, and murder against their opposition. They obstructed train traffic, pushed engines off the rails, and destroyed property. Because of this (and on account of their secret oaths), the Mollies were condemned by Catholic priests and bishops. Agents of the Pinkerton Detective Agency infiltrated the Mollies to obtain evidence against them. Evidence brought by one Pinkerton agent, James McParlan led to the conviction and execution of 19 men said to be Mollies in June 1877. Other Mollies ended up serving prison time. These convictions broke the power of the Molly Maguires.

31. The Great Strikes of 1877 and their results

The Great Strikes began after the Baltimore and Ohio Railroad announced that it was cutting wages. Strikes and demonstrations broke out in Martinsburg, West Virginia; Philadelphia and Pittsburgh; Columbus and

Cincinnati; Chicago; and St. Louis, Missouri. Strikers not only paralyzed the railroads of the North but created considerable unrest in the cities. By July 30, the strikes had spread to the coal fields, crippling industries and foundries that relied on coal. Railroad workers in Trenton and Newark, New Jersey, quit work. The Great Strikes ended when President Rutherford Hayes decided to treat the strikes as an insurrection and sent the United States army into Pittsburgh. Hundreds of millions of dollars of property had been destroyed because of the Great Strikes, and many Americans now grew fearful of communist and socialist infiltration.

32. Whether labor organizations were communist or socialist

Some unions were affiliated with the Communist International, which was working for a general, worldwide proletarian revolution. Other unions were affiliated with the Black International, an anarchist organization. Such leftist organizations generally flourished wherever German immigrants had settled – in Wisconsin, for instance, or Chicago. But they hardly represented the majority of the American labor force.

33. What the Knights of Labor were

The Knights of Labor, founded in 1869, was the first labor organization that tried to unite all workers in one big union. The Knights proposed an end to the wage system in favor of an "industrial cooperative system" where workers would share in the ownership and profits of companies. Terence Powderly, an Irish Catholic who became grand knight of the union in 1881, wanted the Knights to ally themselves with causes that promoted "personal liberty and social equality." Powderly also wanted his union to unite with the temperance movement and encouraged local union councils to form cooperative business enterprises. Under Powderly, the Knights of Labor gained some victories; but Powderly's opposition to clemency for the Haymarket anarchists and his impracticality severely weakened the Knights of Labor at the height of their influence and membership in the 1880s.

34. What the American Federation of Labor (AFL) was

Key Terms at a Glance

trust: a combination in which companies or firms hand over, or entrust, their securities and power to a central board of trustees

evolution: a theory in biology that postulates that various types of plants, animals, and other living things have originated from other preexisting types and that the differences that distinguish them come from modifications in successive generations

laissez-faire: French phrase meaning, "let do"; the idea that the businessman should be able to persue his economic interest as he wishes with little or no government interference

labor union: a combination of workers in various industries who unite to bargain over wages, benefits, and working conditions

The AFL was a labor union formed in 1886 that, under the leadership of Samuel Gompers, eschewed ideas on how to change the economic and social order and concentrated only on goals that could be immediately achieved – such as the eight-hour work day and higher wages. The AFL was a national federation of craft unions that represented only skilled workers. In part because of AFL agitation, various state legislatures began passing laws to regulate the treatment of workers.

35. General Christian attitudes toward the labor question

Most Protestant Christians in the United States maintained a conservative attitude towards the labor question and tended to side with the men who controlled capital. Some other Protestants saw wealth as the reward of virtue, especially industriousness. But the late 19th century saw a growing number of Christian justifications for unionism and even socialism. Other Christian thinkers began to think that sin was not merely individual but that societies had sinful structures that fostered and perpetuated sin in the lives of individuals. Some North American Catholic bishops, priests, and laity objected to labor unions because they thought unions espoused ideas and encouraged practices that could harm the faith of their Catholic members. The bishops of Quebec, for instance, sought from Rome a condemnation of the Knights of Labor because members were required to take secret oaths modeled on the rituals of Freemasonry. But James Cardinal Gibbons, the archbishop of Baltimore, came to the defense of the Knights of Labor and staved off a Vatican condemnation of the group.

36. Pope Leo XIII's contribution to the labor question

The chief contribution of the Catholic Church to the labor question came in Pope Leo XIII's encyclical, *Rerum Novarum*. In *Rerum Novarum*, Leo came out in opposition to socialism; but, he also condemned many of the principles of *laissez-faire* capitalism. Unlike the socialists, Leo asserted the right to private, productive property; but, against the capitalists, he asserted the worker's right to a just wage. According to Leo, God gave the earth to all of mankind but left the determination of the exact character of private property to the industry of men and the institutions of peoples. Workers, he said, should not be treated like machines or cattle, nor should children be forced to labor like adults or work be placed upon females as if they were adult males. Workers, Leo said, have the right to organize themselves into unions and engage in peaceful strikes. Wealth production, he asserted, has the ultimate purpose of helping men live a virtuous life. Because of the moral dimension of economics, Leo said the Church has to be involved in solving social problems.

Questions for Review

1. **What did Americans in the West think of the Indians?**

The white setters in the West thought the Indians were shiftless, intent only on hunting and war, and was wasteful of the land. White men also thought the Indians were treacherous, bloodthirsty, and cruel. The Indian, they thought, must submit to the white man or die.

2. **Explain the general character of the treaties made with the Indian nations.**

The treaties the United States made with the Indians offered them reservations and government subsidies of food in return for land across which whites could travel or on which they could settle. The intent was to get the Indian out of the way.

3. **What made Pierre De Smet's mission to the Indians so successful?**

The Indians deeply trusted Pierre De Smet. It was clear to them that he was genuinely interested in their welfare and that he would stand up for them against injustice.

4. **How did the transcontinental railroad affect the fate of the Indians of the West?**

With increased white settlement, the question of what to do with the Indians became more pressing than ever before. Indian hostilities had not ceased on the plains. The railroads frightened away game and, most importantly, buffalo; they brought professional hunters who killed buffalos by the hundreds The loss of buffalo inspired new revolts among the Southern Cheyenne, the Comanche, and the Kiowa, halting westward traffic on the trails. The railroads accelerated the need whites felt to get Indians out of the way.

5. **Why didn't the reformers' goal of assimilating the Indians into western civilization succeed?**

The problem with Indian policy reform proposals was that the Indians, with their tribal culture, could not easily adjust to western civilization. Indians had no tradition of private property that characterized European society. Another problem was that Indian men thought it an indignity to farm; they were hunters and warriors, not farmers. Whatever farming was done was left to the women.

6. **Why didn't the Indians benefit from the homesteads they received under the Dawes Act?**

The Indians did not benefit from the homesteads they received because they had no tradition of private property ownership – all property belonged communally to the tribe. They did not understand the role of property and were thus easily chated by unscrupulous whites.

7. **How did the cowboy and the cattle drive embody the American ideal?**

The cowboy and the cattle drive embodied the American ideal because they were an image of freedom and strenuous action that inspired the American imagination.

8. **How did technology change the agricultural economy of the United States?**

Except for the great plantations, most farms had been subsistence farms – growing a number of different crops, first, for the consumption of the farmer's family, then for sale on the market. To use the new farming machinery, farms had to become larger (for the machinery was expensive) and produce almost solely for the market. Instead of growing a number of crops, farmers increasingly specialized in one or a few crops – wheat and corn, for example.

9. **Explain what a "trust" is and how it affected the economy of late 19th-century America.**

A trust is a combination in which companies or firms hand over, or "entrust," their securities and power to a central board of "trustees." Such trustees did not form a company incorporated under the laws of any state; thus, they were not subject to the same restraints as other companies. Thus, trusts, if they grew large enough, could dominate and control markets – and some trusts did dominate and control markets.

10. **Explain Darwin's natural selection theory and how proponents of *laissez-faire* used it to justify their economic theory.**

The evolutionary theory of the English naturalist Charles Darwin seemed a justification for the unregulated competition of the business world. According to Darwin, more complex life forms develop from less complex ones through a process of natural selection in which only the fittest, most adaptable, species survive. Many in the late 19th century thought that economics operated in the same manner; in business, they thought, only the fittest should survive. Far from implying any injustice, such survival led, it was thought, to the progress of human society.

Proponents of *laissez-faire* believed that businessmen should be able to pursue their economic interest as they wished with little or no government interference. Those who succeeded were the fittest and deserved to succeed. An influential proponent of the Darwinian and *laissez-faire* school of economics, William Graham Sumner thought that to interfere with the natural cycle of economics – say, by coming to the aid of the less fortunate – said Sumner, is to diminish man's potential.

11. **How did *laissez-faire* and Darwinian natural selection affect the lot of workers in the late 19th century?**

These ideas led to the spirit of free, untrammeled enterprise without government interference. This spirit tended to reduce workers to the status of machines, mere means to an end. Workers, including women and children, were dispensable to their employers, and worked many long hours for little pay in dirty and dangerous conditions.

12. **What is a labor union? How do craft unions (like the AFL) differ from unions like the Knights of Labor?**

A labor union is a combination of workers in various industries wh unite to bargain over wages and working conditions. Craft unions represent only skilled workers. Unions such as the Knights of Labor try to unite all workers in one large union, not just skilled laborers.

13. **Outline the major ides of of Pope Leo XIII's encyclical, *Rerum Novarum*.**

In *Rerum Novarum*, Leo came out in opposition to socialism; but, he also condemned many of the principles of *laissez-faire* capitalism. Unlike the socialists, Leo asserted the right to private, productive property; but, against the capitalists, he asserted the worker's right to a just wage. According to Leo, God gave earth to all of mankind but left the determination of the exact character of private property to the industry of men and the institutions of peoples. Workers, he said, should not be treated like machines or cattle, nor should children be forced to labor like adults or work be placed upon females as if they were male adults. Workers, Leo said, have the right to organize themselves into unions and engage in peaceful strikes. Wealth production, he asserted, has the ultimate purpose of helping men live a virtuous life. Because of the moral dimension of economics, Leo said the Church has to be involved in solving social problems.

Ideas in Action

1. **Read and discuss Pope Leo XIII's encyclical, *Rerum Novarum*. Examine labor issues of**

the late 19th century and our time in light of the encyclical.

(*Rerum Novarum* can be found at www.vatican.va)

2. Read Owen Wister's *The Virginian*, a story of the cowboy legend. How has the legend of the cowboy influenced how Americans think of themselves and their natio?

3. Research one of the Indian nations in this chapter, looking at such things as traditions, religion, and how the nation changed over the course of history.

4. The Franciscan historian of the California missions, Zephyrin Engelhardt, thought that in certain respects the reservation system worked out by the United States government was similar to the Spanish mission system as exemplified by the California missions — but, he thought, there were very fundamental differences as well. What were those similarities? What were the differences? Which system was better in terms of treatment of the native Americans?

Sample Quiz I (pages 537-555)

Please answer the following in complete sentences.

1. What were the actual effects of the U.S. government's intent in settling Indians on reservations?

2. What were Father Pierre De Smet's ideas on how to help the Indians?

3. What were the effects of the transcontinental railroad on American society?

4. What effect did the transcontinental railroad have on the Indians?

5. What were some problems with the Indian reform proposals?

6. What resulted from the Dawes Act?

7. Identify four of the following:
   a. Kientpoos
   b. George Armstrong Custer
   c. Crazy Horse
   d. Sitting Bull
   e. Chief Joseph
   f. Cochise
   g. Geronimo

Answers to Sample Quiz I

Students' answers should approximate the following.

1. The moving of the Indians to reservations proved to be the beginning of their decline. It became harder for Indians to support themselves in the customary manner – by hunting wild game. They increasingly relied on government subsidies of food and clothing; but these were often not sufficient, and the Indians began to suffer hunger and want.

2. Father De Smet thought it was best for the Indians to abandon their nomadic, hunter life for the settled existence of farmer folk. Besides the benefits an agricultural life would bring in terms of civilization, De Smet thought that it was the only way the Indians could survive in a world increasingly dominated by white men. He favored the model of the Reductions of Paraguay – settled, self-ruled communities of Indians, separated from the influence of white men.

3. The railroads brought increased white settlement to the West. Railroad companies advertised for settlers to whom they sold land on credit, and whom they then transported to their property. Many new towns sprang up along the rail routes, and many older towns grew into cities.

4. With increased white settlement, the question of what to do with the Indians became more pressing than ever before and accelerated the

movement to put them on reservations. The railroads frightened away game and, most importantly, buffalo; they brought professional hunters who killed buffalos by the hundreds. The loss of buffalo inspired new revolts among the Southern Cheyenne, the Comanche, and the Kiowa, halting westward traffic on the trails.

5. The problem with Indian policy reform proposals was that the Indians, with their tribal culture, could not easily adjust to western civilization. Indians had no tradition of private property ownership – all property belonged communally to the tribe. Another problem was that Indian men thought it an indignity to farm; they were hunters and warriors, not farmers. Whatever farming was done was left to the women.

6. Though Indians received homesteads from the Dawes Act, they did not benefit from them. They knew nothing of the value of land, and land speculators easily took advantage of them. Though passed ostensibly to "improve" the Indians, the Dawes Act set in motion forces that would reduce tribes to even greater destitution.

7.

  a. *Kientpoos*: called "Captain Jack" by white settlers in northeastern California and southeastern Oregon, Kientpoos was a chief of the Modoc. Kientpoos and his Modoc followers refused to abandon their ancestral lands to make way for white settlement.

  b. *George Armstrong Custer*: a colonel of the Seventh Cavalry, he had distinguished himself as an Indian fighter in the West. He is most remembered for his attempts to take a Sioux village on the Little Bighorn River in what is now Montana. In the ensuing battle, where he and all his men were slaughtered in June 1876 in the famous Battle of the Little Bighorn.

  c. *Crazy Horse*: a Sioux chief who refused to accept any sale of the sacred Black Hills to the U.S. government. Crazy Horse defeated Custer at the Battle of the Little Bighorn; but he and his allied chiefs suffered various defeats in the summer and fall of 1876.

  d. *Sitting Bull*: a Sioux shaman who joined Crazy Horse and other Sioux and Cheyenne chiefs in resistance to the U.S. government.

  e. *Chief Joseph*: a chief of the Nez Percé and a Christian, who tried to keep peace with white settlers and the U.S. government while trying to keep his ancestral homeland, the Wallowa Valley in northeastern Oregon.

  f. *Cochise*: the leader of the Chiracahua Apache in Arizona who, following an altercation over a kidnapping in which he was held complicit, went on the warpath, laying waste to white settlements in the region of the Gila River.

  g. *Geronimo*: a Chiracahua Apache shaman who led a resistance to the U.S. government when it ordered his people to remove to the barren San Carlos reservation in Arizona.

Sample Quiz II (pages 555-574)

Please answer the following in complete sentences.

1. **Describe the Homestead Act.**

2. **What is a trust?**

3. **What is John D. Rockefeller known for?**

4. **What is Andrew Carnegie known for?**

5. **What was Carnegie's view on the role of the wealthy?**

6. How did Darwin's theory of natural selection influence economic thought in the late 19th century?

7. Why did state government attempts to control trusts fail?

8. How did emigration and immigration change in the late 19th century?

9. What were the goals of the Knights of Labor and the American Federation of Labor?

Answers to Sample Quiz II

Students' answers should approximate the following.

1. The Homestead Act, passed by Congress in 1862 and signed by President Abraham Lincoln, opened up the Great Plains to settlers. Under this act, the federal government granted 160 acres of public land to any settler who could afford to pay a small fee and resided on the land for five years.

2. A trust is a combination in which companies or firms hand over, or "entrust," their securities and power to a central board of "trustees." Such trustees did not form a company incorporated under the laws of any state; thus, they were not subject to the same restraints as other companies. Thus, trusts, if they grew large enough, could dominate and control markets.

3. John D. Rockefeller was a late 19th century businessman who built the Standard Oil Trust. By 1878 he had gained control of over 90 percent of the oil refineries in the United States.

4. A Scottish emigrant, Andrew Carnegie rose in the business world. Carnegie invested in iron and in 1875 built the Edgar Thomson Steel Works near Pittsburgh. There he produced steel rails. By 1888, Carnegie had bought out the steel works in Homestead, Pennsylvania, and had gained control of coal and iron fields, a 425-mile long railway, and a line of Great Lakes steamships. In his lifetime, Carnegie set up the Carnegie trusts to fund cultural and intellectual endeavors.

5. Though he opposed personal charity because he thought it violates the law of competition, Carnegie thought the wealthy should administer their wealth to form ties of brotherhood with the workers. The rich, he said, should use their excess wealth for the good of society. They should endow schools, museums and other cultural establishments to help the poor to better themselves.

6. Darwin's evolutionary theory seemed a justification for the unregulated competition of the business world. According to Darwin, more complex life forms develop from less complex ones through a process of natural selection in which only the fittest, most adaptable, species survive. Many in the late 19th century thought that economics operated in the same manner; in business, they thought, only the fittest should survive. Far from implying any injustice, such survival led, it was thought, to the progress of human society.

7. State government attempts to regulate business were largely unsuccessful. Some companies sued, and regrouped later under a new organization and a new name. Governments failed to force big companies to sell off many of their holdings. Beginning in 1886, too, courts began to overturn state attempts to regulate business on the basis that they violated the freedom of contract.

8. After the war, new laborers, such as farmers' sons escaping to the city and discharged soldiers, entered the industrial workforce. In the 1860s, the number of immigrants from the British Isles began to decrease while the number of immigrants from the European continent grew. Russians, other Slavs, Italians, and southern and eastern Europeans, as well as laborers from China, made up an

increasing share of the swelling number of immigrants entering the United States.

9. The Knights proposed an end to the wage system in favor of an "industrial cooperative system" where workers would share in the ownership and profits of companies. The

AFL eschewed ideas on how to change the economic and social order and concentrated only on goals that could be immediately achieved, such as the eight-hour work day and higher wages.

Essays

Instructions to be given to the students: Write in complete sentences. Underline your thesis. Give three supports or examples that explain why you think what you do and that support your thesis.

1. Using specific examples, describe how Darwinism and *laissez-faire* contributed to the decline of working conditions in the United States. Students should research other sources than this textbook.

2. Do you think labor unions are beneficial or detrimental? Explain why or why not, using specific examples.

3. Compare and contrast the Catholic view on labor and working conditions with the *laissez-faire* view. Which view is more in keeping with the nature of man, and why?

Sample Test

Please answer the following in complete sentences

I. Short Essay – Answer two of the following:

1. What were the different opinions about what to do with the Indians? What resulted from these different ideas?

2. What were the goals of those who wanted to reform the U.S. Indian policy?

3. How did western cattle raising, the transcontinental railroads, and new farm machine technology change the agricultural economy of the U.S.?

4. Describe the business climate of post-war America.

5. Describe the *laissez-faire* and Darwinian theories of William Graham Sumner, and the sociological theories of Lester Ward.

6. Describe the main ideas of *Rerum Novarum*.

II. Short Answer:

1. What did President Grant and the U.S. government see the purpose of the reservation system to be?

2. What is the significance of Wounded Knee?

3. What caused the growth of the steel industry in the United States?

4. Name two 19th century American inventions using electricity.

Answer Key to the Chapter Test

Students' answers should approximate the following:
I.
1. Father De Smet thought that peace with the Indians could be achieved if the government employed honest agents. The old abolitionist guard agreed with De Smet; but, since they

had never lived amongst the western Indians, their prescriptions were more idealistic than the priest's. They favored a different tactic than that of the military, which believed that Indians had first to be pacified (conquered), then treated with fairness. The Eastern reformers wanted the government to take a conciliating approach towards the Indian – a position which earned them the ire of many a western settler who believed the only good Indian was a dead Indian. On the heels of the news of the Fetterman Massacre, Congress created a non-governmental organization called the Indian Peace Commission. The members of the commission included prominent reformers and General Sherman. In 1868, the commission came out with a report that recommended a "hitherto untried policy of endeavoring to conquer [the Indian] by kindness," while it warned of the serious threat that a "handful of savages" posed to the march of civilization and progress.

2. The reformers pointed out how the U.S. government had broken treaty after treaty with the Indians and settled them on the poorest lands. Indians were not improving, the reformers said, but growing more degraded. These reformers, who included the Colorado author, Helen Hunt Jackson, clergymen, and statesmen like Carl Schurz, said the government should strive to civiliize the Indians. Civilization meant Christianization. It meant teaching the Indians to read and write and cipher. It meant getting them to settle down as farmers. Many reformers thought this goal could best be achieved if the tribes were broken up and individuals were given their own plots of land to cultivate. Property ownership was the means, they said, to make the Indians into American citizens and, ultimately, assimilate them into white American culture.

3. Traditionally, both in Europe and America, cattle had been raised in the areas where the people who consumed them lived. Now, with cattle shipped from the West, cattle raising declined in the East. Not just railroads, but industrial development in the East, would have its effect on agriculture as a whole. Except for the great plantations, most farms had been subsistence farms – growing a number of different crops, first, for the consumption of the farmer's family, then for sale on the market. To use the new farming machinery, farms had to become larger (for the machinery was expensive) and produce almost solely for the market. Instead of growing a number of crops, farmers increasingly specialized in one or a few crops – wheat and corn, for example.

4. The post-war era was a time of wild speculation, of rapid production, of ruthless competition. Railroads lowered rates and fares to drive each other out of business. Railroad and other companies manipulated state governments to control markets. Mining companies bribed judges who heard suits over rival claims. Since railroads had practically unlimited control over the regions through which they ran, they could raise and lower their rates at will, and the farmer or merchant had no other recourse than to pay them. Such activities helped bring instability to the market – companies rose and fell, the value of bonds plummeted, the rivalry of manufacturers led to overproduction, which brought a glut of products to the market resulting in dramatic falls in prices. These factors combined to create a financial "panic" (as depressions were then called) in 1873 and, another one twenty years later. Corporations formed trusts to avoid regulation by state laws. A trust is a combination in which companies or firms hand over, or "entrust," their securities and power to a central board of "trustees." Such trustees did not form a company incorporated under the laws of any state; thus, they were not subject to the same restraints as other companies. Thus, trusts, if they grew large enough, could dominate and control markets.

5. Proponents of *laissez-faire* believed that businessmen should be able to pursue their economic interest as they wished with little or no government interference. An influential

proponent of the Darwinian and *laissez-faire* school of economics was William Graham Sumner, a professor of sociology at Yale University. Sumner thought that populations inevitably grow too large for their food supply and thus suffer want and starvation. In order to overcome this natural state of affairs, he said, men invent things and engage in activities that lead to the further progress of the human race. To interfere with this natural cycle – say, by coming to the aid of the less fortunate – said Sumner, is to diminish man's potential. Sumner thought men should maintain the social institutions they have inherited and eschewed ideals, declaring that they (and religion, for that matter) were in conflict with science. Hard-nose scientific facts, thought Sumner, pointed to the soundness of the developing economic order.

Lester Ward – called the father of American sociology – rejected the Darwinian, *laissez-faire* view of society. Ward thought that men by scientific investigation could come to understand how society works and learn how to order and direct it to ameliorate the disorderly effects of economic competition and diminish suffering. Religion, he thought, could not accomplish this, since it had hindered true morality by trying to make men good through fear. Ward thought society (that is, government), armed with scientific knowledge, could create an "organization of happiness." "It is the duty of society, in its collective capacity," he wrote, "so to regulate the phenomena of the social aggregate as to prevent, as far as possible, the advancement of a small class at the expense of a large one."

6. The chief contribution of the Catholic Church to the labor question came in Pope Leo XIII's encyclical, *Rerum Novarum*. In *Rerum Novarum*, Leo came out in opposition to socialism; but, he also condemned many of the principles of *laissez-faire* capitalism.

Unlike the socialists, Leo asserted the right to private, productive property; but, against the capitalists, he asserted the worker's right to a just wage. According to Leo, God gave the earth to all of mankind but left the determination of the exact character of private property to the industry of men and the institutions of peoples. Workers, he said, should not be treated like machines or cattle, nor should children be forced to labor like adults or work be placed upon females as if they were male adults. Workers, Leo said, have the right to organize themselves into unions and engage in peaceful strikes. Wealth production, he asserted, has the ultimate purpose of helping men live a virtuous life. Because of the moral dimension of economics, Leo said the Church has to be involved in solving social problems.

II.

1. The U.S. government saw moving Indians to reservations as the first step in civilizing them. President Grant saw the reservation system as a means to civilize the Indians.

2. Wounded Knee was the last violent encounter between American Indians and the U.S. military. It marked the end of America's Indian wars.

3. The Bessemer converter, invented in the 1850s by the English engineer Sir Henry Bessemer, converted iron ore into steel at a relatively low cost. This invention caused an increase in the steel industry in the United States.

4. *Possible answers:* American inventions using electricity: Alexander Graham Bell's telephone, Charles Bush's dynamo capable of providing power to arc lamps, Thomas Alva Edison's phonograph and incandescent light bulb.

CHAPTER 22: The End of the Century

Chapter Overview

- American Protestantism faced new struggles in the latter half of the 19th century: Darwinism and the materialist worldview.

- Protestantism continued to split into different groups, including New Thought, Christian Science, and Theosophy.

- New movements were entering American society. Among these were Free Love, Free Thought, and anarchism.

- In the Catholic Church a controversy arose as to whether Catholic and American ideals are reconcilable when Pope Pius IX condemned certain errors that seemed strike at the heart of American civic life. Despite this, the Catholic population grew, and the Catholic Church became the single largest Christian group in the country.

- Tensions between German and Irish Catholics began to shake the unity of the Catholic Church in the U.S. in the latter part of the 19th century. Among the controversies of the time was the question of to what degree Catholics should assimilate into American culture.

- The "progressives" and the "preservationists" in the Catholic Church in America waged war on the question of education. Some wanted a Catholic school system free from state control and aid, while others would accept state aid and even partial state control of Catholic schools.

- At the World's Fair, an ecumenical Parliament of World Religions was held. Cardinal Gibbons encouraged Catholic participation. But others,

such as Bishop McQuaid, disagreed. Pope Leo XIII forbade future participation in such ecumenical gatherings.

- Archbishop Ireland preached that in order to conquer the new world to Christ, the Church must be new, adapting herself to the new order. At first, Ireland and the progressives received favor from Rome, but in 1895 the tide turned against them when Pope Leo XIII issued the apostolic letter to the Church in the United States, *Longinqua Oceani*.

- The controversy between the progressives and their opponents came to a head when Abbé Felix Klein published a French translation of *The Life of Father Hecker*. Conservatives both in the United States and France condemned the Hecker biography, and critics began to call Klein, Ireland, and Keane "Americanists," and their alleged ideas, "Americanism." The controversy grew so heated that Pope Leo decided to look into it. Leo issued the encyclical, *Testem Benevolentiae Nostrae*, condemning Americanism.

- The Republicans nominated James A. Garfield as their presidential candidate, and he won the election of 1880. Four months after his inauguration, a disappointed office seeker shot Garfield, and his vice president, Chester A. Arthur,became president.

- Grover Cleveland won the election of 1884, the first Democratic candidate to win the presidency in 28 years. The Republican Benjamin Harrison, however, won the presidential election of 1888. Under President Harrison Congress passed the Sherman Silver Purchase Act and the McKinley Tariff. When the price of domestic goods rose, people blamed the tariff, and the Republicans took a big hit in congressional elections. Grover Cleveland triumphed in the presidential election of 1892.

- President Cleveland opened the World's Fair on May 1, 1893. Weeks later, a series of bank failures collapsed the country into the Panic of 1893.

- Farmers suffered during the panic, especially in Kansas. The introduction of machinery had increased farm productivity, and demand from consumers was not keeping up with the rate of production. As farms went bust, the holdings of those who survived grew larger.

- Farmers began forming alliances, such as the National Grange of the Patrons of Husbandry, to protect their interests.

- In 1892 delegates from the farmers' alliances, the Knights of Labor, and other groups formed a new political party, the People's or Populist Party. In the South there was an attempt to unite poor whites and blacks in a common political movement. This attempt failed, and the Populists soon realized that they could attain power by appealing to the white lower class hatred of the blacks. In the 1890s, southern state governments began to pass segregation laws, known as "Jim Crow" laws.

- Andrew Carnegie retired to his castle in Scotland, leaving the operation of his Homestead, Pennsylvania steel company to Henry Frick. In 1892, Frick proposed a new contract that would cut the workers' wages. When the union demanded more, Frick shut down the factory and sent for Pinkertons. When the Homestead workers heard the Pinkertons were coming, they threw up barricades and armed themselves. A fight ensued, and the governor of Pennsylvania sent in state militia.

- Meanwhile, Alexander Berkman, an anarchist and immigrant from Russia, was determined to carry out the supreme revolutionary sacrifice, political assassination. On July 23, 1892, he walked into Frick's office and attempted to kill him. Frick survived, and Berkman was sentenced to 22 years in prison.

- President Cleveland committed himself to a sound and stable currency, the gold standard. A month after opening the World's Fair, he summoned Congress to repeal the Sherman Silver Purchase Act.

- During the Panic of 1893, three million men and women were out of work. Jacob Coxey dreamed of the United States as a Christian commonwealth and believed the federal government should undertake measures to relieve the poor. In 1894 Coxey formed plans for an Industrial Army that would march from Ohio to Washington, D.C., and stage a peaceful demonstration to call on the federal government to do something for workers. The army left on Easter Sunday 1894. When it reached the steps of the capitol, Coxey was arrested before he could deliver his address.

- In 1894, a strike broke out at the Pullman rail car works outside of Chicago. When Pullman fired three members of a committee of protest, the Pullman workers voted to strike, and Pullman closed the factory. This caused the American Railway Union to call on its members to refuse to handle Pullman cars.

- On July 2, 1894, the federal circuit court in Chicago issued a blanket injunction against obstructing the operation of railroads and holding up the mail. President Cleveland authorized the swearing-in of special deputies. This caused the strikers to riot, and Cleveland sent in federal troops. When the AFL refused to support the strikers, the strike was broken.

What Students Should Know

1. **The religious culture of the U.S. at the end of the 19th century**

   Most Americans still adhered to a "conservative" Protestant religiosity that was centered around Bible reading, personal devotions such as private and family prayer, and "Sabbath" observance. It was a religion still heavily tinged with the Puritan ethic that glorified hard work and sobriety and frowned on "vain" pleasures (card playing, for instance, drinking intoxicating liquors, dancing, and other "carnal" pastimes). Despite the emotional excesses of the revival meetings still popular in the countryside, in small towns, and even on college campuses, the mainstream Protestantism of America was a pretty stiff and rigid affair that identified piety with a narrow and work-a-day middle class propriety. But despite its common character, Protestantism continued to splinter into more and more groups. Among the new groups spawned in America were the Watchtower Bible and Tract Society, or the Jehovah's Witnesses, founded by Charles Taze Russell.

   A sign of American Protestantism's vibrancy was American involvement in the foreign missions. By 1888, American missionaries (most of whom were women) in large numbers could be found in Japan, China, and India. American missionaries spread not only their faith but their notions of equality and democracy.

2. **Tensions of American religion with science**

   Relying on an overly simplistic interpretation of Biblical texts, traditional American Protestantism faced new struggles in the latter half of the 19th century. Darwinists mocked religious belief that insisted that God created the earth in seven, 24-hour solar days, because Genesis seemed to say so. Darwinists told believers it was absurd to hold that the earth was only around 6,000 years old, as the Bible seemed to indicate. Unable to defend their beliefs on scientific grounds, believers attacked science itself as diabolic. Without an adequate philosophical or theological tradition, many Protestants shrank from the task of reconciling science with the faith that it seemed to contradict. For devotees of science, religion was nothing but superstition and had to give way to reason and science. Many had begun to think empirical science – knowledge derived from measurement, observation and experimentation – was the highest form of knowledge and could lead mankind to untold heights of power, prosperity, and happiness. Such optimism belonged to the heirs of Enlightenment thinkers such as Thomas Paine and Thomas Jefferson.

3. **Other religious movements and philosophical/political movements that characterized American life in the late 19th century**

   a. *New Thought:* Many Americans of this period were attracted to the New Thought movement. New Thought held that all unhappiness was merely a mental state that right thinking could overcome. New Thought practitioners spoke of a "mind cure" in which, by meditation in tranquil and harmonious surroundings, one was brought into contact with "that Divine Energy we call God." New Thought tapped into the late 19th century's craze for science. Though essentially non-Christian, it eventually took on some Christian overtones. An example of such a Christianized New Thought movement that was particularly successful in the late 19th century is

Church of Christ, Scientist, or Christian Science. The founder of this group, Mary Baker Eddy, taught that sickness and death are only deceptions and that the mind could control matter and bring about healing of the body. Her principal book, *Science and Health with Key to the Scriptures*, was widely read.

b. *Syncretism:* This, the combining of religious or other beliefs or practices, was represented by Swami Vivekananda who held that science and religion must forge a new union with each other and that material progress was not contrary to spiritual enlightenment. Vivekananda held that no religion has an exclusive hold on the truth or to holiness. This kind of syncretism found many adherents in the United States. Many Americans had become interested in eastern religions, particularly Hinduism, and had taken up the practice of yoga. In 1873, the Polish Madame Blavatsky had come to New York City, bringing with her Theosophy. The Theosophical Society, which she and others founded, sought to create a new religion that brought together Hindu, Buddhist, and Christian beliefs. To the Theosophist, God's workings in man are primarily internal; anything external, religions and churches included, are but shadows of this interior work of God.

c. *Free Love*: this movement, which had a number of divisions, generally held that traditional marriage bonds are oppressive and that men and women should be joined only by the "affinity" they feel for one another. Free lovers did not necessarily espouse promiscuity, but they held that men and women should speak openly about sexuality and not establish any artificial rules governing their relations with one another. Free lovers wanted to place male female relationships on a more "scientific" footing, and so they favored widespread use of contraception. The Free Love movement promoted eugenics – the theory that only the fittest men and women (and often the fittest races) should be allowed to breed in order to produce a master race. So many were the Free Love journals that in 1873 Congress passed the Comstock Act, prohibiting the sending of obscene material through the mail system.

d. *Free Thought*: this movement championed science against what it deemed religion's oppression of the human mind.

e. *Anarchism:* Anarchists hoped for a society wherein the individual conscience would be the final judge of the justice of all laws. They favored the destruction of class government by all means, including violence. Some anarchists stressed the independence of the individual; others hoped for a condition in which all property was held in common.

f. *Utopianism:* this movement was represented by various communitarian attempts to create an alternative to capitalism.

4. Tensions in between Catholics and non-Catholic Americans in the 19th century

Except for the period of the Revolution, when Americans seemed to feel some benevolence toward Catholics, tensions had existed between Catholics and the mostly Protestant population of the United States. The intolerance and hostility Catholics experienced increased when non-English Catholics came to the United States; then, racial bigotry intensified religious intolerance. Protestants suspected and alleged that Catholics were working under secret orders from the pope to subvert American institutions. Actions undertaken by Pope Pius IX, whose reign began in 1846, made life in America more difficult for Catholics. For instance, the pope's "Syllabus of Modern Errors," appended to his 1864 encyclical, *Quanta Cura*, listed as condemned certain ideas that were embraced by Americans. For instance, the pope condemned the notion that "the Church ought to be separated from the State, and the State from the Church." In condemning the proposition, "the Roman Pontiff can, and ought to, reconcile himself, and come to terms with progress, liberalism and modern civilization," the pope seemed to make himself an enemy of all "progress." Another source of tension was the unquestioning confidence American Catholics seemed to repose in their clergy. Protestant Americans found this sort of obedience hard to understand; religious individualists, they thought such obedience nothing but abject slavery. The bishops in the United States, recognizing these tensions, at times tried to downplay certain aspects of Catholic teaching that could irritate Protestants. For instance, some bishops opposed as "inopportune" the definition of papal infallibility at the Vatican Ecumenical Council, held in 1870, because they thought it would create a greater rift between Catholics and Protestants.

5. **The patterns of Catholic immigration in the late 19ᵗʰ century**

Though the cultural center of Catholicism in the United States for a long time remained in the South and, thus, was dominated by the old English Catholic society, the mass immigration of Irish Catholics in the first half of the 19ᵗʰ century had given the Catholic Church in America a decidedly Irish tone. The Irish generally worked in factories in the cities, in mines, or on the railroads. Bigotry against them, especially in New England, was intense. In metropolises like New York City, the Irish by sheer force of numbers gained control of city politics and were able to attain some social advancement. Their Boss Tweed-style politics, though, did not endear the Irish to the hearts of "native" Americans. Irish immigration began to dwindle following the Civil War, and the number of German and continental European Catholic immigrants to the United States increased. As in the years before the war, German immigrants who came to America generally were wealthy enough to buy land, and they crossed the Alleghenies to settle in German communities in the Midwest. These German communities were either mixed, with Protestants and Catholics, or of a single religion. German Catholics brought over their own priests and proved quite successful in building churches and parish schools. They maintained German as their primary spoken language and formed cultural enclaves separated from the Anglo American population.

In 1852, Catholics in the United States numbered about 1,600,000; according to the census of 1880, that number had increased to 6,832,954. The Catholic Church became the single largest denomination in the United States. But, said some in the 19ᵗʰ century, the U.S. Catholic population may have been considerably larger had not so many immigrants fallen away from the Church upon coming to America.

6. **The "progressive" and "preservationist" factions in the U.S. Catholic Church and what they represented**

The "progressive" wing of the Catholic Church in America was represented by James Cardinal Gibbons, archbishop of Baltimore, John Ireland, archbishop of Saint Paul, Minnesota, and Bishop John Keane. These bishops wanted Catholics to embrace American culture. They praised American political institutions, American liberty, and American progress and material civilization. They thought that though America could learn much from the Catholic Church, the Church, too, could benefit by her association with democratic American society. Thus, they favored cultural assimilation and opposed foreign enclaves amongst the faithful. Among the particular issues which the addressed, the progressives supported (at least under certain circumstances) Catholic partnership with public schools, even if this meant that religion was relegated to after-school hours; inter-religious dialogue, as represented by the Parliament of World Religions; the adaptation of the Catholic Church's "manner of life and its method of action to the conditions of the new order" (Archbishop Ireland); separation of Church and state as it was found in the United States (Archbishop Ireland and Bishop Keane).

The preservationists (who included Bishop Bernard McQuaid of Rochester, New York, and much of the German clergy and episcopacy) generally opposed the signature positions of the progressives. They attacked common schools as godless ad thus opposed any Catholic school union with them. They opposed interreligious dialogue as represented by the Parliament of World Religions. They upheld the traditional Church teaching about the relation of Church and state.

7. **What Pope Leo XIII wrote of America in** *Longinqua Oceani*

In this 1895 apostolic letter to the Church in the United States, Leo praised American liberty and the freedom the United States accorded the Catholic Church; but with this praise, came a warning: "It would be very erroneous to draw the conclusion that in America is to be sought the type of the most desirable status of the Church or that it would be universally lawful or expedient for State and Church to be, as in America, dissevered and divorced."

8. **Who Isaac Hecker was and what ideas he held**

Isaac Hecker, who had lived at Brook Farm and Fruitlands in the 1840s, having become disillusioned with the Transcendentalists, converted to the Catholic Church. He was ordained a Redemptorist priest but eventually founded his own religious congregation, the Paulists, dedicated to converting America to the Catholic faith. Isaac Hecker died in 1888. Hecker loved America's institutions and believed that his country had a quasi-messianic destiny to spread free government to the world. He thought that by permitting its citizens a large degree of freedom, the United States was ushering in a new era where the Holy Spirit would inspire and strengthen individuals as never before. He thought the U.S. form of government of the United States was the best possible for Catholics because it is granted a larger margin for liberty of action, and hence for co-operation with the guidance of the Holy Spirit.

9. **How** *The Life of Father Hecker* **led to the Americanist controversy; what the tenets of Americanism were**

The Life of Father Hecker ran as a series in the Paulist publication, *The Catholic World*. But the French priest, Abbé Felix Klein, published a shorter version of the *Life*, translated into French. According to the French biography, Hecker asserted that the Church must adjust herself to modern civilization and should deemphasize such "passive" supernatural virtues as humility and obedience and emphasize the "active" natural virtues, such as courage, prudence, and justice. Individuals, too, according to the French biography, had less need of external guidance from the Church than in former times, since the Holy Spirit had been poured out abundantly in the modern world. The Church, according to the biography, must grant greater freedom to individuals to follow the lead of their own minds and consciences – though it asserted that the external guidance of the Church remained necessary.

Conservatives, both in the United States and France, roundly condemned the French Hecker biography. Critics called Klein, Ireland, and Keane (who had become associated with the ideas set forth in the biography), "Americanists," and their ideas, "Americanism." The controversy over the Hecker book and Americanism grew so rhetorically violent that at last, the pope himself decided to look into it.

10. **How Pope Leo XIII intervened in the Americanist controversy and the results of his intervention**

Pope Leo's response to the crisis was to issue, on January 22, 1899, the encyclical, *Testem Benevolentiae Nostrae*. In *Testem*, the pope assailed Americanism. He said he disapproved of any attempt to deemphasize any Catholic doctrine in order more easily to reconcile the Church with the modern age, because it "would tend rather to separate Catholics from the Church than to bring in those who differ." Leo said it was false to say that the Church's "supervision and watchfulness" should be "in some sense lessened" to give the faithful more freedom to follow the leading of their minds. Rather, said Leo, in the modern age, the Church's guidance was more needed. He dismissed the distinction between "active" and "passive" virtues, saying all virtues are active, he said. The "disregard" of supernatural virtues in favor of natural ones was, the pope said, a short step "to a contempt of the religious life which has in some degree taken hold of minds." One may not hold that religious "vows are alien to the spirit of our times, in that they limit the bounds of human liberty; that they are more suitable to weak than to strong minds; that so far from making for human perfection and the good of human organization, that they are hurtful to both." *Testem Benevolentiae* effectively killed Americanism, at least for a time. American bishops were quick to repudiate the doctrine, though some said that no one in America, at least, held to Americanism.

11. **What political issues occupied the Democratic and Republican parties in the 1880s and 1890s**

One controversy – whether to reform the civil service to minimize political patronage in the rewarding of offices – pitted the "Stalwarts" (who wanted to maintain the status quo) and the reformers. Some in both parties called for the free coinage of silver to put more money into circulation, while others (such as the Democratic president Grover Cleveland) wanted to maintain a strict gold standard. Some, particularly the Republicans, wanted to keep a high tariff on foreign imports both for revenue and to protect American business interests from foreign competition. Others (such as Cleveland) wanted to reduce the tariff.

12. The cause and effects of the Panic of 1893

A series of bank failures in 1893 collapsed the county into a deep depression – the Panic of 1893. Over the next several months, millions lost their jobs, and thousands wandered homeless. Many who, only months before, proudly strutted their prosperity, found themselves bankrupt and ruined.

13. Causes of the farmers' plight in the late 19th century

Farmers were experiencing hard times before the Panic of 1893. Kansas was a case in point. A drought in 1887 destroyed the corn crop in arid western Kansas. Banks foreclosed on farmers who had taken out large loans, and about half the population of Kansas returned to the east. Not only Kansans, but farmers across the country were suffering by the late '80s. With the introduction of machinery, such as McCormick's mechanical reaper, farmers became more productive. But increased production meant more crops on the market; and without a corresponding growth in consumer demand came lower prices for farm produce, and these led to a growing number of farm failures. Increasing railroad transportation costs, unpredictable markets, the money supply, and high interest rates on loans played their part in this, but so did the farmer's desire to "get ahead" – taking out mortgages to gamble on farm produce prices.

14. Effects of the farm crisis

Gradually, as more and more farms went bust, the holdings of those that survived grew larger. Those who could afford machinery, and thus, replace labor, fared better than those who had to pay "hands" to work their fields. In the Deep South, where land was given to a single cash crop – cotton – the farmer's plight was extreme. The merchants, from whom farmers had to borrow money, often demanded that the land be put to cotton instead of other crops – thus perpetuating cultivation practices that destroyed the fertility of the soil. The farmers sold their cotton cheaply to mill owners (who, themselves, sold it again for high prices); thus, a drastic fall in prices meant the farmer had to sell his cotton for even less and so did not make enough money to pay his mortgages. The merchants who had made the loans would then foreclose on the land. Often, they kept the farmer on as a tenant – working land that had formerly been his own.

15. Farmers Alliances and what they did

Like laborers in the cities, farmers had been forming alliances to protect their interests. One such alliance was the National Grange of the Patrons of Husbandry, founded in 1867. The Grange proved an effective way of organizing farmers to resist both the middlemen, who bought their crops, and the railroads, who shipped them. Granges supported political candidates who took control of state legislatures, which then passed laws regulating freight rates. Much of this legislation, though, was not well conceived and so it was easy for courts to rule against it in favor of the railroads. The Grange and others farmers' alliances undertook direct action by organizing cooperative enterprises to cut out middlemen. Farmers organized cooperative stores, marketing arrangements, and, in a few cases, cooperative manufacturing plants for farm equipment – but the opposition of the railroads forced most of these to close. In some cases, railroads refused service to communities that they thought particularly uppity. For the elections of 1890, farmers' alliances organized candidates for state and national elections.

16. The Populist Party and what it stood for; why it was significant

Some farmers' alliance members thought it necessary for farmers to unite with industrial labor against the common enemy. On July 4, 1892, delegates from farmers' alliances, the Knights of Labor, and other groups gathered in Omaha, Nebraska to form a new political party – the People's or Populist Party. Populists called for the popular election of United States senators; the government ownership of railroads, telegraphs, and telephone systems; a graduated income tax, initiative and referendum; the free and unlimited coinage of silver; the prohibition of both speculation in land and its monopolization. Like many third parties, the Populists championed issues that, later, one or both of the major parties would adopt and have enacted into law.

17. The origins of "Jim Crow" and what it was

Some members of Southern farmers' alliances thought the best way to wrest power was to unite blacks and whites in a common front against the mercantile, manufacturing, and railroad interests. But this was doomed to failure. The poor southern white man, who occupied the lowest rung of the white social ladder, bitterly feared blacks. As long as they were slaves, blacks had posed no threat to the poor white's social status, however lowly that was; but, now black freedmen jostled with the poor white for his place, and to keep the black man out, the poor white had to keep him down. Between 1875 and 1890, Southern governments had by and large maintained

the black franchise. There was even little social segregation. Blacks could ride on the same trolleys, eat in the same restaurants, and generally mingle freely with whites. What segregation there was – in churches and schools – was largely of the blacks' own choosing. There was unjust prejudice and racial tension, but under the rule of the old planter class, state governments recognized and maintained black rights. But Populist demagogues realized that they could attain power by appealing to the poor whites' hatred of blacks. Throughout the 1890s, racist Populists took control of state governments in the lower South. Between 1890 and 1908, Populist-controlled state governments altered their constitutions without submitting them to popular vote and enacted poll taxes, literacy tests, and other measures that hindered black people from voting. In the 1890s, first the governments in the deep South, and gradually other southern state governments, began passing segregation laws. These came to be known as "Jim Crow" laws after a black character in musical shows, who danced to a song with the refrain, "Jump, Jim Crow." Restaurants, churches, schools, and public conveyances were, thenceforth, segregated by law. To prevent racial mixture, some laws forbade whites and blacks to enter each other's houses – unless of course the blacks served the whites as servants. Blacks, too were subjected to extralegal lynchings by whites, not only in the South, but in Ohio, Indiana, and Illinois. Whites who perpetrated these lynchings went unarrested and unpunished.

18. *Plessy v. Ferguson* and its significance

Plessy v. Ferguson was an 1896 decision of the U.S. Supreme Court ruled that a Louisiana law forbidding blacks to ride with whites in the same parts of a public conveyance was constitutional, as long as the accommodations provided blacks were equal to those provided whites. The question of constitutionality, said the court, came down to whether "the statute of Louisiana is a reasonable regulation, and with respect to this there must necessarily be a large discretion on the part of the legislature. In determining the question of reasonableness it [the legislature] is at liberty to act with reference to the established usages, customs and traditions of the people, and with a view to the promotion of their comfort, and the preservation of the public peace and good order."

19. The Homestead Strike and its results

The origin of the steel workers strike at Andrew Carnegie's steel plant in Homestead, Pennsylvania was the proposal by Henry Frick (who operated Carnegie's factory) that the workers (organized in a union) accept a new contract that would cut their wages by $22 a month. In July 1892, when the workers remained obdurate (and burned Frick in effigy), Frick closed down the factory. Later he sent armed Pinkertons to guard the factory – whom the workers took prisoner after a standoff lasting 12 hours. On July 23, 1892, the Russian anarchist, Alexander Berkman attempted to murder Frick; but Frick survived. The 143-day-long strike at Homestead ended in a victory for the company. Carnegie, his reputation somewhat tarnished by the episode and chastened by Frick's actions, offered pensions to the leaders of the strike, who had lost their jobs; and, after his retirement, Carnegie established a relief fund for Homestead workers.

20. The Pullman Strike and its results

George Pullman, the owner of the luxury railcar company, had cut the number of workers in his factory from 5,500 to 3,300 and then lowered the wages of those that remained by 25 percent. He then refused to lower the rents workers paid in the company town he had built and which he touted as a model community. When three workers who protested Pullman's refusal to lower rents were fired, the Pullman workers, on May 10, 1894, voted to strike. A day later, Pullman closed the factory. Following the closing of the factory, the American Railway Union (which represented 465 local unions), at the urging of its president, Eugene V. Debs, called on its members to refuse to handle Pullman cars on railways across the country. Meanwhile, Pullman met with the General Managers Association, a "union" of the owners of 24 railroads, and convinced them to resist the ARU's boycott of Pullman cars. When railroad workers refused to handle Pullman cars, members of the General Managers Association promptly fired them. Then at the urging of President Cleveland's attorney general, the federal circuit court in Chicago issued a "blanket injunction" against obstructing the operation of the railroads and holding up the mail. President Cleveland himself authorized the swearing-in of 3,600 special deputies, to be armed and paid by the General Managers' Association. When news of this action reached the strikers, rioting broke out. With the pretext of the riots, Cleveland ordered federal troops into Chicago. The first troops arrived on Independence Day, July 4, 1894. Illinois' governor, John Altgeld, however, protested Cleveland's action, saying it violated "a fundamental principle of our Constitution" – local self-government

The Pullman strike convinced many Americans that the struggle of labor and capital could have revolutionary repercussions if nothing were done about it. Class conflict, they feared, could lead to revolution and, perhaps, to the overthrow of American institutions. While the Pullman strike turned many against the claims of labor, others began to study how to harmonize the conflicts between capital and labor within the prevailing capitalist system. The question, for most concerned Americans was not whether to overthrow the capitalist system but how to save society from the upheavals resulting from the struggle of labor and capital.

21. The election of 1896 and its significance

The presidential election of 1896 pitted the Republican nominee, William McKinley, against the Democrat populist, William Jennings Bryan. The 36-year old Bryan won his nomination after giving the stirring "Cross of Gold" speech (defending silver bimetallism) at the Democratic convention. Bryan's victory turned the Democratic party towards populism. McKinley, however, ran on a strict big business-friendly platform, and called for maintaining the gold standard and protective tariffs. Through Mark Hanna, the Republicans received large contributions from metropolitan banks, insurance companies, and railroads. In some cases, employers ordered their workers to vote for McKinley or lose their jobs. Bryan, for his part, went on a speaking tour around the country, traveling 13,000 miles, making 600 speeches. In the end, Bryan took the South and West, but won only176 electoral votes to McKinley's 271.The election of 1896 made it appear that Americans had landed firmly on the side of capitalism and had rejected the measures that populists proposed.

22. Identify:

a. **Booker Taliaferro Washington:** Born a slave in Virginia, Booker T. Washington had attended night school after the Civil War while working in a salt furnace and then a coal mine in West Virginia. He attended the Hampton (Virginia) Normal and Agricultural institute from 1872 to 1875, where he later taught. In 1881, Washington became the director of a new school for blacks at Tuskegee. Under Washington, the "Tuskegee Normal and Industrial Institute" went from a small school meeting in a small building and a church to become the nation's foremost industrial school for blacks. Booker T. Washington believed that only by educating themselves could blacks attain any true equality in white society. He believed blacks shouldn't demand that equality but prove themselves worthy of it.

b. **Mary "Mother" Jones:** a labor leader and a member of the Knights of Labor. Among her many other activities, in 1899-1900 she was an organizer of the United Mine Workers strike in Arnot, Pennsylvania, which she helped bring to a successful conclusion.

c. **Jacob Coxey:** Jacob Coxey of Massillon, Ohio, was a Civil War veteran, farmer, horse breeder, and owner of a quarry that produced silica sand (used in the production of steel). Identifying himself with the unfortunate poor during the Panic of 1893, Coxey dreamed of the United States as a Christian commonwealth and believed that the federal government should take measures to relieve the poor. Coxey said Washington should issue government bonds to fund national work programs to employ the unemployed – programs such as building roads and other public works. In 1894, he organized a march from Ohio to Washington, D.C., the publicize the plight of the poor. The march of "Coxey's Army," however, ended in Coxey's arrest.

Questions for Review

1. **Describe the two strains of Protestantism prevalent in America in the latter half of the 19th century.**

    One strain was the more "conservative" which centered around Bible reading, personal devotions, and "Sabbath" observance. It was a religion still heavily tinged with the Puritan ethic that glorified hard work and sobriety and frowned on "vain" pleasures. The other strain of Protestantism was one that became increasingly less traditional and began to mix with non-Christian movements, such as spiritism and mind cure.

2. **How did Dwight L. Moody contribute to either of these strains?**

    Moody preached in the style of the old revivalists while encouraging his converts to seek out the church of their preference where the good work, begun by the revival, might be completed. His message was a traditional Protestant message; thus, it did not directly foster the syncretist frms of Proestantism, excpet in that it did not direct conerts to specific religious groups.

3. **What did the science-religion controversy center on? Explain the views of each side.**

    It centered on a supposed opposition between faith and raeason. Relying on an overly simplistic interpretation of Biblical texts, traditional American Protestantism faced new struggles in the latter half of the 19th century. Darwinists mocked religious belief that insisted that God created the earth

---

Key Terms at a Glance

New Thought: a mind-healing movement that held that all unhappiness was merely a mental state that right thinking could overcome

syncretism: a combining of religious or other beliefs and practices

theosophy: a religious philosophy that sought to bring together differing religions

Free Thought: a movement that championed science against religion's oppression of the human mind

Free Love: a movement that held that traditional marriage bonds were oppressive and that men and women should be joined only by the affinity they feel for one another

anarchism: a cluster of doctrines and attitudes centered on the belief that government is both harmful and unnecessary

graduated income tax: a tax the rate of which increases as the income of the taxpayer increases; those who make a higher income pay the tax at a higher rate, while those who make a lower income, pay at a lesser rate.

initiative and referendum: legal provisions where voters can initiate legislation directly and directly repeal existing legislation

Jim Crow law: any of the laws that enforced racial segregation in the South between 1877 and the 1950s

in seven, 24-hour solar days, because Genesis seemed to say so. Darwinists told believers it was absurd to hold that the earth was only around 6,000 years old, as the Bible seemed to indicate. Unable to defend their beliefs on scientific grounds, believers attacked science itself as diabolic. Without an adequate philosophical or theological tradition, many Protestants shrank from the task of reconciling science with the faith that it seemed to contradict. For devotees of science, religion was nothing but superstition and had to give way to reason and science. Many had begun to think empirical science – knowledge derived from measurement, observation and experimentation – was the highest form of knowledge and could lead mankind to untold heights of power, prosperity, and happiness.

4. **Briefly describe each of the new religious movements in the late 19th century.**

New Thought: New Thought held that all unhappiness was merely a mental state that right thinking could overcome. New Thought practitioners spoke of a "mind cure" in which, by meditation in tranquil and harmonious surroundings, one was brought into contact with "that Divine Energy we call God." New Thought tapped into the late 19th century's craze for science. Though essentially non-Christian, it eventually took on some Christian overtones. An example of such a Christianized New Thought movement that was particularly successful in the late 19th century is Church of Christ, Scientist, or Christian Science. The founder of this group, Mary Baker Eddy, taught that sickness and death are only deceptions and that the mind could control matter and bring about healing of the body.

Syncretism: This, the combining or religious or other beliefs or practices, was represented by Swami Vivekananda who held that science and religion must forge a new union with each other and that material progress was not contrary to spiritual enlightenment. Vivekananda held that no religion has an exclusive hold on the truth or to holiness.

Theosophy: In 1873, the Polish Madame Blavatsky brought Theosophy to the United States. The Theosophical Society, which she and others founded, sought to create a new religion that brought together Hindu, Buddhist, and Christian beliefs. To the Theosophist, God's workings in man are primarily internal; anything external, religions and churches included, are but shadows of this interior work of God.

5. **What tensions existed between Catholic doctrine and American ideals in the late 19th century?**

Protestants suspected and alleged that Catholics were working under secret orders from the pope to subvert American institutions. Actions undertaken by Pope Pius IX, whose reign began in 1846, made life in America more difficult for Catholics. The pope's "Syllabus of Modern Errors" condemned certain ideas Americans held dear – the separation of Church and state, the certain desirability of progress and "modern civilization, and Liberalism.

6. **What were the main issues in the German-Irish controversy in the American Catholic Church of the late 19th century.**

German Catholics had, on the whole, remained resolutely separate from the mainstream of America by segregating themselves in German-speaking communities in rural areas and, in cities, by maintaining

German national parishes. Though most members of the American hierarchy were Irish, German bishops ruled in such centers as Milwaukee, Cincinnati, and other midwestern dioceses. German priests, too, had the reputation for being better trained than their English-speaking counterparts, partly because the German priests belonged to religious orders and had studied in Europe. Yet, because the Church in America had taken on such an Irish character, Germans complained that Irish and other English-speaking bishops were marginalizing them. For instance, German priests complained that their national churches were not accorded regular parish status and thus did not have the security that English-speaking parishes had. John Ireland, archbishop of St. Paul, Minnesota, Bishop John Keane, and James Gibbons, archbishop of Baltimore, opposed the German claims. In 1887, Rome ruled that German parishes should be made permanent but ignored other demands made by the German clergy.

7. **Explain the views of the progressives and the preservationists in the American Catholic Church in the late 19th century.**

The "progressive" wing of the Catholic Church in America wanted Catholics to embrace American culture. They praised American political institutions, American liberty, and American progress and material civilization. They thought that though America could learn much from the Catholic Church, the Church, too, could benefit by her association with democratic American society. Thus, they favored cultural assimilation and opposed foreign enclaves amongst the faithful. Progressives supported (at least under certain circumstances) Catholic partnership with public schools, even if this meant that religion was relegated to after-school hours; inter-religious dialogue, as represented by the Parliament of World Religions; the adaptation of the Catholic Church's "manner of life and its method of action to the conditions of the new order" (Archbishop Ireland); separation of Church and state as it was found in the United States (Archbishop Ireland and Bishop Keane).

The preservationists (who included Bishop Bernard McQuaid of Rochester, New York, much of the German clergy and episcopacy) generally opposed the signature positions of the progressives. The attacked common schools as godless and thus opposed any Catholic school union with them. They opposed interreligious dialogue as represented by the Parliament of World Religions. They upheld the traditional Church teaching about the relation of Church and state.

8. **What is Americanism? Was it merely a "phantom heresy"? Please explain.**

Americanism was purported to be a set of ideas held by the followers of Isaac Hecker that asserted that the Church must adjust herself to modern civilization and should deemphasize such "passive" supernatural virtues as humility and obedience and emphasize the "active" natural virtues, such as courage, prudence, and justice. Individuals, too, according to the French biography, had less need of external guidance from the Church than in former times, since the Holy Spirit had been poured out abundantly in the modern world. The Church, according to the biography, must grant greater freedom to individuals to follow the lead of their own minds and consciences – though it asserted that the external guidance of the Church remained necessary. Pope Leo XIII's *Testem Benevolentiae* effectively killed Americanism, at least for a time. American bishops were quick to repudiate the doctrine, though some said that no one in America, at least, held to Americanism. (Students should assess for themselves whether Americanism was merely a "phantom heresy" based on evidence found the in the textbook.)

9. **Explain Father Hecker's views about the Catholic Church in the modern world and how he influenced such men as Archbishop Ireland.**

Isaac Hecker loved America's institutions and believed that his country had a quasi-messianic destiny to spread free government to the world. He thought that by permitting its citizens a large degree of freedom, the United States was ushering in a new era where the Holy Spirit would inspire and strengthen individuals as never before. He thought the U.S. form of government of the United States was the best possible for Catholics because it is grants a larger margin for liberty of action, and hence for co-operation with the guidance of the Holy Spirit. Archbishop Ireland held Hecker up as an example of the reconciliation of the Church and the modern age.

10. **What were the effects of the Panic of 1893? What movements came out of it?**

The Panic of 1893 collapsed the county into a deep depression – the Panic of 1893. Over the next several months, millions lost their jobs, and thousands wandered homeless. Many who, only months before, proudly strutted their prosperity, found themselves bankrupt and ruined. The Panic of 1893 gave new impetus to populist groups that called for policies such as a graduated income tax and the government ownership of railroads, among others, and   Farmers Alliances. An example of this was Coxey's march on Washington, D.C. In 1893.

11. **How and why were Jim Crow laws instituted in the South?**

The poor southern white man, who occupied the lowest rung of the white social ladder, bitterly feared blacks. As long as they were slaves, blacks had posed no threat to the poor white's social status, however lowly that was; but, now black freedmen jostled with the poor white for his place, and to keep the black man out, the poor white had to keep him down. Populist demagogues realized that they could attain power by appealing to the poor whites' hatred of blacks. Between 1890 and 1908, Populist-controlled state governments altered their constitutions without submitting them to popular vote and enacted poll taxes, literacy tests, and other measures that hindered black people from voting. In the 1890s, first the governments in the deep South, and gradually other southern state governments, began passing segregation laws, that became known as Jm Crow laws.

12. **What did the Pullman strike reveal about the status of laborers in late 19th-century America?**

The Pullman strike revealed that Americans were more concerned about how to save society from the upheavals resulting from the struggle of labor and capital than about the issues of justice labor groups were bringing forward. Some Americans, however, began to study how to harmonize the claims of labor and capital, but within the prevailing capitalist system.

Ideas in Action

1. Why do you think American culture gave rise to or fostered so many religious, philosophical, and social movements?

2. Read and discuss *Testem Benevolentiae Nostrae*. Is its message still relevant today?

   The document is available online.

3. Read accounts of the World's Columbian Exhibition and how it influenced American society.

4. Think about and discuss the constitutionality of President Grover Cleveland's sending of troops into Illinois to quell the Pullman strike. Do you think that Governor John Altgeld was right — that Cleveland violated the Constitution by sending in troops even though Altgeld did not request them? Or was what Cleveland did in accord with the Constitution, because, as the Supreme Court argued, he was intervening to protect interstate commerce? Is it clear which side was right?

Sample Quiz I (pages 579-596)

Please answer the following in complete sentences.

1. Describe the "conservative" Protestant religiosity of the late 19th century.

2. How did Darwinists and devotees of science view religion?

3. How did Christians view the reconciliation of science with faith?

4. Name two sources of tension between Catholics and non-Catholic Americans in the 19th century?

5. How did American bishops respond to these tensions?

6. What did Pope Leo XIII write of America in *Longinqua Oceani*?

7. What ideas did Isaac Hecker hold?

8. Describe the tenets of Americanism.

Answers to Sample Quiz I

Students' answers should approximate the following.

1. "Conservative" Protestant religiosity was centered around Bible reading, personal devotions such as private and family prayer, and "Sabbath" observance. It was a religion still heavily tinged with the Puritan ethic that glorified hard work and sobriety and frowned on "vain" pleasures. Despite the emotional excesses of the revival meetings still popular in the countryside, in small towns, and even on college campuses, the mainstream Protestantism of America was a pretty stiff and rigid affair that identified piety with a narrow and work-a-day middle class propriety.

2. Darwinists mocked religious belief that insisted that God created the earth in seven, 24-hour solar days because Genesis seemed to say so. Darwinists told believers it was absurd to hold that the earth was only around 6,000 years old, as the Bible seemed to indicate. For devotees of science, religion was nothing but superstition and had to give way to reason and science. Many had begun to think empirical science was the highest form of knowledge and could lead mankind to untold heights of power, prosperity, and happiness.

3. Unable to defend their beliefs on scientific grounds, believers attacked science itself as diabolic. Without an adequate philosophical or theological tradition, many Protestants shrank from the task of reconciling science with the faith that it seemed to contradict.

4. *Possible Answers:* In the 19th century, Protestants suspected and alleged that Catholics were working under secret orders from the pope to subvert American institutions. Actions undertaken by Pope Pius IX, whose reign began in 1846, made life in America more difficult for Catholics. For instance, the pope's "Syllabus of Modern Errors" listed as condemned certain ideas that were embraced by Americans. Another source of tension was the unquestioning confidence American Catholics seemed to repose in their clergy; Protestant Americans found this sort of obedience hard to understand.

5. The bishops in the United States, recognizing these tensions, at times tried to downplay certain aspects of Catholic teaching that could irritate Protestants.

6. Pope Leo praised American liberty and the freedom the United States accorded the Catholic Church; but with this praise, came a warning: "It would be very erroneous to draw the conclusion that in America is to be sought the type of the most desirable status of the Church or that it would be universally lawful or expedient for State and Church to be, as in America, dissevered and divorced."

7. Isaac Hecker loved America's institutions and believed that his country had a quasi-messianic destiny to spread free government to the world. He thought that by permitting its citizens a large degree of freedom, the United States was ushering in a new era where the Holy Spirit would inspire and strengthen individuals as never before. He thought the U.S. form of government of the United States was the best possible for Catholics because it granted a larger margin for liberty of action, and hence for co-operation with the guidance of the Holy Spirit.

8. Americanism asserted that the Church must adjust herself to modern civilization and should deemphasize such "passive" supernatural virtues as humility and obedience and emphasize the "active" natural virtues, such as courage, prudence, and justice. Individuals were said to have less need of external guidance from the Church than in former times, since the Holy Spirit had been poured out abundantly in the modern world. The Church, according to Americanism, must grant greater freedom to individuals to follow the lead of their own minds and consciences – though it asserted that the external guidance of the Church remained necessary.

Sample Quiz II (pages 597-614)

Please answer the following in complete sentences.

1. **What were the causes of the farmers' plight in the late 19th century?**

2. **What did Farmers Alliances do for the farmers?**

3. **List three positions the Populist Party stood for.**

4. **Describe how Jim Crow laws came about?**

5. **Why was *Plessy v. Ferguson* significant?**

6. **What was the significance of the election of 1896?**

Answers to Sample Quiz II

Students' answers should approximate the following.

1. Farmers were experiencing hard times before the Panic of 1893. With the introduction of machinery, such as McCormick's mechanical reaper, farmers became more productive. But increased production meant more crops on the market; and without a corresponding

growth in consumer demand came lower prices for farm produce, and these led to a growing number of farm failures. Increasing railroad transportation costs, unpredictable markets, the money supply, and high interest rates on loans played their part in this, but so did the farmer's desire to "get ahead" – taking out mortgages to gamble on farm produce prices.

2. One alliance, the National Grange of the Patrons of Husbandry, proved an effective way of organizing farmers to resist both the middlemen, who bought their crops, and the railroads, who shipped them. Granges supported political candidates who took control of state legislatures, which then passed laws regulating freight rates. The Grange and others farmers' alliances undertook direct action by organizing cooperative enterprises to cut out middlemen. Farmers organized cooperative stores, marketing arrangements, and, in a few cases, cooperative manufacturing plants for farm equipment. For the elections of 1890, farmers' alliances organized candidates for state and national elections.

3. *Possible answers:* Populists called for the popular election of United States senators; the government ownership of railroads, telegraphs, and telephone systems; a graduated income tax, initiative and referendum; the free and unlimited coinage of silver; the prohibition of both speculation in land and its monopolization.

4. The poor southern white man, who occupied the lowest rung of the white social ladder, bitterly feared blacks. As long as they were slaves, blacks had posed no threat to the poor white's social status, however lowly that was; but, now black freedmen jostled with the poor white for his place, and to keep the black man out, the poor white had to keep him down. Populist demagogues realized that they could attain power by appealing to the poor whites' hatred of blacks, and state legislatures made laws that encouraged black segregation and "put blacks in their place."

5. *Plessy v. Ferguson* was significant because the Supreme Court said the question of constitutionality of racial segregation came down to whether a state statute is judged reasonable by a state legislature in accord with "established usages, customs and traditions of the people, and with a view to the promotion of their comfort, and the preservation of the public peace and good order."

6. The election of 1896 was significant because it made it appear that Americans had landed firmly on the side of capitalism and had rejected the measures that populists proposed.

Essays

Instructions to be given to the students: Write in complete sentences. Underline your thesis. Give three supports or examples that explain why you think what you do and that support your thesis.

1. Do you think that there was one source or problem from which all of the new political movements (free love, free thought, anarchism, and Utopianism) came from? What is that source or problem, and how do each of the movements stem from it?

2. Can the Catholic Church function in the United States without resorting to a set of ideas sich as Americanism? Explain your reasons in full detail.

3. Was it possible to harmonize the conflicts between capital and labor within the prevailing capitalist system of the 19th century? Why or why not?

Sample Test

Please answer the following in complete sentences.

I. Short Essay – Answer two of the following:

1. Describe three of the new religions and philosophical/political movements that characterized American life in the late 19th century.

2. What did the "progressive" and "preservationist" factions in the U.S. Catholic Church represent?

3. Give a brief outline of *Testem Benevolentiae Nostrae*, and the results of this encyclical.

4. What was the farm crisis? What were its effects?

5. What effect did the Pullman Strike have on American opinion?

II. Short Answer:

1. What showed American Protestantism's vibrancy in the 19th century?

2. What were the two largest groups of immigrants in the 19th century?

3. What was the cause of the Panic of 1893?

4. What was the effect of the Panic of 1893?

5. Identify the following:
   a. Booker T. Washington
   b. Mary "Mother" Jones
   c. Jacob Coxey

Answer Key to the Chapter Test

Students' answers should approximate the following:

I.

New Thought: New Thought held that all unhappiness was merely a mental state that right thinking could overcome. New Thought practitioners spoke of a "mind cure" in which, by meditation in tranquil and harmonious surroundings, one was brought into contact with "that Divine Energy we call God." New Thought tapped into the late 19th century's craze for science. Though essentially non-Christian, it eventually took on some Christian overtones. An example of such as Christianized New Thought movement that was particularly successful in the late 19th century were the Church of Christ, Scientist, or Christian Science. The founder of this group, Mary Baker Eddy, taught that sickness and death are only deceptions and that the mind could control matter and bring about healing of the body.

Syncretism: This, the combining or religious or other beliefs or practices, was represented by Swami Vivekananda who held that science and religion must forge a new union with each other and that material progress was not contrary to spiritual enlightenment. Vivekandanda held that no religion has an exclusive hold on the truth or to holiness. In 1873, the Polish Madame Blavatsky had come to New York City, bringing with her Theosophy. The Theosophical Society, which she and others founded, sought to create a new religion that brought together Hindu, Buddhist, and Christian beliefs. To the Theosophist, God's workings in man are primarily internal; anything external, religions and churches included, are but shadows of this interior work of God.

Free Love: this movement, which had a number of divisions, generally held that traditional marriage bonds were oppressive and that men and women should be joined only by the "affinity" they feel for one another. Free lovers did not necessarily espouse promiscuity, but they held that men and women should speak openly about sexuality and not establish any artificial rules governing their relations with one another. Free lovers wanted to place male/female relationships on a more "scientific" footing, and so they favored widespread use of contraception. The Free Love movement promoted eugenics – the theory that only the fittest men and women (and often the fittest races) should be allowed to breed in order to produce a master race.

Free Thought: this movement championed science against what it deemed religion's oppression of the human mind.

Anarchism: Anarchists hoped for a society wherein the individual conscience would be the final judge of the justice of all laws. They favored the destruction of class government by all means, including violence. Some anarchists stressed the independence of the individual; others hoped for a condition in which all property was held in common. *Utopianism*: this movement was represented by various communitarian attempts to create an alternative to capitalism.

2. The "progressive" wing of the Catholic Church in America wanted Catholics to embrace American culture. They praised American political institutions, American liberty, and American progress and material civilization. They thought that though America could learn much from the Catholic Church, the Church, too, could benefit by her association with democratic American society. Thus, they favored cultural assimilation and opposed foreign enclaves amongst the faithful. Among the particular issues which they addressed, the progressives supported (at least under certain circumstances) Catholic partnership with public schools, even if this meant that religion was relegated to after-school hours; inter-religious dialogue, as represented by the Parliament of World Religions; the

adaptation of the Catholic Church's "manner of life and its method of action to the conditions of the new order"; separation of Church and state as it was found in the United States .

The preservationists generally opposed the signature positions of the progressives. They attacked common schools as godless and thus opposed any Catholic school union with them. They opposed interreligious dialogue as represented by the Parliament of World Religions. They upheld the traditional Church teaching about the relation of Church and state.

3. In *Testem Benevolentiae Nostrae*, Pope Leo XIII assailed Americanism. He said he disapproved of any attempt to deemphasize any Catholic doctrine in order more easily to reconcile the Church with the modern age, because it "would tend rather to separate Catholics from the Church than to bring in those who differ." Leo said it was false to say that the Church's "supervision and watchfulness" should be "in some sense lessened" to give the faithful more freedom to follow the leading of their minds. Rather, said Leo, in the modern age, the Church's guidance was more needed. He dismissed the distinction between "active" and "passive" virtues, saying all virtues are active, he said. The "disregard" of supernatural virtues in favor of natural ones was, the pope said, a short step "to contempt of the religious life which has in some degree taken hold of minds." One may not hold that religious "vows are alien to the spirit of our times, in that they limit the bounds of human liberty; that they are more suitable to weak than to strong minds; that so far from making for human perfection and the good of human organization, that they are hurtful to both." *Testem Benevolentiae* effectively killed Americanism, at least for a time. American bishops were quick to repudiate the doctrine,

though some said that no one in America, at least, held to Americanism.

4. Gradually, as more and more farms went bust, the holdings of those that survived grew larger. Those who could afford machinery, and thus, replace labor, fared better than those who had to pay "hands" to work their fields. In the Deep South, where land was given to a single cash crop – cotton – the farmer's plight was extreme. The merchants, from whom farmers had to borrow money, often demanded that the land be put to cotton instead of other crops – thus perpetuating cultivation practices that destroyed the fertility of the soil. The farmers sold their cotton cheaply to mill owners (who, themselves, sold it again for high prices); thus, a drastic fall in prices meant the farmer had to sell his cotton for even less and so did not make enough money to pay his mortgages. The merchants who had made the loans would then foreclose on the land. Often, they kept the farmer on as a tenant – working land that had formerly been his own.

5. The Pullman strike convinced many Americans that the struggle of labor and capital could have revolutionary repercussions if nothing were done about it. Class conflict, they feared, could lead to revolution and, perhaps, to the overthrow of American institutions. While the Pullman strike turned many against the claims of labor, others began to study how to harmonize the conflicts between capital and labor within the prevailing capitalist system. The question, for most concerned Americans was not whether to overthrow the capitalist system but how to save society from the upheavals resulting from the struggle of labor and capital.

II.
1. A sign of American Protestantism's vibrancy was American involvement in the foreign missions.
2. The two largest groups of immigrants in the 19th century were Irish and German.
3. A series of bank failures in 1893 collapsed the county into a deep depression – the Panic of 1893.
4. Because the Panic of 1893, millions lost their jobs, and thousands wandered homeless. Many found themselves bankrupt and ruined.
5.
   a. **Booker T. Washington:** the director of a new school for blacks at Tuskegee. Under Washington, the "Tuskegee Normal and Industrial Institute" went from a small school meeting in a small building and a church to become the nation's foremost industrial school for blacks. Booker T. Washington believed that only by educating themselves could blacks attain any true equality in white society. He believed blacks shouldn't demand that equality but prove themselves worthy of it.
   b. **Mary "Mother" Jones:** a labor leader and a member of the Knights of Labor. Among her many other activities, in 1899-1900 she was an organizer of the United Mine Workers strike in Arnot, Pennsylvania, which she helped bring to a successful conclusion.
   c. **Jacob Coxey:** a man who identified himself with the unfortunate poor during the Panic of 1893, Coxey dreamed of the United States as a Christian commonwealth and believed that the federal government should take measures to relieve the poor. In 1894, he organized a march from Ohio to Washington, D.C., to publicize the plight of the poor.

At the Crossroads

CHAPTER 23:

Chapter Overview

• Discontent and factions divided the people of Cuba, and separatists sparked a revolt against Spanish rule. Because of this and a depressed economy, Cubans emigrated to the United States where they formed *juntas* to foster revolution in Cuba. Americans in the United States were in favor of the revolutionaries, but President McKinley was hesitant to go to war because business interests opposed it.

• The explosion of the *Maine*, an American battleship, in Havana harbor stirred up war fever in the United States. McKinley tried to avoid war, but Congress pushed for it. Finally, on April 11, 1898, McKinley asked Congress for a declaration of war against Spain. The House of Representatives passed a resolution demanding that Spain grant Cuba its independence. When McKinley ordered the blockading of all Cuban ports, Spain declared war on the United States.

• Roosevelt and his Rough Riders captured San Juan Hill, which made them national heroes. In July the American army besieged the city of Santiago. The Spanish surrendered, thus ending the fighting in Cuba.

• The American army invaded the island of Puerto Rico on July 25. Meanwhile. Commodore Dewey, with the help of Filipino rebel forces, took the city of Manila in the Philippines on August 13.

• On July 26, the Spanish government asked for terms of peace. McKinley issued his terms, and though they were hard, Spain signed a preliminary peace on August 12, 1898.

• In July of 1898, the United States Senate approved the treaty annexing Hawai'i. A discussion about whether the Philippines should be annexed or not was taken up. Some thought it necessary to subjugate peoples like the Filipinos in order to achieve world progress, while some opposed an imperial America. Mark Twain formed the Anti-Imperialist League. Despite protests, however, the United States agreed to pay $20 million to Spain for the Philippine islands in December 1898. The Filipino insurgents did not want annexation, however; they wanted independence. This situation resulted in a struggle between United States forces and Filipino insurgents in the Philippines.

• After occupying the Philippines, the United States began exerting its influence in the Far East. U.S. Secretary of State John Hay announced an "open door policy" in regards to China in 1899 to assure Americans that they would not be edged out of the Chinese market by other nations. During the Boxer Rebellion in 1900, the United States participated in an expeditionary force to relieve Peking.

• In the elections of 1900, McKinley was reelected, with Theodore Roosevelt as his vice president. In 1901 an anarchist's bullet killed President McKinley, and Roosevelt was sworn in as president.

• President Roosevelt represented an ideology that called for protections for workers and a regulation of business for the sake of justice but conceded that big industry was here to stay. Roosevelt thought the best anyone could hope for was a bettering of the conditions of labor instead of an overthrow of or any radical change to the social order.

- In 1905 industrial workers formed the Industrial Workers of the World, an industrial union organization that united workers of all trades and industries, both skilled and unskilled. Socialism, too, began to attract adherents in America.

- Throughout his political career, Roosevelt promoted reform in favor of the common man against corruption. When he became president, he announced that he would enforce the laws to break up trusts. When J.P. Morgan moved to consolidate three railroads in a trust called the Northern Securities Corporation, Roosevelt prosecuted him, and on April 9, 1903, the United States Circuit court dissolved the Northern Securities Corporation. Roosevelt next brought suit against the American Tobacco Company and Standard Oil, and set up departments of commerce and of labor, with a bureau to gather facts for enforcing anti-trust laws.

- A strike amongst coal workers in Pennsylvania in 1902 brought the labor question to the forefront of the public mind once again. John Mitchell, the leader of the strike, asked Roosevelt to set up a tribunal where representatives of both labor and management could arbitrate the strike. The owners derided the request and wanted Roosevelt to send in federal troops. Roosevelt did not send in troops but set up an arbitration board that investigated the situation, returned the workers to their jobs, and decided that the workers would receive a ten percent increase in their pay and a decrease in work hours.

- Roosevelt was a strong proponent of the family and critical of those who encouraged small families. He promoted policies that he thought would strengthen the material basis of family life.

- Roosevelt was reelected to a second term in 1904. During his second term he tempered his trust-busting ways somewhat. He continued and accelerated a tendency toward the centralization of power in the federal government.

- The Roosevelt administration was eager to build a canal connecting the Atlantic and the Pacific. On June 20, 1907, the Senate passed the Spooner Act that authorized the president to pay a French company for the concession to build the canal across the Isthmus of Panama. The only thing needed was the approval of the Colombian government, but the Colombian government refused to cooperate. Fortunately for Roosevelt, revolutionaries in Panama wanted their state to secede from Colombia, and the United States offered its support to the revolutionaries. On November 3, 1903, the new Republic of Panama declared its independence, and on November 18, Panama leased the canal zone to the United States.

- Roosevelt wielded his "big stick" policy not only over Colombia. When Great Britain, Germany, and Italy blockaded the coast of Venezuela, Roosevelt intervened, negotiating with Kaiser Wilhelm II of Germany to submit his claims to the Hague Tribunal.

- In 1904, Roosevelt developed his corollary to the Monroe Doctrine that would allow the United States to assume what Roosevelt thought was its rightful place as a world power. When the United States had to provide fiscal and military protectorates over the small nations of Latin America, the government formally revoked the Roosevelt Corollary in 1930.

- In 1908, Roosevelt did not run again, and the presidency went to his friend, William Howard Taft. President Taft alienated Roosevelt's allies, the progressives, though his administration is noted for progressives policies.

♦ In 1910 Roosevelt returned from hunting in Africa, where he had refined and developed his political ideas into what he called the "New Nationalism." Though he said he did not want the Republican nomination for president in 1912, various entreaties and circumstances won him over to the idea. He lost to Taft. The presidency went to the Democrats with the election of Woodrow Wilson.

♦ The 16th amendment, ratified in February 1913, amended Article 1, Section 9 of the Constitution and so nullified an 1895 Supreme Court decision that declared an income tax unconstitutional.

♦ President Wilson passed two pieces of legislation that have been called his most important achievements. Under Wilson, Congress passed the Underwood Tariff on October 3, 1913, which enacted not only the lowest rates on foreign imports to date, but a graduated federal income tax as well. On December 23, Congress passed the Federal Reserve Act.

What Students Should Know

1. **The background to the Spanish-American War**

   Conditions had not been good in Cuba since 1825, when the Spanish government granted the military governors of the island special powers to prevent Cuba from falling into the hands of newly independent Mexico or Colombia. Throughout the 1850s, Cuba had suffered from a corrupt government that had inspired revolutionary opposition. Three rival factions divided the Cuban people: the separatists, who favored independence from Spain; the reformists, who simply wanted a

reform of colonial government; and the defenders of the status quo. These last were mostly *peninuslares*. In 1868, separatists instigated a revolt against Spanish colonial and established Liberal republican rule. After ten years of bloody war, the rebels in February 1878 accepted the Convention of Zanjón that, while maintaining Cuba as a Spanish colony, granted amnesty to the insurgents, called for reforms in government (including autonomy for Cuba – or dominion status, as Canada had with Great Britain), and proclaimed the gradual abolition of slavery. But Cubans remained discontent; they wanted true autonomy, separation of military and civil power, and assurance of personal and property rights. Cuban émigrés to the United States formed *juntas* (under a *Gran Junta* in New York City) to foster a revolution in Cuba. In 1895 separatists under José Julián Martí and other leaders instigated a rebellion against Spain. Spain sent General Valeriano Weyler y Nicolau to Cuba to crush the rebellion. Weyler earned the title, "Butcher," for the brutal way he suppressed the rebellion. The rebels laid waste to the countryside until it was desolate. In 1897, Spain withdrew Weyler, offered Cuba a measure of home rule, and corrected the worst abuses.

2. **Opinion in the U.S. about the Cuban rebellion**

   Opinion in the United States was solidly on the side of the rebels because Americans saw them as fighting for independence, just as the English colonists had done in 1776. Newspapers owned by William Randolph Hearst and his rival, Joseph Pulitzer pushed for American intervention in the Cuban war. Many Americans saw war as a way of spreading America's "enlightened" institutions and commerce to the "benighted"

Cuban people. Some members of the president's administration wanted war, including the assistant secretary of the navy, Theodore Roosevelt. Business interests, however, were opposed to war, and therefore so was President William McKinley.

3. **How Hawai'i became a republic, and its relations with the U.S.**

In the late 19th century, wealthy owners of pineapple plantations (themselves the descendants of New England missionaries) in 1893 overthrew the last Hawai'ian queen, Liliuokalani and made Hawai'i a republic under President Sanford Dole. Following the coup, President Harrison had introduced an annexation treaty into the Senate. President Cleveland withdrew the treaty after he discovered the Hawai'ian revolution was not a popular uprising but the work of a few A-mericans with the aid of United States troops. But in 1897, President McKinley submitted to the Senate a second treaty for the annexation of Hawai'i.

4. **The events leading to the U.S. declaration of war on Spain**

The American consul to Havana, General Fitzhugh Lee, had asked that the battleship *Maine* be dispatched to Havana harbor – technically an act of war, though Spain ignored the provocation. On February 15, 1898, the *Maine* exploded, with a great loss of life. Though there was no proof the Spanish were responsible, pro-war Americans used the explosion to whip up public animus against Spain. A popular call to avenge the *Maine* began to move Republicans in the direction of war. The decision of a naval court of inquiry that an external submerged mine destroyed the *Maine* convinced most Americans that the Spanish were responsible. McKinley wired demands to Madrid, Spain,

that the Spanish government deemed excessive. Though Spain promised an armistice on April 9, Congress still pressed for war. On April 11, 1898, President McKinley asked Congress for a declaration of war against Spain. Six days later, the House of Representatives passed a resolution demanding that Spain grant Cuba its independence. The Senate soon concurred, and on April 22 McKinley ordered the blockade of all Cuban ports – an act of war. On April 24, Spain declared war on the United States, and, the next day, the United States issued a declaration of war saying Spain must "relinquish its authority and government in the Island of Cuba and withdraw its land and naval forces from Cuba and Cuban waters."

5. **Events of the Spanish-American War**

U.S. Commodore George Dewey's fleet defeated a Spanish fleet in the Philippines on May 1, 1898 and captured Manila Bay.

United States marines landed and established a beachhead at Guantanamo Bay, 40 miles from Santiago.

The first battle between American and Spanish troops occurred at the stronghold of Las Guásimas outside Santiago, on June 24. Though Spanish troops defended themselves with Mauser rifles, they soon abandoned their entrenchments.

On July 1, 1898 an assault of U.S. troops on El Caney, a village outside of Santiago, began. Though numbering only 520 men (against the 4,500 under Lawton) the Spanish fought bravely and doggedly and held off the American forces for many hours. The U.S. forces at last drove the Spanish from their position

The same day, about 700 Spanish troops were holding the roughly 15,000 Americans at bay on San Juan Hill, outside Santiago. The standoff continued until about 12:30 p.m., when the American line began to advance without orders. Theodore Roosevelt and the Rough Riders, together with the 9th and 10th cavalry, black units, finally took San Juan Hill.

On July 3, Admiral Cevera tried to break out of Santiago harbor with his fleet, but the American navy sank the four ships that made up the Spanish squadron and Cervera himself was taken prisoner.

On July 17, the Spanish garrison at Santiago surrendered. The fighting in Cuba had ended.

The U.S. invaded Puerto Rico on July 25.

August 12, 1898: Spain signed a preliminary peace with the United States.

On August 13, U.S. forces took Manila in the Philippines.

December 10, 1898: the United States signed a peace treaty in Paris.

6. Events following the Spanish-American War

The Spanish-American War made Dewey, the Rough Riders, and Theodore Roosevelt national heroes. It also assured for Roosevelt the governorship of New York and the Republican vice-presidential nomination in 1900. More importantly, the war had made the United States an imperial power. In July 1898, the United States Senate approved the treaty annexing Hawai'i, and the course of the war had brought into America's possession the former Spanish Pacific island of Guam. The United States made conquered Puerto Rico a territory with the right to become a state or to declare for independence. U.S. troops occupied Cuba for three years after the war. In 1900, a constitutional convention drew up a constitution for Cuba patterned on that of the United States, agreed to grant the U.S. Guantanamo Bay for a naval base, and

adopted the Platt Amendment, which gave the U.S. the right to "intervene" in Cuban affairs to preserve Cuban independence or to keep order. The annexation of the Philippines was controversial in the U.S.; it was economic and strategic arguments that moved McKinley to deny Filipino independence. McKinley said the Filipino republic (established by Filipino rebels against Spanish rule) could not keep order, and he pushed for annexation. The United States paid Spain $20 million for the Philippine islands.

7. The debate over U.S. imperialism

Though Commodore Dewey had welcomed back exiled Filipino insurgent Emilio Aguinaldo, who, with other rebel leaders, had begun organizing a republic, some Americans argued that if the U.S. did not annex the Philippines, Germany would. The debate over the annexation of the Philippines broadened into a debate over U.S. imperialism. Pro-imperialists argued that the United States needed a base of operations in the Far East, while others claimed that the United States economy required colonial expansion and new markets for American manufacturers. Henry Demarest Lloyd added that "inferior nations" needed the protection of "greater" nations. Other Americans (among whom were Mark Twain, William Jennings Bryan, and Andrew Carnegie), said that the imperialism violated a colonized people's right to freedom and self-government, and was thus immoral. Imperialism they said, was theft. Most Catholics, it seems were anti-imperialist, at least in regards to the Philippines, for they thought American Liberal institutions would threaten the Catholic Church there. Prominent hierarchs, such as Placide Chapelle, archbishop New Orleans, James

Cardinal Gibbons, and Bishop John Ireland supported the annexation of the Philippines.

8. U.S. intervention in China

With the occupation of the Philippines, the United States began to exert its influence in the Far East. In 1899, secretary of state John Hay announced an "open door policy" in regards to China to assure that the United States would not be edged out of the Chinese market by Russia, Great Britain, France, and Japan. When the Boxer Rebellion – an uprising on the part of traditional elements in Chinese society – broke out in June 1900, the United States participated in a joint expeditionary force to relieve Peking. In July of that year, Secretary Hay declared that China was not to be divided up between the European powers, nor was the principle of equality between trading countries to be violated.

9. Progressivism and its divisions

Progressivism was a political ideology that had its roots in Populism but had abandoned Populism's rejection of the industrial order. Progressivism represented those who had become convinced that big industry was here to stay and that the best anyone could hope for was a bettering of the conditions of labor, not an overthrow of or any radical change in the existing order. President Roosevelt represented Progressivism. He accepted the "inevitableness of combination in business" and thought it was necessary to "meet it be a corresponding increase in governmental power over big business." He thought government had to be as big or bigger than business, in order to regulate business.

William Jennings Bryan represented another strain of Progressivism – one that Roosevelt thought was not really Progressivism at all. Bryan and the "tories" (as Roosevelt called them) wanted to see break-up of large trusts and large businesses. They objected as much to big government as they did to big business.

Socialists occupied what might be called the "far left" of Progressivism. Less radical than the communists and the anarchists, the socialists worked at the local level to promote municipal ownership of public utilities, such as waterworks and gas and electric plants. Throughout the first decade of the 20th century, Socialists increased their political clout. By 1911 they had won mayorships in about 18 cities; and they nearly took the mayoral seats of Cleveland and Los Angeles.

10. Who the "Muckrakers" were

A number of journalists furthered the progressive agenda. Dubbed "muckrakers" by Roosevelt, these journalists wrote articles that uncovered corruption in industry and politics. Their number included Lincoln Steffens, Ida Tarbell (who took on Standard Oil), and Upton Sinclair.

11. Who Eugene V. Debs was and how his idea of a labor union differed from that of Samuel Gompers

Debs advocated industrial unionism as opposed to the craft union model championed by Samuel Gompers and the AFL. Debs, and others, argued that, since industry was growing increasingly more centralized, so must unions. Under the Gompers' model, unions, divided up among the various crafts or trades, did not always work in concert together if one or a few went on strike. Such a policy, said Debs, allowed industry to take a divide-and-conquer approach to labor activity and provided no representation for unskilled laborers. If all workers were united under one union, Debs argued, then a strike could cripple a particular industry, thus forcing owners to meet the union's demands. Gompers countered that such an approach had never worked (he referenced the Pullman strike) and always brought more repressive measures against workers in its wake. Only craft union strikes had succeeded, he said.

12. What the Industrial Workers of the World (IWW) was and what it stood for

In 1905, the Western Federation of Miners and other unions united in a union called the Industrial Workers of the World. The "Wobblies," as the Industrial Workers were nicknamed, adopted an industrial union organization that united workers of all trades and industries, both skilled and unskilled. The leaders of this movement were William D. "Big Bill" Haywood, Daniel DeLeon, W.E.Trautman, Eugene V. Debs, and a Catholic priest, Father Thomas J. Hagerty. Both Mother Jones and Emma Goldman became supporters of the IWW. The Industrial Workers of the World grew rapidly. By their second convention in 1906, the Wobblies numbered 100,000 workers. Political differences among the members (there were socialist, anarchist, and trade unionist Wobblies) led eventually to major splits in the IWW's ranks. In 1909 the IWW split into two rival groups, each calling itself the IWW: one based in Chicago; the other, in Detroit. The Chicago-based IWW, the only branch finally to survive, adopted a platform for action that favored class conflict between workers and owners and called for worker ownership of productive property and an end to the wage system.

13. Catholic contributions to the social question in America

Though many Catholics were workers and union members, Catholic leaders had not been conspicuous in efforts to solve the labor crisis. Some bishops were friendly to labor unions; others, fearing what they saw as the unions' socialist and anarchist tendencies, opposed them. But a few American Catholics involved themselves in the labor question. One of these was Father John A. Ryan of the archdiocese of Saint Paul, Minnesota, who wrote a book, *A Living Wage*, on the Church's teaching about just wages. Father Peter E. Dietz of Cleveland sought to apply the ideals of *Rerum Novarum* to the American scene. Dietz was convinced that Catholic priests could help Catholic laymen form Catholic worker organizations to aid in a just resolution of the labor question. Dietz was for a time a member of a German Catholic social justice organization, the St. Louis-based German Roman Catholic Central Union of North America. Dietz later left the organization for a Catholic laborers society called the Militia of Christ for Social Service that met in conjunction with conventions of the American Federation of Labor, and its membership was made up of Catholic AFL members. Dietz came into conflict with the central figure of the Central Union, Frederick P. Kenkel over how *Rerum Novarum* should be applied to the American scene. Dietz has been called a "reformist"; he did not favor any fundamental changes in the organization of the American economy but simply a bettering of the worker's status in the existing system. Kenkel envisioned a more radical transformation of the American economy, proposing what is called a "corporatist" model of industrial organization, where cooperative unions would be formed that included both owners and workers in a given industry, somewhat along the lines of medieval guilds. The cooperative unions would be controlled and directed by workers and owners both and would oversee any conflicts that arose between them, without strikes. Government would step in only when the internal structure of the union was unable to bring a conflict to resolution.

14. Roosevelt and the role of government in relation to business

President Roosevelt thought that a failure to solve the problems associated with capitalism would collapse "the cause of free self-government." Where the states were powerless to deal effectively with the inequalities of capitalism, there the federal government should step in to secure the general welfare of the nation. In his first message to Congress on December 3, 1901, the new president announced that he would not only enforce existing laws to break up trusts but would push for legislation that would give the federal government more power to inspect and regulate business involved in interstate trade. He followed his ideas with action, as when he broke the Northern Securities Company Trust and took on the American Tobacco Company and Standard Oil. But in his second term Roosevelt was less willing to bust trusts. He came to think that trusts were here to stay, and that there were good trusts and bad trusts. The problem with trusts was not their size but their underhandedness and dishonesty. The challenge, he believed, was to regulate bad trusts, not destroy them. Roosevelt's view would be echoed by the Supreme Court in the coming years. In future decisions, the court would rule that a monopoly violated the Sherman Anti-Trust Act, not simply because of its size, but because it "unreasonably" affected interstate trade, and so was in "restraint of trade."

15. Roosevelt and conservation

Roosevelt, was convinced of the need of conserving the country's forests and regions of great natural beauty. He believed forests had to be preserved from ranchers and timber companies that were looting federal public lands of their rich harvest of wood. Certain areas of natural beauty Roosevelt believed were national treasures that had to be kept pristine for the edification of future generations. At Roosevelt's urging, Congress set aside 150 million acres of unsold federal lands as national forest reserve. Roosevelt fostered federal irrigation projects that by 1915 would add a million and quarter new acres to the nation's arable land. Under the Roosevelt presidency, five national parks and two national game reserves were established.

16. How the 1902 coal strike illustrated Roosevelt's constitutional views

In 1902, striking workers in the anthracite coal region of Pennsylvania were demanding higher pay and better working conditions; but owners, led by J.P. Morgan and George F. Baer of the Philadelphia and Reading Railroad, refused to negotiate with them. With the looming threat of a winter without coal, Roosevelt determined that he had to intervene – even though he thought he had no constitutional authority to interfere, since the coal miners were not a trust. He said he could not "more see misery and death come to the great masses of the people in our large cities, and sit by idly, because under ordinary conditions a strike is not a subject for interference by the President, than I could sit by idly and see one man kill another without interference because there is no statutory duty imposed upon the President to interfere in such cases." When the owners derided a proposal of Roosevelt's for arbitration, he, like Grover Cleveland before him, threatened to send in federal troops to operate the mines. Met with a protest that he had no constitutional authority to do this, Roosevelt retorted that "the Constitution was made for the people and not the people for the Constitution."

17.   Roosevelt's ideas on the family

Roosevelt saw the family as the cornerstone of the nation, the basic unit of society. The family, springing from the union of man and woman in marriage, he thought, demanded the assiduous care of both husband and wife. The good of their offspring, he said, is their highest calling. Roosevelt saw the American family in his day as threatened by two evils: a decrease in the birthrate among the "native," Anglo population, and divorce. These, in Roosevelt's mind, presaged disaster for the nation. Roosevelt blamed social conditions – uncontrolled industrialization and urbanization – in part for the decline of family life. He deplored the "ruin of motherhood and childhood by the merciless exploitation of the labor of women and children." And though he asserted that women had a right to education and to careers that hitherto had been closed to them, he wanted to protect their role in the home. He thus opposed those feminists who despised the role of the stay-at-home mother and promoted contraception.

18.   Roosevelt's second-term achievements

In his second term, Roosevelt was able to push through Congress some important progressive legislation. The Hepburn Act, passed in 1906, extended federal regulation from interstate railroads to steamship, express, and sleeping car companies. The bill allowed the Interstate Commerce Commission to determine maximum rates such companies could charge. The companies could appeal the commission's decision to the courts, but the burden of proof was put on the companies. After reading the novel, *The Jungle*, by Upton Sinclair, which exposed

conditions in the meatpacking industry, Roosevelt decided to have that industry investigated. The result was a report of what Roosevelt called the "hideous" conditions in the meatpacking plants. The president wanted a meat inspection act; and though Congress was reluctant, Roosevelt finally prevailed. On June 30, 1906, Congress passed Roosevelt's "Pure Food and Drug Act," providing for federal inspection of the food and drug industry and forbade the manufacture, sale, or transportation of adulterated food or drugs.

19.   Theodore Roosevelt's foreign policy

Roosevelt thought that because the United States had become "a great nation," it was "forced by the fact of its greatness into relations with the other nations of the earth" and so "must behave as beseems a people with such responsibilities." It should offer other nations "cordial and sincere friendship" in "a spirit of just and generous recognition of all their rights." Nevertheless, the U.S. should demand respect from other nations and thus build up its military strength so that its rights will be respected. This he encapsulated in the adage, 'Speak softly, and carry a big stick; you will go far.'" Roosevelt, though, was not belligerent. The fear expressed when he took over from McKinley, that he would draw the nation into war, proved unfounded. Once he became president, Roosevelt did all he could to avoid war. He had granted Cuba her independence, as McKinley had promised, and had only intervened once to restore order on the island, as the Platt Amendment allowed the United States president to do. Roosevelt allowed the Philippines to establish a degree of self-rule, though a United States governor still presided over the island nation. Roosevelt supported the formation of The

Hague Tribunal, a court to settle international quarrels before they erupted into war. In 1904, he appended the "Roosevelt Corollary" to the Monroe Doctrine that allowed the U.S. to intervene in the affairs of nations in the Americas as an "international police power" if "chronic wrongdoing" occurred in them. He applied this corollary in 1904 when the Dominican Republic reneged on its debts to European creditors. In 1907, the Root-Takahira agreement with Japan stipulated that the Japanese would discourage further immigration to the United States and specified that the United States, Japan, and the European powers would maintain equal trading status with China (the "Open Door" policy) and that the military status of the United States and Japan would remain unchanged in the Pacific. Roosevelt was a peace maker: he brought Russia and Japan to negotiate an end to their war and sign a peace treaty at Portsmouth, New Hampshire, on September 5, 1905. At Algeciras in 1906, Roosevelt mediated a dispute between France and Germany over Morocco.

20. How Roosevelt obtained for the U.S. the Panama canal zone

Roosevelt was in favor in building a canal, connecting the Carribean and Atlantic with the Pacific, through the isthmus of Panama. Others wanted a canal built through Nicaragua, and Roosevelt wanted to make sure this did not happen. He wanted to take advantage of an offer from a French company that had attempted build a canal through Panama, to sell rights to the canal zone to the United States. In 1902, the U.S. Senate approved the Spooner Act that authorized the president to purchase these rights, but only if Colombia ceded the land across the isthmus to the United States "within a reasonable time." If it did not, the president

was to pursue the Nicaragua option. An offer by the Colombian *charge d'affairs* in Washington to sell the rights to the Isthmus, however, did not win the approval of the Colombian government. When the Colombians failed to respond to veiled threats, Roosevelt met with Philippe Bunau-Varilla, the leader of revolutionaries in Panama who wanted their state to secede from Colombia. Bunau-Varilla asked Roosevelt if the United States military would prevent Colombian troops from landing in Panama in the event of a revolution, and Roosevelt in a veiled way said it would. On October 19, 1903, three United States vessels of war were ordered to anchor off the coast of Panama. Then, U.S. military commanders were instructed to occupy the Panama Railroad if a revolution broke out – thus preventing the advance of Colombian troops into Panama. When the Panamanian revolutionaries carried out their designs on November 3, 1903, the Colombian government was unable to intervene. On November 3, the new Republic of Panama declared its independence, which the U.S. recognized. On November 18, the new Republic of Panama leased the canal zone "in perpetuity" to the United States "to the entire exclusion of the exercise by Panama of any … sovereign rights, power or authority."

21. President William Howard Taft's progressive record

Taft was a disappointment to progressives who had supported Roosevelt. He signed into law the Payne-Aldrich Tariff bill that placed higher rates on imports; and, despite provisions added by Taft, this tariff was roundly condemned by progressives. When Gifford Pinchot (Roosevelt's old friend and supported by the Muckrakers), the head of the Forestry Service, leveled accusations against Richard Ballinger, the secretary of the Interior, Taft supported Ballinger and fired Pinchot.. Still, in some ways, Taft's progressive record was at least as good as Roosevelt's. Taft supported a bolstering of the Interstate Commerce Commission by granting it the power to suspend transportation rate increases until the railroads could prove the increases were reasonable. The number of prosecutions for violations of the Sherman Anti-Trust Act under Taft's attorney general were double those under Roosevelt's. Taft supported the progressive-inspired amendments to the Constitution – the 16th Amendment, to establish an income tax, and the 17th Amendment, that provided for the popular election of United States senators. He protected federal oil lands from exploitation, asked Congress to place coal lands in reserve, and established a bureau of mines. But Taft's appointments to the Supreme Court ruled against certain progressive-inspired legislation.

22. The platform of the Progressive ("Bull Moose") Party during the campaign of 1912

The Roosevelt that returned from his big-game hunting expedition in Africa was more radically progressive than he was during his presidency. His Square Deal insisted that the rich man "holds his wealth subject to the general right of the community to regulate its business use as the public welfare requires." Roosevelt's Progressive Party called for the popular election of United States senators; the adoption by states of initiative, referendum, and recall; equal suffrage for men and women; popular recall of judicial decisions; and automatic Supreme Court review of any rulings made by lower federal courts declaring a business policing act of a

state legislature was unconstitutional. The Progressives favored laws "looking to the prevention of industrial accidents, occupational diseases, overwork, involuntary unemployment, and other injurious effects incident to modern industry."They wanted to give to state and federal governments authority over the "fixing of minimum safety and health standards for the various occupations." They called for the "prohibition of child labor"; "minimum wage standards for working women"; the "general prohibition of night work for women"; an eight-hour work day for women and young workers; the establishment of the eight-hour day "in continuous twenty four-hour industries"; and the "protection of home life against the hazards of sickness, irregular employment and old age through the adoption of a system of social insurance adapted to American use." As for conservation, the Progressive platform called for public control of the "remaining forests, coal and oil lands, water powers and other natural resources still in state or National control (except agricultural lands.)"

23. The realignment of parties after the election of 1912

The victory of Woodrow Wilson, a progressive Democrat, in the election of 1912 led to the defection of progressives from the Republican party ; and this defection proved to be permanent. In the coming years, the Republicans would become the conservative party, while the Democrats drew all the progressive elements in American politics. Roosevelt's Progressive Party, though it won 12 seats in Congress, did not survive the election of 1912.

24. The significance of Theodore Roosevelt's presidency

Roosevelt championed progressive policies that were taken up and carried forward by Woodrow Wilson. Roosevelt fairly established progressivism in U.S. politics and thus turned the nation in a new direction – a progressive one.

25. Woodrow Wilson's views on government

Woodrow Wilson was essentially a moderate progressive. He praised the industrial and material development of the United States, though he thought it had dire effects on the natural world and came with a large human cost. The government, he said, sided with selfish interests and too often forgot the people. He wanted changes that would make the industrial order serve the people, but he wanted to preserve the economic order of the United States as it was. He thus championed the progressive policies favored by progressive Democrats and Republicans, as well as members of the Progressive Party.

26. The Underwood Tariff and what it accomplished

On October 3, 1913, Congress passed the Underwood Tariff, which Wilson signed, that enacted the lowest rates on foreign imports since the Civil War. But the most significant part of Underwood was not its tariff provisions (though these were significant),

but the fact that a graduated federal income tax was appended to the bill and became law. The new Underwood income tax was levied on individuals (with incomes over $3,000 a year) and married couples (with incomes over $4,000 a year), with an added tax (surtax) on incomes exceeding $20,000 a year. Corporations were taxed at one percent a year. Most Americans, however, were unaffected by the income tax.

27. The background of the 16th Amendment and what it accomplished

This Underwood federal income tax was not the first of its kind. During the Civil War, both the Union and the Confederacy levied income taxes. The federal tax was abolished in 1872. In 1894, during the panic, the federal government levied an income tax on businesses and individual incomes over $4,000, but the tax never went into effect because the Supreme Court declared an income tax unconstitutional in *Pollock v. Farmers' Loan and Trust Company*, the Supreme Court declared the federal income tax to be a direct tax on individuals and this, it said, was forbidden by Article 1, Section 9 of the Constitution: "No Capitation, or other direct, Tax shall be laid unless in Proportion to the Census or Enumeration herein before directed to be taken." Taxing income on personal property, said the court, is the same

---

Key Terms at a Glance

imperialism: the policy of extending a nation's power and dominion by acquiring territory or indirect control of the political life of another country

Progressivism: an American political movement that, like Populism, sought the regulation of business through government action to remedy abuses and to benefit workers and the citizenry as a whole. Unlike Populists, however, Progressives did not seek any radical change for the social order.

as taxing property, and the Constitution only allows a direct federal tax on property to be levied in proportion to the population of each state. The income tax of 1894 laid a direct tax on citizens, regardless of state boundaries. The Sixteenth Amendment, ratified in February 1913, amended Article 1, Section 9 of the Constitution and so nullified the Supreme Court's 1895 decision.

28. The background of the Federal Reserve Act and what it did

The Federal Reserve Act, passed under a special session of Congress in 1913, has been called, with the Underwood Tariff, one of Wilson triumphs. Since the days of Andrew Jackson, the United States, unlike other industrial countries, had no central bank that governed the activities of local banks. Many claimed the lack of a central bank made the supply of money "inelastic" – that is, unable to adjust to the needs of production and consumption. Lack of elasticity, it was said, led to periodic panics and depressions. Local and state banks maintained no uniformity with one another. Thus, many argued, a central bank was needed to maintain uniformity in the issuing of money and credit across the nation. Because, particularly in the Democratic party, many Americans objected to a central bank, the challenge was to create a central bank that, at least, didn't appear to be centralized. The Federal Reserve Act divided the country into 12 districts, each with its own Federal Reserve bank. These banks were private but were governed by a Federal Reserve Board, whose members were to be appointed by the president. The Federal Reserve could issue bank notes or paper currency. It could also govern the amount of credit local member banks could issue and the amount of interest they could charge on loans. The Federal Reserve was created to regulate the supply of money and credit so they could expand when production slowed and remain stable when production increased.

29. The Clayton Anti-Trust Act and its significance

In 1914, Congress passed the Clayton Anti-Trust Act of 1914, which Samuel Gompers called "labor's charter of rights," since it declared that labor unions had never been, in themselves, unlawful combinations; that strikes, boycotts were not, as such, violations of federal law; and that federal courts could not use injunctions (as during the Pullman strike) in labor disputes. Other legislation included a law granting workman's compensation for the federal civil services and a law forbidding interstate commerce in products derived from child labor. This last law the Supreme Court declared unconstitutional.

Questions for Review

1. **Why did the United States go to war with Spain?**

    Many Americans thought the U.S. should go to war with Spain to free Cuba from repressive government. The incident that set off the war, however, was the explosion of the *U.S.S. Maine* in Havana harbor in February 1898. Any Americans were convinced that Spain was responsible for the explosion. When Spain refused a U.S. demand that Cuba be granted independence, Congress declared war. Many Americans saw the war as a way of spreading America's "enlightened" institutions and commerce to the "benighted" Cuban people,

2. **What did the war with Spain achieve for the United States?**

The Spanish-American war had made the United States an imperial power. Besides the annexation of Hawai'i in July 1898 (not direcly related to the war), the course of the war had brought into America's possession the former Spanish Pacific island of Guam, Cuba, Puerto Rico, and the Philippines.

3. **Why was the United States so interested in the annexation of Hawai'i and the Philippines, but not Cuba?**

The United States was interested in Hawai'i because it was a profitable trade center, and the Philippines for similar reasons. Other reasons for annexing the Philippines were that some thought the United States needed a base of operations in the Far East, and that the subjugation of peoples like the Filipinos was necessary for world progress. Some warned that if the U.S. did not annex the Philippines, Germany would.

4. **Explain how the International Workers of the World differed from unions like the American Federation of Labor.**

The International Workers of the World (IWW) adopted an industrial union organization that united workers of all trades and industries, both skilled and unskilled. The IWW brought workers from all different trades together in a common purpose. It was unlike the AFL, which organized only skilled workers according in separate unions according to their trades.

5. **Describe the contributions American Catholics made to the labor question.**

Though many Catholics were workers and union members, Catholic leaders had not been conspicuous in efforts to solve the labor crisis. Some bishops were friendly to labor unions; others, fearing what they saw as the unions' socialist and anarchist tendencies, opposed them. But a few American Catholics involved themselves in the labor question. One of these was Father John A. Ryan of the archdiocese of Saint Paul, Minnesota, who wrote a book, *A Living Wage*, on the Church's teaching about just wages. Father Peter E. Dietz of Cleveland sought to apply the ideals of *Rerum Novarum* to the American scene. Frederick Kenkel promoted the "corporatist" model of industrial organization, where cooperative unions joined owners and workers in a given industry, somewhat along the lines of medieval guilds.

6. **How did Progressivism differ from Populism**

Progressivism had its roots in Populism. It favored many of the same policies that Populism did, but it rejected Populism's opposition to the industrial order. Progressives thought the industrial order could not be overcome and that the best anyone could hope for was a bettering of the conditions of labor within the existing order.

7. **What were Roosevelt's policies on industry and trusts?**

President Roosevelt thought that a failure to solve the problems associated with capitalism would collapse "the cause of free self-government." Where the states were powerless to deal effectively with the inequalities of capitalism, there the federal government should step in to secure the general welfare of the nation. He said he would not only enforce existing laws to break up trusts but would push for legislation that would give the federal government more power to inspect and regulate business involved in interstate trade. But in his second term Roosevelt was less willing to bust trusts. He came to think that trusts were here to stay, and that there were good trusts and bad trusts. The problem with trusts was not their size but their underhandedness and dishonesty. The challenge, he believed, was to regulate bad trusts, not destroy them.

8. What two evils did Roosevelt see as threatening the American family? How did he think the country might address those threats?

The two evils Roosevelt saw as threatening the American family were a decrease in the birthrate among the "native," Anglo population, and divorce. Though he asserted that women had a right to education and to careers that hitherto had been closed to them, he wanted to protect their role in the home. He thus opposed those feminists who despised the role of the stay-at-home mother and promoted contraception. Roosevelt believed the country could address the problems besetting the family by Americans abandoning selfishness and welcoming children. But he promoted policies that would strengthen the material basis of family life – such as a living wage and tax rate that favored families.

9. Why were Roosevelt and others eager to build a canal in Panama?

It was important to build the Panama canal in order to connect the Carribean and Atlantic with the Pacific. This would shorten considerably the distance ships had to travel between the east and west coasts of America and greatly aid trade.

10. What are some of Roosevelt's achievements in international affairs?

Once he became president, Roosevelt did all he could to avoid war. He had granted Cuba her independence and had only intervened

once to restore order on the island, as the Platt Amendment allowed the United States president to do. Roosevelt allowed the Philippines to establish a degree of self-rule, though a United States governor still presided over the island nation. Roosevelt supported the formation of The Hague Tribunal. In 1904, he appended the "Roosevelt Corollary" to the Monroe Doctrine that allowed the U.S. to intervene in the affairs of nations in the Americas as an "international police power" if "chronic wrongdoing" occurred in them. He applied this corollary in 1904 when the Dominican Republic reneged on its debts to European creditors. Roosevelt brought Russia and Japan to negotiate an end to their war and sign a peace treaty in 1905. At Algeciras in 1906, Roosevelt mediated a dispute between France and Germany over Morocco.

11. Why did progressives disapprove of President Taft? Were their criticisms entirely just? Please explain.

Taft was a disappointment to progressives who had supported Roosevelt. He signed into law the Payne-Aldrich Tariff bill that placed higher rates on imports; and, despite provisions added by Taft, this tariff was roundly condemned by progressives. When Gifford Pinchot (Roosevelt's old friend and supported by the Muckrakers), the head of the Forestry Service, leveled accusations against Richard Ballinger, the secretary of the Interior, Taft supported Ballinger and fired Pinchot. But Taft's progressive record was, in some ways at least, as good as Roosevelt's, for he promoted and supported a number of progresive policies while in office.

12. Describe Roosevelt's "New Nationalism."

At the basis of Roosevelt's New Nationalism was what he called the "Square Deal." His

Square Deal insisted that the rich man "holds his wealth subject to the general right of the community to regulate its business use as the public welfare requires." The Square Deal favored the popular election of United States senators; the adoption by states of initiative, referendum, and recall; equal suffrage for men and women; popular recall of judicial decisions; and automatic Supreme Court review of any rulings made by lower federal courts declaring a business policing act of a state legislature was unconstitutional. It backed laws "looking to the prevention of industrial accidents, occupational diseases, overwork, involuntary unemployment, and other injurious effects incident to modern industry." It wanted to give to state and federal governments authority over the "fixing of minimum safety and health standards for the various occupations." It called for the "prohibition of child labor"; "minimum wage standards for working women"; the "general prohibition of night work for women"; an eight-hour work day for women and young workers; the establishment of the eight-hour day "in continuous twenty four-hour industries"; and the "protection of home life against the hazards of sickness, irregular employment and old age through the adoption of a system of social insurance adapted to American use." The Square Deal called for public control of the "remaining forests, coal and oil lands, water powers and other natural resources still in state or National control (except agricultural lands.)"

13. **What, according to Woodrow Wilson's inaugural address, was the duty that lay before the American people? How does this duty tie into Wilson's agenda of reform?**

The duty that lay before the American people, said Wilson, "is to cleanse, to reconsider, to restore, to correct the evil without impairing the good, to purify and humanize every process of our common life without weakening or sentimentalizing it." Wilson's agenda of reform was a reformed tariff, aid to agriculture, conservation of forests and water-courses, the study and perfection of the means of putting government "at the service of humanity." The "first duty of law," he said, "is to keep sound the society it serves."

Ideas in Action

1. **Research the ideas of the American imperialists and anti-imperialists (such as Mark Twain) of the late 19th and early 20th centuries. Stage a debate between proponents of American imperial expansion and those opposed to it.**

2. **Roosevelt justified the use of the United States military as a "police power" to intervene when grave imbalances occurred in neighboring North and South American nations. He thought that it was time for the United States to take its rightful place in the world. If, as the Declaration of Independence says, all government must arise from the consent of the governed, how can Americans justify intervening in the political and economic affairs of foreign nations?**

3. **Discuss Roosevelt's opinion that, at times, the president must go beyond the powers granted him by the Constitution to address a crisis in national life. Recall, that Roosevelt cited the example of Abraham Lincoln in support of his position. Are such actions by a president every justified? Why or why not?**

4. **Roosevelt thought the powers of the federal government needed to be as extensive, or more extensive, than the power of business, in order to regulate business. Given that**

governments exist to promote and protect the common good, was Roosevelt correct?

5. Research the culture of either Puerto Rico, Cuba, Hawai'i, or the Philippines and what effect the United States has had on the culture.

Sample Quiz I (pages 619-638)

Please answer the following in complete sentences.

1. Name the three factions that divided the Cuban people.

2. How did the battleship *Maine* contribute to war with Spain?

3. What were some arguments against imperialism?

4. How did the United States intervene in China?

5. What was Progressivism?

6. Describe Eugene V. Debs' ideas on labor.

7. What were the Industrial Workers of the World?

8. How did Father John A. Ryan and Father Peter E. Dietz, and Frederick Kenkel contribute to the Catholic view on the labor question?

9. What did President Roosevelt think was the role of the government in regards to big business?

10. Why did Roosevelt urge conservation?

Answers to Sample Quiz I

Students' answers should approximate the following.

1. Three rival factions divided the Cuban people: the separatists, who favored independence from Spain; the reformists, who simply wanted a reform of colonial government; and the defenders of the status quo. These last were mostly *peninuslares*.

2. The American consul to Havana, General Fitzhugh Lee, had asked that the battleship *Maine* be dispatched to Havana harbor – technically an act of war, though Spain ignored the provocation. On February 15, 1898, the Maine exploded, with a great loss of life. Though there was no proof the Spanish were responsible, pro-war Americans used the explosion to whip up public animus against Spain. A popular call to avenge the *Maine* began to move Republicans in the direction of war.

3. Some Americans (among whom were Mark Twain, William Jennings Bryan, and Andrew Carnegie), said that the imperialism violated a colonized people's right to freedom and self-government, and was thus immoral.

Imperialism they said, was theft. Most Catholics, it seems were anti-imperialist, at least in regards to the Philippines, for they thought American Liberal institutions would threaten the Catholic Church there.

4. In 1899, secretary of state John Hay announced an "open door policy" in regards to China to assure that the United States would not be edged out of the Chinese market by Russia, Great Britain, France, and Japan. When the Boxer Rebellion – an uprising on the part of traditional elements in Chinese society – broke out in June 1900, the United States participated in a joint expeditionary force to relieve Peking. In July of that year, Secretary Hay declared that China was not to be divided up between the European powers, nor was the principle of equality between trading countries to be violated.

5. Progressivism was a political ideology that had its roots in Populism but had abandoned Populism's rejection of the industrial order. Progressivism represented those who had become convinced that big industry was here

to stay and that the best anyone could hope for was a bettering of the conditions of labor, not an overthrow of or any radical change in the existing order.

6. Debs advocated industrial unionism as opposed to the craft union model championed by Samuel Gompers and the AFL. Debs, and others, argued that, since industry was growing increasingly more centralized, so must unions. Under the Gompers' model, unions, divided up among the various crafts or trades, did not always work in concert together if one or a few went on strike. Such a policy, said Debs, allowed industry to take a divide-and conquer approach to labor activity and provided no representation for unskilled laborers. If all workers were united under one union, Debs argued, then a strike could cripple a particular industry, thus forcing owners to meet the union's demands.

7. In 1905, the Western Federation of Miners and other unions united in a union called the Industrial Workers of the World. The "Wobblies," as the Industrial Workers were nicknamed, adopted an industrial union organization that united workers of all trades and industries, both skilled and unskilled. There were trade-unionists, socialists, and anarchists represented in the IWW.

8. Father John A. Ryan of the archdiocese of Saint Paul, Minnesota wrote a book, A Living Wage, on the Church's teaching about just wages. Father Peter E. Dietz of Cleveland sought to apply the ideals of Rerum Novarum to the American scene. Kenkel envisioned a more radical transformation of the American economy, proposing what is called a "corporatist" model of industrial organization, where cooperative unions would be formed that included both owners and workers ina given industry, somewhat along the lines of the medieval guilds.

9. President Roosevelt thought that a failure to solve the problems associated with capitalism would collapse "the cause of free self-government." Where the states were powerless to deal effectively with the inequalities of capitalism, there the federal government should step in to secure the general welfare of the nation.

10. Roosevelt, was convinced of the need of conserving the country's forests and regions of great natural beauty. He believed forests had to be preserved from ranchers and timber companies that were looting federal public lands of their rich harvest of wood. Certain areas of natural beauty Roosevelt believed were national treasures that had to be kept pristine for the edification of future generations.

Sample Quiz II (pages 638-657)

Please answer the following in complete sentences.

1. How did the Pure Food and Drug Act come about?

2. Why did Roosevelt recognize Panama's independence?

3. What was the significance of Roosevelt's presidency?

4. What were President Wilson's views on government?

5. What was the Underwood Tariff bill? What did it include?

6. What did the 16th Amendment achieve?

7. Describe the Federal Reserve Act.

8. Describe the Clayton Anti-Trust Act.

Answers to Sample Quiz II

Students' answers should approximate the following.

1. In his second term, Roosevelt was able to push through Congress some important

progressive legislation. The Hepburn Act, passed in 1906, extended federal regulation from interstate railroads to steamship, express, and sleeping car companies. After reading the novel, *The Jungle*, by Upton Sinclair, which exposed conditions in the meatpacking industry, Roosevelt decided to have the meat industry investigated. The result was a report of what Roosevelt called the "hideous" conditions in the meatpacking plants. The president wanted a meat inspection act; and though Congress was reluctant to pass such legislation, Roosevelt finally prevailed. On June 30, 1906, Congress passed Roosevelt's "Pure Food and Drug Act," which provided for federal inspections of the food and drug industry and forbade the manufacture, sale, or transportation of adulterated food or drugs.

2. Roosevelt wanted to take advantage of an offer from a French company that had attempted build a canal through Panama, to sell rights to the canal zone to the United States. In 1902, the U.S. Senate approved the Spooner Act that authorized the president to purchase these rights, but only if Colombia ceded the land across the Isthmus to the United States "within a reasonable time. When Colombia refused to cede the land, Roosevelt backed Panama's revolution against Colombia and then recognized Panama's independence. After Roosevelt recognized Panama's independence, the country leased the canal to the United States.

3. Roosevelt championed progressive policies that were taken up and carried forward by Woodrow Wilson. Roosevelt fairly established progressivism in U.S. politics and thus turned the nation in a new direction.

4. Woodrow Wilson was essentially a moderate progressive. He praised the industrial and material development of the United States, though he thought it had dire effects on the natural world and came with a large human cost. The government, he said, sided with selfish interests and too often forgot the people. He wanted changes that would make the industrial order serve the people, but he wanted to preserve the economic order of the United States as it was. He thus championed the progressive policies favored by progressive Democrats and Republicans, as well as members of the Progressive Party.

5. The Underwood Tariff enacted the lowest rates on foreign imports since the Civil War. Underwood included a graduated federal income tax.

6. In 1894, during the panic, the federal government levied a tax of two percent per year on businesses and individual incomes over $4,000, but the tax never went into effect because the Supreme Court declared an income tax unconstitutional in *Pollock v. Farmers' Loan and Trust Company*. The court said declared the federal income tax to be a direct tax on individuals and this, they said, was forbidden by the Constitution. Taxing income on personal property, said the court, is the same as taxing property, and the Constitution only allows a direct federal tax on property to be levied in proportion to the population of each state. The income tax of 1894 laid a direct tax on citizens, regardless of state boundaries. The Sixteenth Amendment, ratified in February 1913, amended the Constitution and so nullified the Supreme Court's 1895 decision.

7. The Federal Reserve Act divided the country into 12 districts, each with its own Federal Reserve bank. These banks were private but were governed by a Federal Reserve Board, whose members were to be appointed by the president. The Federal Reserve could issue bank notes, or paper currency. It could also govern the amount of credit local member banks could issue and the amount of interest they could charge on loans. The Federal Reserve was created to regulate the supply of

money and credit so they could expand when production slowed and remain stable when production increased.

8. In 1914, Congress passed the Clayton Anti-Trust Act of 1914, which Samuel Gompers called "labor's charter of rights," since it declared that labor unions had never been, in themselves, unlawful combinations; that strikes, boycotts were not, as such, violations of federal law; and that federal courts could not use injunctions (as during the Pullman strike) in labor disputes. Other legislation included a law granting workman's compensation for the federal civil services and a law forbidding interstate commerce in products derived from child labor. This last law the Supreme Court declared unconstitutional.

Essays

Instructions to be given to the students: Write in complete sentences. Underline your thesis. Give three supports or examples that explain why you think what you do and that support your thesis.

1. What is your view on imperialism, particularly U.S. imperialism? Is it a good or an evil? Why?

2. Do we see any of the effects of Roosevelt's presidency and ideas in our own day? Has the country moved away from Roosevel'ts progressivism?

3. What is your view on the social and labor question as described in this chapter? Are the solutions presented realistic? Why or why not?

Sample Test

Please answer the following in complete sentences.

I. Short Essay – Answer two of the following:

1. Describe the different kinds of Progressivism

2. How did the 1902 coal strike illustrate Roosevelt's constitutional views?

3. Describe Roosevelt's views on the family and the dangers that threatened it.

4. Describe Roosevelt's foreign policy.

5. What was the platform of the Progressive party during the election of 1912?

II. Short Answer:

1. Why was American opinion on the side of the Cuban rebels?

2. What sorts of arguments led McKinley to deny Filipino independence?

3. How did the IWW's ranks eventually split?

4. Why did many people think a central bank was needed?

5. How did the Republican Party become the the "conservative" party in America?

Answer Key to the Chapter Test

Students' answers should approximate the following:

I.

1. President Roosevelt perhaps represented on strain of Progressivism. He accepted the "inevitableness of combination in business" and thought it was necessary to "meet it be a corresponding increase in governmental power over big business." He thought government had to be as big or bigger than business, in order to regulate business. William Jennings Bryan represented another strain of Progressivism – one that Roosevelt thought was not really Progressivism at all.

Bryan wanted to see break-up of large trusts and large businesses. He objected as much to big government as he did to big business. Socialists occupied what might be called the "far left" of Progressivism. Less radical than the communists and the anarchists, the socialists worked at the local level to promote municipal ownership of public utilities, such as waterworks and gas and electric plants.

2. In 1902, striking workers in the anthracite coal region of Pennsylvania were demanding higher pay and better working conditions; but owners, led by J.P. Morgan and George F. Baer of the Philadelphia and Reading Railroad, refused to negotiate with them. With the looming threat of a winter without coal, Roosevelt determined that he had to intervene – even though he thought he had no constitutional authority to interfere, since the coal miners were not a trust. He said he could not "more see misery and death come to the great masses of the people in our large cities, and sit by idly, because under ordinary conditions a strike is not a subject for interference by the President, than I could sit by idly and see one man kill another without interference because there is no statutory duty imposed upon the President to interfere in such cases." When the owners derided a proposal of Roosevelt's for arbitration, he, like Grover Cleveland before him, threatened to send in federal troops to operate the mines. Met with a protest that he had no constitutional authority to do this, Roosevelt retorted that "the Constitution was made for the people and not the people for the Constitution." This event indicated that Roosvelt saw the Constitution as a rule that could be set aside when circumstances arose that seriously threatened the good of society.

3. Roosevelt saw the family as the cornerstone of the nation, the basic unit of society. The family, springing from the union of man and woman in marriage, he thought, demanded the assiduous care of both husband and wife. The good of their offspring, he said, is their highest calling. Roosevelt saw the American family in his day as threatened by two evils: a decrease in the birthrate among the "native," Anglo population, and divorce. These, in Roosevelt's mind, presaged disaster for the nation. Roosevelt blamed social conditions – uncontrolled industrialization and urbanization – in part for the decline of family life. He deplored the "ruin of motherhood and childhood by the merciless exploitation of the labor of women and children." And though he asserted that women had a right to education and to careers that hitherto had been closed to them, he wanted to protect their role in the home. He thus opposed those feminists who despised the role of the stay-at-home mother and promoted contraception.

4. Roosevelt thought that because the United States had become "a great nation," it was "forced by the fact of its greatness into relations with the other nations of the earth" and so "must behave as beseems a people with such responsibilities." It should offer other nations "cordial and sincere friendship" in "a spirit of just and generous recognition of all their rights." Nevertheless, the U.S. should demand respect from other nations and thus build up its military strength so that its rights be respected. But Roosevelt was not belligerent. Once he became president, Roosevelt did all he could to avoid war. He had granted Cuba her independence had only intervened once to restore order on the island, as the Platt Amendment allowed the United States president to do. Roosevelt allowed the Philippines to establish a degree of self-rule, though a United States governor still presided over the island nation. Roosevelt supported the formation of The Hague Tribunal, a court to settle international quarrels before they erupted into war. In

1904, he appended the "Roosevelt Corollary" to the Monroe Doctrine that allowed the U.S. to intervene in the affairs of nations in the Americas as an "international police power" if "chronic wrongdoing" occurred in them. He applied this corollary in 1904 when the Dominican Republic reneged on its debts to European creditors. In 1907, the Root-Takahira agreement specified that the United States, Japan, and the European powers would maintain equal trading status with China (the "Open Door" policy) and that the military status of the United States and Japan would remain unchanged in the Pacific. Roosevelt was a peace maker: he brought Russia and Japan to negotiate an end to their war and sign a peace treaty at Portsmouth, New Hampshire, on September 5, 1905. At Algeciras in 1906, Roosevelt mediated a dispute between France and Germany over Morocco.

5. The Progressive Party called for the popular election of United States Senators; the adoption by states of initiative, referendum, and recall; equal suffrage for men and women; popular recall of judicial decisions; and automatic Supreme Court review of any rulings made by lower federal courts declaring a business policing act of a state legislature was unconstitutional. The Progressives favored laws regulating safety and health standards in industry as well as providing for involuntary unemployment.

They called for the "prohibition of child labor"; minimum wage standards; an eight-hour work day for women and young workers; ; and a system of social insurance. The Progressive called for public control of the "remaining forests, coal and oil lands, water powers and other natural resources still in state or National control (except agricultural lands.)"

II.

1. Opinion in the United States was solidly on the side of the rebels because Americans saw them as fighting for independence, just as the English colonists had done in 1776.

2. Economic and strategic arguments moved McKinley to deny Filipino independence. McKinley said the Filipino republic could not keep order and he pushed for annexation.

3. Political differences among the members (there were socialist, anarchist, and trade unionist Wobblies) led eventually to major splits in the IWW's ranks.

4. Many people believed a central bank was needed to maintain uniformity in the issuing of money and credit across the nation.

5. The victory of Woodrow Wilson, a progressive Democrat, in the election of 1912 led to the defection of progressives from the Republican party; and this defection proved to be permanent. Thenceforth, conservatives dominated the Republican Party.

CHAPTER 24: The Second Mexican Revolution

Chapter Overview

♦ Under President Porfírio Díaz, Mexico enjoyed a period of peace. Díaz invited in foreign capital into Mexico and gave American landowners rights to land. He made peace with the Catholic Church, making a secret agreement with the Church in Mexico that would allow him to approve all Church appointments. Due to this, the Church became subservient to the government and alienated herself from the people by allying herself with Díaz. Sectors of the Church in Mexico, however, began to take a serious and critical look at Díaz's society, and Catholics formed Catholic Worker circles and held social justice congresses.

♦ A new transformation came about in Díaz's government due to a group of young men called *científicos*. As a consequence, workers were in grievous want and working conditions were poor. Workers were growing revolutionary, however, as new ideas, including anarchism and socialism, spread to Mexico, inspiring the formation of unions and strikes.

♦ In the south of Mexico, resistance to Díaz's regime was beginning, led by Emiliano Zapata. Zapata organized a defense committee in 1909, after which the villagers of Anencuilco peacefully seized hacienda lands and divided them amongst themselves.

♦ More resistance arose in the form of words from Francisco Madero, who wrote that the country should return to the Constitution of 1857 and Díaz not seek re-election. In 1910, anti-re-electionists nominated Madero as their presidential candidate. *Maderistas* converged on the National Palace in Mexico City to protest the Díaz regime, and Madero was arrested. Two weeks later, Díaz was re-elected.

♦ On his release from prison, Madero fled to Texas, where he declared the elections null and void and published the Plan de San Luis Potosí, calling on the people of Mexico to rise against Díaz. Forces began to gather under Pascual Orozco and Pancho Villa, and on November 27, 1910, they defeated federal troops, thus beginning a full-fledged rebellion.

♦ The *científico* leader, José Limantour, took control of the government in Mexico City, and sought an armistice with the rebel leaders. Madero was willing to sign an armistice but was persuaded not to, and laid down more demands. The revolution ran swiftly towards victory. Díaz's friends and family finally convinced him to resign.

♦ The provisional president, Francisco de la Barra, was not able to carry out the radical provisions of Madero's plan, and many people came to distrust Madero himself. Catholics in Mexico, dissatisfied with the state of things in Mexico, formed the National Catholic Circle and the Guadalupan Workers.

♦ Zapata decided it was time to reignite the revolution. On November 25, 1911, he published the *Plan de Ayala* as the standard of the renewed struggle. On February 9, 1913, the rebellion began.

- After the capture and execution of Madero, Victoriano Huerta became president. Huerta was dissipated and cruel and inspired a new uprising, led by Venustiano Carranza, Alvaro Obregón, and Pancho Villa.

- The revolution began to take an anti-clerical turn. Carranza and Obregón were from the North, where there was little contact with the Catholic Church. Revolutionaries opposition to traditional Mexican culture drew them int an attack on the Church, which they believed hampered Mexico's entrance into American-style prosperity.

- Woodrow Wilson, the president of the United States , disapproved of President Huerta, and began arming Carranza and the Constitutionalist forces. With the aid of the United States, the revolutionaries forced the federal garrison in Mexico City to surrender, and five days later, Obregón marched his army in triumph into the city.

- The overthrow of Huerta, however, did not bring peace to Mexico, and divisions that had plagued the revolutionary forces became clearly pronounced. The Villisats and the Carranzistas accused each other of betraying the struggle. Carranza suggested holding a convention of rebel leaders in Mexico City where he could control it. General Obregón told Villa agreed to hold the convention in Aguascalientes, where Villa could control it. Villa and Zapata then marched on Mexico City, beginning a civil war.

- In the United States, business interests with property in Mexico, as well as Catholics, urged President Wilson to intervene in the Mexican civil war. President Wilson gave his support to Carranza, causing Villa to turn on the Americans, who, he thought, had betrayed him.

- By the spring of 1916, most regions recognized Carranza as provisional president, but the country was far from peaceful. Carranza could not keep order and alienated many of his cabinet. In the autumn Carranza called for a constitutional convention to revise the Constitution of 1857. The new Constitution of 1917 was very controversial, especially in regards to the Church. The government from then on became anti-clerical.

- Carranza used his power against the radicals, which caused the radical elements to flare up. When Carranza tried to break a railroad strike in Sonora, the Sonoran governor, Adolfo de la Huerta, declared his state's independence, and he and Plutarco Calles issued a plan calling for the removal of Carranza. Carranza fled, and Obregón and his army marched into Mexico City, where Obregón was sworn in as president.

- Obregón appeared to be a friend to labor and radical agrarian aspirations, and businessmen in the United States complained he was a "Bolshevist." Obregón needed U.S. support if his hand-picked candidate for president, Plutarco Calles, were to succeed him without trouble in 1923, so he gave in to Washington's demands, and President Calvin Coolidge recognized his government in August 1923. A rebellion broke out over the election of 1923. The rebellion was quickly crushed with the aid of the United States, and Calles became president.

- Calles ruled as an absolute dictator and remained resolutely in opposition to the Church. He vigorously applied the anti-clerical articles of the 1917 constitution. On June 14, 1926, he decreed that priests who wore their clerical garb in public were to be fined, and he closed seminaries, monasteries, and Church-run institutions.

- Faithful Catholics refused to submit to this violence. The lawyer Anacleto Gonzáles Flores formed the Union Popular to unite Catholics. In the autumn of 1925, Pope Pius XI denounced Mexico's government but did not call on Mexican Catholics to undertake political resistance. Some Catholics, however, thought no peaceful resistance was possible, and Rene Capistrán Garza founded the *Liga Defensora de Libertad Religiosa* (National League for the Defense of Religious Liberty) in 1924 against the government's anti-Catholic measures.

- When a newspaper published an interview with the archbishop of Mexico City wherein he condemned the anti-clerical legislation of the Constitution of 1917, Calles was outraged and issued a penal code that laid down penalties for those who violated the anti-clerical articles. The Church responded with defiance, and on July 14, the bishops gave their support to an economic boycott. When that did not work, the bishops received the approval of the pope to place an interdict on Mexico, causing all public worship to cease.

- Beginning in August 1926, spontaneous armed uprisings occurred throughout Mexico. On January 1, 1927, the *Liga Defensora* issued a call to arms. Under leaders such as Miguel Hernandez and Victoriano Ramirez, insurgent forces fought the federal army. The federals named the insurgents *Cristeros*.

- The rebellion suffered from setbacks and would have died in the summer of 1927 had not Victoriano Ramirez, nicknamed *El Catorce*, rekindled the rebellion. The *Liga* decided the scattered Cristero forces needed coordination and military discipline, and Enrique Gorostieta Velarde took on the command of the rebellion, training the *Cristeros* into a disciplined army.

- In 1929, the American ambassador, Dwight Morrow, encouraged Calles to come to an agreement with the *Cristeros*. With the support of the pope, the government and the Mexican Church came to an agreement, the *arreglos*, announced on June 17, 1929. The Mexican Church's woes were far from over, however, as the government violated the *arreglos* by executing Cristero leaders.

- Though new presidents came into office, Calles remained the sole power in Mexico. In 1931 the federal government enacted a new wave of anticlerical legislation, closing churches and enforcing "socialist education." This inspired a new revolt among former *Cristeros*, waged also against the Church, which they thought had betrayed them.

- A new party formed with the elections 1929, the *Partido Nacional Revolucionario* (PNR). A new power structure in the PNR began to diminish Calles' power in 1933. When Lázaro Cárdenas became president, he waged political war against Calles. In 1936 Cárdenas deported Calles and Luis Morones to Texas.

- In 1936, representatives of Mexico, the United States, and other Latin American countries met in conference, agreeing that no American states should intervene in the internal affairs of another American state.

- Though anti-Catholic himself, Cárdenas in 1936 denounced those who placed the religious problem above all the problems of the national program, allowing churches to reopen throughout Mexico. It still remained a crime for priests to appear in public in clerical attire, however. This inspired a new movement among Catholics, *Sinarquismo*. The *Sinarquistas* and other groups formed a political party, the *Partido Acción Nacional* (National Action Party), or PAN.

- The election of Ávila Camacho in 1940 was the first peaceful transition of power in Mexico in many years. With the election of Camacho, the Mexican revolution effectively ended.

What Students Should Know

1. **The achievements of Porfirio Díaz**

Díaz's dictatorship began in 1876 and continued (except for one four-year period when he did not hold office but still possessed political power) until 1911. During this period, there was mostly peace: Mexico did not suffer from any major civil wars. Díaz paid foreign railroad companies to lay down track in Mexico. The railroads built, however, benefited North American commerce rather than the people of Mexico. Díaz gave over most public lands to real estate corporations, generals, politicians, and U.S. capitalists, thus enriching foreigners and rich and powerful Mexicans. Because Díaz's policies, most of the mineral and oil wealth of Mexico passed into the hands of U.S. capitalists.

Díaz's government enforced laws that forbade anyone but individuals to own land and this led to a loss of their communal lands (*ejidos*) by Indian tribes. When tribes resisted, the government crushed them. The sale of government lands and the confiscation of Indian lands led to a great disparity of wealth in Mexico. Though a few native Mexicans profited, foreigners controlled most of the plantations. Because Díaz placated members of the middle class by giving them well-paying government jobs, the government bureaucracy in Mexico grew dramatically during the Díaz years.

2. **The state of the Church in Mexico under Díaz**

Under the influence of his wife, and her father, the interior secretary, Díaz even made peace with the Church. Díaz and Mexico's archbishop, Antonio Pelagio Labastida y Dávalos, reached a secret agreement. In return for non-enforcement of the anti-clerical Laws of the Reform, Labastida agreed to allow Díaz to approve all church appointments. The archbishop would also see to it that priests preached submission to the Díaz government. The secret agreement allowed the Church in Mexico once again to acquire property. The Church built schools; men's and women's monasteries and convents spread across the land; the number of clergy rose dramatically. These clergy began mobilizing the laity, oversaw the expansion of the Catholic press as well as of Catholic education. Yet, the Church became subservient to the dictator, who could enforce the Laws of the Reform against her any time the bishops or priests fell out of line. Allying herself with Díaz, too, eventually alienated the Church from many of the people who suffered under the dictatorship. But if the Catholic Church in Mexico did not directly challenge the Díaz regime, sectors of it began taking a serious and critical look at the society Don Porfirio had created. Inspired by German Catholic social thought and, more importantly, Pope Leo XIII's 1890 social encyclical, *Rerum Novarum*, the younger generation of priests and laity began to turn their attention to questions of social justice. They formed Catholic Workers Circles and held social justice congresses in first decade of the 20th century.

3. **Who the *científicos* were**

The científicos were young men (of the creole class) who thought the good of Mexico lay in the material progress that came through the application of science to social and economic life. Believing the Mexican people incapable of Liberal democracy, the *científicos* enthusiastically embraced the Díaz dictatorship. Civilization they thought could only come to Mexico through the rule of the creole aristocracy and the importation of foreign capital. José Ives Limantour, the director of the treasury, was the leader of the *científicos* after 1895. Under Limantour, the Mexican economy prospered. For the first time in history, the Mexican government was bringing in more revenue than it was paying out. Railroads were nationalized; public works were built. Illiteracy decreased. Poetry and the arts flourished. Still, Mexico was beset by dire poverty and an extreme concentration of wealth into the hands of a very few, largely because of the policies favored by the *científicos*

4. The condition of the Mexican rural poor and proletariat under Díaz

The rural poor were reduced to practical slavery and suffered from ignorance, want, and hunger. Without their *ejidos*, Indian peons had only the pittance paid them by rich *hacendados* to rely on for their subsistence. Under Limantour prices had doubled; and with their buying power drastically decreased, the peons sank into wretched poverty. The poor, working in the factories, though better paid than the rural workers, were still in grievous want. But they were growing revolutionary, embracing anarchism and socialism. Between 1900 and 1910, these movements inspired the formation of unions and strikes. The Díaz government brutally suppressed these strikes.

5. Who Emiliano Zapata was and how he rose against the Díaz regime

Emiliano Zapata was the son of a *mestizo* sharecropper and small landowner in Morelos, a state just south of Mexico City. He was a successful horse trainer, but he abandoned this profession to fight for justice

for peons of Morelos. Though devoted to *Juárismo*, Zapata did not disdain the Catholic faith. Elected to lead the defense committee of Anencuilco in September 1909, Zapata decided to meet head on the threat of the hacienda, *El Hospital*, which was encroaching on Indian lands. Under Zapata's lead, the villagers peacefully reoccupied land the hacienda had seized and then divided it among themselves.

6. Who Francisco Madero was, and the course of the revolution he led

Francisco Madero came from a rich Mexican family that controlled vast lands in the northern state of Coahuila. In 1908, Madero wrote a book in which he suggested that the country return to the Constitution of 1857 and that Díaz not seek reelection. The book made Madero a popular figure. In April 1910, a convention of anti-re-electionists nominated Madero as their presidential candidate. A month after 30,000 *Maderistas* converged on the National Palace in Mexico City to protest the Díaz regime. In June, Díaz had Madero arrested and imprisoned. But in October 1910, Madero, released on bail, fled to Texas. There he declared the elections null and void, published the *Plan de San Luis Potosí*, and proclaimed November 20 as the day the people of Mexico should rise against Díaz. But when the rebellion did not come off, Madero went to New Orleans to set sail for Europe. But then, in the northern desert state of Chihuahua, Pascual Orozco organized *vaqueros* into a guerilla force. He was joined by the bandit leader, Pancho Villa (Doroteo Arango), and together they scored an important victory against federal forces. On February 14, 1911, Madero joined the rebels in Chihuahua. In the south, on March 11, Zapata was scoring victories in Morelos. By April 1911, guerilla forces throughout

Mexico had risen against Díaz. While the government (under Limantour's direction) tried to negotiate with the rebels, Orozco and Villa took Ciudad Juárez, Zapata seized the city of Cuautla, and state capitals fell to rebel *guerrilleros*. At last, Díaz resigned and on May 26, 1911, Díaz left Mexico City.

7. **Agrarian reform and it role in the revolution**

Agrarian reform referred to the redistribution of land to the poor from whom, by government polices and the machinations of capitalists, it had been taken. Agrarian reform became one of the central issues of the Mexican revolution. Madero's *Plan de San Luis Potosi* called for agrarian reform, but, given his connections with the wealthy families of Mexico and the *científicos*, it was unlikely that he would carry it out. Zapata, for one, did not think Madero was serious about reform.

8. **Catholic response to the social question in Mexico**

Not all Catholics were dissatisfied with the state of things under Díaz; some looked upon Don Porfirio as a defense against those forces that would seek to destroy the Church. Other Catholics, however, hoped to form a political party; but these Catholics, being socially prominent and politically well-connected, were mistrusted by Catholics who sought to apply the social doctrine of the Church to Mexico. These formed the *Operarios Guadalupanos* (OG – Guadalupan Workers), which, between 1909 and the end of 1911, spread to 20 states and federal territories, mostly in central and western Mexico. These groups, formed of small member cells, were not under centralized control; but, rooted as they were in local parish structures, they were able to form a network that allowed

them to take concerted action. Parish OG groups provided study groups on social problems, artisan and worker circles, and health care services. Some cells promoted public morality through theater, while others published newspapers. In 1909, the OG opened two rural credit and savings establishments to provide affordable credit to the poor. The OG journal, *Restauración Social* (Social Restoration), discussed such social justice issues as what constitutes a just family wage. OG members studied the social encyclicals of Pope Leo XIII and published newsletters analyzing Mexico's social problems in light of Catholic social justice teaching. Some solutions were radical; for instance, in June 1914, an OG leader, José Encarnación Preciado, suggested that social Catholics espouse an agrarian reform that would divide large haciendas among workers, who would contribute to bonds that would reimburse former owners. Politically, the OG hoped for a more democratic state structure, resting on universal manhood suffrage. It hoped for a government, controlled by Catholic laity, that would respect the institutional Catholic Church in Mexico as a freely operating body in the greater society. In a word, the OG favored what has been called "Christian democracy" – a form of society where the Church and state have clearly defined spheres but are united in mutual cooperation and recognition. Shortly after Díaz's fall from power, members of the OG and other Catholics formed what has been called Mexico's first modern political party – the *Partido Católico Nacional* (PCN – the National Catholic Party). During the brief period of its existence (1910-1913), the PCN was able to take advantage of the OG's parish-based network to form an effective political movement.

Since 1918, Anacleto Gonzáles Flores, a lawyer in Jalisco, had been writing books and articles detailing his vision of a Catholic social and political order for Mexico. Flores opposed democracy (he thought Mexico was not ready for it) but called for the popular methods of individual sacrifice and non-violent civil disobedience to oppose the government. To unite Catholics, he formed the *Union Popular*, whose journal, *Gladium* (Latin for "sword"), was reaching 80,000 readers by 1924.

9. How Madero's policies inspired new uprisings

Madero was committed to a restoration of the freedoms guaranteed under the Constitution of 1857 – freedom of the press, of conscience, of assembly, etc. – and he wanted all Mexicans to exercise full voting rights. He wanted to prune back severely the privileges of foreign capitalists. But Madero was heavily influenced by his family, wealthy landowners. Though Madero himself did not proceed violently against his enemies, his brother, Gustavo, took up the repressive policies of Díaz. Madero's relatives carried on the *científico* policies from the days of Díaz. Yet, Madero's freedom of speech and of the press encouraged more radical elements to organize. Trade unions again appeared. In the capital, the House of the World Worker became a center for intellectuals who promoted socialist and Marxist ideas. The toleration of such radicalism alarmed wealthy Mexicans and foreign investors. Zapata's conviction that Madero was not serious about agrarian reform led him to publish the *Plan de Ayala* on November 25, 1911. the plan called for the redistribution of one-third of lands, timber, and water to the landless, with compensation to the owners. But those "landlords, *cientificos*, or bosses" who opposed the plan in any way would lose all their lands, which would go to pensions for widows and orphans of those who died in the revolution. Government manipulation of the election of 1912 turned the National Catholic Party against the president when Liberals persuaded the Mexican government to annul the results of many of the elections where the PCN had prevailed. Anti-Madero forces had the support of the U.S. ambassador, Henry Lane Wilson (who was associated with American business interests opposed to Madero). He backed a coup led by Bernardo Reyes in association with Madero's general, Victoriano Huerta. On February 18, 1913, the palace guard arrested Madero, and Huerta, Diaz, and Wilson signed the Compact of the Citadel in the U.S. embassy. Huerta became provisional president. Madero was killed while allegedly attempting to escape.

10. The character of Huerta's regime and the rebellion that arose against him

Victoriano Huerta was a drunkard, treacherous, and cruel. To assure his absolute sway over Mexico, Huerta replaced several state governors with generals faithful to him. He conducted a purge of congress, jailing over a hundred representatives who opposed his regime. Huerta secured the PCN's acquiescence to his regime by promising the party 100 seats in the congress and pledging to uphold the results if a PCN candidate won the planned presidential election in October 1913. Though the party had expressed disapproval of Huerta, it struck a bargain with him, thus assuring its demise. Huerta's brutality inspired new uprisings. Venustiano Carranza, the governor of Coahuila in the north, a conservative constitutionalist, issued his *Plan de Guadalupe* demanding the overthrow of Huerta and the restoration of the Constitution of 1857. In Sonora, General

Alvaro Obregón organized a revolutionary army. To assert his leadership of the revolution, Carranza called himself "First Chief of the Constitutionalist Army." Still, he forged an alliance with Obregón and established his government at Nogales in Sonora. Pancho Villa joined the rebellion, but operated independently. With his *dorados*, Villa seized control of all Chihuahua and established his government at Chihuahua City. In the south Emiliano Zapata operated alone and extended his sway towards the Pacific seacoast, into Puebla and the state of México, and into the federal district itself. Throughout Mexico, small-time generals were rising, overthrowing their local *hacendados* and political bosses. In Mexico City, Huerta's closing of the House of the World Worker in May had either forced radical intellectuals into hiding or into revolutionary ranks. A number of radicals went north to Carranza to serve him in what became known as the "Red Battalion." Others went over to Zapata. These intellectuals forced Carranza to adopt radical goals for his revolution. When in the summer of 1913, Villa acknowledged Carranza as his revolutionary chief, the two leaders declared that the revolution would be directed against both the dominance of the wealthy landholders and the power of the Church. When Huerta refused to recognize the October 1913 elections, President Woodrow Wilson decided to support Carranza's "Constitutionalist" forces. With American arms, the Constitutionalists were able to defeat Huerta's federal forces. When Villa broke with Carranza, the combined armies of Alvaro Obregón and Carranza's general, Pablo Gonzalez, advanced against the capital, capturing it on August 10, 1914.

11. The anti-clericalism of the northern revolutionaries

Both northerners, Carranza and Obregón came from a population that in many areas had had little contact with the Catholic Church. The influence of both Spanish culture and the Church had been intense in what is called "Old Mexico," but had been vestigial in the regions of the far northern frontier – Sonora, Chihuahua, Coahuila, and Nuevo León. Because of their isolation from Spanish culture and the Church, the men of the north were inclined to admire the United States. To make Mexico more like Anglo-America, the northern revolutionaries thought they had to weaken and destroy the power of the Catholic Church. The men of the north thought Protestantism was responsible for the political, and economic prosperity of the U.S.; thus, Carranza and Obregón encouraged Protestant proselytisizing and the establishment of Protestant congregations in Mexico, and supported legislation to weaken the power of the Church.

12. Divisions among the revolutionary forces and how Carranza took control of the revolution

Following the overthrow of Huerta, the divisions among the revolutionary forces became more pronounced. Obregón installed Carranza as provisional president, but then agreed with Villa that Carranza should hold power only until elections could be held. Obregón and Villa agreed, too, to hold a convention in Aguascalientes (within Villa's sphere of influence); but after Villa attempted to have Obregón killed, the general joined Carranza. The *Villistas* and *Zapatistas* held a convention at Aguascalientes and named a provisional president of the republic. In late 1914, they captured Mexico City; and while Zapata withdrew back to Morelos, Villa remained in the capital with his puppet president. Needing the support of the people, on January 6, 1915, Carranza decreed a series of agrarian reforms and formed an alliance with the House of the World Worker, which provided six "red battalions" to fight for Carranza. These moves induced U.S. President Wilson to throw his support to Villa. But with Obregón's decisive defeat of Villa at Celaya in April 1915, the U.S. switched its support to Carranza. With Villa now become a bandit annoyance and Zapata forced into the *sierra* of Morelos, most regions of Mexico by spring 1916 recognized Carranza as provisional president.

13.   The Constitution of 1917 and its provisions

In the autumn of 1916, President Carranza called for a constitutional convention to revise the Constitution of 1857. Carranza merely wanted to strengthen the power of the president, but he was unable to dominate the convention, which met at Querétaro in December. The party backed by Alvaro Obregón controlled the convention and, in six short weeks, produced a constitution notable for its rejection of old Liberal *laissez-faire* business doctrines, its espousal of agrarian reform, and its bitter anti-clericalism. The constitution promulgated in 1917 decreed that no individuals or corporate entities could directly own land, and especially, water and subsoil minerals in Mexico. All land belonged to the whole people of Mexico, even if it was divided up among many users. This meant that the state (the representative of the Mexican people) could take land (though with compensation) from its current owners if the good of "the people" demanded it. The constitution declared that seizures of *ejidos* under *Ley Lerdo* were null and void, and, if they needed to, *ejideros* could take land from neighboring haciendas. Article 123 of the new constitution

established some of the most progressive labor legislation in the world. Among other measures, the article limited the workday to eight hours, abolished child labor, declared the right of workers to organize unions, and called on employers to give workers a share in profits. Both articles 27 and 123 assured that workers and peasants would support the new government. The Constitution of 1917 allowed the state to seize Church property, decreeing church buildings the property of the state. Priests had to register with the government; state governments could limit the number of priests within their jurisdictions, and foreigners could not serve as priests in Mexico. The constitution prohibited monastic vows, outlawed monastic orders, forbade the holding of public religious ceremonies outside of church buildings, and sought to eradicate the influence of religion in education.

14.   Why the Constitution of 1917 was anti-clerical

Since the days of Díaz, the Church had gone far in restoring her fortunes in Mexico, and just as important, many Catholics, inspired by Leo XIII's *Rerum Novarum*, were turning their attention to the needs and concerns of modern men. The formation of the Catholic Party had been part of this awakening, as was the founding of its auxiliary association, the League of Catholic Students. The League established youth centers in cities throughout Mexico, as well as the Catholic Student Center in Mexico City. In January of 1913, the Catholic Great Workers' Diet that met at Zamora suggested labor reforms similar to those later enshrined in Article 123 of the 1917 constitution; and in Mexico City the Jesuit priest, Alfredo Méndez Medina, founded Mexico's first real trade union. The bishops moreover were strongly supportive of such labor organizing. Also in 1913, Catholics had formed the *Asociacion Catholica de la Juventud Mexicana* (ACJM – the Catholic Association of Mexican Youth) whose brightest lights were to be two young laymen: Anacleto Gonzáles Flores and Rene Capistrán Garza. Yet, despite this evident concern with social justice, the revolutionaries (with the exception of Zapata) opposed the Church, pointing to the bishops' alliance with Díaz and the Catholic Party's agreement with Huerta. As has been noted (summary point 11, above), the revolutionaries saw the Church as a hindrance to progress in Mexico.

15. Carranza as president and his fall from power

Carranza was not the author of the more radical provisions of the Constitution of 1917, and he did nothing to enforce them – both to avoid conflicts with foreign governments and because he had no desire to do so. Both the Church and the landowners resisted the government's reforms. Carranza did nothing to redistribute lands to the peasants and he actively suppressed workers' attempts to organize unions. He closed the House of the World Worker in Mexico City and arrested one of its most powerful leaders, Luis Morones. But in 1918, Luis Morones, released from prison, travelled to Coahuila, helped organize a labor union that was to function as an arm of Carranza's power. Morones became the leader of this union, the *Confederación Regional Obrera Mexicana* (Regional Confederation of Mexican Workers – CROM). Morones and a secret cadre of leaders, called *Grupo Acción*, came to control CROM. With Villa no longer a power broker and Zapata dead (Carranza's government arranged the treachery by which Zapata was killed in April 1919), Carranza prepared to

make sure his chosen candidate won the election in 1920. But when he tried to break a railroad strike in Sonora, the governor, Adolfo de la Huerta, declared his state's independence. In April 1920, de la Huerta and Plutarco Elías Calles, the former governor of Sonora, issued a plan calling for the removal of Carranza and the appointment of a provisional president until elections could be held. They were joined by Obregón and met no opposition, for Carranza's closest allies had deserted him. Carranza fled the capital and later was murdered in a remote Indian village. De la Huerta was sworn in as provisional president and served until November, when Alvaro Obregón became president.

16. The government under President Obregón

President Obregón was able to make peace with the *Zapatistas* and buy off Pancho Villa. He a friend to labor and radical agrarian aspirations – for which businessmen in the United States complained that he was a "Bolshevist." But though Obregón did not suppress organized labor, he recognized only one legal union, the CROM of Luis Morones, who used murder and violence against rivals and business owners, and enriched himself and his *Grupo Acción* members at the expense of workers. Though Obregóm established the *Confederación Nacional Campesina* (National Farm Workers' Confederation), he did little more to further agrarian reform. In all, Obregón's government distributed to Indian villages only a small portion of the lands that remained in private hands. Obregón encouraged education and entrusted his program to José Vasconcelos, who was committed to *Hispanidad,* the ideal of Spanish culture, built over 1,000 schools in rural villages throughout Mexico, and had translated great European classics into

Spanish. Though Obregón and the men who surrounded him used socialist terminology, their policies were anything but Marxist or Bolshevist. Under Obregón, a new class of Mexican capitalists sprang up; and though many *hacendados* held on to their wealth, a new ruling class merely replaced the old. Obregón formed a dictatorship that was native-born Mexican. He ruled in a manner reminiscent of Don Porfirio, playing off rival groups against each other. In the states his governors were, more often than not, corrupt. The military maintained its time-honored privileges. Though he had been among the principal supporters of the anti-clerical provisions of the Constitution of 1917, as president, Obregón adopted a more or less tolerant attitude toward the Church. Yet, Obregón continued to back Protestant missionary endeavors in Mexico, and his government gave direct support to Protestant missions. Obregón long had a rocky relationship with the U.S. government, which refused to recognize his presidency because he wouldn't formally guarantee that the Mexican government (in accordance with the 1917 constitution) would not seize lands held by foreigners. Finally, to assure that his hand-picked successor, Plutarco Elías Calles, could succeed him, Obregón agreed to Washington's demands. President Calvin Coolidge recognized Obregón's government in August 1923.

17.   The government of Plutarco Elías Calles

At first, Calles was more determined to realize the radical goals of the Constitution of 1917 than Obregón had been. For instance, Calles distributed eight million acres to 1,500 villages, he established agricultural banks to provide loans for the new farmers, and more firmly allied himself with labor than had Obregón. But it was not long before the basic corruption of Calles' regime undid his would-be radicalism. Calles ruled as an absolute dictator and was ruthless to those who opposed him. Though he called himself a socialist, Calles little by little warmed to Liberal capitalist ideas and policies. His closest associates were wealthy capitalists, and so it was not surprising that he began to promote a native Mexican capitalism instead of the agrarianism for which the revolution had supposedly been fought. This change was wrought, in part, through Calles' friendship with the new U.S. ambassador to Mexico, Dwight Morrow. Partly through Morrow's influence, Calles redirected the revolution away from agrarianism and towards the interests of the middle class and the wealthy. The benefits of Calles' native capitalism accrued largely to his closest associates. Even Calles' agricultural banks benefited mainly wealthy landowners. CROM's Luis Morones, whom Calles appointed secretary of industry, used his office to enrich himself and his *Grupo Acción* cronies. Calles vigorously applied the anti-clerical articles of the constitution. Priests could be imprisoned for five years if they criticized the government. Calles closed seminaries, seized Church-run orphanages and homes for the aged, closed monasteries of male and female religious, and attempted to establish a national, nonpapal Church. Governors in states followed Calles' example. Calles had intended Obregón to succeed him in the presidency; but though Obregón won the election in the summer of 1928, he was assassinated on July 17, 1928. Calles faced the crisis by summoning state governors and military leaders to the capital where he pledged that, from thenceforth, Mexico would not be ruled by personalities but by laws. Calles pledged to steer Mexico toward true democracy. Congress then appointed Emilio Portes Gil, as provisional president of the republic. Calles, however, remained at the center of power — self-dubbed the *jefe maximo* (supreme leader) of the revolution.

Gil appeared more revolutionary than Calles had been. He supported independent unions, but this was only to crush CROM. Once CROM was severely weakened, the government (really, Calles) proceeded to smash independent unions. In the election of 1929, *Obregonistas* and *Callistas* formed the *Partido Nacional Revolucionario* (PNR) to be the sole political party of Mexico. It would run presidential candidates who would be mere fronts for Plutarco Calles. In 1930, having fallen fully under Morrow's influence, Calles declared the revolution's agrarian policy a failure, and the ruling president, Órtiz Rubio, ended further land distribution to Indian villages.

18. How Catholics and the Catholic Church responded to Calles' anti-clerical measures

Faithful Catholics refused to submit to Calles' violence. In the autumn of 1925, Pope Pius XI denounced Mexico's revolutionary government, but he did not call on Mexican Catholics to undertake direct political resistance; rather he said they should concentrate on actions of a more religious, social, and cultural character. Some Mexican Catholics, however, concluded that nothing but political action would stop Calles from destroying the Catholic Church in Mexico. The *Liga Nacional Defensora de Libertad Religiosa* (National League for the Defense of Religious Liberty), founded by René Capistran Garza in 1924, took a combative stance against the government's anti-Catholic measures. On July 2, 1926 the government issued a penal code that laid down penalties for those who violated the constitution's anti-clerical articles. He insisted that all priests in Mexico register with the government – a

measure preparatory to exile, or worse. He deported 200 foreign born priests and religious. In response, the *Liga* (supported by the bishops) called for an economic boycott. When this did not work, Mexico's bishops (with the pope's support) placed an interdict on Mexico, beginning July 31, 1926.

19. The course of the *Cristero* rebellion

In response to the interdict, from August to September 1926, spontaneous armed uprisings occurred, north of the capital, in west-central Mexico. The *Liga* decided to try to organize a full-scale rebellion, and on January 1, 1927, Capistran Garza issued a call to arms. Anacleto González Flores, though he had been urging peaceful means, gave his approval to the rebellion, and thus the *Union Popular* entered the fight, as did many ranchers and peasants. The insurgents could not at first beat the federal army until, in the Pacific coastal state of Colima, the ex-seminarian and leader of the ACJM, Enrique de Jesús Ochoa, repulsed a federal army. Under leaders such as José Reyes Vega and Victoriano Ramirez, *Cristero* forces (so called because of their battle cry, *Viva Cristo Rey!*) won significant victories in Guanajuato and Jalisco. To gather arms, an underground arms network grew up in Mexico City to supply the insurgents. Women, members of the "Brigades of St. Joan of Arc," strapped gun belts under their dresses, passed through federal check points, and crossed the lines to deliver ammunition to the rebels. Capistrán Garza went to the United States to solicit funds to purchase more arms. In the regions they controlled, some *Cristero* leaders levied taxes on the people. They requisitioned the goods of large landowners. They attacked trains. Some *Cristero* commanders (but not all) abducted wealthy men and demanded ransom for them. But, beginning in March

392 Chapter 24: The Second Mexican Revolution

1927, the *Cristero* rebellion began suffering setbacks. In March 1927 police apprehended Flores in Guadaljara. On April 1, 1927, Flores, with four comrades, was executed. Then On April 19, 1927, Padre José Reyes Vega lost his brother in a raid the priest led against a train and in revenge ordered several train cars doused with gasoline and set afire, killing 51 civilians. This act turned public opinion against the *Cristeros* and the rebellion nearly came to end, in part because of Garza's inability to raise funds in the U.S. (on account of which he resigned from the *Liga* in July 1927). Without arms, the rebellion could not continue, and by summer it appeared that it was over. But then Ramirez rekindled the rebellion in the Los Altos region of Jalisco There he found ready followers; for, not only had Los Altos all along been the center of the rebellion, but its people had suffered harsh repression by the government. The *Liga Defensora* turned thus to a retired general, Enrique Gorostieta Velarde, to take on overall command of the rebellion, though Gorostieta did not embrace the aims of the *Cristeros*. Nevertheless, he turned the ragged bands of *Cristeros* into a disciplined army and their forces grew to between 40,000 and 50,000 men and, throughout 1928, defeated federal forces time and again on the field of battle – and this, despite the fact that the United States was supplying the federals with arms. But U.S. ambassador Dwight Morrow urged Calles and President Portes Gil to come to an understanding with the Church. Father John J. Burke, the legal advisor to the United States bishops, supported Morrow's reconciliation effort. In 1929, Morrow and Burke arranged a secret meeting between themselves, the pope's delegate, exiled Msgr. Leopoldo Ruiz y Flores, bishop of Michoacán, and Portes Gil. With Morrow as facilitator and the warm support of Pope Pius XI, the government and the Mexican Church

at last came to an agreement – *los arreglos*, "the arrangements." If the rebellion ended, the government said it would grant amnesty to all *Cristeros* who laid down arms; it pledged to restore their residences to priests and bishops, require civil registry of only some of the clergy, and allow religious instruction in churches (though not in schools). The *arreglos* were announced on June 27, 1929, and the interdict was lifted. The rebellion ended in the summer of 1929.

20. **The character of the *Cristeros***

Some *Cristero* leaders joined the insurgents to further their own aims. Even some of the rebellion's true adherents had mixed motives. But it was the religious motive that was paramount. And though middle class, professional men were central to the rebellion; the rank and file of the *Cristero* insurgent army were drawn mostly from the peasant classes. Though most were not formally educated, the *Cristeros* had a rich and evocative oral culture. Many of them taught themselves to read and indulged, not only in devotional books, but textbooks on law and even astronomy. Some among the peasant *Cristero* leaders – when circumstances called them to it – discovered an aptitude for political organization. To maintain order in the liberated regions of Jalisco, Colima, Zacatecas, and Michoacán, *Cristero* leaders had to establish governments that, though led by military men, were nevertheless democratic in character. Religion inspired these civil governments to crackdown on immoral behavior, including speculation in trade. "Sacrificing themselves for the Cause of God" – this phrase aptly sums up how the *Cristeros* saw themselves. And though not all *Cristeros* were strict in their observance of their faith, they were men committed to their Catholic religion, which they encapsulated in the phrase, "Kingship of

Christ." They did not rise up against the government because of any natural proclivity for revolution, for these peasants had a deep regard for constituted authority and were profoundly patriotic. They rose because the civil authority had dared to assert itself against *Cristo Rey*. Calles, they thought, was the servant of Freemasonry, Protestantism, and the United States. The *Cristeros* saw themselves as the defenders of the Church, joined in the epic battle that had first pitted the Archangel Michael against the enemy of mankind.

21. The aftermath of the *Cristero* rebellion

No sooner had the *arreglos* been issued, ending the *Cristero* rebellion, than the government violated them by ordering the execution, on July 3, 1929, of the *Cristero* leader, Padre Aristeo Pedroza. By the end of 1929, the government had executed all but two of the *Cristero* leaders in Guanajuato and Zacatecas. Between 1929 and 1935, 5,000 *Cristeros*, officers and men, were executed. Many of those who survived fled into the desert, tried to lose themselves in large cities, found refuge in states with governors sympathetic to their plight, or crossed the border into the United States.

In 1931, the federal government undertook to limit the number of priests in Mexico. In response, Pope Pius XI issued the encyclical, *Acerba Animi*, condemning the violation of the *arreglos* while calling on the faithful to submit to the government. But riots and priest shootings increased. State governors closed churches. By 1935, only 305 authorized priests remained to minister to the millions of Catholics throughout the entire Republic of Mexico. In 1934, Calles issued his *Grito de Guadalajara*, calling on the government to enforce "socialist education." This inspired a new revolt among about 7,500 former *Cristeros* called the "Second," in which they waged war not just against the state, but the Church, which many *Cristeros* felt had betrayed them in 1929 by signing on to the *arreglos*. The Second was both a terrorist and guerrilla struggle. Among its victims were school teachers.

22. How Calles fell from power

Younger men who had grown up during the revolution were not content to see the struggle end in a triumph for capitalism.

Key Terms at a Glance

interdict: a sanction or punishment placed by the Church on a city or region. When a land is under interdict, no public rites of the Church, including public Masses, may lawfully be said. Priests, however, may privately administer necessary sacraments.

Bolshevism: the doctrine of the Bolshevists, who espoused Marxist Communism and sought the violent overthrow of capitalism

científico: a member of a group of officials in Mexico who advocated the practical application of scientific methods to problems in society and industry

Plan de Ayala: Emiliano Zapata's plan that called for land redistribution in favor of the peons

Cristero: a member of the insurgent army which fought against Calles' enforcement of the anti-clerical articles of the Constitution of 1917

Beginning in 1933, these men, who were heavily influenced by Communist theories, grew more influential in the PNR. Seeking to appease these young leftists, Calles lent his support to the candidacy of Lázaro Cárdenas in the election of 1934. President Cárdenas undertook an all-out war against the *Callistas*. The new president pushed agrarian reform, sympathized with strikes, and closed illegal gambling houses owned by Calles' friends. Cárdenas dismissed Calles' hand-picked cabinet members, and by forming coalitions with various anti-Calles groups, gradually isolated the *jefe maximo* in the PNR. In April 1936, Cárdenas deported both Calles and Luis Morones to Texas.

23. The presidency of Lázaro Cárdenas

Cárdenas returned to the more radical roots of the revolution. He reorganized the PNR, renaming it *Partido Revolucionario Institutional* (PRI) – the Institutional Revolutionary Party – to represent peasants, workers, and the army. Cárdenas advanced agrarian reform like no other Mexican president had before him. In 1910, 95 percent of the land had been held by *hacendados*; by 1940, that percentage had shrunk to 60 percent. To increase Mexico's ability to feed its population, Cárdenas encouraged better agricultural methods and established cooperatives. Bolstered by the conclusion of the Buenos Aires conference in 1936, where the United States agreed that no American state should intervene in the internal affairs of another American state, Cárdenas proceeded against foreign-owned petroleum companies who refused to appoint Mexicans to managerial positions, and in May 1938, he confiscated all foreign-owned oil properties in Mexico, nationalizing them into Mexican Petroleum. Though a virulent anti-clerical, Cárdenas denounced those who focused overly much on the religion question, and this

denunciation led in several states to a lifting of some of the restrictions against the Church. Though anti-clerical laws remained, most were not enforced. Indeed, relations between the government and the Church improved in the late '30s, with the Church coming out in favor of many government policies, including the nationalization of oil. Though Cárdenas was accused of being a Communist, he did not call for state ownership of all industries and seemed to favor employee ownership of business.

24. What *Sinarquismo* was

Sinarquismo was movement that arose among former *Cristeros* and other Catholics. The *Sinarquistas* insisted that Mexico should acknowledge the Catholic religion and the country's Spanish heritage. They favored hierarchical government rather than democracy and called for the establishment of industrial organizations that included both workers and owners. In the matter of industrial organization, they followed Pope Pius XI, who, in his encyclical *Quadragesimo Anno*, proposed that in such organizations workers and employers could peacefully arbitrate their differences without the rancor that leads to and results from strikes. The *Sinarquistas* and other groups formed a political party, the *Partido Acción Nacional* (PAN, National Action Party). But since the PRI controlled national and state elections, the PAN served as little more than an avenue for dissent – dissent that was often put down by violence.

25. The presidency of Ávila Camacho and its significance

Camacho, elected president in 1940, was the PRI candidate but a centrist. For one thing, he favored industrial growth according to capitalist principles. But though he proclaimed himself a Catholic and did not strictly enforce anti-clerical legislation, he did not change the essentially anti-clerical character of Mexican government. Camacho's presidency represented the effective end of the revolution.

26. The fruits of the Mexican Revolution

Under the PRI, the party of the revolution, Mexico was a sham democracy, a one party government whose legitimacy rested on the pretence of popular suffrage. The struggle for the poor and downtrodden masses had ended only in setting up new oppressors. But the cultural and economic effects of the revolution were significant. It had allowed more of the poor to own land. By the 1940s, over one-half of Mexico's arable land was held by *ejidos* and by small farmers. The revolution however did little to change the traditional condition of the Mexican people. Because of the revolution, Mexicans, most of whom were at least part Indian, began to identify themselves with their Indian heritage unlike the Liberals and conservatives of the 19th century, who had embraced European models as their guide. And, despite itself, the revolution had made Mexico more Catholic. It has been said that Mexicans were more Catholic in 1925 than they were in 1910. The revolution had forced many to embrace the religion in which they had been born. Still, the revolution had shackled the Church. With dramatically fewer priests, many Mexicans, though devout, remained poorly catechized. Yet, the Faith remained strong in Mexico and, in the years to come, inspired new calls for social justice against a repressive regime.

Questions for Review

1. **What problems troubled Mexico during Porfirio Díaz's regime?**

Under Díaz, many *mestizos* rose to wealth and prominence, in part through the confiscation of Indian lands. Díaz enforced the *Ley Lerdo* which forbade any but individuals to own land, and many Indian tribes suffered, especially when they tried to revolt. The sale of government lands and the confiscation of Indian lands led to a great disparity of wealth in Mexico. Díaz controlled the government, and it was filled with his yes men. The rural poor were reduced to practical slavery and suffered from ignorance, want, and hunger. The poor, working in the factories, though better paid than the rural workers, were still in grievous want. Though under Díaz, railroads were built, they benefited chiefly the foreign interests that built them. Díaz gave over most public lands to real estate corporations, generals, politicians, and U.S. capitalists, thus enriching foreigners and rich and powerful Mexicans. Most of Mexican mineral and oil wealth passed into the hands of U.S. capitalists.

2. **How did the policies of the *científicos* affect the Mexican government and society during the years of Porfirio Díaz's regime?**

The *científicos* believed that civilization could only come to Mexico through the rule of the creole aristocracy and the importation of foreign capital. José Ives Limantour, the director of the treasury, was the leader of the *científicos* after 1895. Under Limantour, the Mexican economy prospered. For the first time in history, the Mexican government was bringing in more revenue than it was paying out. Railroads were nationalized; public works were built. Illiteracy decreased. Poetry and the arts flourished. Still, Mexico was beset by dire poverty and an extreme concentration of wealth into the hands of a very few, largely because of the policies favored by the *científicos*.

3. What situation caused Emiliano Zapata to lead a revolt in Morelos?

Since the 1880s, haciendas had been seizing the lands of small farmers and Indian *ejidos*, forcing their owners to work as peons on the ever-growing sugar-cane plantations. One such hacienda was *El Hospital*, which threatened lands held by the peasants and the village of Anencuilco in Morales. *El Hospital* would have successfully absorbed the small property around Anencuilco as it, and other haciendas, had done with Indian lands before but for Emiliano Zapata. Elected the lead the defense committee of Anencuilco, Zapata decided to meet head on the threat of *El Hospital*. Under Zapata's lead, the villages peacefully reoccupied land the hacienda had seized and then divided it among themselves.

4. How did Catholics respond to societal problems in Mexico both during the years of Díaz's regime and afterward?

Not all Catholics were dissatisfied with the state of things under Díaz; some looked upon Don Porfirio as a defense against those forces that would seek to destroy the Church. Other Catholics, however, hoped to form a political party. Others formed the *Operarios Guadalupanos* (OG – Guadalupan Workers). Parish OG groups provided study groups on social problems, artisan and worker circles, and health care services. Some cells promoted public morality through theater, while others published newspapers. In 1909, the OG opened two rural credit and savings establishments to provide affordable credit to

the poor. The OG journal, *Restauración Social* (Social Restoration) discussed such social justice issues as what constitutes a just family wage. OG members studied the social encyclicals of Pope Leo XIII and published newsletters analyzing Mexico's social problems in light of Catholic social justice teaching. The OG favored what has been called "Christian democracy" – a form of society where the Church and state have clearly defined spheres but are united in mutual cooperation and recognition. Shortly after Díaz's fall from power, members of the OG and other Catholics formed what has been called Mexico's first modern political party – the *Partido Católico Nacional* (PCN – the National Catholic Party). During the brief period of its existence (1910-1913), the PCN was able to take advantage of the OG's parish-based network to form an effective political movement. Since 1918, Anacleto Gonzáles Flores, a lawyer in Jalisco, had been writing books and articles detailing his vision of a Catholic social and political order for Mexico. Flores opposed democracy (he thought Mexico was not ready for it) but called for the popular methods of individual sacrifice and non-violent civil disobedience to oppose the government. To unite Catholics, he formed the *Union Popular*.

5. Why did those who had supported President Madero at last stir up a revolution against him?

Though Madero himself did not proceed violently against his enemies, his brother, Gustavo, took up the repressive policies of Díaz. Madero's relatives carried on the *científico* policies from the days of Díaz. Yet, Madero's freedom of speech and of the press encouraged more radical elements to organize. Trade unions again appeared. In the capital, the House of the World Worker became a center for intellectuals who promoted socialist and Marxist ideas. The toleration of such radicalism alarmed wealthy Mexicans and foreign investors. Zapata's conviction that Madero was not serious about agrarian reform led him to publish the *Plan de Ayala* on November 25, 1911. Government manipulation of the election of 1912 turned the National Catholic Party against the president when Liberals persuaded the Mexican government to annul the results of many of the elections where the PCN had prevailed.

6. **Why and how did the revolution against Huerta turn anti-clerical?**

The influence of both Spanish culture and the Church had been intense in what is called "Old Mexico," but had been vestigial in the regions of the far northern frontier – Sonora, Chihuahua, Coahuila, and Nuevo León. Because of their isolation from Spanish culture and the Church, the men of the North were inclined to admire the United States. To make Mexico more like Anglo-America, the northern revolutionaries thought they had to weaken and destroy the power of the Catholic Church. The men of the north thought Protestantism was responsible for the political, and economic prosperity of the U.S.; thus, Carranza and Obregón encouraged Protestant proselytizing and the establishment of Protestant congregations in Mexico and supported legislation to weaken the power of the Church.

7. **How did the United States affect the course of the revolution?**

Woodrow Wilson, the president of the United States, disapproved of President Huerta, and began arming Carranza and the Constitutionalist forces. With the aid of the United States, the revolutionaries forced the federal garrison in Mexico City to surrender.

8. **What were the principles of the Constitution of 1917?**

The constitution promulgated in 1917 decreed that no individuals or corporate entities could directly own land, and especially, water and subsoil minerals in Mexico. All land belonged to the whole people of Mexico, even if it was divided up among many users. This meant that the state (the representative of the Mexican people) could take land (though with compensation) from its current owners if the good of "the people" demanded it. The constitution declared that seizures of *ejidos* under *Ley Lerdo* were null and void, and, if they needed to, *ejideros* could take land from neighboring haciendas. Article 123 of the new constitution established some of the most progressive labor legislation in the world. Among other measures, the article limited the workday to eight hours, abolished child labor, declared the right of workers to organize unions, and called on employers to give workers a share in profits. Both articles 27 and 123 assured that workers and peasants would support the new government. The Constitution of 1917 allowed the state to seize Church property, decreeing church buildings the property of the state. Priests had to register with the government; state governments could limit the number of priests within their jurisdictions, and foreigners could not serve as priests in Mexico. The constitution prohibited monastic vows, outlawed monastic orders, forbade the holding of public religious ceremonies outside of church buildings, and sought to eradicate the influence of religion in education.

9. **Describe the events that caused the *Cristero* uprising.**

On July 2, 1926, President Calles issued a penal code that laid down penalties for those who violated the constitution's anti-clerical articles. He insisted that all priests in Mexico register with the government – a measure preparatory to exile, or worse. He deported 200 foreign born priests and religious. In response, the *Liga* (supported by the bishops) called for an economic boycott. When this did not work, Mexico's bishops (with the pope's support) placed an interdict on Mexico, beginning July 31, 1926. In response to the interdict, from August to September 1926, spontaneous armed uprisings occurred, north of the capital, in west-central Mexico.

10. **What chiefly motivated the *Cristeros* in their uprising?**

The *Cristeros* chiefly rose because the civil authority had dared to assert itself against Christ the King. Calles, they thought, was the servant of Freemasonry, Protestantism, and the United States. The *Cristeros* saw themselves as the defenders of the Church, joined in the epic battle that had first pitted the Archangel Michael against the enemy of mankind.

11. **Why were the bishops of Mexico hesitant to back the *Cristeros*?**

In part this was because of a reticence to ally themselves with any political movement that they feared could compromise their position. Too, it was far from clear that the *Cristero* uprising could succeed – if for no other reason than that the U.S. government was backing Calles with money and arms. If the *Cristeros* were victorious, would the U.S. tolerate a Catholic government in Mexico, if such a regime came to be? And if they did not succeed, the prospect of a guerrilla war

without any foreseeable end could jeopardize the interests of the Church, not help them.

12. **How did the PNR weaken Calles' power?**

Younger men who had grown up during the revolution were not content to see the struggle end in a triumph for capitalism. Beginning in 1933, these men, who were heavily influenced by Communist theories, grew more influential in the PNR. Seeking to appease these young leftists, Calles lent his support to the candidacy of Lázaro Cárdenas in the election of 1934. President Cárdenas undertook an all-out war against the *Callistas*. The new president pushed agrarian reform, sympathized with strikes, and closed illegal gambling houses owned by Calles' friends. Cárdenas dismissed Calles' hand-picked cabinet members, and by forming coalitions with various anti-Calles groups, gradually isolated the *jefe maximo* in the PNR. In April 1936, Cárdenas deported both Calles and Luis Morones to Texas.

13. **What was the significance of the Buenos Aires non-intervention agreement?**

At the Buenos Aires convention, the United States agreed that no American state should intervene in the internal affairs of another American state. This, albeit temporary, agreement served Cárdenas' purposes, for foreign capitalists with property in Mexico opposed his economic policies.

14. **What were the cultural, religious, and economic effects of the Mexican Revolution?**

Under the PRI, the party of the revolution, Mexico was a sham democracy, a one party government whose legitimacy rested on the pretence of popular suffrage. The struggle for the poor and downtrodden masses had ended only in setting up new oppressors. But the cultural and economic effects of the revolution were significant. It had allowed more of the poor to own land. The revolution however did little to change the traditional condition of the Mexican people. Because of the revolution, Mexicans, most of whom were at least part Indian, began to identify themselves with their Indian heritage unlike the Liberals and conservatives of the 19th century, who had embraced European models as their guide. And, despite itself, the revolution had made Mexico more Catholic. It has been said that Mexicans were more Catholic in 1925 than they were in 1910. The revolution had forced many to embrace the religion in which they had been born. Still, the revolution had shackled the Church. With dramatically fewer priests, many Mexicans, though devout, remained poorly catechized. Yet, the Faith remained strong in Mexico.

Ideas in Action

1. Study maps of Mexico and identify the regions and places mentioned in this chapter.

2. Listen to *corridos* (Mexican ballads) that tell of events and persons of the Second Mexican Revolution and the *Cristero* uprising. What do these ballads tell us about how the Mexican people view these struggles?

3. Read literature about the *Cristero* war, such as Elizabeth Borton de Treviño's *The Fourth Gift*.

4. Read the lives of the martyrs of the *Cristero* war.

5. How did the policies pursued by Plutarco Elías Calles epitomize the ideals of Liberalism, especially Mexican Liberalism?

6. Was the *Cristero* uprising a just war, according to the principles of Catholic just war doctrine? (See the *Catechism of the Catholic Church*, 2258–2317)

Sample Quiz I (pages 661-680)

Please answer the following in complete sentences.

1. Name three of Porfirio Díaz's achievements – good or bad.

2. How did the secret agreement between Díaz and the Church benefit the Church?

3. How was the secret agreement a detriment to the Church?

4. Who were the *científicos* and what did they believe?

5. What was the condition of the Mexican rural poor and proletariat under Díaz?

6. What did the *Plan de Ayala* call for?

7. How and why was the rebellion kindled against Victoriano Huerta?

8. Why were the northern revolutionaries anti-clerical?

9. Briefly describe Carranza's policies as president.

10. Describe how Catholics, inspired by *Rerum Novarum*, turned their attention towards the needs and concerns of modern men.

Answers to Sample Quiz I

Students' answers should approximate the following.

1. *Possible answers:*

   a. During Díaz's dictatorship, there was mostly peace: Mexico did not suffer from any major civil wars.

   b. Díaz paid foreign railroad companies to lay down track in Mexico. The railroads built, however, benefited North American commerce rather than the people of Mexico.

c. Díaz gave over most public lands to real estate corporations, generals, politicians, and U.S. capitalists, thus enriching foreigners and rich and powerful Mexicans.

d. Díaz's government enforced laws that forbade anyone but individuals to own land and this led to a loss of their communal lands (*ejidos*) by Indian tribes. When tribes resisted, the government crushed them.

e. Because Díaz placated members of the middle class by giving them well-paying government jobs, the government bureaucracy in Mexico grew dramatically during the Díaz years.

f. Díaz came to an agreement with the Catholic Church in Mexico, which granted a good deal of liberty of ation to the Church, though anti-clerical laws remained.

2. The secret agreement allowed the Church in Mexico once again to acquire property. The Church built schools; men's and women's monasteries and convents spread across the land; the number of clergy rose dramatically. These clergy began mobilizing the laity and oversaw the expansion of the Catholic press as well as of Catholic education.

3. Because of the secret agreement, the Church became subservient to the dictator, who could enforce the Laws of the Reform against her any time the bishops or priests fell out of line. Allying herself with Díaz, too, eventually alienated the Church from many of the people who suffered under the dictatorship.

4. *The científicos* were young men (of the creole class) who thought the good of Mexico lay in the material progress that came through the application of science to social and economic life. Believing the Mexican people incapable of Liberal democracy, the *científicos* enthusiastically embraced the Díaz dictatorship. Civilization they thought could only come to Mexico through the rule of the creole aristocracy and the importation of foreign capital.

5. Under Díaz, the rural poor were reduced to practical slavery and suffered from ignorance, want, and hunger. Without their *ejidos*, Indian peons had only the pittance paid them by rich *hacendados* to rely on for their subsistence. Prices had doubled; and with their buying power drastically decreased, the peons sank into wretched poverty. The poor, working in the factories, though better paid than the rural workers, were still in grievous want.

6. The *Plan de Ayala* called for the redistribution of one-third of lands, timber, and water to the landless, with compensation to the owners. But those "landlords, *científicos*, or bosses" who opposed the plan in any way would lose all their lands, which would go to pensions for widows and orphans of those who died in the revolution.

7. Victoriano Huerta was a drunkard, treacherous, and cruel. To assure his absolute sway over Mexico, Huerta replaced several state governors with generals faithful to him. He conducted a purge of congress, jailing over a hundred representatives who opposed his regime. Huerta's brutality inspired new uprisings.

8. The influence of both Spanish culture and the Church had been intense in what is called "Old Mexico," but had been vestigial in the regions of the far northern frontier. Because of their isolation from Spanish culture and the Church, the men of the north were inclined to admire the United States. To make Mexico more like Anglo-America, the northern revolutionaries thought they had to weaken and destroy the power of the Catholic Church. The northern revolutionaries thought Protestantism was

responsible for the political, and economic prosperity of the U.S.

9. Carranza was not the author of the more radical provisions of the Constitution of 1917, and he did nothing to enforce them – both to avoid conflicts with foreign governments and because he had no desire to do so. Carranza did nothing to redistribute lands to the peasants and he actively suppressed workers' attempts to organize unions.

10. The formation of the Guadalupan Workers had been part of this awakening, as was the League of Catholic Students. The Guadalupan Workers studied social encyclicals, published newsletters, set up worker circles, and healthcare services. The Guadalupan Workers helped form Mexico's first Catholic political party. The League established youth centers in cities throughout Mexico, as well as the Catholic Student Center in Mexico City. In January of 1913, the Catholic Great Workers' Diet that met at Zamora suggested labor reforms similar to those later enshrined in Article 123 of the 1917 constitution; and in Mexico City the Jesuit priest, Alfredo Méndez Medina, founded Mexico's first real trade union. The bishops moreover were strongly supportive of such labor organizing. Also in 1913, Catholics had formed the *Asociacion Catholica de la Juventud Mexicana* (ACJM – the Catholic Association of Mexican Youth).

Sample Quiz II (pages 680-695)

Please answer the following in complete sentences.

1. Briefly describe the government under President Obregón.

2. Briefly describe the government of Plutarco Calles

3. How did the Catholics respond to Calles' anti-clerical measures?

4. How did many *Cristeros* see themselves?

5. Why did many *Cristeros* fight?

6. How did the second *Cristero* rebellion come about?

7. What caused Calles to fall from power?

8. Briefly describe the presidency of Lázaro Cárdenas.

9. Explain *Sinarquismo*.

10. Briefly describe the presidency of Ávila Camacho.

Answers to Sample Quiz II

Students' answers should approximate the following.

1. President Obregón was able to make peace with the *Zapatistas* and buy off Pancho Villa. He was a friend to labor and radical agrarian aspirations. Though Obregón established the *Confederación Nacional Campesina* (National Farm Workers' Confederation), he did little more to further agrarian reform. Obregón formed a dictatorship that was native-born Mexican. He ruled in a manner reminiscent of Don Porfirio, playing off rival groups against each other. In the states his governors were, more often than not, corrupt. The military maintained its time-honored privileges. As president, Obregón adopted a more or less tolerant attitude toward the Church. Yet, Obregón continued to back Protestant missionary endeavors in Mexico, and his government gave direct support to Protestant missions.

2. Plutarco Calles ruled as an absolute dictator and was ruthless to those who opposed him. Though he called himself a socialist, Calles little by little warmed to Liberal capitalist ideas and policies. His closest associates were wealthy capitalists, and so it was not surprising that he began to promote a native

Mexican capitalism instead of the agrarianism for which the revolution had supposedly been fought. Calles vigorously applied the anti-clerical articles of the constitution.

3. In the autumn of 1925, Pope Pius XI denounced Mexico's revolutionary government, but he did not call on Mexican Catholics to undertake direct political resistance. The National League for the Defense of Religious Liberty took a combatitive stance against the government's anti-Catholic measures. In response to Calles' penal code, the *Liga* (supported by the bishops) called for an economic boycott. When this did not work, Mexico's bishops (with the pope's support) placed an interdict on Mexico, beginning July 31, 1926.

4. The *Cristeros* saw themselves as the defenders of the Church, fighting for Christ the King just as the Archangel Michael had fought against the enemy of mankind.

5. Though not all *Cristeros* were strict in their observance of their faith, they were men committed to their Catholic religion, which they encapsulated in the phrase, "Kingship of Christ." They did not rise up against the government because of any natural proclivity for revolution, for these peasants had a deep regard for constituted authority and were profoundly patriotic. They rose because the civil authority had dared to assert itself against *Cristo Rey*. Calles, they thought, was the servant of Freemasonry, Protestantism, and the United States.

6. In 1931, the federal government undertook to limit the number of priests in Mexico. In response, Pope Pius XI condemned the violation of the *arreglos* while calling on the faithful to submit to the government. But riots and priest shootings increased. State governors closed churches. In 1934, Calles issued his *Grito de Guadalajara*, calling on the government to enforce "socialist education."

This inspired a new revolt among about 7,500 former *Cristeros* called the "Second," in which they waged war not just against the state, but the Church.

7. Young men who had grown up during the revolution and were not content to see the struggle end in a triumph for capitalism grew more influential in the PNR. President Cárdenas undertook an all-out war against the *Callistas* and finally deported Calles.

8. Cárdenas returned to the more radical roots of the revolution. He reorganized the PNR to represent peasants, workers, and the army. Cárdenas advanced agrarian reform like no other Mexican president. Cárdenas encouraged better agricultural methods and established cooperatives. Cárdenas confiscated all foreign-owned oil properties in Mexico, nationalizing them into Mexican Petroleum. Though a virulent anti-clerical, Cárdenas denounced those who focused overly much on the religion question, and this denunciation led in several states to a lifting of some of the restrictions against the Church. Though anti-clerical laws remained, most were not enforced.

9. *Sinarquismo* was a movement that arose among former *Cristeros* and other Catholics. The *Sinarquistas* insisted that Mexico should acknowledge the Catholic religion and the country's Spanish heritage. They favored hierarchical government rather than democracy and called for the establishment of industrial organizations that included both workers and owners.

10. Camacho, elected president in 1940, was the PRI candidate but was a centrist. For one thing, he favored industrial growth according to capitalist principles. But though he proclaimed himself a Catholic and did not strictly enforce anti-clerical legislation, he did not change the essentially anti-clerical character of Mexican government.

Essays

Instructions to be given to the students: Write in complete sentences. Underline your thesis. Give three supports or examples that explain why you think what you do and that support your thesis.

1. Mexico's history is full of strife and upheaval, while the United States' is relatively peaceful. What do you think is the reason for this?

2. Compare and contrast the constitutions of 1857 and 1917. How did Mexico change from one constitution to the next? Were the changes for better or for worse?

3. Mexico's revolution of 1911 was inspired by certain social goals. The revolution, however, did not attain many of the goals for which they supposedly fought. Why was this so? How might the Mexican revolution been successful? Could it have been successful?

4. **What were the fruits of the Mexican Revolution?**

Sample Test

Please answer the following in complete sentences.

I. Short Essay – Answer two of the following:

1. **How did the *Operarios Guadalupanos* address the social issues in Mexico and what policies did the group favor?**

2. **What did the Constitution of 1917 legislate in regards to the ownership of land, workers' rights (give two examples), the rural power, and the Catholic Church (give two examples).**

3. **Describe the *Cristeros*. Who were they? What social classes were represented among them? For what did they fight? How did they characterize their enemy?**

II. Short Answer:

1. **Why did Emiliano Zapata rise against the Díaz regime?**

2. **What is agrarian reform?**

3. **Why did the northern revolutionaries oppose the Church?**

4. **What was the significance of the presidency of Ávila Camacho?**

5. **Idenfity:**
   a. **Porfirio Díaz**
   b. **Venustiano Carranza**
   c. **Pancho Villa**
   d. **Alvaro Obregón**
   e. **Plutarco Calles**

Answer Key to the Chapter Test

Students' answers should approximate the following:

I.

1. *Operarios Guadalupanos* (OG – Guadalupan Workers) groups provided study groups on social problems, artisan and worker circles, and health care services. Some cells promoted public morality through theater, while others published newspapers. In 1909, the OG opened two rural credit and savings establishments to provide affordable credit to the poor. The OG journal, *Restauración Social* (Social Restoration) discussed such social justice issues as what constitutes a just family wage. OG members studied the social encyclicals of Pope Leo XIII and published newsletters analyzing Mexico's social problems in light of Catholic social justice teaching. Some solutions were radical; for instance, in June 1914, an OG leader, José

Encarnación Preciado, suggested that social Catholics espouse an agrarian reform that would divide large haciendas among workers, who would contribute to bonds that would reimburse former owners. Politically, the OG hoped for a more democratic state structure, resting on universal manhood suffrage. It hoped for a government, controlled by Catholic laity, that would respect the institutional Catholic Church in Mexico as a freely operating body in the greater society. In a word, the OG favored what has been called "Christian democracy" Shortly after Díaz's fall from power, members of the OG participated in what has been called Mexico's first modern political party – the *Partido Católico Nacional* (PCN – the National Catholic Party).

2. The constitution promulgated in 1917 decreed that no individuals or corporate entities could directly own land, and especially, water and subsoil minerals in Mexico. All land belonged to the whole people of Mexico. This meant that the state (the representative of the Mexican people) could take land (though with compensation) from its current owners if the good of "the people" demanded it. The constitution declared that seizures of *ejidos* under *Ley Lerdo* were null and void, and, if they needed to, *ejideros* could take land from neighboring haciendas. Article 123 of the new constitution established some of the most progressive labor legislation in the world. Among other measures, the article limited the workday to eight hours, abolished child labor, declared the right of workers to organize unions, and called on employers to give workers a share in profits. The Constitution of 1917 allowed the state to seize Church property, decreeing church buildings the property of the state. Priests had to register with the government; state governments could limit the number of priests within their jurisdictions, and

foreigners could not serve as priests in Mexico. The constitution prohibited monastic vows, outlawed monastic orders, forbade the holding of public religious ceremonies outside of church buildings, and sought to eradicate the influence of religion in education.

3. Though some *Cristero* leaders joined the insurgents to further their own aims, and some of the rebellion's true adherents had mixed motives, it was the religious motive that was paramount among them. And though middle class, professional men were central to the rebellion; the rank and file of the *Cristero* insurgent army were drawn mostly from the peasant classes. Though most were not formally educated, the *Cristeros* had a rich and evocative oral culture. "Sacrificing themselves for the Cause of God" – this phrase aptly sums up how the *Cristeros* saw themselves. And though not all *Cristeros* were strict in their observance of their faith, they were men committed to their Catholic religion, which they encapsulated in the phrase, "Kingship of Christ." They did not rise up against the government because of any natural proclivity for revolution, for these peasants had a deep regard for constituted authority and were profoundly patriotic. They rose because the civil authority had dared to assert itself against *Cristo Rey*. Calles, they thought, was the servant of Freemasonry, Protestantism, and the United States. The *Cristeros* saw themselves as the defenders of the Church, joined in the epic battle that had first pitted the Archangel Michael against the enemy of mankind.

4. Politically, after the revolution, Mexico became a sham democracy, a one party government whose legitimacy rested on the pretence of popular suffrage. But the cultural and economic effects of the revolution were significant. It had allowed more of the poor

to own land. By the 1940s, over one-half of Mexico's arable land was held by *ejidos* and by small farmers. The revolution however did little to change the traditional condition of the Mexican people. Because of the revolution, Mexicans, most of whom were at least part Indian, began to identify themselves with their Indian heritage unlike the Liberals and conservatives of the 19th century, who had embraced European models as their guide. And, despite itself, the revolution had made Mexico more Catholic. It has been said that Mexicans were more Catholic in 1925 than they were in 1910. The revolution had forced many to embrace the religion in which they had been born. Still, the revolution had shackled the Church. With dramatically fewer priests, many Mexicans, though devout, remained poorly catechized.

II.
1. Zapata rose against the Díaz regime because in Mexico haciendas were seizing land from the Indians.
2. Agrarian reform refers to the redistribution of land to the poor from whom it had been taken.
3. The northern revolutionaries opposed the Church because they saw her as a hindrance to progress in Mexico.
4. Camacho's presidency was significant because it represented the effective end of the revolution.

5.
a. Díaz was the president of Mexico for over 30 years against whose policies sparked the Mexican revolution in 1911.
b. Venustiano Carranza was the governor of Sonora who led the the revolution against President Victoriano Huerta. When he became president, Carranza betrayed the ideas of the revolution he had led. He was driven from power and assassinated.
c. Pancho Villa was a bandit and revolutionary leader from Chihuahua who briefly captured Mexico's capital, Mexico City.
d. Alvaro Obregón was a general from northern Mexico who established Carranza in power and later himself became president of Mexico. He died from an assassin's bullet when he, once again, stood for election to the presidency.
e. Plutarco Calles followed Obregón as president and became the powerful master of Mexico's revolutionary party. His anti-clericalism brought about the *Cristero* rebellion. Calles was later driven from power by Cárdenas.

CHAPTER 25: The War to End All Wars

Chapter Overview

- In Sarajevo in Bosnia, a member of the Black Hand, a Serbian terrorist group, assassinated Archduke Franz Ferdinand of Austria and his wife. Austria-Hungary made harsh demands of Serbia in reparation for the assassination of the archduke. When Serbia refused to accede to the demands and began a partial mobilization of its army, Austria-Hungary declared war on July 28, 1914. Russia backed Serbia, and was allied to France. Germany, which was allied with Austria-Hungary and Italy, declared war on Russia as well as France. When Germany invaded Belgium on August 4, Great Britain entered the war. On August 19, 1914, President Wilson declared that the United States must remain neutral in the conflict.

- German forces were doing well at the beginning of the war; in the east, the German army defeated Russian armies, and in the west, the German offensive had pushed within a few miles of Paris. Throughout the rest of the year, however, the war on the Western Front developed into a bloody slugging match with neither side gaining any significant advantage.

- Britain gained a superiority at sea, and British naval ships stopped all neutral ships bound for Europe. This intensified feeling against Great Britain in the United States, which was allayed when Britain began placing large orders for food and munitions in the United States, thus relieving an economic recession.

- Germany began to dive undersea in U-boats as a response to Britain's blockade of German ports. At first these attacks were only directed against British warships, but in order to cripple British trade, the Germans began to direct U-boat warfare against all commercial shipping. Kaiser Wilhelm announced that the waters around the British Isles were a war zone and that all merchant ships bound for Allied ports within these waters would be sunk. The first American ship to be sunk was the *Gulflight*. On May 7, 1915, a British liner, *R.M.S. Lusitania*, with Americans on board, was sunk by a German U-boat. This incident, coupled with anti-German propaganda, aroused American opinion against Germany.

- While President Wilson did nothing to prepare the country for war, civilians made their own preparations. Following the sinking of the passenger liner, *Arabic*, carrying three Americans, Wilson demanded that Germany abandon warfare of this sort. The German government agreed, and on September 19 withdrew all U-boats from the English Channel.

- Wilson took up the cry for preparedness in the Fall of 1915, facing stiff opposition. Wilson's case was furthered by German war policies. On March 13, Allies began arming merchant ships, and Germany loosened restrictions on sinking non-military vessels. Allied actions, however, soured some Americans against the Entente, while news of battle losses in Europe bolstered the desire to remain neutral. After the Battle of the Somme in 1916, Americans wanted no part in the war. Despite that, Congress passed the "Big Navy Act" on August 29.

- Wilson was re-elected in 1916, and began to pursue peace initiatives. He sent a note to all the belligerent countries asking them to state what they required for peace. Wilson's peace efforts came to nothing when Germany would not reply, though Wilson still continued to press his peace initiative.

- In late January of 1917, the German government communicated its minimum terms for peace as well as an announcement that it would commence unrestricted submarine warfare against Allied and neutral ships sailing in restricted war zones. This caused Wilson to break off diplomatic relations with Germany.

- When German U-boats sunk the passenger liner *Laconia*, many Americans were jolted from their neutrality. Wilson tried, and failed, to get Congress to arm merchant ships. Then a revolution took place in Russia, changing the face of the war for Wilson. The sinking of three unarmed American merchant ships on March 18 gave Wilson further reason to enter the war. On April 4, 1917, the Senate voted to declare war on Germany. The House followed on April 6.

- On May 18, 1917, Congress passed the Selective Service Act in order to increase army enlistment. Anti-German propaganda increased in the United States, and rumors that anarchists, communists, and other radicals were subverting the war effort caused Congress to pass the Espionage and Sedition Acts.

- After the Bolsheviks in November of 1917 overthrew the Russian government, the new Communist government made a separate treaty with Germany on March 3, 1918 and withdrew from the war.

- Pope Benedict XV had been exhorting leaders of Europe to abandon the war since 1914 when he issued his encyclical letter, *Ad Beatissimi*. He refused to take sides and continued to call for peace. Benedict drew up four points for peace

that he sent to Germany. Kaiser Wilhelm II indicated his pleasure, and the pope laid out his peace proposal in seven points. President Wilson would not accept the pope's peace plan. Though the German government was in accord with the pope's peace efforts, the peace negotiations went no further.

- Soon after, Wilson offered a peace proposal of his own, on January 9, 1918, that were very similar to Pope Benedict's, which the president had dismissed as unrealistic. Benedict's plans, however, did not call for breaking up existing political units or forming new states as Wilson's did.

- Emperor Karl I of Austria-Hungary, a devout Catholic, was against the war and sent a secret note to his brothers-in-law, the princes of Bourbon-Parma, who fought on the Allied side, expressing his willingness to support the restoration of Serbia and German withdrawal from Belgium as well as the return of Alsace-Lorraine to France. Despite the note's secrecy, the French government publicized it, creating a rift between German and Austria-Hungary. Emperor Karl tried to negotiate with President Wilson, but Wilson would not accede to any of the emperor's requests.

- The Germans opened their last great series of offensives on the Western Front in the spring of 1918. In desperation the Allies requested additional troops from President Wilson, and these arrived in July. At Soissons, two American divisions struck the German lines in a battle that turned the tide of war. Following the Meuse-Argonne offensive in September, the cause of Germany was lost. On November 9, Prince Max of Baden, Wilhelm's chancellor, declared that the *kaiser* would abdicate. He then formed a Liberal government, and on November 11, 1918, representatives of Germany and Allied leaders met to sign an armistice.

- The armistice was to last only 60 days, but those 60 days turned into six months during which the British maintained their blockade of German ports and the Allies prepared their strategy of revenge against Germany and her allies. When the warring nations finally met in January 1919, it was clear that the Fourteen Points were scrapped and Germany had to pay.

- To cool the thirst for vengeance, President Wilson presented the Allied nations with his dream of a League of Nations. He was able to convince Allied leaders to accept the principle of a League of nations, and on February 14, the peace conference approved the preliminary draft for the convening of the League of Nations.

- Wilson directed the redrawing of the boundaries of Eastern Europe. Meanwhile, developments in Russian shook the confidence of the victors and the Versailles Peace Conference. The Bolsheviks had established a "dictatorship of the proletariat," threatening worldwide Communist revolution. By the time the Treaty of Versailles was signed by Germany on June 28, 1919, the Bolsheviks were in undisputed control of Russia.

- Theodore Roosevelt died on January 6, 1919, symbolizing the eclipse of progressivism. In 1918, voters gave the Republicans control of the Senate, and President Wilson failed to push through the Senate the ratification of the Versailles treaty and the League of Nations covenant. Wilson tried to appeal to the American people by going on a speaking tour. In the fall of 1920, Warren G. Harding was elected president.

What Students Should Know

1. **President Wilson's views on the Great War in 1914**
Addressing the war in an August 19, 1914 message to Congress, President Woodrow Wilson declared that "the United States must be neutral in fact as well as in name…. We must be impartial in thought as well as in action, must put a curb upon our sentiments."

2. **American opinion about the war in 1914** As of August 1914, American opinion was largely for staying out of the war. Most Americans seemed to embrace the policy of George Washington and of Thomas Jefferson, that the United States should remain free of foreign entanglements. Too, almost everyone, both in Europe and America, thought the war would be over in a matter of months; there was no point in intervening in a short-lived conflict overseas. Yet, American opinion about the war was not entirely neutral. College-educated and prosperous Americans favored intervention on the side of the Entente; and in the South, where there was strong pro-English sentiment, many were in favor of aiding Great Britain. Some American college graduates tried to land commissions in the British army. Others joined the French foreign legion and formed a division of the French air force called the Lafayette Escadrille or organized an American ambulance service for the Entente. The greatest anti-war sentiment was found in the Midwest, where were many settlements of Germans whose sympathies lay with Germany. There, too, Populist sentiment, still strong, saw the war as the work of commercial interests vying for foreign markets, with bankers and munitions makers standing to profit from the conflict.

3. **American reactions to acts of war by the Entente and the Central Powers**

Americans first reacted to the British Royal Navy's tight blockade of German ports and the British navy's stopping of all neutral ships bound for Europe and and its confiscation of all cargo marked for Germany. President Wilson and Secretary of State William Jennings Bryan condemned this "highhanded" policy. Feeling against Great Britain intensified and was only allayed when the Entente began placing large orders for food and munitions in the United States. The United States had been suffering from an economic recession in 1914, which this increased buying relieved. The Entente nations also took out direct loans from American banks. Germany's response to the British blockade – U-boat warfare – in the end, did more to irritate America than the blockade itself. In order to cripple British trade like the British had crippled Germany's, the German high command decided to direct U-boat warfare against commercial shipping. After Kaiser Wilhelm announced in February 1915 that all waters around the British Isles were a war zone and that all merchant ships bound for Allied ports within those waters would be sunk, President Wilson told the German government that the United States would hold them "to a strict accountability" for any American "property damaged or lives lost." On May 1, 1915, a U-boat sank an American tanker, the *Gulflight*, without warning. The United States accepted Germany's offer of an apology and reparations for what the German government called an "unfortunate accident"

4. **The *Lusitania* incident and its effects on American opinion**

The *R.M.S Lusitania* was a British passenger liner that sailed from New York, bound for England, on May 1, 1915. Though a passenger ship, the *Lusitania* carried, among other cargo, munitions – shrapnel shells and rifle shells. On April 22 the Imperial German Embassy in the United States had issued the following notice to travelers, warning them of the dangers of sailing into the German war zone around Great Britain. On May 7, near Queenstown, Ireland, the *Lusitania* met a German U-boat. The U-boat commander, without warning, fired his last torpedo at the liner. A great explosion from the hold of the *Lusitania* followed the smaller detonation of the torpedo. In the sinking of the *Lusitania*, over 1,100 civilian passengers lost their lives; 128 of them were American. The sinking of the *Lusitania* aroused American opinion against Germany. Still, many Americans preferred that the United States not join the war against Germany. Some of these were German-Americans; others were Irish-Americans who hated the English. Almost a week after the sinking of the *Lusitania*, Wilson, through Secretary of State Bryan, demanded that the German government take responsibility for the sinking and make reparations in order to "prevent the recurrence of anything so obviously subversive of the principles of warfare." Wilson said that, though Germany undertook her submarine warfare as retaliation for the British blockade, still the "Imperial German Government" must accept – as Wilson was sure it did – that "the lives of noncombatants, whether they be of neutral citizenship or citizens of one of the nations at war, cannot lawfully or rightfully be put in jeopardy by the capture or destruction of an unarmed merchantman." Germany, said Wilson, must, like other nations, "take the usual precaution of visit and search to ascertain whether a suspected merchantman is in fact of belligerent nationality or is in fact carrying contraband of war under a neutral flag." Wilson's message did recognize the fact that "it is practically impossible for the officers of a submarine to visit a merchantman at sea and examine her papers," and so, "manifestly submarines cannot be used against merchantmen." The German government delayed returning a reply. On June 9, Wilson composed another note to the German government in which he denied the legality of forming a war zone around an enemy country. The sinking of the *Lusitania* was a crisis moment. While it didn't bring the United States into the European war, it certainly led to significant policy changes in Wilson's administration. Forced to attend to the international arena, Wilson began to think that war, though undesirable, was a real possibility. America's army and navy, he began to believe, must be made ready just in case war proved to be the country's lot.

5. **The effect of Allied war propaganda on American opinion**

Allied reports to the United States told of German atrocities against civilians in Belgium. Whatever truth there was to these reports, they were vastly exaggerated by the Allies; and since Great Britain had cut Germany's transcontinental cable, the Germans had no way of telling their side of the story to Americans. Thus, the sinking of the *Lusitania,* coupled with French and English propaganda, embittered Americans against the German *Reich.* Theodore Roosevelt, who had earlier admired the Germans, began to call for war against Germany. He was critical of President Wilson's policy of neutrality. "In a really tremendous world struggle, with a great moral issue involved," Roosevelt said, "neutrality does not serve righteousness, for to be neutral between right and wrong is to serve wrong."

6. **The preparedness movement in America**

Wilson did nothing immediately to prepare the country for the event of war. Instead, civilians provided the catalyst for military preparedness. General Leonard Wood had, in 1913, established a military training camp at Plattsburg, New York, to train civilians in the techniques of modern warfare. Theodore Roosevelt went about the country promoting the camps and military preparedness in general. The sinking of the passenger liner *Arabic* on which three Americans were killed on August 19, 1915 encouraged the military preparedness movement. But then the German government agreed to Wilson's demand and forbade the sinking of passenger liners and then withdrew all U-boats from the English Channel. Still, in the Fall of 1915, Wilson himself took up the cry of preparedness, on account of which he faced stiff opposition from progressives such as William Jennings Bryan and Senator La Follette, who said Wilson was the dupe of men who wanted to profit off the production of armaments, as well as farm and labor groups. To drum up support for preparedness, Wilson toured the country, stumping for his policies. German war policies in the winter and spring of 1916 – especially the sinking of the passenger liner *Sussex*, in which American passengers were killed – gave greater impetus to preparedness. Nevertheless, Allied actions in the war soured some Americans against the Entente, and news of battle losses in Europe bolstered the desire of Americans to remain neutral. Still, the efforts of Wilson and his new secretary of war, Newton D. Baker, to push preparedness were successful. On August 29, 1916, Congress passed the "Big Navy Act," a ten-year plan to make the United States navy the equal to any other in the world. The United States Shipping Board

Act, passed September 7, allocated $50 million for the purchase or construction of merchant ships that would form a national merchant marine.

7. Wilson's peace efforts and "peace without victory"

In early 1916, Wilson sent Colonel Edward Mandell House on a secret mission to England, France, and Germany to feel out whether the warring powers would accept Wilson's mediation to help end the war. None of the powers were interested. Following the election of 1916, Wilson continued his peace initiatives. The Germans seemed ready to negotiate with the allies. On December 18, 1916, Wilson sent a note to all the belligerent countries, asking them to state "the precise objects which would … satisfy them and their people that the war had been fought out." He received a reply from Lloyd George, prime minister of Great Britain, that Great Britain sought "complete restitution, full reparation, and effectual guarantees" that in the future Germany would maintain peace with her neighbors. But Germany's chancellor. Bethmann-Hollweg did not reply, and Wilson's peace effort came to nothing.

On January 22, 1917, Wilson addressed Congress, laying out his ideas on how peace could be achieved in Europe without any side being the victor. He wanted, in his words, a "peace without victory." Wilson claimed he spoke for the "silent mass of mankind everywhere" when he said that peace should be attained through compromise. But the attainment of peace, he said, required a guarantee of peace, which could only come through recognition of the equality of nations. In the future, no nation should seek to dominate another nation, no one power should rule the seas or the lands, and all nations should agree on limiting their armaments. In the future, said Wilson, nations should avoid "entangling alliances" but should join together in a "concert of power." Wilson proposed that "a force be created … so much greater than the force of any nation now engaged or any alliance hitherto formed or projected that no nation, no probable combination of nations could face or withstand it" – a league of nations.

8. Progressive legislation in 1916

In the summer of 1916, Wilson and congressional Democrats prepared several pieces of progressive legislation. In June, against opposition from conservative Republicans and the business interests, the Senate approved Wilson's appointment of Louis D. Brandeis to the Supreme Court. Brandeis was a progressive pro-labor and social justice lawyer. On July 17, Congress passed the Rural Credits Act, which created 12 federal farm loan banks that would offer low interest mortgages to farmers. In August, Congress passed a Workmen's Compensation Act that assured federal employees' pay in the event of injury or sickness. In September, Congress won for railroad workers the eight-hour workday and other benefits.

9. Why the United States declared war on Germany

In response to the British blockade of Germany, the German government decided it must resume its blockade of Great Britain. In late January, the German government communicated, along with its minimum terms for peace, an announcement that on February 1, 1917 it would commence unrestricted submarine warfare against Allied and neutral ships sailing into the restricted "war zone." On February 3, President Wilson broke off diplomatic relations with Germany. On February 25,

1917, a German U-boat sank the Cunard passenger liner *Laconia*, bound from New York harbor to England. Then, on February 26, the British Naval Intelligence Service presented the United States Department of State with a note, a decoded message from the German foreign secretary Zimmerman to the German minister in Mexico that said if the United States entered the war on the Allied side, the German government would ally itself with Mexico and allow it "to reconquer the lost territory in New Mexico, Texas, and Arizona." The news turned American opinion toward war. In February, after Congress refused to allow Wilson to arm merchant ships, the president ignored Congress and ordered the arming of merchant ships. Following the Russian Revolution in March 15 (which established a republican government in Russia) Wilson called the new Congress into special session. On April 2, before Congress, Wilson called the "warfare against commerce … a warfare against mankind," and asked Congress to declare war on Germany. Wilson said the war's aim would be "to vindicate the principles of peace and justice in the life of the world." He said the U.S. would fight Germany for "the ultimate peace of the world and for the liberation of its peoples, the German peoples included: for the rights of nations great and small and the privilege of men everywhere to choose their way of life and of obedience. *The world must be made safe for democracy...*" On April 4, 1917, the Senate voted to declare war on Germany, followed by the House on Friday, April 6.

10.   Early U.S. contributions to the war and preparations for war

The United States could not send troops to the theater of war right away, but it did help in the war at sea. The United States secretary of the Navy sent destroyers to Queenstown, Ireland, as an anti-submarine patrol. The destroyer patrol and the convoy would dramatically cut down on shipping losses to U-boats: from 850,000 tons in April, to 293,000 tons in November. Meanwhile, Wilson and Congress worked to build up U.S. land forces. On May 18, 1917, Congress passed, and Wilson signed, the Selective Service Act, which required all men between the ages of 21 and 30 to register for service. By June 5, 1917, 9.6 million men had registered for the draft; in 1918, when registration was extended between the limits of 18 and 45 years of age, this number increased to 24.2 million men. The number of men actually inducted into service from the two registrations, however, only amounted to 2.2 million. Wilson advocated centralization policies that increased federal presence in the life of Americans. Taxes, including the new income tax, were raised to meet war expenditures. In August 1917, Congress, at the urging of the president, passed the Lever Act, which gave the federal government the power to create a food and a fuel administration that would regulate industry in the United States. The first American troops arrived in Paris on July 4, 1917; but, by the end of 1917, only 180,000 American soldiers had arrived in France.

11.   Government propaganda efforts during the war and its effects

The federal government waged a war of propaganda against Germany. The congressional committee on public information issued printed material, sent out 75,000 "four minute men" to deliver anti-German oratory at movie houses, and commissioned movies to portray for citizens the barbarity of the "Huns." Though Wilson had asserted that the United States' quarrel was with the German government, not the German people, government-sponsored propaganda, purportedly written by "experts," argued that the German race itself had always been depraved. The propaganda stirred up public sentiment against Americans of German ancestry. In some places, laws were passed forbidding the teaching of the German language in schools and colleges. German books were thrown out of public libraries; the playing of German music was forbidden. German-Americans who supported the Allied side in the war were held suspect.

12. The Espionage and Sedition Acts, and what they accomplished

Acting on the belief that secret agents of the *kaiser* were infiltrating all sectors of American society, Congress, on June 15, 1917, passed the Espionage Act, which punished with a $10,000 fine and 20 years in prison anyone who interfered with the draft or who spread information to the enemy. In May 1918, Congress passed the Sedition Act, which punished anyone who criticized, in writing, speech or action, "the conduct or actions of the United States government or its military forces, including disparaging remarks about the flag, military uniforms, similar badges or symbols." Over 1,500 persons were arrested under the Espionage and Sedition Acts. Most of these were peace advocates, among whom were numbered many anarchists and socialists. Eugene Debs was arrested and convicted under the Sedition Act for an anti-war speech he delivered in Canton, Ohio, on June 16, 1918.

13. What the Red Scare was

Fear of communists and other leftists – called the "Red Scare" – was occasioned by the establishment of the Bolshevik government in Russia. The scare became especially virulent after the war when, in June 1919, Wilson appointed A. Michael Palmer attorney general. Palmer thought Bolshevism threatened the United States with unrest and revolution. The scare was fueled by race riots in East St. Louis, Chicago, and Washington, D.C., by a general strike in Seattle, which was said to be Communist-inspired, and by bombs set off in eight U.S. cities. Palmer's agents raided communist, socialist, IWW, and other leftist headquarters, and broke into union halls, arresting suspected Red revolutionaries. Palmer's primary targets were foreigners, who, since they were not American citizens, could be deported. It influenced the court trial of two Italian anarchists, Nicola Sacco and Bartolomeo Vanzetti. Sacco and Vanzetti, who were arrested and convicted for the murder of Alesandro Berardelli in Braintree, Massachusetts, a suburb of Boston, on April 15, 1920. The Red Scare dissipated after Palmer issued a series of warnings that the Reds would launch a revolution to overthrow the United States government on May 1, 1920 – an event that never transpired.

14. What Pope Benedict XV said in *Ad Beatissimi* and his attitude toward the warring sides

Shortly after he was elected pope, Benedict XV issued, on November 1, 1914, the feast of All Saints, an encyclical letter, *Ad Beatissimi* – a declaration that war violated the mystical union of men in the Communion of Saints. In *Ad Beatissimi*, Pope Benedict insisted that the war came about because of a lack of mutual love among men. He spoke of disregard for divinely established authority in state and church – particularly, the divorce of public authority from the religion of Christ – as well as strife among classes; but ultimately, according to Benedict, greed for money and the search for honors and the pleasures of this life were the ultimate cause of war: Pope Benedict never ceased calling for peace. Criticized for not condemning Germany, Benedict replied that men on both sides of the conflict were his children. Besides, he had received news of alleged German atrocities only from the mouths and pens of Germany's enemies and thus would hold his peace until better evidence was proffered him. The pope did not want to jeopardize the possibility of bringing Germany to the peace table by any undue and hasty condemnation.

15. Pope Benedict's seven peace points and President Wilson's response

After his peace intervention of 1917 had received something of a positive response from Germany, Benedict issued "seven points" that could serve as a basis for peace. In these points, Benedict called on nations to replace the "material force of arms" with the "moral force of right" and, on all sides, simultaneously, to reduce armaments. He said nations should establish an "institution of arbitration" to decide international questions, that would have the power to level sanctions against a state that refused to submit international questions to it for arbitration, or which refused to accept its decision. The pope called for the elimination of "all obstacles to the free intercourse of people" by assuring "true liberty and common rights over the sea." The warring nations, he said, should reciprocally renounce war indemnities for the damages and cost of the war, as "the continuation of such carnage solely for economic reasons would be inconceivable." All occupied territories, said Benedict, should be evacuated and restored to their nations, and rival claims of territory should be considered "in a conciliatory

spirit," giving "due weight, within the limits of justice and feasibility… to the aspirations of the populations, and, on occasion, bringing their particular interests into harmony with the general welfare of the great community of mankind."

When Wilson received the seven points, he replied, through Secretary of State Lansing, that the pope's proposals were unrealistic, especially since the enemy (Germany) had an "irresponsible government" that "secretly planned to dominate the world." Wilson said the United States could not "take the word of the present rulers of Germany as a guaranty of anything that is to endure" unless the "will and purpose of the German people" supported it. Thus, Wilson said he could not accept the pope's peace plan.

16. Wilson's Fourteen Points and what they called for

The "Fourteen Points" for peace Wilson delivered to Congress on January 8, 1918 were very similar to Pope Benedict's seven points, which the president had dismissed as unrealistic. For instance, Benedict's second point, calling for reciprocal decrease of armaments, was essentially Wilson's fourth point. The pope's third point was Wilson's 14th point, where the president called for a "league of nations." Wilson's second point was Benedict's fourth, calling for freedom and community of the seas. Benedict, however, did not call for breaking up existing political units or for forming new states along national lines, as did Wilson.

17. The U.S. contributions to the Allied war effort

U.S. contributions to the Allied war effort became decisive in the Spring of 1918 when the Germans opened a series of offensives on the Western Front. In July 1918, Americans were a decisive factor in the failure of the Germans to meet their objectives in the Second Battle of the Marne. Following the Meuse-Argonne offensive in late September, in which 896,000 Americans (out of combined Allied force of 1,031,000) participated, the cause of Germany was lost.

In August 1918, a German Crown Council, over which Wilson presided, called for peace negotiations.

18. **Wilson's attitude toward Germany's *kaiser* and Austria-Hungary's emperor**

Point ten of Wilson's Fourteen Points dealt with the multicultural, multinational Austro-Hungarian Empire and said essentially that it should be broken up along national lines. When Emperor Karl I of Austria-Hungary sent Wilson a direct appeal to open talks between representatives of their governments, pledged that he would relinquish territories, and asked Wilson to clarify the Fourteenth Point, Wilson refused to deal with him. At war's end, Wilson declared that he would not negotiate with Kaiser Wilhelm II of Germany because he

was not an elected official. The same policy applied to Karl of Austria. Wilson's response led to the deposition of Kaiser Wilhelm II and Emperor Karl's withdrawal from power. The governments established in both Germany and Austria were republics.

19. **How the Great War ended**
On November 11, 1918, representatives of Germany met Allied leaders in a dining car on a rail siding in the forest of Compiègne in France. At 11 a.m. both sides signed an armistice, which ended the war.

20. **Wilson's interventions at Versailles** During the peace negotiations at the French palace of Versailles in January 1919, it was clear that the Fourteen Points had been scrapped and that Germany would be made to pay. In January 1919, when peace negotiations began, Wilson was able to convince Allied leaders to accept the principle of a league of nations. On February 14, the peace conference approved the preliminary draft for the covenant of the League of Nations. But the actual peace

---

Key Terms at a Glance

Entente: a name for the British, Russian, and French alliance in World War I

Seven Points: Pope Benedict XV's proposal to end the First World War and to provide for a future peace

Fourteen Points: President Woodrow Wilson's proposal to end of the First World War and to provide for a future peace. The Fourteen Points were to be the basis of the Treaty of Versailles but were abandoned by the Allies.

League of Nations: an organization composed of representatives of the world's nations for the peaceful solution of international disputes

Communism: a revolutionary socialist movement that aims at creating a classless social order based on common ownership of productive property

negotiations did not go entirely as Wilson wanted. Wilson's fellow negotiators – Georges Clemenceau of France and Lloyd George of Great Britain – wanted vengeance, and they wanted to keep Germany weak. Italy, too, and Japan wanted territorial concessions. Wilson was able to lessen the severity of some Allied demands. Still, the Allies enacted stern measures against their defeated enemy. Wilson directed the redrawing of the boundaries of Eastern Europe in order to assure the "self-determination" of various racial groups. His ideal was that peoples of like language and nationality should be grouped in nations together. Thus, Austria-Hungary was divided into two republics, Austria and Hungary, and the Southern Slav regions (including Bosnia and Herzegovina) of the Habsburg domain were joined to Serbia to form the kingdom of Yugoslavia. But though he favored nations being formed along the lines of common race and language, he opposed Austria's union with Germany because, then, Germany would have a Catholic majority, and that, said Wilson, "would mean the establishment of a great Roman Catholic nation which would be under the control of the Papacy."

21. Indications of the future of progressivism after the Great War

The first evidence that the American pendulum was swinging away from the progressive legacy was the congressional elections of 1918, when voters gave the Republicans control of the Senate. The second was President Wilson's failure to push through the Senate the ratification of the Versailles treaty and the League of Nations covenant. Another sign of the failure of progressivism was the election of 1920, in which the Democrats (the progressive party) lost to the conservative Republican candidate, Warren G. Harding, by an enormous landslide. But one sign that progressivism was not entirely dead was the respectable showing in the polls by the Socialist candidate, Eugene V. Debs, in prison under a Sedition Act conviction.

Questions for Review

1. **How did the assassination of Archduke Franz Ferdinand spark the Great War?** After the assassination of Franz Ferdinand, Franz Josef, emperor of Austria and King of Hungary, acting on the assumption that the government of Serbia was responsible for the assassination, made impossible demands of Serbia. When Serbia refused to accede to all of the demands and began a partial mobilization of its army, Austria-Hungary declared war.

2. **What were President Wilson's reasons for remaining neutral at the beginning of the war?** Addressing the war in an August 19, 1914 message to Congress, President Woodrow Wilson declared that "the United States must be neutral in fact as well as in name…. We must be impartial in thought as well as in action, must put a curb upon our sentiments." Wilson in part was responding to American public opinion, which opposed "foreign entanglements" and participation in foreign wars.

3. **Explain the significance of the sinking of the *Lusitania*.** The sinking of the *Lusitania* aroused American opinion against German, and led to significant policy changes in Wilson's administration. Forced to attend to the international arena, Wilson began to think

that war, though undesirable, was a real possibility. America's army and navy, he began to believe, must be made ready just in case war proved to be the country's lot.

4. **How did Theodore Roosevelt view the war, and how did his opinion compare to those of the American people?**

Roosevelt was against taking sides in the war, and this opinion was similar to that of the American people in that they wanted no entanglement in foreign affairs. But in response to Allied propaganda and the sinking of the *Lusitania*. Roosevelt, who had admired the Germans, began to call for war against Germany. "Neutrality," he said, "does not serve righteousness."

5. **What did Wilson think was the United States' duty in the war?**

Wilson thought it the United States' duty in the war was to continue to follow the same object in war as she had in peace --- "to vindicate the principles of peace and justice in the life of the world as against selfish and autocratic power and to set up amongst the really free and self-governed peoples of the world such a concert of purpose and of action as will henceforth insure the observance of those principles."

6. **Why, according to Wilson, was the United States going to war?**

Wilson said the United States was going to war to vindicate the principles of peace and justice in the life of the world, liberate the German people, to fight for the rights of nations great and small and the privilege of men everywhere to choose their way of life and their government, and to make the world safe for democracy.

7. **What did Pope Benedict XV think was the cause of the war?**

Pope Benedict XV said that the war came about because of a lack of mutual love among men. He said man had disregarded divinely-establihsed authority – particularly the Church of Christ – and had fallen into class strife, greed for money, and desire for honors and the pleasures of this life.

8. **Describe Pope Benedict's Seven Points. How were they similar to, and how different from, Woodrow Wilson's Fourteen Points?**

In the Seven Points points, Benedict called on nations to replace the "material force of arms" with the "moral force of right" and, on all sides, simultaneously, to reduce armaments. He said nations should establish an "institution of arbitration" to decide international questions, that would have the power to level sanctions against a state that refused to submit international questions to it for arbitration, or which refused to accept its decision. The pope called for the elimination of "all obstacles to the free intercourse of people" by assuring "true liberty and common rights over the sea." The warring nations, he said, should reciprocally renounce war indemnities for the damages and cost of the war, as "the continuation of such carnage solely for economic reasons would be inconceivable." All occupied territories, said Benedict, should be evacuated and restored to their nations, and rival claims of territory should be considered "in a conciliatory spirit," giving "due weight, within the limits of justice and feasibility… to the aspirations of the populations, and, on occasion, bringing their particular interests into harmony with the general welfare of the great community of mankind."

The "Fourteen Points" for peace Wilson delivered to Congress on January 8, 1918 were very similar to Pope Benedict's seven points, which the president had dismissed as unrealistic. For instance, Benedict's second point, calling for reciprocal decrease of armaments, was essentially Wilson's fourth point. The pope's third point was Wilson's 14th point, where the president called for a "league of nations." Wilson's second point was Benedict's fourth, calling for freedom and community of the seas. Benedict, however, did not call for breaking up existing political units or for forming new states along national lines, as did Wilson.

9. **Explain Wilson's concept of a League of Nations.**

Wilson thought the attainment of peace required a guarantee of peace, which could only come through recognition of the equality of nations. In the future, said Wilson, nations should avoid "entangling alliances" but should join together in a "concert of power." Wilson proposed that "a force be created … so much greater than the force of any nation now engaged or any alliance hitherto formed or projected that no nation, no probable combination of nations could face or withstand it" – a league of nations.

10. **What American liberties were curtailed during the war?**

During the war, because of a fear of sedition, Congress punished anyone who criticized, in writing, speech or action, the conduct or actions of the United States government or its military forces.

11. **What were the signs that Americans had rejected Progressivism after World War I?**

The first evidence that the American pendulum was swinging away from the progressive legacy was the congressional elections of 1918, when voters gave the Republicans control of the Senate. The second was President Wilson's failure to push through the Senate the ratification of the Versailles treaty and the League of Nations covenant. Another sign of popular rejection of progressivism was the election of 1920, which Republican Warren G. Harding won.

Ideas in Action

1. Study and discuss the poetry of the Great War. (A good source is *The Penguin Book of First World War Poetry*, Jon Silkin, ed.)

2. Listen to the songs of the Great War, and discuss how they embodied the spirit of the time.

3. Consider President Lincoln and President Wilson's curtailment of cherished American liberties during wartime and their reasons for doing so. Is such a curtailment of these liberties ever justified? Stage a debate on the question.

4. As we have seen in this chapter, both President Wilson and Pope Benedict XV supported the formation of a world authority to curtail war. This world authority would exercise powers that we normally associate with national governments. Popes since Benedict XV have continued to favor the existence of such a world authority. Research the question of why they have supported it and discuss why or why not such an authority is desirable. And if it is desirable, what should be the extent of its powers. Should it concern itself only with war or with other matters as well?

Sample Quiz I (pages 701-711)

Please answer the following in complete sentences.

1. What were President Wilson's views on the Great War as stated in his message to Congress in 1914?

2. Describe the different views on the war in the various parts of the United States in 1914.

3. How was American bad feeling towards Great Britain allayed, and why?

4. What effects did the *Lusitania* incident have on American opinion?

5. What was the effect of Allied war propaganda on American opinion?

6. Describe Wilson's peace efforts.

7. Describe the progressive legislation of 1916.

8. Why, according to Wilson, was the United States fighting Germany?

Answers to Sample Quiz I

Students' answers should approximate the following.

1. Addressing the war in an August 19, 1914 message to Congress, President Woodrow Wilson declared that "the United States must be neutral in fact as well as in name…. We must be impartial in thought as well as in action, must put a curb upon our sentiments."

2. In 1914, the majority of Americans favored remaining neutral. College-educated and prosperous Americans favored intervention on the side of the Entente; and in the South, where there was strong pro-English sentiment, many were in favor of aiding Great Britain. The greatest anti-war sentiment was found in the Midwest, where were many settlements of Germans whose sympathies lay with Germany. Populists, who thought the war the work of commercial interests vying for foreign markets, with bankers and munitions makers, were opposed to entering the war.

3. Bad feeling against Great Britain was only allayed when the Entente began placing large orders for food and munitions in the United States. The United States had been suffering from an economic recession in 1914, which this increased buying relieved. In January 1917, Wilson laid out his idea of peace without victory and the germ of his idea for a league of nations.

4. The sinking of the *Lusitania* aroused American opinion against German, and led to significant policy changes in Wilson's administration. Forced to attend to the international arena, Wilson began to think that war, though undesirable, was a real possibility. America's army and navy, he began to believe, must be made ready just in case war proved to be the country's lot.

5. Allied reports to the United States told of German atrocities against civilians in Belgium. Whatever truth there was to these reports, they were vastly exaggerated by the Allies; and since Great Britain had cut Germany's transcontinental cable, the Germans had no way of telling their side of the story to Americans. Thus, the sinking of the *Lusitania*, coupled with French and English propaganda, embittered Americans against the German *Reich*. Theodore Roosevelt, who had earlier admired the Germans, began to call for war against Germany.

6. In early 1916, Wilson sent Colonel Edward Mandell House on a secret mission to England, France, and Germany to feel out whether the warring powers would accept Wilson's mediation to help end the war. On

December 18, 1916, Wilson sent a note to all the belligerent countries, asking them to state "the precise objects which would ... satisfy them and their people that the war had been fought out."

7. On July 17, Congress passed the Rural Credits Act, which created 12 federal farm loan banks that would offer low interest mortgages to farmers. In August, Congress passed a Workmen's Compensation Act that assured federal employees' pay in the event of injury or sickness. In September, Congress won for railroad workers the eight-hour workday and other benefits.

8. Wilson said the United States was fighting Germany to vindicate the principles of peace and justice in the life of the world, liberate the German people, to fight for the rights of nations great and small and the privilege of men everywhere to choose their way of life and government, and to make the world safe for democracy.

Sample Quiz II (pages 711-725)

Please answer the following in complete sentences.

1. **Name some ways the United States contributed to make preparations for the war.**

2. **What were the effects of government propaganda efforts during the war?**

3. **Describe the Espionage Act.**

4. **Describe the Sedition Act.**

5. **What were the main points in *Ad Beatissimi*?**

6. **How did Pope Benedict XV respond to those who criticized him for not condemning Germany?**

7. **Why did Pope Benedict finally decide to issue the Seven Points?**

8. **What was Wilson's response to Pope Benedict's Seven Points?**

9. **What were some indications that progressivism was dying after the Great War?**

Answers to Sample Quiz II

Students' answers should approximate the following.

1. The United States could not send troops to the theater of war right away, but it did help in the war at sea. The United States secretary of the Navy sent destroyers to Queenstown, Ireland, as an anti-submarine patrol. Meanwhile, Wilson and Congress worked to build up U.S. land forces. On May 18, 1917, Congress passed, and Wilson signed, the Selective Service Act, which required all men between the ages of 21 and 30 to register for service. Wilson advocated centralization policies that increased federal presence in the life of Americans. Taxes, including the new income tax, were raised to meet war expenditures. In August 1917, Congress, at the urging of the president, passed the Lever Act, which gave the federal government the power to create a food and a fuel administration that would regulate industry in the United States.

2. Government propaganda stirred up public sentiment against Americans of German ancestry. In some places, laws were passed forbidding the teaching of the German language in schools and colleges. German books were thrown out of public libraries; the playing of German music was forbidden. German-Americans who supported the Allied side in the war were held suspect.

3. Acting on the belief that secret agents of the *kaiser* were infiltrating all sectors of American society, Congress, on June 15, 1917, passed

the Espionage Act, which punished with a $10,000 fine and 20 years in prison anyone who interfered with the draft or who spread information to the enemy.

4. In May 1918, Congress passed the Sedition Act, which punished anyone who criticized, in writing, speech or action, "the conduct or actions of the United States government or its military forces, including disparaging remarks about the flag, military uniforms, similar badges or symbols."

5. In *Ad Beatissimi*, Pope Benedict declared that war violated the mystical union of men in the Communion of Saints. He insisted that the war came about because of a lack of mutual love among men. He spoke of disregard for divinely established authority in state and church – particularly, the divorce of public authority from the religion of Christ, as well as strife among classes, but said, ultimately, greed for money and the search for honors and the pleasures of this life were the ultimate cause of war: Pope Benedict never ceased calling for peace.

6. Criticized for not condemning Germany, Benedict replied that men on both sides of the conflict were his children. Besides, he had received news of alleged German atrocities only from the mouths and pens of Germany's enemies and thus would hold his peace until better evidence was proffered him. The pope did not want to jeopardize the possibility of bringing Germany to the peace table by any undue and hasty condemnation.

7. After his peace intervention of 1917 had received something of a positive response from Germany, Benedict issued "seven points" that could serve as a basis for peace.

8. When Wilson received the seven points, he replied that the pope's proposals were unrealistic, especially since the enemy (Germany) had an "irresponsible government" that "secretly planned to dominate the world." Wilson said the United States could not "take the word of the present rulers of Germany as a guaranty of anything that is to endure" unless the "will and purpose of the German people" supported it.

9. The first evidence that the American pendulum was swinging away from the progressive legacy was the congressional elections of 1918, when voters gave the Republicans control of the Senate. The second was President Wilson's failure to push through the Senate the ratification of the Versailles treaty and the League of Nations covenant. Another sign of the failure of progressivism was the election of 1920, which the conservative Republican Warren G. Harding won

Essays

Instructions to be given to the students: Write in complete sentences. Underline your thesis. Give three supports or examples that explain why you think what you do and that support your thesis.

1. Compare and contrast Pope Benedict XVI's Seven Points and President Wilson's Fourteen Points. Which do you think is better, and why?

2. The Entente and the United States seemed to think they were fighting a great war for a great cause. Do you think this was true? Why or why not? How did the events of the war deny or affirm this idea? (Students may reference outside sources.)

3. Read the poetry of the Great War from the beginning, the middle, and the end of the war. (A good source is *The Penguin Book of First World War Poetry*, Jon Silkin, ed.). How do the views and ideas of the authors change over the course of the war?

Sample Test

Please answer the following in complete sentences.

I. Short Essay – Answer two of the following:

1. Describe President Wilson's ideas on how peace could be achieved.

2. What events caused the United States to declare war on Germany?

3. Describe Pope Benedict XVI's seven peace points.

4. How did Wilson intervene during the peace negotiations at Versailles?

II. Short Answer:

1. In which direction did American opinion go about the war in 1914?

2. What three things encouraged the preparedness movement in America?

3. When did the United States declare war on Germany?

4. What was the "Red Scare"?

5. When did the Great War end?

6. What was one sign that progressivism was not dead in the United States, despite the conservative victory in the election of 1920?

....

Answer Key to the Chapter Test

Students' answers should approximate the following:
I.

1. On January 22, 1917, Wilson addressed Congress, laying out his ideas on how peace could be achieved in Europe without any side being the victor. He wanted, in his words, a "peace without victory." Wilson said that peace should be attained through compromise. But the attainment of peace, he said, required a guarantee of peace, which could only come through recognition of the equality of nations. In the future, no nation should seek to dominate another nation, no one power should rule the seas or the lands, and all nations should agree on limiting their armaments. In the future, said Wilson, nations should avoid "entangling alliances" but should join together in a "concert of power." Wilson proposed that "a force be created … so much greater than the force of any nation now engaged or any alliance hitherto formed or projected that no nation, no probable combination of nations could face or withstand it" – a league of nations.

2. On February 1, 1917, Germany answered that it would commence unrestricted submarine warfare against Allied and neutral ships sailing into the restricted "war zone." On February 3, President Wilson broke off diplomatic relations with Germany. On February 125, 1917, a German U-boat sank the Cunard passenger liner *Laconia*, bound from New York harbor to England. Then, on February 26, the British Naval Intelligence Service presented the United States Department of State with a note, a decoded message from the German foreign secretary Zimmerman to the German minister in Mexico that said if the United States entered the war on the Allied side, the German government would ally itself with Mexico and allow it to reconquer the lost territory in New Mexico, Texas, and Arizona." The news turned American opinion toward war. Following the Russian Revolution in March 15 (which established a republican government in Russia) Wilson called the new Congress into special session. On April 2, before Congress, Wilson called the "warfare against commerce … a warfare against mankind," and asked Congress to declare war on Germany.

3. In his "seven points," Pope Benedict XV called on nations to replace the "material force of arms" with the "moral force of right" and, on all sides, simultaneously, to reduce armaments. He said nations should establish an "institution of arbitration" to decide international questions, that would have the power to level sanctions against a state that refused to submit international questions to it for arbitration, or which refused to accept its decision. The pope called for the elimination of "all obstacles to the free intercourse of people" by assuring "true liberty and common rights over the sea." The warring nations, he said, should reciprocally renounce war indemnities for the damages and cost of the war, as "the continuation of such carnage solely for economic reasons would be inconceivable." All occupied territories, said Benedict, should be evacuated and restored to their nations, and rival claims of territory should be considered "in a conciliatory spirit," giving "due weight, within the limits of justice and feasibility… to the aspirations of the populations, and, on occasion, bringing their particular interests into harmony with the general welfare of the great community of mankind."

4. In January 1919, when peace negotiations began, Wilson was able to convince Allied leaders to accept the principle of a league of nations. On February 14, the peace conference approved the preliminary draft for the covenant of the League of Nations. But the actual peace negotiations did not go entirely as Wilson wanted. Wilson's fellow negotiators – Georges Clemenceau of France and Lloyd George of Great Britain – wanted vengeance, and they wanted to keep Germany weak. Italy, too, and Japan wanted territorial concessions. Wilson was able to lessen the severity of some Allied demands. Still, the Allies enacted stern measures against their defeated enemy. Wilson directed the redrawing of the boundaries of Eastern Europe in order to assure the "self-determination" of various racial groups.

II.
1. As of August 1914, American opinion was largely for staying out of the war.
2. The three things that encouraged the preparedness movement in America were the sinking of the passenger liner *Arabic* on which three Americans were killed on August 19, 1915, German war policies in the spring of 1916, and the sinking of the passenger liner *Sussex* in which American passengers were killed.
3. The United States Senate declared war on Germany on April 4, 1917, followed by the House on April 6.
4. The "Red Scare" was fear of communists and other leftists, occasioned by the establishment of the Bolshevik government in Russia.
5. The Great War ended on November 11, 1918.
6. One sign that progressivism was not entirely dead was the respectable showing in the polls by the Socialist candidate, Eugene V. Debs, in prison under a Sedition Act conviction.

CHAPTER 26: The Roaring Twenties and the Great Crash

Chapter Overview

- The temperance movement, led by people such as Billy Sunday, Frances Willard, Carrie Nation, and others, took on new life in the early 20th century. On December 18, 1917, Congress approved the 18th Amendment, forbidding the manufacture, sale, and transportation of alcohol in the United States. Andrew Volstead introduced a prohibition bill that Congress approved in 1919; it went into effect on January 16, 1920.

- Women began to demand the suffrage, led by Susan B. Anthony and Elizabeth Cady Stanton. Despite opposition on all sides, in 1917 New York gave women the suffrage, and two years later Congress approved the 19th Amendment, giving women the right to vote. It became part of the Constitution on August 26.

- The National Woman's Party introduced into Congress the Equal Rights Amendment, forbidding all discrimination on the basis of sex.

- Henry Ford made his first automobile in 1896 and formed the Ford Motor Company in 1903. In 1908 he came up with a simple, affordable design, the "Model T." His production was greatly increased by his institution of the assembly line in 1914.

- The automobile transformed American society and increased the tendency to urbanization. It had adverse effects on other forms of transportation, and exacerbated the American tendency to rootlessness.

- Orville and Wilbur Wright developed their first glider plane design in 1900, and their first self-propelled plane in 1903. By 1919, the first transatlantic flight was made.

- By the 1920s many Americans were convinced that the United States received more than its share of immigrants. Congress passed the Johnson Act in 1921, limiting immigration. Another Johnson Act in 1924 further limited immigration.

- A census in 1920 showed that for the first time there were more city dwellers than farm dwellers in the United States.

- During the '20s, Americans looked to the great cities for their culture. Tin Pan Alley in New York City began to market music on a mass scale, and soon all of America was singing the same music. This was helped by the Gramophone and the radio. Jazz became popular, and motion pictures were influential in forming the mass-produced culture of the '20s.

- The '20s were a prosperous time in which the American dream was more and more defined as the possession of "things." Salesmanship and advertising became more aggressive, and people began to buy things they didn't know they needed or even wanted.

- Following the Volstead Act, the government began to send agents to inspect every house and cellar in America for alcohol. Bootleggers took industrial alcohol and converted it into gin and whiskey, selling it to clandestine drinking holes called "speakeasies." Crime syndicates arose in big cities to coordinate illegal trade in alcohol and bootlegging. The most famous gangster of this period was Al Capone.

♦ The '20s ushered in new "freedoms," and young people reveled in a culture of sexual promiscuity expressed through dress, music, courtship, and conversation. These young people called themselves the "lost generation" because they didn't fit into or sympathize with the world that had died in the trenches of France.

♦ New educational ideas came to the fore in '20s. John Dewey's educational theories attacked all forms of authoritarianism, including parental and religious authority.

♦ Distorted versions of Psychoanalysis in the United States justified all manner of behavior. Such philosophies weakened further the hold religious belief had on Americans.

♦ Margaret Sanger founded the American Birth Control League, later renamed Planned Parenthood, and encouraged the use of contraceptives. She saw birth control as an instrument to produce a race free of "defectives"and to perfect womanhood. Her thought began to make more parents believe it their moral duty not to bear too many children.

♦ Warren G. Harding's administration was fraught with political corruption. The president himself was not involved in the corruption of his cabinet, though he may have known of it and turned a blind eye to much of it.

♦ President Harding attacked "factions of hatred and prejudice and violence," including a new Ku Klux Klan that terrorized not only blacks but Catholics and Jews, as well. Harding showed himself a foe to a rising Anti-Semitism in the United States.

♦ Harding held the National Disarmament Conference in 1921-22 in which delegates from different countries met to reach an agreement on naval disarmament. The conference resulted in a treaty in which the three major naval powers, Great Britain, the United States, and Japan, agreed to limit their naval tonnage.

♦ Harding died on August 2, 1923, and his vice-president, Calvin Coolidge, took office. A year later Coolidge won the presidential election. In his term, Coolidge stressed strict economy.

♦ In the late 1920s, the economy boomed. Things were not so good under the surface, however. Agriculture had taken a big hit, and speculation schemes brought instability to the market. Operators of companies led "bear raids" on smaller companies, driving them out of business. The wealth in America was not well distributed.

♦ In October of 1929, stock prices began to fall, and investors began frantically to sell off their stock. People stopped buying on credit, industrial production fell, and workers were laid off. By 1932 unemployment had reached 12 million. Men withdrew their deposits from banks, which caused many of them to fold.

♦ In 1932 Franklin Delano Roosevelt became president by promoting what he called his "New Deal" in an attempt to turn the country towards recovery.

What Students Should Know

1. **About the Temperance Movement and the 18th Amendment**

The temperance movement went back a long way in American history. Frances Willard organized women into the Women's Christian Temperance Union in 1874. Twenty years later, temperance activists formed the Anti-Saloon League of America. Both organizations believed the consumption of alcohol led to innumerable social ills, such as poverty, disease, crime, and insanity. Members of the Women's Christian Temperance Union used moral persuasion to convince people to abandon drink. Carrie Nation of Medicine Lodge, Kansas, from 1900 until about 1910, began destroying bottles, kegs and furniture in saloons. Temperance was widely supported by evangelical Protestant churches and preachers (such as Billy Sunday). They received the support of women who wanted their husbands to give up drink and by business leaders. By 1917, 27 states had passed laws making the production, sale, and consumption of alcoholic beverages illegal. Other states passed "local option" legislation that allowed towns and counties "go dry" if they chose. But states complained that unless all states went dry, state and local prohibition laws were useless. In December 1917, Congress approved (and in little more than a year, the required number of states approved) the 18th Amendment to the Constitution that forbade "the manufacture, sale, or transportation of intoxicating liquors within, the importation thereof into, or the exportation thereof from the United States and all territory subject to the jurisdiction." In the meantime, Congress approved, in October 1919 the "Volstead Act" prohibiting the production, sale, and manufacture of all liquors that contained over one-half of one percent of alcohol. The Volstead Act went into effect January 16, 1920, one year after the ratification of the 18th Amendment.

2. **The women's suffrage movement and the 19th Amendment**

By the time of Wilson's inauguration as president in 1913, proponents of granting women the right to vote (called "suffragettes") had become a powerful political force in the United States. The two movements, woman's suffrage and temperance, so overlapped with one another that liquor companies opposed women's suffrage, in part it seems, because they feared votes for women equaled votes for prohibition. The two most prominent leaders of the women's suffrage movement, Susan B. Anthony and Elizabeth Cady Stanton, were prominent in the temperance movement and, before the Civil War, in the abolitionist movement. The suffragette movement had been demanding the vote as the key and guarantee of other natural rights that the movement believed belonged to women. Suffragettes rejected traditional notions of male authority, both in the state and the family. Many of them held that all professions, including law, political office, and the ministry, should be open to women. Anthony applied to women arguments she had used to defend the right of blacks to vote. The freedom to secure their naturals rights, she said, belonged to blacks before governments were ever created, and blacks did "not barter away their natural rights" when they entered into political society. Anthony held that the suffrage was a woman's inalienable right and so to deprive women of the right to vote was an act of tyranny. Not all suffragettes went as far as Anthony and Stanton. In 1895, more conservative elements in the women's suffrage movement distanced themselves from Stanton when she published *The Women's Bible.* In this work, Stanton argued that one had to look at God in a new light – not as masculine only, but as feminine as well; not only as Heavenly Father, but as Heavenly Mother.

Not everyone, not even all women, supported the women's suffrage movement. Many opposed the suffragette movement because they thought that giving woman the right to vote would remove her from her proper sphere, the home. The notion of equality espoused by proponents of women's suffrage was in opposition to the traditional notion that the father represented his family in society. To give women the suffrage assumed that wives had interests opposed to their husbands' interests. Opponents of women's suffrage formed, in 1911, the National Association Opposed to Woman Suffrage, led by Mrs. Arthur Dodge. Cardinal Gibbons was a prominent member of the National Association. He thought giving women the suffrage would remove them from the sphere of the home, which in turn would diminish women's dignity. Mother Mary Jones also opposed giving women the suffrage. Speaking of feminism, she said that "women are out of place in political work. There already is a great responsibility upon women's shoulders – that of rearing rising generations. It has been in part their sad neglect of motherhood which has filled reform schools and which keeps the juvenile courts busy." Jones held that women "can begin now to be more useful than they have been by studying these economic problems and helping toward industrial peace … Home training of the child should be her task, and it is the most beautiful of tasks. Solve the industrial problem and the men will earn enough so that women can remain at home and not leave it."

Yet, despite opponents, in 1917, New York gave women the suffrage. Two years later, the United States Congress approved the 19th Amendment: "The right of citizens of the United States to vote shall not be denied or abridged by the United States or by any State on account of sex." By August 26, 1920, the required 36 states had approved the amendment, and it became part of the Constitution.

3. The Equal Rights Amendment

In 1923, the National Women's Party (NWP) introduced into Congress the Equal Rights Amendment (ERA), which forbade all discrimination on the basis of sex. The NWP opposed legislation directed to protecting women workers because such legislation treated them as a special class, not as equals to men – thus allying itself with the *laissez-faire* National Association of Manufacturers (which endorsed the ERA). Unlike suffrage, the ERA never even made it through Congress.

4. Who Henry Ford was and what he accomplished

Ford, a native of Dearborn Michigan, became interested in mechanics as a young man. After learning about the internal combustion engine (developed by the German Nikolaus August Otto in 1870), Ford became interested in understanding and building his own version of the new invention called the automobile. He completed his first model automobile in 1896 and by 1899 had built three more. His first attempt to form an automobile company failed in 1900, and for the next three years he built racers. The fame of one of these racers, the "999," attracted the interest of several investors, with whom Henry formed the Ford Motor Company in 1903. Ford wanted to produce cars that the typical working man could afford. In 1908 he came up with a simple design for a car that would require low maintenance and would be easy to repair – the "Model T." By 1916, Ford Motor Company had sold over 500,000 cars and, by 1923, about 2,500,000. In 1927, the company reached the 15 million mark in cars sold worldwide. Ford's institution of the assembly line in 1914 greatly accelerated the manufacturing of cars. The assembly line allowed for continuous production, making it possible for one car to be built in just 93 minutes. In the coming years, other industries would adopt the assembly line, significantly reducing the cost of manufactured goods. In order to attract better workers (and to increase their buying power) Ford raised wages in his industries from $2.40 for a nine-hour day to $5 for an eight-hour day. Workers that increased in skill and speed could see their wages raised to six or seven dollars a day. Such wages assured for the auto tycoon a steady and loyal workforce and increased his factory output. It also allowed (through greater efficiency) for a gradual decrease in the price of the Model T.

5. The automobile and its social effects

Ford was not the only automobile manufacturer in the United States. Though New England was, at first, the center of the auto industry in the United States, the success of Ford brought more and more auto manufacturers to the Detroit area, making that city the center of the auto industry. Gradually, larger manufacturers absorbed the smaller ones. The automobile transformed American life perhaps more than any other single invention. Since the Ford car was so inexpensive, many could buy one, and this led, eventually, to the building of suburban communities outside of large cities and to a gradually spreading urbanization of the countryside. Trucks benefitted Farmers. State governments began funding the construction of roads. By 1925, states began paying for hardtop roads, and the following year the federal government offered funds to match whatever the states raised themselves. Thus, increasingly, distant parts of the country began to be connected by a network of highways. Automobile production had an adverse effect on other forms of transportation and the industries that

supported them. In time, the bus would replace the rural trolley car. Coastal steamboat and freight traffic would give way to truck transportation. With the increasing use of oil and petroleum, coal-mining regions languished while oil producing areas (such as California and Texas) increased in population and prosperity. With the expansion of good roads and the growing abundance of gasoline, Americans began taking road trips. This growing ease of transportation exacerbated the American lack of rootedness and of fidelity to one's native soil. Indeed, the automobile would become the symbol of individual freedom and would take its place as a constituent part of the "American dream" of individual autonomy and material prosperity.

6. The invention of the airplane and its social effects

In December 1903, the two brothers, Orville and Wilbur Wright of Dayton, Ohio, came to Kitty Hawk on the coast of North Carolina with a glider to which they had fixed a four-cylinder, 200-pound, 12-horsepower engine that they had designed. On the morning of December 17, the Wrights made four powered flights on the beach at Kitty Hawk. The Wrights continued to perfect their airplane design. Two years after Kitty Hawk, Wilbur flew a Wright plane 24 miles in 38 minutes. Wilbur took a 35 horsepower plane he and Orville had designed to France in 1908 and flew it 62 miles, 361 feet above the ground, in one hour and 54 minutes. World War I accelerated airplane design, replacing stick and canvas for strong steel for the bodies of planes. Beginning in 1919, pilots began making transatlantic flights, and two army lieutenants made the first non-stop transcontinental flight from New York to San Diego in a German Fokker monoplane in 26 hours and 50 minutes. Lieut. Commander Richard E. Byrd made the first flight over the North Pole on May 9, 1926. A Wright engine powered the Ryan monoplane, the "Spirit of St. Louis," in which the young Charles A. Lindbergh made his non-stop flight from Roosevelt Field on Long Island to the Le Bourget airdrome in Paris on May 20-21, 1927. Lindbergh had flown the longest distance yet: 3,735 miles in 33 hours and 39 minutes. The development of passenger airlines would eventually end the reign of the railroad and of passenger ships in long-distance passenger transportation. The first passenger air service began in 1927, between New York and Boston. In the early 1930s, Trans World Airlines would initiate the age of modern airline transportation.

7. **Why the United States began restricting foreign immigration in the 1920s, and the effects of such restrictions**

By the 1920s, many Americans had become convinced that the United States should reform its past liberal immigration policies. Labor leaders didn't want gains they had made for workers lost by an influx of laborers who could work for much lower wages. Some intellectuals argued that, since most of the immigrants were now coming from southern and eastern Europe, their political traditions would corrupt American freedom. In 1921, Congress passed the Johnson Act, which President Warren Harding signed. The Johnson Act limited the number of immigrants to three percent of the number of the foreign born of each nationality in the U.S. according to the 1910 census. The Johnson Act also set quotas according to the immigrants' countries of origin: the majority, from Northern Europe; the remainder, from southern and eastern Europe. Subsequent congressional acts

further lowered immigration quotas and were clearly seeking to cut off southern and eastern European immigration. In 1924, Congress approved the visa system, which required immigrants to prove that they would not end up on the public dole and that they were not communists or anarchists. The immigration laws did not apply to Canadians, Mexicans, or immigrants from the West Indies. Limiting immigration led to a decline in foreign ghettoes in the cities and of foreign language publications and journals. Formerly European ethnic ghettoes became increasingly black and Puerto Rican, as these peoples moved north to take advantage of industrial jobs in the cities.

8. **Increasing urbanization, its causes and effects**

The United States Census of 1920 reported that, for the first time in American history, city dwellers outnumbered those who lived on farms and in small towns. The rural population had decreased to 48.6 percent of a population numbering 117.8 million. Some rural people came to cities to seek their fortunes. The increase in monoculture and the dependence on distant centers for the processing and sale of farm produce had already altered farming culture. The mechanization of farming was undermining the viability of farming society. Mechanical harvesters and reapers, steam tractors and then gasoline-driven tractors enhanced productivity even more, decreasing the number of laborers needed in the fields. Unemployed farm laborers swelled the population of urban areas. Farms grew larger as lands formerly reserved for growing feed for draft animals could now be tilled for cash crops. Mechanization made it easier to work more and more land. The increased productivity resulted in the overproduction of farm products; and since the supply of food exceeded the demand for food, the price of crops fell. Soon, only farmers who could afford the machinery to work the ever-growing farmsteads could compete on the market. Those who could not afford the machinery were forced out of business and moved to the cities. The move from the country to the city had tremendous social significance. Farming communities tend to be conservative, are slow to change, and so preserve traditions. Moving to the city, country folk were thrown into the maelstrom of an ever-changing American culture where old values were being questioned and new ones were being created to replace the old. With the dwindling of the country population, America lost an important bastion of conservatism needed to withstand an ever-swelling tide of new-fangledness, not only in mechanical inventions, but in the social and moral life of the people as well.

9.   American mass culture in the 1920s

A popular, mass culture characterized the United States in the 1920s. Manners, habits of dress, music, cuisine, and other aspects of culture were developed in the cities and aped in rural communities. Indigenous, local forms of music were being replaced by popular songs produced by composers and publishers on what was called Tin Pan Alley in New York City. This mass-produced popular music, though not exactly something new in America, undermined local traditions and helped destroy all musical variety. Everyone, everywhere, was listening to the same music. Recorded music accelerated this trend and made stars out of individual singers. Recordings also helped spread another sort of music: Jazz. Equally influential in forming the mass-produced culture of the '20s were motion pictures, produced in Hollywood, California.

The 1920s were a prosperous time. The stock market continued to rise to unprecedented heights throughout the decade. It seemed as if everyone was entering the middle class and could enjoy the comforts of life. The American dream was more and more defined as the possession of "things" – of cars, radios, factory-made furniture, and clothing of the latest fashion. Such possessions defined the middle-class family. Salesmen peddled big city standards of "respectable" and comfortable living. Salesmanship and advertising were more aggressive in the '20s than in any previous decade of American history. The mass production of automobiles and other products required a vigorous sales effort to convince people to buy, and this contributed to mass culture. Advertising convinced Americans to define their lives by material standards – to keep up with their neighbors in the race toward prosperity and comfort. Companies convinced people to "buy on time" – that is, to go into debt – to purchase items that they could well do without. Most Americans purchased their Fords by paying them off over time. Mass production and advertising influenced even American cuisine, making it everywhere the same. Manufacturers produced foods that required a minimum of preparation. Except for a few isolated souls, the men of the 1920s wanted no causes, desired no struggles; they wanted "normalcy," they longed only for a comfortable, prosperous life.

10.   The effects of Prohibition

Prohibition did not end the buying, selling, transportation, and consumption of alcohol in the United States. Rather, it seemed to accelerate these activities. In the years following the passage of the Volstead Act, bootleggers ran distilleries and smugglers criss-crossed the Mexican and Canadian borders to bring in foreign liquor. Ships from foreign countries, anchored off the three-mile limit of the American coastline, awaited motor launches that would carry smuggled alcohol to shore. People brewed their own beer and hard cider for personal use, or took industrial alcohol and converted it into "bathtub gin" and whiskey – "hooch" – some of which was sold to clandestine drinking holes called "speakeasies." Prohibition didn't decrease the drinking of hard liquor; with the closing of breweries and wineries, drinkers turned instead to hard beverages like gin and whiskey. Speakeasies were raided by government agents, their liquor destroyed, and their owners jailed. Yet speakeasies benefited from the patronage of large crime syndicates in the cities that bribed police and government officials to turn a blind eye to speakeasy traffic or to deal gently with speakeasy operators. After the passage of Prohibition, crime syndicates arose in big cities such as New York and Chicago to coordinate the illegal trade in alcohol and bootlegging. Gangsters and the mafia grew rich and powerful off the illegal traffic in alcohol.

11. The "Lost Generation" and its character

Suffrage was not the only new "freedom" women enjoyed in the 1920s. The decade witnessed a loosening of age-old standards of feminine decorum that, in turn, had its effects on the relationship between the sexes. Young people, especially, of the 1920s, rejected what they thought was the over-rigid morality of the late 19th century (the "Victorian Age"). Instead, they reveled in a culture of sexual promiscuity that expressed itself in dress, music, courtship, and conversation. The young people of the post-war era called themselves the "lost generation" because they didn't fit into or sympathize with the world that had died in World War I. Old

standards of courtship were collapsing. Various new ideas that were floating about aided in the decline of morality during the decade of the '20s. John Dewey's educational theories attacked all forms of "authoritarianism," including in that term parental authority and the authority of religion. For Dewey, there was no absolute right or wrong, but, he said, ethics must be adjusted to the peculiar conditions of each time and place. Knowledge, too, according to Dewey, was not about truth but about dealing with practical difficulties in the here and now. Closely allied with Dewey's Pragmatism was Permissiveness, which held that parents should not restrict their children's behavior but allow them to follow the thrust of their desires as much as possible. Popularized and distorted versions of Psychoanalysis, developed by the Austrians Sigmund Freud and Carl Jung, and introduced to the English speaking world by Havelock Ellis, taught that it was psychologically "unhealthy" for people to "repress" their sexual desires; that by doing so, they would develop "neuroses."

12. Changes in the religious and family life in the 1920s

The new philosophies weakened further the hold religious belief had on Americans. Religious belief had been declining before the 1920s and, with it, the institution of the family. For decades, the family had suffered various strains. The industrial world had reduced many families to grinding poverty. It had divorced economic activity from the home and so separated fathers for long periods of time from their families. These strains, together with the new permissive philosophies, wreaked havoc on family life. Along with the burdens placed on the traditional family, the 1920s witnessed a campaign waged against the large family. Margaret Sanger and her American Birth

Control League (later renamed Planned Parenthood) led the charge in this war. She founded the American Birth Control League to disseminate the idea that women could only be free if they were able to control their reproductive faculties. Sanger saw birth control as instrumental in producing a race free of "defectives," as she called those with mental and physical disabilities. Sanger's thought would in time make more and more parents think that they had a moral duty not to bear too many children. Many would come to think that the way to stop poverty and other social ills was to limit the increase of the population.

13.   Anti-social movements in the 1920s

The 1920s saw the rise of a new Ku Klux Klan. This new Klan hated not only blacks, but Catholics and Jews as well. Swathed in the white robes and hoods of the older Klan, the new Klan had added another symbol – the burning cross – which it ignited before the houses of its victims. The new Ku Klux was not just a southern phenomenon; the organization throve in the Midwest, where blacks were moving in great numbers for work, and in the Far West. The Klan was able to get sympathetic governors elected in Oklahoma and Oregon and nearly took control of the government of Indiana. Anti-Semitism was on the rise in the 1920s, and one of its chief proponents was none other than Henry Ford. The Ford-controlled Dearborn, Michigan newspaper published the spurious "Protocols of the Elders of Zion," which purported to be a document written by Jews, in which they planned a subversion of Christian civilization. In 1920, Ford published a book, *The International Jew*. In this book he argued that Jews were at the bottom of war and all its ills.

14.   The Harding administration

Harding has gone down in history as perhaps the worst president the United States has had, because of the corruption of his administration. Yet, there is more to said of Harding besides the corruption of the men closest to him. In domestic policy, Harding worked to curtail government expenditures and to cut taxes, including dramatically slashing income tax rates. The president was in favor of tariffs with rates flexible enough to rise and fall according circumstances. Harding opposed joining the League of Nations because he thought it would form a super-state that would rob member states of their sovereignty. Harding's great foreign policy triumph was the National Disarmament Conference, held in Washington, D.C. in 1921-22. Delegates from the United States, Britain, Japan, France, Italy, Belgium, Holland, Portugal, and China met to reach an agreement on naval disarmament. In the treaty that resulted, the three major naval powers, Great Britain, the United States, and Japan, agreed to limit their naval tonnage. Japan benefited most from the treaty because, though her navy was to be smaller than the navies of either the United States or Great Britain, she had only one ocean to govern, while the United States had to divide her fleets over two seas, and Great Britain over three. The Harding administration answered the plea of the Soviet Union for food relief; the American Relief Association in 1922 began directing 18,000 relief stations in the Soviet Union, which fed four million children and six million adults. Medical aid was also given. The Harding administration oversaw similar relief efforts in other countries. Still, in 1921, criticism of Harding's corrupt aides grew. Farmers, who were suffering the effects of low prices for their crops, were not happy with Harding because he opposed extending government relief to them. Harding died of pneumonia on August 2, 1923.

15. Corruption in the Harding administration

The Harding administration was rife with political corruption. The president was not involved in this corruption; still he did nothing to stop it, when he knew of it. With the death of Harding, news of the scandals in his administration became public. It became known that Albert B. Fall, Harding's secretary of the interior, and Edwin M. Denby, the secretary of the navy, had received the president's permission to transfer naval petroleum deposits from the naval to the interior department. Fall illegally leased the public oil reserve, Elk Hill, to the oil magnate, Edward Doheny, and the Teapot Dome reserve in Wyoming to another oil man, Harry Sinclair, in return for some oil storage tanks the oil men agreed to build at the naval base at Pearl Harbor. On top of that, Fall received $300,000 from Sinclair and $100,000 from Doheny. The "Teapot Dome Scandal" was but the beginning of the scandals discovered in the Harding administration.

16. Calvin Coolidge and his administration

Coolidge, who, as vice president under Harding, succeeded the latter as president in 1923 was a taciturn man who continued the "conservative" Republican policies of his predecessor. Coolidge favored maintaining the tariff, but without frequent revisions. He was for tax reduction. He disapproved of government aid to relieve farmers as well as any bonuses to war veterans, though he signed an act that doubled the amount of money the federal government gave to the builders of merchant ships. He opposed joining the League of Nations but agreed to U.S. participation in the World Court.

Coolidge stressed strict "economy" in government, which meant, in part, a reduction and, even, elimination of the national debt. Coolidge supported cutting taxes. He opposed the Veterans Bonus Bill, but the Republican Congress overrode his veto. The Coolidge administration furthered the peace-making policies of Harding. Secretary of State Kellogg and Aristide Briand of France in 1928 drew up the Kellogg-Briand Peace Pact, to which 62 nations, including Italy, Japan, and Germany signed on. In the pact, the signing powers pledged that they would "renounce war as an instrument of national policy," and that they would solve "all disputes or conflicts of whatever nature or of whatever origin" by peaceful means.

17. The condition of the economy in the 1920s

During the 1920s, the American economy was booming. The stock market was rising to unprecedented heights; common people could buy such "luxuries" as an automobile, a radio, and the accoutrements for the "modern kitchen." Widespread optimism assured the nation that, soon, every American could achieve the "American dream" of middle class comfort. Coolidge claimed, in 1928, that prosperity had come to America precisely because government had taken a hands-off policy toward business. But not all sectors of the economy had been doing well. The biggest industries were those that produced automobiles and radios, along with those industries tied to automobiles and radios (for instance, the rubber and tire-making industries). Other industries, though, languished. Agriculture, for instance, had taken huge hits after the war. During the war, the government had encouraged farmers to expand their fields and to buy machinery to produce surpluses for the army and the war-devastated peoples of Europe. The government artificially hiked the prices of wheat and other grains to $2 a bushel. By 1920, however, the price of wheat had fallen to 67 cents a bushel, and farmers fell deep into debt. Neither Harding nor Coolidge, would do anything to help the farmers.

The farmers' problem was overproduction. Overproduction would have plagued even the auto industry and its related industries, but for several factors. For one, these industries extended credit to consumers to buy cars, radios, toasters, and other items. The European market – devastated during the war – was another source of growth for American industries in the 1920s. After the war, the United States had made many large loans to Europe, a large percentage of which returned to the United States in the form of purchases for manufactured goods. High U.S. tariffs, however, kept reviving European industries from competing in the American market, and European industry languished. Eventually, Europe could not pay off debts to America; loans from the United States thereafter decreased as did European purchases of American goods.

Perhaps the biggest boom in American business resulted from widespread speculation in stocks. Participation in the stock market spread throughout society.

Stock brokers allowed investors to buy stocks "on margin," a scheme that worked well as long as stocks continued to rise, but could be devastating if stocks fell dramatically. Enough investors selling their stocks could quickly depreciate the value of the stocks. Speculation schemes brought instability to the market. – Stock pools, "bear raids," and purchase of stocks in a smaller company and its subsequent closure.

Another source of instability for the economy of the booming '20s was the ill distribution of wealth. In 1929, only 0.1 percent of the people had income that equaled the combined income of the lowest 42 percent of the people; this same 0.1 percent controlled one third of the savings, while 80 percent of the people had no savings at all.

18. The Crash of 1929 and its effects

On September 3, 1929, stock prices began to fall and then plummeted on Monday, October 21. Panicky investors began selling. Though over the next two days prices stabilized, on "Black Thursday," October 24, prices took another dive. Prices stabilized again on Friday and Saturday, when major bankers intervened to shore up the market; but on Monday, prices plummeted, and the market fell by 13 percent. The next day, Tuesday, October 29, 1929 terrified investors frantically

---

Key Terms at a Glance

suffragette: an advocate for woman's suffrage

speakeasy: a clandestine drinking hole where alcohol was illegally sold in the Prohibition era

Pragmatism: a school of thought that holds that knowledge is not about truth but is to be directed toward dealing with practical difficulties

Permissiveness: an opinion in psychology that says parents should not restrict their children's behavior but allow them to follow the thrust of their desires as much as possible

sold off their stocks. Over 16 million stocks changed hands that "Black Tuesday."

The panic of Wall Street spread across the nation. Consumers, both rich and middle class, stopped buying on credit, and industrial production fell by nine percent between October and December 1929. Industrial downturn led to worker layoffs, and those laid off could not afford to make further payments on the items they had bought on credit. Instead, they returned such items to manufacturers, only exacerbating the glut of manufactured goods and leading to yet further layoffs. By 1930, unemployment reached five million; by 1932, it had climbed to 12 million – 25 percent of the normal working force. As people withdrew their deposits from banks, many banks folded. Shantytowns began springing up to house those who had been turned out of their houses. Farmers resorted to arms to resist in the repossession of their farms by banks. While many of the rich could weather the hard times, a large number of the middle class and the poor were in a desperate condition. They felt they had no place to turn to find protection from the forces that threatened to overwhelm them.

19. President Herbert Hoover's ideas on how to address the "Great Depression"

Herbert Hoover maintained his confidence in the Liberal economic system he had espoused in more prosperous times. In his mind, the president must give encouragement to the country; he should promote policies to help business revive, but he must never support measures that give direct relief to the suffering nor suffer the government to interfere in the economy beyond what is necessary to maintain equal opportunity and the freedom of individual enterprise. Despite the deepening crisis, Hoover continued to

speak as if all would soon be well. Yet, despite Hoover's optimistic prognostications, the depression deepened. Hoover did sign a measure passed by Congress in March 1932, the Reconstruction Finance Corporation (RFC), which could lend money to railroads, banks, agricultural agencies, and to industrial and commercial companies. The philosophy behind the RFC was that aid given to corporations would eventually "trickle down" to everyone else. The RFC was instrumental in saving many banks from going bust.

20. What Franklin Delano Roosevelt's "New Deal" entailed

Roosevelt, the Democratic presidential nominee in the election of 1932, proposed active government intervention in the economy. He called for federal unemployment relief, for legislation directly to aid agriculture and railroads and to protect consumers and investors. He wanted to lower tariffs and to repeal Prohibition. All this he called the "New Deal," which was really not all that new, being an extension of Teddy Roosevelt's "Square Deal," Wilson's "New Freedom," and the policies promoted by the Progressive Bull Moosers.

21. How Roosevelt reconciled the expansion of presidential and federal powers with the United States Constitution

Roosevelt said emergency measures were needed to meet the crisis of the Great Depression. He said that if "the normal balance of executive and legislative authority" was not adequate for the purpose, he would ask Congress for "broad executive power" to attack the crisis. Roosevelt said, "Our Constitution is so simple and practical that it is possible always to meet extraordinary needs by changes in emphasis and arrangement without loss of essential form."

Questions for Review

1. **Why did people such as Cardinal Gibbons and Mother Jones oppose woman's suffrage?**

   Cardinal Gibbons thought giving women the suffrage would remove her from the sphere of the home, which in turn would diminish women's dignity. Mother Mary Jones also opposed giving women the suffrage because she said that women are out of place in political work, and that there is already a great responsibility upon women's shoulders – that of rearing rising generations. Jones held that home training of the child should be the women's task, and it is the most beautiful of tasks.

2. **How did the assembly line affect the worker as a craftsman?**

   While the assembly line greatly increased production, it had the mind numbing effect of reducing each worker to a mere cog in a wheel. Before, an individual worker was involved in the manufacturing process from beginning to end and so would do a number of different tasks and be able to see the fruits of his labor; on the assembly line, however, he performed one simple task over and over and over again. Little skill was, therefore, required of the worker; he became merely one easily replaceable part of a great manufacturing machine. In the coming years, other industries would adopt the assembly line, significantly reducing the cost of manufactured goods, but at the high price of further demeaning the workman in his dignity as craftsman.

3. **What effects did the automobile have on American life?**

   The automobile transformed American life perhaps more than any other single invention. Since the Ford car was so inexpensive, many could buy one, and this led, eventually, to the building of suburban communities outside of large cities and to a gradually spreading urbanization of the countryside. Trucks benefitted farmers. State governments began funding the construction of roads. By 1925, states began paying for hardtop roads, and the following year the federal government offered funds to match whatever the states raised themselves. Thus, increasingly, distant parts of the country began to be connected by a network of highways. Automobile production had an adverse effect on other forms of transportation and the industries that supported them. In time, the bus would replace the rural trolley car. Coastal steamboat and freight traffic would give way to truck transportation. With the increasing use of oil and petroleum, coal-mining regions languished while oil producing areas (such as California and Texas) increased in population and prosperity. With the expansion of good roads and the growing abundance of gasoline, Americans began taking road trips. Indeed, the automobile would become the symbol of individual freedom and would take its place as a constituent part of the "American dream" of individual autonomy and material prosperity.

4. **What American traits did the automobile exacerbate?**

   The automobile exacerbated the American lack of rootedness and of fidelity to one's native soil.

5. **Why did Americans became so opposed to immigration by the 1920s?**

    By the 1920s, many Americans had become convinced that the United States should reform its past liberal immigration policies. Labor leaders didn't want gains they had made for workers lost by an influx of laborers who could work for much lower wages. Some intellectuals argued that, since most of the immigrants were now coming from southern and eastern Europe, their political traditions would corrupt American freedom.

6. **What social forces led to the decline of the farm population and the growth of cities?**

    Industrialism and the mechanization of farming, along with the rest of life, began to undermine the viability of farming society. Mechanical harvesters and reapers, steam and gasoline tractors, enhanced productivity but decreased the number of laborers needed in the fields. Unemployed farm laborers left the country for the city, swelling the population of urban areas.

7. **How did increased urbanization influence and change American society?**

    The move from the country to the city had tremendous social significance. Farming communities tend to be conservative, are slow to change, and so preserve traditions. Moving to the city, country folk were thrown into the maelstrom of an ever-changing American culture where old values were being questioned and new ones were being created to replace the old. With the dwindling of the country population, America lost an important bastion of conservatism needed to withstand an ever-swelling tide of newness, not only in mechanical inventions, but in the social and moral life of the people as well.

8. **Explain Chesterton's claim that "the problem with rural Americans was that they were not peasants."**

    Chesterton said that "the defect by which [Americans] fall short of being a true peasantry is that they… do not, like some peasantries, create other kinds of culture besides the kind called agriculture. Their culture comes from the big cities; and that is where all the evil comes from."

9. **What were some of the "freedoms" enjoyed by the Lost Generation?**

    The Lost Generation enjoyed such "freedoms" as suffrage and a loosening of age-old standards of feminine decorum that, in turn, had its effects on the relationship between the sexes. Young people, especially, of the 1920s, rejected what they thought was the over-rigid morality of the late 19th century (the "Victorian Age"). Instead, they reveled in a culture of sexual promiscuity that expressed itself in dress, music, courtship, and conversation.

10. **How did Pragmatism, Permissiveness, and Psychoanalysis affect religion and family in America?**

    These philosophies weakened the hold religious belief had on Americans. Religious belief had been declining before the 1920s and, with it, the institution of the family. Pragmatism and Permissiveness influenced parents who were told by various "authorities" that they should not restrict their children's behavior but allow them to follow the thrust of their desires as much as possible. Psychoanalysis justified all manner of behavior. American youth were told that it was psychologically "unhealthy" to "repress" their sexual desires.

11. **Briefly lay out the causes of the economic crash of 1929.**

During the 1920s, America's economy was booming. The stock market rose to unprecedented heights. But not all sectors of the economy had been doing well. Farmers suffered from overproduction. After the war, the United States had made many large loans to Europe. Because high U.S. tariffs, however, kept reviving European industries from competing in the American market, European industry languished. Eventually, Europe could not pay off debts to America; loans from the United States thereafter decreased as did European purchases of American goods.

Perhaps the biggest boom in American business resulted from widespread speculation in stocks. Participation in the stock market spread throughout society. Stock brokers allowed investors to buy stocks "on margin," a scheme that worked well as long as stocks continued to rise, but could be devastating if stocks fell dramatically. Enough investors selling their stocks could quickly depreciate the value of the stocks. Speculation schemes brought instability to the market. – Stock pools, "bear raids," and purchase of stocks in a smaller company and its subsequent closure.

Another source of instability for the economy of the booming '20s was the ill distribution of wealth. In 1929, only 0.1 percent of the people had income that equaled the combined income of the lowest 42 percent of the people; this same 0.1 percent controlled one third of the savings, while 80 percent of the people had no savings at all.

Ideas in Action

1. Read Chesterton's *What I Saw in America*. Discuss whether his description of America in the 1920s remains true today.

2. Read more about Henry Ford and the Wright brothers and how they made their inventions.

3. Obtain a copy of the American bishops' 1919 pastoral letter. Discuss whether their diagnosis of American culture remains true today.

4. Read Franklin Delano Roosevelt's first inaugural address (available on the internet). Would a modern politician speak as he did? Why or why not?

Sample Quiz I (pages 729-739)

Please answer the following in complete sentences.

1. What are some reasons the Women's Christian Temperence Union and the Anti-Saloon League of America opposed the consumption of alcohol?

2. Describe the 18th Amendment and the Volstead Act.

3. Why did some Americans oppose the women's suffrage movement?

4. What was the Equal Rights Amendment? What did its supporters, the Naitonal Women's Party, oppose legislation to protect women in the workplace?

5. Identify the following and what they are known for:
   a. Henry Ford
   b. Orville and Wilbur Wright

6. Why did the United States begin to restrict foreign immigration?

7. What were the cultural effects of limiting foreign immigration?

8. How did the mechanization of farm equipment lead to urbanization

9. What was the effect of urbanization?

Answers to Sample Quiz I

Students' answers should approximate the following.

1. Both organizations the consumption of alcohol because they believed it led to innumerable social ills, such as poverty, disease, crime, and insanity.

2. The 18th Amendment to the Constitution forbade "the manufacture, sale, or transportation of intoxicating liquors within, the importation thereof into, or the exportation thereof from the United States and all territory subject to the jurisdiction thereof for beverage purposes..." The Volstead Act prohibited production, sale, and manufacture of all liquors that contained over one-half of one percent of alcohol.

3. Many opposed the suffragette movement because they thought that giving woman the right to vote would remove her from her proper sphere, the home. The notion of equality espoused by proponents of women's suffrage was in opposition to the traditional notion that the father represented his family in society. To give women the suffrage assumed that wives had interests opposed to their husbands'. Cardinal Gibbons thought giving women the suffrage would remove her from the sphere of the home, which in turn would diminish women's dignity. Mother Mary Jones also opposed giving women the suffrage because she said that women are out of place in political work, and that there is already a great responsibility upon women's shoulders – that of rearing rising generations. Jones held that home training of the child should be the women's task, and it is the most beautiful of tasks.

4. In 1923, the National Women's Party (NWP) introduced into Congress the Equal Rights Amendment (ERA), which forbade all discrimination on the basis of sex. The NWP opposed legislation directed to protecting women workers because such legislation treated them as a special class, not as equals to men.

5.
   a. Henry Ford a mechanic who designed the "Model T" automobile and founded the Ford Motor Company. He also invented the assembly line.
   b. Orville and Wilbur Wright were two brothers who invented and built the world's first successful airplane.

6. By the 1920s, many Americans had become convinced that the United States should reform its past liberal immigration policies. Labor leaders didn't want gains they had made for workers lost by an influx of laborers who could work for much lower wages. Some intellectuals argued that, since most of the immigrants were now coming from southern and eastern Europe, their political traditions would corrupt American freedom.

7. Limiting immigration led to a decline in foreign ghettoes in the cities and of foreign language publications and journals. Formerly European ethnic ghettoes became increasingly black and Puerto Rican, as these peoples moved north to take advantage of industrial jobs in the cities.

8. The mechanization of farming was undermining the viability of farming society. Mechanical harvesters and reapers, steam tractors and then gasoline-driven tractors enhanced productivity even more, decreasing the number of laborers needed in the fields. The increased productivity resulted in the overproduction of farm products; and since the supply of food exceeded the demand for food, the price of crops fell. Soon, only farmers who could afford the machinery to work the ever-growing farmsteads could compete on the market. Those who could not afford the machinery were forced out of business and moved to the cities.

9. The move from the country to the city had tremendous social significance. Farming

communities tend to be conservative, are slow to change, and so preserve traditions. Moving to the city, country folk were thrown into the maelstrom of an ever-changing American culture where old values were being questioned and new ones were being created to replace the old. With the

dwindling of the country population, America lost an important bastion of conservatism needed to withstand an ever-swelling tide of new-fangledness, not only in mechanical inventions, but in the social and moral life of the people as well.

Sample Quiz II (pages 739-757)

Please answer the following in complete sentences.

1. What were some of the effects of prohibition?

2. Who was Margaret Sanger and what did she do?

3. Describe the events that led to the Teapot Dome Scandal.

4. Identify two factors of instability in the U.S. economy that led to the Crash of 1929.

5. Identify two effects of the Crash of 1929?

6. How did Herbert Hoover want to address the "Great Depression"?

7. What did Franklin Delano Roosevelt's "New Deal" entail?

8. How did Roosevelt reconcile the expansion of presidential and federal powers with the United States Constitution?

Answers to Sample Quiz II

Students' answers should approximate the following.

1. Prohibition did not end the buying, selling, transportation, and consumption of alcohol in the United States. Rather, it seemed to accelerate these activities, and bootlegging and smuggling occurred often. People brewed their own beer and hard cider for personal use, or took industrial alcohol and converted it into "bathtub gin" and whiskey – "hooch" – some of which was sold to clandestine drinking holes called "speakeasies." Prohibition didn't decrease the drinking of hard liquor; with the closing of breweries and wineries, drinkers turned instead to hard beverages like gin and whiskey. After the passage of Prohibition, crime syndicates arose in big cities such as New York and Chicago to coordinate the illegal trade in alcohol and bootlegging. Gangsters and the mafia grew rich and powerful off the illegal traffic in alcohol.

2. Margaret Sanger founded the American Birth Control Leaugle (later renamed Planned Parenthood) and led the campaign against the large family in the 1920s. She founded the American Birth Control League to disseminate the idea that women could only be free if they were able to control their reproductive faculties.

3. The Teapot Dome Scandal began with Albert B. Fall, Harding's secretary of the interior, and Edwin M. Denby, the secretary of the navy, had received the president's permission to transfer naval petroleum deposits from the naval to the interior department. Fall illegally leased the public oil reserve, Elk Hill, to the oil magnate, Edward Doheny, and the Teapot Dome reserve in Wyoming to another oil man, Harry Sinclair, in return for some oil storage tanks the oil men agreed to build at the naval base at Pearl Harbor. On top of that, Fall received $300,000 from Sinclair and $100,000 from Doheny..

4. *Possible answers:* During the 1920s, America's economy was booming. The stock market rose to unprecedented heights. But not all sectors of the economy had been doing well. Farmers suffered from overproduction. After the war, the United States had made many large loans to Europe. Because high U.S. tariffs, however, kept reviving European industries from competing in the American market, European industry languished. Eventually, Europe could not pay off debts to America; loans from the United States thereafter decreased as did European purchases of American goods.

Perhaps the biggest boom in American business resulted from widespread speculation in stocks. Participation in the stock market spread throughout society. Stock brokers allowed investors to buy stocks "on margin," a scheme that worked well as long as stocks continued to rise, but could be devastating if stocks fell dramatically. Enough investors selling their stocks could quickly depreciate the value of the stocks. Speculation schemes brought instability to the market. Stock pools, "bear raids," and purchase of stocks in a smaller company and its subsequent closure.

Another source of instability for the economy of the booming '20s was the ill distribution of wealth. In 1929, only 0.1 percent of the people had income that equaled the combined income of the lowest 42 percent of the people; this same 0.1 percent controlled one third of the savings, while 80 percent of the people had no savings at all.

5. *Possible answers:* The panic of Wall Street spread across the nation. Consumers, both rich and middle class, stopped buying on credit, and industrial production fell by nine percent between October and December 1929. Industrial downturn led to worker layoffs, and those laid off could not afford to make further payments on the items they had bought on credit. Instead, they returned such items to manufacturers, only exacerbating the glut of manufactured goods and leading to yet further layoffs. Unemployment grew. As people withdrew their deposits from banks, many banks folded. Shantytowns began springing up to house those who had been turned out of their houses. Farmers resorted to arms to resist these possession of their farms by banks. While many of the rich could weather the hard times, a large number of the middle class and the poor were in a desperate condition. They felt they had no place to turn to find protection from the forces that threatened to overwhelm them.

6. Herbert Hoover maintained his confidence in the Liberal economic system he had espoused in more prosperous times. In his mind, the president must give encouragement to the country; he should promote policies to help business revive, but he must never support measures that give direct relief to the suffering nor suffer the government to interfere in the economy beyond what is necessary to maintain equal opportunity and the freedom of individual enterprise. Despite the deepening crisis, Hoover continued to speak as if all would soon be well.

7. Roosevelt proposed active government intervention in the economy. He called for federal unemployment relief, for legislation directly to aid agriculture and railroads and to protect consumers and investors. He wanted to lower tariffs and to repeal Prohibition. All this he called the "New Deal," which was really not all that new, being an extension of Teddy Roosevelt's "Square Deal," Wilson's "New Freedom," and the policies promoted by the Progressive Bull Moosers.

8. Roosevelt said, "Our Constitution is so simple and practical that it is possible always to meet extraordinary needs by changes in emphasis and arrangement without loss of

essential form." He thus thought he could greatly expand federal and presidential power without compromising the basic integrity o the Constitution.

Essays

Instructions to be given to the students: Write in complete sentences. Underline your thesis. Give three supports or examples that explain why you think what you do and that support your thesis.

1. Do you think women should have the suffrage? Why or why not?

2. It has been posited that the Great War contributed to the loosening of morals and new social evils seen in the 1920s. Do you think this is true? Why or why not? If it is true, how did the Great War?

3. G.K. Chesterton said the problem with rural Americans was that they are not peasants. Explain why he said that, and if you think it is true or not as applied to the 1920s. How does it apply to our culture today?

4. How does music affect a society? How did the music of the 1920s affect America's society? (Students can use outside sources. Good sources: *Man the Musician* by Viktor Zuckerkandl; "Mass Culture or Popular Culture" by Thomas Storck (available on the internet); *The Closing of the American Mind*: "Music" by Allan Bloom)

Sample Test

Please answer the following in complete sentences.

I. Short Essay – Answer two of the following:

1. **Describe the suffrage movement and what the suffragettes believed.**

2. **What effect did the automobile and the airplane have on society?**

3. **Describe American mass culture in the 1920s.**

4. **What was the "Lost Generation"? How was it characterized?**

5. **What changes in family life (including the expectation of family size) occurred in the 1920s?**

II. Short Answer:

1. **What constitutional amendment gave women the suffrage?**

2. **List the racist, anti-social movements that arose in the 1920s.**

3. **Why is Harding known the worst president in the history of the United States?**

4. **According to Herbert Hoover, how far should the government intervene directly in the economy?**

5. **Why was the "New Deal" not really new?**

Answer Key to the Chapter Test

Students' answers should approximate the following:

I.

1. The suffragette movement had been demanding the vote as the key and guarantee of other natural rights that the movement believed belonged to women. Suffragettes rejected traditional notions of male authority, both in the state and the family. Many of them held that all professions, including law, political office, and the ministry, should be open to women. Anthony applied arguments she had applied to the right of blacks to vote to women. The freedom to secure their

naturals rights, she said, belonged to blacks before governments were ever created, and they did "not barter away their natural rights" when they entered into political society. Anthony held that the suffrage was a woman's inalienable right and so to deprive women of the right to vote was an act of tyranny. Not all suffragettes went as far as Anthony and Stanton. In 1895, more conservative elements in the women's suffrage movement distanced themselves from Stanton when she published *The Women's Bible.* In this work, Stanton argued that one had to look at God in a new light – not as masculine only, but as feminine as well; not only as Heavenly Father, but as Heavenly Mother.

2. The automobile transformed American life perhaps more than any other single invention. Since the Ford car was so inexpensive, many could buy one, and this led, eventually, to the building of suburban communities outside of large cities and to a gradually spreading urbanization of the countryside. Trucks benefitted Farmers. State governments began funding the construction of roads. By 1925, states began paying for hardtop roads, and the following year the federal government offered funds to match whatever the states raised themselves. Thus, increasingly, distant parts of the country began to be connected by a network of highways. Automobile production had an adverse effect on other forms of transportation and the industries that supported them. In time, the bus would replace the rural trolley car. Coastal steamboat and freight traffic would give way to truck transportation. With the increasing use of oil and petroleum, coal-mining regions languished while oil producing areas (such as California and Texas) increased in population and prosperity. With the expansion of good roads and the growing abundance of gasoline, Americans began taking road trips. This growing ease of transportation exacerbated the American lack of rootedness and of fidelity to one's native soil. Indeed, the automobile would become the symbol of individual freedom and would take its place as a constituent part of the "American dream" of individual autonomy and material prosperity.

3. A popular, mass culture characterized the United States in the 1920s. Manners, habits of dress, music, cuisine, and other aspects of culture were developed in the cities and imitated in rural communities. Indigenous, local forms of music were being replaced by popular songs produced by composers and publishers on what was called Tin Pan Alley in New York City. This mass-produced popular music, though not exactly something new in America, undermined local traditions and helped destroy all musical variety. Everyone, everywhere, was listening to the same music. Recorded music accelerated this trend and made stars out of individual singers. Recordings also helped spread another sort of music: Jazz. Equally influential in forming the mass-produced culture of the '20s were motion pictures, produced in Hollywood, California. The 1920s were a prosperous time. The stock market continued to rise to unprecedented heights throughout the decade. It seemed as if everyone was entering the middle class and could enjoy the comforts of life. The American dream was more and more defined as the possession of "things" – of cars, radios, factory-made furniture, and clothing of the latest fashion. Such possessions defined the middle-class family. Salesmen peddled big city standards of "respectable" and comfortable living. Salesmanship and advertising were more aggressive in the '20s than in any previous decade of American history. The mass production of automobiles

and other products required a vigorous sales effort to convince people to buy, and this contributed to mass culture. Advertising convinced Americans to define their lives by material standards – to keep up with their neighbors in the race toward prosperity and comfort. Companies convinced people to "buy on time" – that is, to go into debt – to purchase items that they could well do without. Most Americans purchased their Fords by paying them off over time. Mass production and advertising influenced even American cuisine, making it everywhere the same. Manufacturers produced foods that required a minimum of preparation. Except for a few isolated souls, the men of the 1920s wanted no causes, desired no struggles; they wanted "normalcy," they longed only for a comfortable, prosperous life

4. The 1920s witnessed a loosening of age-old standards of feminine decorum that, in turn, had its effects on the relationship between the sexes. Young people, especially, of the 1920s, rejected what they thought was the over-rigid morality of the late 19th century (the "Victorian Age"). Instead, they reveled in a culture of sexual promiscuity that expressed itself in dress, music, courtship, and conversation. The young people of the post-war era called themselves the "lost generation" because they just didn't fit into or sympathize with the world that had died in World War I. Old standards of courtship were collapsing. Various new ideas that were floating about aided in the decline of morality during the decade of the '20s. Educational theories attacked all forms of "authoritarianism," including in that term parental authority and the authority of religion as well as objective morality. Permissiveness held that parents should not restrict their children's behavior but allow them to follow the thrust of their desires as much as possible began to influence society.

Popularized and distorted versions of Psychoanalysis taught that it was psychologically "unhealthy" for people to "repress" their sexual desires; that by doing so, they would develop "neuroses."

5. The new philosophies weakened further the hold religious belief had on Americans. Religious belief had been declining before the 1920s and, with it, the institution of the family. For decades, the family had suffered various strains. The industrial world had reduced many families to grinding poverty. It had divorced economic activity from the home and so separated fathers for long periods of time from their families. These strains, together with the new permissive philosophies, wreaked havoc on family life. Along with the burdens placed on the traditional family, the 1920s witnessed a campaign waged against the large family. Margaret Sanger and her American Birth Control League (later renamed Planned Parenthood) led the charge in this war. She founded the American Birth Control League to disseminate the idea that women could only be free if they were able to control their reproductive faculties. Sanger saw birth control as instrumental in producing a race free of "defectives," as she called those with mental and physical disabilities. Sanger's thought would in time make more and more parents think that they had a moral duty not to bear too many children. Many would come to think that the way to stop poverty and other social ills was to limit the increase of the population.

II.
1. The 19th Amendment gave women the suffrage.
2. The anti-social movements that arose in the 1920s were a new Ku Klux Klan and anti-Semitism.

3. Harding is known as the worst president in the history of the United States because of the corruption of his administration.

4. Hoover believed that government should not intervene in the economy beyond what is necessary to maintain equal opportunity and the freedom of individual enterprise.

5. The "New Deal" was not really real because it was an extension of Teddy Roosevelt's "Square Deal," Wilson's "New Freedom," and the policies promoted by the Progressive Bull Moosers.

CHAPTER 27: Depression and War

Chapter Overview

- With government inaction regarding the Depression under Hoover, people took matters into their own hands and withdrew their savings from banks, causing bank failures to proliferate. When he became president, Roosevelt ordered the closing of all banks for four days. He submitted an emergency bank bill to Congress, and when the banks reopened on March 13, there was no run on savings. Two days later, the stock market began to climb slowly.

- During the first hundred days of his administration, Roosevelt and his advisers worked out the policies that formed the first onslaught of the New Deal. Congress passed 13 bills between March 9 and June 16, 1933. These bills were either emergency measures to take care of immediate problems or were meant to be permanent.

- One of the emergency measures passed was the National Recovery Administration, which applied to industry codes that governed relations between labor and management.

- One of the most significant acts of legislation was Roosevelt's decision, on April 19, 1933, to abandon the gold standard. Some criticized this policy, but Wall Street praised it because, they said, it would make American industries more competitive in the world market.

- After the adjournment of Congress on June 16, 1933, Roosevelt continued to promote programs that he said would restore prosperity. The first lady, Eleanor Roosevelt, ardently supported her husband's crusade, and breaking tradition, addressed audiences across the country.

- Roosevelt intended his New Deal not only for whites. It included blacks and Indians in its reach. Roosevelt awarded blacks with public office posts and abolished segregation in federal offices. The Commission of Indian Affairs adopted policies that encouraged the strengthening of tribal government and the preservation of native culture. The Indian Reorganization Act repealed the Dawes Act.

- On August 14, 1935, Congress passed the Social Security Act, perhaps the most significant and far-reaching of the New Deal measures.

- New Deal legislation racked up huge amounts of debt, and despite Roosevelt's emphasis on a slow and steady business recovery, the number of unemployed was still between 10 and 12 million. These failures emboldened Roosevelt's political opponents. Opposition came sometimes from the Supreme Court, and even from his own party, the Democrats. Another Roosevelt opponent, a Catholic priest, Father Charles Coughlin, organized the National Union for Social Justice to promote his ideas, and gave talks over the radio. The National Union for Social Justice converged with the "Share-Our-Wealth" program of Senator Huey P. Long. Despite opposition, however, Roosevelt was re-elected in 1936.

- Although the economy seemed to be gaining steam in 1937, a recession hit in the fall of that year. Roosevelt tried to push through more New Deal measures, but Congress was not responsive, though it did approve the Fair Labor Standards Act in 1938.

- Catholics addressed the economic and social ills of the 1930s, including Father John Augustine Ryan. The New Deal era saw Catholics making their first clear contribution to the public life of the United States; and for the first time in American history, the Catholic voice was heard with some respect.

- Dorothy Day, who had been a communist and free-love radical, became Catholic in 1927. Over the following years she worked with Peter Maurin to create the Catholic Worker Movement.

- Even after the optimism of the '20s was dispelled, Americans still thought the United States should and could isolate itself from the rest of the world. Such isolation was becoming more difficult, since the United States was in fact involved in the world. The world in which it was involved was racked with problems. Totalitarian regimes brought great instability to Europe. In Russia, Vladimir Ilyich Lenin organized the Union of Soviet Socialist Republics. When Lenin died, Josef Stalin became dictator and instituted a "Five Year Plan" which made Russia the fourth greatest industrial power in the world.

- Communist agitation shook the republic of Italy. In 1919 Benito Mussolini formed the Fascist party and in 1922 took over the government. In Germany, Adolf Hitler founded the National Socialist party in 1920. In 1934, Hitler became president of Germany, initiating what he called the Third *Reich*. Meanwhile, Japan was engaged in a war with China

- In 1934, Japan renounced the Washington naval disarmament agreements and began to build up her navy. The following year Hitler renounced Germany's post war agreement and initiated his program of rearmament. Hitler then commenced the military occupation of the Rhineland, the demilitarized buffer between

France and Germany. In July 1936, Germany and Italy entered into an accord, forming the "Rome-Berlin Axis."

- Americans were not eager for war, and Congress passed a series of neutrality acts forbidding the sale or transport of arms or munitions to warring nations. In 1937, Hitler informed foreign powers that he would seek new territories for Germany. Great Britain and France did nothing while Germany invaded several countries. When Mussolini invaded and occupied Albania, Great Britain and France guaranteed they would protect Poland and Romania against German aggression.

- On August 24, 1939, Adolf Hitler and Josif Stalin signed a non-aggression pact. On September 1, 1939, Hitler and Stalin invaded Poland. Two days later Great Britain and France declared war on Germany.

- When Paris fell to the Axis, Roosevelt declared a "Short of War" policy, and Congress passed a bill to build up and expand the navy. On December 7, 1941, a Japanese fleet attacked Pearl Harbor in Hawai'i. On December 8, Congress declared war on Japan. Three days later, Germany and Italy declared war on the United States.

What Students Should Know

1. **Roosevelt's first 100 Days and the legislation it produced**

   During the first 100 days of his administration, Roosevelt introduced a flurry of legislation into Congress in an attempt to address the challenge of the Great Depression. Roosevelt showed himself to be a decisive leader, and this filled people with a confidence in government they had not known for years. The first hundred days of

Roosevelt's administration were a dizzying whirlwind of activity. The men he had gathered around him as advisers (called the "brain trust" because most were from college and universities) with the president worked out the policies that formed the first onslaught of the New Deal. Between March 9 and June 16, 1933, the president presented Congress with 13 bills, each of which the Senate and House passed in record time. The bills of the first hundred days were either emergency measures to take care of immediate problems or were meant to be permanent. Among the most significant measures of this "New Deal" legislation was the Civilian Conservation Corps (CCC). Established under army control, the CCC employed young men to help conserve natural resources. Another significant measure was the National Industrial Recovery Act (NIRA), which established the Works Projects Administration (WPA) that employed men in reforestation and flood control projects, in building schools and in clearing slums. The WPA also employed "white collar" workers and college graduates to write guides for regions and states and hired out-of-work librarians to staff government-run libraries. The NIRA as well the National Recovery Administration (NRA). The purpose of the NRA was to apply to industry codes that governed relations between labor and management. These codes set maximum hours of work and, in some cases, maximum prices for goods. The codes determined minimum wages and forbade child labor. Industries that volunteered could negotiate their own codes with representatives of government and labor, while those that refused were governed by blanket codes imposed by the government. Among the permanent legislation of the 100 Days was the Tennessee Valley Authority (TVA). The TVA governed the valley of the Tennessee River, that ran through Tennessee, Alabama, Mississippi, and Kentucky. The TVA, an independent public body, built dams for flood control and for production of electricity; it erected power plants and nitrate plants for fertilizer. The dams and power plants brought electrical power to most of Tennessee and to portions of Georgia, Alabama, Mississippi, and Kentucky. One of the most significant acts of the Hundred Days was Roosevelt's decision, on April 19, to abandon the gold standard. (Congressional ratification followed on June 5.) This, and the subsequent Thomas amendment to the Agricultural Adjustment Act, would allow the president to determine at will the value of the dollar up to 50 percent of the value it had in 1933. Abandoning the gold standard meant the government would no longer redeem greenbacks with their equivalent value in gold. Another significant piece of legislation was the Glass-Steagall Banking Act of June 16. Besides ruling that banks might no longer use investors' funds to speculate on the stock market, Glass-Steagall established the Federal Deposit Insurance Corporation (FDIC) which guaranteed all bank deposits up to $5,000.

2. **The ideas guiding the New Deal**

The New Deal did not establish a system of public assistance in which the beneficiaries received direct, gratuitous government support. Roosevelt did not believe that it was good for a man's sense of self-dignity to receive handouts, so he pushed through Congress measures that would provide work for the unemployed – such as the Civilian Conservation Corps. The New Deal, too, seemed guided by a very progressive loose constructionist theory of constitutional interpretation. The NRA, for instance, went far beyond the commerce clause in the

Constitution that allowed the federal government to regulate commerce between states. Relations between labor and management had, before, been a state concern. By forbidding child labor, the federal government was entering into the realm of the family by making decisions regarding child welfare. Such decisions had, traditionally, been reserved to parents. But the New Deal was in some ways very supportive of the traditional family structure and motivated by a sense of social justice. Among the chief concerns of the architects of the New Deal (many of whom were women, including the secretary of labor, Frances Perkins, and the first lady, Eleanor Roosevelt) was to provide heads of families with a living wage so that, not only children, but even mothers of families need not leave the home in search of gainful employment. Roosevelt himself said the NRA codes would "guarantee living wages."

3. Other important New Deal Legislation

The New Deal did not end with the adjournment of Congress on June 16, 1933. In fireside chats, in addresses to Congress, Roosevelt continued to promote programs that he said would restore prosperity "by reestablishing the purchasing power of half the people," would bring about a better balance between agriculture, manufacturing and commerce, and would eliminate abuses and excesses in the economy. Among this significant legislation was the formation of the Securities and Exchange Commission by Congress in June 1934, establishing federal oversight of the stock market. Perhaps the most significant and far-reaching of New Deal measures was the Social Security Act, establishing a payroll tax of one percent – that is, the self-employed would pay the government one percent of his earnings;

The monies collected went as a bonus to boost state old-age pensions and as grants to states for children's health and welfare, to the blind, and to expand the state public health systems. In June 1938, Congress passed the Fair Labor Standards Act, which finally established a 40-hour work week as well as a federal minimum wage of 40 cents per hour.

4. The role of Eleanor Roosevelt

The first lady, Eleanor Roosevelt, ardently supported her husband's measures. Breaking tradition, she addressed audiences across the country, and, though herself a patrician, met and conversed easily with common folk. Other first ladies had taken active roles in their husbands' presidency – Wilson's wife ran the country during her husband's sickness; still, none of these were ever *public* in their involvement. Eleanor Roosevelt, in contrast, not only spoke publicly in person and over the radio, but gave press conferences. She, with Frances Perkins, was one of the several women who were among the chief architects of the New Deal.

5. The New Deal and racial minorities

Roosevelt intended his New Deal to benefit not only whites. He awarded office posts to blacks and abolished segregation in federal offices. While trying to push integration in the military, Roosevelt made equal opportunity for employment part and parcel of New Deal industry measures. Such polices, together with Eleanor's very apparent concern for the plight of blacks, affected the balance of political power. Blacks began moving from the Republican party into the Democratic party in ever increasing numbers. The New Deal included Indians in its reach. Native Americans had not fared well since the Dawes Act in the 1880s tried to turn them into individual proprietors by breaking up tribal lands. By the end of the Hoover's administration, boarding schools in which Indian children were segregated from their families had been abolished. Under Roosevelt, the Commission of Indian Affairs adopted policies that encouraged the strengthening of tribal government and the preservation of native culture. The Indian Reorganization Act, passed June 18, 1934, repealed the Dawes Act and allowed reservations to purchase more land if they needed to.

6. The Supreme Court and the New Deal

The United States Supreme Court included both opponents and supporters of the New Deal – the former, the "conservatives"; the latter, the "progressives." The progressives followed the judicial philosophy laid down by the late chief justice, Oliver Wendell Holmes, Jr. Holmes, who had held that the interpretation of the Constitution should be flexible enough to allow government to respond to current needs and circumstances. Law, he said, "corresponds at any given time with what is understood to be convenient. That involves continual change, and there can be no eternal order." Progressives like Holmes saw the courts as another avenue of Constitutional change. The four "conservative" justices of the Supreme Court were essentially proponents of *laissez-faire* – the federal government, they believed, had no place in regulating business activities. The swing vote was Chief Justice Charles Evans Hughes, who at different times sided with the conservatives and the progressives, making Supreme Court decisions on the constitutionality of New Deal legislation confusing and inconsistent. For instance, Hughes joined with conservatives in declaring the NRA unconstitutional because it went beyond the powers vested in the federal government by the commerce clause of the Constitution. However, Hughes joined Justice Benjamin J. Cardozo in his decision in a case challenging the Social Security Act as a violation of the 10th Amendment. Writing for the six to three majority, Cardozo said that the Social Security Act did not violate state sovereignty since states did not have to comply with the act. Cardozo then noted that the Depression had necessitated the Social Security Act.

After securing a second term, Roosevelt asked Congress to authorize him to appoint one new justice to the Supreme Court for every Supreme Court justice over 70 who would not retire. Since six justices were over 70, Roosevelt wanted to increase the size of the Supreme Court to 15. His intent was clear. Since the Supreme Court had declared so many New Deal acts unconstitutional, Roosevelt would pack the court with six new justices who were amenable to his policies. But public opposition to the measure induced Congress to refuse the president's request. Roosevelt, however, ultimately triumphed. After his attempt to pack the court, the Supreme Court justices began rubber-stamping all New Deal legislation brought before them. Moreover, over the next four years, on account of justices dying or resigning, Roosevelt could appoint men to the court who shared his progressive and "broad construction" reading of the Constitution. By 1941, Roosevelt had created a new, progressive court.

7. Opponents of the New Deal

Aside from business leaders and the wealthy, the president's opposition was composed of sundry groups who widely disagreed among themselves. Some were "conservative" and *laissez faire*; some were just more conservative than Roosevelt, though progressive. Some groups were more progressive, while others were radical.

Some Democrats opposed Roosevelt. Al Smith and others, including the wealthy industrial Du Pont family, formed the American Liberty League in 1934 to counteract what they saw as the New Deal's erosion of personal and property rights.

One of the most powerful voices against Roosevelt was Father Charles Coughlin. Coughlin, a popular homilist, began broadcasting over the radio in the late 1920s. Blaming the Depression on President Hoover's policies, Coughlin had supported the candidacy of Roosevelt. Coughlin had believed Roosevelt shared his conviction that greed and profit mongering lay at the root of the Depression; that the country must adopt principles of "social justice," of a Christian economy, to restore prosperity. The United States had plenty of resources for all its people, but, said Coughlin, government "had not faced the problem of distribution" of the nation's wealth. Father Coughlin thought that in order to assure a living wage to the worker, the government needed to restrain the greed of money-lenders and revalue the dollar so that workers could have a living annual salary, even when not working. Coughlin's National Union for Social Justice (formed in 1934) called as well for the nationalization of important resources, the abolition of the Federal Reserve System and its replacement with a government-controlled national bank, among other measures.

Another of Roosevelt's opponents was the former governor of, and then senator from, Louisiana, Huey Long. In the Senate he dubbed himself the "Kingfish" and offended Senators, even those from his own Democratic party. He supported Roosevelt's bid for the presidency in 1932 but later turned against him. In the Senate, Long came

up with his "Share-Our-Wealth" program. The government, he said, should tax fortunes and inheritances in order to assure to every American family a $5,000 house and an annual income of $2,000 a year. His fellow senators, of course, gave him no heed, but that didn't bother the Kingfish. He used his position as a pulpit to trumpet his program to the American people.

In the first years of the Depression, the membership of the American Communist party doubled. The leader of the party, Earl Browder, under orders from Moscow, told party members to infiltrate various political movements and political parties. Some members obtained federal posts and passed on any government information they could to Moscow. The Communist *Daily Worker* in New York attacked Roosevelt as a tool of the capitalist powers.

8. The Dust Bowl, its causes and effects

With profits to be made in farming following the Great War, the grasslands of the Plains (in the region west of the 100th meridian) had been turned from cattle raising to wheat growing. These regions, however, enjoyed little rainfall and relied on the native grasses growing there to anchor the soil against erosion. Already in the 1920s, over cultivation had so eroded soils in 100 counties in the western plains that they were declared "dust bowls" – unfit for further cultivation. But on November 11, 1933, strong wind storms hit drought stricken fields in South Dakota, driving before them the exposed soil and turning fields to drifting sand. From South Dakota, the winds continued into the south, toward Texas, spreading similar destruction. By 1934, the "Dust Bowl" included 756 counties in 19 states. Farmers in the Dust Bowl regions had already been suffering from falling prices, foreclosures, and unemployment. Larger farms, run with farm machinery, had displaced thousands of workers. Now, drought and destructive winds forced a vast migration of the poverty-stricken from the region stretching from the Dakotas to Texas. Families piled all their earthly belongings in ramshackle cars and headed west. Arriving in California, these migrants (derisively called "Okies" because many came from Oklahoma) glutted the migrant farm labor market. Paid low wages and suffering violence from organized police resistance in support of California growers, the migrants discovered that they had not left poverty, suffering, and injustice behind them.

9. Roosevelt and his view of the U.S. Constitution

In January 1937, Roosevelt told Congress that the authors of the U.S. Constitution had intended that a liberal interpretation of the Constitution in the years to come would give the Congress "the same relative powers over new national problems as they themselves gave Congress over the national problems of their day." Roosevelt said he did not want to alter "our fundamental law" but give it a more enlightened interpretation. He argued that there needed to be a more flexible interpretation of the Constitution lest the American people should conclude that democracy was too inflexible to handle crises of the complex modern world and so would opt for more totalitarian forms of government.

10. Catholics and the New Deal

Not all Catholics agreed with Father Coughlin's analysis of, or solutions to, the social questions. One prominent authority on Catholic social teaching, Father John Augustine Ryan of the Catholic University of America in Washington, D.C., disagreed violently with Father Coughlin. Since the publication of his book, *A Living Wage*, in 1906, Father Ryan had written, taught, and spoken on social justice themes in light of Catholic doctrine. With Father Raymond A. McGowan, Ryan headed the Social Action Department of the National Catholic Welfare Conference, a body formed by the bishops in the 1920s to coordinate national Catholic life. The Social Action Department had distributed thousands of pamphlets detailing social programs based on papal encyclicals. Because of Leo XIII's *Rerum Novarum* and the work of Father Ryan and other American Catholics in explaining it, Catholics were able to make their first clear contribution to the public life of the United States. Some Catholics thought that New Deal policies accorded well with the means and aims of the papal social encyclicals, *Rerum Novarum* and *Quadragesimo Anno*. Father Coughlin, at first, seemed to think so. Other Catholic social justice leaders, such as Father Ryan, did not categorically condemn Roosevelt's program. But most rank and file Catholics probably didn't even think about the question. They were of peasant stock or of the working class and not usually well-educated. The Democratic party had for many years been their party, and Roosevelt had effectively worked them into his coalition.

One unique response to the challenges of the era came from a Catholic convert, Dorothy Day and a French acti-vist/intellectual, Peter Maurin, who in 1933 founded the newspaper, the *Catholic Worker*, around which a movement arose. Peter provided the ideas for the movement, while Dorothy provided the practical leadership. Peter wanted a social order where it was easy for men to be good. To achieve this, he wanted "round table discussions" where men and women could discuss the principles of a just social order. Next, would come "houses of hospitality" where the poor and needy could come to find help in their material needs and where they would learn to work cooperatively. He hoped bishops would establish such houses in their dioceses. The next step would be "agronomic universities" or farming colonies. "People will have to go back to the land," said Maurin. "The machine has displaced labor, the cities are overcrowded. The land will have to take care of them." The Catholic Worker was a purely lay movement within the structure and obedience of the Catholic Church. Both Dorothy Day and Peter Maurin held tenaciously to Catholic orthodoxy and were obedient to the bishops and the pope. Still, the movement followed its own initiatives and never became an official Church movement in the way religious orders of priests, brothers, and nuns have been. Some Catholic Worker ideas were held suspect by rank and file Catholics, most especially the movement's position on non-violence. Dorothy Day and, it seems, Peter Maurin held that, because of the destructiveness of modern weaponry, no modern war could be just. War-making, especially modern war-making, they believed, violated the Christian's call to be a peacemaker. Thus, many Catholic Workers refused to serve in the military and, when the Second World War came, they became conscientious objectors. Yet, Catholic Workers went farther than this. They rejected all forms of violence, even in self-defense. Day and Maurin were critical of the capitalist system and trumpeted a wider distribution of private, productive property as an alternative. They were equally critical of such governmental welfare schemes as the New Deal because they thought it does not belong to the government to practice the works of mercy but to smaller, decentralized

bodies. They emphasized personal responsibility.

11. Catholic social teaching and the New Deal

In a 1930 letter, the United States bishops had addressed the problem of unemployment. "The failure" leading to the current crisis, wrote the bishops, "is not due to lack of intelligence nor any more to ignorance. It is due to lack of good will. It is due to neglect of Christ." The solution lay, said the bishops, in almsgiving but also in trying "to remold the institutions that surround work, ownership and trade to the image of the Savior of the world." One such "institution" the bishops cited was the wage system. It is not enough, said the bishops, merely to assure workers a minimum wage; morality *and* economic security demanded a living wage – a wage sufficient enough to allow a laborer becomingly to support a family.

In 1930, on the 40th anniversary of Pope Leo XIII's *Rerum Novarum*, Pope Pius XI published a social encyclical, *Quadragesimo Anno.* In this encyclical, Pius reaffirmed that men have a right to private property but emphasized that the possession of property carried with it certain social obligations. In order that property might meet those social obligations, the state had a role in regulating its use. Though in *Quadragesimo Anno*, Pope Pius asserted that "no one can be at the same time a good Catholic and a true socialist," he condemned the basic tenet of laissez-faire capitalism – that free competition should be considered the right ordering principle of economic life. While reasserting the right of workers to organize unions, Pius emphasized that workers must respect the rights of owners. Thus, in the struggle for a living wage, workers must consider how much an employer can actually pay. Like Leo XIII, however, Pius XI saw the living wage as a means for workers to acquire "by skill and thrift" a "certain moderate ownership." But Pius went further than Leo and called for industries to provide workers a participation in the ownership, management, and profits of business. Like the American bishops, Pope Pius called for a "reform of the social order" – "principally the state." His alternative vision was of a society made up not mostly of large businesses (though these were not excluded), but more characteristically of small farmers, craftsmen, shopkeepers, and merchants. Each group would be organized in a guild or corporation that negotiated disputes between employers and employed (the state only stepping in when the corporation hit an impasse) and looked out for members and their families, made sure they received a just wage or charged a just price for their goods, and protected their interests. Such corporations would not be arms of the government; and though they would receive recognition from the government, they would serve as effective intermediary bodies between the government and the people.

In *Quadragesimo Anno*, Pius XI enunciated what became known as the "principle of subsidiarity": "just as it is wrong to withdraw from the individual and commit to the community at large what private enterprise and industry can accomplish, so, too, it is an injustice, a grave evil and a disturbance of right order for a larger and higher organization to arrogate to itself functions which can be performed efficiently by smaller and lower bodies."

12. Isolationism and the United States' place in the world

Even after World War I, many Americans believed that the United States could, and should, isolate itself from the rest of the world. They believed that America,

surrounded as she was by great oceans, like moats about a castle, had nothing to fear from the disturbances of Europe or Asia. America had her own problems. But the United States *was* involved in the world. She had colonies and military bases in the Pacific. She was a creditor to European nations. Her policy of maintaining a high tariff on imports had caused other nations to follow suit, though it only retarded their industrial development since they had become dependent on American loans and exports. The abandonment of the gold standard by Great Britain in 1931 and, subsequently, by Roosevelt in 1933, to inflate the currency (and so artificially raise prices) lessened the value of currency and disrupted international exchange.

13. World totalitarian movements

In Europe, nations were falling under totalitarian governments. In 1917, in Russia, Vladimir Ilyich Lenin and the Bolsheviks had established a Communist regime in Russia. In 1923, Lenin organized Russia, Ukraine, White Russia, and Georgia into a confederation of four Soviet Socialist Republics, called the Union of Soviet Socialist Republics. The regime was nominally democratic, but in reality was controlled by the Communist Party, and, ultimately by Lenin, the head of the party. Though under the Soviet constitution the party and the state were formally separate, in practice the All Union Congress of Soviets merely rubberstamped party decisions. Josef Stalin followed Lenin as head of the Communist Party and of the government. In the mid '30s, though Stalin adopted certain capitalistic measures to spur industrial production, he actively promoted Communist revolution throughout the world. Centered in Moscow, the Third International (called *Komintern*) coordinated Communist

Party action in Europe, the United States, Mexico, and China. In theory, Communism was anti-nationalistic, for it sought the worldwide union of all workers, regardless of race or nationality. Yet, despite the Soviet threat, Great Britain and Italy both recognized the Soviet Union in 1924. The United States, under Harding, Coolidge, and Hoover continued to recognize the Russian government in exile; but under Roosevelt, in 1934, the United States recognized the Soviet Union.

In Italy, economic woes in the 1920s led to widespread discontent, and Soviet-inspired socialists instigated a number of paralyzing strikes. Militarists, upset that Italy had not secured territories in Africa and the Near East after the war, also stirred up discontent. The Liberal government, under the nominal leadership of King Vittorio Emanuele III, was powerless. Into this uncertainty came Benito Mussolini. In 1919, Mussolini formed in Milan a club centered around what became known as Fascism. Mussolini's Fascism was like Stalinism in that it espoused state control of all commercial and social life. It was the opposite of Communism in that it was nationalistic, glorying in and seeking to glorify the Italian nation, at the expense of other nations and peoples, when necessary. In 1921, Mussolini organized his and allied clubs (called *Fasci*) throughout Italy into a political party. Mussolini, called *Il Duce* (the Leader) by his followers, used violence and intimidation to achieve his ends. In 1922, he and his Fascists took control of the Italian government and drove out the Socialists. Mussolini became dictator and instituted a number of public works programs to relieve unemployment. Abolishing labor unions, he set-up 13 syndicates to handle disputes between management and labor.

Socialists, Liberals, and Soviet-inspired Communists disturbed the unstable German republic established at Weimar in 1919. Germany had suffered serious economic collapse after the war. Unreasonable war reparation payments weighed heavily on the country. The value of the German *Mark* became extraordinarily inflated. Though prosperity began to return in the late 1920s, it collapsed in the crash of 1929. Poverty in Germany was exacerbated by a sense of the humiliation of the Treaty of Versailles. The treaty had placed the whole blame for the Great War on Germany. Versailles had so demilitarized Germany that she had not sufficient forces to defend her borders if attacked. The glory of the second German *Reich* or "empire" (the first being the Holy Roman Empire of the Middle Ages) had been humbled to the dust. Germany was ripe for any demagogue who would promise to revive her prosperity and restore her power. Like Italy, Germany throughout the '20s was torn between left-wing Socialist and right-wing nationalist factions. The National Socialist Party, founded by Adolf Hitler in 1920, was similar to those of Mussolini's Fascists and promoted the superiority of the German "Aryan" race over all others, Hitler and the "Nazis" promised to restore Germany to her glory. In 1932, Hitler ran for president against Hindenburg, but lost. But fearing the growth of the Communist party, Hindenburg formed a coalition with the Nazis. In 1933, he appointed Hitler as chancellor of Germany. On March 23, the German *Reichstag* voted to delegate all power to Hitler's government. Hitler hailed this as the beginning of what he called the Third *Reich*. When Hindenburg died in 1934, Hitler became president as well as chancellor of Germany. Like Stalin and Mussolini, he crushed all political opposition, promoted his doctrine of German racial superiority, instigated a persecution against Jews, and imprisoned any Protestant or Catholic clergy who opposed his policies. Politically, Hitler centralized the government at Berlin; the *Reichstag* transferred all the powers held by the individual German states to the central government. To end the Depression and to put men to work, Hitler instituted government programs of public works. But nothing was more effective in reviving German prosperity than Hitler's program of rebuilding the German military.

14. What conflicts were occurring in Europe and Asia

Japan was engaged in an undeclared war with China in the latter's province of Manchuria. This was part of a bid to establish Japanese hegemony over East Asia: India, Burma, Indonesia, Indochina, and the Philippines – a policy that could spell war with France, Great Britain, and the United States, all of whom had East Asian colonies and dependencies. The League of Nations was powerless to do anything about Japanese aggression, and the governments of France, the United States, and Great Britain, absorbed by domestic problems, issued only protests. By 1932, Japan had set-up a puppet government in Manchuria (which it renamed Manchukuo), and the following year forced a truce from the Chinese government of Chiang Kai-shek. In 1934, Japan renounced the Washington naval disarmament agreements of 1921-22 and began to build up her navy. In 1935, further Japanese invasions of Chinese provinces forced the Chinese government of Chiang Kai-shek to make peace with Communist rebels in the northwest, and an actual, if undeclared, war erupted between Japan and China.

In Europe, in 1935, Hitler denounced the disarmament clauses in the Treaty of Versailles and initiated his program of rearmament. The following year, Hitler commenced the military occupation of the Rhineland – the region in western Germany which, according to the Treaty of Versailles, was to remain a demilitarized buffer between France and Germany. Germany's actions brought France, Great Britain, and Italy, briefly, into an alliance. France also concluded an alliance with Russia and Czechoslovakia. The alliance of these nations might have been sufficient to check any further German aggression, but other tensions dissolved it. Because of her alliance

---

Key Terms at a Glance

parens patriae: a principle derived from common law that allows the public authority to provide for orphaned minor children. It has been extended to include state power over children raised by what are deemed unfit parents, as well as government care over all citizens.

subsidiarity: the organizing principle that political and social matters should be handled by the smallest competent authority and higher authorities should only perform tasks which cannot be performed at a local level.

Fascism: a nationalistic regime which espouses state control of all commercial and social life

Nazism: (from the German *Nationalsozialismus*) a form of Fascism that incorporates racism and anti-Semitism

with Italy, France had agreed to Mussolini's designs on Ethiopia. By May 1936, superior Italian forces defeated the primitive Ethiopian military, drove Ethiopian emperor, Haile Selassie, from his throne in Addis Ababa, and occupied the country. When England and France backed League of Nations' sanctions against Italy, Hitler courted Mussolini by giving him military aid. In October 1936, Italy and Germany entered into an accord, forming the "Rome-Berlin Axis." Hitler and Mussolini continued their acts of aggression. Hitler convinced Great Britain and France's leaders that he merely wanted the Sudetenland, and then, without international opposition, invaded the region. But in a few months after occupying the Sudetenland, Hitler took Prague, the capital of Czechoslovakia. Bohemia and Slovakia became satellite states of the Third *Reich*. For his part, Mussolini invaded and occupied Albania. Following these last acts of aggression, Great Britain and France guaranteed that they would protect Poland and Romania against German aggression.

15. How World War II began

Hitler and Stalin's non-aggression pact, signed in August 1939, was followed by a secret agreement to divide up Poland between them. On September 1, 1939, Hitler invaded Poland from the west, while Stalin invaded from the east. Great Britain and France then declared war on Germany. Germany, Italy, and Japan formed the "Triple Axis," a mutual defensive alliance. In May 1940, Germany invaded neutral Belgium and Holland and then turned into France. On June 14, 1940, Paris fell to the Germans.

16. The American response to the war in Europe

With the fall of Paris, Roosevelt, who favored the Allied cause, came up with the "Short of War" policy that would help Great Britain gain time while the Americans rearmed and restrain Japan in the Far East by diplomatic measures and naval deterrence. In June 1940 Congress passed a bill to build up and expand the navy and build up a two-ocean navy. In September, Congress established the first peace-time draft in the history of the United States.

Roosevelt faced opposition from isolationists in America, who were opposed to U.S. intervention in Europe. The America First Committee, under the leadership of aviator Charles Lindbergh, led the opposition to war. After Roosevelt's victory in the election of 1940, Congress passed the Roosevelt-introduced Lend-Lease Act, which authorized the president to "sell, transfer, lease, lend" war materials to any nation the president deemed "vital to the defense of the United States." Because of Lend-Lease, $50 billion in army foodstuffs and other services went to the Allies, and American industry turned to the production of war material.

On August 14, 1940, Roosevelt and Great Britain's prime minister, Winston Churchill, signed the Atlantic Charter in which they pledged themselves to common principles, which included the right of peoples to choose their own form of government and looked to the formation of "a permanent system of general security" – something like the League of Nations.

17. How the United States entered World War II

While Germany and Russia were waging war in Europe, Japan was working to establish a "protectorate" over French Indochina. To meet the threat Japan posed to the Philippines, Congress authorized the president to establish a partial embargo against Japan and to restrict the shipment of war materials to that country. Roosevelt froze all of Japan's financial assets in the United States. Great Britain and the Netherlands joined the United States in cutting off Japan's source of financial credit (so she could not borrow money) as well as all imports of rubber, scrap iron, and fuel oil to the island country. These moves induced the Japanese generals to decide that these countries should restore the flow of credit and oil or face war. When in November 1941, Roosevelt refused to consider a Japanese ultimatum, the Japanese generals prepared to strike a U.S. target in the Pacific. On December 7, 1941, Japanese war planes attacked the U.S. fleet at Pearl Harbor in Hawai'i. On December 8, 1941, the U.S. Congress followed the president's urging and voted to declare war on Japan. Three days later, in fidelity to their pact with Japan, Germany and Italy declared war on the United States.

Questions for Review

1. **Why might some Americans have doubted that Roosevelt's New Deal measures were constitutional? Why, according to Roosevelt, were they constitutional?**

    Some Americans may have doubted Roosevelt's New Deal measures were constitutional because they believed the New Deal legislation went beyond the powers vested in the federal government the commerce clause of the Constitution, and that it invaded the reserved rights of states. Roosevelt thought the New Deal measures were constitutional because he believed the Constitution should be flexible enough to allow government to respond to current needs and circumstances.

2. **What were the goals of the National Recovery Administration (NRA)? How was the NRA geared to helping the family?**

    The NRA's goal was to apply to industry codes that governed relations between labor and management. It helped the family by implementing child labor laws and guaranteeing heads of families living wages so that mothers and children would not have to work.

3. **What were the benefits of the Social Security Act, and what were its problems?**

    The Social Security Act established a payroll tax. The proceeds of the tax benefited state old-age pensions and provided grants to states for children's health and welfare, to the blind, and to expand the state public health systems. But it established the federal government – not local communities, not the states – as the primary guardian of public welfare. It also undermined the importance of the family by removing one of its important function, that of caring for the elderly.

4. **Explain the views of Roosevelt's opponents (both conservative and progressive) to the New Deal.**

    Some of Roosevelt's opponents wre "conservative" and *laissez faire*; some were just more conservative than Roosevelt, though progressive. Some groups were more progressive, while others were radical.

    Among Democrats opposed Roosevelt. Al Smith and others, including the wealthy industrial Du Pont family, formed the American Liberty League in 1934 to counteract what they saw as the New Deal's erosion of personal and property rights.

    Father Charles Coughlin, a popular homilist and radio broadcaster, blamed the Depression on President Hoover's policies, but came to believe that Roosevelt had betrayed social justice principles. Coughlin had supported the candidacy of Roosevelt. Coughlin believed government "had not faced the problem of distribution" of the nation's wealth. Father Coughlin thought that in order to assure a living wage to the worker, the government needed to restrain the greed of money-lenders and revalue the dollar so that workers could have a living annual salary, even when not working. Coughlin called for the abolition of the Federal Reserve System and its replacement with a government-controlled national bank, among other measures.

The Democratic governor of, and then senator from, Louisiana, Huey Long, proposed, against Roosevelt, the "Share-Our-Wealth" program. The government, he said, should tax fortunes and inheritances in order to assure to every American family a $5,000 house and an annual income of $2,000 a year.

Communists opposed Roosevelt, attacking him as a tool of the capitalists.

5. What did Catholics think about the New Deal?

Many Catholics thought that New Deal policies accorded well with the means and aims of the papal social encyclicals, *Rerum Novarum* and *Quadragesimo Anno.* Other Catholic social justice leaders, such as Father Ryan, did not categorically condemn Roosevelt's program. But most rank and file Catholics probably didn't even think about the question. Some Catholics agreed with Father Charles Coughlin that Roosevelt did not go far enough to assure "social justice" to all citizens. Others followed Dorothy Day and Peter Maurin (and the Catholic Worker Movement) in insisting that it does not

belong to the government to practice the works of mercy but to decentralized bodies.

6. What did the American bishops think the solution to the crisis of the Depression necessarily involved?

The American bishops said the solution to the crisis of the Depression necessarily involved remolding the institutions that surround work, ownership and trade to the image of the Savior of the world. The bishops promoted social justice based on papal social encyclicals , which called for living wages and other justice measures.

7. Lay out the main points of Pope Pius XI's encyclical, *Quadragesimo Anno,* and what it called for.

In this encyclical, Pius reaffirmed that men have a right to private property but emphasized that the possession of property carried with it certain social obligations. In order that property might meet those social obligations, the state had a role in regulating its use. Though in *Quadragesimo Anno,* Pope Pius asserted that "no one can be at the same time a good Catholic and a true socialist," he condemned the basic tenet of laissez-faire capitalism – that free competition should be considered the right ordering principle of economic life. While reasserting the right of workers to organize unions, Pius emphasized that workers must respect the rights of owners. Thus, in the struggle for a living wage, workers must consider how much an employer can actually pay. Like Leo XIII, however, Pius XI saw the living wage as a means for workers to acquire "by skill and thrift" a "certain moderate ownership." But Pius went further than Leo and called for industries to provide workers a participation in the ownership, management, and profits of business. Like the American bishops, Pope

Pius called for a "reform of the social order" – "principally the state." His alternative vision was of a society made up not mostly of large businesses (though these were not excluded), but more characteristically of small farmers, craftsmen, shopkeepers, and merchants. Each group would be organized in a guild or corporation that negotiated disputes between employers and employed (the state only stepping in when the corporation hit an impasse) and looked out for members and their families, made sure they received a just wage or charged a just price for their goods, and protected their interests. Such corporations would not be arms of the government; and though they would receive recognition from the government, they would serve as effective intermediary bodies between the government and the people.

In *Quadragesimo Anno*, Pius XI enunciated what became known as the "principle of subsidiarity": "just as it is wrong to withdraw from the individual and commit to the community at large what private enterprise and industry can accomplish, so, too, it is an injustice, a grave evil and a disturbance of right order for a larger and higher organization to arrogate to itself functions which can be performed efficiently by smaller and lower bodies."

8. **Explain Dorothy Day and Peter Maurin's ideas about how to best to bring reform to society.**

Dorothy Day and Peter Maurin wanted a social order where it was easy for men to be good. To achieve this, they wanted "round table discussions" where men and women could discuss the principles of a just social order. Next, would come "houses of hospitality" where the poor and needy could come to find help in their material needs and where they would learn to work cooperatively. They hoped bishops would establish such houses in their dioceses. The next step would be "agronomic universities" or farming colonies. "People will have to go back to the land," said Maurin. "The machine has displaced labor, the cities are overcrowded. The land will have to take care of them." The Catholic Worker was a purely lay movement within the structure and obedience of the Catholic Church.

9. **Explain the course of events that led the United States to declare war against the Axis powers.**

While Germany and Russia were waging war in Europe, Japan was working to establish a "protectorate" over French Indochina. To meet the threat Japan posed to the Philippines, Congress authorized the president to establish a partial embargo against Japan and to restrict the shipment of war materials to that country. Roosevelt froze all of Japan's financial assets in the United States. Great Britain and the Netherlands joined the United States in cutting off Japan's source of financial credit (so she could not borrow money) as well as all imports of rubber, scrap iron, and fuel oil to the island country. These moves induced the Japanese generals to decide that these countries should restore the flow of credit and oil or face war. When in November 1941, Roosevelt refused to consider a Japanese ultimatum, the Japanese generals prepared to strike a U.S. target in the Pacific. On December 7, 1941, Japanese war planes attacked the U.S. fleet at Pearl Harbor in Hawai'i.

Ideas in Action

1. **Listen to Roosevelt's Fireside Chats and discuss them. (These can be found on the Internet.)**

2. Discover what projects sponsored by the NRA (such as murals) or the WPA (such school buildings, libraries, parks, and airports) can be found in your own region, town, or city.

3. Read and discuss some of the writings of Dorothy Day and Peter Maurin. Their writings (including the *Easy Essays*) can be found at:: http://www.catholicworker.org

4. Read and discuss Pope Pius XI's encyclical, *Quadragesimo Anno*. It may be found on the website of the Holy See.

5, What would Thomas Jefferson have said about Franklin Delano Roosevelt's flexible interpretation of the Constitution? Did Roosevelt capture the intention of the authors of the Constitution? Why or why not?

6. If there is a Catholic Worker House of Hospitality near your home, visit it and learn more about it.

Sample Quiz I (pages 762-773)

Please answer the following in complete sentences.

1. Describe the ideas guiding the New Deal in terms of government-provided assistance, constitutional theory, and the family.

2. What did the Social Security Act entail? How much did employers and employees pay into the tax? What did the tax fund?

3. What did the Fair Labor Standards Act establish?

4. What was Eleanor Roosevelt's role in promoting the New Deal?

5. How did the New Deal benefit blacks? How did blacks respond to Roosevelts measures in their favor?

6. How did Roosevelt's presidency help the Indians?

7. Describe the judicial theory of Oliver Wendell Holmes, Jr.

8. How did "conservatives" on the Supreme Court view New Deal measures?

9. What caused the Dust Bowl?

Answers to Sample Quiz I

Students' answers should approximate the following.

1. Roosevelt did not believe that it was good for a man's sense of self-dignity to receive handouts, so he pushed through Congress measures that would provide work for the unemployed. New Deal, too, was guided by a very progressive loose constructionist theory of constitutional interpretation.

2. The Social Security Act established a payroll tax of one percent – that is, the self-employed would pay the government one percent of his earnings. The monies collected went as a bonus to boost state old-age pensions and as grants to states for children's health and welfare, to the blind, and to expand the state public health system.

3. The Fair Labor Standards Act established a 40-hour work week as well as a federal minimum wage of 40 cents per hour.

4. The first lady, Eleanor Roosevelt, ardently supported her husband's measures. Breaking tradition, she addressed audiences across the country, and, though herself a patrician, met and conversed easily with common folk. Other first ladies had taken active roles in their husbands' presidency, but none of these were ever *public* in their involvement. Eleanor Roosevelt, in contrast, not only spoke publicly in person and over the radio, but gave press conferences. She, with Frances Perkins, was one of the several women who

were among the chief architects of the New Deal.

5. Roosevelt intended his New Deal to benefit not only whites. He awarded office posts to blacks and abolished segregation in federal offices. While trying to push integration in the military, Roosevelt made equal opportunity for employment part and parcel of New Deal industry measures. These policies, together with Eleanor's very apparent concern for the plight of blacks, encouraged blacks to move from the Republican party into the Democratic party in ever increasing numbers.

6. Under Roosevelt, the Commission of Indian Affairs adopted policies that encouraged the strengthening of tribal government and the preservation of native culture. The Indian Reorganization Act repealed the Dawes Act and allowed reservations to purchase more land if they needed to.

7. The progressives followed the judicial philosophy laid down by the late chief justice, Oliver Wendell Holmes, Jr. Holmes, who had held that the interpretation of the Constitution should be flexible enough to allow government to respond to current needs and circumstances. Law, he said, "corresponds at any given time with what is understood to be convenient. That involves continual change, and there can be no eternal order." Progressives like Holmes saw the courts as another avenue of Constitutional change.

8. Conservative justices of the Supreme Court were essentially proponents of *laissez-faire* – the federal government, they believed, had no place in regulating business activities.

9. With profits to be made in farming following the Great War, the grasslands of the Plains had been turned from cattle raising to wheat growing. These regions, however, enjoyed little rainfall and relied on the native grasses growing there to anchor the soil against erosion. Already in the 1920s, over cultivation had so eroded soils in 100 counties in the western plains that they were declared "dust bowls" – unfit for further cultivation. But on November 11, 1933, strong wind storms hit drought stricken fields in South Dakota, driving before them the exposed soil and turning fields to drifting sand. From South Dakota, the winds continued into the south, toward Texas, spreading similar destruction.

Sample Quiz II (pages 773-791)

Please answer the following in complete sentences.

1. **How did Catholics view the New Deal?**

2. **What were Peter Maurin's ideas on how to reform society?**

3. **According the Unites States bishops, what was the root of the unemployment crisis of the 1930s?**

4. **How did Pope Pius XI describe the principle of subsidiary in *Quadragesimo Anno*?**

5. **What is Isolationism?**

6. **How did did the U.S. first respond to the war in Europe?**

7. **Describe the Atlantic Charter.**

8. **How did the United States enter the war?**

Answers to Sample Quiz II

Students' answers should approximate the following.

1. Some Catholics thought that New Deal policies accorded well with the means and aims of the papal social encyclicals, *Rerum Novarum* and *Quadragesimo Anno*. Father Coughlin, at first, seemed to think so, but later thought the New Deal did not go far enough. Other Catholic social justice leaders,

such as Father Ryan, did not categorically condemn Roosevelt's program. But most rank and file Catholics probably didn't even think about the question. They were of peasant stock or of the working class and not usually well-educated. Some Catholics followed Dorothy Day and Peter Maurin, holding that works of charity should not be left to government programs.

2. Peter wanted a social order where it was easy for men to be good. To achieve this, he wanted "round table discussions" where men and women could discuss the principles of a just social order. Next, would come "houses of hospitality" where the poor and needy could come to find help in their material needs and where they would learn to work cooperatively. He hoped bishops would establish such houses in their dioceses. The next step would be "agronomic universities" or farming colonies, to return more people to the land.

3. "The failure" leading to the current crisis of unemployment, wrote the bishops, "is not due to lack of intelligence nor any more to ignorance. It is due to lack of good will. It is due to neglect of Christ."

4. Pope Pius XI's principle of subsidiary: "just as it is wrong to withdraw from the individual and commit to the community at large what private enterprise and industry can accomplish, so, too, it is an injustice, a grave evil and a disturbance of right order for a larger and higher organization to arrogate to itself functions which can be performed efficiently by smaller and lower bodies."

5. Even after World War I, many Americans believed that the United States could, and should, isolate itself from the rest of the world. They believed that America, surrounded as she was by great oceans, like moats about a castle, had nothing to fear from the disturbances of Europe or Asia. America had her own problems. Thus, they held that the United States should not intervene in world crises or be involved in the problems of the world outside the United States..

6. With the fall of Paris, Roosevelt came up with the "Short of War" policy that would help Great Britain gain time while the Americans rearmed and restrained Japan in the Far East by diplomatic measures and naval deterrence. In June 1940 Congress passed a bill to build up and expand the navy and build up a two-ocean navy. In September, Congress established the first peace-time draft in the history of the United States. In 1940, Congress passed the Roosevelt-introduced Lend-Lease Act, which resulted in American industry turning to the production of war material.

7. On August 10, 1940, Roosevelt and Great Britain's prime minister, Winston Churchill, signed the Atlantic Charter in which they pledged themselves to common principles, which included the right of peoples to choose their own form of government and looked to the formation of "a permanent system of general security" – something like the League of Nations.

8. To meet the threat Japan posed to the Philippines, Congress authorized the president to establish a partial embargo against Japan and to restrict the shipment of war materials to that country. Roosevelt froze all of Japan's financial assets in the United States. These moves induced the Japanese generals to decide that the U.S. and other countries should restore the flow of credit and oil or face war. When in November 1941, Roosevelt refused to consider a Japanese ultimatum, the Japanese generals prepared to strike a U.S. target in the Pacific. On December 7, 1941, Japanese war planes attacked the U.S. fleet at Pearl Harbor in Hawai'i. On December 8, 1941, the U.S. Congress followed the president's urging and

voted to declare war on Japan. Three days later, in fidelity to their pact with Japan, Germany and Italy declared war on the United States.

Essays

Instructions to be given to the students: Write in complete sentences. Underline your thesis. Give three supports or examples that explain why you think what you do and that support your thesis.

1. Do you think the New Deal helped the United States at all? Why or why not?

2. Was Dorothy Day and Peter Maurin's Catholic Worker Movement a realisitic response to the problems of the 1930s? (Students might consider what they and others mean by "realistic.")

3. If you were an American living in 1940, would ou have supported an isolationist or interventionist policy in relation to the war in Europe? Please give reasons to support your position.

4. Read Pope Pius XI's *Quadragesimo Anno*. Do you think that what he wrote in 1930 stlll applies to the world today? Why or why not?

Sample Test

Please answer the following in complete sentences.

I. Short Essay – Answer two of the following:

1. **Describe three of the New Deal measures passed in the first hundred days of Roosevelt's presidency.**

2. **What were Roosevelt's views on the U.S. Constitution?**

3. **Lay out the main ideas of *Quadregesimo Anno*.**

4. **What was the U.S. Supreme Court's response to the New Deal? How did Roosevelt deal with the court?**

II. Short Answer:

1. **In terms of the family, why did Eleanor Roosevelt and Frances Perkins support a living wage?**

2. **Why did many American Catholics not think about the question of whether New Deal policies were in accord with the social encyclicals?**

3. **According the U.S. bishops, in what did the solution to the unemployment problem lie?**

4. **What regimes were taking over in Europe?**

5. **What attack brought America into the second world war?**

Answer Key to the Chapter Test

Students' answers should approximate the following:

I.

1. *Possible answers:* The Civilian Conservation Corps (CCC) employed young men to help conserve natural resources. The National Industrial Recovery Act (NIRA) established the Works Projects Administration (WPA) that employed men in reforestation and flood control projects, in building schools and in clearing slums. The Tennessee Valley Authority (TVA), an independent public body, built dams for flood control and for production of electricity; it erected power plants and nitrate plants for fertilizer. The dams and power plants brought electrical power to most of Tennessee and to portions of Georgia, Alabama, Mississippi, and Kentucky. One of the most significant acts of the Hundred Days was Roosevelt's decision,

on April 19, to abandon the gold standard. This, and the subsequent Thomas amendment to the Agricultural Adjustment Act, would allow the president to determine at will the value of the dollar up to 50 percent of the value it had in 1933. Another significant piece of legislation was the Glass-Steagall Banking Act of June 16. Besides ruling that banks might no longer use investors' funds to speculate on the stock market, Glass-Steagall established the Federal Deposit Insurance Corporation (FDIC) which guaranteed all bank deposits up to $5,000.

2. In January 1937, Roosevelt told Congress that the authors of the U.S. Constitution had intended that a liberal interpretation of the Constitution in the years to come would give the Congress "the same relative powers over new national problems as they themselves gave Congress over the national problems of their day." Roosevelt said he did not want to alter "our fundamental law" but give it a more enlightened interpretation. He argued that there needed to be a more flexible interpretation of the Constitution lest the American people should conclude that democracy was too inflexible to handle crises of the complex modern world and so would opt for more totalitarian forms of government.

3. In *Quadragesimo Anno*, Pius reaffirmed that men have a right to private property but emphasized that the possession of property carried with it certain social obligations. In order that property might meet those social obligations, the state had a role in regulating its use. Though in *Quadragesimo Anno*, Pope Pius asserted that "no one can be at the same time a good Catholic and a true socialist," he condemned the basic tenet of laissez-faire capitalism – that free competition should be considered the right ordering principle of economic life. While reasserting the right of workers to organize unions, Pius emphasized

that workers must respect the rights of owners. Thus, in the struggle for a living wage, workers must consider how much an employer can actually pay. Like Leo XIII, however, Pius XI saw the living wage as a means for workers to acquire "by skill and thrift" a "certain moderate ownership." But Pius went further than Leo and called for industries to provide workers a participation in the ownership, management, and profits of business. Like the American bishops, Pope Pius called for a "reform of the social order" – "principally the state." His alternative vision was of a society made up not mostly of large businesses (though these were not excluded), but more characteristically of small farmers, craftsmen, shopkeepers, and merchants. Each group would be organized in a guild or corporation that negotiated disputes between employers and employed (the state only stepping in when the corporation hit an impasse) and looked out for members and their families, made sure they received a just wage or charged a just price for their goods, and protected their interests. Such corporations would not be arms of the government; and though they would receive recognition from the government, they would serve as effective intermediary bodies between the government and the people.

4. The four "conservative" justices of the Supreme Court were essentially proponents of *laissez-faire* – the federal government, they believed, had no place in regulating business activities. The swing vote was Chief Justice Charles Evans Hughes, who at different times sided with the conservatives and the progressives, making Supreme Court decisions on the constitutionality of New Deal legislation confusing and inconsistent.

After securing a second term, Roosevelt asked Congress to authorize him to appoint one new justice to the Supreme Court for every Supreme Court justice over 70 who would not retire. Since six justices were over 70, Roosevelt wanted to increase the size of the Supreme Court to 15. His intent was clear. Since the Supreme Court had declared so many New Deal acts unconstitutional, Roosevelt would pack the court with six new justices who were amenable to his policies. But public opposition to the measure induced Congress to refuse the president's request. Roosevelt, however, ultimately triumphed. After his attempt to pack the court, the Supreme Court justices began rubber-stamping all New Deal legislation brought before them. Moreover, over the next four years, on account of justices dying or resigning, Roosevelt could appoint men to the court who shared his progressive and "broad construction" reading of the Constitution. By 1941, Roosevelt had created a new, progressive court.

II.

1. Eleanor Roosevelt and Frances Perkins) wanted to provide heads of families with a living wage so that, not only children, but even mothers of families need not leave the home in search of gainful employment.

2. Many Catholics didn't think about the question because they were of peasant stock or of the working class and not usually well-educated. The Democratic party had for many years been their party, and Roosevelt had effectively worked them into his coalition.

3. The solution to the unemployment problem lay, said the bishops, in almsgiving but also in trying "to remold the institutions that surround work, ownership and trade to the image of the Savior of the world.

4. The regimes taking over in Europe were Communism, Fascism, and the National Socialist Party.

5. The Japanese attack on Pearl Harbor brought America into the second world war.

CHAPTER 28: World War II and the Cold War

Chapter Overview

* With preparations for the war, the Depression in the United States was buried for good. By 1942, Japan had conquered the Philippines and almost all of East Asia. The Japanese set their sights on New Guinea but abandoned attempts to conquer it when they met the U.S. Navy in the Coral Sea. The U.S. then won an important victory against the Japanese at Midway Island.

* Throughout the first half of 1942, Great Britain's prime minister, Winston Churchill, and President Roosevelt discussed where Allied forces should initiate their strike into Europe. They agreed on "Operation Torch," a strike into North Africa.

* In February 1943 the Americans took Guadalcanal in the Solomon Islands, punching an opening in the Japanese wall of defense.

* Once Roosevelt and Churchill had North Africa in their possession, they met in January 1943 to discuss the further conduct of the war. The Allied leaders agreed on demanding nothing short of "unconditional surrender" from the Axis powers. They adopted the "Combined Bomber Offensive," which wreaked destruction on Germany's civilian population.

* By August 17, 1943, Allies had taken the entire island of Sicily and got set to invade Italy. The Italians were sick of war, however, and under the new premier, Marshal Badaglio, Italy sought peace with the Allies. Italy formally surrendered on September 3, 1943. The Germans still occupied Italy, however, and after a long fight, the Allies liberated Rome on June 4, 1944.

* In the United States, many Catholics were opposed to the war before the bombing of Pearl Harbor. Afterward, many Catholics supported the war, although the bishops warned against excesses and outlined the conditions for lasting peace. The war saw the stirrings of a pacifist movement among Catholics, among them Dorothy Day and the Catholic Workers.

* The air war weakened the German *Luftwaffe* so much that control of the air passed to the Allies. Gradually the Allies began to beat back the weakening German army, beginning with "D Day" on June 6, 1944. On August 25, the Americans liberated Paris, and the German army began melting away before the Allies. In the Pacific, in October, the Americans began the liberation of the Philippines.

* In late January of 1945, the Allies advanced to the Rhine. On February 13, Allied planes dropped incendiary bombs on Dresden, laying waste to the city. After April 14, when the Allies broke through German defensive lines, all effective German opposition ended. Adolf Hitler and his mistress, Eva Braun, committed suicide on April 30. The Allies crushed German resistance in Italy on May 4, and three days later the German government signed an agreement of unconditional surrender with the Allies, ending the war in Europe.

* On April 12, 1945, President Roosevelt died, leaving the presidency to his vice-president, Harry Truman. It still remained to defeat the

Japanese. On March 14, 1945, the American army took Iwo Jima. Now the Allies faced the prospect of a land invasion of Japan to secure Japan's unconditional surrender. The United States, however, had a new secret weapon. On July 26, Allied leaders gave the Japanese an ultimatum: they were to surrender unconditionally. When Japan refused to comment, Colonel Paul W. Tibbets headed out for an expedition over the Japanese city of Hiroshima on August 6, 1945. He dropped the atomic bomb on Hiroshima, leveling four square miles of the city and killing thousands of people. Three days later the United States dropped the second atomic bomb on nearby Nagasaki. On August 14, 1945, the Emperor Hirohito surrendered.

- The Allies divided Germany and Austria into four occupation zones. Josef Stalin imposed Communist governments over nearly all the countries in Russia's sphere of influence. The division of Europe and the world between the Communist bloc of nations and the "free world" led to a state of undeclared conflict, called the "Cold War."

- The United Nations General Assembly, founded in 1945, assembled in 1946 for its first session to discuss the future use of atomic energy. The Lilienthal-Acheson Report presented a plan to channel atomic research in the ways of peace. The United States endorsed a modified version of this report, which the Soviets rejected. Meanwhile, Stalin was moving ahead on his own atomic program.

- During the post-war occupation of Europe and Japan, the United States did a great deal to help Europe restore its prosperity. When Great Britain, France, and Italy suffered a severe economic collapse, the United States proposed the Marshall Plan, which gave European countries economic help. With the help of the United States, Western Europe once again became one of the most prosperous regions in the world.

- On March 12, 1947, President Truman outlined the objectives of his foreign policy in what became known as the "containment" policy to support freed peoples who were resisting attempted subjugation by Communists. To protect the nations of Western Europe from Soviet aggression, the United States, Canada, and ten nations of Western Europe signed the North Atlantic Treaty Organization, NATO, on April 4, 1949.

- In August 1949, the Soviet Union successfully tested its first atomic bomb, thus beginning the nuclear arms race.

What Students Should Know

1. **Course of the war in the Pacific from December 1941 to February 1943**

Between December 1941 and May 1, 1942, the Japanese had conquered the Philippines and almost all East Asia. But Japan's entire attempt to conquer New Guinea was halted in the Battle of the Coral Sea in May. Hoping to destroy the American Pacific fleet in 1942 (before U.S. Production in ships and planes would outstrip the Japanese), Admiral Yamamoto order an assault on the U.S. Airbase on Midway Island in June 1942. Midway, however, was a victory for the United States, and Yamamoto sustained important losses. The Japanese however held strong positions along the probable route the American navy would take in its push toward Japan -- a ribbon of islands that began in the South Pacific and included the Philippines, Formosa (Taiwan), and the Ryukyus. To break through this Japanese "wall" of islands, in August 1942, U.S. Marines landed at Guadalcanal in the Solomons, where the Japanese were building an air base. Over the next several months, so many naval battles were fought in the waters about Guadalcanal that soldiers named them Ironbottom Sound, for all the ships that sank there. On February 9, 1943, the Japanese evacuated their troops from Guadalcanal. By capturing Guadalcanal, the Americans had punched an opening in the Japanese wall of defense. By the end of January, 1943, American and Australian soldiers had driven the Japanese from the coast of New Guinea, from Papua to Huon Gulf. The tide had turned. The United States could now take the offensive in the Pacific war.

2. American mobilization for the war effort

Because of preparations before the war, the United States military was in better shape than it had been at its entry into the First World War, but still much needed to be done. Conscription of men into the army, navy, and coast guard began in earnest. Though the United States refused to conscript women, as many as 250,000 women served the war effort as nurses or as female auxiliaries of the army and navy. Women went to work in factories. By war's end in 1945, about 15 million men and women had served in the American armed forces. American industrial output supplied, not only American needs, but those of her allies. There were shortages in oil, steel, and rubber; but the United States and Venezuela stepped up oil drilling and refinement. The United States instituted a rationing system for steel and rubber, and citizens held collection drives. The shortage of rubber was met by the production of synthetic rubber. Production of war commodities buried the Depression for good. The American government paid for all this war preparation by raising taxes but by going into deep debt.

3. Japanese relocation

Fearing that the large number of Japanese who lived in the Pacific Coast states would, by espionage and sabotage, aid a Japanese invasion, President Roosevelt, in February 1942, issued an order authorizing the establishment of "military areas ... from which any or all persons may be excluded" and where their right to enter or remain could be restricted. Though not specifically, this order was directed toward the 112,000 Japanese (two-thirds of whom were citizens) who lived in Washington, Oregon, and California. After registering themselves with the government, the Japanese went to "relocation centers" and were forbidden to return to their homes. The United States Supreme Court eventually upheld the Roosevelt Administration's argument that the order did not violate the civil rights of Japanese because they were not compelled to remain at relocation centers. The court argued that it fell under the power of the "national government ... to wage war successfully." Though the court conceded that "distinctions between citizens solely because of their ancestry are by their very nature odious to a free people whose institutions are founded upon the doctrine of equality," it argued that the emergency of war allows the government to take precautions it could not take in peacetime.

4. What happened in the European Theater in 1942

Beginning in January, 1942, German U-boats prowled the waters off the coast of North America, sinking merchant ships they found. Between January and June 1942, U-boats struck about 382 ships, including oil tankers. The U.S. met the emergency by building small, armed escort vessels and by establishing inshore and offshore patrols and convoy systems for merchant ships. These eventually decreased the U-boat threat. Hitler had invaded Russia in 1940, and by the spring of 1942 the Germans were again advancing toward Moscow. Stalin called on his allies to open a second front in Europe to draw part of Hitler's strength from Russia. Roosevelt and Churchill agreed on what became known as "Operation Torch," a combined American and British assault on North African port cities of Oran and Algiers on the Mediterranean coast and Morocco on the Atlantic coast.

5. **The general events of the invasion of North Africa**

In early November 1942, British and American task forces landed at Oran in Algiers and at Casablanca in Morocco. The Germans and Italians were completely surprised. The troops from Vichy France, which held North Africa, gave only a weak resistance, and General Eisenhower was able to persuade the Vichy commander of the French in Algiers to issue a cease-fire. The Germans met the Allied threat in North Africa by flying 20,000 men to North Africa and establishing fighter and bomber bases in Tunisia. In February, the German General Rommel (called "Desert Fox" for his wiliness) maneuvered his *Nord Afrika* Corps to cut the Allied forces in two. But though General Rommel defeated American troops in the battle of the Kasserine Pass in February 1943, five days later, American General George Patton with American and British forces forced Rommel to retreat into Tunisia. In May, Rommel surrendered the cornered German army of 275,000 men to Patton. Tunisia had been secured for the allies.

6. **The conference at Casablanca and its results**

With North Africa in their possession, Roosevelt and Churchill met in Casablanca in January 1943 to discuss the further conduct of the war. Josef Stalin, occupied with the German invasion of Russia, could not attend the conference. At Casablanca, the Allied leaders agreed on policies that would have profound effects on the war effort. Churchill embraced Roosevelt's proposal that the Allies accept nothing short of "unconditional surrender" from the Axis powers. They also agreed on the "Combined Bomber Offensive," which included strategic bombing. Before the American entry into the war, the British Royal Air Force (RAF) had been engaged in night air raids on German cities with war industries, oil refineries, synthetic rubber factories, etc. Because the raids were carried out at night, civilian centers in cities, as well as the military targets, suffered destruction. The Combined Bomber Offensive would continue and expand this war policy: the RAF would bomb cities by night, while the United States Army Air Force carried on more precise strikes during the day. The targets would not be purely military, but civilian, as well. Allied bombing raids wreaked destruction on Germany's industrial cities. Beginning in March 1943, the RAF began bombing cities in the industrial Ruhr region of Germany. Because it was difficult to spot industrial complexes at night, British planes dropped their bombs on city centers, which burned more quickly than outlying areas. Bombing laid waste old, beautiful works of art and architecture in German cities. In July, the RAF began firebombing cities. In Hamburg the bombing created a firestorm that destroyed one-half of the houses in the city and killed 50,000 inhabitants. In November, the RAF and the United States Army Air Force began round-the-clock bombing of the German capital, Berlin, destroying three and one-half square miles of the city.

7. The events of the Invasion of Italy

In July 1943, an Allied force of 250,000, commanded by General Dwight David Eisenhower, landed on Sicily, surprising the island's German and Italian defenders. The Allies commanded by General Patton swept across Sicily, entering Palermo on the north coast of Sicily in less than month. After securing the entire island in August, the Allies crossed over into Italy. In July, after 560 Allied planes had bombed Rome, Italy's King Vittorio Emanuele III forced Benito Mussolini to resign as premier and appointed Marshal Badoglio in his place. Badoglio immediately began to seek peace terms with the Allies; but because of the Allies' policy of unconditional surrender, negotiations dragged out to early September – enough time for the Germans to move reinforcements into Italy. Thus, though Italy formally surrendered on September 3, 1943, German forces held key positions in Italy, including Rome. German forces bitterly contested the Allied advances but were forced to retire. On October 1, Allied forces seized Naples. Only 100 miles lay between Naples and Rome, but stiff German resistance bogged down the Allied advance for eight months. The Germans held a stout defensive line anchored at the monastery of Monte Cassino. The Allies were unable to break the this "Gustav" line. In May, 1944 the Allies finally pushed the Germans from the Gustav line. Retiring, the Germans formed another line (the "Gothic Line") to the north of the Arno River. The Allies liberated Rome on June 4, 1944.

8. Events in the Pacific Theater, 1943-1944

After Guadalcanal, the American commander in the Pacific, General Douglas MacArthur worked out a strategy that he called "leap-frogging." Instead of attacking heavily fortified Japanese positions, MacArthur decided to seize less strongly fortified islands between Japanese positions and the home island. In this way he hoped to sever the limbs of the Japanese military from their trunk and so neutralize them. MacArthur himself would move by way of the Bismarck Islands, and Admiral Nimitz, through the Gilberts, Marshalls, and the Carolines. Their forces would meet and together make a drive into the Philippines, China, or Japan itself. The campaign began in mid 1943. In June 1943 U.S. B-29 bombers bombed not only military and industrial targets in Japan, but civilian centers as well. On June 19 and 20, Japan's Admiral Ozawa engaged the American fleet in the Philippine Sea but was decisively defeated.

9. What the Allies decided at Teheran

1943, Roosevelt, Churchill, and Stalin met at Teheran in Iran to discuss the progress of the war and, after victory had been won, how to rebuild Europe. Stalin agreed to some of Roosevelt's desires: the establishment, after the war, of a United Nations organization and Russian entrance into the war against Japan. But Stalin demanded much in return: a "security belt" (to include the Baltic states, and eastern Poland) to protect Russia from future invasion. In private talks, Roosevelt agreed to Stalin's demands and said he was willing to give Stalin German East Prussia and further agreed to a new eastern border for Germany, at the Oder River, and to the deportation, "on a voluntary basis," of Poles from eastern Poland. Among Roosevelt's proposals at Teheran was the post-war division of Germany into five small zones.

10. Catholic response to the war

At first, the American bishops gave little support for a U.S. role in the European war, urging the government to pay heed as a first responsibility to the welfare of the American people. The bishops had been strongly opposed to atheistic Communism; and, after Jewish refugees, fleeing Germany, came to America, the American bishops, besides establishing an aid committee for them, spoke out publicly against the Nazi government of Germany and condemned anti-Semitism. After the bombing of Pearl Harbor, in a letter to Roosevelt the bishops voiced their support for the war. Most Catholics agreed. In their minds, Japan and Germany were unjust aggressors, and stopping their predations was obviously a just cause. The American bishops, however, warned against excesses. In a November 1942 pastoral letter they declared that the war must maintain the high moral purpose enunciated by Roosevelt in his war aims. That young men, merely teenagers, were being drafted and that women left their homes to work in factories was a matter of concern for the bishops. Then, the lack of a religious dimension to the struggle disturbed the bishops. "Secularism," they wrote, "cannot write a real and lasting peace." In November 1943, the bishops issued another statement outlining the conditions for a lasting peace. The recognition of the sovereignty of God and of the primacy of the moral law, the bishops wrote, were the necessary foundations of peace. All men, regardless of race, said the bishops, have natural rights that cannot be violated. The

sovereignty of all nations, the bishops said, must also be respected.

The Second World War saw the first stirrings of a pacifist movement among Catholics. Some Catholics, including a few priests, had come to the conclusion that, because of its destructiveness, modern war could not possibly be justified by traditional just war criteria. At the center of the Catholic pacifist movement was Dorothy Day and the Catholic Worker Movement. But though Dorothy Day and other Catholic pacifists appealed to the writings of Popes Pius XI and Pius XII for a justification of their pacifism, the popes never went so far as to absolutely condemn modern war. Pius XII spoke out against the "homicidal instruments of war" that indiscriminately targeted military and civilian targets and the violations of the "limits of legitimate warfare." The pope condemned "Marxist socialism," but he spoke out against the Liberal economic system that oppressed workers, depriving them of a just wage for their labor and robbing them of their dignity. Liberal ideas about the state, said Pius, had destroyed a true idea of the state and led finally to the belief that the state has complete power over everyone and everything in society.

11. The course of the war in the European theatre in 1944

The Allied air war on Germany, though harsh, had not seriously affected Germany's war production or weakened German civilian morale. Rising civilian death tolls only steeled German resistance against that the Allies. The air war, though, so weakened the German *Luftwaffe* (air force) that control of the air passed to the Allies. The allies had been building up their forces in southern England in preparation for an invasion of Normandy. On June 6, 1944, code named "D

Day," the Battle for Normandy began. By late July, the Allies had occupied Normandy and the Battle for France began. In August, the Allies invaded southern France from the ports of Toulon and Marseilles, and pushed, by way of the Rhone Valley to Lyons. On August 25, General Patton's army liberated Paris, and Charles de Gaulle took up the presidency of restored France. In September 4, the Allies entered Belgium, liberated Luxembourg, crossing into Germany. In the east, in June, Josef Stalin's Soviet forces had opened an 800 mile front, from Leningrad to the Carpathians. In five weeks, Russian forces had crossed Ukraine and Poland, to the outskirts of Warsaw. Further south, the Red Army forced the surrender of Romania. In Italy, the Allies had driven the Germans to their last line of defense in the Po Valley.

12. The course of the war in the Pacific in 1944

In October 1944, two thrusts of American forces in the Pacific coalesced in the Leyte Gulf in the Philippines. The Japanese occupation of the Philippines had been cruel. Japanese soldiers had reduced the Filipino people to poverty. At times, Japanese soldiers marched groups of Filipino men into the jungles and murdered them. General MacArthur landed on Leyte Island, but the winning of the Philippines would not be easy. The Japanese high command, staking all to drive MacArthur and Nimitz from the Philippine islands, sent the entire Japanese fleet south. The Battle of Leyte Gulf, October 25, 1944, proved to be the largest sea battle history has seen. The American navy and air force were able to defeat a formidable foe and drive the Japanese navy from Philippine waters.

13. What happened in the invasion of Germany

The Allied onslaught in Europe bogged down along the fortifications that guarded the German fatherland. Dreading the dishonor of unconditional surrender (a policy Pope Pius XII had asked the Allies to abandon) and fearing the vengeful violence of the invading armies, the Germans put up the stubborn defense of despair. In mid-December, the German army made one last desperate gamble to break the Allied lines. In the Battle of the Bulge, the German army assaulted the Allied lines around Bastogne. The Allies succeeded in saving Bastogne. By mid January, the lines had returned to what they were before mid-December. In late January, the Allies resumed their advance to the Rhine while the Russians, in the east, were directing an invasion along a 1,000-mile front. To hamper German troop movements, the Allies decided to bomb eastern German cities. B-29s assaulted Dresden, a city with no military significance, no anti-aircraft defenses, but filled with hundreds of thousands of war refugees. In February 1945, Allied planes dropped incendiary bombs that ignited firestorms that laid waste the city. Three hours later came more B-29s and more incendiary bombs. The fires that consumed Dresden claimed an estimated 135,000 lives. In early February, the Russian army was parked outside of Berlin.

Beginning in late March 1945, Allied armies began crossing the Rhine and advanced to the Ruhr River. After April 14 all effective German opposition ended. Allied armies marched through Bavaria in the South, discovering the concentration camps where Nazis had imprisoned Jews and Gypsies, along with Germans, including Catholic and Protestant clergy, who had opposed the Nazi regime. From the west, Allied armies pierced to the Elbe while the

Russians attacked Berlin. On April 30, Adolf Hitler and his longtime mistress, Eva Braun, committed suicide in a bunker in Berlin and, soon after, the Russians captured the German capital. Admiral Doenitz, the new head of the German government, approached Eisenhower to discuss surrender, but the American general insisted, in the spirit of Yalta, that Doenitz instead surrender to the Russians. On May 4, the Allies crushed all German resistance in Italy, and three days later, the German government signed an agreement of unconditional surrender with the Allies. The war in Europe had ended.

14. The Yalta conference and what was decided there

Churchill and Roosevelt met with Stalin at Yalta on the Black Sea on February 4, 1945. Roosevelt wanted assurance from Stalin that Russia would support the formation of an international organization called the United Nations. In return, F.D.R. was willing to grant Stalin's demands – three votes in the United Nations, the right to regulate the formation of the government of Poland (Stalin promised democratic elections there), and the right to the use of forced German labor for a period of ten years. In return for his promise to enter the war against Japan, Churchill and Roosevelt gave Stalin control of the Manchuria railroad, of the port of Darien and of naval bases at Port Arthur, the Kurile Islands, and South Sakhalin. Meanwhile, on the western front, the Allies were finally able to break through the German defensive lines.

15. How the Allies triumphed in the Pacific

The American army and navy in the Pacific were making steady advances against the Japanese. From the island of Saipan, American bombing raids pounded Japanese cities to dust, progressively destroying Japan's industrial capability to make war, as well as killing tens of thousands of Japanese civilians – men, women and children. By late February 1945, American marines drove the Japanese from the island of Iwo Jima. By late June, Americans overwhelmed Japanese resistance on Okinawa. The British joined the Americans in the Pacific after the fall of Germany. The Japanese, it seems, were willing to agree to all Allied demands, but wanted assurance that the emperor Hirohito would remain head of government; but the Allies insisted on unconditional surrender, without any conditions – something to which the Japanese would not agree. On July 26, Truman, Churchill, and the Combined Chiefs of Staff at Potsdam sent Japan an ultimatum of unconditional surrender or face "utter destruction." After the Japanese returned an answer of "no comment," the United States dropped two atomic bombs, one on Hiroshima (August 6, 1945) and the other on Nagasaki (August 9). The bombings had their desired effect. On August 14, the Emperor Hirohito, long an advocate of peace, surrendered. The formal act of unconditional surrender was signed aboard the *U.S.S Missouri* on September 2, 1945. The Second World War was finished.

16. The development of the atomic bomb

When Harry Truman became president following Roosevelt's death, he learned for the first time that the United States had been working on a new, secret weapon. Refugee scientists from Europe had warned President Roosevelt that German scientists were working on the concept of uranium fission to produce a bomb that could wipe out large sections of cities. To beat the Germans, the United States commenced the Manhattan Project. In centers throughout the country, this top-secret project worked to master the splitting of the atom. On December 2, 1942,

Enrico Fermi and other physicists had produced the first self-sustaining nuclear chain reaction. By 1944, J. Robert Oppenheimer, at the laboratories at Los Alamitos, New Mexico, had developed the first atomic bomb. On July 16, 1945, this atomic bomb was successfully exploded at Los Alamos.

17. Reactions to the atomic bomb

The American people, for the most part, greeted the bombings of Hiroshima and Nagasaki with enthusiasm; the terrible ordeal of war was over. But some voices protested what they saw as the ruthlessness of the bomb. Some American Protestants thought the churches of America should reckon the bomb as a clear departure from Christian principles. Like their countrymen American Catholics, for the most part, approved of the bombings, but some Catholics vociferously condemned them – the Catholic journal, *Commonweal,* for instance, and Dorothy Day and the Catholic Worker Movement. Pope Pius XII did not directly address the atomic bombings, but in the course of the war he had condemned terror bombings. The day after the bombing of Hiroshima, however, the Vatican's newspaper, *L'Osservatore Romano*, summed up the war and made a dire prediction. "This war," it said, "provides a catastrophic conclusion. Incredibly this destructive weapon remains a temptation for posterity, which, we know by bitter experience, learns so little from history."

18. Potsdam and what it decided

Allied leaders met at Potsdam in July 1945, following the end of the war in Europe. At Potsdam, Stalin was able to win important concessions from Truman and Britain's new prime minister, Clement Attlee. The Allies divided Germany and Austria into four occupation zones: one each for the United States, Great Britain, Russia, and reconstituted France. The cities of Berlin and Vienna were likewise parceled out to the victorious powers. Truman and Attlee agreed that Russia should establish interim governments, to be "broadly representative of all democratic elements," in Austria, Hungary, Czechoslovakia, Bulgaria, and Romania. Stalin pledged that these interim governments would eventually allow for free elections. The British and the Americans agreed to Soviet annexation of eastern Poland and to Stalin's request that the Soviet-established government of Poland be given East Prussia and a large swath of German territory from the Oder River eastward. Though Russia's contribution in the Pacific theater amounted to only five days of fighting, the Allies agreed to Russia's control of Manchuria.

19. The Cold War

After Potsdam, with the exception of Austria and Czechoslovakia, which set up democratic governments, Russia imposed Communist governments over all the countries in her "sphere of influence." Any elections held were only pretenses to give the Communist governments a semblance of legitimacy. It soon became apparent to everyone that the "western" democratic nations had a new and formidable enemy; that the Soviet Union had succeeded Nazi Germany as the new threat to "freedom," not only in Europe, but, indeed, the world over. War with the Soviets was, in 1945, unthinkable; indeed, many progressives in the United States thought the only way to ensure world peace was continually to appease Stalin. Truman decided that the way to deal with him was to make it clear that the Soviets would gain nothing by any act of war. This were the beginnings of what came to called the "Cold War," for never was there actual war between the U.S. and her allies and the Soviet Communist powers, but they represented opposing political blocs threatening each other with destruction. The division between East and West came to be called the "Iron Curtain," from a 1946 speech by Winston Churchill.

Truman's policy came to be called "containment." Truman sought to prevent more countries from falling prey to Communist groups from within, or to Soviet pressures from without by actively supporting anti-Communist governments and even by direct intervention – though without directly engaging with the Soviet Union itself. Examples of this intervention was the U.S. support of pro-Western governments in Greece and Turkey and the Berlin Airlift.

To protect the nations of Western Europe from Soviet aggression, the United States, Canada, and ten nations of Western Europe signed a treaty of mutual protection, the North Atlantic Treaty Organization (NATO), on April 4, 1949. Under NATO, the United States pursued her policy of containment by shipping arms to Western Europe and by organizing the armed forces under the single command of Dwight Eisenhower, who became supreme commander of NATO. In 1954, West Germany (those non-Russian sectors organized in 1949 as the Federal Republic of Germany) was allowed to join NATO. Though in Europe it was a success, containment failed in the Far East, when the Communist forces of Mao Zedong drove the government of Chiang Kai-shek from the Chinese mainland to Taiwan.

20. The formation of the United Nations

In April 1945, representatives of 50 nations met in San Francisco, California and drafted a charter for the United Nations Organization. The United Nations Charter established a world organization, divided into two bodies: the Security Council and the Assembly. Five nations sat on the Security Council: the United States, Great Britain, the Soviet Union, China, and France. Each Security Council member had veto power over any resolution approved by the other council members. Alongside the Security Council, the charter established an Assembly in which member nations each had one vote and unlimited time for discussion and debate. The charter gave the United Nations powers that the League of Nations never possessed. The organization could approve the use of force against nations that defied its decrees; it could establish economic sanctions and even call for war measures against the recalcitrant. The United Nations could establish its own permanent armed forces.

21. The UN and the atomic bomb

At its first session in 1946, the United Nations General Assembly took up the question of the future use of atomic energy. The General Assembly voted to establish the United Nations Atomic Energy Commission to look for ways to control atomic energy throughout the world. Two reports on how to do this were introduced. The Lilienthal-Acheson Report, published in the United States in March 1946, and authored by David Lilienthal, called for the establishment of an international authority that would own the raw materials (plutonium and uranium) used in the production of atomic energy, as well as all the reactors and facilities connected to the production and use of atomic energy. This atomic authority would be under the control of the nations of the world and thus, it was hoped, would assure that nuclear materials would not fall under the control of any nation. President Truman sent Bernard Baruch to present a modified version of the Lilienthal-Achison plan to the first meeting of the UN Atomic Energy Commission in June 1946. In Baruch's proposal, the international authority would not own the world's plutonium and uranium but simply have oversight of them. It specified that oversight must extend to every country of the world before the United States would divest itself of its atomic arsenal and raw materials. The international authority, according to the Baruch plan, would have the power to levy sanctions against nations that refused to participate in the inspection. The veto power of members of the Security Council, said Baruch, would not apply to the international authority. The Soviets and Poland opposed the Baruch plan. A Soviet plan called for the immediate dismantling of all atomic arsenals (at that time, only the United States possessed atomic weapons) and the establishment of an international authority with only limited powers of inspection. The Soviets were working on their own atomic bomb program at the time, and the United States did not seem willing to give up its arsenal.

The United Nations Atomic Energy Commission continued to hold meetings to discuss the Baruch and Soviet plans, as well as other plans, for future atomic policy. These discussions closed on July 29, 1949 with no agreement. A month later, the Soviet Union successfully tested its first atomic bomb, thus beginning what came to be called the nuclear arms race.

22. The U.S. and post-war Europe

Germany had been devastated by the war and the Allies who held joint custody of the government disagreed among themselves on how to govern it. Though initially, the Allies had determined to leave Germany to her own devices, to keep her weak for a good time to come, faced with mass starvation and in epidemics, the United States and Great Britain began shipping food into Germany. The Allies introduced tribunals to try and convict men accused of "war crimes" and other atrocities. Trials held at Nürnberg in Bavaria convicted twelve leading Nazis. The Allies worked to stamp out any remaining vestiges of Nazism from Germany, to prepare, at least, the western sectors of the country to adopt a republican form of government. The United States funded 68 percent of relief efforts to bring food to Europe, helping resettle displaced persons, and transporting Jews from Europe to their new homeland (established by Great Britain) in Palestine. Trade restrictions were eased between the United States and European countries. The United Nations, with U.S. aid, established two financial institutions to help with recovery: the International Monetary Fund (IMF) and the International Bank for Reconstruction and Development. To forestall such financial collapses as had occurred in Great Britain, France, and Italy in 1947, the United States proposed the Marshall Plan that said if European countries came up with economic reconstruction plans that would "permit the emergence of political and social conditions in which free institutions can exist," the United States would give them the money to institute these plans. Sixteen countries approved the plan, while those countries under Communist governments turned to Russia. The U.S Congress resisted approving the plan until a Communist *coup d'état* overthrew the democratic government

Key Terms at a Glance

containment: the American policy announced under President Truman to check the advancement of Communism

Cold War: the period of open rivalry waged diplomatically, politically, and culturally, but not in full scale war, between the United States and its allies and the Soviet Union and its allies

of Czechoslovakia. Then Congress approved the plan.

23. The U.S. and post-war Japan

The occupation of Japan fell to the United States alone. Truman appointed General Douglas MacArthur Supreme Commander of Allied Powers with the authority to oversee the occupation of Japan. MacArthur wanted his government to be a shining example of justice and of Christian charity. MacArthur worked assiduously to inculcate American political and social principles in Japanese society. He ended the secret police. He instituted land reform, breaking up large estates and distributing over 4.5 million acres to Japanese peasants. Under his aegis, Japan adopted a democratic and representative government, and allowed women to vote in the first general election. Under MacArthur, Japan disestablished its state religion; the Emperor cast off all the divine attributes that, for over 2,000 years, had been associated with his office. Yet it was during MacArthur's command of the American Occupational Force that the Japanese Diet legalized abortion. In May 1948, the Japanese parliament passed the Eugenic Protection Law that allowed abortion in cases of fetal abnormality and where a pregnancy resulted from rape or could gravely harm a woman's health. The bill received MacArthur's approval because he was convinced that

population growth posed a threat to the Japanese economy. Following the passage of the Eugenic Protection Law, the abortion rate in Japan climbed dramatically, while the birthrate began the steady decline from which Japan has never recovered.

Questions for Review

1. **How did the decisions made by the Allies in Casablanca in 1943 affect the war effort?**

Roosevelt proposed the Allies accept nothing short of "unconditional surrender" from the Axis powers. The Allies agreed on the "Combined Bomber Offensive," which included strategic bombing. Before the American entry into the war, the British Royal Air Force (RAF) had been engaged in night air raids on German cities with war industries, oil refineries, synthetic rubber factories, etc. Because the raids were carried out at night, civilian centers in cities, as well as the military targets, suffered destruction. The Combined Bomber Offensive would continue and expand this war policy: the RAF would bomb cities by night, while the U.S. Army Air Force bombed them by day. The targets would not be purely military but civilian as well.

2. **What was the objective of the Combined Bomber Offense? Did it achieve this objective?**

The CBO's objective, according to a general directive issued from Casablanca, was "the progressive destruction and dislocation of the German military, industrial and economic system, and the undermining of the morale of the German people to the point where their capacity for armed defense is fatally weakened."

3. Why were American Catholics hesitant to support the war before the Japanese attack on Pearl Harbor? What was their attitude to the war after the attack?

At first, the American bishops gave little support for a U.S. role in the European war, urging the government to pay heed as a first responsibility to the welfare of the American people. After the bombing of Pearl Harbor, in a letter to Roosevelt the bishops voice their support for the war. Most Catholics agreed. In their minds, Japan and Germany were unjust aggressors, and stopping their predations was obviously a just cause. Some, though a very few, Catholics (such as those belonging to the Catholic Worker Movement) refused to participate in the war. Modern war and its destructiveness, they said, could not be moral.

4. Describe the American Catholic bishops' conditions for lasting peace in 1943.

The bishops said the recognition of the sovereignty of God and of the primacy of the moral law were the necessary foundations of peace. All men, regardless of race, said the bishops, have natural rights that cannot be violated. The sovereignty of all nations, the bishops said, must also be respected.

5. What was Dorothy Day's defense of pacifism?

Dorothy Day wrote in defense of pacifism that "theologians have laid down conditions

for a just war ... and many modern writers, clerical and lay, hold that these conditions are impossible of fulfillment in these present times of bombardment of civilians, open cities, the use of poison gas, etc."

6. What effect did the Allied war on Germany have on its civilians?

The Allied war on Germany did not weaken German civilian morale. The rising civilian death tolls only convinced the Germans that the Allies were brutal enemies and steeled German resolve to resist the Allies to the last extremity.

7. What important decisions were made by the Allies at Teheran in 1943?

At Teheran the Allies decided on the establishment, after the war, of a United Nations organization and Russian entrance into the war against Japan. Roosevelt agreed to Stalin's demands of a "security belt" (to include the Baltic states, and eastern Poland) to protect Russia from future invasion and said he was willing to give Stalin German East Prussia and further agreed to a new eastern border for Germany, at the Oder River, and to the deportation, "on a voluntary basis," of Poles from eastern Poland. Among Roosevelt's proposals at Teheran was the post-war division of Germany into five small zones.

8. Describe the course of events that led to the atomic bombings of Hiroshima and Nagasaki.

After the fall of Germany, the Japanese, it seems, were willing to agree to all Allied demands, but wanted assurance that the emperor Hirohito would remain head of government; but the Allies insisted on unconditional surrender, without any conditions – something to which the Japanese would not agree. On July 26, Truman, Churchill, and the Combined Chiefs of Staff at Potsdam sent Japan an ultimatum of unconditional surrender or face "utter destruction." When the Japanese returned an answer of "no comment," the United States dropped two atomic bombs, one on Hiroshima and the other on Nagasaki.

9. **How did the American public opinion greet the atomic bombings of Hiroshima and Nagasaki?**

    The American people, for the most part, greeted the bombings of Hiroshima and Nagasaki with enthusiasm; the terrible ordeal of war was over. But some voices protested what they saw as the ruthlessness of the bomb. Some American Protestants thought the churches of America should reckon the bomb as a clear departure from Christian principles. Like their countrymen American Catholics, for the most part, approved of the bombings, but some Catholics vociferously condemned them.

10. **Explain how the United Nations sought to deal with the threat of the atomic bomb.**

    The United Nations General Assembly voted to establish the United Nations Atomic Energy Commission to look for ways to control atomic energy throughout the world. This atomic authority would be under the control of the nations of the world and thus, it was hoped, would assure that nuclear

materials would not fall under the control of any nation.

11. **Describe Truman's containment policy. What events led to the institution of this policy?**

    Truman sought to prevent more countries from falling prey to Communist groups from within, or to Soviet pressures from without by actively supporting anti-Communist governments and even by direct intervention – though without directly engaging with the Soviet Union itself.

Ideas in Action

1. Discuss how the decisions made by world leaders during World War II have affected our world and the nature of warfare today.

2. Learn about the splitting of the atom and atomic power. To what uses is this technology put to today? What controversies surround its use?

3. Read news accounts of the activities and policies of the United Nations Organization. Discuss whether the UN has been or is an effective force for world peace.

4. Discuss the morality of the warfare policies of both the Axis and Allied powers in World War II in light of the discussion on the Fifth Commandment in the *Catechism of the Catholic Church*, paragraphs 2258-2317.

Sample Quiz I (pages 795-807)

Please answer the following in complete sentences.

1. What was the significance of the capture of Guadalcanal?

2. What was the purpose of President Roosevelt's Japanese relocation?

3. Why did the United States Supreme Court uphold the Roosevelt Administration's argument that the relocation order did not violate the civil rights of Japanese?

4. What was "Operation Torch"?

5. Describe the "Combined Bomber Offensive."

6. Describe MacArthur's "leap-frogging" strategy in the Pacific. What did Mac Arthur hope to achieve by "leap-frogging"?

7. Why did some Catholics become pacifists at the time of Second World War?

8. How did Pope Pius XII view modern war?

Answers to Sample Quiz I

Students' answers should approximate the following.

1. By capturing Guadalcanal, the Americans had punched an opening in the Japanese wall of defense. By the end of January, 1943, American and Australian soldiers had driven the Japanese from the coast of New Guinea, from Papua to Huon Gulf. The United States could take the offensive in the Pacific war.

2. President Roosevelt instituted Japanese relocation because he feared that the large number of Japanese who lived in the Pacific Coast states would, by espionage and sabotage, aid a Japanese invasion.

3. The United States Supreme Court eventually upheld the Roosevelt Administration's argument that the order did not violate the civil rights of Japanese because they were not compelled to remain at relocation centers. The court argued that it fell under the power of the "national government … to wage war successfully." The court argued that the emergency of war allows the government to take precautions it could not take in peacetime.

4. Roosevelt and Churchill agreed on what became known as "Operation Torch," a combined American and British assault on North African port cities of Oran and Algiers on the Mediterranean coast and Morocco on the Atlantic coast.

5. The "Combined Bomber Offensive" included strategic bombing in which the British Royal Air Force would bomb cities by night, while the United States Army Air Force carried on more precise strikes during the day. The targets were both military and civilian

6. "Leap-frogging was a strategy that General Douglas Mac Arthur worked out in which instead of attacking heavily fortified Japanese positions, American forces would seize less strongly fortified islands between Japanese positions and the home island. By using this strategy of "leap-frogging, MacArthur hoped to sever the limbs of the Japanese military from their trunk and so neutralize them.

7. Some Catholics became pacifists because they had come to the conclusion that, because of its destructiveness, modern war could not possibly be justified by traditional just war criteria.

8. Pius XII did not directly condemn modern war, but he spoke out against the "homicidal instruments of war" that indiscriminately targeted military and civilian targets and the violations of the "limits of legitimate warfare."

Sample Quiz II (pages 807-820)

Please answer the following in complete sentences.

1. What were the effects of the Allied invasion on Germany?

2. How did the war in Europe end?

3. Why did the United States drop atomic bombs on Hiroshima and Nagasaki?

4. Lay out the events that led to the development of the atomic bomb.

5. What agreements were made at Postdam?

6. What was President Truman's policy of containment.

7. What is NATO, and why was it formed?

8. How did the Lilien-Atcheson Report propose to control nuclear weapons? How

were these recommendations modified by the Baruch proposal?

9. **What did the Marshall Plan propose?**

Answers to Sample Quiz II

Students' answers should approximate the following.

1. The Allied air war on Germany, though harsh, had not seriously affected Germany's war production or weakened German civilian morale. Rising civilian death tolls only steeled German resistance against that the Allies. The air war, though, so weakened the German *Luftwaffe* (air force) that control of the air passed to the Allies.

2. The war in Europe ended when the Allies had taken most of Germany, Hitler had committed suicide, and the Russians had conquered Berlin. With these events, and when all German resistance ended in Italy, the German government signed an agreement of unconditional surrender with the Allies.

3. After the fall of Germany, the Japanese, it seems, were willing to agree to all Allied demands, but wanted assurance that the emperor Hirohito would remain head of government; but the Allies insisted on unconditional surrender, without any conditions – something to which the Japanese would not agree. On July 26, Truman, Churchill, and the Combined Chiefs of Staff at Potsdam sent Japan an ultimatum of unconditional surrender or face "utter destruction." When the Japanese returned an answer of "no comment," the United States dropped two atomic bombs, one on Hiroshima and the other on Nagasaki.

4. To beat the Germans, who were working on the concept of uranium fission, the United States commenced the Manhattan Project. In centers throughout the country, this top-secret project worked to master the splitting of the atom. On December 2, 1942, Enrico Fermi and other physicists had produced the first self-sustaining nuclear chain reaction. By 1944, J. Robert Oppenheimer, at the laboratories at Los Alamitos, New Mexico, had developed the first atomic bomb.

5. At Postdam, the Allies divided Germany and Austria into four occupation zones: one each for the United States, Great Britain, Russia, and France. The cities of Berlin and Vienna were likewise parceled out to the victorious powers. Truman and Attlee agreed that Russia should establish interim governments, to be "broadly representative of all democratic elements," in Austria, Hungary, Czechoslovakia, Bulgaria, and Romania. Stalin pledged that these interim governments would eventually allow for free elections. Great Britain and the United States agreed to Russia's control of Manchuria.

6. Truman sought to prevent more countries from falling prey to Communist groups from within, or to Soviet pressures from without by actively supporting anti-Communist governments and even by direct intervention – though without directly engaging with the Soviet Union itself.

7. NATO, the North Atlantic Treaty Organization, was formed as a treaty of mutual protection to protect the nations of Western Europe from Soviet aggression.

8. Two reports on how to do this were introduced. The Lilienthal-Acheson Report, published in the United States in March 1946, and authored by David Lilienthal, called for the establishment of an international authority that would own the raw materials (plutonium and uranium) used in the production of atomic energy, as well as all the reactors and facilities connected to the production and use of atomic energy. This atomic authority would be under the control of the nations of the world and thus, it was hoped, would assure that nuclear materials

would not fall under the control of any nation.

9. The Marshall Plan said if European countries came up with economic reconstruction plans that would "permit the emergence of political and social conditions in which free institutions can exist," the United States would give them the money to institute these plans.

Essays

Instructions to be given to the students: Write in complete sentences. Underline your thesis. Give three supports or examples that explain why you think what you do and that support your thesis.

1. What makes a war just? Was World War II a just or unjust war? Explain. (Sources on the just war issue:

2. People often speak of the Allies having the "moral high ground" in the war. Is this true? Why or why not? Students can use outside sources to answer this question.

3. How did the culture and institutions of the American people change between the two world wars? What brought about these changes? How did modern warfare contribute to these changes?

Sample Test

Please answer the following in complete sentences.

I. Short Essay – Answer two of the following:

1. **What were the results of the Combined Bomber Offensive?**

2. **What did the Allies decided at Teheran and Yalta?**

3. **What was the U.S. Catholic bishops' response to the war?**

4. **What were the reactions to the atomic bomb, both in the U.S. and the Vatican?**

5. **Describe the formation and charter of the United Nations.**

II. Short Answer:

1. **What ended the Depression for good?**

2. **What two things did the Allies agree on at Casablanca?**

3. **Why did some Catholics think modern war was unjust?**

4. **When was the formal act of Japan's unconditional surrender signed?**

5. **Why was the "Cold War" so called?**

Answer Key to the Chapter Test

Students' answers should approximate the following:

I.

1. Allied bombing raids wreaked destruction on Germany's industrial cities. Beginning in March 1943, the RAF began bombing cities in the industrial Ruhr region of Germany. Because it was difficult to spot industrial complexes at night, British planes dropped their bombs on city centers, which burned more quickly than outlying areas. Bombing laid waste old, beautiful works of art and architecture in German cities. In July, the RAF began firebombing cities. In Hamburg the bombing created a firestorm that destroyed one-half of the houses in the city and killed 50,000 inhabitants. In November, the RAF and the United States Army Air Force began round-the-clock bombing of the German capital, Berlin, destroying three and one-half square miles of the city.

2. From November 28 to December 1, 1943, Roosevelt, Churchill, and Stalin met at Teheran in Iran to discuss the progress of the war and, after victory had been won, how to rebuild Europe. Stalin agreed to some of Roosevelt's desires: the establishment, after the war, of a United Nations organization and Russian entrance into the war against Japan. But Stalin demanded much in return: a "security belt" (to include the Baltic states, and eastern Poland) to protect Russia from future invasion. In private talks, Roosevelt agreed to Stalin's demands and said he was willing to give Stalin German East Prussia and further agreed to a new eastern border for Germany, at the Oder River, and to the deportation, "on a voluntary basis," of Poles from eastern Poland. Among Roosevelt's proposals at Teheran was the post-war division of Germany into five small zones. Churchill and Roosevelt met with Stalin at Yalta on the Black Sea on February 4, 1945. Roosevelt wanted assurance from Stalin that Russia would support the formation of an international organization called the United Nations. In return, F.D.R. was willing to grant Stalin's demands – three votes in the United Nations, the right to regulate the formation of the government of Poland (Stalin promised democratic elections there), and the right to the use of forced German labor for a period of ten years. In return for his promise to enter the war against Japan, Churchill and Roosevelt gave Stalin control of the Manchuria railroad, of the port of Darien and of naval bases at Port Arthur, the Kurile Islands, and South Sakhalin.

3. At first, the American bishops gave little support for a U.S. role in the European war, urging the government to pay heed as a first responsibility to the welfare of the American people. The bishops had been strongly opposed to atheistic Communism; and, after Jewish refugees, fleeing Germany, came to America, the American bishops, besides establishing an aid committee for them, spoke out publicly against the Nazi government of Germany and condemned anti-Semitism. After the bombing of Pearl Harbor, in a letter to Roosevelt the bishops voiced their support for the war. Most Catholics agreed. In their minds, Japan and Germany were unjust aggressors, and stopping their predations was obviously a just cause. The American bishops, however, warned against excesses. In a November 1942 pastoral letter they declared that the war must maintain the high moral purpose enunciated by Roosevelt in his war aims. That young men, merely teenagers, were being drafted and that women left their homes to work in factories was a matter of concern for the bishops. Then, the lack of a religious dimension to the struggle disturbed the bishops. "Secularism," they wrote, "cannot write a real and lasting peace." In November 1943, the bishops issued another statement outlining the conditions for a lasting peace. The recognition of the sovereignty of God and of the primacy of the moral law, the bishops wrote, were the necessary foundations of peace. All men, regardless of race, said the bishops, have natural rights that cannot be violated. The sovereignty of all nations, the bishops said, must also be respected.

4. The American people, for the most part, greeted the bombings of Hiroshima and Nagasaki with enthusiasm; the terrible ordeal of war was over. But some voices protested what they saw as the ruthlessness of the bomb. Some American Protestants thought the churches of America should reckon the bomb as a clear departure from Christian principles. Like their countrymen American Catholics, for the most part, approved of the bombings, but some Catholics vociferously condemned them – the Catholic journal,

Commonweal, for instance, and Dorothy Day and the Catholic Worker Movement. Pope Pius XII did not directly address the atomic bombings, but in the course of the war he had condemned terror bombings. The day after the bombing of Hiroshima, however, the Vatican's newspaper, *L'Osservatore Romano,* summed up the war and made a dire prediction. "This war," it said, "provides a catastrophic conclusion. Incredibly this destructive weapon remains a temptation for posterity, which, we know by bitter experience, learns so little from history."

5. In April 1945, representatives of 50 nations met in San Francisco, California and drafted a charter for the United Nations Organization. The United Nations Charter established a world organization, divided into two bodies: the Security Council and the Assembly. Five nations sat on the Security Council: the United States, Great Britain, the Soviet Union, China, and France. Each Security Council member had veto power over any resolution approved by the other council members. Alongside the Security Council, the charter established an Assembly in which member nations each had one vote and unlimited time for discussion and debate. The charter gave the United Nations powers that the League of Nations never possessed. The organization could approve the use of force against nations that defied its decrees; it could establish economic sanctions and even call for war measures against the recalcitrant. The United Nations could establish its own permanent armed forces.

II.

1. Production of war commodities ended the Depression for good.

2. At Casablanca, the Allied leader agreed on the policy of unconditional surrender and the Combined Bomber Offensive.

3. Some Catholics had come to the conclusion that, because of its destructiveness, modern war could not possibly be justified by traditional just war criteria.

4. The formal act of Japan's unconditional surrender was signed aboard the *U.S.S Missouri* on September 2, 1945.

5. The "Cold War" was so called because there never was there actual war between the U.S. and her allies and the Soviet Communist powers, but they represented opposing political blocs threatening each other with destruction.

CHAPTER 29: The Atomic Age

Chapter Overview

- Before, during, and after the Second World War, the congressional House Un-American Activities Committee investigated "subversive groups," especially Nazis and Communists.

- On June 25, 1950, Korea erupted in a war instigated by Communists in North Korea. On June 27, President Truman gave his support to the United Nations Security Council's declaration of war on North Korea. The United Nations sent in troops, and soon U.N. forces compelled more than half of the North Korean army to surrender. On October 7 the United Nations General Assembly approved an invasion of North Korea, and by the end of the month North Korean resistance had been broken. When Chinese forces came into the fight, U.N. Forces withdrew from North Korea until they were able to stabilize their lines, and began a new counter-offensive. Peace negotiations began in July 1951 and continued for two years.

- The invasion of South Korea heightened American fears of Communism, and Senator Joseph McCarthy led a crusade to weed out Communists, who, he said, were infiltrating the United States government. In 1954, McCarthy was accused of conduct "unbecoming a member of the United States Senate" and formally censured.

- In the presidential election of 1952, Dwight D. Eisenhower became president, giving the Republicans control of the executive branch again after 20 years. Eisenhower chose big businessmen to fill the chief posts in his administration. Eisenhower's "dynamic conservatism" was more openly in favor of private big business while still maintaining and even expanding federal social programs.

- During Eisenhower's administration, covert operations were conducted in other countries, under the auspices of the Central Intelligence Agency (CIA). The CIA helped topple and establish foreign governments. When the Democrats regained control of Congress in the elections of 1954, Eisenhower had a hard time getting his policies approved. Even after the death of Stalin, U.S. military spending remained massive, and more powerful and deadly weapons were developed.

- In October 1957, the Soviets launched the world's first earth-orbiting satellite, *Sputnik*. In January 1958, the United States launched a satellite, *Explorer I*. This led to the passage of the National Aeronautic and Space Act in July 1958 and the founding of the National Aeronautics and Space Administration (NASA).

- President Eisenhower appointed Earl Warren as Chief Justice of the Supreme Court, an act that would have long lasting effects. During Warren's term, the Supreme Court overthrew racial segregation in schools. Following this, a black woman, Rosa Parks, fought segregation by refusing to give up her seat on a bus to a white man. In November 1956, the Supreme Court ruled segregation in local transport unconstitutional. Eisenhower became involved in the segregation issue in 1957, and on September 9, Congress passed the first civil rights act since 1870, creating a federal Civil Rights Commission.

- After the Second World War, prosperity dawned on the United States, including an upsurge in population called the "Baby Boom," increased production, and more jobs. The working man's wage rose, and a GI bill that allowed more men to go to college, lead to an increase in the number of "white collar" workers. The rise in wages brought more people into the middle class. An increase in housing led to suburbanization, which in turn led to an increase in private transportation and highways. American culture grew even more homogenous through the proliferation of "chain" stores and popular entertainment, such as television. In the 1950s the youth became consumers, and an entire youth culture arose.

♦ In 1960, John Fitzgerald Kennedy became president and introduced his federal aid program called the "New Frontier." Kennedy was unable to get Congress to approve most of his New Frontier legislation, however. Many Americans found the Kennedy vitality and idealism invigorating.

♦ In 1961, the Soviets sent a manned spacecraft around the earth. The United States sent its first astronaut, Alan Shepard, into space a month later. The arms race continued when the Soviets broke the verbal agreement to stop nuclear testing. Kennedy followed suit on April 25, 1962 and ordered the resumption of nuclear testing. Fearing the long-term health effects of nuclear radiation, the United States, the Soviet Union, and Great Britain signed the Nuclear Test Ban Treaty on August 5, 1963.

♦ Following Martin King Luther, Jr.'s call for non-violent resistance, students began to challenge racial segregation through "sit-ins." Consequently, many eating establishments removed segregated seating, and the Interstate Commerce Commission prohibited racial segregation on buses and in terminals used in interstate commerce. In the spring of 1963,

mass demonstrations for racial equality were held in the North as well as the South.

♦ On November 22, 1963, President Kennedy was shot while on a speaking trip in Texas. His vice-president, Lyndon Johnson, was sworn in as president on the plane on the way back to Washington. Johnson called on Congress to carry out Kennedy's plans and programs, and at his urging Congress passed the Civil Rights Act of 1964. Johnson was re-elected in 1964.

♦ When in August 1964 North Vietnamese torpedo boats attacked U.S. destroyers, President Johnson pushed the "Tonkin Resolution" which gave him authority to halt further aggression. He then launched retaliatory air strikes on North Vietnam and increased military aid to South Vietnam. When Communist guerillas attacked U.S. bases in South Vietnam, Johnson ordered an all-out bombing of North Vietnam and sent more troops into Vietnam.

♦ During the 1960s, the youth of the baby boom generation became disillusioned with the American dream and what they deemed the hypocrisy of society. The civil rights movement gave them a cause to fight for. The Vietnam war further radicalized American youth, and they began protesting the bombings and atrocities of the war. The youth began questioning not only government but all the institutions of society.

♦ The Vietnam War affected other groups. Media coverage of the war and the rising death count of American soldiers made the war highly unpopular and caused unrest amongst blacks in the ghettos of American cities. Malcolm X, a spokesman for the Nation of Islam movement, encouraged rioting and violence against segregation.

♦ Feminism arose as a facet of the "sexual revolution." Feminists formed the National

Organization for Women to fight for women's rights. They promoted contraception and abortion and full legal, economic, and social equality with men.

◆ After the Tet Offensive in Vietnam in January 1968, President Johnson called a partial halt to the bombing of North Vietnam and said he would pursue peace negotiations. On October 31, Johnson ordered an end to all bombing in North Vietnam.

◆ On October 11, 1962, Pope John XXIII called an ecumenical council in order to "update" the Church. When the media started covering the council, it seemed as if revolutionary changes were afoot. In 1963 Cardinal Spellman of New York brought the long-silenced John Courtney Murray to Rome as a *peritus*, and Murray became a chief architect of the conciliar document, *Dignitatis Humanae*, the *Declaration on Religious Liberty*. In defense of the declaration, Murray published a paper for the council fathers called, "The Problem of Religious Freedom."

◆ Though the Church did not change any teaching in Vatican II, many authors gave the impression that she had, especially in regards to artificial contraception. Thousands of priests and women religious abandoned their vocations. John XXIII's successor, Paul VI, addressed the question of contraception in the encyclical letter, *Humanae Vitae*. Following this, many Catholic theologians criticized the pope and his encyclical. Some Catholic theologians denied the authority of the pope.

◆ Richard Nixon, who had become president in 1968, resumed peace talks with North Vietnam, but they were going nowhere. To unite Americans around a common issue, he addressed environmental problems. Then on July 20, 1969, Neal Armstrong landed on the moon. Nixon began making friendly overtures to both Communist China and Russia.

◆ In 1965, the Supreme Court struck down a Connecticut law that penalized the use of contraceptives, based on a constitutional "right to privacy." Eight years later, the Supreme Court invoked the "right to privacy" in *Roe v. Wade* that struck down not only Texas statutes restricting abortion, but all such statutes nationwide. Critics of the decision coalesced in a new movement for justice, the right-to-life or "pro-life" movement.

What Students Should Know

1. **Why the House Un-American Activities Committee was formed and what it did**

   The House Un-American Activities Committee had been founded in 1938 to investigate "subversive groups," particularly Nazis, in the United States. After the war, the committee turned its attention to Communists because of fears that Communist espionage and infiltration had made it possible for the Soviets to progress so quickly in developing an atomic bomb. In 1947, the committee investigated alleged Communist infiltration in the Hollywood film industry. But of more lasting effect in dealing with Communists in Hollywood was the blacklist of suspected persons that the studios voluntarily adopted. Those whose names were blacklisted could find no work in the movie capital. The Committee's subpoenaing of Whittaker Chambers in 1948 led to the famous trial of Alger Hiss. Hiss had been one of Roosevelt's chief advisers at Yalta and one of the chief architects of the United Nations, and was, then, president of the Carnegie Endowment for World Peace. Chambers said that in the 1930s, he and Hiss had been members of the same Communist group and that Hiss had passed secret state documents to Moscow. Hiss couldn't be convicted of treason, but the jury found him guilty of perjury and sentenced him to five years in prison.

2. What happened with the Julius and Ethel Roseberg case

A closely watched case was that of Julius and Ethel Rosenberg, who were convicted of giving nuclear secrets to the Soviets. Though neither were convicted of treason but of conspiracy to commit espionage (a lesser charge that normally only carried a penalty of imprisonment), the Rosenbergs were condemned to death. When they had exhausted all attempts for appeal and had been refused pardon by President Truman (among others, Pope Pius XII had, without commenting on the merits of the case, directly appealed to the president for clemency), the couple were executed by electric chair on April 5, 1951.

3. The causes of the Korean War

On June 25, 1950, Korea erupted in a war instigated by Communists. At the end of the Second World War, Korea had been divided along the 38th parallel into two nations. The north was Communist, while the south, called the Republic of Korea, was not Communist but was highly unstable. The South Korean army melted before the advance of North Korean troops (supported by Communist China), who crossed the 38th parallel on June 25, 1950. The war was a surprise, for it had been assumed that the next war would be worldwide and atomic, and this was conventional. President Truman gave his full support to the United Nations Security Council's declaration of war on North Korea on June 27. (This was the first war the United States entered without a formal declaration of war by Congress.) Ten nations responded to the U.N.'s appeal for what it called a "police action" against North Korea, and the UN's forces were placed under the command of General Douglas MacArthur.

4. The course of the Korean War

During the first months of the war, as United Nations forces were gathering, the North Koreans were able to push South Korean and what U.N. forces there were in Korea into the southeastern corner of the country. U.N. navy bombarded the coasts of Korea, while air force carried on round-the-clock bombing strikes in support of U.N. forces. On September 15, 1950, U.N. troops made an amphibious landing behind enemy lines at Inchon on the west coast of Korea and captured Seoul, the capital of South Korea. Then U.N. forces forced more than half the North Korean army to surrender. The United Nations General Assembly on October 7 approved an invasion of North Korea, and U.N. forces on October 19, captured Pyongyang, and by the end of October 1950, broke North Korean resistance. On November 24, MacArthur commenced an offensive to the north; but after two days, Communist Chinese forces forced U.N. forces to take the defensive. The Chinese were so successful against the U.N. Forces that, in mid December, they were forced to withdraw from North Korea. In early January, 1951, Communist forces took Seoul. In March, U.N. troops began a new counter-offensive. By March 14, U.N. forces retook Seoul and on April 3, pushed across the 38th parallel. MacArthur now wanted to support a Chinese Republican invasion of the Chinese mainland from Taiwan, but Truman opposed him. When MacArthur publicly criticized the president, Truman in April replaced him with General Matthew B. Ridgeway. By the end of May 1951, the battle lines once again lay along the 38th parallel. They would change little for the remainder of the war. Peace negotiations between the warring sides began in July of 1951 and continued for nearly two years. The guns fell silent on July 27, 1953 when both sides signed a cease-fire.

5. Senator Joseph McCarthy and anti-Communism

Responding to heightened American fears of a world-wide spread of Communism and of Communist infiltration of the United States government, the media, and university intelligentsia, Wisconsin Senator Joseph McCarthy, a German-Irish Catholic, led a crusade to weed out Communists who, he said, were infiltrating the United States government – particularly the highly sensitive state department, which dealt with international affairs. In February 1950, McCarthy told the Senate that he knew the names of a number of Communists in the state department. The Senate then established a special committee to investigate McCarthy's charges, placing it under the leadership of Democratic Senator Millard Tydings of Maryland. When the Tydings Committee report came out, it condemned McCarthy rather than those he had accused. But by July 1950 McCarthy had become one of the most powerful men in the Senate. His charges were often exaggerated and, at times, untrue. In 1951, McCarthy attacked the Truman administration, declaring that the president was the dupe of men in his cabinet. When Eisenhower became president, McCarthy said he was soft on Communism. McCarthy investigated the Voice of America and attacked the Protestant clergy. His allegations against the United States Army led to the two-month long "Army-McCarthy" hearings that resulted in a tightening of security on army bases. But in July 1954, a resolution in Congress accused McCarthy of conduct "unbecoming a member of the United States Senate." In November 1954, the

Senate formally censured McCarthy. Thereafter, his influenced waned.

6. The Eisenhower Administration and "Dynamic Conservatism"

Unlike Roosevelt, who had chosen progressive intellectuals to fill his cabinet, President Eisenhower picked leaders of big business to fill the chief posts in his administration. Only the secretary of labor was from the working class; but he soon resigned. Eisenhower characterized his policies as "dynamic conservatism"; for though it did not abandon the big government model of Roosevelt; it more openly favored private big business, while still maintaining and even expanding federal social programs.

7. Changes in capitalism in the 1950s

In the 1950s, business leaders were no longer calling for *laissez-faire* competition but were willing to accept the government as their referee. But big business profited from its cooperation with government. By 1956, 135 corporations had come to own 45 percent of all industrial assets in the United States. In such industries as oil refining, meat packing, iron and steel, a few companies, banded together, controlled the pricing of raw materials and of manufactured goods, and so set the pace for smaller competitors. Most competition was not within industries but between competing products. Talented, ambitious young men were less likely to open new businesses but were content with working for corporations.

8. U.S. foreign interventions in the 1950s

The Eisenhower administration conducted covert operations in other countries. The chief instrument in these operations was the Central Intelligence Agency, or CIA, founded during the Roosevelt years. Though no war was declared, nor U.N. police action voted on, the United States, through the CIA, helped topple and establish governments as far away as Asia and as close to home as Central America. One such intervention was carried out against Mohammad Mosaddeq, the premier of Iran. The CIA was involved in training insurgent troops to overthrow the government of Jacobo Árbenz, the president of Guatemala in behalf of the United Fruit Company. In June 1954, a force of Guatemalan exiles and foreign recruits, in a coup orchestrated by the CIA, overthrew Árbenz and established a new government more friendly to United Fruit and the United States.

9. What the U.S. Supreme Court decided in *Brown v. Board of Education of Topeka*, and its significance.

Brown v. Board of Education concerned one Oliver Brown, a black man residing in Topeka, Kansas, who brought the Topeka Board of Education to trial for refusing to allow his third-grade daughter to attend a white school. When the United States District Court ruled against Brown, citing the 1896 Supreme Court decision, *Plessy v. Ferguson*, which decided that racially "separate but equal" accommodations on public transportation did not contradict the equal protection clause of the 14th Amendment to the Constitution," Brown and the NAACP appealed the decision to the United States Supreme Court. In the decision he wrote for the court in 1954, Chief Justice Earl Warren said what the authors of the amendment, members of Congress and of state legislatures, "had in mind" when they adopted the 14th Amendment "cannot be determined with any degree of certainty." Warren asked whether segregation in 1954

deprived students of equal protection? Though black and white schools were becoming equal, Warren said that segregation itself gave blacks a sense of inferiority, "Separate educational facilities are inherently unequal," he said; thus, segregation deprived people "of the equal protection of the laws guaranteed by the Fourteenth Amendment." In 1955, the Supreme Court made a ruling that desegregation must proceed with "all deliberate speed."

10. Southern reaction to the *Brown* decision

In March 1956, 96 Southern congressmen issued a declaration denouncing *Brown* as a violation of the Constitution and called upon states to, in effect, nullify it. The judicial branch, they said, was acting as the legislative branch and encroached "upon the reserved rights of the states and the people." The debates that preceded the submission of the 14h Amendment in the 1860s, wrote the congressmen, "clearly show that there was no intent that it should affect the systems of education maintained by the states." The Warren court "substituted their personal political and social ideas for the established law of the land."

11. Rosa Parks and what she did

In 1955, in Montgomery, Alabama, a black woman, Rosa Parks, refused to give up her seat on a bus to a white man – for which she was arrested. Parks' defiance of segregation led the black Baptist minister, Martin Luther King, Jr., to organize blacks in Montgomery to form carpools and boycott public transportation. The boycott continued for about a year; then, in November 1956, the Supreme Court ruled that segregation in local public transportation was unconstitutional.

12. **How Eisenhower enforced the Supreme Court's segregation decisions in Little Rock Arkansas**

In the fall of 1957, nine black children were prevented to enter a white public high school in Little Rock, Arkansas by the national guard, called out by the governor of Arkansas. Though the Constitution allows the president to protect a state "against domestic violence" only "on application of the legislature, or of the executive," Eisenhower sent national guard units into Little Rock to maintain order. "When a state refuses," declared Eisenhower, "to utilize its police powers to protect persons who are peacefully exercising their rights under the Constitution as defined in such [federal] court orders, the oath of office of the President requires that he take action to give that protection. Failure to act in such a case would be tantamount to acquiescence in anarchy and the dissolution of the Union."

13. **The Civil Rights Act of 1957 and what it entailed**

The Civil Rights Act of 1957 created a federal Civil Rights Commission and a civil rights division in the office of the United States Attorney General. The latter would have the power to prosecute those who placed any obstacles to any citizen's exercise of his constitutional rights. Offenders, even if they were state officials, could be fined or imprisoned if they ignored the orders of federal judges in these matters.

14. **Post-war American prosperity and on what it was based**

The Marshall Plan helped bring prosperity to Western European nations and thus opened up markets for American goods. The postwar "Baby Boom" meant the necessity for increased production and thus more jobs. But among the chief causes of the post-war prosperity was the dramatic rise in government military spending, especially after the Korean War. Unions insisted that companies pay working men a wage sufficient to support a family, thus raising the real weekly earnings of factory workers by 50 percent. A GI bill passed by Congress allowed more men to go to college and so increased the number of those working for prosperous corporations. The rise in wages brought many more people into the middle class, though poverty still remained.

15. **The causes of suburbanization and its effects**

Federal aid for housing allowed many Americans to achieve home ownership. Because of federal policy that favored the purchase of new houses over existing houses in cities, much new housing went up on the outskirts of cities thus bringing about the growth of suburban neighborhoods – suburbanization. A pioneer of the mass housing production that came to characterize suburbs was Levitt and Sons, Inc. Levitt and Sons laid out vast neighborhood tracts upon a general plan that included spaces for shopping centers and for schools. The houses, built after a very limited number of models, though comfortable, made for architecturally monotonous neighborhoods. Many people, however, welcomed this development, for it allowed them to leave the crowded conditions of the cities.

16. **The character of the new suburban culture**

Suburban culture was characterized by the automobile – it was, in fact, automobiles and federal and state improved highways that made suburbs possible, since workers now had to commute longer distances to their jobs. Automobile ownership became a hallmark of American life. Highways allowed suburbs to be built ever farther from city centers, creating, in time, large, sprawling urban landscapes. Because of suburban development, American culture grew ever more homogenous. Everywhere, suburbs shared common characteristics. Television destroyed much of what remained of homespun entertainment and spread mass fads that influenced dress, speech, and social mores nationwide. Industrialism had already undermined home-based industries and so separated the father from his family for long periods throughout the day. Suburbanization exacerbated separation of the father from the family brought about by industrialism by increasing the distances between home and work. Wives, separated from husband and children (who went to school) for long hours, found their lives increasingly occupied in house cleaning, shopping, and socializing. Many women began to suffer from boredom and dissatisfaction. The wealth of the 1950s allowed even youth to become consumers, and an entire youth culture arose to meet (and create) the demand.

17. The character of the general culture in the 1950s

The culture of the 1950s was, at least externally, religious, conservative, and family-centered. Most Americans attended religious services and upheld a morality that valued family cohesiveness, self reliance, honesty, hard work, and patriotism. But the media and advertising spread the notion that happiness lay in the possession of material goods. Indeed, the "American dream" was increasingly defined in material terms – home ownership, the possession of consumer goods, and the freedom to better one's condition. The mass-produced culture was not only shallow, it could be sexually

suggestive. In the end, the morality of the Eisenhower era would be seen as a morality of respectability. American youth would come to conclude that their parents' ethics were a mere veneer to make them appear "upstanding" in the eyes of their neighbors.

18. What the Supreme Court decided in *Abington School District v. Schempp*

In 1963, the Warren Supreme Court heard a case, *Abington School District v. Schempp,* challenging the right of public schools to carry on religious exercises. The Warren court agreed with the litigants, Madeline Murray and Edward Schempp. The court basically said that, though the First Amendment only binds Congress from erecting an "establishment of religion" (that is, a state-sponsored church), it went further and erected (in the words of Thomas Jefferson) a "wall of separation" between church and state." Prayer and other religious exercises in public schools, argued the court, violated the First Amendment. All state acts, said the court, must be religiously neutral.

19. The highlights of president John F. Kennedy's presidency and domestic policies

Kennedy, the first Catholic to be elected president of the United State, had, during the 1960 election, met a good deal of suspicion because of his religion. But Kennedy assured voters that he wouldn't deliver the United States over to papal rule. To the Greater Houston Ministerial Alliance, he said: "whatever issue may come before me as president, if I should be elected – on birth control, divorce, censorship, gambling, or any other subject – I will make my decision … in accord with what my conscience tells me to be in the national interest, and without regard to outside religious pressure or dictation, and no power or threat of punishment could cause me to decide otherwise." Kennedy came into office with his own federal aid program, called the "New Frontier." But conservative Democrats joined with Republicans to block most New Frontier legislation. Congress did approve increased military spending and eventually passed such New Frontier measures as an increase in the minimum wage from one dollar to $1.25 an hour and a housing act that gave grants to towns and cities for local transportation systems and middle-income housing. Congress approved the formation of the Peace Corps.

Kennedy positioned himself as a champion of civil rights. In 1962, he sent federal troops to the University of Mississippi to protect James Meredith, a black man, who had enrolled there. In 1963 he sent the national guard to the University of Alabama when Governor George Wallace prohibited the enrollment of black students.

John F. Kennedy was assassinated on November 22, 1963 in Dallas, Texas. His vice-president, Lyndon Baines Johnson, succeeded to the presidency.

20. The course of American involvement in Vietnam

In 1954, Communist Vietnamese rebels defeated French forces at Dien Bien Phu in French Indochina, and the now independent Vietnam was divided between a Communist state under rebel leader Ho Chi Minh and a southern republic under the autocratic Ngo Dinh Diem. When North Vietnam began a guerrilla war against the south, Eisenhower in 1955 sent in military advisers and supplies. By the time Kennedy took office, the number of Americans in Vietnam had grown to 12,000. Kennedy continued Eisenhower's policy and expanded it, sending "Green Berets" as a special counter-insurgency force to South Vietnam.

When Lyndon Johnson became president, he said the U.S. was involved in Vietnam because its ally, South Vietnam, had asked for help against Communist aggression. Under Johnson, the U.S. presence in Vietnam expanded greatly. In the summer of 1964, the government claimed that North Vietnamese torpedo boats had, within a two-day period, attacked U.S. destroyers in the Gulf of Tonkin. (U.S. attacks in North Korea had prompted the first violent exchange; at the second of these Tonkin incidents, no North Vietnamese sea craft were present.) Johnson pushed the "Tonkin Resolution" through Congress, giving him authority to halt further aggression. Johnson then launched retaliatory air strikes on North Vietnam and increased military aid to South Vietnam. When Communist guerrillas attacked U.S. bases in South Vietnam. Johnson ordered an all-out bombing of North Vietnam, south of the 20th parallel. When it became clear that air power alone could not overcome guerrilla forces, Johnson, in June 1965, ordered more U.S. ground troops into Vietnam. By 1968, about a half a million Americans were fighting in a war that, to many Americans, would seem a hopeless morass from which the country would not be able to extricate itself. Coverage by the television media of the war, coupled with the rising American death count made the war highly unpopular. The war in Vietnam was splitting America down generational lines, with parents by and large supporting the war, their children opposing it.

On January 30, 1968, the North Vietnamese launched the "Tet Offensive," their largest offensive against South Vietnam and her American ally. The North Vietnamese and the Viet Cong attacked 30 South Vietnamese cities and drove American troops from 100 major positions, inflicting heavy casualties. The Tet offensive led many to believe Vietnam was a costly and hopeless war. On March 31, 1968, Johnson, in a television address to the American people, announced that he was calling a partial halt to the bombing of North Vietnam and that he would pursue peace negotiations with the North Vietnamese. When these peace talks in Paris yielded no results because North Vietnam insisted on a complete cessation of American bombing, Johnson, in October 1968, announced that he had ordered an end to all bombing of North Vietnam and had decided to include representatives of South Vietnam and the Viet Cong in the negotiations. When Richard Nixon became president, the U.S. and South Vietnam resumed peace talks with North Vietnam and the Viet Cong. In June, however, Nixon announced he would begin withdrawal of American troops from the war zone as long as the South Vietnamese increased their capability to defend their country and the North Vietnamese did not increase their attacks on remaining American forces. But despite troop withdrawals, the war continued into Nixon's second term, which began in 1973. The Vietnam War ended for the United States in 1973.

21. **Relations between Cuba, the United States, and the Soviet Union in the late 1950s and early 1960s**

In 1956, in Cuba, Fidel Castro and Ernesto "Che" Guevara initiated a revolution against the regime of the Cuban dictator, Fulgencio Batista. Though the revolution began with only a handful of men, it soon swelled with peasant recruits wishing to overthrow Batista's oppressive regime. On New Year's Day, 1959, Batista fled Havana, and soon after, Castro became dictator. While, in the beginning, Castro's objectives called for an end to political imprisonment, the restoration of popular elections, a congress, and a free press, under the influence of his brother, Raúl and Che, Castro gravitated towards Communism. After the revolutionary government began confiscating sugar plantations and major industries (many owned by Americans), President Eisenhower broke off diplomatic relations with Cuba and forbade Americans to trade with the island. In 1961, Castro proclaimed himself a Marxist-Leninist, and his closure of Catholic churches earned him excommunication. Nikita Khruschev, the Soviet premier, extended credit to Cuba and agreed to buy the island's sugar crop, thus cementing an alliance between Cuba and the Communist block of nations. Like Eisenhower, Kennedy wanted Castro overthrown. In April 1961, a force of anti-Castro Cubans who had been trained by the CIA landed at the Bay of Pigs on the southwestern coast of Cuba, hoping to foment a revolution; but Castro was still popular, and the insurgents were routed. But in the late summer, early fall of 1962, the U.S. government learned that the Russians were building missile sites on the island of Cuba, which placed major American cities in the range of atomic missile attack. Though the Russian minister said the missile sites were "purely defensive," Kennedy demanded their removal, hinting that if the Soviets didn't comply, the U.S. would launch a missile strike on Cuba. On October 23, the Organization of American States voted to approve a blockade of Cuba suggested by Kennedy, while U.S. nuclear armed B-52s, submarines armed with polaris missiles, and ICBMs were made ready, and the army, navy, and marines were mobilized in Florida and in the Gulf ports. On October 26, Khrushchev offered to evacuate the missile sites if

Kennedy agreed not to invade Cuba. The crisis had been averted.

22. The course of the "Space Race" and the nuclear arms race during the early 1960s

Rivalry between the superpowers continued in the space race. In April 1961, the Soviets became the first to send a manned spacecraft around the earth. A month later, the United States rocketed its first "astronaut," Alan Shepard, into space. On February 20, 1962, American astronaut John Glenn orbited the earth thrice in five hours. When a Russian satellite photographed the dark backside of the moon, Congress voted more money for what was dubbed "Project Apollo." Kennedy promised that the United States would be the first to land a man on the moon. In the nuclear arms race, Khrushchev in 1961 broke a verbal agreement he made with Eisenhower and resumed nuclear open-air testing, exploding 50 nuclear devices. On April 25, 1962, Kennedy ordered the resumption of nuclear testing. Fear over the long-term health effects of nuclear radiation fall-out in the atmosphere finally brought the Americans and the Soviets to the negotiating board. On August 5, 1963, the United States, the Soviet Union, and Great Britain met in Moscow and signed the Nuclear Test Ban Treaty, agreeing that both sides would end open-air nuclear testing.

23. Sit-Ins and Freedom Riders, and what they accomplished

Following Dr. Martin Luther King, Jr.'s call for non-violent resistance, in February 1960, four black college students from the Agricultural and Technical College of North Carolina in Greensboro peacefully sat at a "whites only" lunch counter at Woolworth's variety store in Greensboro and requested service. When refused, they continued sitting. Soon students and others throughout the South staged similar "sit-ins," as well as "read-ins" in segregated libraries, and "wade-ins" on segregated beaches. By 1961, many eating establishments had removed segregated seating. In May 1961, groups of blacks called "Freedom Riders" tested federal laws against segregation in public transportation. They set out by bus from Washington, D.C. toward New Orleans. Mobs attacked the Freedom Riders at several stops. Following the Freedom Rides, the Interstate Commerce Commission in September 1961 prohibited racial segregation on buses and in terminals used in interstate commerce.

24. The character of civil rights demonstrations

In the spring of 1963, mass demonstrations for racial equality were held both in the North and the South. The demonstrations were peaceful but sometimes met violence, as in Birmingham, Alabama, where police used high-pressure fire hoses, electric cattle prods, and dogs against demonstrators. The city and the protestors reached an agreement on desegregation, but in September 1963, a bomb, thrown into a black church in Birmingham, killed four girls attending a Sunday school class.

25. Martin Luther King, Jr., the March on Washington, and its effects

When southern representatives in Congress blocked a civil rights bill that Kennedy had introduced in June 1963. Martin Luther King, Jr., organized a massive march on Washington, D.C. In August 1963, 200,000 demonstrators (60,000 of them white) marched into Washington, D.C., processing from the Washington to the Lincoln memorials. In a speech before the Lincoln Memorial in Washington, King enunciated the goals of the mainstream Civil Rights Movement. He said he hoped for a day when people "will not be judged by the color of their skin but by the content of their character." Among the effects of the March on Washington was the passing of the Civil Rights Act of 1964. Besides strengthening voting rights protection, the act prohibited segregation in places of "public accommodation" – restaurants, hotels, terminals, etc.; required the federal government to withhold assistance to state or county programs that favored racial discrimination; gave the attorney general authority to institute lawsuits against segregation in schools; and established the Equal Employment Opportunity Commission (EEOC) to fight racial preferences in employment.

26. What the "Great Society" was

The Great Society was President Johnson's program to address poverty in the United States. At the president's urging, Congress approved a multi-billion dollar federal aid to schools and libraries bill; expanded Social Security to include "Medicare" (medical care for people over age 65); and added anti-poverty programs.

27. The Voting Rights Act and what it did

The Voting Rights Act was a law passed by Congress that secured the right to vote for black people. The act abolished most literacy tests for voting and authorized the sending of federal examiners to register voters in any county that practiced racial discrimination.

28. Causes and results of the radicalization of youth in the 1960s

Kennedy's idealism had inspired youth of the early 1960s. The civil rights movement had

given them a cause for which to fight. Many youth, it seems, had become disillusioned with an American dream that seemed to promise only more material prosperity, ease, and comfort; they had grown impatient with a society that proclaimed freedom and equality but denied them to some simply because they were not white. Beginning in 1960, student groups fighting for civil rights and other radical causes began to form throughout the country. One example of these groups was the Free Speech Movement (FSM) at the University of California, Berkeley, which organized a student sit on the Berkeley campus, for which 800 students were arrested in December 1964. The Vietnam War further radicalized many American youth, who protested U.S. bombing and its effects on the Vietnamese civilian population. Military conscription of young men, too, made the war unpopular. Some fled to Canada or Europe. Men publicly burned their draft cards. The decade of the '50s had created a youth culture; the '60s gave rise to a youth counterculture. Youth did not merely question the war but the entire adult world they had inherited. Their parents, they declared, were materialistic; they were hypocrites, espousing a code of conduct they violated in their daily lives. Youth began to question not only government but all the institutions of society – the church, marriage, and the family. A "hippie" culture developed among youth who wanted to live according to ideals of peace, anarchic freedom, and free love.

29. Racial Unrest in the 1960s

By the mid '60s, nearly 70 percent of American blacks lived in cities, particularly in the North. Though northern cities had no segregation laws, the fact that blacks earned much less than whites meant that they lived separated from whites in the poorest and most run-down sections of the cities. Many blacks began to think that the government was diverting promised funds from them to the war effort. Dissatisfaction among blacks was, in some cases, fanned by radical black groups, such as the Nation of Islam. Founded in 1930 by Elijah Muhammad, the Nation of Islam favored the complete separation of the races in their own geographical regions. By the 1960s, Elijah Muhammad's disciple, Malcolm X, became the spokesman for the movement. Malcolm X rejected Martin Luther King, Jr.'s call for non-violent resistance as naïve and advocated that blacks meet white violence with violence. In the summers of 1966 and 1967, rioting occurred in the ghettos of Newark, New Jersey, Los Angeles, California, and Detroit, Michigan. In April 1968, white violence took the life of Martin Luther King, Jr., who had come to Memphis Tennessee to lead a peaceful rally in support of the city's striking garbage workers. He was shot dead while standing on the balcony of his hotel room.

30.   The resurgence of Feminism

American Feminism returned in 1962 with the book, *The Feminine Mystique* by Betty Friedan, which claimed that society had reduced women to mere servants of men and so questioned what many considered the middle class achievement of the post-war world: the middle-class family. In 1966, Friedan and others formed the National Organization for Women (NOW) to fight, both socially and politically, for women's rights. Feminists demanded full legal, economic and social equality with men. They trumpeted the cause of inexpensive, readily available abortion.

31.   The character of Catholic life in America after World War II

Despite peculiarly religious differences of cult, American Catholics, after World War II, became hardly distinguishable from other Americans. American Catholics were entering the middle class, moving to the suburbs, buying and enjoying consumer goods. Besides embracing a more pronounced anti-Communism, Catholics had no common set of political goals on which they all agreed. The post-war Catholic Church in America seemed to be thriving in a material way. There was a large core of priests to serve the faithful, the vast majority of whom attended Mass weekly. A number of Americans, attracted to the Church, converted. New contemplative monasteries were springing up around the country. Catholic authors, journals, and the television personality, Archbishop Fulton Sheen, influenced culture and popular culture. Catholic lay movements like Catholic Action were gaining momentum. In the early '60s, American Catholics felt that they had "arrived" and that the world could be changed for the better. Pope John XXIII's call for *aggiornamento*, or the "updating" of the Church, ended, it seemed, the state of war that had existed between the Church and the modern world since before the days of Pius IX.

32.   What happened to the Catholic Church in the U.S. following the Second Vatican Council

Catholics eager to know what the council was up to gleaned little from the official reports of the American bishops. But then the *New York Times* published an account of the council that revealed deep divisions between "liberal" and "conservative" council fathers and began running daily accounts of council happenings. American Catholics began to think that the Church was doing more than updating, but making revolutionary changes. Though the Church did not change any teaching in any of the council documents, many authors gave the impression that she had. American Catholics were told that the Church had altered her teaching on religious liberty, on the relationship between the Catholic Church and other churches and religions, and in other areas as well – including artificial contraception. When a commission established by Pope John XXIII concluded that the Church should change her teaching on artificial contraception, many Catholic theologians and priests began saying that it was permissible for Catholic married couples to use artificial contraceptives to limit the size of their families. But then in July 1968, the Pope Paul VI in the encyclical letter *Humanae Vitae* ("Of Human Life") reiterated traditional Church teaching on artificial contraception. Priests, prominent theologians, and journalists publicly criticized *Humanae Vitae, and some and* some questioned the very doctrine of papal infallibility. A statement, signed by 200 theologians and published in the *New York Times* denied the authority of *Humanae Vitae*. More and more Catholic voices were calling for a new, democratic Church. Thousands of men left the priesthood, and many women religious abandoned their orders. The number of men in seminaries dwindled dramatically. Millions of Catholic faithful, too, dropped out of the Church.

33. Richard Nixon's domestic policies

Nixon ignored peace protests and did little to further black civil rights. Though he vetoed a number of health and education bills the Democratic-dominated Congress sent him, Nixon expanded certain social programs. In 1970, he called for the appropriation of $10 million to clean the nation's rivers and lakes. It was by Nixon's urging that Congress created both the Occupational Safety and Health Administration (OSHA) and the Environmental Protection Agency (EPA). After Nixon's reelection in 1972, revelations of scandals in his administration surrounding the break-in and bugging of the Democratic national headquarters at the Watergate building in Washington, D.C. During the 1972 campaign ultimately forced Richard Nixon to resign the presidency in August 1974.

34. Richard Nixon's foreign policy achievements

President Nixon in 1972 began making friendly overtures to both Communist China and Russia. In February 1972, Nixon became the first U.S. president to visit China. The United States and China agreed to expand their cultural, educational, and journalistic contacts and to broaden trade between their

---

Key Terms at a Glance

dynamic conservatism: the program of the Eisenhower administration that openly favored private big business while maintaining and even expanding federal social programs.

suburbanization: the growth of residential and business areas on the edges of cities

two nations. Though the United States still formally recognized Taiwan's government as the government for all China, the Nixon administration, in October 1972, agreed to remove its objections to Red Chinese membership in the United Nations. Subsequently, the United Nations admitted Red China and expelled Taiwan. Nixon traveled to Moscow to meet with Soviet premier Leonid Ilyich Brezhnev in May 1972 to discuss progress in the Strategic Arms Limitation Treaty (SALT) talks between the two countries, but they forged other agreements as well: on limiting atomic weapons; protecting the natural environment; on sharing medical, space and technological knowledge; on forming a joint trade commission.

35. What the Supreme Court decided in *Roe v. Wade*, and why

The Supreme Court decision, *Roe v. Wade*, that declared unconstitutional a Texas law that banned abortions except to save the life of a mother, depended, in part, on an earlier Supreme Court decision, *Griswold v. Connecticut*, in which the majority of justices argued that the Constitution guarantees a right to privacy. The majority opinion argued that rights enumerated in the Constitution have "penumbras" – non-enunciated rights "that help give [enumerated rights] life and substance." One of these penumbras was privacy. In *Roe,* Justice Harry A. Blackmun argued for the court that the Texas law was unconstitutional because it violated Jane Roe's right to privacy, under which it located "a woman's qualified right to terminate her pregnancy." Though 14th Amendment declares a state shall not "deprive any *person* of life, liberty, or property," Blackmun said that, since society is not agreed as to whether the definition of "person" includes unborn human life, the life of unborn children is not protected by the Constitution. Blackmun drew the line for a legal definition of person at "viability" – the point where an unborn child is able to survive on its own, independent of the mother. Blackmun, however, declared that the right to privacy is not absolute; that the state, at some point, may have an interest in protecting the unborn before viability. In a dissenting opinion, Justice William Rehnquist wrote that the 14th Amendment doesn't protect citizens against being deprived of their liberty simply but only says that one cannot be deprived of liberty unless he be convicted of a crime in a court of law; it says nothing about state laws which, inevitably, limit some freedom. Rehnquist argued that when the court decides to do things, such as "break pregnancy into three distinct terms," it is not acting like a court but like a legislature. The role of the Supreme Court, said Rehnquist, is not to decide when and where a state has a compelling interest in restricting abortion but simply to determine the intent of the men who drew up the 14th Amendment.

Questions for Review

1. Why did the United States participate in the Korean War?

The United States participated in the Korean War because the U.S. government under President Truman was intent on "containing" Communism – keep it from spreading. U.S. participation in the war was in response to the United Nations' appeal for what it called a "police action" against North Korea.

2. What effects did the policies of the Eisenhower administration have on society?

President Eisenhower picked leaders of big business to fill the chief posts in his administration, thus showing it more openly favored large business. Because of this, business leaders were no longer calling for *laissez-faire* competition but were willing to accept the government as their referee. Big business profited from its cooperation with government. By 1956, 135 corporations had come to own 45 percent of all industrial assets in the United States. At the same time, Eisenhower still maintained and even expanded federal social programs.

3. **What was the role of the CIA in U.S. foreign interventions in the 1950s?**

The United States, through the CIA, helped topple and establish governments as far away as Asia and as close to home as Central America.

4. **Lay out Chief Justice Earl Warren's reasoning in his decision in** *Brown v. Board of Education of Topeka.* **On what grounds did 96 southern congressman criticize the decision in March 1956?**

Chief Justice Earl Warren held that what the authors of the 14th Amendment, members of Congress and of state legislatures, "had in mind" when they adopted the 14th Amendment "cannot be determined with any degree of certainty." But the question of intent, said Warren, was unimportant. The question for Warren was: did segregation, in 1954, deprive students of equal protection? Though black and white schools were becoming equal, Warren said that segregation itself gave blacks a sense of inferiority, "Separate educational facilities are inherently unequal," he said; thus, segregation deprived people "of the equal protection of the laws guaranteed by the Fourteenth Amendment." Ninety-six southern congressmen criticized the decision on the grounds that the judicial branch, they

said, was acting as the legislative branch and encroached "upon the reserved rights of the states and the people."

5. **Explain the effects the phenomenon of suburbanization had on the culture of the United States in the 1940s-1960s.**

Because of suburban development, American culture grew ever more homogenous. Everywhere, suburbs shared common characteristics. Television destroyed much of what remained of homespun entertainment and spread mass fads that influenced dress, speech, and social mores nationwide. Suburbanization exacerbated separation of the father from the family brought about by industrialism by increasing the distances between home and work. Wives, separated from husband and children (who went to school) for long hours, found their lives increasingly occupied in house cleaning, shopping, and socializing. The "modern" wife began to seem increasingly ornamental. Many women began to suffer from boredom and dissatisfaction. The wealth of the 1950s allowed even youth to become consumers, and an entire youth culture arose to meet (and create) the demand.

6. **Describe the "middle class" culture of the United States in the 1950s and early 1960s.**

The culture of the 1950s was, at least externally, religious, conservative, and family-centered. Most Americans attended religious services and upheld a morality that valued family cohesiveness, self reliance, honesty, hard work, and patriotism. But the media and advertising spread the notion that happiness lay in the possession of material goods. Indeed, the "American dream" was increasingly defined in material terms – home ownership, the possession of consumer goods, and the freedom to better one's condition. The mass-produced culture was not only shallow, it could be sexually suggestive. In the end, the morality of the Eisenhower era would be seen as a morality of respectability. American youth would come to conclude that their parents' ethics were a mere veneer to make them appear "upstanding" in the eyes of their neighbors.

7. **What "dream" did Martin Luther King, Jr. have?**

Martin Luther King, Jr.'s dream was "that one day this nation will rise up and live out the true meaning of its creed: 'We hold these truths to be self-evident: that all men are created equal' … I have a dream that my four children will one day live in a nation where they will not be judged by the color of their skin but by the content of their character."

8. **Why, according the President Johnson, was the United States in Vietnam?**

President Johnson said the U.S. was involved in Vietnam because a U.S. ally, South Vietnam, had asked for help against Communist aggression.

9. **How did the culture of the 1960s and the Vietnam War serve to radicalize the American youth and bring about the hippie movement?**

Kennedy's idealism had inspired youth of the early 1960s. The civil rights movement had given them a cause for which to fight. Many youth, it seems, had become disillusioned with an American dream that seemed to promise only more material prosperity, ease, and comfort; they had grown impatient with a society that proclaimed freedom and equality but denied them to some simply because they were not white. The Vietnam War further radicalized many American youth, who protested U.S. bombing and its

effects on the Vietnamese civilian population. Military conscription of young men, too, made the war unpopular. '60s gave rise to a youth counterculture. Youth did not merely question the war but the entire adult world they had inherited. Their parents, they declared, were materialistic; they were hypocrites, espousing a code of conduct they violated in their daily lives. Youth began to question not only government but all the institutions of society – the church, marriage, and the family. A "hippie" culture developed among youth who wanted to live according to ideals of peace, anarchic freedom, and free love.

10. **What were the goals of the feminist movement of the 1960s?**

Feminists demanded full legal, economic, and social equality with men. They trumpeted the cause of inexpensive, readily available abortion.

11. **What was the character of the post-World War II Catholic Church in the United States?**

Despite peculiarly religious differences of cult American Catholics, after World War II, became hardly distinguishable from other Americans. Americans Catholics were entering the middle class, moving to the suburbs, buying and enjoying consumer goods. Besides embracing a more pronounced anti-Communism, Catholics had no common set of political goals on which they all agreed. The post-war Catholic Church in America seemed to be thriving in a material way. There was a large core of priests to serve the faithful, the vast majority of whom attended Mass weekly. A number of Americans, attracted to the Church, converted. New contemplative monasteries were springing up around the country.

Catholic authors, journals, and the television personality, Archbishop Fulton Sheen, influenced culture and popular culture. Catholic lay movements like Catholic Action were gaining momentum. In the early '60s, American Catholics felt that they had "arrived" and that the world could be changed for the better. Pope John XXIII's call for *aggiornamento*, or the "updating" of the Church, ended, it seemed, the state of war that had existed between the Church and the modern world since before the days of Pius IX.

12. Explain the reasons Pope John XXIII gave for calling the Second Vatican Ecumenical Council.

Pope John declared he had called the gathering of the world's bishops to take "into account the errors, the requirements, and the opportunities of our time" so that the eternal truths of the Church "might be presented in exceptional form to all men throughout the world."

13. What led to the upheavals in the Catholic Church in the United States after the Council?

Catholics began to think that the Church was doing more than updating at Vatican II, but making revolutionary changes. Though the Church did not change any teaching in any of the council does, many authors gave the impression that she had. But then in July 1968, Pope Paul VI in the encyclical letter *Humanae Vitae* ("Of Human Life") reiterated traditional Church teaching on artificial contraception. Priests, prominent theologians, and journalists publicly criticized *Humanae Vitae*, and some questioned the very doctrine of papal infallibility. A statement, signed by 200 theologians and published in the *New York Times* denied the authority of *Humanae Vitae*. More and more Catholic voices were calling for a new, democratic Church. Thousands of men left the priesthood, and many women religious abandoned their orders. The number of men in seminaries dwindled dramatically. Millions of Catholic faithful, too, dropped out of the Church.

14. How did the Supreme Court in *Abington School District v. Schempp* interpret the First Amendment in regards to religion?

Though the First Amendment only binds Congress from erecting an "establishment of religion" (that is, a state-sponsored church), the Supreme Court decided it did more – it erected (in the words of Thomas Jefferson) a "wall of separation" between church and state. Prayer and other religious exercises in public schools, argued the court, violated the First Amendment. All state parties, said the court, must be neutral in regards to religion.

15. What is the "right to privacy"? Where did Justice William O. Douglas in the *Griswold* decision say he found this right in the Constitution? How was the "right to privacy" used in the Supreme Court decision, *Roe v. Wade*?

The "right to privacy" is a person's right to privacy in one's associations. The justices knew that "privacy" was not among the enumerated constitutional rights; but in his decision for the majority, Justice William O. Douglas argued that the enumerated rights have "penumbras" – non-enunciated rights "that help give [enumerated rights] life and substance." In *Roe v. Wade*, a single woman, "Jane Roe" (a pseudonym) who wanted to have an abortion challenged a Texas law that banned abortions except to save the life of the mother. Justice Harry A. Blackmun argued for the court that the Texas law was unconstitutional because it violated Jane Roe's right to privacy.

Ideas in Action

1. Read about and watch videos of the first moon landing.

2. Interview someone who lived during the cultural revolution of the 1960s. Ask his or her opinion of the changes and how they have affected our society today.

3. Discuss Justice William O. Douglas' understanding of penumbral rights in the Constitution. Does, for instance, the right to freedom of association imply a right to privacy? If it does, is it the business of courts to define such a penumbral right? And if penumbral rights exist, how do we determine which rights are more fundamental?

4. We have seen in our study that the conviction that the United States has a special mission to the world as a sort of City on a Hill was common in American history. How was this conviction apparent in the post-World War II world? Who upheld it? Did anyone question it?

5. Read documents of the Second Vatican Council (*Lumen Gentium* and *Gaudium et Spes* recommended) and compare what the council fathers said to what is happening in the Church now.

Sample Quiz I (pages 823-837)

Please answer the following in complete sentences.

1. Why was the House Un-American Activities Committee formed?

2. What caused the Korean War?

3. How did Eisenhower characterize his policies?

4. How did the culture of capitalism change in the 1950s?

5. Why, according to Chief Justice Warren in *Brown v. Board of Education of Topeka,* was racial segregation unconstitutional?

6. How did Eisenhower say justify his enforcement of the Supreme Court's segregation decisions?

7. What was the Civil Rights Act of 1957, and what did it entail?

8. On what was the post-war prosperity of America based, and how was it manifested?

9. How did federal policy promote suburbanization?

10. What did the Supreme Court decide in *Abington School District v. Schempp*?

11. What did President Kennedy say in response to fears that he would deliver the United States over to papal rule?

Answers to Sample Quiz I

Students' answers should approximate the following.

1. The House Un-American Activities Committee had been founded in 1938 to investigate "subversive groups," particularly Nazis, in the United States. After the war, the committee turned its attention to Communists because of fears that Communist espionage and infiltration had made it possible for the Soviet to progress so quickly in developing an atomic bomb.

2. On June 25, 1950, Korea erupted in a war instigated by Communists. At the end of the Second World War, Korea had been divided along the 38th parallel into two nations. The north was not Communist, while the south, called the Republic of Korea, was not but was highly unstable. North Korea, with the

support of Communist China, invaded South Korea.

3. Eisenhower characterized his policies as "dynamic conservatism"; for though his administration did not abandon the big government model of Roosevelt; it more openly favored private big business, while still maintaining and even expanding federal social programs.

4. By 1956, 135 corporations had come to own 45 percent of all industrial assets in the United States. In such industries as oil refining, meat packing, iron and steel, a few companies, banded together, controlled the pricing of raw materials and of manufactured goods, and so set the pace for smaller competitors. Most competition was not within industries but between competing products. Talented, ambitious young men were less likely to open new businesses but were content with working for corporations.

5. Warren asked whether segregation in 1954 deprived students of equal protection? Though black and white schools were becoming equal, Warren said that segregation itself gave blacks a sense of inferiority, "Separate educational facilities are inherently unequal," he said; thus, segregation deprived people "of the equal protection of the laws guaranteed by the Fourteenth Amendment."

6. Eisenhower said "When a state refuses, to utilize its police powers to protect persons who are peacefully exercising their rights under the Constitution as defined in such [federal] court orders, the oath of office of the President requires that he take action to give that protection. Failure to act in such a case would be tantamount to acquiescence in anarchy and the dissolution of the Union."

7. The Civil Rights Act of 1957 created a federal Civil Rights Commission and a civil rights division in the office of the United States Attorney General. The latter would have the power to prosecute those who placed any obstacles to any citizen's exercise of his constitutional rights. Offenders, even if they were state officials, could be fined or imprisoned if they ignored the orders of federal judges in these matters.

8. The Marshall Plan helped bring prosperity to Western European nations and thus opened up markets for American goods. The postwar "Baby Boom" meant the necessity for increased production and thus more jobs. But among the chief causes of the post-war prosperity was the dramatic rise in government military spending, especially after the Korean War. Unions insisted that companies pay working men a wage sufficient to support a family, thus raising the real weekly earnings of factory workers by 50 percent. A GI bill passed by Congress allowed more men to go to college and so increased the number of those working for prosperous corporations. The rise in wages brought many more people into the middle class, though poverty still remained.

9. Federal aid for housing allowed many Americans achieve home ownership. Because of federal policy that favored the purchase of new houses over existing houses in cities, much new housing went up on the outskirts of cities thus bringing about the growth of suburban neighborhoods – suburbanization.

10. In *Abington School District v. Schempp*, the court basically said that the First Amendment erected an "establishment of religion" (that is, a state-sponsored church), it went further and erected (in the words of Thomas Jefferson) a "wall of separation" between church and state." Prayer and other religious exercises in public schools, argued the court, violated the First Amendment. All state acts, said the court, must be religiously neutral.

11. In response to fears that he would deliver the United States over to papal rule, Kennedy said: "whatever issue may come before me as

president, if I should be elected – on birth control, divorce, censorship, gambling, or any other subject – I will make my decision … in accord with what my conscience tells me to be in the national interest, and without

regard to outside religious pressure or dictation, and no power or threat of punishment could cause me to decide otherwise."

Sample Quiz II (pages 837-854)

Please answer the following in complete sentences.

1. What effect did the Tet Offensive have?

2. What concerns led the United States and the Soviet Union to adopt the Nuclear Test Ban Treaty? What did the treaty do?

3. Describe "sit-ins" and what they achieved.

4. What did the Civil Rights Act of 1964 mandate?

5. What was the "Great Society"?

6. What was the Voting Rights Act and what did it mandate?

7. What did the new feminism of the 1960s demand?

8. How did Pope John XXIII's call for *aggiornamento* make Americans feel that the Catholic Church was changing?

9. Describe President Nixon's domestic polices.

10. Describe President Nixon's foreign policies.

11. What did *Roe v. Wade* decide?

Answers to Sample Quiz II

Students' answers should approximate the following.

1. The Tet offensive led many to believe Vietnam was a costly and hopeless war. On March 31, 1968, Johnson, in a television address to the American people, announced that he was calling a partial halt to the bombing of North Vietnam and that he would pursue peace negotiations with the North Vietnamese.

2. Fear over the long-term health effects of nuclear radiation fall-out in the atmosphere brought the Americans and the Soviets to the negotiating board. On August 5, 1963, the United States, the Soviet Union, and Great Britain met in Moscow and signed the Nuclear Test Ban Treaty, agreeing that both sides would end open-air nuclear testing.

3. Following Dr. Martin Luther King, Jr.'s call for non-violent resistance, in February 1960, four black college students from the Agricultural and Technical College of North Carolina in Greensboro peacefully sat at a

"whites only" lunch counter at Woolworth's variety store in Greensboro and requested service. When refused, they continued sitting. Soon students and others throughout the South staged similar "sit-ins," as well as "read-ins" in segregated libraries, and "wade-ins" on segregated beaches. By 1961, many eating establishments had removed segregated seating.

4. Besides strengthening voting rights protection, the Civil Rights Act of 1964 prohibited segregation in places of "public accommodation" – restaurants, hotels, terminals, etc.; required the federal government to withhold assistance to state or county programs that favored racial discrimination; gave the attorney general authority to institute lawsuits against segregation in schools; and established the Equal Employment Opportunity Commission (EEOC) to fight racial preferences in employment.

5. The Great Society was President Johnson's program to address poverty in the United States. At the president's urging, Congress approved a multi-billion dollar federal aid to schools and libraries bill; expanded Social Security to include "Medicare," medical care for people over age 65; and added anti-poverty programs.

6. The Voting Rights Act was a law passed by Congress that secured the right to vote for black people. The act abolished most literacy tests for voting and authorized the sending of federal examiners to register voters in any county that practiced racial discrimination.

7. Feminists demanded full legal, economic and social equality with men. They trumpeted the cause of inexpensive, readily available abortion.

8. In the early '60s, American Catholics felt that they had "arrived" and that the world could be changed for the better. Pope John XXIII's call for *aggiornamento,* or the "updating" of the Church, ended, it seemed, the state of war that had existed between the Church and the modern world since before the days of Pius IX.

9. Nixon ignored peace protests and did little to further black civil rights. Though he vetoed a number of health and education bills the Democratic-dominated Congress sent him, Nixon expanded certain social programs. In 1970, he called for the appropriation of $10 million to clean the nation's rivers and lakes. It was by Nixon's urging that Congress created both the Occupational Safety and Health Administration (OSHA) and the Environmental Protection Agency (EPA).

10. President Nixon in 1972 began making friendly overtures to both Communist China and Russia. In February 1972, Nixon became the first U.S. president to visit China. The United States and China agreed to expand their cultural, educational, and journalistic contacts and to broaden trade between their two nations. Though the United States still formally recognized Taiwan's government as the government for all China, the Nixon administration, in October 1972, agreed to remove its objections to Red Chinese membership in the United Nations. Nixon traveled to Moscow to meet with Soviet premier Leonid Ilyich Brezhnev to discuss progress in the Strategic Arms Limitation Treaty (SALT) talks between the two countries, but they forged other agreements as well: on limiting atomic weapons; protecting the natural environment; on sharing medical, space and technological knowledge; on forming a joint trade commission.

11. The Supreme Court decision, *Roe v. Wade,* that declared unconstitutional a Texas law that banned abortions except to save the life of a mother.

Essays

Instructions to be given to the students: Write in complete sentences. Underline your thesis. Give three supports or examples that explain why you think what you do and that support your thesis.

1. What, do you think, is the ultimate root of the problems facing post-war America? Be sure to connect your points in order.

2. How has feminism affected our society today? What benefits has it brought? What problems stem from it?

3. What effects has suburbanization had on present-day culture and society? Is this good or bad?

Sample Test

Please answer the following in complete sentences.

I. Short Essay – Answer three of the following:

1. Why did Oliver Brown sue the Topeka Board of Education? How did the U.S. District Court decide the case? What was the U.S. Supreme Court's final ruling?

2. Describe the character of the new suburban culture that arose after World War II.

3. Describe the general culture of the 1950s.

4. What were the causes and results of the radicalization of youth in the 1960s?

5. What happened to the Catholic Church in the U.S. following the Second Vatican Council?

6. What did the U.S. Supreme Court decided in *Roe v. Wade*? How was the court's decision based on *Griswold v. Connecticut*? What was Justice Rehnquist's dissent?

II. Short Answer:

1. Identify the following and what they are known for.
   a. Joseph McCarthy
   b. Rosa Parks
   c. Martin Luther King, Jr.
   d. Malcolm X

2. Why, according to President Johnson, was the United States involved in Vietnam?

3. What was Dr. Martin Luther King, Jr.'s dream?

Answer Key to the Chapter Test

Students' answers should approximate the following:

I.

1. *Brown v. Board of Education* concerned one Oliver Brown, a black man residing in Topeka, Kansas, who brought the Topeka Board of Education to trial for refusing to allow his third-grade daughter to attend a white school. When the United States District Court ruled against Brown, citing the 1896 Supreme Court decision, *Plessy v. Ferguson*, which decided that racially "separate but equal" accommodations on public transportation did not contradict the equal protection clause of the 14th Amendment to the Constitution," Brown and the NAACP appealed the decision to the United States Supreme Court. Brown and the NAACP appealed *Brown* to the Supreme Court in 1951. In the decision he wrote for the court in 1954, Chief Justice Earl Warren said what the authors of the amendment, members of Congress and of state legislatures, "had in mind" when they adopted the 14th Amendment "cannot be determined with any degree of certainty." But this question, said Warren, was unimportant. The question for Warren was: did segregation, in 1954, deprive students of equal protection? Though black and white schools were becoming equal, Warren said that segregation itself gave blacks a sense of inferiority, "Separate educational facilities are inherently unequal," he said; thus, segregation deprived people "of the equal protection of the laws guaranteed by the Fourteenth Amendment." In 1955, the Supreme Court made a ruling that desegregation must proceed with "all deliberate speed."

2. Suburban culture was characterized by the automobile – it was, in fact, automobiles and federal and state improved highways that made suburbs possible, since workers now had to commute longer distances to their jobs. Automobile ownership became a hallmark of American life. Highways allowed

suburbs to be built ever farther from city centers, creating, in time, large, sprawling urban landscapes. Because of suburban development, American culture grew ever more homogenous. Everywhere, suburbs shared common characteristics. Television, which by 1953 had invaded two-thirds of American households, destroyed much of what remained of homespun entertainment and spread mass fads that influenced dress, speech, and social mores nationwide. Industrialism had already undermined home-based industries and so separated the father from his family for long periods throughout the day. Suburbanization exacerbated separation of the father from the family brought about by industrialism by increasing the distances between home and work. Wives, separated from husband and children (who went to school) for long hours, found their lives increasingly occupied in house cleaning, shopping, and socializing. The "modern" wife began to seem increasingly ornamental. Many women began to suffer from boredom and dissatisfaction. The wealth of the 1950s allowed even youth to become consumers, and an entire youth culture arose to meet (and create) the demand.

3. The culture of the 1950s was, at least externally, religious, conservative, and family-centered. Most Americans attended religious services and upheld a morality that valued family cohesiveness, self reliance, honesty, hard work, and patriotism. But the media and advertising spread the notion that happiness lay in the possession of material goods. Indeed, the "American dream" was increasingly defined in material terms – home ownership, the possession of consumer goods, and the freedom to better one's condition. The mass-produced culture was not only shallow, it could be sexually suggestive. In the end, the morality of the

Eisenhower era would be seen as a morality of respectability. American youth would come to conclude that their parents' ethics were a mere veneer to make them appear "upstanding" in the eyes of their neighbors.

4. Kennedy's idealism had inspired youth of the early 1960s. The civil rights movement had given them a cause for which to fight. Many youth, it seems, had become disillusioned with an American dream that seemed to promise only more material prosperity, ease, and comfort; they had grown impatient with a society that proclaimed freedom and equality but denied them to some simply because they were not white. Beginning in 1960, student groups fighting for civil rights and other radical causes began to form throughout the country. On example of these groups was the Free Speech Movement (FSM) at the University of California, Berkeley, which organized a student sit on the Berkeley campus, for which 800 students were arrested in December 1964. The Vietnam War further radicalized many American youth, who protested U.S. bombing and its effects on the Vietnamese civilian population. Military conscription of young men, too, made the war unpopular. Some fled to Canada or Europe. Men publicly burned their draft cards. The decade of the '50s had created a youth culture; the '60s gave rise to a youth counterculture. Youth did not merely question the war but the entire adult world they had inherited. Their parents, they declared, were materialistic; they were hypocrites, espousing a code of conduct they violated in their daily lives. Youth began to question not only government but all the institutions of society – the church, marriage, and the family. A "hippie" culture developed among youth who wanted to live according to ideals of peace, anarchic freedom, and free love.

5. Catholics eager to know what the council was up to gleaned little from the official reports of the American bishops. But then the *New York Times* published an account of the council that revealed deep divisions between "liberal" and "conservative" council fathers and began running daily accounts of council happenings. American Catholics began to think that the Church was doing more than updating, but making revolutionary changes. Though the Church did not change any teaching in any of the council does, many authors gave the impression that she had. American Catholics were told that the Church had altered her teaching on religious liberty, on the relationship between the Catholic Church and other churches and religions, and in other areas as well – including artificial contraception. When a commission established by Pope John XXIII concluded that the Church should change her teaching on artificial contraception, many Catholic theologians and priests began saying that it was permissible for Catholic married couples to use artificial contraceptives to limit the size of their families. But then in July 1968, Pope Paul VI in the encyclical letter *Humanae Vitae* ("Of Human Life") reiterated traditional Church teaching on artificial contraception. Priests, prominent theologians, and journalists publicly criticized *Humanae Vitae, and some and some* questioned the very doctrine of papal infallibility. A statement, signed by 200 theologians and published in the *New York Times* denied the authority of *Humanae Vitae*. More and more Catholic voices were calling for a new, democratic Church. Thousands of men left the priesthood, and many women religious abandoned their orders. The number of men in seminaries dwindled dramatically. Millions of Catholic faithful, too, dropped out of the Church.

6. The Supreme Court decision, *Roe v. Wade* declared unconstitutional a Texas law that banned abortions except to save the life of a mother. Roe depended, in part, on an earlier Supreme Court decision, *Griswold v. Connecticut*, in which the majority of justices argued that the Constitution guarantees a right to privacy. The majority opinion argued that rights enumerated in the Constitution have "penumbras" – non-enunciated rights "that help give [enumerated rights] life and substance." One of these penumbras was privacy. In *Roe,* Justice Harry A. Blackmun argued for the court that the Texas law was unconstitutional because it violated Jane Roe's right to privacy, under which it located "a woman's qualified right to terminate her pregnancy." Though 14th Amendment protection of declares a state shall not "deprive any *person* of life, liberty, or property," Blackmun said that, since society is not agreed as to whether the definition of "person" includes unborn human life, the life of unborn children is not protected by the Constitution. Blackmun drew the line for a legal definition of person at "viability" – the point where an unborn child is able to survive on its own, independent of the mother. Blackmun, however, declared that the right to privacy is not absolute; that the state, at some point, may have an interest in protecting the unborn before viability. In a dissenting opinion, Justice William Rehnquist wrote that The 14th Amendment doesn't protect citizens against being deprived of their liberty simply but only says that one cannot be deprived of liberty unless he be convicted of a crime in a court of law; it says nothing about state laws which, inevitably, limit some freedom. Rehnquist argued that when the court decides to do things, such as "break pregnancy into three distinct terms," it is not acting like a court but like a legislature. The role of the Supreme Court,

said Rehnquist, is not to decide when and where a state has a compelling interest in restricting abortion but simply to determine the intent of the men who drew up the 14th Amendment.

II.

1.

   a. Joseph McCarthy was a United States Senator who led a crusade to weed out Communists who, he said, were infiltrating the United States government.

   b. Rosa Parks was a black woman who refused to give up her seat on a bus to a white man – for which she was arrested. Parks' defiance of segregation led the black Baptist minister, Martin Luther King, Jr., to organize blacks in Montgomery to formed carpools and boycott public transportation.

   c. Martin Luther King, Jr., was a civil rights leader who called for non-violent resistance to racism and segregation.

   d. Malcolm X was a disciple of Elijah Muhammad, leader of the Nation of Islam, who favored the complete separation of the races in their own geographical regions. Malcolm X, became the spokesman for the movement. Malcolm X rejected Martin Luther King, Jr.'s call for non-violent resistance as naïve and advocated that blacks meet white violence with violence.

2. President Johnson said the U.S. was involved in Vietnam because its ally, South Vietnam, had asked for help against Communist aggression.

3. Dr. King said he dreamed of a day when people "will not be judged by the color of their skin but by the content of their character."

Resources

I. Supplemental Reading

There is a large jump in ability and maturity between the middle school and high school years with a wide variety of speeds at which students develop. Thus, we've included in the additional resources books that are adult level, but also (especially in the historical fiction) books which can be classified as "young adult." These young adult books are nevertheless well written and can be enjoyed by older students as well. It is advised that the teacher use discretion, being sensitive to each individual student's maturity level, especially regarding realistic books on modern wars.

General Exploration of the New World

* *America As Seen by Its First Explorers: The Eyes of Discovery* by John Bakeless
* *Evangelization of the New World* by James Leek
* *The Great Explorers: The European Discovery of America* by Samuel Eliot Morison (also available in audio book)
* *They Saw America First* by Katherine and John Bakeless (out of print, check library)
* *Great Lives: Exploration* by Milton Lomask

Chapter 1
Primary Sources:
* *The Four Voyages: Being His Own Log-Book, Letters and Dispatches with Connecting Narratives* by Christopher Columbus
* *Select Letters of Christopher Columbus*, with other original documents, relating to his four voyages to the New World
* *The Letters of Amerigo Vespucci and other documents illustrative of his career* (also includes letters from Columbus and Bartolome de las Casas), translated by Clements Markham

* *The Life of Columbus from His Own Letters and Journals and Other Documents of His Time* by Edward Everett Hale
* *The True History of the Conquest of New Spain* by Bernal Diaz del Castillo (eye witness account)

Secondary Sources:
* *Admiral of the Ocean Sea: A Life of Christopher Columbus* by Samuel Eliot Morison
* *Columbus & Cortez, Conquerors for Christ* by John Eidsmoe
* *So Noble a Captain: the Life and Times of Ferdinand Magellan* by Charles McKew Parr (out of print, check library)
* *Cortes and the Downfall of the Aztec Empire* by John Manchip White

Fiction:
* Louise Andrews Kent's "He Went with…" series was originally written for the pre-high school level, but they are still entertaining and engaging stories for older readers.
  ○ *He Went with Christopher Columbus*
  ○ *He Went with Magellan*
  ○ *He went with Vasco da Gama*
* *Captain From Castile* by Samuel Shellabarger (made into a movie with Tyrone Power)
* *The King's Fifth* by Scott O'Dell

Chapter 2
Primary Sources:
* *A Short Account of the Destruction of the Indies* by Fray Bartolome de las Casas, O.P.
* *In Defense of the Indians* by Fray Bartolome de Las Casas, O.P.

Secondary Sources:
* *Our Lady of Guadalupe and the Conquest of Darkness* by Warren H. Carroll

- *Our Lady of Guadalupe* – DVD available from Ignatius Press
- *Maria of Guadalupe: Shaper of History, Shaper of Hearts* by Paul Badde
- *St. Rose of Lima: Patroness of the Americas* by Sr. Mary Alphonsus, O. Ss.R.
- *St. Martin De Porres: Apostle of Charity* by Guiliana Cavallini
- *The History of the Conquest of Peru* by William Prescott

Chapter 3
Primary Sources:
- *Samuel de Champlain, Founder of New France: A Brief History with Documents* by Samuel de Champlain
- *Voyages of Samuel de Champlain, 1604-1618* by Samuel de Champlain
- *Marquette's First Voyage, 1673-1677: Travels and Explorations of the Jesuit Missionaries in New France* by Pere Jacques Marquette (out of print, check library)

Secondary Sources
- *Pere Marquette* by Agnes Repplier (out of print)
- *Father Marquette and the Great Rivers* by August Derleth (written for pre-high school level, but worth reading if the student has not previously been introduced to Fr. Marquette's story)
- *La Salle and the Discovery of the Great West* by Francis Parkman
- *The Jesuits in North America in the Seventeenth Century* by Francis Parkman
- *Pioneers of France in the New World* by Francis Parkman
  The individual Parkman titles are also published together in one volume:
  ◦ *France and England in North America, Vol. 1* (contains *Pioneers of France in the New World, The Jesuits in North America in the Seventeenth Century, La Salle and the Discovery of the Great West, The Old Regime in Canada*)

  ◦ *France and England in North America, Vol. 2:* (contains *Count Frontenac and New France under Louis XIV, A Half-Century of Conflict, Montcalm and Wolfe*)
- *A People's History of Quebec* by Jacques Lacoursiere
- *St Kateri: Lily of the Mohawks* by Matthew Bunson
- *The Life and Times of Kateri Tekakwitha* by Ellen H. Walworth
- *In Her Footsteps: The Story of Saint Kateri Tekakwitha* – documentary DVD
- *Saint in the Wilderness: The Story of Isaac Jogues, Missionary and Martyr in the New World* by Glenn Kittler
- *Saints of the American Wilderness: The Brave Lives And Holy Deaths of the Eight North American Martyrs* by John A. O'Brien
- The Shrine of Our Lady of Martyrs in Fultonville, NY - http://www.martyrshrine.org/
- *Chuiraquimba and Black Robes* by Madeleine Polland

Fiction:
- *Shadows on the Rock* by Willa Cather
- *The Last Fort: A Story of the French Voyageurs* by Elizabeth Coastworth
- *Madeline Takes Command* by Ethel C. Brill (written for pre-high school, but an exciting story, also available on audio)
- *Captured by the Mohawks* by Sterling North (written for pre-high school)

Chapter 4
Primary Sources:
- *Hakluyt's voyages: The principal navigations, voyages, traffiques & discoveries of the English Nation* by Richard Hakluyt, selected by Irwin Blacker

Secondary Sources:
- *The Americans: The Colonial Experience* by Daniel J. Boorstin

- *The Shipwreck That Saved Jamestown: The Sea Venture Castaways and the Fate of America* by Lorri Glover and Daniel Blake Smith

Fiction:
- *The Legend of Sleepy Hollow* by Washington Irving
- *Rip Van Winkle* by Washington Irving
- *This Dear-Bought Land* by Jean Lee Latham

Chapter 5
Primary Sources:
- *Mourt's Relation: A Journal of the Pilgrims at Plymouth*

Secondary Sources:
- *Betty Alden: The First-Born Daughter of the Pilgrims* by Jane Goodwin Austin
- *The Story of Bacon's Rebellion* by Mary Newton Stanard
- Books by artist Edwin Tunis on the Colonial Period.

Fiction:
- *The Witch of Blackbird Pond* by Elizabeth Speare
- *Constance: A Story of Early Plymouth* by Patricia Clapp (out of print, check library)
- *The Scarlet Letter* by Nathaniel Hawthorne
- *Captain Bacon's Rebellion* by Helen Lobdell (written for pre-high school, out of print)

Chapter 6
Secondary Sources:
- *The Colonial Wars* by Howard H. Peckham
- *The Border Wars of New England* by Drake Samuel Adams
- *Flintlock and Tomahawk: New England in King Philip's War* by Douglas Edward Leach
- *King Philip's War: Colonial Expansion, Native Resistance, and the End of Indian Sovereignty* by Daniel R. Mandell
- *When the Forest Ran Red* (French and Indian War) DVD

- *The War That Made America: The Story of the French and Indian War* PBS DVD

Fiction:
- *Calico Bush* by Rachel Field (pre-high school, Newbery Honor Book)
- *The Sign of the Beaver* by Elizabeth George Speare (pre-high school, Newbery Honor)
- *Calico Captive* by Elizabeth George Speare (pre-high school reading level)
- *The Light in the Forest* by Conrad Richter (pre-high school reading level)
- *Muskets Along the Chickahominy* by Gertrude E. Finney (out of print, check library)
- *A High Wind Rising* by Elsie Singmaster (out of print, check library)
- *The Yemassee: A Romance of Carolina* by William Gilmore Simms (out of print)
- *Northwest Passage* by Kenneth Roberts (also made into a movie with Spencer Tracy)
- *The Young Titan* by F. Van Wyck Mason (out of print, check library)
- *The Deerslayer* by James Fenimore Cooper
- *The Pathfinder* by James Fenimore Cooper
- *The Last of the Mohicans* by James Fenimore Cooper

Chapter 7
Primary Sources:
- *Writings of Junipero Serra*, edited by Antonine Tibesar
- *On the Trail of a Spanish Pioneer: The Diary and Itinerary of Francisco Garcés*

Secondary Sources:
- *Serra: Ever Forward, Never Back* DVD (EWTN docu-drama)
- *The Man Who Founded California: The Life of Blessed Junipero Serra* by M.N. Couve de Murville
- *The Last of the Conquistadors: Junipero Serra* by Omer Englebert (out of print)

- *Life And Times Of Fray Junipero Serra: Or The Man Who Never Turned Back, 1713-1784* by Maynard Geiger
- *California Missions: The Earliest Series of Views Made in 1856* by Henry Miller
- *Saints of the California Missions: Mission Paintings of the Spanish and Mexican Eras* by Norman Neuerburg
- *Life in a California Mission: Monterey in 1786* from the journals of Jean Francois de La Perouse
- *The California Missions: History, Art and Preservation*
- **Mission Memories** by John Steven McGroarty
- *San Antonio Missions National Historical Park* by Luis Torres
- *The Spanish Missions of San Antonio* by Lewis Fisher
- *Fray Juan Crespi: Missionary Explorer on the Pacific Coast 1769-1774* by Herbert Eugene Bolton (out of print, check library)
- *Francisco Garces: Pioneer Padre of Kern* by Ardis M. Walker
- *Kino: A Legacy,* by Charles W. Polzer, S.J.

Chapters 8 & 9
Primary Sources:
- *Sketches of Eighteenth-Century America* by J. Hector St. John De Crevecoeur
- *Letters from an American Farmer* by J. Hector St. John De Crevecoeur
- *Diary of the American Revolution from Newspapers and Original Documents* by Frank Moore
- *Thomas Paine: Collected Writings*
- *Autobiography of Benjamin Franklin*
- *The Journal of Major George Washington, 1754* by George Washington
- *Memoirs of General Lafayette: with an Account of His Visit to America and His Reception by the People of the United States*
- *Swamp Fox: General Francis Marion and his Guerrilla Fighters of the American Revolutionary War* by William Dobein James (eye witness account)
- *The American Revolutionaries: A History in Their Own Words 1750-1800* by Milton Meltzer
- Selections from the *World's Great Speeches,* edited by Lewis Copeland and Lawrence Lamm
  The Price of Loyalty: Tory Writings from the Revolutionary Era, edited by Catherine S. Crary

Secondary Sources
- *Founding Brothers: The Revolutionary Generation* by Joseph J. Ellis
- *Daniel Morgan: Revolutionary Rifleman* by Don Higginbotham
- *Joseph Brant, 1743-1807, Man of Two Worlds* by Isabel Kelsay
- *John Paul Jones: A Sailor's Biography* by Samuel Eliot Morison
- *John Adams and the American Revolution* by Catherine Drinker Bowen
- *The Hero of Ticonderoga - or Ethan Allen and his Green Mountain Boys* by John De Morgan
- *Lafayette* by Harlow Giles Unger
- *Life and Times of the Most Rev. John Carroll, Bishop and First Archbishop of Baltimore Embracing the History of the Catholic Church in the United States, 1763-1815* by John G. Shea
- *Princes of Ireland, Planters of Maryland: A Carroll Saga, 1500-1782* by Ronald Hoffman
- *Warrior on Two Continents: Thaddeus Kosciuszko* by David J. Abodaher
- *Thaddeus Kosciuszko: Military Engineer of the American Revolution* by Francis C. Kajencki
- *The Revolutionary War in the Southern Backcountry* by James Swisher
- *1776* by David McCullough

Fiction:
- *My Brother Sam is Dead* by James Lincoln Collier (pre-high school, Newbery Honor)
- *Johnny Tremain* by Esther Forbes (Newbery Medal)
- *John Treegate's Musket* by Leonard Wibberly

- *Peter Treegate's War* by Leonard Wibberly
- *Sea Captain from Salem* by Leonard Wibberly
- *Treegate's Raider's* by Leonard Wibberly
- *Sarah Bishop* by Scott O'Dell
- *April Morning* by Howard Fast
- *Janice Meredith* by Paul Leicester Ford
- *Drums* by James Boyd
- *Oliver Wiswell* by Kenneth Roberts
- *Arundel* by Kenneth Roberts
- *Rabble in Arms* by Kenneth Roberts
- *The Spy* by James Fenimore Cooper
- *The Partisan: A Romance of the Revolution* by William G. Simms
- *The Scout: Tthe Black Riders of Congaree* by William G. Simms
- *Woodcraft: Hawks about the Dovecote* by William G. Simms
- *Israel Potter: His Fifty Years of Exile* by Herman Melville

Chapter 10

Primary Sources:
- *The Life of George Washington* by John Marshall (contemporary of Washington)
- *Notes on the State of Virginia* by Thomas Jefferson
- *James Madison: Writings 1772-1836*
- *The War of 1812: Writings from America's Second War of Independence*, edited by Donald R. Hickey

Secondary Sources:
- *Carry On, Mr. Bowditch* by Jean Lee Latham (pre-high school)
- *The Diary of an Early American Boy* by Eric Sloane
- *A Museum of Early American Tools* by Eric Sloane
- *After the Revolution: Profiles of Early American Culture* by Joseph J. Ellis

Chapter 11

Primary Sources:
- *Memoir, Correspondence, And Miscellanies, From The Papers Of Thomas Jefferson*
- *Autobiography of Thomas Jefferson*
- *The Journals of Lewis and Clark*

Secondary Sources:
- *John Adams* by David McCullough
- *Alexander Hamilton* by Ron Chernow
- Thomas Jefferson's home Monticello - http://www.monticello.org/
- *Thomas Jefferson: A Film by Ken Burns* – PBS DVD
- *Bold Journey: West with Lewis and Clark* by Charles H. Bohner (pre-high school)
- *First Across the Continent: The Story of the Exploring Expedition of Lewis and Clark in 1804-5-6* by Noah Brooks
- *Undaunted Courage: Meriwether Lewis, Thomas Jefferson, and the Opening of the American West* by Stephen Ambrose
- *Bird Woman: Sacagawea's Own Story* by James Willard Schultz
- *Sacagawea Speaks: Beyond the Shining Mountains with Lewis and Clark* by Joyce Badgley Hunsaker
- Lewis & Clark Fort Mandan Foundation - http://www.fortmandan.com/
- *The War of 1812: A Forgotten Conflict* by Donald R. Hickey
- *The War of 1812* - PBS DVD
- *The British at the Gates: The New Orleans Campaign in the War of 1812* by Robin Reilly

Fiction:
- *The Lively Lady* by Kenneth Roberts
- *Captain Caution* by Kenneth Roberts

Chapter 12

Primary Sources:
- *Tales of Mexican California: Cosas De California* by Antonio Franco Coronel

Secondary Sources:

- *Morelos of Mexico: Priest, Soldier, Statesman* by Wilbert H. Timmons
- *The Mexican Wars for Independence* by Timothy Henderson

Chapter 13

- *Elizabeth Seton: Selected Writings*, edited by Annabelle Melville
- *Soul of Saint Elizabeth Seton* by Joseph I. Dirvin, C.M.
- *Mother Seton and the Sisters of Charity* by Alma Powers-Water (pre-high school)
- *A Time for Miracles* (life of St. Elizabeth Seton) DVD
- *American Lion: Andrew Jackson in the White House* by Jon Meacham
- *The Cherokee Nation and the Trail of Tears* by Theda Perdue
- *Cherokee Tragedy: The Ridge Family and the Decimation of a People* by Thurman Wilkins

Chapters 14 & 15

Primary Sources:

- *A Narrative of the Life of David Crockett* by David Crockett
- *The Diary of a Forty-Niner* by Chauncey L. Canfield
- *Democracy in America* by Alexis de Tocqueville
- *Two Years Before the Mast* by Richard Henry Dana
- *A Tour on the Prairies (1835)* by Washington Irving
- *Life Among the Indians* by George Catlin
- *The Prairie Traveler: A Handbook for Overland Expeditions* by Randolph Barnes Marcy
- *Across The Plains In 1844* by Catherine Sager
- *Narcissa Whitman: Diaries and Letters 1836* by Narcissa Whitman

Secondary Sources:

- *The Seasons of America Past* by Eric Sloane
- *Astoria: Anecdotes of an Enterprise beyond the Rocky Mountains* by Washington Irving

- *Simon Brute and the Western Adventure* by Elizabeth Bartlme
- *Saint John Neumann: His Writings and Spirituality* by Rev. Boever, C.Ss.R.
- *John James Audubon* by John Burroughs
- *Bear Flag Rising: The Conquest of California, 1846* by Dale L. Walker
- *A Wicked War: Polk, Clay, Lincoln, and the 1846 U.S. Invasion of Mexico* by Amy S. Greenberg
- *A Country of Vast Designs: James K. Polk, the Mexican War and the Conquest of the American Continent* by Robert W. Merry
- *The Age of Gold: The California Gold Rush and the New American Dream* by H.W. Brands
- *First Girl in the West* by Eliza Spalding Warren

Fiction:

- *A Gathering of Days: A New England Girl's Journal* by Joan W. Blos
- *The Lost Wagon* by Jim Kjielgaard (available on ebook from Bethlehem Books)
- *White Moccasins* by Louis Capron (pre-high school, out of print, check library)
- *Fear in the Forest* by Cateau De Leeuw (pre-high school, out of print, check library)
- *The Kentuckians* by Janice Holt Giles
- *Hannah Fowler* by Janice Holt Giles
- *Johnny Osage* by Janice Holt Giles
- *Death Comes for the Archbishop* by Willa Cather
- *A Lantern in Her Hand* by Bess Streeter Aldrich
- *The Yearling* by Marjorie Kinnan Rawlings (pre-high school level)
- *Carlota* by Scott O'Dell (pre-high school level)
- *Roughing It* by Mark Twain
- *The Adventures of Tom Sawyer* by Mark Twain
- *The Adventures of Huckleberry Finn* by Mark Twain

Chapters 16, 17 & 18

Primary Sources:

- *Abraham Lincoln: Selected Speeches and Writings* by Abraham Lincoln
- *The Complete Personal Memoirs of Ulysses S. Grant* by Ulysses S. Grant

- *Co. Aytch: A Confederate Memoir of the Civil War* by Sam R. Watkins
- *I Rode with Stonewall* by Henry Kyd Douglas
- *The Rise and Fall of the Confederate Government* by Jefferson Davis
- *An Uncommon Soldier: The Civil War Letters of Sarah Rosetta Wakeman, alias Pvt. Lyons Wakeman, 153rd Regiment, New York State Volunteers, 1862-1864* by Sarah R. Wakeman
- *Mary Chesnut's Civil War* by Mary Chesnut
- *Sarah Morgan: The Civil War Diary Of A Southern Woman*, edited by Charles East
- *Brokenburn: The Journal of Kate Stone, 1861-1868.* edited by John Anderson
- *Kate: The Journal of a Confederate Nurse* by Kate Cumming
- *Civil War Hospital Sketches* by Louisa May Alcott
- *Civil War Nurse: The Diary and Letters of Hannah Ropes* by Hannah Ropes
- *Letters of a Civil War Nurse: Cornelia Hancock, 1863-1865*
- *Civil War Letters: From Home, Camp and Battlefield*, edited by Bob Blaisdell
- *Narrative of the Life of Frederick Douglass* by Frederick Douglass
- *The Underground Railroad: Authentic Narratives and First-Hand Accounts* by William Still

Secondary Sources:
- *Lincoln* by David Herbert Donald
- *Lincoln* – DVD, directed by Steven Spielberg, starring Daniel Day-Lewis (PG-13)
- *Lee* by Douglas Southall Freeman
- *Stonewall Jackson* by James Robertson
- *Still Standing: The Stonewall Jackson Story* – DVD
- *Jefferson Davis, American* by Jr. William J. Cooper
- *The Blue and the Gray, the Story of the Civil War as Told by Participants* by Henry Commager
- *The Civil War: A Narrative* by Shelby Foote
- *This Hallowed Ground: A History of the Civil War* by Bruce Catton

- *The Army of the Potomac* trilogy by Bruce Catton
  - *Mr. Lincoln's Army*
  - *Glory Road*
  - *A Stillness at Appomattox*
- *The Civil War: A Film by Ken Burns* – PBS DVD
- *Gettysburg* – DVD, starring Tom Berenger and Martin Sheen
- *Ultimate Civil War Series - 150th Anniversary Edition* DVD, directed by Kevin Hershberger
- *John Brown, Abolitionist: The Man Who Killed Slavery, Sparked the Civil War, and Seeded Civil Rights* by David S. Reynolds
- *Civil War Poetry*, edited by Paul Negri
- *The Irish Brigade In The Civil War: The 69th New York and Other Irish Regiments of The Army Of The Potomac* by Joseph G. Bilby
- *Irish Confederates: The Civil War's Forgotten* by Phillip Thomas Tucker
- *African American Faces of the Civil War: An Album* by Ronald S. Coddingon
- *The Sable Arm: Black Troops in the Union Army, 1861-1865* by Dudley Taylor Cornish
- *A Brave Black Regiment: The History of the Fifty-Fourth Regiment of Massachusetts Volunteer Infantry 1863-1865* by Captain Luis F. Emilio
- *The Massachusetts 54th Colored Infantry* – DVD, narrated by Morgan Freeman
- *Woman of Valor: Clara Barton and the Civil War* by Stephen Oates
- *Cyclone in Calico: The Story of Mary Ann Bickerdyke* by Nina Brown Baker (out of print)
- *Harriet Tubman: The Road to Freedom* by Catherine Clinton
- *Life of Blessed Francis Xavier Seelos* by Rev. Carl Hoergerl, C.Ss.R.
- *Seelos: Tireless Intercessor* (life of Blessed Francis Xavier Seelos) DVD from Ignatius Press
- *American Brutus: John Wilkes Booth and the Lincoln Conspiracies* by Michael W. Kauffman
- *Mr. Lincoln's Camera Man: Mathew B. Brady* by Roy Meredith

Fiction:
- *Uncle Tom's Cabin* by Harriet Beecher Stowe

- *The Red Badge of Courage* by Stephen Crane
- *Across Five Aprils* by Irene Hunt
- *Little Women* by Louisa May Alcott
- *Traveller* by Richard Adams
- *Killer Angels* by Michael Shaara
- *Gods & Generals* by Jeff Shaara
- *Last Full Measure* by Jeff Shaara
- *Civil War Stories* by Ambrose Bierce

Chapter 19
Primary Sources:
- *Recollections of My Life: Emperor of Mexico,* Maximilian 1832-1867
- *With Santa Anna in Texas: A Personal Narrative of the Revolution* by Jose Enrique de la Pena

Secondary Sources:
- *Maximilian and Carlota: Europe's Last Empire in Mexico* by M.M. McAllen
- *Santa Anna of Mexico* by Will Fowler
- *U.S. Mexican War 1846-1848* – PBS DVD

Chapter 20
- *Reconstruction: America's Unfinished Revolution, 1863-1877* by Eric Foner
- *A Short History of Reconstruction* by Eric Foner (abridged version of above book)
- *From Slave to Priest: The Inspirational Story of Fr. Augustine Tolton* by Sr. Caroline Hemesath
- *Up from Slavery* by Booker T. Washington

Fiction:
- *Flight into Spring* by Bianca Bradbury

Chapter 21
Primary Sources:
- *Life, Letters and Travels of Father Pierre-Jean DeSmet, S.J. 1801-1873* by Pierre-Jean DeSmet
- *John Muir: Nature Writings* (includes *The Story of My Boyhood and Youth; My First Summer in the Sierra; The Mountains of California; Stickeen; Essays*) by John Muir

Secondary Sources:
- *The Life of Father De Smet, SJ: Apostle of the Rocky Mountains* by Rev. E. Laveille, S.J.
- *Edison: A Biography* by Matthew Josephson
- *The Wild Muir: Twenty-Two of John Muir's Greatest Adventures* by Lee Stetson
- *Indian Boyhood* by Charles (Ohiyesa) Eastman
- *From the Deep Woods to Civilization* by Charles (Ohiyesa) Eastman
- *Indian Heroes and Great Chieftains* by Charles (Ohiyesa) Eastman

Fiction
- *O Pioneers!* by Willa Cather
- *My Antonia* by Willa Cather
- *Giants in the Earth: A Saga of the Prairie* by O. E. Rolvaag
- *Peder Victorious: A Tale of the Pioneers Twenty Years Later* by O. E. Rolvaag (sequel)
- *The Octopus: A Story of California* by Frank Norris
- *The Pit: A Story of Chicago* by Frank Norris

Chapter 22
- *Meet Katharine Drexel: Heiress and God's Servant of the Oppressed* by Mary Van Balen Holt
- *Saint Katharine: The Life of Katharine Drexel* by Cordelia Frances Biddle
- *Sorrow Build a Bridge: The Life of Mother Alphonsa, Daughter of Nathaniel Hawthorne* by Katherine Burton (out of print, check library)
- *To Myself a Stranger: A Biography of Rose Hawthorne Lathrop* by Patricia Dunlavy Valenti (out of print, check library)
- *George Washington Carver: In His Own Words* – edited by Gary R. Kremer

Fiction:
- *Ramona* by Helen Hunt Jackson
- *Poor White* by Sherwood Anderson
- *Winesburg, Ohio* by Sherwood Anderson
- *Captains Courageous* by Rudyard Kipling
- *The Call of the Wild* by Jack London (pre-high school level)

- *White Fang* by Jack London (sequel)
- *The Song of the Lark* by Willa Cather

Chapter 23

Primary Sources:

- *An Autobiography by Theodore Roosevelt* by Theodore Roosevelt
- *Letters of a Woman Homesteader* by Elinore Pruitt Stewart

Secondary Sources:

- *Crucible of Empire: The Spanish American War-* PBS DVD
- *Mornings on Horseback: The Story of an Extraordinary Family, a Vanished Way of Life and the Unique Child Who Became Theodore Roosevelt* by David McCullough
- *The Rise of Theodore Roosevelt* by Edmund Morris
- *Theodore Rex* by Edmund Morris
- *Colonel Roosevelt* by Edmund Morris
- *TR: The Story of Theodore Roosevelt* – PBS DVD

Fiction:

- *The Virginian* by Owen Wister
- *Little Britches: Father and I Were Ranchers* by Ralph Moody
- *Man of the Family* by Ralph Moody
- *The Fields of Home* by Ralph Moody
- *Mary Emma and Company* by Ralph Moody
- *Daddy Long Legs* by Jean Webster (pre-high school level)

Chapter 24

- *The Cristero Rebellion: The Mexican People Between Church and State 1926-1929* by Jean Meyer
- *La Cristiada: The Mexican People's War for Religious Liberty* by Jean Meyer
- *For Greater Glory* – DVD movie on the *Cristeros*
- *Blood-Drenched Altars* by Francis Clement Kelley
- *The Life and Times of Pancho Villa* – Friedrich Katz

- *Zapata and the Mexican Revolution* – John Womack

Chapter 25

Primary Sources:

- Pope Benedict XV's encyclical *Ad Beattissimi Apostolorum (available at* www.vatican.va)
- *The Red Fighter Pilot: The Autobiography of the Red Baron* by Manfred von Richthofen
- *Poilu: The World War I Notebooks of Corporal Louis Barthas, Barrelmaker, 1914-1918* by Louis Barthas
- *The Burning of the World: A Memoir of 1914* by Bela Zombory-Moldovan

Secondary Sources:

- *The Assassination of the Archduke: Sarajevo 1914 and the Romance That Changed the World* by Greg King
- *A World Undone: The Story of the Great War, 1914 to 1918* by G.J. Meyer
- *A Heart for Europe: The Lives of Emperor Charles and Empress Zita of Austria-Hungary* by Joanna Bogle
- *The Last Empress: Life and Times of Zita of Austria-Hungary, 1892-1989* by Gordon Brook-Shepherd
- *The Unknown Pope: Benedict XV and the Pursuit of Peace* John F. Pollard
- Vatican Radio interview with Professor John F. Pollard on Pope Benedict XV and WWI: http://en.radiovaticana.va/news/2014/06/24/ben edict_xv_and_his_pursuit_of_peace/1102133
- *Benedict XV and World War I: Courageous Prophet of Peace* by Fr. Ashley Beck
- *Stories of World War I: Faith in Action* by Dr. Raymond Edwards and Sr. Fabiola Fernandes (available from the Catholic Truth Society)
- *Fr. Willie Doyle & World War I: A Chaplain's Story* by K.V. Turley (available from the Catholic Truth Society)
- *1917: Red Banners, White Mantle* by Warren H. Carroll
- *Fatima* DVD (available from Ignatius Press)

- *Duffy's War: Fr. Francis Duffy, Wild Bill Donovan, and the Irish Fighting 69th in World War I* by Stephen L. Harris
- *Doughboys, the Great War, and the Remaking of America* by Jennifer D. Keene

Fiction:

- *World War One British Poets: Brooke, Owen, Sassoon, Rosenberg and Others* - edited by Candace Ward
- *Poetry of the First World War: An Anthology* – edited by Tim Kendall
- *All Quiet on the Western Front* by Erich Maria Remarque (graphic, for mature readers, caution advised)
- *The Road Back: A Novel* by Erich Maria Remarque (for mature readers, caution advised)
- *August 1914* by Alexander Solzhenitsyn
- *One of Ours* by Willa Cather
- *Soldier of the Horse* by Robert W. Mackay
- *Memoirs of an Infantry Officer* by Siegried Sassoon

Chapter 26

- *What I Saw in America* by G.K. Chesterton
- *Sidelights on New London and Newer York and Other Essays* by G.K. Chesterton (out of print, check library)
- *The Contrast* by Hilaire Belloc (out of print, check library)
- *The Spirit of St. Louis* by Charles Lindbergh

Fiction:

- *Main Street* by Sinclair Lewis
- *Babbitt* by Sinclair Lewis
- *The Great Gatsby* by F. Scott Fitzgerald
- *The Bridge* by Hart Crane (a poem)
- *Poems* by Robert Frost
- *The Wasteland* by T.S. Eliot (a poem)

Chapter 27

Primary Sources:

- *The Long Loneliness* by Dorothy Day
- *From Union Square to Rome* by Dorothy Day

- *Peter Maurin: Apostle to the World* by Dorothy Day
- *Easy Essays* by Peter Maurin (available on the website of the New York Catholic Worker: www.catholicworker.org)
- *Letters from the Dust Bowl*, by Caroline Henderson
- *I'll Take My Stand* – "Twelve Southerners." A manifesto of American Southern agrarianism.
- *Quadragesimo Anno*, encyclical of Pope Pius XI

Secondary Sources:

- *Between Two Fires: Europe's Path in the 1930s* by David Clay Large
- *A Man of the Beatitudes: Pier Giorgio Frassati* by Luciana Frassati
- *Pier Giorgio Frassati: Sanctity within Reach* – DVD
- *All is Grace: A Biography of Dorothy Day* by Jim Forest
- *The American Way: Family and Community in the Shaping of the American Identiy* – Allan Carlson
- *The New Agrarian Mind: The Movement Toward Decentralist Thought in Twentieth Century America* – Allan Carlson

Fiction:

- *Roll of Thunder, Hear My Cry* by Mildred Taylor (pre-high school level)
- *No Promises in the Wind* by Irene Hunt
- *The Grapes of Wrath* by John Steinbeck.(for mature readers, includes adult themes and language)
- *To Kill A Mockingbird* by Harper Lee

Chapter 28

There are too many additional resources available on World War II to list here, so we have concentrated mostly on the Catholic works that may not be as well known.

Primary Sources:

- *The Shadow of His Wings: The True Story of Fr. Gereon Goldmann, OFM* by Gereon Karl Goldman

- *Priestblock 25487: A Memoir of Dachau* by Jean Bernard
- *Anne Frank: The Diary of a Young Girl*

Secondary Sources:
- *Advent of the Heart: Seasonal Sermons and Prison Writings*, 1941- 1944 by Alfred Delp, S.J.
- *Father Placido Cortese: The Courage of Silence -* DVD
- A Nobel Treason: *The Story of Sophie Scholl and the White Rose Revolt Against Hitler* by Richard Hanser
- *Edith Stein: The Untold Story of the Philosopher and Mystic Who Lost Her Life in the Death Camps of Auschwitz* by Waltraud Herbstrith
- *Edith Stein: The Seventh Chamber* – DVD
- *Edith Stein and Companions* by Fr. Paul Hamans
- *The Courageous Heart of Irena Sendler* – DVD, available from Ignatius Press
- *The Scarlet and the Black: The True Story of Monsignor Hugh O Flaherty, Hero of the Vatican Underground* by J.P. Gallagher
- *The Scarlet and the Black* – movie starring Gregory Peck
- *A Hand of Peace: Pope Pius XII and the Holocaust* – DVD
- *Pius XII: Under the Roman Sky* - DVD
- *God's Mighty Servant: Sister Pascalina Lehnert, Secretary of Pius XII* -- DVD
- *Maximilian Saint of Auschwitz* – DVD, one man play performed by Leonardo Defilippis
- *Kolbe: Saint of the Immaculata* by Francis Kalvelage
- *The Story of the Trapp Family Singers* by Maria Augusta Trapp
- *The Hiding Place* by Corie Ten Boom
- *The Journal of Helene Berr* by Helene Berr
- *The Inn of the Sixth Happiness* by Alan Burgess
- *Farewell to Manzanar* by Jeanne Houston (Japanese internment)

Fiction:
- *The Borrowed House* by Hilda Van Stockum (pre-high school level)
- *Enemy Brothers* by Constance Savery (pre-high school level)
- *On the Edge of the Fjord* by Alta Halverson Seymour (pre-high school level)
- *The Tangled Skein* by Alta Halverson Seymour (pre-high school level)
- *The Ark* by Margot Benary-Isbert (pre-high school level)
- *Rowan Farm* by Margot Benary-Isbert (pre-high school level, sequel to *The Ark*)
- *The Long Way Home* by Margot Benary-Isbert (pre-high school level)
- *Castle on the Border* by Margot Benary-Isbert (pre-high school level)
- *Dangerous Spring* by Margot Benary-Isbert (pre-high school level)
- *A Time to Love* by Margot Benary-Isbert (pre-high school level)

Chapter 29
- *The Miracle of Father Kapaun: Priest, Soldier, and Korean War Hero* by Roy Wenzl
- *A Shepherd in Combat Boots: Chaplain Emil Kapaun of the 1st Cavalry Division* by William K. Maher
- *The Grunt Padre: Father Vincent Robert Capodanno, Vietnam, 1966-1967* by Fr. Daniel Mode
- *We Shall Overcome: Documentary of the March on Washington* (Smithsonian Folkways)

II. Suggested Music

Chapters 1-2
Spain
- Cristóbal de Morales (1500-1553): *Requiem* (performed by the Gabrieli Consort)
- Unknown composer: *Music for Ferdinand and Isabella of Spain* (performed by the Early Music Consort of London)
- Tomas Luis de Victoria (1548-1611) *Jesu dulcis memoria* (motet) *O magnum mysterium* (motet)

France

- Guilliame Dufay (1397-1474): *Missa l'homme armé* (performed by the Oxford Camerata). Dufay was a Franco-Flemish composer who was very influential during the mid 15th century. The "Parody" or "Imitation" Mass, a composition which mimicked the popular songs of the period or pre-existing compositions, was very popular at this time. *L'homme armé* ("The Armed Man") was a popular French song from the Renaissance.
- Josquin des Prez (1455-1521): *Ave Maria, virgo serena* (performed by the Hilliard Ensemble)

Italy

- Giovanni Pierluigi da Palestrina (1525-1594)
  Sicut Cervus (motet)
  Jesu Rex Admirabilis (motet)
  Alma Mater Redemptoris (motet)
  Missa Papae Marcelli

Chapter 3
France

- Jean-Baptiste Lully (1632-1687): *Grands Motets (Te Deum; Miserere; Plaude laetare Gallia)* Performed by *Le Concert Spirituel*. Lully was a Florentine-born French composer who became a French subject in 1661. He spent most of his life composing in the court of Louis XIV of France.
- Louis Couperin (1626-1661): *Harpsichord Suites* (performed by Laurence Cummings). The harpsichord was very popular at this time of history. It was used widely throughout the 15th, 16th, and 17th centuries. In the 18th century it began to be less popular with the invention of the pianoforte.
- Lully/Couperin: *Musique pour le marriage de Louis XIV* (performed by La Simphonie du Marais). This collection was written for the marriage of King Louis XIV of France and Maria Theresa of Spain. King Louis loved music and dance, and he loved a show. The wedding was held on June 9, 1660, and the records say that the procession included "a lot of trumpets…and when we entered the church, Mass was sung. [There were] musicians on each side, [a] symphony, and organ music." The accounts say that Lully directed the violins, and Couperin played the organ.

Chapter 4

- Thomas Tallis (1505-1585): Tallis is considered one of England's greatest composers, and he holds a primary place in the anthologies of English church music.
  If ye love me (motet)
  O Lord give Thy Holy Spirit (motet)
  Verily, verily I say unto you (all performed by the Tallis Scholars
- William Byrd (1540-1623): Byrd worked as Gentleman of the Chapel Royal in 1570 and wrote music for Elizabeth I.
  Ave Verum Corpus (motet)
- Tallis/Byrd: *Cantiones Sacrae 1575* (performed by David Skinner). In 1575 Queen Elizabeth gave Byrd and Tallis together a patent for music publishing, which allowed them to earn some money for every piece of music that was published, printed, or sold in England. They wrote *Cantiones Sacrae* to thank the queen.
- Thomas Weelkes (1576-1623): *Since Robin Hood* (madrigal, performed by the King's Singers)
  Gloria in Excelcis Deo (motet, performed by King's College Choir)

Chapter 5
England

- Henry Purcell (1659-1695): *Music for the Funeral of Queen Mary* (performed by Equale Brass Ensemble, Monteverdi Choir and John Eliot Gardiner). Purcell wrote this march, canzona, and anthem for orchestra and choir in 1695 for the funeral of Queen Mary II of England. Parts of the piece were performed at Purcell's own funeral the same year.

Birthday Odes for Queen Mary (performed by

Equale Brass Ensemble, Monteverdi Choir and John Eliot Gardiner)
- *Dido and Aeneas* (opera)

Italy
- Claudio Monteverdi (1567-1643): *Duo Seraphim* (motet)
  L'Orfeo (oratorio, performed by the English Baroque Soloists)

Chapters 6-10
Spain
- Ignacio de Jerusalem (1707-1769): a Spanish composer who settled in Mexico. His music was performed in the California missions.

  Mass in D Minor (performed by Chanticleer)
  Resopnsorio Segundo de S.S. Jose (performed by Chanticleer)
  Dixit Dominus (performed by Chanticleer)
  Matins for the Virgin of Guadalupe (performed by Chanticleer)
- Manuel de Zumaya (c. 1678-1755):
  Hieremiae Prophetae Lamentationes ("Lamentations of the Prophet Jeremiah")
  Celebren Publiquen (performed by Chanticleer)
  Sol-fa de Pedro (performed by Chanticleer)

Spanish American
- *Hispanic Traditions: The Music of New Mexico* (Smithsonian Folkways)
- *Spanish Folksongs of New Mexico* (Smithsonian Folkways)

Italy
- Antonio Vivaldi (1678-1741)
  The Four Seasons (violin concerto)

Germany
- Johann Sebastian Bach (1685-1750)
  St. Matthew's Passion (oratorio)
- George Frederick Handel (1685-1759)
  Messiah (oratorio)
- Wolfgang Amadeus Mozart (1756-1791):
  Requiem (Mass for the dead)

La Nozze di Figaro ("The Marriage of Figaro") (opera)
Die Zauberflöte ("The Magic Flute") (opera)

English America
- *Early American Roots* (music of English America, performed by Hesperus)
- William Billings (1746-1600): American choral composer, widely regarded as the father of American choral music and creator of what is recognized as a uniquely American style

  Easter Anthem: the Lord is ris'n indeed (performed by Paul Hillier and His Majestie's Clerkes)

  The Continental Harmony (performed by the Gregg Smith Singers)

  David's Lamentation (performed by Paul Hillier and His Majestie's Clerkes)
- *The Birth of Liberty – Music of the American Revolution* (Performed by American Fife Ensemble, The Liberty Tree Wind Players, and the Continental Harmony Singers)

Chapters 11-13
France
- Hector Berlioz (1803-1869)
  Symphonie Fantastique (symphony)
  Te Deum

Spain
- Juan Crisóstomo Arriaga (1806-1826): called the "Spanish Mozart" because like Mozart he was a child prodigy who died young. Arriaga and Mozat share the same birthday, January 27, though they were born 50 years apart.

  The Three String Quartets (performed by Camerata Boccherini): these string quartets are undoubtably Arriaga's greatest work, and they contain notably Spanish elements
- *Stabat Mater Dolerosa* (performed by Euskadiko Orkestra Sinfonikoa)

Germany
- Ludwig van Beethoven (1770-1827): *Symphony*

No. 3 in E-flat major (op. 55), "Eroica": As a young man Beethoven greatly admired the ideals of the French Revolution and dedicated his third symphony to Napoleon Bonaparte, whom he viewed as the embodiment of the French Revolution's ideals. When Beethoven heard that Napoleon had proclaimed himself the emperor of France in May 1804, he was disgusted and changed the dedication of the symphony to Prince Franz Joseph Maximillian Lobkowitz, and the name of the symphony from "Bonaparte" to "Eroica" (heroic).

Namensfeir Overture, Op. 115: a symphonic overture written in 1815. The title of the overture refers to the feast of St. Francis of Assisi, the name day of the Austrian emperor Franz I. The theme at the beginning is similar to that which Beethoven used to set the "Ode to Joy" in his Ninth Symphony.

Symphony No. 9 in D minor, Op. 125: the final complete symphony by Beethoven. It is one of the best-known works of the Western classical repertoire, and is considered to be one of Beethoven's greatest works. It is the first example of a composer using voices in a symphony, which previously had used only instruments. The famous "Ode to Joy" in the fourth movement is taken from a poem written by Friedrich Schiller.

Chapter 14
Mexico
- Joaquín Beristáin (1817-1839): pianist, cellist, and composer, Beristáin was known as the "Mexican Bellini."
  Obertura Primavera (performed by Arcordeón Clásico)
- Ry Cooder and The Chieftains, *San Patricio* (an album telling the story of the San Patricio Battalion, with traditional music)

Germany/Austria
- Johannes Brahms (1833-1897)

Liebeslieder Waltzes
Symphony No. 1 in C Minor, Op. 68

Chapter 15
- Charles Ives (1874-1954): Ives is ones of the first American composers of international renown, and after his death he came to be regarded as an "American original." Many of Ives' tonal imagery sources are hymn tunes, traditional songs, patriotic songs, and the melodies of Stephen Foster.

  The Unanswered Question (performed by the Chicago Symphony Orchestra under Morton Guild). This piece is influenced by the works of Ralph Waldo Emerson and Henry David Thoreau, important influences in Ives' life.

  Piano Sonata No. 2: "Concord, Mass., 1840-60" (performed by Gilbert Kalish). Written between 1909 and 1915, this sonata is also influenced by Emerson and Thoreau. Ives described it as an "impression of the spirit of transcendentalism that is associated in the minds of many with Concord, Mass., of over a half century ago... undertaken in impressionistic pictures of Emerson and Thoreau, a sketch of the Alcotts, and a scherzo supposed to reflect a lighter quality which is often found in the fantastic side of Hawthorne."

- Stephen Foster (1826-1864): an American songwriter known as the "father of American music." Many of Foster's songs were popular with the soldiers on both sides of the Civil War. (*American Dreamer: Songs of Stephen Foster*, performed by Thomas Hanson)

Chapter 16-18
- Edmund Dédé (1827-1903): a free Creole of color, Dédé was born in New Orleans, Louisiana. He began a violin prodigy at a young age, and later studied at the Paris Conservatory where he received instruction

from several noted teachers, and became a good friend of Charles Gounod. He wrote many compositions for violin, orchestra, and voice. He spent most of his life away from the United States because of white hostility against black musicians, but visited once to perform his *Quasimodo Symphony.*

Mon pauvre Coeur, for voice and piano (performed by Richard Rosenberg and the Hot Springs Music Festival)

Chicago, grand valse á l'américaine (performed by Richard Rosenberg and the Hot Springs Music Festival)

- Jay Ungar (1946-present): *The Civil War – Traditional American Songs and Instrumental Music*
- Louis Moreau Gottschalk (1829-1869): a pianist and composer, Gottschalk was very popular during the mid 19ᵗʰ century.
  Bamboula, Op. 2 (Danse des Negres), (performed by Amiram Rigai)
  The Dying Poet (performed by Amiram Rigai)
- *Ballads of the Civil War* (Smithsonian Folkways)
- *A Treasury of Civil War Songs* (sung by Tom Glazer, Smithsonian Folkways)
- *Civil War Naval Songs* (Smithsonian Folkways)

Chapter 19

- Macedonio Alcalá Prieto (1831-1869): Mexican violinist, pianist, and songwriter.

  Dios nunca muere (God never dies) (performed by Cuarteteto Latinoamericano): a delegation from the town of Tlacolula requested that Prieto compose a waltz in honor of the Virgin Mary, the patron of their town. The waltz was a huge success in the town and has become the unofficial state anthem of Oaxaca, from whence Prieto came.

- Melesio Morales (1838-1908): Morales is known as the father of Mexican opera. His success in Florence, Italy, with his opera *Ildegonda* made him famous in his country.

  Ildegonda (performed by Orquesta Sinfónica

Carlos Chávez)
Nezahuacoyotl (performed by Two Harps): a waltz inspired by a 15ᵗʰ century poet-king who ruled the Nahua kingdom

Chapters 20-21

- *An Anthology of American Folk Music* (Smithsonian Folkways)
- Edvard Grieg (1843-1907): a Norwegian composer and pianist who is widely considered as one of the leading Romantic era composers. His use of Norwegian folk music put Norway in the international spectrum.

  Peer Gynt (performed by Paavo Jarvi and Estonian National Symphony Orchestra): incidental music to the play by Henrik Ibsen

  Sigurd Jorsalfar (performed by Ole Kristian Ruud and Bergen Philharmonic Orchestra): incidental music to the play by Bjørnstjerne Bjørnso

- Antonín Dvořák (September 8, 1841 – May 1, 1904)
  Sonatina in G Major for Violin and Piano, Op. 100, B. 183 (performed by Qian Zhou). This sonatina was written in 1893 during Dvořák's sojourn in America, and contains themes which are inspired by Indian melodies and Negro spirituals. These are characterized by pentatonic scales and syncopated rhythms, among other traits. The last movement, which was jotted down on Dvořák's sleeve during a visit to Minnehaha Falls near Saint Paul, Minnesota, is often performed alone as *Indian Lullaby* or *Indian Canzonetta.*

  Symphony No. 9 in E minor, "From the New World," composed by Dvorak when he was director of the National Conservatory of Music of America

Chapter 22-23

- **Giacamo Puccini (1858-1924):** an Italian composer, Puccini has been called the "greatest composer of Italian opera after Verdi." His early work is rooted in traditional late-19th-century romantic Italian opera, but his later work was composed in the realistic *verismo* style. He is the one of the leading exponents of this style.

La Bohéme: first performed in 1896, this opera about the "Bohemian" life in Paris became a great success and was performed across the world, including in the United States

Tosca: this opera is Puccini's first foray into *verismo*

La Fanciulla del West (also called *The Girl of the Golden West*): an opera about Gold Rush California. In this opera, Puccini weaves American folk melodies into his music.

- *Classic Labor Songs* (from the Smithsonian Folkways Recordings)

Chapter 24

- Carlos Chávez (1899-1978): Mexican composer and conductor who founded and directed the Mexican Symphonic Orchestra. Much of his work was influenced by native Mexican cultures.

Sinfonía India No. 2 (performed by the Stadium Symphony Orchestra of New York): this second of six symphonies is probably the most popular of Chávez's works. It uses native Yaqui percussion instruments

Xochipili (performed by La Camerata): suite for double quartet

- *Corridos* (Smithsonian Folkways)
- *Con Corridos y Rancheras* (Smithsonian Folkways)
- *Heroes and Horsemen: Corridos from the Arizona-Sonora Borderlands* (Smithsonian Folkways)
- *Cristero Corridos*: Instituto de los corridos de Zacatecas y Altos de Jalisco, *Corridos de la Rebellion Cristera*, INAH, Disc 20. Ed. Irene Vásquez Valle y José de Santiago Silva. México, 1986.

- Folklyric/Arhoolie Records, *The Mexican Revolution*, Disc IV (CD 7044) Post-Revolutionary *Corridos* and Narratives, 1996.

Chapter 25

- Ralph Vaughn Williams (1872-1958)
  The Lark Ascending (performed by Iona Brown and Academy of St. Martin-in-the-Fields): This tone poem, scored for solo violin and piano, was written in 1914, in the early days of World War I when the pastoral scene of a singing bird on the wing was the opposite of what was happening in the world, and seemed far removed from reality. It was composed as a response to George Meredith's poem of the same name.
- Gustav Holst (1874-1934)
  The Planets (performed by Chicago Symphony Orchestra): written between 1914 and 1916, this suite includes the movement entitled "Mars, the Bringer of War." It is said that Holst was inspired by the First World War in writing this movement.
- Benjamin Britten (1913-1976)
  War Requiem (performed by London Symphony Orchestra): this requiem scored for choir and orchestra is based on the Latin requiem Mass and the poems of Wilfred Owen, one of the great war poets.
- *Songs of World War I: From Original Recordings 1914-1926* (Take Two)

Chapter 26

- Charles Ives (1874-1954) – See Chapter 15, above.
- *American Prohibition and Moonshine Songs* (New Lost City Ramblers, Smithsonian Folkways)
- *The Great Gatsby: Hit Songs of the 1920s* (ABC Classics)
- George Gershwin (1898-1937): An American composer and pianist who composed in both popular and classical styles.
  Rhapsody in Blue for piano and orchestra (1924)
  Porgy and Bess, an opera (1935)

- Ferde Grofé (1892-1972): an American composer, arranger, and pianist.
  Mississippi Suite (Tone Journey) (1925)
  Grand Canyon Suite (1931)

Chapter 27

- Woody Guthrie (1912-1967): the American folksinger and songwriter who chronicled the plight of the common people, especially during the Great Depression.

  Dust Bowl Ballads: this album contains Guthrie's collection of Dust Bowl songs. The songs are semi-autobiographical, and chronicle Guthrie's experiences during the Dust Bowl era. These songs are said to contain an element of social activism, and became an important influence on later musicians such as Pete Seeger and Bob Dylan.
- *Songs of the Depression* (New Lost City Ramblers, Smithsonian Folkways)

Chapter 28

- Igor Stravinsky (1882-1971)
  Symphony in Three Movements (performed by Columbia Symphony Orchestra and CBC Symphony Orchestra): This symphony is considered Stravinsky's first major composition after he emigrated to the United States. Stravinsky referred to the symphony as his "war symphony." He claimed it was a direct response to events of World War II.
- Dmitri Shostakovich (1906-1975)
  Symphony No. 7 in C major, Op. 60, "Leningrad" (performed by London Philharmonic Orchestra): the symphony became very popular in both the Soviet Union and the West as a symbol of resistance to Nazi totalitarian and militarism.
- *Let's Put the Axe to the Axis – Songs of World War II, Vol. I* (Smithsonian Folkways)

Chapter 29

- Arvo Pärt (1935-present): an Estonian composer who developed a style based on the slow modulation of sounds such as bells and pure voice tones, a technique reminiscent of the medieval Notre-Dame school and sacred music of Eastern Orthodoxy. He also experimented with the 12-tone system. During the late 1970s he developed a sound that is distinctly his own, the triad series. He describes the sound of the triad as "like that of pealing bells," and named his new method of composition "tintinnabuli style."

  Für Alina (performed by Dietmar Schwalke, Alexander Malter, and Vladimir Spivakov): this composition marks the start of Pärt's use of tintinnabulation.
- Peter "Pete" Seeger (1919-2014): an American folk singer and activist, Seeger emerged on the public scene during the 1960s as a prominent singer of protest music in support of international disarmament, civil rights, counterculture, and environmental causes.

  Where Have All the Flowers Gone: Seeger got his inspiration for this song from the novel *And Quiet Flows the Don*, which describes the Cossack soldiers galloping off to join the Czar's army, singing as they go. The song is a meditation on war and death.
  We Shall Overcome: this song became the Civil Rights anthem.
- Bob Dylan (1941-present): the American musician and singer-songwriter has been an influential figure in popular music and culture. Most of his work dates from the 1960s and chronicles social unrest. Dylan's lyrics incorporate a variety of political, social, philosophical, and literary influences. His songs defied existing pop music conventions and appealed to the rising counterculture.
  "Blowin' in the Wind": this song became one of the anthems for the civil rights and anti-war movements in the United States

Timeline

15th Century

1418 The Tepanecs conquer Tenochtitlán and Texcuco. They are later driven out by the Aztecs and Nezahualcoyotl, king of Texcuco.

1492 Christopher Columbus makes landfall on San Salvador
Columbus establishes the first Spanish settlement in America at Navidad, on the island of Hispaniola

1493 Pope Alexander VI issues the bull, *Inter Caetera*

1494 Spain and Portugal sign the Treaty of Tordesillas

1497 John Cabot's first exploration of the coast of North America

1498 Columbus discovers the South American continent
John Cabot's second exploration establishes an English claim to North America.

16th Century

1502 Montezuma becomes king of the Aztecs.

1508 Pope Julius II grants the *patronato real* to the king of Spain.

1512 The crown of Spain issues the Laws of Burgos

1513 Juan Ponce de Léon lands on the Florida peninsula
Vasco Nuñez de Balboa first sees the "South Sea" – the Pacific.
The crown of Spain issues the *Requiriemento*.

1521 Juan Sebastián Elcano arrives in Spain after having circumnavigated the globe.
Cortés conquers Tenochtitlán.

1524 Giovanni de Verrazzano establishes a claim for France in North America.

1532 Conquest of Peru

1534 Jacques Cartier's first exploration of the North American coast
On his second voyage (1534-1536), Cartier discovers the Saint Lawrence River and gives the region around the river the name Canada.

1538 The University of Saint Thomas Aquinas established in Santo Domingo

1542 Hernando de Soto dies after having explored southeast North America.
Francisco Vasquez de Coronado and his party return to Mexico after having explored the region of New Mexico.
King Carlos I of Spain issues the *Nuevas Leyes*.
Juan Rodriguez Cabrillo explores the North Pacific, including the coast of Alta California; he discovers San Diego Bay.

1544 Bartolomé de las Casas appointed bishop of Chiapas

1550 Las Casas debates Juan Ginés de Sepulveda at Valladolid.

1565 Pedro Menéndez de Avilés establishes San Agustín in Florida.

1573 The crown of Spain issues the Basic Law.

1579	Francis Drake lands on the west coast of North America
1580	Francis Drake returns to England after having circumnavigated the globe.
1585	First English settlement established on Roanoke Island
1587	Second English settlement established on Roanoke Island
1597	Juanillo's rebellion in the Guale region of Florida
1598	Juan de Oñate takes possession of New Mexico for Spain.

17th Century

1602	Sebastián Vizcaíno explores the coast of Alta California; he discovers Monterey Bay (where the first Mass on the California coast was offered).
1607	Founding of Jamestown, Virginia
1608	Samuel de Champlain establishes Québec.
1609	Champlain with the Huron and Algonquin defeat the Iroquois on the banks of Lake Ticonderoga.
1611	The first missionaries, Jesuits, arrive in New France.
1612	John Rolfe and others plant tobacco in Virginia.
1614-	
1615	First Dutch settlements founded on the Hudson River in North America
1620	Mayflower Compact signed
	Foundation of Plymouth colony
1623	Establishment of New Netherlands
1629	Foundation of the Massachusetts Bay Company
1630	The founding of Santa Fé in New Mexico
1632	King Charles I grants parts of Virginia to Lord Baltimore.
1633	Establishment of Maryland colony
1638	King Louis XIII of France dedicates his lands to Our Lady of the Assumption.
	Foundation of New Sweden on the Delaware River
1641	Massachusetts adopts the Body of Liberties.
1649	Lord Baltimore and the Maryland colonial government issue the Toleration Act.
1655	New Sweden becomes part of New Netherlands.
1663	King Charles II charters Providence Plantation.
1664	New Netherlands becomes an English possession.
1673	Marquette and Joliet find and explore the Mississippi River.
1675	King Philip's War
1676	Nat Bacon's rebellion
1680	Popé's rebellion drives the Spanish out of New Mexico.
1681	King Charles II establishes the proprietorship of Pennsylvania.
1682	La Salle establishes Louisiana for King Louis XIV of France.
1686	Padre Kino establishes his first mission in the Pimería Alta.
1692	The Spanish retake Santa Fé and New Mexico.
	King William III establishes the Church of England in Maryland.
1695	Pima rebellion in the Pimería Alta

18th Century

1702	Queen Anne's War begins.
1704	The Spanish abandon Apalachee in Florida.
1711	Death of Padre Kino
1713	The Peace of Utrecht ends Queen Anne's War.
1717	New Orleans established on the lower Mississippi.
1720	The Spanish crown abolishes the *encomienda* system.
1730s	The beginning of the First Great Awakening
1733	Oglethorpe establishes Georgia.
1739	The War of Jenkins' Ear begins.
1744	The War of Jenkins' Ear merges with King George's War (War of the Austrian Succession).
1748	The Treaty of Aix-la-Chapelle ends King George's War.
1750	Spain and Portugal sign a treaty that leads to the destruction of Reductions of Paraguay.
1754	Meeting of the Albany Congress
1755	The French defeat Braddock at Fort Duquesne.
	Beginning of the French and Indian War (Seven Years' War)
1759	The British capture Québec.
1760	The French governor, the Marquis de Vandreuil, surrenders all of French Canada to the British.
	George III becomes king of Great Britain.
1763	The Peace of Paris ends the French and Indian War (Seven Years' War).
	Spain cedes Florida to the British.
1764	Parliament approves the Revenue Act.
1765	The British Parliament passes the Stamp Act.
	The Virginia Burgesses issues Resolves against the Stamp Act.
	Colonial Stamp Act Congress protests the Stamp Act.
1766	Parliament repeals the Stamp Act but approves the Declaratory Act.
	Parliament approves the Quartering Act.
1767	Fray Junípero Serra made *padre presidente* of the Baja California missions
	Passage of the Townshend Acts
1768	Lord Hillsborough suspends the Massachusetts assembly.
1769	Serra goes into Alta California and arrives at San Diego. He establishes his first mission there.
	Daniel Boone begins to explore Kentucky.
1770	Serra and Portolá claim Alta California for the king of Spain.
	Repeal of the Townshend Acts
	Boston Massacre
1772	*Gaspee* incident
1773	Parliament grants special privileges to the British East India Company.
	Boston Tea Party
1774	Juan Bautista de Anza completes his first exploration of Arizona and southern Alta California.
	Parliament passes the Coercive Acts.

The Second Continental Congress convenes.

Parliament passes the Quebec Act.

Congress issues its Declaration and Resolves and the Association.

Parliament passes the New England Restraining Act.

1775 Battles of Lexington and Concord

Battle of Bunker (Breeds) Hill

1776 Thomas Paine publishes *Common Sense*.

Anza's second expedition reaches San Francisco Bay, where settlers establish a mission and presidio.

The Continental Congress endorses and declares independence (July 3-4)

Washington takes Trenton

1777 Washington takes Princeton.

Americans victorious in the First and Second Battles of Freeman's Farm (Saratoga)

The British take Philadelphia.

Congress approves the Articles of Confederation.

1778 France and the United States sign two treaties of friendship and commerce.

The British take Savannah and Charleston.

1779 Cornwallis restores South Carolina to royal rule.

Americans defeated in the Battle of Camden.

Patriots defeat loyalists at King's Mountain.

1781 The Articles of Confederation go into effect.

Cornwallis surrenders at Yorktown.

1782 The United States and Great Britain sign the first Treaty of Paris, ending the war.

1783 The United States, Great Britain, Holland, France, and Spain sign the formal Treaty of Paris.

1784 The pope appoints John Carroll prefect apostolic of the Church in the United States

Death of Fray Junípero Serra

1786 Virginia approves Jefferson's Statute of Religious Liberty.

1787 Massachusetts' state militia crushes Shays' Rebellion.

The Constitutional Convention convenes in Philadephia.

The U.S. Congress promulgates the Northwest Ordinance.

The Constitutional Convention approves a new federal constitution.

1789 The pope appoints John Carroll first bishop of Baltimore, with jurisdiction over the entire United States.

The U.S. Congress formally promulgates the Constitution. George Washington becomes the first president of the United States.

Congress passes the Judiciary Act.

1791 Congress and the states approve the Bill of Rights.

Washington puts down the Whiskey Rebellion.

Eli Whitney invents the Cotton Gin.

1794 Battle of Fallen Timbers

1797 XYZ Affair

1798 Congress and John Adams approve the Alien and Sedition Act.

Kentucky and Virginia Resolves

1799 The Second Great Awakening begins at the Red River Revival.

19th Century

1800   Thomas Jefferson elected president

1801   Spain secretly cedes the Louisiana Territory to France.

1803   Chief Justice Marshall and the Supreme Court lay down their decision in *Marbury v. Madison.*
The Louisiana Purchase

1804   Lewis and Clark begin their expedition of discovery.
Aaron Burr kills Alexander Hamilton at Weehawken.

1806   Lewis and Clark complete their expedition of discovery.
Napoleon issues the Berlin Decrees.

1807   The British issue the Orders in Council against Napoleon.
The U.S. Congress passes, and Jefferson signs, the Embargo Act.

1808   The Volunteers of Fernando VII imprison the Spanish viceroy in Mexico City.
Benedict Joseph Flaget becomes bishop of Bardstown, Kentucky.

1809   Congress repeals the Embargo Act.
Congress approves an act of non-intercourse with Great Britain.
President Madison revokes and then reinstates non-intercourse with Great Britain.
Insurgents proclaim West Florida independent of Spain.

1810   The United States annexes West Florida
Padre Miguel Hidalgo y Costilla calls for revolution against Spanish rule in Mexico.
Hidalgo's insurgents slaughter royalists in the Alhóndiga de Granaditas in Guanajuato.
Padre José Maria Teclo Morelos y Pavon commences a revolution in Zacatula.
Hidalgo's army lays siege to Mexico City.
Hidalgo establishes a government at Guadalajara.

1811   Hidalgo's army suffers a serious defeat. He withdraws from Guadalajara.
Royalist forces capture Hidalgo and Allende.
Execution of Hidalgo and Allende.
After much controversy, the Distict of Orleans becomes a state, under the name Louisiana.
Tecumseh's people defeated by Amerian troops under William Henry Harrison at the Battle of Tippecanoe.

1812   Congress declares war on Great Britain – the beginning of the War of 1812.
The British force Americans under General Hull to surrender at Detroit.

1813   Oliver Hazard Perry and the American fleet defeat the British in the Battle of Lake Erie.
Morelos and others assemble a revolutionary congress. He issues the *Sentiementos de la Natión.*
Fort Mims Massacre leads Andrew Jackson to wage an unltimately victorious war with the Creek "Red Sticks."

1814   The British surrender York (Toronto) to the Americans.
Naval battle on Lake Champlain stops a British advance through New York.
The British capture and burn Washington.
The Battle of Fort McHenry
The convening of the Hartford Convention
The United States and Great Britain sign the Treaty of Ghent, ending the war.

1815   Morelos captured by royalist forces
Morelos condemned and executed
The Battle of New Orleans

1816   Morelos' revolutionary congress dissolved
End of the Patriot War in East Florida

1817   Ambrose Maréchal becomes archbishop of Baltimore.
The Seminole in Spanish Florida go on the warpath against white settlements in the United States.

1818   The U.S. and Great Britain forge an agreement to occupy Oregon Country jointly.

1819   The Marshal Supreme Court issues *McCulloch v. Maryland*.
A financial panic strikes the United States.
Tallmadge Amendment introduced into Congress

1820   King Fernando VII restores the Liberal Constitution of 1812 in Spain and Mexico.
John England becomes bishop of Charleston.
Congress Approves the Compromise of 1820.

1821   Moses Austin receives a Spanish land grant in Texas.
Agustín de Iturbide publishes his *Plan de Iguala*.
In Veracruz, the Spanish viceroy, Juan de O'Donojú, agrees to the *Plan de Iguala*. Mexico wins her independence.
Iturbide establishes his government in Mexico City.

1822   Iturbide crowned Emperor Agustín I of Mexico
The ruling *junta* of California swears allegiance to Mexico.
Antonio Lopez de Santa Anna leads a rebellion against Emperor Agustín.

1823   The Mexican government grants Stephen Austin and other *empresarios* land grants in Texas.
Iturbide abdicates and goes into exile.
Mexico proclaimed a republic. President James Monroe issues the Monroe Doctrine.
Bishop John England draws up a constitution for his diocese.

1824   Mexico's congress promulgates the Constitution of 1824.
John Quincy Adams elected president of the United States

1825   Indian revolt at La Purísima, Santa Inez, and Santa Barbara in California.

1826   Erie Canal completed

1827   Jedediah Smith begins his first exploration for a route from the Rockies into California.

1828   Jedediah Smith begins his second exploration into California.
John C. Calhoun publishes his "Exposition andProtest," detailing his doctrine, "Nullification."

1829   Congress passes the "Tariff of Abominations"
Andrew Jackson becomes president of the United States.
Vicente Guerrero becomes president of Mexico
Guerrero abolishes slavery in Mexico.
Antonio López de Santa Anna captures Spanish force at Tampico.
In a *coup d'tat*, Vice President Anastasio Bustamante drives Guerrerro from power and establishes a conservative government in Mexico City.

1830   Congress passes the Indian Removal Act.
Mexico limits further Anglo immigration into Texas and orders the collection of customs

duties along the border of Texas and Louisiana.

Publication of the *Book of Mormon*.

1831 Guerrero executed by a firing squad

William Lloyd Garrison founds *The Liberator*

1832 South Carolina issues a order of nullification against Congress's tariff of 1832.

Black Hawk's War

1833 After Bustamante relinquishes power, the Mexican congress elects Santa Anna as president and the Liberal, Valentín Gómez Farías vice president.

Congress passes Force Bill against South Carolina, which repeals its ordinance of nullification

Govenor José Figueroa orders the secularization of the California missions.

Foundation of Oberlin College in Ohio

Theodore Dwight Weld founds the American Antislavery Society.

President Jackson vetoes a congressional bill for an early rechartering of the Bank of the United States.

President Jackson forces the closure of the Bank of the United States.

Gómez Farías and the Mexican congress approve legislation to weaken the power of the Church and the military in Mexico.

Congress approves, and President Jackson signs, a compromise tariff bill and the Force Bill.

1834 Santa Anna drives Gómez Farías from power and establishes a dictatorship.

Santa Anna and his congress abolish the Constitution of 1824 and establish a *Poder Conservador*.

Simon Bruté de Remur becomes bishop of Vincennes.

American Protestant missionaries settle the Willamette Valley in Oregon.

1835 The Seminole under Osceola commence a war against the United States.

Texians defeat Mexican forces in battle at San Antonio de Bexár

1836 Siege and Battle of the Alamo

Texas proclaimed an independent republic

Battle of San Jacinto; Santa Anna grants Texas her independence.

Congress passes first of the "gag resolutions," tabling petitions relative to slavery.

1837 Osceola captured

A financial panic hits the United States.

1838 The U.S. military begins the forced removal of the Cherokee to Indian Territory.

A French fleet blockades the port of Veracruz and bombards the fortress of San Juan de Ulúa.

The beginning of the Pastry War in Mexico.

1839 Pope Gregory XI condemns the slave trade.

1841 Bustamante again becomes president of Mexico, but is soon driven from power by Santa Anna.

1844 Santa Anna driven into exile in Havana

1845 The U.S. Congress, by a joint resolution, annexes Texas.

Frederick Douglass publishes the *Narrative of Frederick Douglass, An American Slave.*

1846 President Herrera of Mexico and then President Paredes refuse President Polk's offer to purchase California.

President Polk orders General Zachary Taylor to advance his detachment to the Río Grande.

Taylor blockades Matamoros.

Mexican cavalry skirmish with Taylor's troops.

The United States declares war on Mexico.

Taylor invades Mexico.

Bear Flag Revolt in California. Insurgents proclaim the "California Republic" in Sonoma.

President Polk and the U.S. Senate agree to a compromise with Great Britain dividing Oregon along latitude 49 degrees.

The U.S. navy captures the port of Monterey in California.

Santa Anna again president of Mexico.

Wilmot Proviso introduced into Congress.

1847 Taylor defeats Santa Anna at Saltillo.

Brigham Young and his Mormon followers settle in the Great Salt Lake basin.

General Winfield Scott lands at Veracruz and begins his invasion of Mexico.

Californio leaders sign the Cahuenga Capitulations, surrendering California to the United States.

Battle of Churubusco

Battle of Chapultepec and Scott's capture of Mexico City.

1848 Discovery of gold at Sutter's mill in California. Beginning of the California Gold Rush.

The United States and Mexico sign the Treaty of Guadalupe Hidalgo.

Lucy Stone begins the women's suffrage movement.

1850 Congress approves the Compromise of 1850.

California admitted as a state

1851 Treaty of Fort Lawrence concluded with the Plains Indian nations.

1852 *Uncle Tom's Cabin* published

1853 Santa Anna returns to power in Mexico.

1854 President Franklin Pierce's administration issues the Ostend Manifesto.

Congress passes, and President Pierce signs, the Kansas-Nebraska Act.

The Know-Nothing Order forms the American Party.

Pro-slavery forces establish a government at Leavenworth, Kansas; Free-Soilers set up their own government in Topeka.

Gadsden Purchase

1855 Mexican Liberals drive Santa Anna from power.

1856 Border violence creates civil strife in Kansas.

The Mexican Liberal government issues the *Ley Juárez* and *Ley Lerdo.*

1857 The U.S. Supreme Court issues its decision in the Dred Scott case.

Pro-slavery Lecompton Constitution for Kansas submitted it to Congress

The Mexican government promulgates a new, Liberal, anticlerical constitution.

Pope Pius IX condemns Mexico's Liberal government.

Félix Zuloaga and the conservatives overthrow Mexico's Liberal government.

1858 Lincoln-Douglas debates

Conservatives remove Zuloaga from power and appoint Miguel Miramón president.

1859 John Brown's assault on Harper's Ferry fails.

John Brown executed.

Liberal leader, Benitor Juárez, issues the Laws of the Reform.

1860 Abraham Lincoln elected president

South Carolina secedes from the union.

1861   Liberals forces in Mexico capture Mexico City. Benito Juárez becomes president.
Six southern states form the Confederate States of America and elect Jefferson Davis president.
Confederate forces in Charleston, South Carolina, fire on Fort Sumter.
Abraham Lincoln calls up volunteers.
Virginia secedes from the union. The Confederate capital moved to Richmond.
First Battle of Manassas (Bull Run)
First the Confederates (under Leonidas Polk) and then the federals (under U.S. Grant) move into neutral Kentucky.
Spanish, British, and French forces capture Veracruz.

1862   Lincoln issues General War Order Number 1.

U.S. Grant captures Forts Henry and Donelson in Kentucky.
The Battle of Shiloh
Federal Admiral Farragut captures New Orleans.
The Confederate congress passes a conscription act.
The Battle of the Seven Days
The French defeated at Puebla – *Cinco de Mayo*
Congress passes the Homestead Act.
Federal General John Pope issues war orders against the civilian population of Virginia.
Second Battle of Manassas (Bull Run)
Battle of Sharpsburg (Antietam)
Lincoln issues the preliminary Emancipation Proclamation.
Lincoln suspends habeas corpus throughout the North.
Battle of Fredericksburg
Sioux uprising in Minnesota ends in defeat.

1863   The Emancipation Proclamation goes into effect.

The French capture Mexico City.
Battle of Chancellorsville
The U.S. Congress passes a conscription act.
Robert E. Lee invades Pennsylvania.
Battle of Gettysburg
Fall of Vicksburg
Battle of Chattanooga

1864   U.S. Grant appointed Lieut. General of the U.S. army

Maximilian von Habsburg accepts the throne of Mexico.
Lee and Grant battle for northern Virginia.
Grant lays siege to Petersburg, Virginia.
Federal General William Tecumseh Sherman takes Atlanta.
Sherman captures Savannah.
Sand Creek Massacre in Colorado

1865   Sherman captures Columbia, South Carolina, and the navy captures Charleston.

The Confederate government evacuates Richmond.

The federal government establishes the Freedman's Bureau.

Lee surrenders at Appomattox Court House.

President Lincoln assassinated

Surrender of Confederate General Joe Johnston

Final battle of the Civil War at Palmito Ranch, Texas.

President Andrew Johnson institutes his reconstruction plan.

Emperor Maximilian of Mexico issues a decree ordering the execution of "bandits."

The U.S. Congress establishes the Joint Committee on Reconstruction.

1866   Congress passes the Freedmen's Bureau Bill, vetoed by President Johnson.

The French forces begin their withdrawal from Mexico.

Congress passes its Civil Rights Act, vetoed by President Johnson. Congress overrides his veto.

The U.S. Supreme Court in *Ex Parte Milligan*, declares Lincoln's wartime suspension of *habeas corpus* unconstitutional – overturning the Civil Rights Act.

Congress approves the 14th Amendment.

President Johnson declares the end of the "insurrection."

Fetterman Massacre near Fort Kearney in Wyoming

1867   Congress passes its Reconstruction Act.

The Ku Klux Klan forms a central organization to counteract Reconstruction.

Congress passes the Tenure of Office Act.

Inauguration of the Dominion of Canada.

The French sail from Veracruz.

Porfirio Díaz takes Puebla.

Emperor Maximilian surrenders at Querétaro.

Benito Juárez resumes the presidency of Mexico.

Execution of Maximilian

1868   The House of Representatives votes to impeach President Johnson.

The Senate fails to convict President Johnson of "high crimes and misdemeanors."

Ratification of the 14th Amendment

Treaty of Fort Laramie

1869   Congress passes the 15th Amendment.

The Central and Union Pacific Railroads meet at Promotory Point in Utah.

Avondale mine disaster

Terence Powderley founds the Knights of Labor.

1870   Congress passes the first of its three force acts.

1871   Election involving Juárez, Porfirio Díaz, and Sebastían Lerdo de Tejada decided in the Congress. Juárez takes a fourth term as president.

Díaz leads a rebellion against Juárez.

1872   The Crédit Mobliier scandal surfaces.

Juárista forces crush the *Porfirista* rebellion.

Death of Juárez. Lerdo de Tejada becomes president of Mexico.

Beginning of the Modoc War in California

1873   A financial panic strikes the United States.

End of the Modoc War.

Congress passes the Comstock Act.

1874   Congress passes, and President Grant signs, the second Civil Rights Act.

1875   The "Long Strike"

1876   Porfirio Díaz instigates a rebellion against President Lerdo.

Battle of the Little Bighorn

Lerdo flees Mexico City. Díaz assumes the provisional presidency of Mexico.

Chief Joseph surrenders to General Nelson Miles.

1877   President Hayes orders the withdrawal of troops from the South, ending Reconstruction.

Surrender of Crazy Horse

The Great Strikes

1879   Thomas Edison develops the light bulb.

1882   John D. Rockefeller forms the Standard Oil Trust.

1885   Geronimo and followers flee the San Carlos Reservation

1886   Geronimo surrenders to General Nelson Miles.

Samuel Gompers separates the AFL from the Knights of Labor.

1887   Congress passes the Dawes Act.

Congress passes the first Interstate Commerce Act.

1889   The Ghost Dance begins to spread among western Indian nations.

1890   Congress approves the Sherman Anti-Trust Act.

Massacre at Wounded Knee

1891   Pope Leo XIII issues *Rerum Novarum.*

1892   Foundation of the Populist Party

Homestead Strike

1893   World's Columbian Exposition and World's Fair held in Chicago

A financial panic hits the United States.

Revolution in Hawai'i and establishment of the Republic of Hawai'i

José Ives Limantour becomes director of the treasury under President Porfirio Díaz.

1894   Pullman Strike

1895   Beginning of the Cuban rebellion against Spain

1896   The U.S. Supreme Court issues its *Plessy v. Ferguson* decision.

1898   Explosion of the *Maine* in Havana harbor

The United States declares war on Spain.

Spain signs a peace treaty with the United, surrendering Cuba, Puerto Rico, and the Philippines to the United States.

Formation of the Anti-Imperialist League

1899   Pope Leo XIII issues *Testem Benevolentiae Nostrae.*

20th Century

1901   President McKinley assassinated. Theodore Roosevelt becomes president.

The Roosevelt administration decides to prosecute J.P. Morgan for violations of the Sherman Anti-Trust Act.

1902   Roosevelt forces the resolution of a coal strike in Pennsylvania.

1903   U.S. Circuit Court in St. Louis orders the dissolution of J.P. Morgan's Northern Securities Company.

The first of the Catholic Worker congresses opens in Puebla.

The first successful air flight by the Wright Brothers at Kitty Hawk in North Carolina

At Roosevelt's urging, Congress establishes a department of commerce and labor.

Colombia refuses to sign the Panama canal treaty with the United States.

With U.S. aid, revolutionaries in Panama win their independence from Colombia.

Panama leases the canal zone to the United States "in perpetuity."

1904   Roosevelt issues his "corollary" to the Monroe Doctrine.

Roosevelt establishes a protectorate over the Dominican Republic.

1905   Roosevelt brings Japan and Russia to sign a peace treaty.

1906   National Monuments Act passes Congress.

The Hepburn Act extends federal regulation from railroads to steamship, express, and sleeping car companies.

Congress, at Roosevelt's urging, passes the Pure Food and Drug Act.

San Francisco earthquake

1907   The United States and Japan sign the Root-Takahira Agreement.

A financial panic hits the United States.

The U.S. Senate passes the Spooner Act.

1908   William Howard Taft elected president

1909   Congress passes, and Taft signs, the Payne-Aldrich Tariff.

Under Emiliano Zapata, peasants reoccupy land seized from them by *El Hospital* hacienda in Morelos.

Formation of the *Operarios Guadalupanos* in Mexico

Ford Motor Company introduces the Model T.

1910   Anti-relectionists in Mexico nominate Francisco Madero as their presidential candidate.

President Díaz has Madero arrested and imprisoned.

Progressive Hiram Johnson wins the governorship of California.

Pascual Orozco and Pancho Villa lead a revolution in Chihuahua against Díaz.

Founding of the *Partido Católico Nacional.*

1911   Madero joins revolutionaries in Chihuahua.

Zapata seizes Ayala in Morelos.

Formation of the National Association Opposed to Women's Suffrage

Robert La Follette and other progressives form the National Progressive Republican League.

Guerilla forces form throughout Mexico.

Porfirio Díaz flees Mexico.

Francisco Madero becomes president of Mexico.

Zapata issues the *Plan de Ayala.*

1912   Roosevelt runs for president on the Progressive "Bull Moose" ticket.

Democrat Woodrow Wilson beats Progressive Roosevelt and the Republican President Taft in the presidential election.

1913   Ratification of the 16th Amendment, permitting the federal government to levy an income tax.

With President Wilson's backing, Congress passes the Underwood Tariff, with a provision for a federal income tax.

Congress approves the Federal Reserve Act.

President Madero imprisoned and executed. General Victoriano Huerta becomes president of Mexico.

1914   Congress establishes the Federal Trade Commission.

Congress passes the Clayton Anti-Trust Act – "labor's bill of rights."

Henry Ford institutes the assembly line.

Venustiano Carranza begins a revolution against Huerta.

Tampico incident in Mexico. The United States seizes the port of Veracruz.

World War I breaks out in Europe.

General Alvaro Obregon takes Mexico City. Huerta flees to the United States.

Venustiano Carranzza appointed president of Mexico.

Aguascalientes convention

Pancho Villa and Emiliano Zapata take Mexico City.

1915   Obregón defeats Villa at Celaya.

Sinking of the *Lusitania*

President Wilson demands that Germany desist from U-boat warfare.

Wilson calls for military preparedness.

1916   Villa attacks Columbus, New Mexico.

The United States Congress passes the Big Navy Act and the United States Shipping Board Act.

Carranza recognized as provisional president of Mexico.

President Wilson begins his peace initiatives with Europe's warring powers.

1917   President Wilson outlines his "peace without victory" plan.

Germany recommences U-boat warfare.

President Wilson breaks off diplomatic relations with Germany.

The Mexican government promulgates the Constitution of 1917.

A German U-boat sinks the *Laconia*.

The British publish the Zimmerman dispatch.

The United States declares war on Germany.

Congress approves the Selective Service Act.

Congress passes the Espionage and Sedition Acts.

The 19th Amendment ratified

President Wilson rebuffs Pope Benedict XV's Seven Points peace initiative.

The U.S. Congress approves the 18th Amendment.

1918   President Wilson issues his Fourteen Points for peace.

The Second Battle of the Marne in France.

The Central Powers and the Entente sign the armistice, ending the First World War.

1919   Peace negotiations open at Versailles.

Assassination of Emiliano Zapata

The United States contributes forces to drive the Bolsheviks from power in Russia.

Signing of the Peace of Versailles

Several bombings in U.S. cities provide the catalyst for the Red Scare.

President Wilson suffers a stroke.

The United States Congress fails to ratify the Versailles treaty and the League of Nations Covenant.

1920 The Volstead Act goes into effect – the beginning of Prohibition in the United States.

Sacco and Vanzetti trial

Carranza driven from power and assassinated

Alvaro Obregón becomes president of Mexico.

Conservative Republican Warren G. Harding elected president of the United States.

1921 A bomb explodes in the basilica in Mexico City.

The first Johnson Act places limits on immigration to the United States.

The National Disarmament Conference held in Washington, D.C.

1923 The National Women's Party introduces the Equal Rights Amendment into Congress.

President Harding dies of pneumonia in San Francisco. Calvin Coolidge becomes president.

The Teapot Dome Scandal breaks.

Plutarco Calles elected president of Mexico

1924 Congress approves the second Johnson Act, further limiting immigration quotas.

1925 Pope Pius XI condemns Mexico's government.

1926 Calles decrees that priests may not wear clerical garb in public.

Calles lays down a penal code to enforce anti-clerical laws and deports foreign-born priests.

The bishops of Mexico lend their support to an economic boycott.

The bishops of Mexico institute an interdict.

Spontaneous armed rebellions break out against Calles' government in west-central Mexico.

1927 Capistrán Garza and the *Liga Defensora* issue a call to arms against Calles' government – the beginning of the *Cristero* revolt.

Execution of Anacleo González Flores

Sacco and Vanzetti executed

Charles A. Lindbergh makes his transatlantic flight in the *Spirit of St. Louis.*

Padre José Reyes Vega orders the burning of train cars, killing 51 civilians.

Obregón assassinated

Victoriano Ramírez, *El Catorce*, rekindles the *Cristero* rebellion.

Enrique Gorostieta Velarde becomes overall commander of *Cristero* forces.

1928 Herbert Hoover elected president of the United States

Signing of the Kellogg-Briand Peace Pact.

1929 Calles' government and the bishops of Mexico agree on the *arreglos*, ending the interdict and the *Cristero* rebellion.

St. Valentine's Day Massacre in Chicago

Callistas and *Obregonistas* form the *Partido Nacional Revolucionario* (PNR).

"Black Tuesday" on Wall Street

1930 The U.S. bishops issue a letter on unemployment.

1931 Pope Pius XI issues *Acerba Animi*, condemning the anti-clerical policies of the Mexican government.

Pope Pius XI issues *Quadragesimo Anno.*

1932 Franklin Delano Roosevelt elected president

1933 Roosevelt and Congress enact 100 days of legislation to counteract the Great Depression.

The Dust Bowl

First number of the *Catholic Worker* published

The 21ˢᵗ Amendment, repealing prohibition, ratified

1934   Calles issues his *Grito de Guadalajara.*

Congress approves the Indian Reorganization Act, repealing the Dawes Act.

The "Second" rebellion of former *Cristeros* breaks out in Mexico.

Lázaro Cárdenas elected president of Mexico.

1935   Cárdenas institutes agrarian reform.

The U.S. Congress approves the Social Security Act.

1936   Roosevelt elected to a second term

Cárdenas denounces extreme anti-clericalism.

Cárdenas deports Calles from Mexico.

Reorganization of the PNR into the *Partido Revolucionario Institutucional* (PRI)

The Buenos Aires agreement forged between the United States, Mexico, and other Latin American countries.

1937   Roosevelt asks Congress to increase the number of Supreme Court justices.

A new downturn in the economy prompts Roosevelt to call for an extension of the New Deal.

1938   The U.S. Congress approves the Fair Labor Standards Act.

Cárdenas nationalizes oil properties into Mexican Petroleum.

Roosevelt renounces the U.S. treaty of commerce with Japan.

1939   World War II begins in Europe.

1940   Roosevelt announces the "Short of War" policy.

Avila Camacho becomes president of Mexico.

Roosevelt wins a third term as president.

1941   Roosevelt delivers his "Four Freedoms" address.

Congress approves the Lend-Lease Act.

Roosevelt and Great Britain's prime minister, Winston Churchill, sign the Atlantic Charter.

Congress authrorizes Roosevelt to enact a partial embargo against Japan.

Roosevelt receives the Philippines' armed forces into the United States army.

Roosevelt freezes Japan's financial assets in the United States.

With the Netherlands and Great Britain, the United States cuts off Japan's source of financial credit.

Japan sends an ultimatum to the United States.

Japan attacks Pearl Harbor.

The United States declares war on Japan.

Germany and Italy declare war on the United States.

1942   President Roosevelt authorizes Japanese relocation.

Battle of Midway

Battle of Guadalcanal

Roosevelt and Churchill implement Operation Torch.

1943   Roosevelt and Churchill meet at Casablanca.

Rommel surrenders in North Africa.

The invasion of Italy begins.

1944   The Allies push the Germans from the Gustav line and liberate Rome.

The United States engages in a massive bombing campaign against mainlaid Japan.

Roosevelt, Churchill, and Josef Stalin meet at Teheran.

Battle of the Phlippine Sea

D-Day: the Allies occupy Normandy.

Soviet forces occupy Warsaw.

Liberation of Paris.

General Douglas MacArthur lands at Leyte Island in the Philippines.

Battle of the Bulge

1945   Dresden bombed

Battle of Iwo Jima

Churchill, Roosevelt, and Stalin meet at Yalta.

Battle of Okinawa

Death of Roosevelt; Harry Truman becomes president.

Inauguration of the United Nations Organization

Germany surrenders.

Truman, Churchill, and Stalin meet at Potsdam.

The United States drops two atomic bombs on Hiroshima and Nagasaki.

Japan surrenders. The end of World War II.

1946   The UN General Assembly establishes the United Nations Atomic Energy Commission.

The UN establishes the International Monetary Fund (IMF) and the International Bank for Reconstruction and Development.

1947   President Truman outlines his Containment policy toward Communism.

The House Un-American Activities Committee tries the "Hollywood Ten."

1948   The U.S. Congress approves the Marshall Plan.

Conviction of Alger Hiss for perjury

1949   The United States, Canada, and ten European nations form the North Atlantic Treaty Organization (NATO).

Berlin airlift

The Soviet Union successfully tests its first atomic bomb.

1950   North Korea invades South Korea.

The United Nations declares war on North Korea.

Senator Joseph McCarthy begins his campaign against Communist infiltration in government.

1951   Execution of Julius and Ethel Rosenberg

Peace negotiations begin between the warring sides in Korea.

1952   Dwight David Eisenhower elected president

1953   Belligerants in the Korean conflict sign a cease fire.

1954   The U.S. Senate formally censures Senator McCarthy.

The U.S. Supreme Court issues its decision in *Brown v. Board of Education of Topeka.*

1955   The U.S. Supreme Court rules that desegregation must proceed "with all deliberate speed."

Eisenhower sends military advisers to South Vietnam.

Rosa Parks refuses to give up her seat on a bus to a white man.

Blacks in Montgomery, Alabama boycott public transportation.

1956   Southern congressmen call on the states to nullify the *Brown* decision.

The U.S. Supreme Court rules that segregation in public transportation is unconstitutional.

1957   The "space race" begins with the launching of the Soviet satellite, *Sputnik.*
President Eisenhower sends the national guard into Little Rock, Arkansas.
Congress passes the Civil Rights Act of 1957.

1959   Fidel Castro establishes his dictatorship in Cuba.

1960   Formation of Students for a Democratic Society at the University of Michigan
John F. Kennedy elected president of the United States

1961   The Bay of Pigs invasion
"Freedom Riders" protest segregation in public transportation.

1962   The Cuban Missile Crisis
Congress approves "Project Apollo."
Opening of the Second Vatican Council in Rome

1963   The U.S. Supreme Court lays down its decision in *Abington School District v. Schempp.*
The United States, Great Britain, and the Soviet Union sign the Nuclear Test Ban Treaty.
President Kennedy sends the national guard to the University of Alabama.
Bombing of a black church in Birmingham, Alabama
Martin Luther King, Jr., leads a massive march into Washington, D.C.
Mass demonstrations for racial equality held in the North and the South.
Assassination of President Kennedy. Lyndon B. Johnson becomes president.

1964   President Johnson calls on Congress to carry President Kennedy's war on poverty forward.
Congress passes the Civil Rights Act of 1964.
The Free Speech Movement (FSM) organizes a sit-in at the University of Berkeley in California.

1965   President Johnson lays out his "Great Society" program.
Gulf of Tonkin incident
Congress approves the Tonkin Resolution.
The Supreme Court lays down its decision in *Griswold v. Connecticut.*
President Johnson approves retaliatory airstrikes on North Vietnam.
Johnson orders more ground troops into Vietnam.
Close of the Second Vatican Council

1966   Formation of the National Organization for Women (NOW)
Rioting in Los Angeles and Newark

1967   Rioting in Detroit

1968   The Tet Offensive
President Johnson announces he will pursue peace negotiations with North Vietnam and that he will not run again for president.
Assassination of Martin Luther King, Jr.
Violence at the Democratic National Convention in Chicago
Pope Paul VI's *Humanae Vitae* inspires protest in the United States.
President Johnson announces a cessation of all bombing of North Vietnam.
Richard M. Nixon elected president of the United States

1969   President Nixon announces he would begin troop withdrawals from Vietnam.
First Apollo landing on the Moon.

1970   President Nixon calls for initiatives to clean up the natural environment.

1972   Nixon visits China.

Nixon visits Russia to discuss the progress of the Strategic Arms Limitation Treaty (SALT) and forges other agreements with Premier Leonid Brezhnev.

Nixon reelected president

1973 Revelation of the Watergate scandal

American troops withdraw entirely from Vietnam.

The Supreme Court lays down its decision in *Roe v. Wade*.

1974 Nixon resigns on account of the Watergate scandal.